Drugs and Behavior

An Introduction to Behavioral Pharmacology

Taken from:

Drugs and Behavior: An Introduction to Behavioral Pharmacology, Sixth Edition
by William A. McKim

Learning Solutions

New York   Boston   San Francisco
London   Toronto   Sydney   Tokyo   Singapore   Madrid
Mexico City   Munich   Paris   Cape Town   Hong Kong   Montreal

Cover Art: Courtesy of PhotoDisc/Getty Images.

Taken from:

Drugs and Behavior: An Introduction to Behavioral Pharmacology, Sixth Edition
by William A. McKim
Copyright © 2007, 2003, 2000, 1997, 1991 by Pearson Education, Inc.
Published by Prentice Hall
Upper Saddle River, New Jersey 07458

This special edition published in cooperation with Pearson Learning Solutions.

Pearson Learning Solutions, 501 Boylston Street, Suite 900, Boston, MA 02116
A Pearson Education Company
www.pearsoned.com

Printed in the United States of America

1 2 3 4 5 6 7 8 9 10 V0ZN 15 14 13 12 11 10

000200010270585977

AM

ISBN 10: 0-558-74927-5
ISBN 13: 978-0-558-74927-9

To Alyssa, Jacob, Nicholas, James, Jillian, and Aiden

Contents

6   ALCOHOL   128

7   TRANQUILIZERS AND SEDATIVE-HYPNOTICS   161

Preface

The field of behavioral pharmacology is always changing. Every day, there are exciting new developments and insights. Often these developments and discoveries are of great interest to people who use drugs both as medicines and for recreation. A great many interesting things have been discovered since the first edition of this book was published in 1987. It has been an exciting challenge to keep up with these new developments and to decide what to include in this text. At the same time, I believe it is important to tell the stories of the pioneers, to describe their groundbreaking research, and to provide the context in which these new discoveries were made. In addition, new drugs and new fashions in drug use have come on the scene, and others have gone out of style. Students are asking new and different questions, and it is important to be able to provide answers. With every edition of the book, I have attempted to keep up with these trends. Unfortunately, these new developments and trends happen too fast to keep pace with, so I am always, frustratingly, condemned to be a little behind the times. I count on the users of this book to supplement it with up-to-date material on new developments and trends. One aim of this book is to provide a background in which the significance of this new material can be understood.

This edition includes material on brain imaging, explaining how it works and giving examples of the insights it provides into the effects of drugs on the operation of the brain. In this regard, I acknowledge the work of Stephanie H. Hancock, who is responsible for much of this new material. I have acknowledged her contribution by listing her as the coauthor of the chapter on neurophysiology, although she has made significant contributions to many other chapters as well.

There has also been a significant change in the final chapter. This chapter, which has always been on hallucinogens, contained a catalog of dozens of hallucinogenic drugs, both well known and obscure. In this edition, I have taken a different approach, concentrating on drugs that are representative of several categories and including a discussion of drugs that are now popular in the rave and club scenes. These drugs are not used as traditional hallucinogens. Rather, modern users are more interested in their effects as phantasticants, empathogens, and entactogens,—and on their possible harmful effects.

This book would not have been possible without the assistance of many people. These include those mentioned in the earlier editions whose influence remains reflected in subsequent editions. In this edition, I would like to acknowledge the help of my wife, Edna McKim, who tolerated my frequent absences, both physical and mental, while the manuscript was being revised. I would also like to mention my colleagues at Memorial University of Newfoundland and many other institutions around the world who have read drafts, sent helpful suggestions, and pointed out a few errors. I also want to acknowledge many students who suffered through many teaching experiments and the office staff of the Psychology Department at Memorial University. These people include but are not limited to Terry Belke, Shola Elabanjo, Robert Gable, Peter Heinen, Barry Jones, Jeff Kushner, Brenda Noftle, and Mark Smith.

I would also like to acknowledge the helpful comments of Susan Dudish-Poulsen, Charles Hickis, Laurence Nolan, James Rothenberger, Debra Spear, and George Taylor who reviewed the 5th edition for the publisher. I also thank the people at Prentice Hall/Pearson Education and GGS Book Services for their excellent and professional help with the editing and production. These include, but are not limited to William Grieco, Jessica Mosher, Eileen O'Sullivan, Bruce Owens, Andrew Roney, and Connie Strassburg.

Apart from taking credit where credit is due, none of these people can be held in any way responsible for errors or problems in the book. Please direct all complaints to me for the benefit of the seventh edition.

William A. McKim
St. John's

Some Basic Pharmacology

WHAT IS A DRUG?

Most people understand what is meant by the term *drug*, but, surprisingly, coming up with a precise definition is not all that easy. The traditional way is to define a drug as any substance that alters the physiology of the body. This definition, however, includes food and nutrients, which are not usually thought of as drugs. Consequently, a drug is sometimes defined as a substance that alters the physiology of the body but is not a food or nutrient. This definition usually works, but it still leaves a lot to be desired. To begin with, the distinction between a drug and a nutrient is not at all clear. Vitamin C, for example, alters physiology, but is it a drug? If it is consumed in the form of an orange, it is clearly food, but if taken as a tablet to remedy a cold, it could be thought of as a drug.

Similarly, some substances that alter the physiology of the body may best be thought of as toxins or poisons rather than as drugs and may not be deliberately consumed. Gasoline and solvent vapors are examples. If they are consumed deliberately to get high, they might be drugs, but when inhaled unintentionally in the workplace, they may be called environmental toxins. The exact distinction between a toxin and a drug is not clear.

One element that complicates the definition appears to be the intention of the drug user. If a substance is consumed to get high or to treat a disorder, it is clearly best to think of it as a drug, but if it is consumed for taste or sustenance, it may not be useful to think of it as a drug. Such a debate has been waged about caffeine. As you will see in Chapter 10, caffeine clearly alters human physiology, but it also has been used as a flavoring agent in products such as soft drinks. If consumers prefer a soft drink that contains caffeine because they like the drink's taste, perhaps caffeine should not be thought of as a drug in that context. If the soft drink is consumed because of the effect caffeine has on the nervous system, then it is appropriate to think of it as a drug. A similar debate has been waged about the role of nicotine in tobacco (see Chapter 9). In these cases, the consequences are important to government regulatory agencies and various manufacturers. Fortunately, it is not necessary for us to form a precise definition of the term *drug*. An intuitive definition will serve our purposes. However, we should never lose sight of the fact that any one definition may not be appropriate in all circumstances.

NAMES OF DRUGS

One of the more confusing things about studying drugs is their names. Most drugs have at least three names—a chemical name, a generic name, and a trade name—and it may not always be apparent which name is being used at any given time.

Chemical Name

All drugs have a *chemical name*, stated in formal chemical jargon. A chemist can usually tell by looking at the name what the molecule of the drug looks like. Here is the chemical name of a drug:

7-chloro-1,3-dihydro-1-methyl-5-phenyl-2H-1, 4-benzodiazepin-2-one

As you can see, it is full of chemical terminology, letters, and numbers. The numbers refer to places where different parts of the drug molecule are joined. To make things more complicated, there are different conventions for numbering these parts of molecules. As a result, the same drug will have different chemical names if different conventions are used.

Generic Name

When a drug becomes established, its chemical name is too clumsy to be useful, so a new, shorter name is made up for it—a *generic name* or *non-proprietary name*. The generic name for the drug whose chemical name we just struggled through is *diazepam*. A drug's generic name bears some resemblance to its chemical name. The conventions for making up generic names are handy to know because they are clues to the nature of the drug. For example, most barbiturate drugs end in *-al*, like secobarbital, and most local anesthetics end in *-caine*, as in procaine.

For the most part, textbooks (including this book) and scientific discussions of drugs use generic names.

Another type of name is being used more and more. New substances created by drug companies may be used extensively before generic names can be established. Instead of their chemical names, these drugs are sometimes referred to by a code using letters and numbers—for example, *SKF 10,047*. The letters refer to the drug company (in this case, Smith Kline and French), and the numbers are a unique code for the drug.

Trade Name

When a drug company discovers and develops a new drug, often at a cost of millions of dollars, it can patent the drug for a number of years so that no other company can sell it. The drug company does not sell the drug under its generic name. Instead, it makes up a new name, called, the *trade name* or *proprietary name*. The trade name is the property of the company that sells the drug, and no other company can use that name (hence, the name is proprietary). The trade name for the drug we have been discussing is Valium. After the patent expires, other companies can sell the drug, or they can make it under license from the owner of the patent, but they frequently sell it under a different trade name. Therefore, one drug can have many different trade names.

Because drug companies sell their products under trade names, people in the medical profession are most familiar with trade names and are most likely to use those names. If a physician gives you a prescription for a drug and you are told the name of the drug, you may not be able to find it listed in this or any other text that uses generic names. Trade names can be distinguished from generic names because the first letter is capitalized.

Strictly speaking, the trade name refers to more than the active ingredient in the medicine; it refers to the *formulation*. The active ingredient is marketed in the form of a pill, tablet, or capsule that may contain a number of other ingredients—fillers, coloring agents, binding agents, and coatings collectively referred to as *excipients*. The excipients and the active ingredient are combined in a particular way, and this is known as the formulation. Different pharmaceutical companies may market the same drug but in different formulations that are given different trade names. It cannot be assumed that all formulations with the same active ingredient are equal. For example, different formulations may dissolve at different rates in different parts of the digestive system and, consequently, may not be equally effective.

DESCRIBING DOSAGES

All of modern science uses the metric system, and drug doses are nearly always stated in *milligrams* (mg). A milligram is 1/1,000 of a gram (there are a little over 28 grams in an ounce).

It is generally true that the effect of a drug is related to its concentration in the body rather than the absolute amount of drug administered. If the same amount of a drug is given to individuals of different sizes, the drug will reach a different concentration in the body of each individual. To ensure that the drug is present in the same concentration in the brains of all subjects or patients, different doses are given according to body weight. For this reason, in research papers, doses are usually reported in terms of milligrams per kilogram (kg) of body weight—for example, 6.5 mg/kg. (A kilogram is equal to 2.2 pounds.)

Reporting doses in this manner also helps when comparing research on different species. If you account for such other factors as metabolic rate and body composition, a dose of 1 mg/kg in a monkey will be roughly comparable to a dose of 1 mg/kg in a human. Interspecies comparisons, however, can be tricky. Generally, smaller organisms have higher metabolic rates than larger animals. As we shall see later, many drugs are destroyed by the body's metabolism. What this means is that drugs are metabolized faster in smaller animals, and so it is often necessary to give them a higher dose if they are to reach an exposure equivalent to that of a human. Thus, a dose of 1.0 mg/kg to a human may be equivalent to a dose of 10.0 mg/kg in a mouse or a rat. For this reason, research done on rats and mice

often uses doses that seem ridiculously high in human terms.

Dose–Response Curves

To get a true picture of the effect of a drug, it is usually necessary to give a range of doses of the drug. The range should cover a dose so low that there is no detectable effect and a dose so high that increases in dose have no further effect. It is usual to plot the effect of this range of doses on a graph, with the dose indicated on the horizontal axis and the effect on the vertical axis. This type of figure is called a *dose–response curve* (DRC). Figure 1-1 shows a typical DRC. It indicates the effect of caffeine on a mouse's rate of responding on an FI (fixed interval) schedule (schedules will be explained in Chapter 2).

Note that the scale on the horizontal axis is graduated logarithmically. It is generally found that a small change in low doses can have a big effect, but an equally small change in a large dose has no effect. Plotting doses on a log scale allows a wide range of doses to be reported and permits greater precision at the low end of the dosage range. Log scales became common when it was found that many physiological effects of a drug showed up as a straight line when plotted on a log scale.

In the example just used, the drug effect was a measure of response rate, but there are other types of DRCs in which the effect is a discrete binary variable rather than a continuous one. For example, we could not use this type of curve if we wanted to report a DRC for the effectiveness of a drug as an anesthetic. Subjects are either anesthetized or they are not. If the vertical axis simply read *Yes* or *No*, we would not have any sort of a curve. When a binary variable is used, DRCs are constructed differently and are sometimes referred to as dose–effect curves.

Problems like these are handled by working with groups of subjects. Each group is given a different dose of the drug, and the percentage of subjects in each group that shows the effect is then plotted. An example of this type of DRC is given in Figure 1-2. This hypothetical experiment

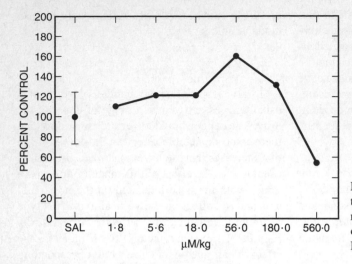

Figure 1-1 The dose–response curve for the effect of caffeine on the rate of responding by a mouse being reinforced on an FI schedule with food (adapted from McKim, 1980).

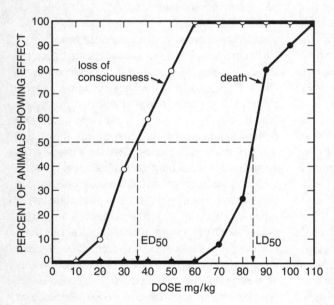

Figure 1-2 Results of a hypothetical experiment using 12 groups of rats. Each group was given a different dose, ranging from 0.0 (a placebo) to 110 mg/kg. One curve shows the percentage of animals in each group that lost consciousness; the other curve shows the percentage that died at each dose. The ED_{50} and the LD_{50} are also indicated.

is designed to establish the DRC for loss of consciousness and the lethal effects of a fictitious new drug, "endital." In this experiment, there are 12 groups of rats. Each group is given a different dose of the fictitious drug endital—from 0 mg/kg, a placebo, to 110 mg/kg. The vertical axis of the graph shows the percentage of rats in each group that showed the effect. The curve on the left shows how many rats lost consciousness, and the

curve on the right shows the percentage of rats in each group that died.

ED_{50} and LD_{50}. A common way of describing these curves and comparing the effectiveness of different drugs is by using the ED_{50}, *the median effective dose*, or the dose that is effective in 50 percent of the individuals tested. The ED_{50} for losing consciousness from endital in Figure 1-2 is

35 mg/kg. By checking the next curve, you can see that the dose of endital that killed 50 percent of the rats was 84 mg/kg. This is known as the *median lethal dose*, or the LD_{50}.

It is also common to use this shorthand to refer to lethal and effective doses that are not at the median. For example, the LD_{50} is the dose at which 50 percent of subjects die, the LD_1 is the dose that kills 1 percent of subjects, and the ED_{99} is the dose that is effective in 99 percent of all cases.

In DRCs where the vertical axis is continuous, the ED_{50} is also used, but in this case, it refers to a dose that produces an effect that is 50 percent of the maximum effect that the drug causes at any dose.

Drug Safety

When new drugs are being developed and tested, it is common to establish the LD_{50} and the ED_{50} to give an idea of the safety of a drug. Obviously, the farther the lethal dose is from the effective dose, the safer the drug. The *therapeutic index* (TI) is sometimes used to describe the safety of a drug. This is the ratio of the LD_{50} to the ED_{50}; $TI = LD_{50}/ED_{50}$. The higher the index, the safer the drug. The TI of endital calculated from Figure 1-2 would be 84/35 = 2.4.

Drug safety may also be described as a ratio of the ED_{99} and the LD_1.

POTENCY AND EFFECTIVENESS

Potency and *effectiveness* (or *efficacy*) are terms that are sometimes used to describe the extent of a drug's effect. The two terms do not mean the same thing. When you are comparing two drugs that have the same effect, *potency* refers to differences in the ED_{50} of the two drugs. The drug with the lower ED_{50} is the more potent. For example, if you compared LSD and a drug called lysergic acid amide, a related hallucinogen found in morning glory seeds, you would find that lysergic acid amide is 10 times less potent than LSD in producing a hallucinatory experience. In other words, the nature and extent of the effect of lysergic acid amide would be the same

as LSD if you increased the dose of lysergic acid amide by a factor of 10.

Effectiveness refers to differences in the maximum effect that drugs will produce at any dose. Both aspirin and morphine are analgesics or painkillers. When dealing with severe pain, aspirin at its most effective dose is not as effective as morphine. To compare these two drugs in terms of potency would not be appropriate. They both might produce analgesia at the same dose and, thus, be equally potent, but the extent of the analgesia would be vastly different.

PRIMARY EFFECTS AND SIDE EFFECTS

It is generally accepted that no drug has only one effect. In most cases, however, only one effect of a drug is wanted, and other effects are not wanted. It is common to call the effect for which a drug is taken the *primary* or *main effect* and any other effect a *side effect*. If a drug is taken to treat a disease symptom, that is its primary effect. Anything else it might do, harmful or otherwise, is a side effect.

Very often, the distinction between the two is arbitrary. Aspirin, for example, has several physiological effects: It brings down fever, it reduces swelling and inflammation, and it slows the blood's ability to clot. If you take aspirin because you have a high temperature, the temperature-reducing effect is the primary effect, and the other two are side effects. The inhibition of blood clotting is a potentially harmful effect because it can cause bleeding into the stomach, which can have serious consequences for some people. Recently, it has been shown that this anticlotting effect can be useful. Strokes are caused by a clot of blood getting caught in the brain. Many physicians believe that taking one aspirin a day can reduce the chances of stroke in people at high risk for stroke. In this case, the anticlotting effect would be the primary effect, and any other effects that the aspirin might be having would be the side effects.

When new behaviorally active drugs are developed to treat diseases, the ability of a drug to be abused or to create an addiction is considered a dangerous side effect. To a drug user, however, this psychological effect of the drug is vitally important, and any other effects the drug may have on the body are considered unimportant or undesirable.

DRUG INTERACTIONS

When two drugs are mixed together, their effects can interact in several ways. If one drug diminishes the effect of another, this interaction is called *antagonism*. Drug antagonism is established by plotting two DRCs: one DRC for the drug alone and a second DRC for the drug in the presence of the other drug. If the DRC for the first drug is shifted to the right (i.e., the ED_{50} increases) by adding the new drug, this result indicates antagonism between the drugs.

If adding the new drug shifts the DRC to the left (i.e., the ED_{50} decreases), this indicates that the drugs have an *additive effect*. If drugs have an effect together that is greater than might be expected simply by combining their effects, this is called a *superadditive effect*, or *potentiation*. It is not always obvious whether a drug interaction is additive or superadditive, but in one situation, the distinction is clear: If one drug has no effect alone but increases the effect of a second drug, potentiation is clearly occurring.

In these examples, drug interaction is defined in terms of shifts in the DRC indicated by changes in the ED_{50}, but interactions may also change the effectiveness of drugs. That is, the ED_{50} may not change, but the maximum effect may increase or decrease.

Careful determination of how drugs interact can tell us a great deal about the mechanism of drug action. For example, if we give a drug that is known to block a certain type of receptor and find that it antagonizes a specific effect of another drug, we can guess that the second drug probably interacts with that type of receptor to produce that effect (see Chapter 4).

PHARMACOKINETICS

The study of how drugs move into, get around in, and are eliminated from the body is called *pharmacokinetics*. The pharmacokinetics of a drug are described in three processes: *absorption*, how a drug gets into the blood; *distribution*, where it goes in the body; and *excretion*, how the drug leaves the body.

Drugs do not have an effect on all body tissues. As a matter of fact, most drugs influence the operation of the body only at specific and limited places, called *sites of action*. A drug may get into the body, but unless it gets to its site of action, it will have no effect. It is, therefore, important to understand how drugs get from their place of administration to the place where they act (i.e., pharmacokinetics).

ROUTES OF ADMINISTRATION

Some foods and medications may contain large amounts of valuable nourishment and medicine, but simply swallowing them or otherwise putting them into the body is no guarantee that they will have the desired effect. It is also true that the way a substance is administered not only can determine whether it gets to its site of action but also affects how fast it gets there and how much of it gets there.

A route of administration refers to the method used to get a drug from outside the body to some place under the skin. This purpose can be accomplished by taking advantage of the body's natural mechanisms for taking substances inside itself (such as digestion and breathing), or the drug can be artificially placed under the skin by means of injection. Some substances can be directly absorbed through the skin, but this is not a common route of administration for recreational or medical purposes.

Parenteral Routes of Administration

Parenteral routes of administration involve injection through the skin into various parts of the body, using a hollow needle and syringe.

Parenteral routes are further subdivided, depending on the specific point in the body where the drug is to be left by the needle.

Vehicle. Before a drug can be injected, it must be in a form that can pass through a syringe and needle—that is, it must be liquid. Because most drugs are in a dry powder or crystalline form (the word *drug* is derived from the French *drogue*, meaning "dry powder"), it is necessary to dissolve a drug in some liquid before it can be injected. This liquid is called a *vehicle*. Most behaviorally active drugs tend to dissolve well in water and remain stable for long periods of time in water solution. Pure water is not totally inert with respect to the physiology of the body, so a weak salt solution is used instead. Because body fluids contain dissolved salts, the most common vehicle is *normal* or *physiological saline*, a solution of 0.9 percent sodium chloride (ordinary table salt), which matches body fluids in concentration and does not irritate the tissues when it is injected.

In some cases, the drug to be injected does not dissolve in water. The active ingredient in marijuana, tetrahydrocannabinol (THC), is an example of such a drug, and it requires a different vehicle.

When a drug is in liquid form and the syringe is filled, the needle can be inserted into various places in the body, and the drug and vehicle is then injected to form a small bubble, or *bolus*. There are four common parenteral routes, depending on the site where the drug is to be placed: (a) subcutaneous, (b) intramuscular, (c) intraperitoneal, and (d) intravenous.

Subcutaneous. The term *subcutaneous* in published material is frequently abbreviated *s.c.* In jargon, it is called "sub-q." As the name suggests, in this route of administration, the drug is injected to form a bolus just under the skin or cutaneous tissue. In most laboratory animals, the injection is usually made into the loose skin on the back, between the shoulders. For medical purposes in humans, s.c. injections are usually done under the skin of the arm or thigh, but the hand or wrist is sometimes used to self-administer heroin, a procedure referred to as *skin popping*.

Intramuscular. In the *intramuscular* (i.m.) route, the needle is inserted into a muscle, and a bolus is left there. In humans, the most common muscle used for this purpose is the *deltoid* muscle of the upper arm or the *gluteus maximus* muscle of the buttock. To receive such an injection, the muscle must be fairly large, so i.m. injections are seldom given to rats and mice. They are more frequently given to monkeys. This route of administration is common also for pigeons; the injection is given into the large breast muscle.

Intraperitoneal. The abbreviation for the *intraperitoneal* route is *i.p.*, and, as the name suggests, the needle is inserted directly into the peritoneal cavity. The *peritoneum* is the sack containing the visceral organs, such as the intestines, liver, and spleen. The aim of an i.p. injection is to insert the needle through the stomach muscle and inject the drug into the cavity that surrounds the viscera. It is not desirable to inject the drug directly into the stomach or any of the other organs. Doing so could be harmful and could cause hemorrhaging and death. At the very least, injection into an organ is likely to alter the reaction to the drug.

Intraperitoneal injections are commonly used with rats and mice because they are easy and safe and cause the animals very little discomfort. They are much less convenient in larger animals and are almost never given to humans. At one time, rabies vaccine was commonly given to humans via this route, but this is no longer the case.

Intravenous. In an *intravenous* (i.v.) injection, the end of the needle is inserted into a vein, and the drug is injected directly into the bloodstream. This procedure is more popularly known as *mainlining*. Before an i.v. injection can be given, it is necessary to find a vein that comes close enough to the surface of the skin that it can be pierced with a needle. In humans, this is usually the vein on the inside of the elbow. The most common procedure is to wrap a tourniquet around the upper arm between the injection site and the heart. Because veins carry blood toward the heart, the tourniquet will dilate or enlarge the vein at the injection site and make injection easier.

When the end of the needle is inserted into the vein, the tourniquet is removed, and the drug is injected when normal blood flow has resumed. This is essentially the reverse of the procedure used when blood is removed for a blood test. One difficulty with i.v. injections, however, is that a vein cannot be used too frequently, or it will collapse and simply stop carrying blood. When veins have collapsed in the arms, other veins in the wrists, hands, and feet may be used, but they are more difficult to strike accurately with a needle.

In laboratory animals, i.v. injections are not commonly used by behavioral pharmacologists because veins close to the surface of the skin are unusual in rats, mice, and pigeons, and the procedure is not easy in unrestrained animals. Fur and feathers also make the location of such veins difficult to find. When i.v. injections are necessary, they are usually accomplished by means of a permanently implanted catheter. A *catheter* is a tube that is surgically implanted into the body. One end of the tube is at a site inside the body, and the other end is outside. In rodents and monkeys, venous (in a vein) catheters are usually inserted in the jugular vein, and the free end of the tube emerges from the animal's back. When an intravenous injection is required, the syringe is attached to the end of the catheter outside the body, and the drug is injected. Researchers frequently use this type of preparation to study self-administration of drugs by animals (the catheter may be attached to a motor-driven pump that the animal can control by pressing a lever; see Chapter 5). Intravenous catheters are fairly permanent and may last for months before they have to be replaced.

Other Parenteral Routes. Experimental research with laboratory animals sometimes involves injections directly into the nervous system. In *intrathecal* injections, for example, the needle is inserted into the nervous system between the base of the skull and the first vertebra. The drug is left in the cerebral-spinal fluid (the fluid that bathes the nervous system) and quickly diffuses throughout the nervous system. An *intraventricular* injection is done through a *cannula* inserted into the ventricles of the brain (chambers filled with cerebral-spinal fluid). A cannula is like a catheter, except it is a rigid tube resembling a hypodermic needle. Cannulas are often attached to the animal's skull. Intrathecal and intraventricular injections are frequently used in attempts to isolate the site of action of a drug to the central nervous system (the brain and spinal cord; see Chapter 4).

Technology has also been developed to permit the injection of small quantities of a drug into specific places in the brain through permanently implanted cannulas.

ABSORPTION FROM PARENTERAL SITES

With intravenous injections, the drug is put directly into the blood, but when other sites are used, the drug must be absorbed into the circulatory system. The rate at which a drug gets into the blood from an injection site is determined by a number of factors associated with blood flow to the area. Generally, the volume of blood flow is greater to the peritoneal cavity than to the muscles, and it is greater to the muscles than under the skin. As a result, absorption is fastest from an i.p. injection and slowest from an s.c. injection.

Heat and exercise can speed absorption from i.m. and s.c. sites because such factors increase blood flow to muscles and skin. Thus, an i.m. injection will be absorbed faster if the muscle is exercised after the injection, and the drug from a subcutaneous site will get into the blood faster if heat is applied to the area and more slowly if the area is chilled.

To be absorbed into the bloodstream, a drug must pass through the walls of the capillaries. A *capillary* is a tiny vessel through which blood flows. Capillaries permeate most body tissues.

They are so small in diameter that red blood cells can barely pass through. It is through the walls of capillaries that nutrients and oxygen pass out of the blood into body tissues, and it is also through these capillary walls that waste products and carbon dioxide pass into the blood and are removed. Blood leaves the heart and is distributed around the body in *arteries*. The arteries divide into smaller and smaller branches until they become capillaries. The blood in capillaries is eventually collected in *veins*, which carry the blood back to the heart and the lungs.

The walls of the capillaries are made up of a single layer of cells. Between these cells are small openings, or *pores*, through which nutrients, waste products, and drugs may pass freely. The only substances in the blood that cannot move in and out of the capillaries through these pores are red blood cells and large protein molecules, which are trapped inside because they are larger than the pores.

Injected drugs pass into capillaries and the bloodstream through these pores by simple *diffusion*. Diffusion is the process by which a substance tends to move from an area of high concentration to an area of low concentration until the concentrations are equal in both areas. If a drop of food coloring is placed in the corner of a tub of still water, it will remain as a highly colored drop for only a short period of time. The forces of diffusion will soon distribute the coloring evenly throughout the tub of water. The same principle determines that a drug injected into a muscle or under the skin will move from the area of high concentration (the bolus at the site of the injection) into the blood, an area of low concentration, until the concentrations in the two places are equal. The drug from an injection site will move through the pores into the blood in the capillaries surrounding the injection site. Because this blood is constantly circulating and being replaced by new blood with a low concentration of drug, more will be absorbed as the blood circulates through the area.

Areas that are serviced by many capillaries will absorb drugs faster than areas that have few capillaries. Because muscles use more oxygen, they have a richer capillary supply than the skin; for this reason, absorption into the blood is faster from i.m. injections than from s.c. injections. Drugs injected into the peritoneum have access to an even greater number of capillaries; consequently, i.p. injections are absorbed even more rapidly.

Absorption through capillary walls is not a factor in intravenous injections because the drug is placed directly into the blood. Blood in the veins is transported to the heart and then redistributed around the body after a short detour through the lungs. The body has about 6 liters of blood, and the heart pumps these 6 liters once a minute, so the drug in most i.v. injections is distributed around the body about a minute after injection.

Depot Injections

Some drugs need to be taken continuously or chronically to prevent the symptoms of a disease or disorder from reappearing. The antipsychotic drugs (see Chapter 13) are examples of drugs that sometimes need to be taken continuously for many years. Often people do not like to take these drugs and do not continue to use them after release from a hospital. As a result, they are readmitted regularly with recurring psychotic symptoms. It is possible to give these people *depot injections*— the drug is dissolved in a high concentration in a viscous oil (often sesame oil), which is then injected into a muscle, usually in the buttock. The drug then slowly diffuses from the oil into the body fluids over a long period of time. A single depot injection of an antipsychotic drug can be effective as long as four weeks. This technique usually works only with drugs that are highly lipid soluble (to be discussed shortly); otherwise, they would be released too quickly. Fortunately, antipsychotic drugs have this property (Lemberger, Schildcrout, & Cuff, 1987).

INHALATION OF GASES

Every cell in the body requires oxygen and gives off carbon dioxide as a waste product. The body has developed a very efficient system for absorbing gases from the air, the lungs, and distributing them quickly and completely throughout the body in the circulatory system. When drugs in the form of gases or vapor are breathed into the lungs, this system gets them into the blood very rapidly.

The lungs are an extremely efficient gas exchange system. Their inside surface is convoluted and contains many pockets of air so that the total surface area exposed to the air is very large. This entire area is richly supplied with blood by capillaries, which are close to the surface. When a gas is inhaled, it is absorbed through the capillary walls and enters the circulating blood. This will happen with gases and with the fumes of volatile substances (substances that evaporate rapidly such as solvents).

Figure 1-3 shows the circulation to and from the lungs. After blood returns to the heart through the veins, it is pumped directly to the lungs. Here the carbon dioxide is released from the blood into the air, and oxygen in the lungs is absorbed into the blood. The blood then returns directly to the heart and is pumped around the body. One of the main arteries from the heart goes directly to the brain. Consequently, drugs dissolved in the blood in the lungs are delivered very quickly to the brain without having to pass through the liver first, where some metabolism takes place.

The principle that governs the movement of gases from inhaled air into the blood and from the blood into the air within the lungs is diffusion. Gases move from areas of high concentration to areas of low concentration. If the concentration of drug in the inhaled air is higher than in the blood, the drug will move from the air into the blood, but if the

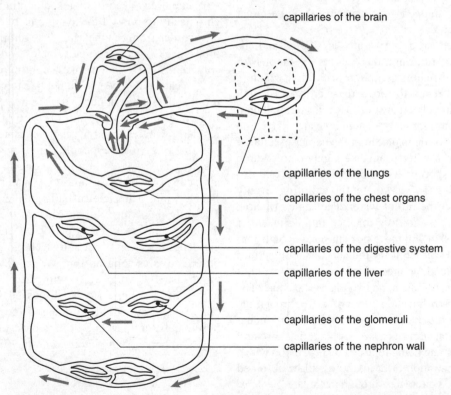

capillaries of the brain

capillaries of the lungs

capillaries of the chest organs

capillaries of the digestive system

capillaries of the liver

capillaries of the glomeruli

capillaries of the nephron wall

Figure 1-3 The circulatory system. The heart circulates blood returning from the body via the veins and the lungs and then sends it out via arteries to the body and the brain.

reverse is true, the drug passes out of the blood into the air and is exhaled. Thus, the inhalation of gases provides a means of controlling drug levels in the blood with considerable precision. This ability is one reason gases are used widely as general anesthetics, and inhalation is the favored route of administration for anesthesia. With volatile substances, this happens as well, although the rate is determined by how rapidly the substance evaporates.

INHALATION OF SMOKE AND SOLIDS

Gases and solvent vapors are not the only substances administered through the lungs. Drugs that occur naturally in some plants may be administered by burning the dried plant material and inhaling the smoke. Tobacco, opium, and marijuana are traditionally ingested in this manner. When the dried plant material is burned, the active ingredient remains in the smoke either as a vapor or in tiny particles of ash that are inhaled into the lungs. When contact is made with the moist surface of the lungs, the drug dissolves and diffuses into the blood. The major difference between smoke and gases is that the drug in the smoke particles will not revaporize after it is dissolved in the blood, and, consequently, it cannot be exhaled. These drugs must stay in the body until they are excreted by other means.

Powdered drugs such as cocaine, heroin, and tobacco snuff are sometimes sniffed into the nostrils. This practice is known as *intranasal administration*. What happens to the drug when given in this manner is unclear. It appears that most of the drug sniffed in the nose is dissolved in the moist mucous membranes of the nasal cavities and is absorbed into the blood from there. Some drug enters the lungs, while more runs down the throat into the stomach and digestive system and may be absorbed there. Although the nasal cavity is not as richly supplied with blood as the lungs and although the area is not designed to transport substances into the blood, it is a reasonably efficient system for getting drugs into the blood.

The problem with administration of solids and smoke by inhalation is the susceptibility to damage of all the tissues in the respiratory system. Smoke from burning marijuana and tobacco contains many substances in addition to the active drug; there are tars, hydrocarbons, and other chemicals created by the burning process. In time, these substances may cause respiratory diseases such as emphysema, asthma, and lung cancer, and they may decrease the ability of the lungs to absorb oxygen and eliminate carbon dioxide from the blood. Other forms of the drug with unknown toxicity may also be created by the burning process. In addition, when most substances burn in air, carbon monoxide gas is given off. Carbon monoxide is a very toxic gas because it blocks the ability of the blood to carry oxygen.

In the experimental laboratory, drugs are seldom administered by inhalation to laboratory animals. This is unfortunate because inhalation is a common method used by humans to administer abused drugs. The major difficulty is that in order to make an animal inhale a gas or smoke, it is usually necessary to confine it in a closed environment filled with gas or smoke, or the experimenter must make it wear some kind of helmet or face mask. The uncertainty about total dose and the technical problems of administration make this a cumbersome and unpopular route of administration in behavioral pharmacology. However, some researchers have had some success in training monkeys to suck smoke or vaporized drugs from a spout inserted into their cage.

ORAL ADMINISTRATION

Figure 1-4 shows the digestive system. Drugs absorbed into the body through the digestive system are taken into the mouth and swallowed—hence the term *peroral* (*p.o.*). Sometimes substances can get into the digestive system by other means. As just explained, snuff from the nostrils can sometimes get down the throat and be swallowed.

A drug may be taken into the mouth and not swallowed, as with chewing tobacco. Although this is technically an oral administration, the

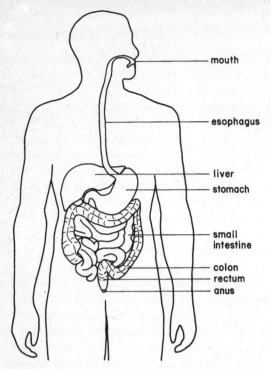

Figure 1-4 The digestive system. Note the location of the liver.

a swallowed drug will be absorbed may be determined by the speed with which it gets through the stomach to the intestines. Because solid food tends to be held in the stomach, taking a drug with a meal generally slows its absorption. When a drug is taken on an empty stomach, it passes quickly into the intestines and is absorbed rapidly.

The walls of the intestines are lined with capillaries to absorb nutrients from food, and these capillaries also absorb drugs. To get to the capillaries and be absorbed into the blood through the pores in the capillary walls, the drug must first pass through the membrane of the intestinal wall.

All body tissue is made of cells, and all cells are surrounded by a membrane. Figure 1-5 shows the cross section of a typical membrane in the body. Most membranes are made up primarily of what is called a *lipid bilayer*. *Lipid* is another name for fat, and the membrane consists of two layers of fat molecules held tightly together. Each lipid molecule has a clump of atoms at one end and two chains of atoms at the other. The lipid molecules in a membrane are organized so that the clumps point to the outside and the tails point inward. Large molecules of protein are embedded in the lipid bilayer, and they have specific functions that will be described in Chapter 4.

Therefore, for a drug molecule to pass through a wall of cells such as that forming the lining of the intestines, it must be able to dissolve in lipids.

absorption into the body is through the *buccal membranes*, or mucous membranes of the mouth, not the digestive system.

The digestive system may also be entered via its other end. Suppositories placed in the rectum also cause the drug to be absorbed into the blood. Such absorption is not as reliable as oral administration, but it can be used to advantage to give medication when it is impossible to give it orally (e.g., when a patient or animal is unconscious or vomiting).

THE DIGESTIVE SYSTEM

After a drug is swallowed, it goes directly to the stomach. The stomach churns and secretes strong acids to break down food pieces and turn them into a liquid that is then released slowly into the intestines, where nutrients are absorbed. Drugs may be absorbed from the stomach, but absorption is most efficient in the intestines. The rate at which

Lipid Solubility

Different drugs have different degrees of lipid solubility that are usually expressed in terms of the *olive oil partition coefficient*. To test lipid solubility, equal amounts of olive oil and water are placed in a beaker, and a fixed amount of drug is mixed in. Later the oil and water are separated, and the amount of drug dissolved in each one is measured. Drugs that are highly lipid soluble are more highly concentrated in the oil. Poorly lipid-soluble drugs mostly end up in the water. This test, although not perfectly accurate, predicts reasonably well the degree to which a drug will dissolve in fat tissue in the body.

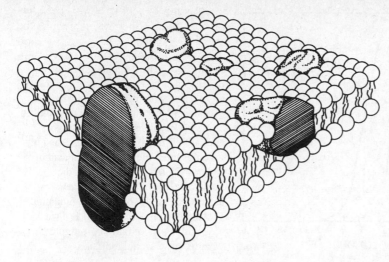

Figure 1-5 A cross section of a typical membrane. It is made up of two layers of lipid molecules with their long chains pointing inward. Embedded in this lipid bilayer are large molecules of protein that serve special functions. (from "The Fluid Model of the Structure of Cell Membranes," S. J. Singer and G. L. Nicholson, *Science*, Vol. 175, pp. 720–731, February 1972.)

All drug molecules vary in their degree of lipid solubility in their normal state, but when a molecule of a drug carries an electric charge, its lipid solubility is greatly diminished. Such a charged molecule is called an *ion.* Ions are not lipid soluble; consequently, they pass through membranes very poorly. When a drug is dissolved in a fluid, some or all of its molecules become ionized. The percentage of ionized molecules in a solution is determined by (a) whether the drug is a weak acid or a weak base, (b) whether it is dissolved in an acid or a base, and (c) its *pKa*. The pKa of a drug is the *pH* at which half its molecules are ionized.

The easiest way to understand pKa is to imagine the following experiment with a fictional drug called "damital." A fixed amount of damital is dissolved in each of 15 bottles; each bottle contains a liquid with a different pH, ranging from 0 to 14. A solution's pH is a number that describes the degree to which it is either an acid or a base. On this scale, 7 is completely neutral. Numbers less than 7 indicate increasing acidity, and numbers greater than 7 indicate increasing alkalinity.

After we dissolve the damital in each bottle, we then determine the percentage of damital molecules that are ionized and plot the results. As shown in Figure 1-6, the pH at which half the damital molecules are ionized is 5.

Most drugs are either weak acids or weak bases. Damital is a weak acid. If we do this experiment again with a drug that is a weak base, we see something different. One line in Figure 1-6 is a plot for an imaginary base, "endital." The curve for the acid damital starts with 0 percent ionization at the acid end of the scale, and ionization increases as it moves toward the base end. Just the opposite is true for endital, the base. It starts with 100 percent ionization in the acids, but its percentage of ionization decreases as the solution gets more basic. The pKa for endital is calculated in the same way as for damital. In this case, the pKa for endital is 8. By knowing whether a drug is an acid or a base and by knowing its pKa, it is possible to predict the degree to which it is likely to be ionized in a solution of known pH. The pH at the lining of the intestine is about 3.5. In Figure 1-6, we can see that damital is about 5 percent ionized at this pH, and endital is completely ionized. Because ionized molecules are not lipid soluble and do not pass through membranes, we can conclude that endital will not be very effective when taken orally, whereas damital will be readily absorbed.

Morphine is a base; its pKa is about 8. Bases are highly ionized at low (acid) pHs, and the curve drops at increasing pHs, so we can predict (correctly) that morphine will be poorly absorbed from the digestive system.

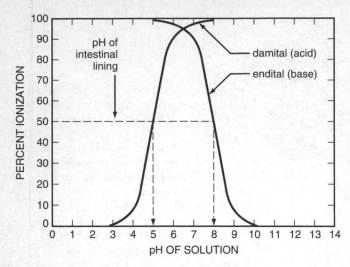

Figure 1-6 The percentage of ionized molecules in two fictional drugs dissolved in solutions with different pHs. Damital, a weak acid, becomes more highly ionized as the pH becomes more basic (higher numbers). Endital is a weak base, and it becomes more highly ionized at acid pHs. By drawing a horizontal line at the 50 percent ionization level, we can determine the pKa of each drug: damital, 5.0, and endital, 8.0. Caffeine is a weak base with a pKa of 0.5. Try to figure out what its curve would look like.

In general, most bases like morphine are poorly absorbed when taken orally, but their absorption depends on their pKa. For example, caffeine is a base, but it has a pKa of 0.5. Its ionization curve drops off quickly at very low pHs; consequently, it is almost entirely nonionized at pHs encountered in the digestive system. Caffeine, therefore, is readily absorbed when taken orally.

It should be pointed out that significant absorption will take place even if only a small percentage of molecules is not ionized. For example, if 97 percent of a drug is ionized at digestive system pHs, only 3 percent will be lipid soluble, but as soon as that percentage diffuses through the membrane and is removed by the blood, 3 percent of the remaining drug loses its charge, so the 97 percent ionization figure will stay constant for the drug remaining in the digestive system. The newly nonionized 3 percent now diffuses into the blood, and 3 percent more can lose its ionization. This process will continue until equilibrium is reached—that is, the concentration of nonionized molecules is the same on either side of the membrane. For this reason, it is not appropriate to think that the percentage of nonionized drug is all that is absorbed. Rather, the percentage of non-ionized molecules determines the number of molecules available for absorption at any period of time and, therefore, determines the rate of absorption.

TRANSDERMAL ADMINISTRATION

Some drugs can be absorbed through the skin. This is called *transdermal administration*. The skin is composed of several layers, but the main barrier to absorption is the *epidermis*, the outer layer of skin. It is made up of a continuous sheet of flattened cells that are densely packed with *keratin*. This layer is virtually impermeable to water and can be penetrated only by lipid-soluble substances. Even then, absorption is very slow. The layer just under the epidermis, however, is made up of connective tissue and serviced by capillaries; therefore, drugs applied to areas where there is a break in the epidermis (as occurs when there is a cut or a wound) can be absorbed.

Considerable research has been aimed at developing ways to make transdermal administration more effective. Traditionally, a drug has been applied in ointments or salves. In this form, absorption of the drug is determined entirely by the lipid solubility of the drug. In some cases, an absorption enhancer may be added to increase the rate of absorption, or the drug may be fixed in a special substance that releases it slowly for absorption. In more advanced systems, the drug is separated from the skin by a special membrane that limits the rate of absorption. Using systems such as this, it is possible to administer a drug at a constant rate and maintain a constant blood level for an extended period of time. One drug that is often administered transdermally is scopolamine, used to treat motion sickness.

Some substances, such as nicotine, are readily absorbed through the skin. This has made it possible to use transdermal nicotine in the form of the nicotine "patch" in the treatment of tobacco addiction (see Chapter 9).

DISTRIBUTION OF DRUGS

Even though most drugs get transported widely around the body by the blood, they tend to become concentrated in particular places and segregated from others. This process is called the *distribution* of a drug.

Lipid Solubility

It has been stressed that lipid-soluble substances can get through membranes easily, but as the olive oil partition coefficient experiment shows, this capacity also means that highly lipid-soluble drugs tend to stay in lipids wherever they encounter them. Consequently, highly lipid-soluble drugs tend to concentrate in body fat outside the central nervous system. Because few drugs have any effect in body fat, all of a drug dissolved in fat is, in effect, inactive. Very often, the body fat acts like a sponge, absorbing a lipid-soluble drug, taking it away from its site of action, and diminishing its effect. Later the drug is slowly released back into the blood from the fat over a long period of time.

Distribution to the Central Nervous System

Many years ago, it was discovered that when certain types of dyes were injected into the blood, they would be distributed to all extracellular fluids except those in the brain and the spinal cord. At that time, it was hypothesized that a special barrier between the blood and the brain protected the central nervous system from free diffusion of many materials out of the blood. This became known as the *blood–brain barrier*. It has now been established that the blood–brain barrier is a result of special cells in the central nervous system that wrap themselves around the capillaries and block the pores through which substances normally diffuse. These cells provide a solid lipid barrier so that non–lipid-soluble substances have great difficulty getting into the brain.

Active and Passive Transport Across Membranes

It is frequently important for the body to get non–lipid-soluble substances across membranes, so special *transport mechanisms* exist. They may be either passive or active.

In the *passive transport mechanism*, it appears that the non–lipid-soluble molecule attaches itself to a carrier or specialized molecule that diffuses across the membrane, releasing the normally non–lipid-soluble substance on the other side. In this way, a substance can move from areas of high to low concentration on either side of a membrane as though it were lipid soluble.

An *active transport mechanism* is similar to a passive mechanism except that it can work against normal diffusion by concentrating a substance on one side of a membrane. This is an active process that requires an expenditure of energy and takes place only in living membranes. Mechanisms such as ion pumps, which maintain electrical potentials of nerve cells (see Chapter 4), are examples of active transport systems. The blood–brain barrier has a number of such systems, many of which actively remove undesirable substances from the brain and some of which selectively concentrate substances in the brain.

Protein Binding

The blood contains a number of large protein molecules that cannot diffuse out of the pores in the capillaries because of their size. Some drugs attach, or bind, themselves to these protein molecules so strongly that they remain attached until metabolized. Consequently, they never get to their site of action.

The Placental Barrier

The blood of the fetus and the blood of the mother are not continuous. Nutrients are transferred to (and waste products are transferred from) the blood of the unborn child through a membrane similar to the blood–brain barrier. This transfer takes place in the *placenta*, the intermediary organ between the fetus and the wall of the uterus. Most behaviorally active drugs can be transferred from the mother's blood through the placenta to the fetus. Highly lipid-soluble substances cross more easily than drugs with low lipid solubility. Drug concentration in the blood of the fetus usually reaches 75 to 100 percent of that of the mother within 5 minutes of administration. Thus, the fetus appears to have very little protection from any drug the mother takes.

EXCRETION AND METABOLISM

There are some substances—for example, heavy metals such as lead and mercury—that the body is not very good at getting rid of. Levels of these substances can build up over time and accumulate to high and toxic concentrations. However, the body has fairly efficient systems to rid itself of most unwanted substances. It has already been described how gases and volatile solvent vapors can be eliminated in exhaled breath. Small amounts of many drugs are eliminated in sweat, saliva, and feces, but the major job of elimination is done by the kidneys and the liver, the "dynamic duo" of excretion.

The Kidneys

The *kidneys* are two organs, each about the size of a fist, located on either side of the spine. Their primary function is to maintain the correct balance between water and salt in body fluids. Along with the excretion of excess water in the form of urine, the kidneys can also excrete molecules of unwanted substances. They function as a complex filtering system that physically removes certain substances from the blood. Figure 1-7 shows the nephron, the functional unit of the kidney. Each kidney has millions of nephrons, all of which work in more or less the same way.

The *nephron* is essentially a long tube. At one end of the tube is a cuplike structure called *Bowman's capsule*, and inside Bowman's capsule is a clump of capillaries called the *glomerulus*. The other end of the nephron empties into collecting tubes, which, in turn, empty into the urinary bladder. The capillaries in the glomerulus have pores in their membranes, and most of the fluid in the blood that flows through these capillaries passes into Bowman's capsule and down the nephron. The remaining blood, which contains red and white cells and large protein molecules that are too large to pass out of the pores, continues out of the glomerulus and then moves through another bed of capillaries that surround the nephron along most of its length. At this point, most of the fluid and other substances are absorbed through the nephron wall back into the blood. Whatever is not reabsorbed passes through the length of the nephron and is excreted from the body in the urine.

The kidney works not by filtering impurities out of the blood but by filtering everything out of the blood and then selectively reabsorbing what is required. Reabsorption in the nephron is accomplished by the mechanisms just described: diffusion, lipid solubility, and active and passive transport. All lipid-soluble substances diffuse through the nephron wall into the blood, unless a selective transport mechanism is working against this diffusion. Desirable substances that are not lipid soluble, such as glucose (blood sugar), have a transport mechanism that successfully reclaims them into the blood. Unless they are reabsorbed by special transport systems, ionized or non–lipid-soluble substances tend to be excreted.

As with the digestive system, pH influences the degree of ionization and, as a consequence, can influence reabsorption. Urine tends to be acidic, and blood is basic, so, much like in the digestive system, acids tend to concentrate on the blood side of the nephron wall, and bases tend to be retained in the urine and are excreted more easily. The pH of the urine can be manipulated and made either more acidic or basic, which means that the excretion of drugs can also be manipulated. A similar process can also be used to facilitate the excretion

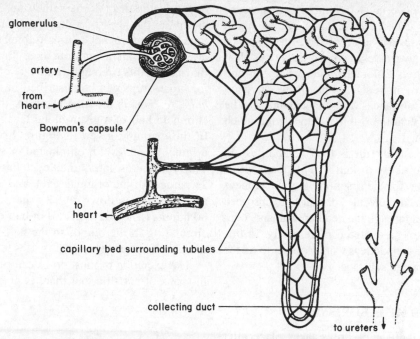

glomerulus

artery

from
heart

Bowman's capsule

to
heart

capillary bed surrounding tubules

collecting duct

to ureters

Figure 1-7 A drawing of a nephron, showing the capillaries of the glomerulus that filter fluid out of the blood into the nephron, and the capillary bed that reabsorbs water, nutrients, and lipid-soluble drugs into the blood. All material that is not reabsorbed is excreted in the urine.

of certain drugs in overdose cases. For example, one of the drug families frequently involved in overdoses is barbiturates, which are weak acids. Making the urine basic tends to ionize the barbiturate molecules, thus preventing their reabsorption. The kidneys can be assisted in the excretion of barbiturates by making the urine basic.

The Liver

The *liver* is a large organ located high in the abdomen, under the diaphragm (see again Figure 1-4). Its function may best be compared to that of a chemical factory where molecules are modified to form new substances useful to the body and where toxic molecules are changed into less harmful substances. These molecular changes are achieved by molecules called *enzymes*. An enzyme is a catalyst, a substance that controls a certain chemical reaction. The enzyme

takes part in the reaction, but when the reaction is finished, the enzyme is released unchanged and is free to participate in another reaction in the same way. Without the presence of the enzyme, the reaction would proceed very slowly or would not take place at all. The body controls chemical reactions by controlling the amount of enzyme available to act as a catalyst.

A good example of an enzyme is *alcohol dehydrogenase*. Someone with a background in chemistry can usually tell, from its name, what an enzyme does. Most enzymes end in the suffix *-ase*. The enzyme alcohol dehydrogenase removes hydrogen from a molecule of alcohol and makes it into acetaldehyde.

The process of restructuring molecules is referred to as *metabolism*, and the products of metabolism are called *metabolites*. In general, metabolites are either more useful to the body or less toxic than the original substance. Where drugs are concerned, the metabolic process is sometimes called *detoxification*. Although this term is appropriate some of the time, metabolites are not always less active or less toxic than the original drug. Chloral hydrate, psilocybin, and THC, the active ingredient of marijuana, are good examples of substances whose metabolites can be more active than the original drugs from which they are formed.

Another general rule is that metabolites are usually more likely to ionize. This tendency is very important for the functioning of the kidneys because ionized molecules cannot be reabsorbed into the blood through the nephron wall and, consequently, can be excreted more easily. In this way, the liver and kidneys work together to rid the body of unwanted substances.

FIRST-PASS METABOLISM

Not all metabolism of drugs takes place after absorption and distribution have occurred. As shown earlier in Figure 1-3, drugs that are absorbed from the digestive system are absorbed into blood that goes to the liver before it returns to the heart. This means that any drug absorbed from the digestive system will pass through the liver before going anywhere else in the body and will be subjected to a certain amount of metabolism by liver enzymes. This is known as *first-pass metabolism*, and it may be responsible for a significant amount of the metabolism of some drugs. Drugs administered by other routes of administration, including drugs absorbed from the nasal cavities and the membranes of the mouth and rectum, are not subjected to first-pass metabolism and may reach higher levels in the body. For a drug such as alcohol, some metabolism takes place in the stomach and intestines even before it is absorbed. This is also referred to as first-pass metabolism.

Rate of Excretion

The kidneys operate most efficiently when the concentration of a drug in the blood is high. As concentration falls off, the kidneys cannot

filter out the drug at the same rate. The curve that plots the level of a drug in the blood over time is, therefore, not a straight line but tends to level off to an asymptote (see Figure 1-8). Because of this trailing off, the rate of excretion for most drugs can be described in terms of a *half-life*. This is the time taken for the body to eliminate half of a given blood level of a drug. In the example given in Figure 1-8, half the original blood level is eliminated in 30 minutes. Thirty minutes later, the level has fallen to 25 percent of the original level, and 30 minutes after that, it is down to 12.5 percent. Every 30 minutes, the body gets rid of half of the drug circulating in the blood, so the half-life of the drug is 30 minutes.

The excretion of most drugs can be described in terms of half-life, but there is one important

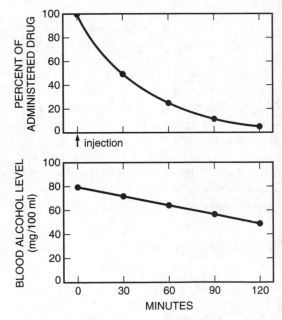

Figure 1-8 The top panel shows a typical excretion curve for a drug like nicotine, which has a half-life of about 30 minutes. The bottom panel shows the excretion function for alcohol, which is excreted at a constant rate (about 15 mg/100 ml of blood per hour). Because the excretion function for alcohol is a straight line, the concept of half-life does not apply.

exception: alcohol. If the blood level of alcohol is above a low minimum level, the excretion curve for alcohol is a straight line, as shown in Figure 1-8. Alcohol does not have a half-life.

FACTORS THAT ALTER DRUG METABOLISM

A number of factors can influence the rate of metabolism of drugs in the liver and, consequently, the intensity and duration of a drug's effect. A great many individual differences in response to drugs can be explained in terms of variations in drug metabolism and enzyme systems that change according to such factors as age, species, and past experience with drugs.

Stimulation of Enzyme Systems

To illustrate how enzymes work, we will use the metabolism of alcohol as an example. The steps in alcohol metabolism are shown in Figure 1-9. In the first two steps, alcohol is converted to *acetaldehyde* by the enzyme mentioned earlier: *alcohol dehydrogenase*. Then the acetaldehyde is converted to *acetyl coenzyme A* by another enzyme called *aldehyde dehydrogenase*.

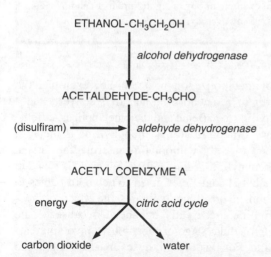

ETHANOL-CH₃CH₂OH

alcohol dehydrogenase

ACETALDEHYDE-CH₃CHO

(disulfiram) ⟶ *aldehyde dehydrogenase*

ACETYL COENZYME A

energy ⟵ *citric acid cycle*

carbon dioxide   water

Figure 1-9 Steps in the metabolism of alcohol. Note that disulfiram (Antabuse) stops this reaction at a point that causes a buildup of acetaldehyde.

Levels of a given enzyme can be increased by previous exposure to a specific drug that uses that enzyme or some other enzyme system. This process, known as *enzyme induction*, is responsible for the development of metabolic tolerance (discussed in Chapter 3). A good example of such a process is an increase in levels of alcohol dehydrogenase in the livers of heavy drinkers. Those who drink a great deal are able to metabolize alcohol slightly faster than nondrinkers and are, therefore, more resistant to its effects.

The effects of repeated exposure to alcohol are not limited to inducing alcohol dehydrogenase. Alcohol can also stimulate the enzymes that metabolize barbiturates; this fact partly explains why heavy drinkers are much less sensitive than nondrinkers to the effects of barbiturates. Box 1-1 gives another example of enzyme induction caused by the herbal antidepressant St.-John's-wort.

Depression of Enzyme Systems

When two drugs that use the same enzyme are introduced into the body at the same time, the metabolism of each will be depressed because both will be competing for the enzyme. Again, we turn to the metabolism of alcohol as an example. Acetaldehyde is converted into acetyl coenzyme A by *aldehyde dehydrogenase*. *Disulfiram* (*Antabuse*) is a drug that competes with acetaldehyde for this enzyme. Acetaldehyde levels then increase in the body because the enzyme is not readily available to metabolize it (see again Figure 1-9). Acetaldehyde is toxic and causes sickness and discomfort, so people who take disulfiram and then drink alcohol will get sick because of the buildup of high acetaldehyde levels. Disulfiram is sometimes used to discourage alcoholics from drinking; alcoholics will feel well and stay that way if they refrain from ingesting alcohol, but as soon as they take a drink, they will feel ill.

Even foods can alter drug metabolism. It was shown in the late 1990s that there are substances in grapefruit juice that can block *cytochrome P4503A4*, which is located in the intestine. This important enzyme is responsible for the significant first-pass metabolism of many drugs.

BOX 1-1   Enzyme Induction Caused by St.-John's-Wort

St.-John's-wort is a plant that is widely used as an alternative medicine for treating depression (see Chapter 14). St.-John's-wort appears to be about as effective as standard antidepressant drugs. It is one of the top 10 natural products used by adults in the United States and has been used by 12 percent of the population. Many believe that it has fewer unwanted side effects than pharmaceutical antidepressant drugs, but it turns out that St.-John's-wort has some potentially serious side effects that may not be readily apparent. It can reduce the effectiveness of many other drugs because it induces production of the enzyme that destroys them.

St.-John's-wort has many potentially active ingredients, including *hyperfortin*, which is a potent activator of something called *PXR* (*pregnane X receptor*). PXR is a protein that can be activated by a variety of chemicals and toxins, including hyperfortin. Its activation is the first step in an elaborate defense mechanism against poisoning by an array of chemicals and toxins. PXR is a transcription factor that stimulates the genes to produce a large number of enzymes responsible for the destruction of many drugs and toxins. One such enzyme stimulated by PXR is cytochrome P4503A4, which alone metabolizes about 60 percent of all clinically relevant drugs.

By taking St.-John's-wort in the recommended doses, you can stimulate the enzymes that destroy many important drugs that you may be taking concurrently. One such drug is the immunosuppressant *cyclosporine,* which is taken widely by organ transplant patients to prevent tissue rejection. Other drugs include atorvastatin, a cholesterol-lowering drug; *indinavir*, a drug used in the treatment of HIV; amytryptaline, an antidepressant; theophylline, a respiratory stimulant; and the tranquilizer alprazolam. St.-John's-wort can also cause unplanned pregnancy by reducing the effectiveness of oral contraceptives.

Thus, while it may appear that St.-John's-wort is an effective antidepressant with few side effects, the picture may not be that simple. In an article describing this effect, Choudhuri and Valerio (2005) conclude,

The case of SJW (St. John's wort) serves as a prototypical example of how a natural product can have far-reaching consequences in health and disease without causing any overt symptomology. (p. 9)

It has been shown that drinking grapefruit juice can significantly increase the blood levels of many drugs. There are a number of drugs that should not be used with grapefruit. They include the antidepressant *busparone* (*BuSpar*), the cholesterol-lowering drugs *lovastatin* (*Mevacor*) and *simvastatin* (*Zocor*), and *sildenafil* (*Viagra*).

Age

Enzyme systems are not fully functional at birth and may take time to develop fully. For this reason, immature members of a species may metabolize drugs differently from adults or may not metabolize them at all. For example, the liver of a newborn human first converts theophylline to caffeine and then metabolizes caffeine very slowly. In adults, theophylline is metabolized directly without this intermediate stage. Theophylline is similar to caffeine and is found in tea but is sometimes given to newborn babies to stimulate breathing. In infants, the effects of theophylline are greatly enhanced because of the intermediate stage of metabolism involving caffeine. For this reason, doses must be small and closely monitored to avoid overdose. A similar problem is encountered when drugs are given to a woman immediately before she gives birth. Drugs given at this time cross the placental barrier and circulate in the blood of the fetus. As long as the child's circulatory system is connected to the mother, the mother's liver can handle the drug, but if the baby is born and the umbilical cord is cut before all the drug is metabolized, the drug remains in the infant's body and is dependent solely on the baby's immature liver for metabolism, a process that may take many days.

There can also be impairments in metabolism at the other end of the life span. Liver functioning is less efficient in elderly people, so physicians prescribing for elderly patients often reduce drug doses accordingly.

Species

The vast majority of research in behavioral pharmacology uses species other than human beings. Studies are usually done on rats, mice, pigeons, or primates. It is important to understand how differences in drug metabolism can alter the intensity and duration of a similar dose in different species. As an example, the levels of alcohol dehydrogenase are quite different in different species. The liver of a rat or mouse contains about 60 percent of the alcohol dehydrogenase per gram in a human liver, but the liver of a guinea pig contains 160 percent of the level in a human liver. The liver of a rhesus monkey has a concentration of alcohol dehydrogenase similar to that of a human liver. As you can see, the same experiment, if performed on a guinea pig, a rat, or a human, might reach quite different conclusions.

COMBINING ABSORPTION AND EXCRETION FUNCTIONS

The effects of a drug change over time. This change reflects increasing and decreasing drug levels after administration. When these varying effects are plotted on a graph, the result is usually called a *time course*. (The drug effect is usually represented on the vertical axis, and time is on the horizontal axis.) Figure 1-10 is a time course for the concentration of a drug in the blood after administration. Note that there are three curves. One shows the time course of absorption of a drug from the site of administration. This curve is hypothetical because it assumes that while the drug is being absorbed, the liver and kidneys are not working and no excretion is going on. The second curve is a hypothetical excretion curve; it shows the rate of excretion of a drug but assumes instantaneous absorption. In reality, neither of these curves would exist. What is usually seen is a combination of the first two curves, shown here as a third curve that has both an ascending and a descending phase, indicating both absorption and excretion. The rate of excretion of any drug (i.e., its half-life) remains constant, but the absorption rate of any given drug can change, depending on the route of administration. Thus, the shape of this curve will vary.

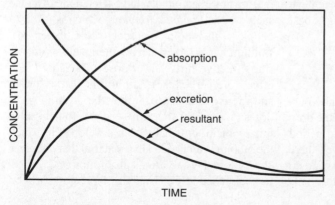

Figure 1-10   A theoretical absorption curve, assuming no excretion; a theoretical excretion curve, assuming instantaneous absorption and distribution; and a third line showing the resultant of these two theoretical processes. The resultant curve is typical of the time course for blood level of most drugs.

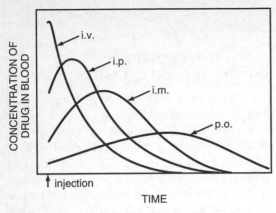

Figure 1-11 The time courses for blood levels of a drug given by different routes of administration.

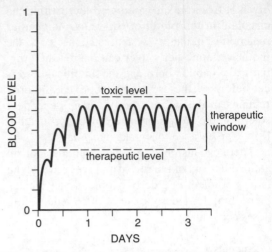

Figure 1-12 The therapeutic window is the range of blood concentrations of a medicine above a level that is ineffective (therapeutic level) and below a level that has toxic side effects (toxic level). When drugs are taken chronically, it is important that the drug be given in the right dose and at the right frequency so that blood levels remain within the therapeutic window.

Figure 1-11 shows typical curves for various routes of administration. When drugs are given intravenously, the absorption phase is very steep; the drug achieves high levels and is metabolized and excreted quickly. When drugs are given orally, the absorption is slow, and blood levels do not reach the same high concentrations seen after i.v. administration, but the drug lasts much longer in the body. Intramuscular and subcutaneous routes are intermediate between i.v. and oral routes. The route of administration can determine whether a drug reaches high levels for a short period or lasts a long time at low levels. If the f   ion of a drug depends on maintaining con-   blood levels, as with antibiotics, oral admin-   tion is preferred. If it is necessary to achieve   high levels for brief periods, the drug is best g   n intravenously.

THE THERAPEUTIC WINDOW

W   n drugs are administered for therapeutic purposes, it is important that the right level of the drug be maintained in the blood for an extended period of time. If the drug reaches too high a level, there will be an increase in unwanted side effects and no increase in the therapeutic effect. If the drug falls below a certain level, it will not have a therapeutic effect at all. This range, called the *therapeutic window*, is illustrated in Figure 1-12. To keep its concentration within this range, a drug must be taken at the correct dose at regular intervals.

For drugs that are absorbed slowly and excreted slowly, it is usually not difficult to achieve a dosing regimen that keeps the blood level within this window, but the task is more complicated for drugs that are absorbed rapidly and excreted rapidly. One such drug is *lithium carbonate*, which is given to people with bipolar disorder (see Chapter 14). Lithium has a rather narrow therapeutic window (the effective dose and a dose that causes side effects are very close). Lithium is also absorbed and excreted rapidly, so it must be given in small doses (as many as four times a day). To help solve this problem, pills have been developed in which the lithium is embedded in a material that dissolves slowly to delay the drug's absorption and, hence, its peak blood level. Using this type of medication makes it easier to keep the blood level within the therapeutic window and reduce the number of doses to two a day.

CHAPTER SUMMARY

- Drugs have three different kinds of names: a chemical name, a generic name, and at least one trade name.

- Doses of a drug are usually described in terms of concentration (i.e., mg of drug/kg body weight).

- Dose–response curves (DRCs) are graph curves that show changes in the effect of a drug that are produced by changes in the dose.

- The ED_{50} (median effective dose) is the dose of a drug that either has a particular effect in 50 percent of the subjects to whom it is given or produces in an individual an effect equivalent to 50 percent of the maximum effect that the drug will have at any dose. The LD_{50} (median lethal dose) is the dose of a drug that will be lethal to 50 percent of the subjects.

- The safety of a drug can be described by the TI (therapeutic index), which is the LD_{50} divided by the ED_{50}.

- When comparing two drugs that have the same effect, the drug with the lower ED_{50} is the more potent. The drug with the greater maximum effect is the more effective.

- All drugs have a number of effects. The effect that the drug is being consumed for is the main or primary effect, and all others are side effects.

- If one drug shifts the DRC of a second drug to the right, the drugs are said to be antagonistic. If the DRC is shifted to the left, the effects are additive. Potentiation or a superadditive effect occurs if the effects of a drug mixture are greater than what might be expected if the effects were simply added together.

- Pharmacokinetics is the study of how drugs move into, around, and out of the body.

- Parenteral administration involves injecting a drug through the skin, using a syringe and a hollow needle. Parenteral injections may be subcutaneous, intramuscular, intraperitoneal, or intravenous. Drugs may also be injected directly into veins through a permanently implanted catheter or into the central nervous system through a permanently implanted cannula.

- Drugs are absorbed from parenteral sites by diffusing into the blood through pores in the walls of capillaries.

- Drugs in the form of gases and/or smoke may be inhaled into the lungs and enter the blood. Drugs that are inhaled reach the brain more quickly than drugs taken by any other route.

- Drugs taken orally must pass through the stomach before they can be absorbed from the small intestine.

- Molecules of drugs that are ionized (i.e., have an electric charge) are not lipid soluble and are absorbed poorly from the digestive system. The rate of absorption of a drug can be altered by changing the pH of the digestive system because this can alter the percentage of ionized molecules.

- More and more molecules of drugs that are weak bases will become ionized as the drug is dissolved in solutions that are increasingly basic and vice versa. The pKa of a drug is the pH at which the molecules of a drug are 50 percent ionized.

- Drugs that are not lipid soluble have difficulty passing through membranes and get into the brain slowly because of the blood–brain barrier. Highly lipid-soluble drugs are sometimes absorbed rapidly into body fat and are released slowly.

- In transdermal administration, drugs are absorbed directly through the skin.

- Factors that affect the distribution of drugs in the body are lipid solubility, the blood–brain barrier, protein binding, and the presence of active and passive transport mechanisms.

- In the kidney, most of the fluid in the blood is released into one end of the nephron. As the fluid passes through, water and nutrients are reabsorbed. Ionized drugs and many drug metabolites are not reabsorbed. They pass through the length of the nephron and are excreted in the urine.

- The liver, the body's chemical factory, uses the process of metabolism to change drug molecules into metabolites, which may then be eliminated by the kidneys. The liver controls metabolism using enzymes, which act as catalysts to speed up certain chemical reactions.

- First-pass metabolism refers to the metabolism of a drug in the digestive system or liver before it gets into general circulation.

- Enzymes can be stimulated by repeated use of a drug or by other drugs, or they can be depressed by age, other drugs, and some foods.

- Half-life is the time taken for the body to get rid of half of a circulating drug.

- The therapeutic window refers to the range of blood levels of a drug between the lowest therapeutically effective blood level and a level that causes undesirable side effects.

2

Research Design and the Behavioral Analysis of Drug Effects

RESEARCH DESIGN

All scientific experimentation can be thought of as a search for a relationship between events. In behavioral pharmacology, the researcher is usually trying to find the relationship between the presence of a drug in an organism and changes that occur in the behavior of that organism. In most true experiments, one of these events is created or manipulated by the experimenter, and the other event is measured. The manipulated event is called the *independent variable*, and the observed event is called the *dependent variable*. The independent variable in behavioral pharmacology is usually the amount of drug put into the organism; that is what the researcher manipulates. The dependent variable is usually some change in the behavior of that organism, and this is what the researcher measures. Later in this chapter we will discuss some of the more commonly used measures of behavior or dependent variables.

Experimental Research Design

Experimental Control. It is not enough to give a drug and observe its effect. For an experiment to be meaningful, the experimenter must be able to compare what happened when the drug was given with what would have happened if the drug had not been given.

A controlled experiment is one in which it is possible to say with some degree of certainty what would have happened if the drug had not been given. This permits comparisons between drug and nondrug states. For example, a researcher could give each person in a group of subjects a pill containing THC, the active ingredient in marijuana, and observe that everyone tended to laugh a great deal afterward. These observations would not be worth much unless the research could demonstrate that the increased laughter was a result of the drug and not a result of the subjects' expectations, their nervousness about being observed, or some factor other than the presence of the drug in their bodies. With most behavioral experiments, many factors could influence the results, so it is essential to be sure that the drug and not something else in the procedure caused the laughter.

The only truly reliable way to do this experiment and eliminate all other possible causes of the laughter would be to have a time machine and, after the experiment, go back and, under exactly the same circumstances, give the same subjects pills identical in appearance but not containing any drug. Comparisons could then be made between the amount of laughter with and without the drug because all other factors (the subjects, the situation, the time of day, and so on) would be the same. Only then could we be sure the laughter was caused by the drug and nothing else.

There is no such thing as a time machine, so the behavioral pharmacologist must compare the behavior of a drugged subject with either (a) the drug-free behavior of that subject under similar conditions (within-subject design) or (b) the behavior of other drug-free subjects under similar conditions (between-subject design).

Within-Subject Design. In this strategy, careful observations are made of a subject's behavior under specific conditions. When the behavior appears to be stable and predictable, it is then possible to give the drug and make comparisons between drugged and nondrugged behavior. In other words, subjects serve as their own controls.

Let us say, for example, that we are interested in the effect of amphetamine on the feeding behavior of rats. In a within-subject design, the researcher carefully measures the daily food consumed by several rats until the measures are constant for each animal. The researcher then injects a dose of amphetamine into each rat and measures food consumption for that day. A meaningful comparison can then be made between food consumption with the drug and without the drug because the researcher has a pretty good idea of how much each animal would have eaten if it had not been given the drug.

Between-Subject Design. The same experiment could be done using a between-subject design. In this strategy, a number of rats are randomly assigned to two groups. One group, the experimental group, would get the amphetamine. The other group, the control group, would not get any drug. The food consumption of both groups could then be compared.

Comparisons of Between- and Within-Subject Designs. The type of design used by a behavioral pharmacologist is usually determined by the type of dependent variable being measured in the experiment. If the measured activity (eating, in this case) is stable from day to day, within-subject designs can be used, but if the dependent variable is subject to systematic change, the researcher is forced to use a between-subject design. Exploratory behavior is a good example of such a measure; on the first exposure to a new cage, a rat will usually spend considerable time moving around and exploring, but on the second day, it may be habituated to the surroundings and may just sit and lick its whiskers. A within-subject design could not be used to study exploratory behavior because the behavior changes from day to day. We would not know whether the change was due to the drug or to habituation. A between-subject design would be appropriate because both the experimental and control groups could be compared on the first exposure to the new cage, and habituation would not be a factor.

The difficulty with the between-subject design is that responses of individuals may vary a great deal. By chance, there may be very curious rats in one group and very lazy rats in another. The differences in the groups would then be due to differences in the rats and not in the effects of the drug. We could get around this difficulty by having larger groups to decrease the likelihood that all the curious rats (or all the lazy ones) would end up in one group. This procedure would require much more work and would have the additional disadvantage that the final results would be in terms of group averages, which sometimes hide important information that is more apparent when working with individual subjects.

The advantage of the within-subject design is that more perfect control conditions can be achieved because each subject is its own control. The disadvantage is that it can be used only with behavioral measures that are not likely to change when repeated. Within-subject experiments usually take more time, but they do not require as many subjects.

Statistical Testing

In some within-subject and most between-subject designs, some statistical tests are needed to determine the probability of differences observed between drug and nondrug measures. Such tests are necessary because differences could be due to chance variations from day to day and from subject to subject. When a researcher finds a difference in the means of the groups, a statistical test can tell how often such a difference would be likely to occur by chance if there were no drug effect. Box 2-1 gives a numerical example of how statistical tests are used.

Placebo Controls

To be completely useful, a control condition must be as similar as possible to the experimental condition, except for one variable: the presence or absence of the drug. In our example in which the effect of amphetamine on rats' eating was determined, the control procedure could have been improved. As you recall, we had two groups: One was injected with amphetamine, and the other was not injected at all. It is quite possible that the anxiety of being stuck with a needle suppressed eating and that the amphetamine had nothing to do with the results. For this reason, behavioral pharmacologists always use a control condition that involves the injection of the vehicle alone (see Chapter 1), that is, a *placebo control*. On control days in within-subject designs and for control subjects in between-subject designs, an injection of normal saline would be given. Subjects in the experimental group or those receiving amphetamine on drug days would be treated identically, except that they would have the drug dissolved in the saline.

Placebo Effects

Such careful controls are especially important with human subjects because of the *placebo effect* phenomenon. A placebo is a totally inert substance that causes no physiological change but is administered as though it were a drug. If people believe they are getting a drug that will have a specific effect, they will frequently show that effect even though the drug does not cause it.

In an interesting experiment by Fillmore and Vogel-Sprott (1992), three groups of subjects were given a cup of coffee before being tested on a psychomotor performance task. One group was told that caffeine would speed their performance, one group was told that caffeine would slow their responding, and the third group was not told anything. The coffee all were given was a placebo: decaffeinated coffee. The groups' performances matched what the subjects had expected; those who were told to expect improvement did better than those who were not told anything, and those told to expect an impairment did worse than those who were not told anything.

This placebo effect makes careful control an absolute necessity when evaluating the clinical effectiveness of newly developed medicines because patients will frequently show an effect they expect the drug to produce. For example, let us suppose that we are testing a new pain reliever. We go to a hospital and give the drug to a group of patients who are in postoperative pain and tell them that this new drug should relieve their distress. The next day, we find that 68 percent of the patients report that their pain was relieved. By itself, this is not a useful experiment because we do not know how many patients would have reported the same thing without the drug. To do this experiment the proper way, it would be necessary to have two groups of patients. Both groups would be told they were getting a pain reliever, but only one group would get the new drug; the other would be given an identical pill containing only an inactive filler. The next day, pain ratings would be taken from all the patients, and comparisons could be made.

The *balanced placebo design* was developed in the mid-1970s by George Marlatt and his colleagues at Washington State University in Seattle (Marlatt & Rohsenow, 1980). It remains the gold standard for research with humans in which the subject's expectations could influence the results in a manner similar to the Fillmore and Vogel-Sprott experiment described previously.

BOX 2-1   An Example of the Use of a Statistical Test

A mythical experiment was done to determine the effect of amphetamine on food consumption in rats. The experiment was a between-subject design with 10 rats in each group. Both groups were treated identically except that the rats in one group were given amphetamine before eating and the rats in the other group were given a placebo injection of the vehicle, normal saline. The amount eaten by each rat is given in the following table:

Control Group		Experimental Group	
Rat Number	Food Eaten (grams)	Rat Number	Food Eaten (grams)
1	18	11	17
2	22	12	14
3	23	13	12
4	17	14	25
5	28	15	15
6	20	16	16
7	16	17	20
8	22	18	21
9	21	19	13
10	18	20	11
Mean	20.5		16.4

The researcher found that the amphetamine (experimental) group ate a mean of 16.4 grams of food and that the control group ate a mean of 20.5 grams of food. On the basis of this difference, could the experimenter conclude that amphetamine reduced food intake? To answer this question, a statistical test is needed.

The most appropriate statistical test for this type of experiment is what is known as a t test. This test takes into account the variability in each group, and, on the basis of certain assumptions, it can tell the experimenter how many times the experiment would have to be repeated to get this big a difference between the means just by chance.

In this case, the t test tells the experimenter that if the drug had no effect and the experiment was done 100 times, a difference this big could occur as often as 10 times just by chance. This result is normally not good enough. Most behavioral researchers insist that their results be explained by chance no more than five times in 100, or, as they say, with a probability of less than 5 percent ($p < .05$). If the probability level is greater than .05, the result is generally considered to be negative. If you read original research reports, you will see the results of statistical tests reported something like this: ($t = 2.09$, $df = 18$, $p < .10$). The first two numbers are values associated with the statistical test, and the final number is the probability level (in this case, it is less than 10 percent).

There are many types of statistical tests for many different research designs. However, they all end up telling you the same thing: how often you would expect to get the results by chance if there were no drug effect (Ferguson, 1966).

When using a within-subject strategy, a statistical test is sometimes not necessary. Most research using operant techniques examines the behavior of three or four experimental subjects in great detail and under carefully controlled experimental conditions. Nondrugged performance is very reliable, so when the drug is given, it is readily apparent whether there are any drug-produced changes in behavior, and statistical analyses are not necessary.

In the balanced placebo design, there are four groups: Two are the same, as in a standard placebo design where subjects in both groups are expecting to get a drug and one group gets a drug and the other gets an identical placebo. In the balanced placebo design, there are two other groups. The subjects in neither expect to get the drug, but one gets the drug, and the other group gets a placebo.

This design is powerful at separating the drug effect from the expectancy or placebo effect because there is a group that does not expect the drug and gets it. Any change in this group must be due entirely to the drug. There is also a group that expects the drug and gets a placebo. Any change seen in this group must be due entirely to the expectation effect and not the drug.

In Chapter 3 there is an extended discussion of the nature of the placebo effect.

Experimenter Bias

Further precautions must be taken in an experiment of this nature. It has been known for some time that an experimenter can influence the outcome of research without knowing it. For example, if the researcher knows which patients have been given a placebo, the researcher might unconsciously change the manner in which the patients are interviewed or even make systematic mistakes in recording data. To eliminate experimenter bias, it is usually necessary to conduct the experiment so that neither the patients nor the researchers giving the drug and interviewing the patients know who has been given the drug and who has been given the placebo. This procedure is called a *double-blind procedure*, and it is essential because it eliminates the possibility of placebo effects and experimenter bias effects.

Three-Groups Design

When a new drug is being tested for use in the treatment of a disease, the standard design is what is known as a *three-groups design*. One group is given the experimental drug to be tested, a second group is given a placebo, and a third group is given an established drug with known therapeutic effect. By having three groups, the researchers can answer a number of important questions. Comparisons between the experimental drug group and the placebo group show whether the drug caused any improvement, comparisons between the placebo group and the established drug group indicate whether the research measures were sensitive enough to detect an improvement, and comparisons between the experimental and established drug groups tell whether the new drug has any advantage over established treatment (Overall, 1987).

In some cases where denying a patient any treatment is known to cause harm, the placebo group may not be used at all, and new treatments are compared only with old established treatments.

NONEXPERIMENTAL RESEARCH

A good deal of what we know about drugs is a result of research that does not involve experiments. As explained earlier, experiments attempt to find relationships between two events: a manipulated event and a measured event. *Nonexperimental research* looks for a relationship between two measured events. A good example is the discovery of a relationship between smoking during pregnancy and infant mortality. It was shown some time ago that there was a higher rate of infant death among babies born to women who smoked during pregnancy than among babies born to nonsmoking mothers (see Chapter 9). In this research, nothing was manipulated; there was no independent variable. The two events, smoking and infant mortality, were measured and found to be related.

One major difficulty with this type of finding is that we cannot assume a causal relationship between the two related events. We know that children born to smoking mothers are more likely to die, but we cannot conclude that smoking causes the infants' deaths. The relationship might be due to some third factor that causes both events. For example, it may be that women smoke because they have a biochemical imbalance that causes their bodies to need the nicotine in cigarettes. This imbalance might also be responsible for the higher infant mortality rates. The only way we could be sure that the smoking caused the infant mortality would be to do a true experiment by finding two groups of nonsmoking pregnant women and forcing one group to smoke. If there were a difference in infant mortality between the two groups, we would be in a good position to propose a causal relationship. Of course, such an experiment is out of the question on ethical grounds and could never be done with humans. For this reason, we must be satisfied with relational rather than causal data on many issues of drug effects in humans.

THE STUDY OF BEHAVIOR

Behaviorism

Contemporary psychology should not really be called "psychology" at all. The name is derived from the Greek word *psyche*, meaning "mind," and it literally means "the study of the mind," which it is not. Modern psychology has its roots in both physiology and philosophy. Its name is derived from philosophy, but its methods and subject matter are closer to physiology.

Early psychologists attempted to study the mind scientifically, but they met with very little success because they used introspection as their method of gathering data. Introspection is the internal observation of what is going on in one's own mind. Introspection failed as a scientific method because it violated one of the principal requirements of science: The subject matter must be public—the data must be available for everyone to observe. Introspection, by its very nature, could not be a source of scientific information.

In the early part of the twentieth century, an American psychologist, John B. Watson, founded a school of psychology known as *behaviorism*, which has become the basis of contemporary Western psychology. Watson rebelled against any study of the mind or of any other concept that could not be defined in terms of observable and measurable events. He claimed that the real subject matter for psychologists should be behavior. Behavior is public, measurable, and reproducible and, consequently, is amenable to the scientific method. As a result of Watson's influence, most experimental psychologists today study overt behavior, although the old terms *psychology* and *psychologist* are still used as widely as ever.

Psychologists and pharmacologists who study the effects of drugs on behavior sometimes refer to their field as *psychopharmacology*, which is simply a combination of the words *psychology* and *pharmacology*. Purists prefer to use the term *behavioral pharmacology*. Today the term *psychopharmacology* is most often used to describe the field that studies the effects of drugs on psychiatric symptoms—a merging of the concerns of both psychiatry and pharmacology.

Introspection

Unstructured Introspection. Introspection, the early psychologists' method of studying internal mental processes, did not succeed as a scientific method and is not particularly helpful as a tool in behavioral pharmacology. This is not to say that unstructured verbal descriptions of drug-produced internal states are not useful to a researcher. On the contrary, they guide and inspire more systematic study. But the accounts themselves are not adequate scientific data unless they are collected in a systematic or structured fashion.

Many chapters in this book provide accounts of the experiences of people who have taken various drugs. These can give us some indication of how a drug affected the writer at that time and can be fascinating, but by themselves they can give readers some indication only of how they might feel if they took a similar dose of the drug. These accounts alone cannot provide data that can be used to predict or understand the action of the drug in terms that scientists can find useful.

Systematic Introspection. Introspection by itself is of no value to the behaviorist, but the acts of introspecting and the subsequent verbalization are behaviors that can be studied. If a psychologist sticks a pin into a subject's finger, the pain will be quite real to the subject but is available only to the subject—not the experimenter—for study. However, if the psychologist asks, "Does it hurt?" and the subject answers, "Yes," the answer is public and scientifically useful. Similarly, when a drug is given to an experimental subject who hallucinates, the visions seen are the subject's own and cannot be studied, but the subject's responses to the visions can be recorded, analyzed, measured, and subjected to any kind of behavioral test. The scientific usefulness of such responses will, to a large extent, depend on the care with which they are collected and the skill with which they are analyzed.

Systematic self-reporting is also useful in human research when studying the effects of drugs on internal states such as moods. Rather than just asking subjects how they feel, the researcher can use scales that measure a particular aspect of how the drug makes a person feel. One example of such a scale is the Profile of Mood States (POMS), a paper-and-pencil test that asks subjects to describe, using a five-point scale, how each of 72 adjectives applies to them at a particular moment. These 72 items yield a score on eight independent subscales: anxiety, depression, anger, vigor, fatigue, confusion, friendliness, and elation. These scales give a reliable and quantifiable measure of a subject's internal state (see Chapter 11 for an example).

The Addiction Research Center Inventory (ARCI) is a similar test developed specifically to assess the abuse potential of drugs. The complete questionnaire consists of 550 true–false items covering a broad range of physical and subjective effects. This scale can be given to a person who has taken a new drug, and the drug's subjective effect can be compared with the effects of these other drug classes (Haertzen & Hickey, 1987). The assumption is that drugs with similar subjective effects, particularly euphoric effects, will be similarly abused (Preston, Walsh, & Sannerud, 1997, pp. 100–103).

LEVEL OF AROUSAL

The concept of *arousal level* has been around for a long time and is the basis for a number of important psychological theories. In the course of a day, we all experience changes in arousal that normally range from deep sleep to mild excitement. Arousal level is thought of as one continuous variable so that the arousal level at a specific time can be characterized as being at a point on a scale and moving in either direction. Figure 2-1 shows the scale of arousal level and indicates the normal range of arousal we encounter in the course of a day.

Arousal can continue above or below the normal ranges, causing pathological or abnormal states. At the low end, arousal goes beyond deep sleep to coma and death; at the high end, excitement ranges into mania, convulsions, and death.

One of the oldest ways of classifying drugs is by whether they increase or decrease arousal. Drugs that increase arousal are "stimulants" or "uppers," and those that decrease arousal are "depressants" or "downers." This distinction, however, is of limited usefulness in behavioral pharmacology because it really describes only the effect of a drug at high doses. Depressants at high doses cause loss of consciousness, and stimulants at high doses cause convulsions. At intermediate doses that are of interest to the behavioral pharmacologist, different stimulants have quite different

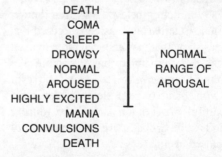

Figure 2-1 The range of arousal levels. Normal arousal varies between deep sleep and excitement, but drugs and disease may cause arousal to move out of the normal range.

effects, and the same is true for depressants. In fact, most "depressant" drugs stimulate spontaneous motor activity at low doses. In fact, it is a principle of behavioral pharmacology that the effect that any drug has on behavior depends far more on the behavior being measured and on the organism and its behavioral history than on the nature and dose of the drug.

The *electroencephalograph* (EEG) is a device that measures electrical waves produced in various parts of the brain. It is described in more detail in Chapter 4 in the section on brain imaging techniques. Apart from detecting activity in different parts of the cortex, it is often used as a measure of arousal. In an alert individual, the EEG will usually show *beta waves*, and a relaxed individual with closed eyes will show smooth, regular waves called *alpha waves*. As a person becomes more relaxed, the waves get larger and the cycles longer.

Sleep

During sleep, these waves become very slow and have a very large amplitude and are called *delta waves* or sleep spindles. As a person goes to sleep, five distinct stages can be recognized with the EEG. These stages are characterized by slower and slower frequency, except the last stage, known as paradoxical or REM sleep. Over the course of a night, the EEG reading shows the brain cycling through these five stages. Every 90 minutes or so, the brain appears to wake up; it shows a normal waking EEG, including beta waves, even though the individual is still sound asleep. Recordings from muscles show that they are even more relaxed than normal, yet the subject has a wide-awake EEG, thus the term *paradoxical sleep*. The term *rapid-eye movement* (REM) sleep is also used because careful observation shows that during these periods, the eyeballs are moving rapidly under the closed eyelids.

The physiological and psychological significance of REM sleep is not understood, but it is known that dreaming is associated with REM, and people deprived of REM sleep suffer from changes in intellectual ability, motivation, and personality. REM sleep can be altered by various drugs.

Arousal and Mood

Drug-produced arousal-level changes are often mistakenly associated with moods. The colloquial classification of drugs as "uppers" and "downers" is based on this presumed relationship between mood and state of arousal; that is, an upper makes you feel up or good, and a downer may not be associated with pleasure or happiness. However, it cannot always be assumed that arousal has anything to do with mood. For example, the stimulation and jitters caused by many stimulant drugs such as caffeine are considered unpleasant, as is the depressed, sedated state caused by the antipsychotic drugs or the confusion caused by benzodiazepines. By contrast, opiates, which cause a depressed, dreamy state, and cocaine, which causes high arousal, produce euphoria and extremely pleasurable mood states called *rushes*.

MEASURING PERFORMANCE IN HUMANS

Some tasks, such as driving a car, are of great interest to behavioral pharmacologists and are studied through elaborate tests and simulations of real-life conditions. Although findings from these tests are directly applicable to the task studied, it is generally better to study the basic intellectual and behavioral processes used in these more complex skills and apply the findings more generally to a greater variety of tasks that use the same basic skills. Most tests of human performance can be categorized according to whether they measure perceptual, cognitive, or motor abilities.

Perception. A number of tests and techniques have been developed to measure the acuity of the senses, particularly sight and hearing. Sensitivity changes are reported as changes in thresholds. The term *absolute threshold* refers to the lowest value of a stimulus that can be detected by a sense organ. It is a measure of the absolute sensitivity of the sense organ. *Difference thresholds* are measures of the ability of a sense organ to detect a change in level or locus of stimulation. If a threshold increases, it means that the intensity of the stimulus must be increased in order for it to be detected. In other words, the sense has become less keen. A lowering in threshold means that a sense has become more sensitive.

An example of how threshold is measured is critical frequency at fusion. If the speed with which a light flickers is increased, eventually a point will be reached where the light appears to be steady. This is the critical frequency at fusion, and it is sensitive to many drugs. The ability to detect flicker is a reliable measure of how well the visual system is functioning. To measure the functioning of hearing, an auditory flicker fusion test has also been developed.

Cognitive Performance. Some very sophisticated tasks have been developed over the years to assess cognitive abilities, that is, the ability to process, store, and retrieve information. Tests of vigilance or attention assess the ability to detect the presence of a specific type of signal in a group of signals, often over an extended period of time. Tests of memory and of learning and recall require a subject to learn a list of items that must be recalled at a later time.

The entire process of learning and testing may take place while the subject is under the influence of a drug, or the effect of a drug on different stages of the process can be determined by giving the drug during either the learning phase or the recall phase.

Other tests of intellectual functioning include the ability to perform addition and subtraction mentally, to sort cards, and to name colors. A commonly used paper-and-pencil task is the *digit symbol substitution test* (DSST). It was originally part of a commonly used intelligence test. At the top of the page in the DSST, the subject is given a table that shows a symbol associated with nine digits. The task is to draw the appropriate symbol next to each number in an array of numbers as fast as possible. It tests memory and psychomotor skills.

Motor Performance. Motor performance is a major concern in assessing the effects of drugs on human performance. Some of the simplest measures of performance are reaction time, tapping rate, hand steadiness, and body sway. Hand–eye coordination is often measured by a device called a *pursuit rotor*. With this device, the subject is instructed to hold the end of a stylus on a point on a rotating disk. The total time the subject is able to hold the stylus on the moving spot is a measure of hand–eye coordination.

Driving. Because driving is such a necessary and common activity, it is important to know the effect many drugs have on the ability of a person to operate an automobile. Determining the effect of a drug on driving ability, however, is not as easy as it might seem. To begin with, driving is a complex activity requiring many skills of perception, motor control, and judgment. There is much more involved than simply moving a car from one place to another. Researchers have tried to assess driving skill by using many different strategies. Some simply have their subjects drive a car through city traffic and have professional driving instructors rate their performance on a number of factors. One difficulty with this approach is that the demands of the task will be different for each person tested because traffic conditions are constantly changing. However, the main problem is that it is unethical to permit subjects to drive in real traffic and endanger their lives and the lives of others if there is any possibility that their skills might be impaired by drugs.

To get around these problems, researchers sometimes have their subjects operate a vehicle around a closed course where various demands are made on the skill of the driver. This approach is more artificial but safer, and because the task is the same for each subject, comparisons are more easily made between and within subjects.

One difficulty with using a real car is that it is sometimes difficult to measure a subject's performance accurately. You can tell if the subject knocks over a pylon, but you will not be able to determine whether the error resulted because the object was not seen, the subject could not estimate the speed of the car, or the reaction time was too slow. To answer such questions, many researchers use computerized driving simulators that are capable of measuring a subject's response time, steering ability, and capacity to react to specific crises. With some simulators, it is even possible to measure the subject's eye movements while driving.

MEASURING BEHAVIOR IN NONHUMANS

Unconditioned Behavior

The simplest measure of behavior in nonhumans is how much of it there is. Such measures are usually referred to as *spontaneous motor activity* (SMA), which may be measured in a number of ways, but usually the animal is placed in an "open field" (a large open box), and its movements are measured either electronically or by drawing a grid on the floor of the open field and counting the number of times the animal crosses a line.

Much can also be learned simply by observing the behavior of animals after they have been given drugs. Some classes of drugs cause animals to exhibit stereotyped behavior—the continuous repetition of a simple act such as rearing or head bobbing. Other drugs may cause sleep or convulsions.

It is also possible to measure other unconditioned behavior using very simple techniques. For example, muscle tone in rats can be measured using an *inclined plane test* where the animal is placed on a board that can be tilted to various degrees. The degree of tilt where the animal is unable to hold on to the surface and slides off is a measure of muscle tone.

A test used to measure anxiety is the *elevated plus maze*, which consists of narrow boards in the shape of a "plus" raised a foot or so off the ground. Two opposite arms of the plus have walls, and the other two do not. Normally, rats spend most of their time on the arms that have walls and only occasionally venture out on the unprotected arms. Drugs that are known to relieve anxiety cause rats to spend more time on the unprotected arms than they normally would.

There are several tests for *analgesia*, or the ability of a drug to block pain. The most common is what is referred to as the *paw lick latency test*. Rats are placed on a metal surface that is heated to about 50 degrees Celsius. This is about the temperature of a hot cup of coffee. When you first pick it up, it feels warm, but the longer you hold it, the hotter it becomes, until you have to put it down. When rats are first placed on the hot surface, they do not react, but within a few seconds, they raise one of their hind paws to their mouth as though they were licking it. The length of time it takes for this to happen is called the *paw lick latency*. Analgesic drugs like morphine lengthen this latency, which is often used as a measure of a drug's analgesic effect. Even if the rat does not show this response, it is removed after a fixed number of seconds to prevent the heat from burning the skin.

Conditioned Behavior

Learned behavior is frequently classified by whether it is a result of *respondent* or *operant* conditioning. This distinction does not represent two types of learning; rather, it arises from attempts to condition two different types of behavior, reflexive and voluntary. Respondent conditioning is also known as *classical* or *Pavlovian* conditioning because it was the first type of learning to be studied systematically and was first investigated by Ivan Pavlov, the great Russian physiologist.

Respondent Conditioning

Respondent behavior is reflexive in the sense that it is under the control of well-defined stimuli in the environment. When a dog salivates at the sight of food, the salivation is respondent behavior under the control of the stimulus of food; that is, it is a reflex. Such a reflex is considered to be unconditioned. Thus, the stimulus, the food, is the *unconditioned stimulus* (UCS), and the salivation is the *unconditioned response* (UCR). Pavlov found that if the sight of food is paired with a neutral stimulus such as a ringing bell, the bell alone eventually elicits the salivation. Thus, the bell becomes a *conditioned stimulus* (CS), and the salivation to the bell in the absence of the food is the *conditioned response* (CR). The process by which stimuli become conditioned has been extensively studied, and a great deal is known about the conditions that control the development and expression of respondent conditioning. Pavlov's studies of drugs' effects on respondent conditioning were some of the very first experiments in behavioral pharmacology. Such studies are rare in behavioral pharmacology today. The importance of respondent conditioning is that it can help us understand many of the effects that drugs have, as we shall see in Chapter 3.

Operant Conditioning

Operant behavior is behavior that appears to be voluntary because it is not elicited by any apparent stimulus in the environment. Operant behavior may be conditioned if it is followed by a *reinforcing stimulus*, such as food. A dog that learns to beg for food at the table is demonstrating operant conditioning. The begging is the operant, and it is maintained by the occasional delivery of food. If begging no longer results in the delivery of food, the begging stops.

The principles of operant conditioning are thought to apply to nearly all behavior of all animals. Operant behavior is usually studied in the laboratory using a *Skinner box*—a small cage attached to an apparatus that will deliver small quantities of food or water. It also contains a *manipulandum*, something that the animal can manipulate or move (e.g., a bar, lever, or knob). Figure 2-2 shows a Skinner box for a rat. In this box, a food delivery system delivers one small pellet of rat food at a time. The manipulandum is a lever on the wall near the food dish.

To study operant conditioning, it is usual to first deprive the subject of food or water so that these can act as rewards for performing the desired operant (in this case, pressing the lever). Each lever press is detected electronically and causes food to be delivered. In this way, the rat is rewarded, or *reinforced*, each time it makes the desired response. When the rat has learned this response, it makes it frequently and reliably. However, the first time it is placed in the box, it may not depress the lever on its own, so a procedure called *shaping* is used. In shaping, the researcher first reinforces the rat for going near the lever. Then, when the rat is approaching the lever reliably, the researcher waits until the rat touches the lever before delivering food. Eventually, the behavior of the rat is shaped by rewarding closer and closer approximations of the desired behavior until the rat is pressing the lever and being rewarded electronically.

Figure 2-2   A Skinner box for a rat. (Courtesy of Gerbrands Corporation, Arlington, Massachusetts 02174)

Schedules of Reinforcement

To maintain this behavior, it is not necessary to reward the rat with food every time it presses the lever. Animals will usually respond many times for one reinforcement, and in most operant research, this is the case. Reinforcement may be given after a specific number of responses or on the basis of time. The term *schedule of reinforcement* refers to the pattern that determines when reinforcements are to be given.

Each schedule of reinforcement engenders a characteristic pattern of responding that will be seen no matter what the species or organism or the type of reinforcer. These patterns are reliable and predictable, and they are sensitive to the effects of many drugs. Behavioral pharmacologists have found them a useful means of analyzing the behavioral effects of drugs because specific schedules are more sensitive to some drugs than others, and similar drugs affect schedule-controlled behavior in a similar manner.

Not only do schedules provide a powerful method for analyzing and classifying drugs, but the study of the effects of drugs on operant behavior is useful in other respects. It is believed that most human behavior, although very complex, is ultimately controlled by reinforcements, just as the behavior of the animal in a Skinner box is. It is believed that by carefully studying the effects of a drug on operant behavior, we can provide valuable information that will help us understand the effects of the drug on the behavior of humans.

Ratio Schedules. When reinforcement is based on the number of responses an animal makes, the schedule is known as a *ratio schedule*. On a *fixed ratio* (FR) schedule, the animal is required to make a fixed number of responses in order to be reinforced. For example, on an FR 30 schedule, every 30th response produces a reinforcement. If only 29 responses are made, the reinforcement is never given. A *variable ratio* (VR) schedule is similar except that the number of required responses varies randomly so that at any given time, the occurrence of a reinforced response cannot be predicted. A VR 30 schedule will produce a reinforcement every 30 responses, on the average.

Interval Schedules. On an *interval schedule*, an animal's responding is reinforced only if a period of time has elapsed since some event, such as a previous reinforcement. Responses that the animal makes during that time are recorded but do not influence the delivery of reinforcement. On a *fixed interval* (FI) schedule, a response is reinforced only after a fixed time has elapsed. A typical example might be an FI 3 schedule; the animal must wait 3 minutes after the delivery of a reinforcement for a response to be reinforced again. On a *variable interval* (VI) schedule, the interval is randomly determined. When a value is specified for a VI, such as VI 2, this indicates that the interval is an average of 2 minutes long.

Avoidance–Escape Task. Not only will animals learn to press a lever to obtain appetitive rewards like food, but they will also learn to avoid and escape from unpleasant stimuli such as electric shocks. On a typical avoidance–escape schedule, the animal is presented with a stimulus such as a buzzer or a light as a warning that a shock is coming. The warning comes several seconds before the shock, and if the animal makes a response during that time, the warning stimulus is turned off, and the shock never comes. If the animal does not respond, the shock comes on, and the animal can then escape from the shock by responding.

This type of task has proved to be a valuable tool in analyzing the effects of drugs. It has been found that drugs useful in treating anxiety in humans interfere with an animal's ability to avoid shock. These drugs block avoidance behavior during the signal but do not have any effect on the animal's ability to turn off or escape from the shock when it does come. This finding shows that the drug has not interfered with the ability of the animal to respond but has selectively blocked the motivation to avoid the shock.

Punishment. Responding that is maintained by appetitive rewards may be suppressed if it is also punished with electric shocks. This behavior is usually measured by having the animal respond on a VI schedule that produces a steady rate of responding. At various times during a session, a stimulus is turned on and lasts for a minute or two. During this stimulus, each response is followed by a shock. Responding during this stimulus will be suppressed. The frequency and intensity of the shock can be manipulated to produce a specific amount of suppression. Some varieties of drugs, such as barbiturates, increase the frequency of behavior that has been suppressed by punishment. Other drugs, such as amphetamine, lack this ability.

As with classical conditioning, a great deal of research has studied the effects of drugs on operant conditioning and schedules, but operant conditioning principles also play a role in understanding the effects of drugs—in particular, why and how organisms use drugs (see Chapter 5).

DISSOCIATION

Material learned while under the influence of a drug may not be easily recalled after the effects of the drug have worn off, and, conversely, information learned while drug free is not easily recalled when intoxicated. This phenomenon, known as *dissociation*, although recognized many years earlier, has been systematically investigated only since 1945.

The first account of dissociation appeared in 1830 in a British medical text. It was related by George Coombe, who stated that "before memory can exist, the organs require to be affected in the same manner, or be in a state analogous to that in which they were, when the impression was first received" (quoted in S. Siegel, 1982, pp. 257–258). As an example of this phenomenon, Coombe cited the case of an Irish porter who had lost track of a valuable parcel while drunk. Later, while sober, he was unable to remember anything about it. The next time he was intoxicated, however, he remembered exactly where he had put it.

Dissociation research often uses the following design. Experimental subjects are assigned to four groups, and they all learn a task on day 1

and are tested for recall on day 2. Group 1 gets a drug on both training and testing days, group 2 gets the drug during training but not during testing, group 3 gets no drug on training days and the drug during testing, and group 4 does not get the drug on either day. The design and results of this type of experiment are shown in Table 2-1. Typically, subjects in groups 1 and 4 on day 2 are able to recall the training they received on day 1, but the subjects in groups 2 and 3 have difficulty remembering what they learned on day 1 because of the change in drug state between these 2 days.

Dissociation has been demonstrated in a number of species, with many drugs, and using a variety of memory tests (Overton, 1972), and it may actually be a cause of much day-to-day forgetting. It has been shown that many drugs we consume regularly every day in moderate doses (e.g., in coffee, tobacco, and alcohol), especially when consumed together, can cause dissociation in a memory task that involved learning a route through a simple map (Lowe, 1988).

Dissociation may play a role in interpreting results of behavioral pharmacology experiments. Performance on a task may deteriorate when drugs are given or taken away. Such effects may be due not to an effect of the drug on the task but rather to a general effect of state change, that is, an inability to transfer learned information from one state (drugged) to another state (undrugged) or vice versa.

TABLE 2-1   The Design of a Typical Dissociation Experiment

On the training day, subjects are taught a task, and on the testing day, they are tested for recall of that task. For groups 1 and 4 the state does not change, but subjects in groups 2 and 3 are tested under drug states different from training. If the drug causes dissociation, subjects in groups 2 and 3 have difficulty remembering.

Group	Training Day	Testing Day	Result
1	Drug	Drug	Memory
2	Drug	Saline	No memory
3	Saline	Drug	No memory
4	Saline	Saline	Memory

It has been speculated that dissociation also may have an important influence on drug use because it means that much of what we learn about drug taking while we are not under the influence of the drug may not be easily remembered after we take the drug. An alcoholic, for example, may experience the adverse and punishing consequences of drinking while sober but may not remember these consequences while drunk. Drug education programs are always aimed at people while they are sober. Information acquired in this state may have little influence on a person after he or she takes a drug.

STIMULUS PROPERTIES OF DRUGS

Another method of analyzing the effects of drugs is by their *stimulus properties*, their ability to act as a discriminative stimulus in a discrimination learning task. In this type of task, a hungry animal, usually a rat, is given a choice of two levers to press. In some sessions lever A will be reinforced, and in other sessions lever B will be reinforced. The reinforcement is on an FR 20 schedule so that without a cue to guide it, the rat will not know which lever will produce the food until it has made at least 20 responses. In this situation, the only cue is the presence of a drug. On days when lever A is reinforced, the rat is injected with a drug, but on days when lever B is reinforced, it is injected with saline. After a short period of training, the rat will learn to discriminate between the drug and saline. On drug days, it will start off responding on lever A, and on saline days, it will start off on lever B. Thus, the first 20 responses on any given day will show whether the rat thinks it has been injected with the drug or saline.

Animals are capable of discriminating even low doses of most drugs, but this is not the most interesting aspect of drug state discrimination. We can do several things in this experiment that will tell us a great deal about the drug. One often-used test is to give the rat a different drug and see how it causes the rat to behave. If the rat makes the response usually made to the training drug, it is said to generalize to that drug, and this result tells us that the two drugs are perceived as similar by the rat. Usually, rats will generalize to drugs that are members of the same class. These responses can be helpful in screening new drugs.

Drug state discrimination studies are also useful in determining the biochemical mechanisms by which a drug produces its subjective effects. This is done primarily through the use of antagonist drugs. For example, it can be demonstrated that the stimulus properties of amphetamine can be blocked by the drug AMPT, which blocks the enzyme that creates the catecholamine neurotransmitters (see Chapter 4). This finding tells us that the subjective effects of amphetamine depend on catecholamines in the brain.

Similar techniques have been used in human research. Subjects are given two capsules and asked if they can tell which one contained a drug similar to a previously administered test drug.

DEVELOPMENT AND TESTING OF PSYCHOTHERAPEUTIC DRUGS

Before any new drug can be put on the market, it must undergo rigorous development and testing to prove that it is effective and safe. Only then will it be approved by governmental agencies for sale as a medicine. In the United States, approval is granted by the federal Food and Drug Administration (FDA). Other countries have similar agencies.

We do not understand the biochemical basis of mental illness well enough to specifically design drugs in the laboratory with any certainty that they will have a desired effect on psychiatric symptoms and will produce a minimum of side effects. Instead, the laboratories of pharmaceutical companies synthesize many new chemicals they think might be effective. These drugs are then screened using nonhumans to determine whether they have effects similar to those of known therapeutically useful drugs, and whether they are safe.

Screening tests, using laboratory animals, can determine whether a drug might have therapeutic properties (Leonard, 1989). It is known, for example, that drugs that are useful in treating anxiety or psychosis will block avoidance responding in doses that have no effect on escape responding. Drugs that are useful in treating depressive illness will block the depression in behavior caused by reserpine. In fact, many of the procedures described earlier in this chapter are used in the initial screening process of behaviorally active drugs.

As described in Chapter 1, toxicity of a drug is assessed by comparing the LD_{50} and the ED_{50} of the useful effect of the drug. The farther the lethal dose is from the effective dose—the higher the therapeutic index (see Chapter 1)—the safer the drug.

When a new drug appears to be reasonably safe and shows interesting behavioral properties in nonhumans, it goes to phase 1 of human testing, which assesses the toxicity and side effects of the drug on healthy human volunteers. In phase 2, the drug is tested on patients under very carefully supervised conditions. If phases 1 and 2 show that the drug has minimal toxic effects and also has a potential therapeutic effect, it then goes to phase 3, expanded clinical trials, which are usually carried out in university teaching hospitals and other institutions and often use the three-groups design discussed earlier. This research is usually carried out by a number of independent investigators under contract to pharmaceutical companies. In 2002 a problem with the reporting of clinical trials came to light. To test the significance of the difference between the treatment group and the placebo group, statistical tests are used. If the difference between the drug treatment group and the placebo group is so great that it would be expected less than 5 percent of the time, the treatment effect is considered meaningful. What this means is that if you repeat the trial 20 times, you would expect to see at least one significant result. If you publish that one trial without mentioning the 19 nonsignificant trials, it makes your drug look like it is effective when it is really not. To get around this problem, drug companies have agreed to register all clinical trials publicly before they are conducted and post the results even if they are negative so that everyone will know about them (see Box 2-2 for a description of how this came about).

If phase 3 investigations are successful, the drug is licensed and marketed. The research, however, does not stop here. Phase 4 involves the

BOX 2-2   Registration of Clinical Trials

It has been estimated that only half of the clinical trials that have been conducted over the past 56 years have ever been reported, and many that were reported did not appear on a searchable index like MEDLINE, so they cannot be easily found (Rennie, 2004). Does this really make a difference? Is it really important that all clinical trials, even those that show negative results, be made public? It certainly is not in the interest of the drug manufacturers if they do an experiment and find that a new drug is no more effective than a placebo. It is also not in the interest of researchers and medical journals to use up valuable page space to publish negative or equivocal data since these findings are not likely to change clinical practice or be cited by other authors. As a result, the studies that do get published have a persistent bias toward positive results.

There are some unfortunate consequences of this tendency for only positive findings to be publicly available, the most serious of which is that harmful effects turned up by these studies are never made public. Here is a recent example.

(Continued)

BOX 2-2

In 2003 and 2004, there was a serious debate as to whether children and adolescents with major depression could be safe and effectively treated with selective serotonin reuptake inhibitors (SSRIs). There was a concern that SSRIs might actually increase the incidence of suicide attempts in this age-group, but no data were available. The drug company that manufactured paroxitine (Paxil), GalaxoSmithKline (GSK), had done two clinical trials on young people in the 1990s that were unable to show that paroxitine was more effective than a placebo. But they were unwilling to share all the results of their clinical trials with other researchers and appeared to have deliberately suppressed making them public for "commercial" reasons (Rennie, 2004).

On June 2, 2004, the attorney general of the state of New York sued GSK saying that the child clinical trials and safety outcome data from other trials had been hidden by GSK and that they had "deprived physicians of the information needed to evaluate the risks and benefits of prescribing paroxitine to children and adolescents with MDD [major depressive disorder]" (Rennie, 2004, p. 1360).

On August 26, 2004, New York Attorney General Eliot Spitzer announced a settlement with GSK where they agreed to putting summaries of the results of all clinical drug trials into a register posted on the Internet with a conspicuous link from their Web site. To see this registry, go to http://ctr.gsk.co.uk/welcome.asp.

In addition, an organization of the publishers of many prestigious medical journals, including the *New England Journal of Medicine* and the *Journal of the American Medical Association* (JAMA), have adopted a new policy that they will not publish any clinical trial that has not been registered in a public registry before it was begun (De Angelis et al., 2004). This is to ensure that drug companies will not "cherry-pick" the best studies for publication and be able to hide studies that do not turn out to be favorable to their product.

accumulation of data on the success of the drug as used in the clinic. Attempts are made to identify adverse effects that were not apparent in the short-term testing during the early stages. In phase 4, improved dosing schedules may be developed, and individuals who are at risk of having adverse reactions to the drug can be identified (Baldessarini, 1985, p. 5).

CHAPTER SUMMARY

- Scientific experiments consist of an independent variable that is manipulated by a researcher and a dependent variable that is measured. In most experimental research in behavioral pharmacology, the independent variable is the presence of a drug

in the body, and the dependent variable is some aspect of behavior.

- Treatment of control subjects in an experiment should be as similar as possible to treatment of experimental subjects. For this reason, control subjects are usually given a placebo, an inactive substance administered in exactly the same way as the drug. This procedure controls for differences that result from the placebo effect.

- The placebo effect refers to the observation that when people expect a drug, they often show the effect of a drug even if they are administered only an ineffective substance.

- Experimental and control conditions may be administered to the same subjects on different occasions (within-subjects design) or to different subjects (between-subjects design).

- To determine whether the differences between experiment and control conditions mean anything, a statistical test is often used. Statistical tests tell the researcher how frequently there would be differences as large as in the experiment if the drug had no effect at all and all differences were due to chance alone.

- A double-blind procedure, where neither the researcher nor the experimental participant knows which group they are in, is used to eliminate the effect of experimenter bias.

- The three-groups design is used in testing new therapeutic drugs. In this design there is a drug group, a placebo group, and a group that receives an established treatment.

- In nonexperimental drug research, when relationships between two measured variables are found, one cannot assume the existence of any causal relationships between variables.

- Although the name *psychology* literally means "the study of the mind," modern psychology is the study of behavior. Introspection may be used as a source of data about drugs, but such data must be collected systematically and interpreted carefully.

- Level of arousal ranges from deep sleep to mild excitement but may extend into pathological states of mania and convulsions at the upper end and coma and death at the low end. Arousal level cannot be assumed to be related to either mood or general activity.

- The performance of the senses is determined by measuring their threshold. Cognitive performance is measured by tests of the ability to process, store, and retrieve information. Motor performance may be measured by simple or choice reaction time, tapping rate, hand steadiness, or pursuit rotor tests.

- Effects of drugs on unconditioned behavior of nonhumans can be measured by observing the amount of activity in an open field or using an inclined plane or an elevated plus maze. Analgesic effects can be measured as paw lick latency on a hot plate.

- Conditioned behavior may be respondent or operant. In respondent conditioning, involuntary reflexive behavior is brought under the control of a previously neutral stimulus. This is also known as classical, or Pavlovian, conditioning. In operant conditioning, voluntary behavior is brought under control by delivery of a contingent reinforcement.

- When reinforcement is not given for every response but is given according to some pattern, the pattern is called a schedule of reinforcement.

- Animals can be trained to avoid and escape a noxious stimulus such as an electric shock.

- Dissociation refers to the fact that information acquired in one drug state may not be readily available in another drug state.

- Animals can be trained to make one response after being given a drug and a different response after being given saline or a different drug. The responses of an animal trained to discriminate a drug can be a useful tool in testing the biochemical mechanisms responsible for the subjective effects of a drug.

- Therapeutic drugs are first screened for effect and safety using nonhumans. They then go through four phases of testing on humans.

3

Tolerance, Withdrawal, Sensitization, and Conditioning of Drug Effects

TOLERANCE

In the year 63 B.C., Mithradates VI, king of Pontus, tried to commit suicide by poisoning himself. Mithradates was a great leader and a great warrior; he had defeated the Roman legions and spread his influence over Asia Minor. But in 63 B.C., he had been defeated by the Roman general Pompey, and his son had just led a successful revolt against him. To end it all, the king took a large dose of poison, but it had no effect on him. He was finally forced to have one of his Gallic mercenaries dispatch him.

What was the source of the king's resistance to poison? King Mithradates was also a good pharmacologist. Throughout his life, he lived in great fear of being poisoned, so, to protect himself, he repeatedly took increasing doses of poison until he could tolerate large amounts without ill effects. This effect has been called *mithradatism* (Lankester, 1889) after the king; today, we know it as *tolerance*. Mithradatism was also practiced by other historical figures, including Vespasia, the mother of the Roman emperor Nero, and the infamous Lucretia Borgia.

Drug tolerance is defined either as the decreased effectiveness (or potency) of a drug that results from repeated administrations or as the necessity of increasing the dose of a drug in order to maintain its effectiveness after repeated administrations. The term *tolerance* is frequently used in a way that suggests that all the effects of a drug diminish at the same rate, but this is usually not the case. Some effects of a drug may develop tolerance very quickly, some other effects may only show tolerance slowly, and some effects may never show tolerance, no matter how often the drug is given. Among the effects of morphine, for example, are nausea and vomiting. These effects show rapid tolerance, but the ability of morphine to constrict the pupils of the eyes shows no tolerance at all, no matter how long the drug is taken. Because tolerance to different effects of a drug develops at different rates, it is apparent that many mechanisms must be responsible for tolerance (Young & Goudie, 1995). For this reason, it is more appropriate to think of tolerance developing to the effect of a drug rather than to the drug itself (J. Stewart & Badiani, 1993).

When tolerance develops, it does not last indefinitely. Tolerance may disappear with the passage of time, after the use of a drug has been discontinued.

As with the development of tolerance, the disappearance of different drug effects may take place at different rates and may depend on the circumstances in which it is administered.

Tolerance to one drug may well diminish the effect of another drug. This phenomenon, called *cross-tolerance*, is usually seen between members of the same class of drugs. All opiate drugs, for example, will show cross-tolerance. Cross-tolerance is sometimes taken as evidence that the drugs may be producing their effect by common mechanisms.

It is usually assumed that a drug must be given repeatedly before tolerance can occur, but some effects of some drugs may show tolerance after only one or two administrations. This type of tolerance is known as *tachyphylaxis*. It is also possible to demonstrate that tolerance may develop during a single administration of a drug. As we have seen in Chapter 1, after a drug is taken into the body, the level of the drug in the blood rises and then falls. With some drugs, it has been shown that their effect is greater at a specific blood level soon after administration, when the level is rising, than at that same point later, when the level of the drug is falling. This indication that tolerance developed during a single administration is called *acute tolerance*. A good example of acute tolerance is given in Chapter 6.

MECHANISMS OF TOLERANCE

Metabolic Tolerance

Metabolic tolerance (also called *dispositional tolerance*) arises from an increase in the rate at which the body is able to metabolize and get rid of a drug. For the most part, this is a result of enzyme induction, an increase in the level of the enzyme the body uses to destroy the drug (see Chapter 1). When a drug is given repeatedly, it may induce or increase the action of the enzyme the body uses to destroy it. With increases in the rate of metabolism, a given amount of a drug will not reach the same peak levels and will not last as long, so that more and more of the drug will be needed to

produce the same effect. When metabolic tolerance takes place, all effects of the drug will be diminished because of the diminished concentration of the drug at the site of action.

Physiological Tolerance

Physiological tolerance is also known as *cellular* or *pharmacodynamic* tolerance. These terms generally describe a type of tolerance that arises from adjustments made by the body to compensate for an effect of the continued presence of a drug. It is generally believed that such adjustments are a result of a process called *homeostasis*. Many of the body's physiological processes are controlled by feedback loops, in much the same way that a thermostat controls the temperature in a room. The thermostat is set to a specific temperature, called a *set point*. It detects the temperature, and when the temperature falls below the set point, it turns the heat on. When the room temperature rises to the set point, it turns the heat off again, thus maintaining an even temperature. Homeostasis provides a flexible system for maintaining a set point in circumstances in which environmental conditions change. For example, if someone were to leave a window open on a cold day, the thermostat would keep the heat on longer in an attempt to maintain the temperature at the set point.

Homeostatic processes work inside the body. They control nearly all the body's operations so that when a drug is taken and it alters some aspect of the body's functioning, the body's response is controlled by a homeostatic mechanism. The disruption or disturbance created by the drug is detected, and this information is sent to the mechanism that controls the disrupted function. The control center responds by compensating for the effect of the drug and restoring normal functioning; that is, it returns the function to its set point. If the drug is repeatedly administered, the body gets better and better at restoring normal function and diminishing the disruptive effect of the drug. This means that the drug will have a smaller and smaller effect the more it is administered. Some of these compensatory processes kick in quickly, but others take longer to develop. Thus, tolerance may appear rapidly to some drug effects and very slowly to others.

When drug administration is stopped and the drug's disruptive effect is removed, the compensatory process is discontinued because it is no longer needed. Again, some compensatory effects may disappear rapidly, but others may go away slowly. Weeks or months may be required for normal functioning to return.

General or Nonspecific Tolerance. To compensate for the effect of a drug, the body may use a variety of physiological mechanisms. Entire physiological systems may be involved, or the compensation may take place at the level of a single cell. For example, if a drug blocks a receptor at a synapse, the body might attempt to compensate for the blockage by creating more receptors so that the transmitter at the synapse can be restored to normal functioning. It might also cause more transmitters to be released from the presynaptic neuron to help overcome the blockage (Nutt, 1997) (see Chapter 4). These changes in sensitivity that take place at the drug's site of action are equivalent to metabolic tolerance because when they occur, all other effects of the drug are diminished to the same extent and may be thought of as *general* or *nonspecific* tolerance.

Specific Tolerance. Physiological adaptations may also take place in any other system in the body that the drug disrupts either directly or indirectly and may be mediated by any number of diverse compensatory mechanisms. If a drug lowers body temperature, for example, the body may use a number of different mechanisms to raise body temperature. These could include altering the metabolic rate or changing the rate of heat loss through the skin by decreasing blood flow to the skin. Because this tolerance is specific to a particular drug effect, it may develop independently of other tolerance mechanisms that may be taking place at the same time and may develop or disappear at different rates.

Functional Disturbances

Constantine Poulos and Howard Cappell (1991), at the Addiction Research Foundation of Toronto, have pointed out that one implication of homeostatic theory is that tolerance will develop only when a drug effect causes a disruption in homeostasis and the disruption is of some significance to the organism. For example, we know that (a) amphetamine causes *anorexia* (loss of appetite) in rats and that (b) this effect will show tolerance when the drug is repeatedly administered to hungry rats in the presence of food. Tolerance to anorexia, however, will not develop if the amphetamine is given repeatedly to rats after they have been fed or given to hungry rats when there is no food available to eat. In other words, no tolerance to the anorexic effect of amphetamine will develop in rats that are not interested in eating or do not have the opportunity to eat at the time they receive the drug. The anorexic effect of the drug does not have a chance to interfere with the functioning of the organism, and there is no feedback to the feeding control mechanism. Similarly, tolerance to the *hypothermic* (body-cooling) effect of alcohol does not develop in rats in a very warm environment, where alcohol does not have a hypothermic effect, and tolerance to the *analgesic* (pain-relieving) effect of morphine develops faster in rats that are subjected to painful stimuli after being given the drug (Poulos & Cappell, 1991). In other words, tolerance will develop (or will develop much faster) only in a circumstance where a drug places a demand on an organism's homeostatic mechanisms. Tolerance to drug effects that are not detected or that do not disrupt functioning does not develop.

Behavioral Tolerance

It has often been demonstrated that tolerance can be influenced by learning and conditioning processes. In other words, through experience with a drug, an organism can learn to decrease the effect that the drug is having. This is called *behavioral tolerance*. This learning, which can involve both instrumental and respondent conditioning processes, is extensively discussed later in this chapter. For now, it is necessary to have a good understanding of how certain types of drug effects become conditioned to environmental stimuli.

WITHDRAWAL SYMPTOMS AND PHYSICAL DEPENDENCE

Withdrawal symptoms are physiological changes that occur when the use of a drug is stopped or the dosage is decreased. Different drugs produce different withdrawal symptoms, but drugs of the same family generally produce similar withdrawal. Withdrawal can be stopped almost instantly by giving the drug that has been discontinued. Often another drug of the same family will also stop withdrawal. This phenomenon is known as *cross dependence*.

Withdrawal usually begins some hours after the use of a drug has been stopped, but it can be produced much more quickly by giving an antagonist drug. Naloxone, a powerful antagonist to morphine, rapidly blocks all morphine effects soon after it is given. When naloxone is given to morphine-dependent humans or nonhumans, severe withdrawal can be seen in minutes.

Probably no word in the field of drug research causes more misunderstanding or has been abused more than *dependence*. It is generally used in two ways: (a) to describe a state in which discontinuation of a drug causes withdrawal symptoms and (b) to describe a state in which a person compulsively takes a drug.

At one point, it was believed that the two states were exactly the same. It was assumed that if you took a drug to the point that withdrawal symptoms would occur when you stopped, you were "dependent," and you would then be driven to seek out and consume the drug in a compulsive manner in order to avoid withdrawal. We now know that this assumption is not correct, but the word *dependence* is still used incorrectly as an explanation for drug abuse. This aspect of dependence will be discussed in more detail in Chapter 5.

More recently, it has been recognized that people will compulsively use drugs that do not cause unpleasant withdrawal symptoms. The term *psychological dependence* is sometimes used to describe this, and the terms *physical dependence* and *physiological dependence* are used to refer only to the state in which withdrawal symptoms occur if the use of a drug is discontinued. This text uses the terms *dependence, physical dependence*, and *physiological dependence* interchangeably to indicate a state in which withdrawal symptoms will occur. Psychological dependence is discussed more thoroughly in Chapter 5.

Tolerance and dependence are believed to be closely related. Withdrawal symptoms are usually thought of as expressions of the adjustment that the body has made to a drug. As described earlier, with repeated administration of a drug, the body changes its functioning and uses homeostatic feedback to compensate for the physiological changes the drug produces. Later, when the drug is discontinued and its effects disappear, it takes some time for the body to readjust to its absence. This readjustment is expressed in the form of withdrawal symptoms. For this reason, the physiological changes seen in withdrawal are usually opposite to the effects of the drug. For example, constipation is one of the more marked effects of heroin use, and one of the major symptoms of withdrawal from heroin is diarrhea.

This sort of idea was first formulated by Solomon and Corbit (1974), who were proposing a theory of addiction and were interested in the *hedonic*, or pleasurable, effects of drugs as an explanation of their use. They hypothesized that drugs of abuse create a highly pleasurable state by a mechanism they called the *A process*. A short time after the A process is initiated by taking the drug, a compensatory unpleasant state is created. They called this the *B process*. Because the state created by the A process is pleasurable and the state created by the B process is unpleasant, they tend to cancel each other. This explains tolerance to drug-induced pleasure. Because the B state lasts longer than the A state, there is a period after the A process ends when the B state dominates, and this causes unpleasant symptoms that we experience as withdrawal. This process is described in Figure 3-1.

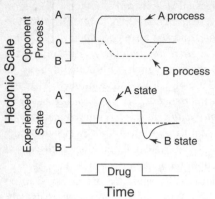

Figure 3-1 The upper panel shows the drug effect on the A process and the opposing B process separately. After the drug is given, the A process increases, but shortly after that, the opposite B process begins. When the drug wears off, the A process diminishes, but the B process continues for a while before disappearing. The lower panel shows the result of combining the A and the B effect. It shows that the A effect will be strongest right after the drug is taken and then diminish. This decreased effect is what would be called acute tolerance. The B effect dominates after the drug has worn off. The B effect would be experienced as a hangover or withdrawal effect. Solomon and Corbit originally proposed this mechanism to explain changes in pleasure (hedonic state) caused by a drug, but the idea can be used to explain many drug effects. Adapted from Solomon and Corbit (1974).

Although Solomon and Corbit's theory was formulated to explain hedonic states created by drugs, it can be applied to understanding any effect of a drug where the A state is any drug effect and the B state is an opposite, compensatory effect.

Hangover. Hangover is a term that is used in different ways. It usually refers to the aftermath of the acute effects of a drug, such as when you go out drinking at night and then feel sick the next day. Often a hangover can be thought of as brief withdrawal symptoms that arise from acute tolerance. Thus, when you take a drug, its effect increases as the blood level increases, but often the effect diminishes faster than the level of the drug in the blood (acute tolerance). This decrease is due to the development of acute tolerance as described earlier. Solomon and Corbit developed the model to describe long-term use of a drug, so that the period of drug administration in the diagram might correspond to a period of weeks or months of continuous use, and the B state at the end of drug use would be unpleasant withdrawal. The process works just as well to describe a single drug administration where the B state as the drug wears off, would be a hangover.

An example of the effect described by Solomon and Corbit within a single administration of the tranquilizer chlordiazepoxide is shown in Box 3-1, where the A process is the tranquilizing

(*anxyolytic*, or *anxiety-relieving*) effect of the drug chlordiazepoxide and the B process is the opposite: anxiety.

If withdrawal and hangover are expressions of compensatory effects that cause tolerance to drugs, you might expect there to be a strong correlation between tolerance and withdrawal symptoms. There is not; it is not unusual for a person to show considerable tolerance to the effects of a drug but to have no withdrawal symptoms when the drug is discontinued. Alcohol is a good example. Many longtime drinkers have a considerable tolerance for some of the effects of alcohol but do not show any signs of physical dependence. There are a number of reasons why this could be so. To begin with, there maybe some tolerance, like behavioral tolerance, that is not created by a physiological compensatory effect, and so there would be no physiological withdrawal. In addition, withdrawal symptoms may not be experienced if the rate of elimination of the drug from the body is very slow, as with THC, the active ingredient in marijuana (see Chapter 15). With slow elimination, the body may be able to "readjust" at the pace of the drug's elimination, and withdrawal symptoms may not be expressed.

Withdrawal symptoms may vary in intensity from one drug to another. With some drugs, withdrawal symptoms may be so slight that they can be detected only by using sensitive instruments, and the individual might not notice them. With other

Using a two-lever, drug discrimination procedure, Barrett and Smith (2005) of Vanderbilt University in Nashville, Tennessee, trained rats to discriminate between a dose of chlordiazepoxide (CDP) and a dose of pentylenetetrazol (PTZ). Chlordiazepoxide is a benzodiazepine tranquilizer that relieves anxiety and has a calming effect (it is an anxiolytic). It works by enhancing the effect of the inhibitory transmitter GABA. Pentylenetetrazol has exactly the opposite effect; it reduces the effects of GABA and causes tension and anxiety (it is an anxiogenic) (see Chapter 7). Barrett and Smith trained their rats to press one lever after being injected with CDP, that is, when they were calm and relaxed, and the second lever after being injected with PTZ, that is, when they were tense and anxious. After being given saline, the rats distributed their responding equally between the two levers.

They then gave their rats an injection of chlordiazepoxide and tested them in the two-lever apparatus at various times after the injection. As can be seen in the diagram below, 8 hours after the CDP injection, rats made 90 percent of their responses in the CDP lever, but by 16 hours after the injection, they made most of their responses on the PTZ lever. Responding slowly returned to the 50 percent level over the next few hours.

What appeared to be happening was that 8 hours after the CDP injection, the rats still felt calm and relaxed and responded on the CDP lever, but all this time, a compensatory response had been developing that was opposite to the CDP effect. After the drug had left the system, the

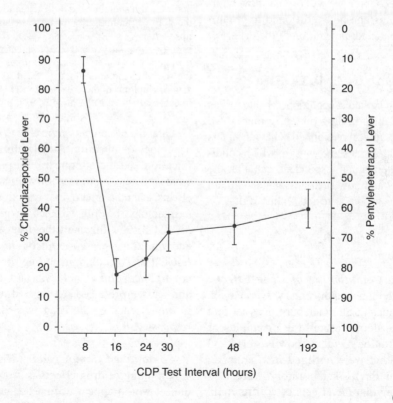

(Continued)

BOX 3-1

compensatory response remained. This made the rats anxious and tense, a feeling like that produced by PTZ, so they pressed the PTZ lever at the 16-hour test. Eventually, this compensatory response diminished, and by 48 hours the rats returned to drug-free response levels, 50 percent on each lever.

It is this sort of process that seems to be responsible for hangovers to many drugs and makes it so that drugs, after they have worn off, sometimes have an effect opposite to their normal effect.

This experiment illustrates the Solomon and Corbit theory described in the text. The A process is the tranquilizing effect of the CDP, and the B process is compensatory anxiety. Compare the lower panel of Figure 3-1 with this Figure.

---

drugs, withdrawal can be so severe as to cause death. The extent of withdrawal may also depend on the dose and administration schedule of the drug. Drugs that are taken intermittently may cause hangover each time they are taken but are unlikely to create withdrawal when their use is discontinued.

Later in this chapter, we will discuss how withdrawal symptoms can be conditioned to stimuli associated with the administration of the drug.

TOLERANCE AND CONDITIONING

In Chapter 2, we looked at conditioned behaviors as dependent variables in drug research; that is, we asked how drugs affect conditioned behavior. In this section, we will look at some ways in which conditioning, both operant and respondent, can alter the effects of drugs and how such effects can explain phenomena such as tolerance and withdrawal.

Behavioral Tolerance Based on Respondent Conditioning

Respondent Conditioning of Drug Effects. At the end of the nineteenth century, Ivan Pavlov and his colleagues in St. Petersburg, Russia, first discovered and demonstrated the principles of respondent conditioning (also known as classical conditioning) that were outlined in Chapter 2. Researchers in Pavlov's laboratory were also the first to show that the effects of a drug could be conditioned to neutral stimuli present at the

time the drug was having its effect. One of these experiments was conducted in the following manner:

A dog was given a small dose of apomorphine subcutaneously and after one to two minutes a note of definite pitch was sounded during a considerable time. While the note was still sounding the drug began to take effect upon the dog: the animal grew restless, began to moisten its lips with its tongue, secreted saliva and showed some disposition to vomit. After the experimenter had reinforced the tone with apomorphine several times it was found that the sound of the note alone sufficed to produce all the active symptoms of the drug, only in a less degree [experiments by Podkopaev]. (Pavlov, 1927, p. 35)

Later the researchers were able to show that after a number of injections, the preliminaries to the injection and the administration procedure itself were sufficient to produce salivation and other drug effects, even though no drug was given. In Pavlov's terminology, the drug was the *unconditioned stimulus* (UCS); the effects of the drug—the salivation and vomiting—were the *unconditioned response* (UCR); the stimulus preceding the drug was the *conditioned stimulus* (CS); and the salivation and nausea produced by these stimuli presented in the absence of the drug was the *conditioned response* (CR).

Conditioned Compensatory Responses. The conditioning of drug effects is more complicated than it would appear at first because the unconditioned response and the conditioned response to the drug are not always the same. Sometimes the stimuli paired with a drug (the conditioned stimulus), when presented in the absence of the drug, produce a physiological response (conditioned response) opposite to that produced by the drug (the unconditioned response). For example, it has been shown in rats that an unconditioned response to morphine is analgesia (a decreased responsiveness to painful stimuli), whereas the conditioned response to stimuli repeatedly paired with morphine injections is *hyperalgesia* (an increased sensitivity to pain). The reasons for this are complex but can be understood if you realize that what is being conditioned is often not the effect of the drug itself but the body's attempt to resist the effect of the drug (Eikelboom & Stewart, 1982).

Earlier it was shown that the body resists drug-induced changes by making adjustments or compensatory changes in its physiology in an attempt to restore normal functioning. These compensations make the body less susceptible to the drug when it is given later, and they are responsible for tolerance. It appears that in many cases, these compensatory responses, not the initial effects of the drug, become conditioned to stimuli that are repeatedly paired with the administration of the drug. Because the compensatory response is in a direction opposite to that of the drug alone, the conditioned drug effect will also be opposite to the initial drug effect.

It is important to understand the nature of conditioned drug effects because they play an important role in how the effects of a drug are expressed when the drug is administered later. An example is conditioned drug tolerance.

Conditioned Drug Tolerance. Early research into tolerance and the development of conditioned compensatory responses to drugs was conducted at McMaster University by Shepard Siegel and his colleagues. Siegel investigated the development of tolerance to the analgesic effect of morphine. To test analgesia, he placed rats on a metal plate that was heated to 54 degrees Celsius. After a few seconds on this plate, rats normally lift a hind paw to their mouth as if they are licking it. This test is known as the *paw lick test*, and the measure of analgesia is the latency or the length of time the rat waits before licking (see Chapter 2). After an injection of morphine, the paw lick latency increases, indicating that the morphine has reduced the animal's sensitivity to pain. With repeated trials, the latency tends to get shorter and shorter as tolerance to the morphine develops (S. Siegel, 1975).

In his experiment, Siegel was able to demonstrate that rats would show tolerance to the analgesic effects of morphine only if they were given the paw lick test in the same room where repeated morphine injections had been experienced earlier. If they were given morphine in the colony room where they were normally housed and were tested in a different room, the animals had long latencies similar to those of animals that had never been given morphine. The tolerance to morphine was dependent on the environment in which the drug had been experienced.

To explain this effect, Siegel proposed that the environment repeatedly associated with the drug acts like a conditioned stimulus, but rather than becoming a conditioned stimulus for the effect the drug is having, it becomes a conditioned stimulus for the physiological changes the body is making to compensate for the effect the drug is having. Thus, the environment associated with the administration of the drug elicits physiological responses opposite to the effect of the drug. These changes help prepare the rat for the drug and diminish its effect; that is, they cause tolerance.

In support of his theory, Siegel was able to show that if he injected a rat with saline and gave it the paw lick test in an environment that had previously been associated with repeated injections of morphine, their latencies would get shorter than normal, that is, the animal would show *hyperalgesia* (an increased sensitivity to pain). This was the compensatory response that had been produced by the morphine environment through conditioning.

Box 3-2 gives an example of how this type of tolerance can protect humans and nonhumans from a heroin overdose.

BOX 3-2   The Mystery of Heroin Overdose

One of the greatest risks of being a heroin addict is death from heroin overdose. Each year about 1 percent of all heroin addicts in the United States die from an overdose of heroin despite having developed a fantastic tolerance to the effects of the drug. In a nontolerant person, the estimated lethal dose of heroin may range from 200 to 500 mg, but addicts have tolerated doses as high as 1,800 mg without even being sick (Brecher & the Editors of *Consumer Reports*, 1972). No doubt, some overdoses are a result of mixing heroin with other drugs, but many appear to result from a sudden loss of tolerance. Addicts have been killed by a dose that was readily tolerated the day before. An explanation for this sudden loss of tolerance has been suggested by Shepard Siegel of McMaster University and his associates Rily Hinson, Marvin Krank, and Jane McCully.

Siegel reasoned that tolerance to heroin was partly conditioned to the environment where the drug was normally administered. If the drug is consumed in a new setting, much of the conditioned tolerance disappears, and the addict is more likely to overdose. To test this theory, S. Siegel and his associates (1982) ran the following experiment. Rats were given daily intravenous injections for 30 days. The injections, either a dextrose placebo or heroin, were given in either the animal colony room or a different room where there was constant white noise. The drug and the placebo were given on alternate days, and the drug condition always corresponded with a particular environment so that some rats always received the heroin in the white-noise room and the placebo in the colony. For other rats, the heroin was always given in the colony, and the placebo was always given in the white-noise room. Another group of rats served as a control. They were injected in different rooms on alternate days but were injected only with dextrose and had no experience with heroin.

All rats were then injected with a large dose of heroin: 15 mg/kg. The rats in one group, labeled the ST group, were given the heroin in the same room where they had previously been given heroin. The other rats, the DT group, were given the heroin in the room where they had previously been given the placebo.

Siegel found that 96 percent of the control group died, showing the lethal effect of heroin on nontolerant animals. Rats in the DT group that received heroin were partly tolerant; 64 percent died. Only 32 percent of the ST rats died, showing that their tolerance was greater when the overdose test was done in the same environment where the drug had previously been administered.

Siegel suggested one reason for addicts' suddenly losing their tolerance: They take the drug in a different or unusual environment, like the rats in the DT group. Surveys of heroin addicts admitted to hospitals and diagnosed as suffering from heroin overdose tend to support this conclusion. Many addicts reported that they had taken the near-fatal dose in an unusual circumstance or that their normal pattern was different on that day (S. Siegel et al., 1982).

Conditioned Compensatory Responses and Withdrawal. Besides explaining some tolerance, learning processes may be responsible for some withdrawal symptoms. We have seen how compensatory responses may be conditioned to a particular environment where the drug is repeatedly given. Later, if an animal is placed in that environment without the drug, it will show conditioned compensatory responses—physiological changes opposite to the drug's effect. When they occur in the absence of the drug, they are withdrawal symptoms, as described earlier in this chapter; therefore, some aspects of withdrawal can be conditioned and may be evoked by specific stimuli previously associated with the use of the drug (S. Siegel, 1983). For example, former heroin addicts who have gone through withdrawal just after they stop using a drug will frequently experience withdrawal symptoms again when they return to places where they have experienced the effects of the drug. As the following example illustrates, there can be little doubt that these conditioned withdrawal symptoms play an important part in relapse to drug use in postdependent addicts:

The patient was a 28-year-old man with a ten-year history of narcotic addiction. He was married and the father of two children. He reported that, while he was addicted, he was arrested and incarcerated for six months. He reported experiencing severe withdrawal during the first four or five days in custody, but later he began to feel well. He gained weight, felt like a new man, and decided that he was finished with drugs. He thought about his children and looked forward to returning to his former job. On the way home after his release from prison, he began thinking of drugs and feeling nauseated. As the subway approached his stop, he began sweating, tearing from his eyes, and gagging. This was an area where he had frequently experienced narcotic withdrawal symptoms while trying to acquire drugs. As he got off the subway he vomited onto the tracks. He soon bought drugs and was relieved.
The following day he again experienced craving and withdrawal symptoms in his neighborhood, and he again relieved the symptoms by injecting heroin. The cycle repeated itself over the next few days and soon he became readdicted. (O'Brien, 1976, p. 533)

The addict's eyes teared, and he began sweating when he came into the subway station, where he had previously acquired drugs. It is likely that his body was preparing itself for an injection of heroin, which it had become conditioned to expect in that environment.

This example shows that conditioned withdrawal symptoms do not disappear when the body makes its initial readjustment to the absence of a drug. Conditioned withdrawal symptoms will go away only through the process of extinction, that is, the presentation of the stimuli when they are not followed by the drug.

Behavioral Tolerance Based on Operant Conditioning

An early experiment in this area was done by Judith Campbell and Lewis Seiden (1973) at the University of Chicago. They trained rats to respond for food reinforcement in a Skinner box on a *differential reinforcement of low rates* (DRL) schedule. On a DRL schedule, the animal is reinforced only if it waits for a fixed period of time between responses. In other words, it is reinforced for responding at a low rate. When amphetamine is given, it stimulates responding, and the rat loses reinforcements because it cannot wait long enough between responses.

For 28 sessions, Campbell and Seiden gave amphetamine to one group of rats immediately before placing them in a Skinner box where they were reinforced on a DRL schedule. Another group of rats was given the same number of injections and the same number of sessions on the DRL schedule, but the amphetamine was given after the DRL trials. Over the period of the experiment, the amphetamine-pretreated rats developed tolerance and were able to obtain more and more reinforcements, but when the other rats were tested on the DRL with amphetamine, they performed as though they had never received the drug; they had no tolerance. If the tolerance shown by the first group had been the result of metabolic or physiological changes that develop in response to the presentation of the drug alone, it should have shown up in both groups because both groups received the same exposures to the amphetamine.

Campbell and Seiden concluded that the difference had only one explanation: The rats had learned to alter their behavior to compensate for the change that the amphetamine caused. This interpretation was supported by the observation that no tolerance develops to the rate-increasing effect of amphetamine on fixed interval (FI) responding (Schuster, Dockens, & Woods, 1966). Increased responding on the FI does not cause the rat to lose reinforcements, whereas it does on the DRL schedule. Thus, it appeared that the rats had developed a particular strategy for overcoming the effect of the amphetamine on DRL. This strategy was learned because it was reinforced by an increase in food presentations.

A similar hypothesis was tested by Muriel Vogel-Sprott (1992) and her colleagues at the University of Waterloo, who have done considerable research on the development of behavioral tolerance to the effects of alcohol on humans. They used a different technique. They reasoned that if tolerance was a result of learning strategies to compensate for the effect of a drug, then the development of tolerance should depend on the occurrence of a reinforcement when a compensatory response is made.

In her experiments, human subjects are trained on a cognitive or motor task such as the pursuit rotor until their performance is stable. Then they are given alcohol for a number of sessions, and this interferes with their performance. Typically, Vogel-Sprott has one group of subjects who are told that they will be given a 25-cent reward immediately after each trial in which they are able to resist the disruptive effects of alcohol and perform in their normal, drug-free range. A second group of subjects is also given a 25-cent reward for each such trial, but the money is saved up and given at the end of the session, and no information is given about which trials were in the drug-free range. A third group is not given any information or money.

Vogel-Sprott has repeated this experiment many times and always finds that subjects given information or feedback about their performance,

whether they are given money or not, always develop tolerance rapidly, and the other groups develop tolerance slowly, if at all (Vogel-Sprott, 1992). It seems that in her experiments, the subjects' knowledge that they are resisting the effects of alcohol is sufficient reinforcement for learning to resist the effects of the alcohol.

The Campbell and Seiden and the Vogel-Sprott studies can be understood in terms of homeostatic theory. In the Campbell and Seiden study, the disruptive effects of the amphetamine caused a loss of reinforcements; consequently, the drug effect had functional significance for the rat. As a result, a homeostatic mechanism kicked in, and a compensatory response was acquired that permitted the animal to respond more slowly and receive more food. No compensatory response developed to the FI responding because the effect of the drug (an increased response rate) did not cause the animal to lose reinforcements and had no biological significance. Similarly, in the Vogel-Sprott experiment, the effect of the alcohol on the pursuit rotor task had no significance for the subjects in the control group, who were not informed that the alcohol was having an effect. The subjects in the experimental group who were paid for good performance, however, found that the disruptive effect of the alcohol had significance for them, and so tolerance developed. Box 3-3 gives an example of how tolerance to alcohol could have played a role in the crash that killed Princess Diana.

BOX 3-3   Did Alcohol Kill Princess Diana?

On August 31, 1997, the world was shocked to learn that Britain's Princess Diana was killed in a car crash in a tunnel in Paris. The reasons for the deadly crash have never been clearly established, but a contributing factor could have been that Henri Paul, the driver of the princess's car, had a blood alcohol level of 175 mg/100 ml of blood—three times the legal limit. Under other circumstances, an accident like this might have been clearly blamed on the intoxicated state of the driver, but the blame is not so readily placed in this case. Diana's car was speeding in an attempt to avoid photographers who were chasing it in other cars and on motorcycles. Reports of witnesses say that Henri Paul "seemed fine" when he took the wheel that night. In fact, videotapes from security cameras in Diana's hotel show Henri Paul walking quite normally, carrying on conversations, and showing no signs of intoxication.

What we know about the development of tolerance to drugs might explain why Henri Paul could "seem fine" and still have such a high level of alcohol in his blood.

Given the reports that Henri Paul had a history of heavy drinking, it is likely that he had developed a considerable tolerance to many of the direct effects that alcohol had on his nervous system (physiological tolerance). In addition, on that day, he had not expected to be called back to work, and he seems to have started drinking early in the morning. He probably had been drinking continuously for an extended period of time. Under these circumstances, extensive acute tolerance has a chance to develop. It may not be surprising, then, that Henri was able to show normal behavior even though his blood alcohol level was excessive.

If Henri Paul was that tolerant, could alcohol have played a role in the accident?

It seems so. To begin with, we know that tolerance does not develop to all the effects of a drug at the same time, and it is possible to be tolerant to some effects of a drug and not others. All we know is that Henri Paul was able to walk and talk normally. On the basis of the work of Vogel-Sprott, we know that tolerance to an effect of alcohol develops if the individual is provided with feedback on the effect of alcohol and is reinforced for making a compensatory response to overcome alcohol's effect. Walking and talking are behaviors that most people who drink regularly are able to practice under the influence of alcohol; very often those behaviors are rewarded with social approval. Because Henri Paul was a professional driver, it would have been disastrous for him to exhibit any effects of alcohol intoxication before driving. Therefore, walking and talking were likely to be the first behaviors restored by both acute and chronic tolerance.

The effects of alcohol on driving might also be subject to learning compensatory strategies that cause tolerance. Indeed, in Vogel-Sprott's laboratory, research on a driving simulator shows such an effect. Diana's driver might possibly have been able to drive safely under normal driving conditions. In fact, he may have done so many times. But it is unlikely that Henri Paul had had a chance, while intoxicated, to practice the skills required to race through a tunnel at high speed in an effort to elude photographers. Such skills may not have had a chance to develop, regardless of his tolerance to all other effects of alcohol.

That fateful night, alcohol may have had a big effect on Henri Paul, but because of his tolerance to some effects, no one, not even Henri Paul himself, was able to detect the debilitating effect. In fact, under most circumstances, it would have gone undetected.

Driving is a complex task requiring many different cognitive and motor skills. In addition, the demands that will be made on a driver on any particular trip cannot be predicted. A person may be able to drive a car safely at a given blood alcohol level, provided that nothing unusual happens. But a driver can never know what demands will be made and whether alcohol, even at a low dose, will be responsible for an accident.

SENSITIZATION

Most of the time, when a drug is repeatedly administered, tolerance to the many effects of the drug develops. In some circumstances, however, an effect of a drug can increase with repeated administrations. This is known as *sensitization* or *reverse tolerance*.

Sensitization is much less common than tolerance, and much less is known about it. Most of what we know about sensitization comes from studies of the activating effects of a variety of drugs, including cocaine, amphetamine, nicotine, alcohol, phencyclidine, and opiates such as morphine. At low doses, all these drugs produce an activating effect when first given to laboratory animals. This effect is characterized by increased motor activity and rearing behavior in rats. At high doses, *stereotyped behaviours* are seen. Stereotyped behaviors are repetitive movements, such as head bobbing and sniffing, that are engaged in for extended periods of time. When repeated low doses are given, there is a progressive increase in activation with each administration. Repeated administration of higher doses will eventually cause stereotyped behavior where only activation was caused by the initial dose (T. E. Robinson & Berridge, 1993, p. 256).

Like tolerance, this sensitization may also be conditioned to a particular environment (J. Stewart & Badiani, 1993). This has been demonstrated in two different ways. First, it has been shown that, as with tolerance, if sensitization is created by repeatedly administering the drug in a specific environment, then sensitization will be greatly diminished or will not appear at all when the drug is given in a different environment. Second, if sensitization results from repeated injections in a specific environment, then that environment will act as a conditioned stimulus for a drug-like conditioned response. In other words, if you place an animal in the environment after a placebo injection, it will show increased activity—the same response that the drug causes (T. E. Robinson & Berridge, 1993, p. 259; P. B. Silverman & Bonate, 1997, p. 124). In this regard, sensitization appears to be a mirror image of tolerance, except that the conditioned response is a drug-like response rather than a drug-opposite response. When the drug-like conditioned response (activation) is elicited in conjunction with the drug effect (also activation), t   is an enhanced drug effect.

 some circumstances, sensitization may also roduced by operant conditioning processes. saw that Vogel-Sprott was able to cause toler- to the disruptive effect of alcohol by paying ects to resist the effects of alcohol on a motor . She was also able to increase the effects of ohol by giving subjects money when their per- mance was further disrupted by alcohol (Zack & Vo l-Sprott, 1995).

Cross sensitization can also be demonstrated. Laboratory animals with a sensitization to morphine will also show increased activation to cocaine and amphetamine and vice versa. In fact, it has been found that stress will also sensitize a

rat to the activating effect of many of these drugs (Piazza & Le Moal, 1998).

Sensitization may differ from tolerance in the fact that it seems to be very persistent. Sensitization conditioned to a particular environment and nonconditioned sensitization have been seen as long as a year after drug exposure in rats (during one-third of their lifetime), and there are no reports of it dissipating over time. In fact, there is evidence that it might *increase* with time (T. E. Robinson & Berridge, 1993, p. 258; P. B. Silverman & Bonate, 1997, p. 125).

From the considerable work directed at discovering the brain mechanisms responsible for the sensitization of behavioral arousal, it has become evident that no single neuronal effect can be responsible (R. C. Pierce & Kalivas, 1997). Sensitization clearly involves the brain's general motivation control system, which is centered in the limbic system. It is responsible for arousal and approach to both conditioned and natural incentives or motivating stimuli such as food and receptive sexual partners. The part of this system that becomes sensitized is the *mesolimbic dopamine system*. As we shall see in Chapters 4 and 5, this mechanism also appears to be responsible for the reinforcing effects of drugs. Sensitization of this system has been proposed as an explanation for drug abuse (T. E. Robinson & Berridge, 2000).

Sensitization of drug-induced activation has not been demonstrated in humans, but sensitization has been linked to the ability of drugs like cocaine and amphetamine to produce symptoms of psychosis in heavy users (see Chapter 11).

EXPECTANCY AND CONTEXT

It is becoming clear that the context in which a drug is administered is capable of having a significant influence on the effect that the drug will have. One of the most powerful contextual effects is whether you know whether the drug is being administered at all, that is, whether you are expecting a drug effect. This the *placebo effect*, and it was discussed in Chapter 2 in a discussion of research design. In recent years the placebo effect has become the subject of considerable interesting research. In 1995 a study was published by Benedetti, Amazino, and Maggi, researchers at the University of Turin Medical School in Italy (Colloca & Benedetti, 2005). They were investigating the effect of the drug promulgide on pain in human subjects. Their results showed that promulgide was better at relieving pain than a placebo and that a placebo was better than no treatment al all. This is not surprising, and these results would normally be interpreted as indicating that promulgide was an effective painkiller, but these researchers included an unusual treatment group in their research. They had a group of participants receive an injection of promulgide through an infusion pump without knowing that they had received any drug at all. Interestingly, in this group, promulgide had no effect on pain. The entire effect of the drug depended on the participants knowing that they were getting the drug. But if all the pain relief was a placebo effect, why did the drug have a stronger effect than the placebo alone?

Colloca and Benedetti explained the effect this way: They proposed that there is a "top-down" pain-relieving pathway from the cortex to a pain control center in the lower brain that is capable of blocking pain when activated. When a person knows that a drug is being administered, this pathway is activated, and pain is diminished. They called this the *expectation mechanism* and it is the reason for the placebo response. They proposed that the promulgide in their experiment had no direct effect on pain. Rather, it directly stimulated this expectation mechanism, and placebo response was enhanced. This is why the promulgide group showed a greater response than the placebo alone.

There are other examples of how the context in which a drug is given can alter the effect of a drug. For example, Volkow and colleagues (2003) used PET scans to measure glucose metabolism (see Chapter 4) and showed that the effect of an injection of methylphenidate (a drug that has similar effects as cocaine) increased glucose metabolism in some parts of the brains of cocaine abusers. Interestingly, the effect was twice as great if the participants were expecting the drug than if they were not expecting the drug. In addition, Volkow and her

associates showed that self-reports of being "high" were also about 50 percent greater when the drug was expected. Their PET scans showed that the increased response in those expecting the drug was probably due to an increased activity in the thalamus.

It has also been shown that drugs may have different effects when they are self-administered than when the person or laboratory animal has no control over the drug administration. Hemby, Koves, Smith & Dworkin (1997) showed that levels of dopamine in the nucleus accumbens (a part of the mesolimbic dopamine system) was higher in rats that were allowed to push a lever to give themselves injections of cocaine than in yolked control rats that received an injection every time the rats in the self-administration group gave themselves an injection.

Novel Environments. It is also clear from research on nonhumans that many drug effects are different when the drug is administered in a novel environment. As discussed in the previous section, stimulant drugs like cocaine and amphetamine tend to cause increases in motor behavior after they are administered, and with repeated administration, this effect shows sensitization. Recent research has shown that if the drug is administered in a novel environment, the amount of locomotor stimulation is considerably more than would be seen if the drug had been administered in a familiar setting. In addition, sensitization of this effect is much more rapid and can be induced at a lower dose if the drug is given in a novel setting. Investigations of this effect have shown that when these drugs are administered in a novel setting, they actually have different effects on the nervous system, effects that are likely to make them more addictive (Badaiani & Robinson, 2004).

CHAPTER SUMMARY

- Tolerance is defined as (a) the decreased effectiveness (or potency) of a drug that results from repeated administrations or (b) the necessity of increasing the dose of a drug in order to maintain its effectiveness after repeated administrations.

- Tolerance develops and dissipates to different effects of drugs at different rates, and so it is likely to be the result of many different processes.

- There are a number of different mechanisms that can cause tolerance. These include metabolic tolerance, changes in metabolism of the drug's physiological tolerance, changes in the physiology to compensate for the effect of the drug, and behavioral tolerance, or conditioned changes in behavior that compensate for the effect of the drug,

- Much tolerance arises from homeostatic mechanisms, but it will develop only where the effect of the drug has some biological significance to the organism.

- Dependence is when withdrawal symptoms occur when the use of the drug is stopped or decreases. For many drugs, withdrawal symptoms will occur when the use of the drugs is stopped. Withdrawal symptoms are thought to be the expression of the compensatory (opposite) effect of the drug, expressed in the absence of the drug.

- Hangover can be thought of as an acute withdrawal symptom.

- Pavlov was the first researcher to demonstrate that stimuli, if paired with the administration of a drug a sufficient number of times, will eventually come to elicit some of the effects of the drug through classical conditioning processes. Later research has shown that, quite often, the effect that becomes conditioned is a physiological response opposite to the unconditioned effect of the drug. It appears as though the compensatory response becomes conditioned.

- Stimuli that are always present when a drug is given will come to elicit conditioned compensatory responses that diminish the effect of the drug. This tolerance does not occur when the drug is given in the absence of these stimuli. When a placebo is administered in the presence of stimuli that predict the drug, a drug compensatory response is sometimes seen. These conditioned compensatory responses are expressed as conditioned withdrawal.

- It has been demonstrated that if a drug interferes with the ability of an organism to obtain reinforcement, tolerance will develop quickly. If there is no reinforcement for compensating for the effect of a drug, tolerance may not develop. Similarly, tolerance to some effects develops only if the organism is reinforced for showing drug compensatory responses.

- Sensitization occurs where a drug effect increases with repeated administrations. Sensitization can be conditioned to specific environments. Sensitization occurs to only some effects of some drugs. These include increases in activity caused by reinforcing drugs, increased stereotyped behaviors caused by psychomotor stimulants, and the reinforcing effects of a drug.

- The expectations of experimental subjects can have a great influence on the effect of a drug. This is the placebo effect. Brain pathways that mediate the expectancy effect have been identified.

- The context in which a drug is administered can also influence its effect. This includes whether the drug is self-administered and whether it is administered in a familiar or a novel environment.

4

Neurophysiology, Neurotransmitters, and the Nervous System

Coauthored by Stephanie D. Hancock

All behavior is under the control of the nervous system, and the effect of behaviorally active drugs can ultimately be traced to a direct or an indirect action on some aspect of the functioning of the nervous system. It is, therefore, necessary to have at least a rudimentary grasp of the normal functioning of the nervous system to understand the behavioral effects of drugs.

THE NEURON

Like all other tissues in the body, the nervous system is made up of cells. Some of these cells, called *glial cells*, are not excitable; they provide structural and metabolic functions in the nervous system. The other cells, called *neurons*, are excitable, and they function to analyze and transmit information. They are responsible for receiving sensory information from outside the body, for integrating and storing information, and for controlling the action of the muscles and glands—in other words, for everything that we see and understand as behavior.

Nerve cells come in many shapes and sizes, but they all have a number of identifiable parts. A typical nerve cell is shown in Figure 4-1. Like all other cells in the body, it has a *nucleus* that contains genetic information. The cell is covered by a *membrane* and is filled with a fluid called *cytoplasm*. All nerve cells have a *cell body*, which is the largest part of the cell and contains the nucleus. Arising from the cell body are several structures. At one end are projections called *dendrites*. These divide into smaller and smaller fibers. The *axon* is a long process attached to the cell body at the *axon hillock*, which is located at the opposite end of the cell body from the dendrites. The axon is usually covered by a layer of fatty material called the *myelin sheath*. The myelin sheath is an extension of a special type of glial cell that wraps itself around the axon.

As we have seen in Chapter 1, cell membranes are made up of two layers of *lipid* molecules (see Figure 1-5) with large protein molecules embedded in them. In nerve cells, these large protein molecules have special functions that make the cells excitable and capable of conveying, storing, and integrating information. These actions are accomplished by controlling the flow of ions through the membrane. These proteins are often a target of behaviorally active drugs.

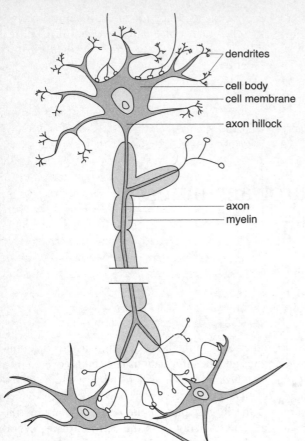

cardinals:
- dendrites
- cell body
- cell membrane
- axon hillock
- axon
- myelin

Figure 4-1 A typical nerve cell. Note that the neuron receives input from synapses from several other nerve cells at its dendrites and cell body and that it also has synapses on other nerve cells.

Resting Potential

If we take two very fine wires, insert one inside a neuron and place the other just outside the membrane, and then attach the wires to a voltmeter, we will see that there is a difference in electrical charge; the inside is slightly negatively charged compared to the outside. A *voltmeter* is a device that measures differences in electrical potential between two places; the same sort of instrument is used to test batteries. The potential difference across the membrane is called the *resting potential*. The resting potential varies from cell to cell but is usually about −70 millivolts. (One millivolt is 1/1,000 volt. A standard flashlight battery has a charge of 1.5 volts.)

The reason for this potential difference is that there is an uneven distribution of ions between the inside and the outside of a cell. *Ions* are particles that possess an electrical charge. The ions described in Chapter 1 were usually large drug molecules; the ions that are responsible for the resting potential of a cell are ionized molecules of the elements potassium (K^+), sodium (Na^+), chlorine (Cl^-), and calcium (Ca^{++}), although some larger molecules of amino acids are also involved.

To understand the resting potential, we need to understand two things: (a) The membrane potential is a relative potential—that is, we are always comparing the inside and the outside of the membrane—and (b) the outside of the membrane is always considered equal to zero. The resting potential exists because there are more positively charged ions than negatively charged ions outside the cell. Because there are fewer positively charged ions inside the cell, the inside of the cell is negative with respect to the outside.

Three processes are responsible for this uneven distribution of ions. The most important process is an *active transport mechanism* known as an *ion pump*. Ion pumps are specialized molecules of protein that selectively move ions from one side of a membrane to another. In nerve cells, an ion pump, known as the Na^+/K^+ pump, moves Na^+ ions to the outside and K^+ ions to the inside, but it moves three Na^+ ions out for every two K^+ ions it moves in, thereby creating an excess of positive ions outside the membrane (see Figure 4-2).

Two other processes are also at work. One is simple diffusion, the tendency for a substance to move from an area of high concentration to an area of lower concentration. The other is *electrostatic charge*, the tendency for similar electrical charges to repel each other and for opposite electrical charges to attract each other. Positive ions are repelled by the net positive charge outside the membrane and attracted to the negative charge inside. The reverse is true for negative ions.

If the membranes were completely permeable to ions, diffusion and electrostatic charge would drive ions unevenly distributed by the ion pumps back across the membrane as fast as the pumps could move them. But membranes are not permeable to ions. The only way that ions can move across the membrane is through specialized holes, or channels, in the membrane. These are called *ionophores* or *ion channels*. Like ion pumps, ion channels are large protein molecules embedded in the cell membrane. They are specialized so that they will allow only certain ions to pass through, and then only at a particular rate. There are ion channels for K^+, Na^+, and Cl^-. (There are also channels for Ca^{++} ions, but these are not involved in the resting potential and have a special function, described later.) There are two types of ion channels: those that are always open (*nongated*), and those that are *gated*. Gated ion channels open and close in response to specific stimuli (see Figure 4-2).

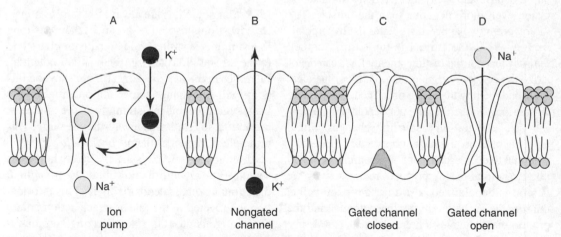

Figure 4-2 (A) An ion pump moving potassium ions (K^+) into a cell and moving sodium ions (Na^+) out of a cell through a membrane. (B) A nongated ion channel that is always open and allows particular ions (in this case, K^+) to move back out of the cell. (C) A closed gated Na^+ ion channel. (D) The open configuration of the same channel shown in C. Note how it allows Na^+ back into the cell.

Normally, the nongated channels do not permit ions to flow through the membrane fast enough to neutralize the ion pumps, so a net positive charge remains outside. This fact explains the resting potential. However, it should be clear that anything that speeds or slows the passage of ions through the membrane can increase or decrease the resting potential.

Stimulation of the Axon

Action Potential. The resting potential of a neuron describes the distribution of ions in the absence of stimulation. In fact, the membrane potential can vary substantially in response to a variety of stimuli. When the membrane potential becomes less negative (i.e., moves toward zero and positive numbers), it is called a *depolarization*. When the membrane potential becomes more negative (i.e., moves further away from zero), it is called a *hyperpolarization*. Normally, changes in ion distribution are responsible for deviation from the resting potential, but to illustrate the process, we can change the resting potential artificially. We can hyperpolarize a cell by inserting a fine electrode (a fine wire similar to the one used to measure the resting potential) into a neuron and applying electricity to make the inside even more negative than the outside. The more current we apply, the greater the hyperpolarization. When the current is turned off, the cell returns to its normal resting potential. We can depolarize the cell by reversing the polarity of the electrode and making the inside of the cell less negative with respect to the outside, but depolarizing a neuron can lead to some startling changes. Small amounts of depolarization simply cause the resting potential to decrease. When the electricity is turned off, the normal resting potential returns. But if the neuron is depolarized past a certain point called the *threshold*, the entire resting potential and the process that maintains it break down.

This breakdown occurs because of special gated ion channels that are sensitive to the number of positive charges inside the cell. These *voltage gated ion channels* open when the potential difference is reduced beyond the threshold. When they open, they allow the free flow of ions across the membrane. First, sodium channels open, and Na^+ ions rush into the cell driven by their concentration gradient (there are many more outside than inside) and their electrostatic charge (they are positively charged, and the outside has a net positive charge). As a result, the resting potential of the membrane is neutralized. In fact, the polarity is actually reversed slightly. When this condition occurs, the sodium ion channels close and potassium channels open. Potassium (K^+) ions rush out of the neuron, driven by their concentration gradient and the transient positive charge created by all the Na^+ ions that just entered. Along with the ion pumps, this process restores the resting potential. The process is illustrated in Figure 4-3.

This breakdown and restoration of the resting potential is known as an *action potential*, and it occurs very quickly. Some cells are capable of producing and recovering from many hundreds of action potentials each second. The term *firing* is often used to indicate an action potential. It is by means of action potentials that the cells in the nervous system integrate and convey information.

The All-or-None Law

Action potentials are always the same, no matter how strong a stimulus produces them. As long as a stimulus is strong enough to depolarize a cell to the threshold, it will cause an action potential. Increases in the depolarizing stimulus beyond this point will not change the action potential in any way; regardless of the strength of the stimulus, the action potential will always be the same. This principle is known as the *all-or-none law*.

If all action potentials are the same, how does a neuron convey information about the strength of the stimulus that is depolarizing it? This information is reflected in the rate at which action potentials are generated. If a depolarizing stimulus is applied continuously to a cell, it will cause the cell to produce repeated action potentials. Weak stimuli that produce low levels of depolarization will permit the membrane a bit of time to recover between action potentials, but more

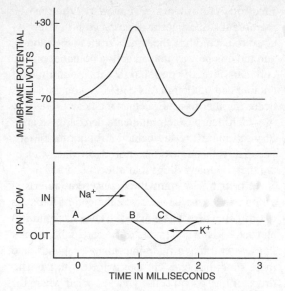

Figure 4-3 The flow of ions during an action potential. The top panel shows a typical action potential. Starting at point A, the resting potential begins to break down. It reaches a peak at B and then returns toward normal. After briefly overshooting −70 mV, the resting potential is restored. The bottom panel shows what happens to ions during the action potential. At point A, sodium channels open, and Na⁺ ions rush in. At point B, the sodium channels close, the potassium channels open, and K⁺ ions rush out. At point C, the potassium ion channels close, and normal resting potential is restored by ion pumps.

intense depolarization caused by stronger stimuli permits less recovery time between action potentials. As a result, the stronger the depolarizing stimulus, the faster the membrane will fire.

Conduction of Action Potentials along the Membrane

When an action potential is generated at a point on the membrane of an axon, it does not stay there. The Na⁺ ions that move into the cell through the ion channels also move sideways along the inside surface of the membrane because of diffusion and electric charge, and this movement reduces the resting potential of the surrounding membrane—that is, it depolarizes it. This depolarization causes the voltage gated ion channels to open and depolarizes the adjacent section of membrane. The action potential will then sweep across the surface of the axon membrane, away from the stimulus that produced it, with undiminished intensity.

Depending on the type of axon, an action potential can move as fast as 100 meters a second. The presence of the myelin coating on the axon greatly speeds the conduction of action potentials along the axon. Myelinated axons can conduct much faster than unmyelinated ones.

Stimulation of the Dendrites and Cell Body

What has just been described is what happens if one depolarizes the membrane of an axon. The action potential is invariable in axons because axons have only voltage gated ion channels and nothing else that can modulate the effect of depolarization. In contrast, the dendrites and cell body contain a great many proteins and enzymes that influence the behavior of ion channels and cell excitability. If you were to insert an electrode into the membrane of a dendrite or a cell body, the same depolarizing stimulus that caused an action potential in an axon can give rise to very different events, depending on which modulating influences are active. Because the form of the depolarization is variable, we refer to depolarization in the cell body and dendrites as *postsynaptic potentials* (PSPs) rather than action potentials. (These potentials are normally created in membranes located at synapses, which will be discussed later.) Postsynaptic potentials are created by the same type of ion flows as action potentials, and they spread across the membrane in a similar manner except that the intensity of PSPs decreases as the distance from the site of stimulation lengthens. The region of the cell known as the axon hillock, where the axon joins the cell body, is the place where variable PSPs are converted to unvarying action potentials. Thus, if the membrane of the cell body and dendrites is highly depolarized, a high rate of action potentials will be produced at the axon hillock.

We will return to the behavior of PSPs in the section on synapses, in which we will discuss how one neuron communicates with another.

Action Potentials from Sensory Neurons

We have seen how action potentials are created when a section of a neuron's membrane is depolarized past its threshold and how the action potential moves along an axon. But the action potentials we have discussed have been artificially created by inserting a stimulating electrode into the cell. Where do natural action potentials come from?

Action potentials arise in neurons from several sources. One of these is the outside world. Sensory neurons are specialized nerve cells that are depolarized or hyperpolarized by events in the environment. In the skin are neurons whose cell bodies are depolarized by pressure, sending action potentials along their axons into the brain and causing us to experience the sensation of touch. The stronger the stimulation, the greater the depolarization and the faster the sensory neurons generate action potentials. The skin also has nerve cells that are specialized to detect heat, cold, and pain. Cells in the ear are depolarized by vibration, and cells in the muscles are depolarized by movement. In fact, all that we know about the outside world comes to our brains in the form of action potentials generated by these specialized receptor neurons.

THE SYNAPSE

We still have not come to the most interesting part: how neurons communicate with one another. A nerve cell is like any other cell in the body; it is completely surrounded by a membrane. For the information received from the outside world to get from the sensory receptor neuron to other neurons in the brain, there must be a mechanism by which one cell is able to communicate with another.

Electron microscopes reveal that although the membranes of adjacent neurons come extremely close to each other, their membranes never touch, and there is no way that an action potential on one cell can directly depolarize the membrane of another cell (although this type of conduction does occur in other tissues, such as the heart). The way in which neurons communicate across this gap is of vital interest to the behavioral pharmacologist because this process is altered, in one way or another, by many drugs that affect behavior.

Information is transferred between neurons at *synapses*. A synapse occurs at the end of the axon of one cell where it terminates close to the dendrites and cell body of another cell. The end of the axon of the first cell may divide into many branches, and these small branches are intertwined with the dendrites of the second cell. Synapses occur where the axons and dendrites come close to each other.

Figure 4-4 is a schematic drawing of a typical synapse. It is characterized by (a) a swelling called the *terminal bouton* at the termination of the branch of the axon of the *presynaptic cell* (the cell sending the information) and (b) a thickening on the membrane of the cell body or dendrite of the postsynaptic cell (the cell receiving the information) immediately beneath the bouton. Between the terminal bouton and the postsynaptic cell is a gap called the *synaptic cleft*. Another feature of the synapse is a number of spherical structures in the terminal bouton called *synaptic vesicles*.

Action at a Synapse

When an action potential arrives at the terminal bouton, calcium (Ca^{++}) channels open, and the flow of calcium ions into the cell causes a chemical called a *neurotransmitter* to be released from the synaptic vesicles into the synaptic cleft. The neurotransmitter is stored in the *vesicles*. When the calcium enters the cell, the vesicles move to the membrane at the synaptic cleft and release the neurotransmitter through the cell wall into the cleft. The neurotransmitter diffuses across the cleft, where it comes in contact with the membrane of the postsynaptic cell.

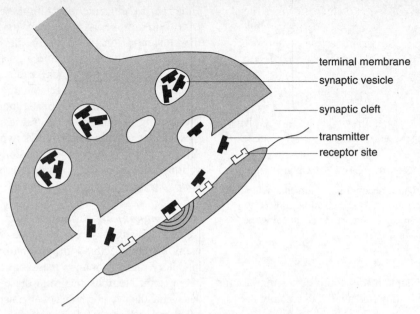

terminal membrane
synaptic vesicle
synaptic cleft
transmitter
receptor site

Figure 4-4 Schematic drawing of a synapse. The molecules of transmitter normally stored in vesicles are released into the cleft in response to the arrival of an action potential. The transmitter molecules diffuse across the cleft and occupy receptor sites on the membrane of the postsynaptic cell. These events cause changes in the excitability of the postsynaptic cell membrane, making it either easier (excitation) or more difficult (inhibition) to fire.

Embedded in the membrane of the postsynaptic cell are specialized molecules called *receptor sites* or *recognition sites*. Receptor sites are designed so that molecules of the neurotransmitter will briefly *bind* to (become attached to) them, much like a key fitting into a lock. When a neurotransmitter with the right configuration (the key) attaches to a receptor site (the lock), it causes certain changes to occur in the postsynaptic cell—changes that can result in a shift in its resting potential or a change in its biochemistry. Such changes can be brought about in a number of direct and indirect ways.

Proteins. It has been mentioned that much of the machinery needed to make a neuron operate, such as ion channels, ion pumps, and receptors, are molecules of *protein*. A protein is actually a long chain of fairly simple molecules called *amino acids*. There are only 20 different amino acids in your body, and every protein is made of these 20 amino acids chained together in a different order. These proteins can be hundreds of amino acids long. What allows proteins to have such special properties is that these chains of amino acids do not remain in a line; rather, they fold up into very complex three-dimensional shapes, allowing them to have the sophisticated mechanical properties they need to function as ion pumps, and so on.

Receptors are proteins, and their configuration means that they can bind to a particular transmitter with the correct complementary shape. When a neurotransmitter of the correct shape binds to a receptor, the receptor changes its shape (we sometimes say the receptor has been activated). This activated receptor has the capacity to alter the functioning of the cell in many different ways.

In some synapses, receptor sites are connected to a gated ion channel and cause it to open or close. This process is illustrated in Figure 4-5. Depending

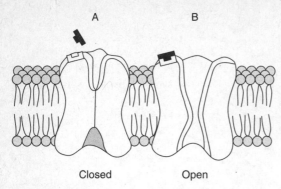

Closed   Open

Figure 4-5 (A) A receptor gated ion channel in the closed configuration. (B) A transmitter molecule occupying the receptor site and the channel in the open configuration.

on the ion channel, this could either increase or decrease the resting potential of the membrane.

Excitation. If the presynaptic cell is producing action potentials at a high rate and it has many synapses on the cell body and dendrites of the postsynaptic cell, the resting potential of the postsynaptic cell will be strongly affected.

When the transmitter causes the receptor sites to open gated ion channels that permit Na^+ into the cell, the resting potential will move closer to the action potential threshold. In other words, the membrane will be depolarized. Depolarization of the postsynaptic membrane has a special name: *excitatory postsynaptic potential* (EPSP). The faster a presynaptic cell fires, the more neurotransmitter it will release at its synapses and the greater the EPSP it will cause. If enough EPSPs are being produced at the same time at many synapses, the postsynaptic cell may be depolarized past its threshold at its axon hillock, and it will create action potentials in its axon. As described in the earlier section on the all-or-none law, the more the postsynaptic cell is depolarized past its threshold, the faster the cell will fire.

Inhibition. There are also synapses at which the neurotransmitter will inhibit the firing of the postsynaptic cell. In this case the neurotransmitter causes the receptor site to open ion channels that

either permit chloride ions into the cell or allow potassium ions out. (K^+ ions leave the cell because the concentration gradient forcing them out is stronger than the electrostatic gradient trying to keep them in. When they leave, they increase the number of positive charges on the outside of the membrane, making the inside more negative.) The resting potential then increases; that is, the postsynaptic membrane becomes hyperpolarized. As a result, it is harder for the cell to produce action potentials. This condition is called an *inhibitory postsynaptic potential* (IPSP).

Summation of Excitation and Inhibition. Neurons have thousands of synaptic contacts from many different cells, some excitatory and some inhibitory, and any or all of these may be active at a given time. Neurons integrate these signals and determine the rate at which action potentials will be generated at the axon hillock or whether any will be generated at all. There are two major types of integration: (a) *spatial summation* and (b) *temporal summation.* Spatial summation occurs when two or more neurons release transmitters onto the same target neuron. The target neuron will have Na^+ ions entering in some regions (excitation) and K^+ ions leaving at other regions (inhibition). These local changes in ion distribution may cancel each other out if they are different or add together if they are the same. The sum of these effects must be able to depolarize the cell beyond the threshold if an action potential is to occur (see Figure 4-6.) Temporal summation occurs when a neuron produces several action potentials closely in time. Although each one may be too small to initiate an action potential, if they arrive closely together, their EPSPs may summate and reach threshold (see Figure 4-6).

Terminating Synaptic Action

The arrival of action potentials at the terminal bouton initiates the release of a transmitter into the synaptic cleft that causes changes in the membrane of the postsynaptic cell, but it is important to have some mechanism to get rid of the transmitter when the presynaptic terminal bouton stops receiving

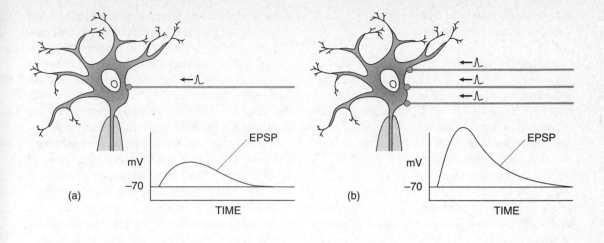

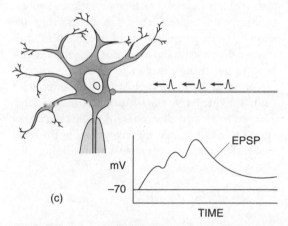

Figure 4-6 Temporal and spatial summation of PSPs on a dendrite. (a) A single impulse arrives at a synapse and causes a PSP. (b) Three impulses arrive at the same time at three different synapses. Their effects summate, causing a much bigger PSP (spatial summation). (c) Three impulses arrive in quick succession at one synapse. Their effects are summed to cause a greater PSP than if only one had arrived (temporal summation).

action potentials. Otherwise, the transmitter would stay in the cleft and continue to influence the post-synaptic cell. Every synapse has some system to accomplish this purpose. It is usually accomplished in one of two ways: (a) The synapse contains an enzyme that destroys the transmitter if it stays in the cleft for any length of time, or (b) the presynaptic cell has a means of reabsorbing the transmitter and then recycling it. The latter process, called *reuptake*, is accomplished by a sort of active transport mechanism embedded in the membrane of the presynaptic cell.

Speed and Duration of the Effects of Neurotransmitters

As we have seen in some synapses, receptor sites are connected to a gated ion channel and cause it to open or close. When this happens the effect occurs very rapidly, in the order of milliseconds, and lasts only briefly. In other cases, the effects do not occur as fast but last longer.

Second Messengers. Some receptor sites are not connected directly to a gated ion channel; their influence on ion channels is indirect and, consequently, somewhat slower. In this case, when the transmitter interacts with the receptor site, a cascade of events is initiated. The ultimate effect of this cascade depends on when it ends, and its ending is influenced by many factors. The first step of the cascade occurs when a special molecule is released inside the postsynaptic cell. This molecule, called a *second messenger*, can do a number of things inside the postsynaptic cell. The most common second messenger is *cyclic AMP* (cAMP). Often a second messenger interacts with gated ion channels from the inside, with effects similar to the directly gated ion channels, as shown in Figure 4-7. Or the second messenger can alter the operation of nongated ion channels in a way that changes the resting potential or its sensitivity to other stimuli.

Second messengers may also have even longer-term or permanent effects because they activate a type of protein called a *kinase*. A kinase is much more persistent than a second messenger and can remain active for many minutes or even for hours. Kinases alter the functioning of both ion channels and receptors, but they do so for a much longer time than second messengers. Kinases also influence many other regulatory processes in the cell, including the release of second messengers from other receptors and the efficiency of ion pumps.

Kinases may also activate (phosphorylate) transcription factors such as *CREB* and *c-fos*. Genes in the cell nucleus have switches that can turn them on or off. These switches are turned on and off by chemicals called *transcription factors*. Whether a particular gene is active at any given time is determined by the presence or absence of particular transcription factors. Thus, when kinases activate transcription factors, they are controlling the expression of particular genes in the cell. Genes contain the code for the order in which amino acids need to be strung together to create a particular protein, and the process of creating these proteins from the genetic code is called *transcription*. The proteins created by the DNA could be receptor sites, ion channels, ion pumps, or any of the other molecules used by the cell in receiving and

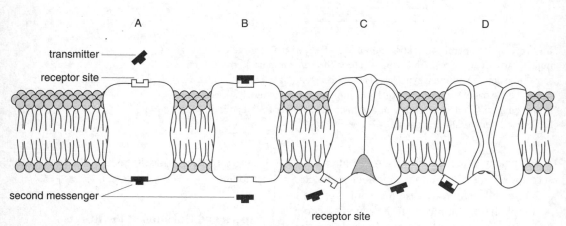

A   B   C   D

transmitter

receptor site

second messenger

receptor site

Figure 4-7 How second messengers work. (A and B) When a receptor outside the cell membrane is occupied by a transmitter molecule, it causes the release, inside the cell, of a molecule of a second messenger. (C and D) The second messenger then interacts with a receptor on the inside of a gated ion channel, in this case causing it to open. Second messengers may do a great many other things in the postsynaptic cell.

transmitting information, or they could be transcription factors for other genes. Thus, a transcription factor may turn on the gene that makes receptor sites for a given transmitter. With more receptor sites, the cell will become more sensitive to that neurotransmitter. In the same way, some ion channels may become more numerous, and others may become less numerous. Second messengers (via kinases and transcription factors) can even cause a synapse to be made or removed, thus permanently altering the connections of a cell. Changes in neuron excitation or sensitivity that arise from changes in gene expression can be very long lasting and are thought to be responsible for the formation and storage of memories in the brain.

Figure 4-8 illustrates the cascade of possible events that can occur after a receptor site is occupied by a neurotransmitter.

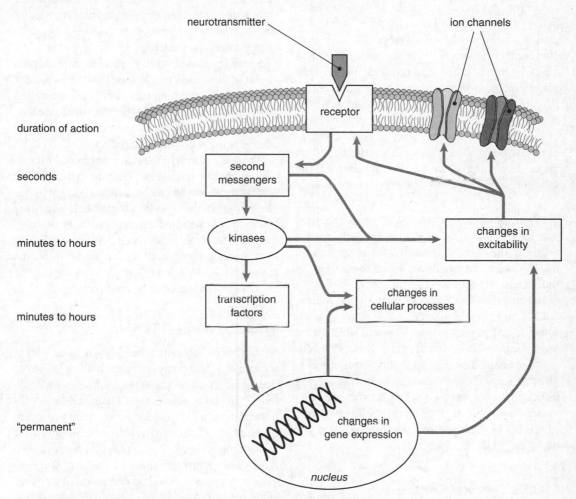

Figure 4-8 The relation between a signal cascade and the resulting effects on cell excitability. As the cascade progresses, the duration of the effect increases. No matter how many steps there are in the cascade and how long those steps are active, all the alterations have common end points. Every change in excitability is the result of alterations to ion channels or receptors or of a change in the biochemical processes of the cell.

Presynaptic Effects of Neurotransmitters

Receptor sites are not located only on the postsynaptic neuron. In fact, there are often many receptor sites for the neurotransmitter located on the presynaptic neuron. These are called *autoreceptors*. They serve to provide feedback on the amount of neurotransmitter in the synaptic cleft and control its release. If levels of the neurotransmitter get too high, the autoreceptors will cause a reduction in the release of the transmitter. It is believed that it is a mechanism such as this that causes a delay in the effectiveness of some psychotherapeutic drugs, such as antidepressants (see Chapter 14). These drugs cause the buildup of crucial neurotransmitters, but autoreceptors detect this excess and block the release of the neurotransmitter, thus blocking the effectiveness of the drug. It sometimes takes a week or two to exhaust the autoreceptors before the drug can make any change in the functioning of the synapse (see Chapter 14).

Neuromodulators. In describing a chemical that has long-lasting effects on the activity of a synapse, the term *neuromodulator* is sometimes used. A neuromodulator can affect the activity or the release of a neurotransmitter by making it either more or less effective at the postsynaptic cell. Neuromodulators may act within the postsynaptic cell, or they may also have an effect on the presynaptic cell and modify the release of a neurotransmitter. They may have short- or long-term effects. Substances that act as neurotransmitters in one synapse may also act as neuromodulators of transmission at a different synapse. Some of the ways that neuromodulators operate are described in the next section.

Other Chemical Signaling Between Neurons

The release of transmitters from the presynaptic cell altering the excitability of a postsynaptic cell is the most common and best-understood mechanism by which cells communicate, but it is not the only one. In addition to autoreceptors, we now know that the presynaptic cell also has receptor sites on the terminal bouton that can respond to chemicals released by the postsynaptic cell or other nearby cells when they become depolarized. This is called *depolarization-induced suppression of excitation* (DSE) or *depolarization-induced suppression of inhibition* (DSI) (depending on whether activity of the synapse was excitatory or inhibitory). In fact, receptors for THC, the active ingredient of cannabis, are located presynaptically and respond to a chemical released by the postsynaptic neuron (see Chapter 15).

Synapses are not always located on dendrites or cell bodies. They can also be located on or near other axons or terminal boutons. These are called *axo-axonal synapses*, and the chemical released at these synapses serves to modulate transmitter release at the receiving synapse.

There are places in the brain where neurotransmitters are not released directly at synapses, but rather are secreted in the general vicinity of a number of cells and diffuse to their synapses where they have an effect on the activity of many cells at the same time. Such release is usually long lasting compared to the brief impulses of activity at synapses. Thus, the excitability of entire brain systems can be modulated.

NEUROTRANSMITTERS

A number of substances are known to be neurotransmitters, and many more are believed to serve that function. In recent years, as many as 50 different substances have been identified as neurotransmitters, and it is likely that there are many others. One of the earliest discovered and best understood is *acetylcholine* (ACh). There also is a family of neurotransmitters called *biogenic amines* or *monoamines*. It is composed of the *catecholamines* (CA), which include *epinephrine* (E), *norepinephrine* (NE), *dopamine* (DA), and one *indoleamine, serotonin*, which is often called *5-hydroxytryptamine* (5-HT).

Some transmitters are amino acids. Three of the most common are (a) *gamma-aminobutyric acid*

(GABA), (b) *glycine*, and (c) *glutamate*. Many of these amino acids are found normally in all cells in the body, where they serve metabolic and other biochemical functions. In some neurons, they can be transmitters as well.

Peptides consist of a number of amino acids linked together in a chain. As you know, receptor sites are made of long chains of peptides folded into a specific shape. Some neurotransmitters are also peptides. These include *somatostatin, vasopressin, oxytocin, prolactin, growth hormone, substance P*, and *insulin*. A number of other peptides, known as *enkephalins* or *endorphins*, are also used. Table 4-1 lists some of the substances believed to be neurotransmitters. You may recognize many of these names because they have been known for years as *hormones*. A hormone is a chemical messenger released into the body by a gland. It circulates throughout the body and has an effect on some biological process distant from the place where it is released. Many peptides were first identified as hormones and given appropriate names, such as growth hormone. It is now clear that the body uses many of these substances as both hormones and neurotransmitters. The two functions are similar: Hormones carry messages over long distances, and neurotransmitters carry messages over very short distances. The distinction between a hormone and a neurotransmitter may not always be clear. In the previous section there was a discussion of how a neurotransmitter may be secreted near a brain structure and has effects on many synapses simultaneously. These substances are acting more as a hormone than a transmitter and are sometimes called *neurohormones* when they act in that capacity.

A number of other chemicals are known to be used as neurotransmitters, neuromodulators, or neurohormones. These include *carbon monoxide* (CO) and *nitric oxide* (NO) (not to be confused with nitrous oxide, NO_2, discussed in Chapter 8).

For a very long time it was believed that a neuron always produced the same neurotransmitter at every one of its synapses. This principle, known as *Dale's law*, is named after Sir Henry Dale, its proposer. The law needed to be modified when it was discovered that some neurons may release

TABLE 4-1   Neurotransmitters in the Central Nervous System

Acetylcholine (Ach)
Biogenic amines (monoamines)
  Catecholamines
    Norepinephrine (NE)
    Dopamine (DA)
    Epinephrine (E)
  Indoleamine
    Serotonin (5-hydroxytryptamine, 5-HT)
  Others
    Histamine
Amino acids
  Gamma-aminobutyric acid (GABA)
  Glycine
  Glutamate
  Proline
Peptides
  Substance P
Morphine-like substances
  Enkephalins
  Endorphins
  Thyrotropin-releasing factors
  Somatostatin
  Vasopressin
  Growth hormone
  Prolactin
  Insulin

more than one chemical, usually an amino acid (a neurotransmitter) and a peptide (a neuromodulator), from their synapses. Although it is not common, we now know that some cells in some circumstances can release different chemicals at different synapses.

Neurons are classified according to the primary neurotransmitter they release. Those that release acetylcholine are called *cholinergic* neurons. Epinephrine is also known as adrenaline (the name used primarily in Europe), so synapses that use epinephrine and norepinephrine are called *adrenergic* and *noradrenergic*, respectively. Those that use dopamine are *dopaminergic*, those that use serotonin are *serotonergic*, and so on.

Even though each neuron almost always releases the same transmitter(s), its effect on various cells can be quite different. The effect of a transmitter depends on the nature of the receptor site it binds to. Because any transmitter may have a number of different receptor sites, activity at its synapses may have many different effects. These receptor sites may cause IPSPs or EPSPs; they may be directly connected to an ion channel, or they might use a second messenger. Thus, a substance released from the vesicles into the cleft can be either an excitatory or inhibitory neurotransmitter or a neuromodulator. Using the lock-and-key analogy, whatever lurks behind a locked door does not depend on the size or shape of the key.

Drugs and Neurotransmission

The transmission between nerves is a chemical process, and it is primarily at synapses that drugs have the opportunity to interfere with the process. Substances administered from outside the body can find their way to synapses and alter their function in many different ways. Externally administered drugs can mimic neurotransmitters by occupying some or all of the receptor sites that cause the drugs' effect (*agonism*). Drugs sometimes occupy receptor sites but have no effect. This action blocks the transmitter from having its normal effect (*antagonism*), as illustrated in Figure 4-9. Other ways that drugs can alter synaptic transmission include (a) decreasing the activity of enzymes that either create or destroy a transmitter, (b) altering the reuptake of a transmitter, (c) altering the activity of a second messenger, (d) interfering with the operation of ion channels, or (e) changing the amount of transmitter that a neuron releases in response to an action potential.

Modulating all this is the function of autoreceptors. If a drug is given that blocks receptors, both the postsynaptic receptor site and the autoreceptors will be blocked. There is, consequently, a decrease in neurotransmission to the postsynaptic

cell, but there is also a decrease in activity in the autoreceptor. This decrease in autoreceptor activity stimulates the cell to produce more neurotransmitter that can compensate for the decreased activity at the postsynaptic site, thus canceling the effect of the receptor blocker on the postsynaptic cell. Such a drug would have no net effect on neurotransmission. If the blocker has a greater effect on the autoreceptor than the postsynaptic receptor, then the net result might be an increase in transmission across the synapse because the presynaptic cell will overcompensate by releasing too much transmitter.

As you can see, things can get very complicated.

Acetylcholine

Acetylcholine (ACh) is synthesized in cholinergic cells and stored in the synaptic vesicles. When an action potential arrives at the terminal bouton, the vesicle releases the ACh into the synaptic cleft, where it interacts with receptor sites on the surface of the postsynaptic cell. The synaptic cleft also contains an enzyme called *acetylcholinesterase* (AChE), which breaks down the ACh whenever it comes in contact with it. Thus, the ACh does not remain in the synaptic cleft for very long. Several drugs interfere with the activity of the AChE; consequently, they interfere with transmission across cholinergic synapses. This is the mechanism of action of many commonly used insecticides and even some older nerve gases, such as sarin.

Some drugs alter the functioning of cholinergic synapses by acting at the ACh receptor sites. Although all ACh receptor sites are stimulated by ACh, they can be classified according to other

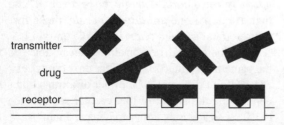

transmitter

drug

receptor

Figure 4-9 Drug transmitter molecules compete for the transmitter's receptor sites. A receptor site may be occupied by the drug molecule, keeping the transmitter molecule out, but the drug is not the correct shape to activate the receptor in the same way the transmitter would. Therefore, the drug blocks the receptor, and the effectiveness of the transmitter is minimized.

substances that can affect them. *Nicotinic* cholinergic receptors are stimulated by nicotine and blocked by a drug called *curare*, a poison that some South American Indians place on the point of their spears and arrows. *Muscarinic* cholinergic receptors are stimulated by muscarine and blocked by drugs like atropine and scopolamine (see Chapter 8).

Interestingly, muscarinic and nicotinic receptor sites differ in the way they alter the postsynaptic cell. Nicotinic receptors are directly connected to a gated ion channel; muscarinic receptors use a second messenger.

Biogenic Amines (Monoamines)

The catecholamines—E, NE, and DA—and the indoleamine 5-HT all work in a similar way, so we will consider them together. The catecholamine neurotransmitters are made by the body from *tyrosine*, a substance found in food. The tyrosine is converted into *L-dopa*, which is then converted to DA and used by dopaminergic neurons. Some DA is converted into NE, and E is created from the NE by another step. Each step in the conversion of tyrosine to E is controlled by a special enzyme. 5-HT is converted from *tryptophan*, another substance found in food, in two steps, using two enzymes.

The biogenic amines—E, NE, DA, and 5-HT—are stored in vesicles in the terminal bouton, where they are protected from two enzymes that destroy them: *monoamine oxidase* (MAO) and *catechol-O-methyltransferase* (COMT). Like ACh, these neurotransmitters are released into the cleft when an action potential arrives, but they are deactivated by a slightly more complex mechanism. After the neurotransmitters diffuse across the synapse and interact with receptor sites, they are reabsorbed into the terminal bouton, where they are again stored in the vesicles and recycled. Any transmitter not protected in this way is destroyed by MAO and COMT.

Other drugs, such as the amphetamines, stimulate these synapses by causing a leakage of the neurotransmitter into the cleft and increasing the amount of neurotransmitter released when an action potential arrives. Drugs such as cocaine and some antidepressants block reuptake so that the transmitter stays in the cleft longer. Activity at synapses that use monoamines as neurotransmitters are also stimulated by drugs that block the activity of MAO (see Chapter 13).

Each biogenic amine can have a number of different receptor sites. Epinephrine and norepinephrine work at two types of receptors: *alpha* (α) and *beta* (β) adrenergic receptors. Each of these has two subtypes, α_1 and α_2 and β_1 and β_2. Dopamine has at least six receptor types; the two main ones, D_1 and D_2, are found in different dopaminergic brain systems. Drugs used to treat psychotic disorders selectively block D_2 receptors, but some of the newer antipsychotic drugs also have effects on other dopamine receptors (see Chapter 13).

Serotonin has four main types of receptors: $5\text{-}HT_1$, $5\text{-}HT_2$, $5\text{-}HT_3$, and $5\text{-}HT_4$. In addition, there are four subtypes of the $5\text{-}HT_1$ receptor (known as $5\text{-}HT_{1a}$, $5\text{-}HT_{1b}$, and so on). The $5\text{-}HT_3$ receptors are connected to a gated ion channel, but the rest use a second messenger system.

This book indicates receptor subtypes using a subscript (e.g., D_1 or D_2), but in other books and papers, you may sometimes see receptor subtypes designated without subscripts (e.g., D1 or D2). Don't be confused—these refer to the same thing.

Gamma-Aminobutyric Acid (GABA)

Most of the neurotransmitters mentioned so far are either excitatory or inhibitory, depending on the nature of the receptor site; GABA, however, is believed to be a universal inhibitory neurotransmitter in all parts of the brain. It produces its inhibitory effect by directly opening a Cl^- ion channel, permitting negatively charged chloride ions to flow inward along their concentration gradient. This action stabilizes the membrane and makes it more difficult to create an action potential. Like the other amino acid transmitters, GABA is removed from the cleft by a reuptake mechanism.

Depressant drugs like the barbiturates and the benzodiazepines (e.g., Valium; see Chapter 7) enhance these inhibitory properties of GABA by increasing its ability to open the chloride ion channel. Convulsant drugs like bicuculline block GABA by occupying its receptor.

There are two classes of GABA receptors: $GABA_A$ and $GABA_B$. $GABA_A$ receptors are directly linked to an ion channel and have immediate inhibitory effects, but $GABA_B$ receptors use a second messenger and are slower acting. The $GABA_A$ receptor is made up of five subunits that show considerable variation in configuration in different brain systems. This makes them deferentially sensitive to different benzodiazepines and other drugs. Different benzodiazepines may have different affinities for some of these variations, and this makes it possible for different benzodiazepines to have different effects in behavior. Some are more potent tranquilizers, some are better sedatives, and so on. By identifying the variations in the GABA receptor molecule and designing drugs that activate only those receptors, it might be possible to create benzodiazepines with very specific effects (Möhler, Fritschy, Crestani, Hensch, & Radolph, 2004).

Glutamate

Glutamate is the major excitatory transmitter in the brain. It has a number of receptor sites that work in a complex fashion and are dependent on the presence of several other substances. The best-understood glutamate receptor is the *NMDA receptor*. One of its receptors operates through a second messenger system, but glutamate causes excitation primarily using the NMDA receptor by directly opening ion channels that allow positively charged ions to cross the membrane. This channel can be blocked by alcohol, solvents, and the hallucinogenic drug phencyclidine (PCP; see Chapter 16).

Peptides

Neurotransmitter peptides are chains of amino acid molecules attached in a specific order. They can be as short as four or five amino acids or as long as 30 or more. Because most other neurotransmitters are built around a single amino acid precursor, peptide molecules are physically much larger than traditional neurotransmitters. Unlike other neurotransmitters that can be synthesized directly in the terminal bouton, these transmitters are formed in the cell body and transported to the synapse before they are stored in vesicles. Peptides are often released with other transmitters; for instance, a neuron may release glutamate and a peptide.

Peptides can be classified into several groups. One group is the *opioid-type* peptides. These are generally formed from a chain of amino acids manufactured elsewhere in the body. Some chains, varying in length from 16 to 30 amino acids, are known as *endorphins*, and shorter chains of five amino acids are called *enkephalins*. There are known receptor sites for these peptides in the brain and elsewhere in the body. Opiates such as morphine activate these same receptors. Opioid peptides have several types of receptors: *mu* (m), *kappa* (κ), and *delta* (δ) receptors. Most of the analgesic and reinforcing effects of morphine are mediated by the mu receptor, although some analgesia is associated with all of the opioid receptor types.

Almost all peptide receptors generate their effects through second messenger systems. In some cases, the peptide/receptor complex may be taken inside the cell (*endocytosis*) where it activates kinases directly. Sometimes the peptide/receptor complex can act directly as a transcription factor. The ways in which these actions are accomplished are very different from traditional neurotransmitters, but the end results are similar.

THE NERVOUS SYSTEM

The nervous system can be divided into various parts, but the most basic distinction is between the *central nervous system* (CNS) and the *peripheral nervous system* (PNS). The CNS is made up of the brain and spinal cord, and the PNS is everything outside the brain and spinal cord. In both systems, neurons are organized in a similar manner; cell bodies tend to be located together, and the axons from these cells also tend to stay together. They form a bundle of axons, which connects to other clusters of cell bodies. We, therefore, find that the nervous system is made up of groups of cell bodies and bundles of axons running between these groups of cell bodies. In the PNS, these groups of cell bodies are called *ganglia* (singular is ganglion), and the bundles of axons are called *nerves*. In the CNS, the cell body groups are called *nuclei* (singular is nucleus) or *centers*, and the bundles of axons are called *tracts*. Because axons are generally covered with myelin, which is white, the nerves and tracts usually appear white and are called *white matter*. The unmyelinated cell bodies are called *gray matter*.

The PNS

Somatic Nervous System. The PNS may be divided into two functional units: (a) the *somatic nervous system* and (b) the *autonomic nervous system*. The somatic system is made up of all the sensory nerves from most of the conscious senses, such as the nerves running from the sensory receptors in the eyes, ears, and skin to the CNS. The somatic nervous system also contains the motor nerves, which have their cell bodies in the spinal cord and send axons directly to the *striated muscles* (muscles over which we normally have voluntary control). The motor nerves control these muscles at neuromuscular junctions, which are very much like synapses. Acetylcholine is the transmitter at most neuromuscular junctions, and the receptor sites are of the nicotinic cholinergic type.

Autonomic Nervous System. Whereas the somatic system usually carries information into the CNS from our conscious senses, the autonomic nervous system is concerned with sensory systems that we are not usually aware of: information about blood pressure and blood gases, the functioning of the intestines, and levels of hormones. The somatic system controls the muscles over which we have voluntary control; the autonomic nervous system controls the muscles of the

heart and intestines, the secretions of glands, and other regulatory systems over which we normally have no conscious control.

The autonomic nervous system really has two divisions. The one that is dominant most of the time and generally keeps the internal functioning of the body operating smoothly is called the *parasympathetic nervous system*. The other autonomic system, called the *sympathetic nervous system*, is connected to the same internal organs as the parasympathetic system, but at times of stress and danger, it comes into operation and takes over from the parasympathetic system. Its function is to prepare the body for a sudden expenditure of energy, as is required for fighting or running. Blood is directed away from the digestive system to the arms and legs, the pupils dilate, and the heart rate and breathing rate increase. This series of changes is called the *fight-or-flight response*.

The parasympathetic and sympathetic nervous systems are anatomically, functionally, and neurochemically distinct. Both systems are influenced by a number of drugs. The parasympathetic system uses ACh as a transmitter to control glands and muscles. Consequently, drugs that alter transmission at cholinergic synapses interfere with parasympathetic functioning. Perhaps the best example of such drugs is atropine, which is a cholinergic muscarinic blocker, otherwise called an *anticholinergic*. Atropine has been used by optometrists to dilate the pupils in the eye so that the retina of the eye can be examined. When atropine is placed in the eye, it blocks the receptor sites at the parasympathetic neuromuscular junctions. Because the parasympathetic system can no longer control the size of the pupils, they dilate. The muscles that control the lens are also under parasympathetic control, so the atropine makes vision blurry as well. Some drugs, such as tricyclic antidepressants and antipsychotics (see Chapters 13 and 14), have anticholinergic side effects that include blurred vision and a dry mouth.

The primary transmitter in the sympathetic system is epinephrine (adrenaline). In times of stress, the adrenal gland secretes epinephrine into the blood, directly stimulating receptors in the sympathetic system and causing the fight-or-flight response. Drugs such as amphetamine and cocaine that stimulate adrenergic synapses will also cause sympathetic arousal.

The CNS

Spinal Cord. The CNS has two basic parts: the *brain* and the *spinal cord*. Some integration of information and reflex activity goes on within the spinal cord, but it functions primarily as a relay station. It transmits information from the sensory nerves into the brain and carries motor commands from the brain to the muscles. The central part of the spinal cord is composed of gray matter and shaped, in cross section, somewhat like a butterfly, as seen in Figure 4-10. It is made up of cell bodies and synapses. Axons from sensory nerves enter the gray matter of the spinal cord from the side nearest the back (dorsal side), and motor axons leaving the spinal cord do so from the side nearest the front (ventral side), as illustrated in Figure 4-10. The *ventral horn* of the gray matter of the spinal cord contains the cell bodies of the *motoneurons*, the neurons that directly control the

action of muscles. This area also mediates many reflexes. The *dorsal horn* contains cells that convey sensory information. Surrounding the gray matter are a number of tracts of axons running both up and down the spinal cord, connecting the brain to various parts of the body.

Brain. It has been estimated that the brain contains 10^{11} (i.e., 100 billion) neurons. On average, each neuron has synapses on 1,000 other neurons and receives an average of 10,000 synapses (Costa, 1985). For many years, it was thought that the number of brain cells was fixed at birth and that cells were lost as aging progressed. We now know that new nerve cells can form throughout life in species as diverse as canaries, rats, and humans. Not all areas of the brain grow new neurons, however. In humans, a region of the hippocampus (see the section "Limbic System" later in this chapter) is the only area known to give rise to new brain cells (Eriksson et al., 1998).

The brain is a complicated structure made up of numerous nuclei and complex fiber tracts that connect the nuclei in many ways. For this reason, the brain has been called a "great raveled knot."

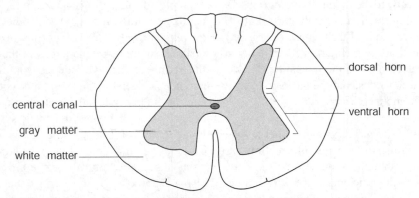

Figure 4-10 A cross section of the spinal cord, showing the white matter and gray matter. Axons of sensory nerves come in through the dorsal horn (toward the back) and form synapses in the gray matter. Cell bodies in the ventral horn (toward the front) send axons to the muscles out the ventral side of the cord. The white matter consists of bundles or tracts of myelinated axons running between the brain and different parts of the body.

In recent years, neuroscientists have made great strides in unraveling the knot, but it still contains many mysteries and is the subject of intensive study. The brain is too complex a structure to be explained in a simple fashion, but we will introduce some of the features that appear to be important in an understanding of many drug effects. Figure 4-11 represents the brain and identifies some of its structures.

Medulla. The area at the base of the brain, where the spinal cord arises, is called the *medulla*. For the most part, it is made up of fiber tracts running to and from the spinal cord and connecting it to higher centers in the brain. A number of nerves of the autonomic nervous system enter and leave the brain at the medulla, and many of them have control centers located there. The proper functioning of these centers depends on the general level of arousal in this area of the brain. The respiratory center, which controls breathing, is very sensitive to many drugs. Barbiturates, opiates, and alcohol depress this center and, consequently, depress breathing. Death from a drug overdose is usually a result of suffocation because the respiratory center becomes depressed to the point where breathing stops. Quite often people who survive drug overdoses have brain damage because low oxygen levels in their blood resulted from extended depression of their respiratory center. If you are ever in a position to help someone who has taken an overdose of a drug, it is important to stimulate or maintain breathing, either by keeping the person aroused and awake or by artificial respiration.

Another center that is located in this part of the brain and is sensitive to drugs is the *vomiting center*. This center is able to monitor the blood and can initiate vomiting, presumably to rid the digestive system of a poison that has just been ingested. Some drugs, such as opiates and nicotine, stimulate this center and cause nausea and vomiting even though the drug was inhaled or injected.

Reticular Activating System and Raphé System. Two diffuse projection systems originate in the medulla and run forward into the higher parts of the brain: the *reticular activating system* (RAS) and the *Raphé system*.

The RAS is a complicated interconnection of diffuse centers and branching fiber tracts connected in such a way that when one part is excited, the entire system becomes activated. The RAS receives input from axons of sensory nerves that run past the RAS on their way from a sense organ

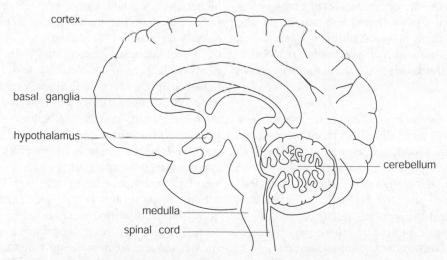

Figure 4-11 A cross section of a human brain. Note the locations of some of the structures mentioned in the text.

to the sensory areas of the cortex. Thus, the RAS is activated by incoming stimulation and projects a diffuse net of axons forward into the entire cortex and higher parts of the brain so that when the RAS becomes active, so does the entire brain. One function of the RAS is to maintain levels of activation in the cortex and thereby control the level of arousal. Because GABA is an inhibitory neurotransmitter, drugs such as barbiturates, which enhance GABA activity, decrease the ability of neurons in the RAS to fire repeatedly and, consequently, decrease arousal. If the RAS of an animal is damaged, it will fall into a coma.

Unlike the RAS, which causes arousal, parts of the Raphé system cause sleep. The Raphé system is also made up of a number of nuclei, but they are not interconnected in the same way as the RAS. Artificial stimulation of some Raphé nuclei causes sleep, and damage to them produces an animal that seldom sleeps. This finding shows that sleep is not just a lack of stimulation in the RAS but an active process as well. The Raphé nuclei use serotonin as a neurotransmitter, and drugs that alter serotonin activity also seem to interfere with sleep.

A number of centers in the Raphé system send axons forward to the limbic system and the forebrain through the *medial forebrain bundle*. These projections are thought to be part of a monoamine system that governs mood and may be the site of action for a class of antidepressants called *selective serotonin reuptake inhibitors* (SSRIs), of which fluoxetine (Prozac) is the best-known example.

Locus Coeruleus. The *locus coeruleus* is a nucleus in the lower brain that receives input from many sources both inside and outside the CNS and diffusely projects axons to the limbic system and cortex and many other higher-brain centers. Its synapses use NE as the transmitter. It is believed that the locus coeruleus contains about 50 to 70 percent of the noradrenergic neurons in the brain. This system, along with several other similar systems (such as the serotonergic forebrain projections of the Raphé system), projects to the higher-brain centers through the medial forebrain bundle and is known to be involved in the control of mood. Depression is believed to be a result of abnormal functioning of these systems.

The activity of the locus coeruleus is controlled by a large inhibitory input of synapses that releases GABA. In addition to mood, activity in the locus coeruleus is believed to be associated with fear, panic, and anger. *Positron emission tomography* (PET) shows that the locus coeruleus and the places in the brain where it sends its axons become highly active when people are having panic attacks. Drugs like the benzodiazepines (e.g., Valium), which increase the inhibitory effect of GABA, are known to relieve anxiety (see Chapter 7), and drugs like amphetamine and cocaine, which stimulate adrenergic synapses, can cause anxiety (see Chapter 12).

The locus coeruleus has also been shown to be involved in the processing of sensory information and has an alerting function when a novel stimulus is experienced.

Cerebellum. Just inside the skull, above the medulla, is a structure known as the *cerebellum*. The cerebellum functions as part of the motor system. Voluntary actions are initiated and controlled by an area of the cortex (discussed later) higher up in the brain, known as the *motor cortex*. Cell bodies in the motor cortex send axons directly to the spinal cord through fiber bundles that travel through the brain stem. There is, however, much more to the motor system than this. Signals from the cortex to the muscles are refined and modified by two other locations in the brain: the *basal ganglia* and the cerebellum. The cerebellum receives direct input from the motor cortex and from the muscles themselves via the spinal cord. It compares these two signals and modifies the output of the cortex both by direct actions on its signals as they pass through the brain stem and by fibers connected back to the cortex. These feedback loops make possible smooth and accurate muscle movements. Another function of the cerebellum is control of the movement of the eye from one fixation point to another. The cerebellum also seems to be involved in learning.

People with damage to the cerebellum are slow and clumsy and often appear to be intoxicated with alcohol. It is quite likely that many of the motor effects of alcohol are due to a specific effect on the cerebellum.

Basal Ganglia. The basal ganglia, located just under the cortex, are important in controlling voluntary movement. Although they contain several nuclei, in a broad sense the basal ganglia can be divided into an input side and an output side. The *striatum* is the input side; it receives axons from the cortex and *thalamus*. The striatum includes the *caudate nucleus* and *putamen*. Projections from the striatum are sent to the *globus pallidus* (or *pallidum*), which is the output side of the basal ganglia. The globus pallidus sends projections back to the cortex via the thalamus. Together, the basal ganglia, the thalamus, and the cortex make up the "motor loop" and control all voluntary movement.

Parkinson's disease is a result of a malfunction of the basal ganglia. People suffering from Parkinson's disease have tremors, rigidity in the limbs, and difficulty initiating movement. It has been demonstrated that Parkinson's is caused by a depletion of DA in the synapses of axons that terminate in the basal ganglia from a center known as the *substantia nigra*. This pathway is known as the *nigrostriatal system*. In many people, the symptoms of Parkinson's disease can be alleviated if the patient is given L-dopa, the metabolic precursor of DA. The L-dopa is absorbed into the brain and transformed into DA, which then increases activity at these synapses in the basal ganglia. We also know that drugs like the antipsychotics, which block DA receptors, have side effects that resemble Parkinson's disease (see Chapter 13).

The system that directly connects the motor cortex to the muscles is called the *pyramidal motor system*; consequently, the system involving the basal ganglia is sometimes called the *extrapyramidal motor system*.

In addition to motor control, the basal ganglia have other functions. They include control of eye movement, memory for locations in space, and some thought processes.

Periaqueductal Gray. Another system that runs through the central part of the brain is the *periaqueductal gray* or *central gray*. It has two functions of interest. The first is involved in the perception of pain. The periaqueductal gray serves as one of several relays for axons that carry pain signals from the dorsal horn of the spinal cord to the cortex. This area is rich in receptor sites for opiate drugs (e.g., morphine) and their endogenous counterparts, endorphins and enkephalins. These neurons send axons to the spinal cord, where they inhibit the neurons that convey pain signals from the body to higher levels of the brain. They do so both by direct inhibition and by stimulating other neurons that release endogenous opiates in the spinal cord. Thus, opiate drugs can block pain by stimulating cells in the periaqueductal gray and the spinal cord.

Also located in the periaqueductal gray is a system that has been described as a "punishment" system. These are sites where electrical stimulation appears to have a punishing effect on experimental animals. Animals will learn to perform a task in order to avoid stimulation in this area. It has not been determined whether the pain perception and the punishment functions of these systems are related, but it is certainly tempting to speculate that they are. The periaqueductal gray also receives input from the *amygdala*, a center that mediates fear and fear conditioning.

Limbic System. Just under the cortex is a series of interconnected nuclei known as the *limbic system*. Among other complex functions, the structures in the limbic system are involved in the control of motivations and emotions and seem to be the site of action of many drugs. One of the more complex structures in the limbic system is the *hypothalamus*. Lesions in specific parts of the hypothalamus can either induce excessive eating or drinking or abolish eating or drinking in experimental animals.

Some reinforcement or pleasure centers are also located in the hypothalamus. Humans and nonhumans will learn to press levers or engage in activities that are followed by electrical stimulation in these areas of the brain. It is thought that the reinforcement centers are stimulated by natural reinforcing stimuli like food and water. The function of such systems is to ensure that the organism will repeat actions that have led to the satisfaction of the drive. They have been called *pleasure centers* because humans sometimes report experiencing pleasure when these areas of the brain are stimulated electrically.

Many reinforcement centers of the brain are associated with the fiber tract called the *medial forebrain bundle*, which carries axons that run in both directions between lower centers in the brain and the hypothalamus and other limbic system structures.

One important reinforcement system, the *mesolimbic dopamine system*, has been identified as a fiber tract whose cell bodies are located in the *ventral tegmental area* (VTA) in the midbrain. The axons of these neurons run through the medial forebrain bundle and terminate in synapses in the limbic system, forebrain, and other structures. In the limbic system, many fibers from the VTA have synapses in the *nucleus accumbens*. Because these fibers use DA as a neurotransmitter and some are known to have receptor sites for morphine-like transmitters on their cell bodies in the VTA, drugs like amphetamine, cocaine, and morphine can stimulate them. This stimulation is probably the source of the *rushes* or intense feelings of pleasure that these drugs cause as well as the powerful tendency to repeat actions that lead to the administration of the drug (see Chapter 5). Malfunctions of the mesolimbic dopamine system also appear to be an important cause of schizophrenia (see Chapter 13).

The *hippocampus* is a large limbic structure that has been implicated in learning and memory. Removal of the hippocampus in humans (as was done years ago to treat epilepsy) causes amnesia. In rats, the hippocampus is important for spatial memory, and destruction of the hippocampus will prevent an animal from learning even a very simple maze consisting of an open field with no walls. Most drugs have effects on the hippocampus, although they can be difficult to spot in traditional behavioral tests. Drug effects on the hippocampus may be related to state dependency and long-term effects rather than acute effects. Place preference, created by associating a place with a drug (discussed in Chapter 5), is also probably mediated, at least in part, by the hippocampus.

Other limbic system structures include the amygdala and the *septum*. Among other connections, these centers receive serotonergic input from the Raphé nuclei. Lesions in the amygdala cause normally aggressive experimental animals to become calm and placid, but when the amygdala is stimulated, animals become aggressive and attack other animals. The amygdala also is active in fear and fear conditioning and is known to be active when people are afraid or have panic attacks. Lesions in the septum also cause emotional changes.

Although it is not known how drugs affect neurotransmitters in the limbic system, it appears that many benzodiazepine receptors are located in this region. The benzodiazepines enhance the inhibitory effects of GABA, and this increased inhibition in the limbic system may be one mechanism by which the benzodiazepines, such as chlordiazepoxide (Librium) and diazepam (Valium), reduce aggression in nonhumans and produce a calming effect (see Chapter 7).

Cortex. The *cortex* makes up the uppermost surface of the brain and virtually covers the rest of the brain. It is convoluted and gives the brain the appearance of a walnut. Because of its convolutions, most of the cortex cannot be seen. If it were flattened out, it would cover an area of 2.5 square feet.

The cortex is undoubtedly the most complex and advanced part of the brain. Its neurochemistry is not well understood, but glutamate and GABA are known to be its prominent excitatory and inhibitory transmitters. Dissociative anesthetics like PCP and ketamine (see Chapter 16) are known to act at these NDMA receptors for glutamate, and these drugs probably have their effects directly on the cortex.

One of the functions of the cortex is to handle the integration of sensory information. Information from each sense is projected to a different part of the cortex, where it is analyzed. Visual information is processed in the *visual cortex* at the back of the brain, and hearing is processed in the *temporal lobes*, as in language and speech. The *somatosensory cortex* handles sensory input from the body. The motor cortex is the area that is responsible for voluntary motor control and is located close to the somatosensory cortex. The motor cortex sends axons directly to the interneurons in the spinal cord that control the motor neurons and, consequently, the muscles (pyramidal motor system). Other axons from this area go to the basal ganglia and the cerebellum, which modify the direct output of the motor cortex and coordinate bodily movement (extrapyramidal motor system). Many of these areas of the cortex are shown in Figure 4-12.

While sensory and motor functions are handled by the central and posterior parts of the cortex, higher mental processes of thought and cognition are carried out in areas of the *frontal cortex* and the *prefrontal cortex*. The frontal cortex monitors the relationship between stimuli and reinforcer availability (including cues that predict the availability of drugs), provides inhibition or control over actions, and appears to regulate expression of emotional behavior. Located ventral to (below) the frontal cortex is the *orbitofrontal cortex*, which is involved in the learning and relearning of stimulus–reward associations and in behavioral control following rewarding or punishing feedback. The prefrontal cortex is the most rostral (toward the front) region of the cortex and is involved in working memory functions, including directing attention, decision making, task switching, deductive reasoning, planning, judgment, and memorization. The *dorsolateral prefrontal cortex* (higher and to the side) has been implicated in the representation, manipulation, and maintenance of attentional demands of a task. The *anterior cingulate* is part of the medial prefrontal cortex that is thought to mediate attention, response competition and selection, suppression of prepotent response tendencies, conditioned drug seeking, and craving.

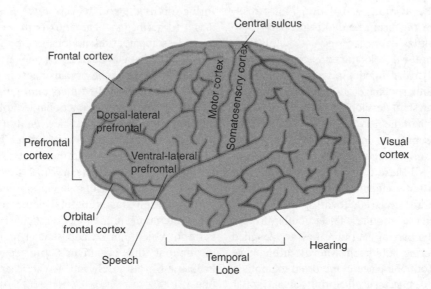

Figure 4-12 The cortex showing the major areas.

Understanding the anatomy and neurochemistry of these complex cortical structures is still elusive, but modern imaging studies (discussed shortly) have provided a great deal of information on their role in the expression of many complex cognitive and behavioral functions, including the effects of drugs and the process of addiction.

DEVELOPMENT OF THE NERVOUS SYSTEM

In the early 1960s, a drug called *thalidomide* was prescribed to many pregnant women to treat the nausea of morning sickness. Unfortunately, the drug interfered with the developing fetus, and many of these mothers gave birth to babies with missing or severely malformed limbs. Since the time of thalidomide, it has become widely recognized that drugs consumed by a mother during pregnancy can alter the development of the fetus. Drugs that cause such malformations are called *teratogens* (literally, "monster makers").

The developing nervous system is particularly vulnerable to disruption by drugs, and there are two reasons to believe that behaviorally active drugs are especially potent teratogens. First, in order to be behaviorally active, drugs must readily penetrate the brain, and this property also gives these drugs easy access across the placenta to the body of the developing fetus. Second, drugs that act to alter the functioning of neurotransmitters are particularly dangerous because of the way the nervous system develops.

The growth of the nervous system is a complex and delicate process involving the formation, migration, and interconnection of billions of nerve cells. All these cells form during the first 12 weeks after conception. During this time, therefore, brain cells are forming at a rate of 150,000 cells a minute. These cells do not develop in the part of the brain they are destined to occupy during adulthood. Many neurons have to migrate from one place in the brain to another. This journey must take place only at particular times in the development of the brain and in the appropriate order, or the brain will develop incorrectly. When these cells reach their target area, their growth is still not completed. They must attach themselves to their neighbors and send out their axons along prescribed paths to make contact with other cells in the developing brain. In addition, they must then form synapses with these other cells.

The formation, differentiation, and migration of cells; the projection of axons; and the formation of synapses are under chemical control. Chemicals are released by different parts of the developing brain, and the migrating cells and axons move either toward or away from these sources of chemicals. It is now believed that these control chemicals are similar to substances used as neurotransmitters in the adult brain. Consequently, if a mother consumes a psychoactive drug at crucial times during the development of the fetal brain, it could interfere with the delicate chemical signaling taking place in the developing brain of the fetus. If these chemical control signals are altered, masked, or inhibited, the development of the fetal brain may be disrupted (Abel & Sokol, 1989).

Such disruptions may cause severe brain malformation of the sort seen in *fetal alcohol syndrome* (described in Chapter 6), or they may cause much less apparent disruptions in the functioning of the brain that can be detected only after careful systematic study of the organism's behavior. This kind of damage is called *functional teratology* or *behavioral teratology*. Functional teratology is an exciting and comparatively new field of research. Most functional teratology research has been done on laboratory animals, and the exact significance for humans is still not clear. What is clear is that exposure to low levels of behaviorally active drugs during certain stages of fetal development can cause alterations in the functioning of the nervous system, which can be apparent at many stages throughout the organism's life span (Boer, Feenstra, Mirmiran, Swaab, & Van Haaren, 1988; Spear, 1997).

BRAIN IMAGING OF DRUG EFFECTS

Electroencephalography and Event-Related Potentials

Electroencephalography. In Chapter 2, we discussed how changes in level of arousal, from alertness to sleep, correspond to variations in brain wave activity. These changes are measured using a device called an *electroencephalograph* (EEG). Invented in 1929 by a German neuropsychiatrist named Hans Berger, the EEG is the oldest technique used to monitor brain activity.

The EEG works by measuring electrical activity originating in the cerebral cortex and subcortical nuclei. Generally, 21 electrodes are adhered to the scalp at specific locations that are determined using standard landmarks on the skull, and a reference electrode is attached to a neutral part of the body, usually the earlobe or cheek, where there is very little electrical activity. This electrode provides an electrically neutral point against which to measure the electrical potential differences at the other 21 electrodes. The potential differences between the points on the scalp and the neutral part of the body are amplified and recorded by pens on a roll of paper that moves at a constant rate. The changes in the potential detected by these electrodes show up as wavy lines on the paper, and these tracings indicate the simultaneous firing of neurons in the brain in the vicinity of the electrode. The EEG provides a direct measure of brain activity. It is analyzed in terms of *frequency* (the number of oscillations or waves per second, measured in hertz [Hz]) and *amplitude* (or the magnitude of waves in millivolts). Frequency reflects the rate of firing, and amplitude reflects the number of neurons firing in synchrony and the distance between the neurons and the recording electrode.

The slowest-frequency waves are called *delta waves*, ranging from approximately 1 to 3 Hz. *Theta waves* are 4 to 8 Hz, and *alpha waves* are from 8 to 13 Hz. *Beta waves* are from 12 to 35 Hz.

EEG is a very useful tool in psychopharmacology. In addition to being a direct measure of arousal, EEG changes can also be correlated with changes in subjective state or mood. By asking participants to report their mood while under the influence of a particular drug, their subjective state can be correlated with EEG recordings.

EEG recordings can also be used to compare alterations in brain activity during a drug-free baseline measure or in a control group versus participants under the influence of a particular drug. Such alterations may include the appearance of a new waveform that differs from that of the control state, spikes in amplitude of waveforms (characteristic of seizure activity), or stabilization of normal waveform fluctuations that occur between varying levels of arousal.

Classification of newly developed drugs can also be accomplished using EEG by comparing electrophysiological characteristics of known drugs and categorizing new drugs according to similarities in frequency and amplitude of waveforms. Drug tolerance and drug dependence (discussed in Chapter 3) can also be quantified by assessing changes in EEG recordings over repeated sessions. Decreases in drug-induced changes in the amplitude or frequency of EEG waves across repeated drug sessions indicate tolerance to the neurophysiological effects of a drug. Similarly, researchers can use EEG to assess the rate at which tolerance occurs as well as the degree of cross-tolerance between various drugs of the same class. Physical dependence can also be assessed by the appearance of withdrawal symptoms once the effects of a drug have worn off. Physical dependence, like tolerance, can be quantified by correlating EEG recordings with somatic and autonomic withdrawal symptoms. Finally, there is evidence that the EEG can detect differences in brain wave patterns between people with a predisposition to become addicted to certain drugs. By analyzing the EEGs of these individuals after exposure to a drug, it may be possible to identify individuals at risk of drug dependence. It may also be possible to identify how changes in brain activity in high-risk individuals can cause addiction to certain drugs.

Event-Related Potentials. To assess genetic vulnerabilities to drug addiction, researchers most commonly analyze *evoked potentials*, also referred to as *event-related potentials* (ERP), within an EEG paradigm. Commonly occurring events, such as visual or auditory stimuli presented by an experimenter, evoke characteristic deflections in the waveform being plotted on the EEG recording. An unexpected stimulus evokes a very different ERP with a characteristic positive deflection in amplitude at approximately 300 milliseconds (ms) but ranging from 250 to 500 ms following stimulus presentation. This ERP is known as the *P300* (a positive deflection at approximately 300 ms post-stimulus). The paradigm used to evoke the P300 is called the *oddball paradigm*, in which a participant is presented with two stimuli that differ along some dimension, such as the color of visual stimuli or the tone of auditory stimuli. One of these stimuli is rarely presented (the low-probability stimulus), whereas the other occurs frequently (the high-probability stimulus). The participant is instructed to ignore the high-probability stimulus and to attend only to the low-probability stimulus (the oddball). Presentation of the oddball evokes the P300 potential. The amplitude of the P300 provides an index of the amount of cognitive energy or resources the participant is devoting to perception of the stimulus. Decreases in P300 amplitude, therefore, indicate a reduced capacity or an impairment in the ability to pay attention to the stimulus. The latency of the P300 (i.e., the amount of time that elapses between presentation of the oddball and the occurrence of the P300 potential) provides an index of the time required for the participant to evaluate and recognize the stimulus as the oddball. Longer P300 latencies, therefore, indicate that the participant needs more time to process the stimulus. There is some evidence that the P300 wave is different in those who have a high genetic susceptibility to become an alcoholic.

The P300 is also useful in assessing the acute effects and duration of action of different classes of drugs on participants' cognitive capacity. These measures can be more sensitive than behavioral or neuropsychological assessments and are useful in discovering some of the more subtle impairments in the cognitive processing of events. ERP can also be used to measure tolerance and dependence in drug-using participants. Intoxicated participants with a history of drug abuse often display P300 amplitudes and latencies similar to control participants who are naive to the particular drug, This suggests that the brain of a drug abuser can compensate for the effects of the drug (i.e., that the participant has developed tolerance to the drug-induced cognitive impairments). When the same participants stop using the drug, however, reductions in P300 amplitude and increases in latency appear, suggesting the development of drug dependence.

Problems with EEG and ERP. Both EEG and ERP are useful techniques that continue to inform researchers of the effects of drug intoxication. These techniques are extremely reliable when testing conditions are strictly maintained but are sensitive to factors such as time of day, season of the year, age of the participant, and the recency of food intake. These factors must, therefore, be carefully controlled when performing EEG or ERP techniques. It has been suggested that EEG and ERP have limited diagnostic ability given that the distinctiveness of drug effects can be very small. For example, increases in alpha activity is common to many classes of drugs and is similarly observed in participants practicing transcendental meditation. Similarly, decreases in P300 amplitude that indicate drug withdrawal are also evident in individuals diagnosed with dementia, schizophrenia, depression, and borderline personality disorder. These similarities could possibly lead to misinterpretation of EEG or ERP data because these changes in brain activity may be caused by some factor other than the drug effect under investigation.

Positron Emission Techniques

Positron Emission Tomography. *Positron emission tomography* (PET) makes use of the unstable, chemical properties of *radioactive tracer isotopes* (*radiotracers*) to produce three-dimensional images of the brain. Radioisotopes most commonly used in PET imaging of the brain include ^{15}oxygen (^{15}O), ^{13}nitrogen (^{13}N), ^{11}carbon (^{11}C), and ^{18}fluorine (^{18}F). Participants ingest a radiotracer made up of a metabolically active agent, such as glucose, water, or a drug of abuse, that has been made radioactive by being combined with a radioactive isotope. For example, when a stable carbon atom in a molecule of cocaine is replaced by the unstable isotope of carbon, ^{11}C, the result is the radiotracer [^{11}C]-cocaine, which can be detected in the brain. A machine called a *cyclotron* is needed to create these radiotracers.

Radiotracers can be given by injection, inhalation, or orally, depending on the agent that is being administered. Participants must wait for a short period while the radiotracer becomes concentrated in brain areas where the metabolically active agent or drug is distributed. They are then placed in the PET imaging scanner, which is shaped like a cylinder and contains a series of connected radiation detector cameras. Radioisotopes such as ^{15}O, ^{13}N, ^{11}C, and ^{18}F are short lived, with half-lives ranging from 2 to 110 minutes, and decay by emitting positrons. The emitted positrons are antimatter that travel a distance of less than 1 mm before meeting an electron, which is matter. As a result, they annihilate each other, and this produces high-energy *gamma rays* that pass out of the brain in exactly opposite directions, at which point they are detected by special cameras.

Radiation detector cameras used in PET imaging are comprised of a ring of *scintillator crystals* that fluoresce momentarily when struck by high-energy gamma rays. Bursts of light produced by gamma rays that hit the ring of crystals at exactly 180 degrees apart and at exactly the same time are detected and amplified by photomultiplier tubes. This information is then transmitted to a computer. Gamma rays detected even slightly off of 180 degrees apart or at a difference of nanoseconds are ignored. By measuring where gamma rays hit the scintillator crystals, researchers can plot the origin of positron emission to create an image of exactly where the radiotracer activity is within the brain.

PET scans can be used for a wide range of purposes. First, they allow researchers to directly measure the brain distribution and activity of stimulant drugs such as cocaine, methamphetamine, and amphetamine; opioids such as heroin and morphine; hallucinogens such as PCP and ketamine; and other commonly used drugs, such as nicotine, alcohol, and marijuana.

Second, local concentrations of drug receptor sites can be determined by administering tiny doses of radiotracers that contain pharmacologically inactive amounts of a drug and occupy only a small fraction of available receptor sites. This allows researchers to estimate drug receptor density in specific brain areas and to keep track of changes in the number of receptors that might occur over time, for example, because of tolerance.

Third, PET scanning can be used to assess competition for receptor binding sites, as when molecules of a drug or radiotracer compete with a neurotransmitter for binding on the same receptor site. Competition between a drug and a radiotracer that occupies the same receptor site but produces no changes in mood can provide an index of the degree of drug binding required to produce subjective feelings of drug-induced euphoria. This method can also be used to measure the actions of naturally occurring chemicals, such as neurotransmitters, or to assess potential treatments (antagonists) that might block or reverse the effects of an abused drug.

Fourth, PET scanning can be used to isolate areas of the brain that are active during a mental activity, such as drug craving, by measuring changes in metabolic activity and blood flow to these areas. Using the glucose-mimicking radiotracer 2-deoxy-2-[^{18}F]fluoro-D-glucose (abbreviated ^{18}FDG), changes that occur in regional glucose metabolism as neurons are activated and deactivated can be traced to particular brain regions that are active during drug craving, and changes in regional cerebral blood flow (which is correlated with glucose metabolism) can be assessed using [^{15}O]-water.

Finally, PET scanners for laboratory animals, such as rats and apes, aid in the preclinical assessment of newly developed drug treatments. Animal researchers use this technology to radio-label and monitor drug absorption, distribution, and excretion more efficiently compared to the time and cost involved in sacrificing multiple animals and analyzing brain tissue.

PET scanning of the human brain was developed in 1973 by researchers at Washington University in St Louis, Missouri. It was superior to other techniques used at that time, such as EEG, because PET could isolate areas of drug activity and glucose and oxygen use deep within the brain and could be completed in as little as 30 seconds. Currently, radiolabeling allows researchers to locate the sites of action of a virtually unlimited number of biologically active compounds.

Problems with PET. PET imaging does have its limitations. Compared to newer technologies, such as *magnetic resonance imaging*, PET offers a low degree of spatial resolution, and it is sometimes difficult to distinguish between two structures very close together in the brain. Ideally, a PET scanner would be able to isolate the location of gamma ray emission within 0.5 mm, something that has not yet been achieved. The most state-of-the-art PET scanners achieve a reconstructed image resolution of 4 to 4.5 mm because of the necessary size of scintillator crystals, which measure approximately 3 to 4 mm in width. PET scanning also poses a health risk in that radioactive agents are administered into a patient's body. The total dose of radiation during a scanning session is usually 7 millisieverts (mSv), comparable to 70 chest X-rays. This amount seems relatively large. However, when we consider that 7 mSv is approximately equal to 1 year of radiation exposure for the aircrew of a commercial jetliner, the risk can be put in better perspective. Nevertheless, the health costs and benefits of radiation exposure inherent in conducting PET scans must be weighed carefully, especially if multiple scans are to be performed on a single patient.

Finally, the expense of PET scanning, in terms of medical personnel and equipment required, limits its use. Because the radioisotopes used to create radiotracers decay so quickly, they must be produced on-site. This means that a cyclotron, which produces the radioisotopes, must be bought (at a price of $2.5 million to $4.6 million, plus an additional $1 million setup cost) or located very nearby.

SPECT. As an alternative to PET, brain imaging can be completed using its sister technique, *single photon emission computed tomography* (SPECT). SPECT uses a *collimator*, consisting of lead blocks containing many tiny holes that allow gamma rays to pass through and hit scintillator crystals that detect rays that project from the brain in parallel. This information is then amplified by photomultiplier tubes and transmitted to a computer. Nonparallel gamma rays are undetected and are absorbed by the lead. Compared to PET scanning, SPECT uses radioisotopes that are much longer lasting, such as ^{99m}technetuim (^{99m}Tc), ^{123}iodine (^{123}I), and ^{133}xenon (^{133}Xe), with half-lives ranging from 6 hours to 5 days. This allows for more long-lasting brain functions to be measured and also eliminates the need for having a cyclotron on-site, greatly reducing the cost of scanning. However, compared to coincident detection of gamma rays in PET, detection of parallel rays in SPECT can be technically challenging and more susceptible to error. Furthermore, the spatial resolution of SPECT is even less than that of PET, generating an even less precise image of active brain regions.

Magnetic Resonance Techniques

Magnetic resonance imaging (MRI) is a technique that takes advantage of the magnetic charge of billions of hydrogen atoms that exist in the body. The nucleus of the hydrogen atom has a single proton (which has a positive electrical charge) and a large *magnetic moment*, making it ideal for the purposes of MRI. Having a large magnetic moment means that when hydrogen atoms are placed within a magnetic field, they will align with the field, similar to the way in which iron filings scattered randomly on a sheet of paper will align parallel to a bar magnet placed beneath the paper. Although they are aligned with the magnetic field, this does not mean that hydrogen nuclei stand still. In fact, the atoms are in constant movement, each spinning on its axis like a child's toy top. It is this spinning of positively charged protons that produces the magnetic property of hydrogen nuclei.

The most fundamental component of an MRI machine is the very powerful magnet that creates an external magnetic field, forcing the alignment of hydrogen nuclei within the body. The MRI machine looks like a giant cube, typically measuring 2 meters tall by 2 meters wide and 3 meters long. It contains a horizontal tube, called the *bore* of the magnet, in which a participant is placed. Two units of measurement are commonly used to describe the intensity of a magnetic field within the bore: *gauss* and *tesla* (where 1 tesla = 10,000 gauss). The magnetic pull of the earth is 0.5 gauss, whereas the magnetic field that runs through the bore of the MRI machine measures 1.5 to 2.0 tesla, or up to 40,000 times more intense than the magnetic field of the earth. The type of magnet most commonly used to create this amazingly powerful field is called a *superconducting magnet*. It consists of many coils of wire, wrapped around the bore of the magnet, that conduct an electric current and create the magnetic field. You can imagine that the amount of electricity required to generate and maintain a magnetic field of 1.5 tesla would be prohibitively expensive. To overcome this obstacle, the coils of wire are bathed in liquid helium, bringing the temperature of the wire to more than 452 degrees Fahrenheit (269 degrees Celsius) below zero. This extreme cold eliminates the electrical resistance of the wire and makes using the MRI scanner much more economically feasible.

Once the participant is placed within the *isocenter* (exact center) of the bore and the magnetic field is turned on, the spinning hydrogen protons within the participant's body align in the direction of the field, which, running from head to toe, is called the *z-axis*. Because of the complex laws of quantum mechanics, approximately half the protons will line up in the direction of the participant's feet and half in the direction of the participant's head. However, they largely cancel each other out and produce a net magnetization *angle of alignment* (a) of 0 degrees. While they are aligned, spinning hydrogen protons also rotate, or *precess*, around the axis of the externally created magnetic field, somewhat similar to how the earth revolves around the sun. The precession frequency of an atom (how quickly the protons precess) is specific to the type of atom and is known as the *Larmor frequency*. For the hydrogen proton, the Larmor frequency in a magnetic field of 1.5 tesla is 63.9 megahertz (MHz), where 1 MHz equals 1 million Hz, or 1 million cycles per second. Although all hydrogen nuclei precess at this frequency, at any given time the protons may be at any *phase* of their precession around the axis of the externally created magnetic field. It helps to think of phase in terms of an analog clock. Imagine that multiple clocks are purchased in an airport shop and taken by the purchasers to various parts of the world. Once they arrive in their particular time zone, each purchaser sets the clock to the proper time of day. The second hand, minute hand, and hour hand on each of the clocks should move (precess) around the center (axis) of the clock at the same speed. However, each of the clocks would be at a different phase of its precession since each time zone is different. So while the frequency of precession for each clock is identical, each clock would be at a different phase of their precession around the axis of the clock at any given time. Phase is an important component in obtaining an MRI image, which we will review shortly.

So far we've discussed the "magnetic" component of MRI, but what about *resonance*? Resonance is defined as the transfer of energy, at a particular frequency, between two systems. Every material has a natural frequency at which it resonates. If you've ever rubbed a moist fingertip around the rim of a crystal wine glass, you'll have noticed that the glass seems to "sing." This phenomenon is produced by the transfer of energy from the friction generated by the contact of your moving fingertip with the glass, causing the molecules of the crystal to vibrate at their natural resonant frequency. If a singer could produce a tone of the exact resonant frequency of crystal and of a great enough amplitude (volume), the glass would absorb enough energy from the sound waves produced by the singer that it would shatter under the strain. In MRI, electromagnetic energy in the form of *radiofrequency* (RF) *waves* is directed into the body. Electromagnetic energy is a combination of electric and magnetic fields that travel at the speed of light. In addition to RF waves, other forms of electromagnetic energy include X-rays, microwaves, gamma rays, and all forms of light, including ultraviolet and infrared. When directed into the body, pulses of RF energy that are at the precise Larmor frequency of hydrogen protons cause the protons to absorb the energy and resonate. As the protons resonate, their net magnetization, or angle of alignment (a) with the z-axis (the external magnetic field), diverges from 0 degrees and, if enough energy is applied, approaches 90 or even 180 degrees. When a = 90 degrees, the RF pulse is referred to as a 90-degree pulse; at 180 degrees, it is referred to as a 180-degree pulse. As RF waves are applied through the coils of the MRI machine, hydrogen protons not only increase their angle of alignment from the z-axis but also acquire the same phase of precession a nd the axis of the external magnetic field. king back to our clock analogy, it's as if all ks all over the world suddenly began to display same time of day and rotate in step with each r. When the RF pulse is turned off, the protons n to return to their 0-degree alignment with the is and also begin the process of *dephasing*, or r ating out of step. As they do so, the protons re ase the excess of energy (in the form of RF wa s) that was stored during resonation, creating a signal that is picked up by the coil of the MRI machine and sent to a computer.

It is these two components of relaxation—proton realignment with the z-axis and proton dephasing—that are used to create an MRI image of the body. These two components of proton relaxation are characterized by *relaxation times* that will be used to describe MRI data. The first is called *spin-lattice relaxation time* (T1) and is the amount of time in milliseconds for the strength of the net magnetization (e.g., a = 90 or 180 degrees) to return to 63 percent of its value before RF waves were applied. This measure will vary according to the type of tissue being resonated. The second component of proton relaxation is called *spin-spin relaxation time* (T2) and is the amount of time required for protons to complete their dephasing (or to stop rotating in step) once the RF waves have been stopped. A T1-weighted image (where spin-lattice relaxation is the dominant source of the MR signal) produces a clear image of neuroanatomy in which gray matter appears gray, white matter appears white, and cerebrospinal fluid is dark. A T2-weighted image (where spin-spin relaxation is the dominant source of the MR signal) highlights areas of pathology in which gray matter appears dark, white matter appears bright, and cerebrospinal fluid is even brighter.

When an MRI exam is being administered, the most widely used methodology is called the *spin echo sequence*, which allows researchers to construct three-dimensional images of the body. A series of 90-degree RF pulses are repeatedly applied to the participant at a constant repetition time. As protons relax following the cessation of the 90-degree RF pulse, a 180-degree RF pulse is applied that reverses proton relaxation, causing an increase in the angle of alignment and a rephasing of protons, thereby increasing the emitted signal. The images created have a high spatial resolution in the order of 0.5 to 2.0 mm, making the produced image visually superior to that produced in PET imaging.

The MRI room must be specially constructed with a reinforced floor and a magnetic shield not only to block the effects of the superconducting magnet but also to prevent interference from other sources of radiofrequency waves (such as FM radio) that can be picked up and sent by the machine and interfere with data acquisition.

fMRI. Like PET scanning, magnetic resonance can also be used to link changes in cerebral blood flow with activity in specific areas of the brain using a technique called *functional magnetic resonance imaging* (fMRI). Rather than injecting radioactive tracers, however, fMRI relies on the intravenous injection of a magnetic agent (the *contrast technique*) or the magnetic properties of iron-rich deoxygenated hemoglobin (the *noncontrast technique*). A commonly used contrast technique requires the injection of gadolinium, a silvery-white metal that is highly magnetic. Injection of gadolinium increases the strength of the magnetic field only in those regions of the brain that are activated by a particular stimulus (such as a word, picture, or sound broadcast to the participant in the MRI machine) or a particular emotional or mood state. The change in magnetic field strength alters spin-spin (T2) relaxation time, thereby producing a visually contrasting image in active versus inactive areas of the brain.

The most commonly used noncontrast fMRI technique is referred to as *blood oxygen level–dependent* (BOLD) *imaging*, which uses T2-weighted images to assess changes in local concentrations of deoxygenated hemoglobin. During brain activation, changes in blood flow and volume exceed the speed at which oxygen is consumed from the blood. This leads to increased quantities of oxygenated hemoglobin (and a reduction in the ratio of deoxygenated to oxygenated hemoglobin) in the brain, thereby producing changes in fMRI signal intensity.

fMRI frequently uses a methodology called *gradient echo sequence*, which is very similar to spin echo sequence used in MRI. In fact, both spin echo and gradient echo sequences can be used in both MRI and fMRI data acquisition. In gradient echo sequence, series of RF pulses are applied at the Larmor frequency of hydrogen, and T1 and T2 relaxation times are used to produce an image, as in spin echo sequence. In gradient echo sequence, however, as RF pulses are applied to the brain through the coil, a gradient magnet, much weaker in intensity compared to the

superconducting magnet (ranging in strength from 180 to 270 gauss), produces an additional magnetic field that is superimposed on the main magnetic field. Brief application of this gradient field accelerates the dephasing of hydrogen protons (i.e., spin-spin relaxation). A second gradient is then applied to reverse the process of dephasing, causing rephasing of protons. The purpose of using gradient magnets is to cause brief disturbances in the external magnetic field rather than administering additional RF pulses, as is the case in spin echo imaging. The gradient magnets excite only a small slice of tissue rather than the entire volume and are thereby used to alter the resonance of hydrogen protons at very precise areas of the brain that researchers are interested in imaging. As such, multiple gradients can be applied to different regions of the brain in succession, thereby significantly reducing the amount of time required for scanning.

Advantages and Problems with MRI. Magnetic resonance techniques are superior to many other forms of brain imaging because they produce images with very high contrast resolution (the ability to distinguish two similar but not identical tissues in a very small area) and spatial resolution in relatively little time. They are also quite safe in that they do not require the injection of radioactive materials, as does PET scanning. However, MRI and fMRI are not without shortcomings. Like PET scanning equipment, MRI equipment is very expensive to purchase and use. In addition, the physical setup of the MRI machine can be problematic for certain individuals. People weighing more than 134 kg (295 pounds) cannot be handled by most MRI machines, although newer machines are being constructed to accommodate heavier individuals. Furthermore, a significant number of participants (approximately 10 percent) also report feeling high levels of discomfort or anxiety, with 1 percent of participants exhibiting severe claustrophobic or panic attacks inside the small confinement of the MRI bore. The loud clanking noise created by the scanner and scanning sessions ranging from 20 to 90 minutes only exacerbate this problem. An additional problem is the need for participants to remain entirely motionless throughout the session, which is especially difficult if they are feeling anxious or uncomfortable. Even very slight head movements can create significant loss of spatial resolution and distortion in the created image.

Because of the extreme intensity of the superconducting magnet, participants and medical personnel are checked carefully for any metal objects they may be carrying before they enter the MRI room. Paper clips, keys, hemostats, stethoscopes, hair clips, and any other small magnetic objects can be pulled off the body and become dangerous flying projectiles, getting sucked into the bore of the MRI where the participant is lying. In addition to external objects, metallic objects inside the body, such as aneurysm clips in the brain, some dental implants, heart pacemakers, and metal objects not secured in place by the growth of scar tissue (e.g., newly inserted staples or fragments of metal in the eye, which does not form scar tissue), can be dislodged or heated to scalding temperatures by the magnet, causing severe internal damage. Pacemakers are particularly sensitive and can malfunction even if the wearer goes near the scanning room. In addition, heart monitors, oxygen tanks, IV poles, and many other forms of lifesaving and life-monitoring equipment that contain metal cannot enter the MRI room.

fMRI is also affected by issues that do not apply to MRI. Changes in blood flow and volume measured by fMRI BOLD imaging are interpreted to result from experimentally controlled stimuli or induction of a particular mood or emotional state. However, activation of certain brain regions could represent noise in the data created by boredom, anxiety, or simply thinking about something outside the experimental context. Standard lag times of 4 to 8 seconds between stimulus onset and signal acquisition, dictated by the relationship between neuronal activation and changes in blood flow and volume, make it all the more difficult to correlate the presentation of stimuli with changes in regional blood flow.

Table 4-2 provides a comparison of the advantages and disadvantages of these brain imaging techniques, and Color Plates A to D give examples of the images they can produce.

TABLE 4-2   Summary of the Advantages and Disadvantages of Different Brain Imaging Techniques

EEG and ERP

Advantages

- Provides a direct measure of brain activity and thereby records timing of activity very precisely
- Noninvasive
- Inexpensive

Disadvantages

- Poor spatial resolution
- Does not directly record interior of brain
- Susceptible to noise from head movements
- Susceptible to variations in testing condition

PET and SPECT

Advantages

- Ability to radio-label an almost infinite number of naturally occurring and synthetic chemicals
- Can be completed very quickly
- Good spatial resolution
- Can image any region of the brain

Disadvantages

- Uses radioactive chemicals
- High cost of cyclotron, scanner, and numerous medical personnel
- Provides an indirect measure of brain function, thereby reducing temporal resolution

MRI and fMRI

Advantages

- Superior spatial resolution
- Can be completed very quickly
- Can image any region of the brain
- Thought to be noninvasive

Disadvantages

- Cannot accommodate individuals with metallic implants
- Increases in regional blood flow may be altered by mood or even daydreaming
- Only a moderate level of temporal resolution in fMRI

CHAPTER SUMMARY

- Nervous tissue is made up of nerve cells called neurons, which are excitable. Their excitability depends on the breakdown of the resting potential, which is the difference in electrical charge between the inside and the outside of the membrane of each cell. The resting potential is a result of uneven distribution of ions on either side of the membrane.

- There are more positively charged ions outside the neuron than inside. This uneven distribution of ions is created by the K^+/Na^+ ion pump. Ion channels permit the flow of specific ions across the cell membrane at a specific rate. Some ion channels may be opened either by the presence of a chemical or by a change in the resting potential.

- When the cell membrane on an axon is depolarized to a certain point (called the threshold), ion channels open, and the resting potential can no longer be maintained and breaks down. This condition is called an action potential. The resting potential then quickly restores itself.

- Action potentials are not generated when the resting potential of the dendrites and cell body are depolarized. Instead, an excitatory postsynaptic potential is generated that passively spreads over the surface of the membrane.

- Action potentials move away from the cell body, along the cell's axon, to synapses very near the cell body and dendrites of another neuron. They stimulate the second neuron by releasing a chemical called a neurotransmitter into the tiny gap between the cells.

- The transmitter interacts with receptor sites on the membrane of the postsynaptic cell. Depending on the nature of the receptor site, the effect will be to cause either depolarization (an increase in the excitability of the postsynaptic cell called an EPSP) or hyperpolarization (a decrease in the excitability of the postsynaptic cell called an IPSP).

- Neurotransmitters may cause other longer-acting effects on the postsynaptic cell by causing the release of second messengers and by modifying the expression of genes that create receptor sites and ion channels.

- Production of action potentials at a cell's axon depends on the sum of the excitation and inhibition at all the synapses on its dendrites and cell body at any given time.

- Autoreceptors are located on the presynaptic membrane and regulate the concentration of neurotransmitter, and sometimes the postsynaptic cell and other nearby cells release chemical messengers that can modify the release of neurotransmitters.

- Acetylcholine, epinephrine, norepinephrine, dopamine, serotonin, GABA, glutamate, and some peptides can act as neurotransmitters. Some can also act as neuromodulators and neurohormones.

- Drugs have their effect by interfering with some aspect of synaptic transmission. Among other things, they can block receptor sites, stimulate receptor sites, block the metabolism or reuptake of neurotransmitters, and interfere with second messengers.

- Each neurotransmitter can have a number of different receptor sites and the effect of the neurotransmitter is determined by the type of neurotransmitter.

- The nervous system has two major divisions. The central nervous system is made up of all the neurons in the brain and spinal cord; all other neurons make up the peripheral nervous system, which is further divided into the somatic and the autonomic nervous systems. The autonomic nervous system also has two parts: the parasympathetic system, which controls the vegetative involuntary functions of the body on an ongoing basis, and the sympathetic nervous system, which prepares the body for the sudden expenditure of energy, or the fight-or-flight response.

- The central part of the spinal cord is gray matter (cell bodies) surrounded by white matter (myelinated axons), which consists of fiber bundles of axons running to and from the brain.

- The medulla, located at the base of the brain, controls breathing and other autonomic functions. The cerebellum controls the smooth movement of muscles. The reticular activating system controls arousal. The Raphé system, conversely, is important in causing sleep.

- The locus coeruleus is a center in the lower brain that sends norepinephrine projections to the limbic system and the cortex. It is associated with anxiety and panic, and it seems to be responsible for withdrawal from opiates. The central gray is important in mediating responses to pain. It contains opiate receptors and is one site of action for the analgesic effects of the opiates.

- The basal ganglia form part of the extrapyramidal motor system. The striatum is the input side of the basal ganglia, and the pallidum is the output side. Together with the cortex, they form a loop that controls motor activity.

- The limbic system controls emotions and motivation. It is made up of a number of centers, including the hypothalamus, which controls eating and drinking and contains reinforcement centers.

- The nucleus accumbens receives dopaminergic input from the ventral tegmental area. This is the mesolimbic dopamine system, which is important in motivation and reinforcement of natural motivations and drug self-administration.

- The cortex makes up the uppermost surface of the brain and receives direct input from many senses. It also has direct control over voluntary movement. The cortex contains centers that permit us to recognize speech and written language and enable us to speak and write.

- The frontal and prefrontal cortex are important in thinking and decision making, attention, and working memory.

- The development of the brain is a complex process that involves the formation, migration, and connection of billions of neurons. Because migration and synapse formation are controlled by substances that resemble neurotransmitters, drugs that affect the functioning of the central nervous system can be teratogens and can severely disrupt the development of the nervous system.

- A number of neuroimaging techniques are now widely used to study the effects of drugs. These include EEG and ERP, PET, and its variation SPECT, and MRI and fMRI.

5

Dependence, Addiction, and the Self-Administration of Drugs

Why do people use drugs? On the surface it may seem like an easy question to answer, but like most "easy" questions, the more you think about it, the more difficult it becomes. To people who take drugs, the reasons may seem obvious, at least to themselves, but can we depend on these insights to formulate a scientific theory of drug taking? When we drink a beer, smoke a cigarette, or drink a cup of coffee, we are taking a drug, and if we are asked why we do this, most of us can come up with an answer that sounds reasonable: "Because I like it," "It wakes me up," or "I need to unwind after a long, hard day." These are reasonable statements, but even though they may satisfy us and those around us, the history of research into drug use shows that self-analysis and "obvious" explanations have led researchers down many dead-end paths and should be approached with caution.

A more difficult question is why people abuse drugs; why do some people insist on taking a drug to the point where it jeopardizes their health, finances, family life, and comfort? There may be equally obvious reasons for the overuse of drugs:

"Losing his wife drove him to drink" or "She started smoking pot because of peer pressure but soon became hooked." Once again, such explanations seem reasonable, but is there any scientific basis for them?

Even though drug use and addiction have been the object of scientific investigation since the middle of the nineteenth century, it is only in the past 50 years that real progress has been made. In this chapter we will look at some of the attempts that have been made to answer these questions over the years and examine some of the more widely held ideas about drug use and addiction.

Early attempts to understand drug use were directed strictly at addiction. No one thought of studying the normal drug use. People were content to assume that the use of drugs that did not create problems for the user could be explained in the same way one might use to understand any activity. Whether the drug was alcohol, tobacco, or cocaine, drug use was just another pleasurable activity that people might choose to pursue, like eating a good meal or having sex. Because it is considered "normal" to seek pleasure and avoid pain, the reason for using drugs was obvious and did not require further explanation. For this reason, "normal" drug use was never studied systematically until the middle of the twentieth century.

Addiction, on the other hand, did not seem normal. Addicted people often caused themselves great personal, financial, and social harm, which they acknowledged, yet in spite of knowing the damage they were doing, they continued to use their drug. Because addiction did not appear to follow normal rules, addiction has received the bulk of scientific attention over the years.

HISTORY OF ADDICTION RESEARCH

Addiction as a Disease

Background. Until the middle of the nineteenth century, people who had problems with drugs were considered to be deficient in character, moral fiber, willpower, and/or self-control; in other words, they were sinners or criminals. Consequently, addiction to drugs was a problem for priests and clerics to understand and for the legal system to deal with. Excessive or destructive use of drugs was not considered a medical problem and received no scientific attention. In the mid-nineteenth century, these ideas were challenged on two fronts.

A powerful social reform movement under way in England and North America advocated reform for a variety of social problems of the time: child labor, slavery, poverty, and the treatment of criminals, including "inebriates" (alcoholics). The American Association for the Cure of Inebriates was established in 1870 and became the forerunner of the temperance movement. Its first principle was, "Inebriety is a disease." The idea that alcoholism was a disease was not based on any medical research at the time but was motivated strictly by humanitarian concerns. They were concerned with the welfare of inebriates. By describing excessive drinking as a disease rather than a sin, they were able to convince governments and the rest of society to offer treatment rather than punishment.

In addition to the social reform movement and its zeal to help inebriates, the medical profession was already involved in other drugs of abuse at the time: morphine and opium. Opium, the raw extract of the opium poppy, was usually consumed in the form of laudanum, a mixture of opium and alcohol. Morphine, the principal active ingredient in opium, was usually injected. Laudanum was sold as a patent medicine, and morphine was widely used by physicians to treat a number of ailments (see Chapter 12). It was logical, then, to think of abuse of these drugs as a problem that physicians should solve, that is, as a medical problem (Berridge & Edwards, 1981).

This revision of the perception of drug abuse as a disease rather than a sin led to the adoption of a new terminology. Toward the end of the nineteenth century, the temperance and antiopium social movements started using the term *addiction* to refer exclusively to the excessive use of drugs and to replace terms such as *intemperance* and *inebriety* (Alexander & Schweighofer, 1988). The medical profession also adopted the term *addiction* and started using it as a diagnosis and an explanation of excessive drug use, thereby giving addiction the implication of a disease. This use is still common.

The *disease model*, as we shall call it, seemed to fade until the middle of the twentieth century, when the Alcoholics Anonymous movement gained prominence and influence. One of its most articulate theorists, E. M. Jellinek, focused attention on the issue and eventually wrote a book called *The Disease Concept of Alcoholism* (Jellinek, 1960).

Thanks to Jellinek, the idea that addiction is a disease became formalized first with alcoholism, which was declared a disease by the World Health Organization in 1951 and the American Medical Association in 1953 (Room, 1983). By implication, then, all forms of drug addiction became a disease. This new status of addictions was formalized by recognition in the American Psychiatric Association's *Diagnostic and Statistical Manual of Mental Disorders (DSM)*. This book lists conditions considered to be mental disorders and presents standardized criteria by which these disorders may be recognized and diagnosed.

The fourth edition of the *DSM* (*DSM-IV*), published in 1994, does not use the term *disease*, but it defines *disorder* as a clinically significant behavioral or psychological syndrome or pattern that occurs in an individual and that is associated with present distress (e.g., a painful symptom) or disability (impairment in one or more important areas of functioning), or with a significantly increased risk of suffering death, pain, disability, or an important loss of freedom (American Psychiatric Association, 1994, p. xxi). The *DSM-IV* does not use the term *disease*, but *disorder* is clearly a synonym for *disease*.

The *DSM-IV* does not use the term *addiction* either. Instead, it uses the terms *substance dependence* and *substance abuse* and provides very specific criteria by which these conditions can be diagnosed (see Box 5-1). Being recognized in the *DSM-IV* is important for a number of reasons. Their inclusion in the *DSM-IV* gives dependence and substance abuse the status of "diseases" under the law, at least insofar as physicians in the United States are able to charge for treating them.

Similarly, the tenth revision of the *International Statistical Classification of Diseases and Related Health Problems* (*ICD-10*) is a similar catalog of diseases issued by the World Health Organization (1993). The *ICD-10* distinguishes between harmful use and a dependence syndrome; the criteria are similar to those for substance dependence and substance abuse in the *DSM-IV*.

What Is the Disease Like? In spite of this insistence that addiction (or dependence or abuse) is a disease, there have been few attempts to describe exactly what sort of a disease it is. This is unfortunate because simply declaring that something is a disease does little to help us understand it and even less to help us treat it.

There are two sorts of suggestions: (a) predisposition theories, which say that people are either born with the disease or acquire it at some time before they begin abusing the drug and that this disease predisposes people to become addicts whenever they start using the drug, and (b) exposure theories, which suggest that addiction is a disease that is caused by repeated exposure to the drug.

Predispositions. The earliest scientific attempt to formulate a disease theory was made by E. M. Jellinek in a series of papers in the 1950s and his book *The Disease Concept of Alcoholism*. His theory explained only addiction to alcohol, not all addictions, but some of his ideas have been widely applied to other drugs. As we shall see in greater detail in Chapter 6, Jellinek proposed that alcoholism is not caused by alcohol. It is a disease that is inherited; people are born with it. Jellinek suggested that it is like an allergy. People with an allergy to cats will have no problems with the allergy if they do not go near cats. Similarly, if alcoholics do not drink alcohol, they will never have a problem, but if they did drink it, the disease will make them lose control of their drinking. His ideas have been widely adopted by the Alcoholics Anonymous movement and are believed by millions of people.

Since Jellinek, there have been other attempts to explain addictions in terms of a predisposition, usually genetic, which makes some people vulnerable to the addictive properties of specific drugs. Many involve metabolic variations that either increase or decrease a person's sensitivity to a drug and, consequently, their motivation to consume it. Whether these alterations are diseases depends largely on the point of view of the theorist.

Drug Exposure Diseases. There are some disease theories that claim that people are not born with the disease of addiction, nor do they acquire it somehow before using the drug. These theories propose that addiction is caused by exposure to the drug. Alan Leshner, a past director of the U.S. National Institute of Drug Abuse (NIDA), has expressed this idea as follows:

This unexpected consequence of drug use [addiction] is what I have come to call the oops phenomenon. Why oops? Because the harmful outcome is in no way intentional. Just as no one starts out to have lung cancer when they smoke, or no one starts out to have clogged arteries when they eat fried foods, which in turn usually

BOX 5-1 Psychoactive Substance Dependence and Abuse Criteria. Reprinted with permission from American Psychiatric Association. © 1994, DSM-IV Criteria for Substance Dependence.

Criteria for Substance Dependence

A maladaptive pattern of substance use, leading to clinically significant impairment or distress, as manifested by three (or more) of the following, occurring at any time in the same 12-month period:

1. tolerance, as defined by either of the following:
   (a) a need for markedly increased amounts of the substance to achieve intoxication or desired effect
   (b) markedly diminished effect with continued use of the same amount of the substance
2. withdrawal, as manifested by either of the following:
   (a) the characteristic withdrawal syndrome of the substance
   (b) the same (or a closely related) substance is taken to relieve or avoid withdrawal symptoms
3. substance is often taken in larger amounts or over a longer period than was intended
4. there is a persistent desire or unsuccessful efforts to cut down or control substance use
5. a great deal of time is spent in activities necessary to obtain the substance (e.g., visiting multiple doctors or driving long distances), use of the substance (e.g., chain smoking), or recovering from its effects
6. important social, occupational, or recreational activities are given up or reduced because of substance use
7. the substance use is continued despite knowledge of having a persistent or recurrent physical or psychological problem that is likely to have been caused or exacerbated by the substance (e.g., current cocaine use despite recognition of cocaine-induced depression, or continued drinking despite recognition that an ulcer was made worse by alcohol consumption)

Specify if:
With Physiological Dependence: evidence of tolerance or withdrawal (i.e., either item 1 or 2 is present)
Without Physiological Dependence: no evidence of tolerance or withdrawal (e.g., neither item 1 nor 2 is present)

Criteria for Substance Abuse

1. A maladaptive pattern of substance use leading to clinically significant impairment or distress, as manifested by one (or more) of the following, occurring within a 12-month period:
   (a) recurrent substance use resulting in failure to fulfill major role obligations at work, school, or home (e.g., repeated absences or poor work performance related to substance use; substance-related absences, suspensions, or expulsions from school; neglect of children or household)
   (b) recurrent substance use in situations in which it is physically hazardous (e.g., driving an automobile or operating a machine when impaired by substance use)
   (c) recurrent substance-related legal problems (e.g., arrests for substance-related disorderly conduct)
   (d) continued substance use despite having persistent or recurrent social or interpersonal problems caused or exacerbated by the effects of the substance (e.g., arguments with spouse about consequences of intoxication, physical fights)
2. The symptoms have never met the criteria for Substance Dependence for this class of substance.

cause heart attacks, no one starts out to become a drug addict when they use drugs. But in each case, though no one meant to behave in a way that would lead to tragic health consequences, that is what happened just the same, because of the inexorable, and undetected, destructive biochemical processes at work.

While we haven't yet pinpointed precisely all the triggers for the changes in the brain's structure and function that culminate in the "oops" phenomenon, a vast body of hard evidence shows that it is virtually inevitable that prolonged drug use will lead to addiction. From this we can soundly conclude that drug addiction is indeed a brain disease. (**http://www.nida. nih.gov/Published_Articles/Oops.html**)

As we shall see later, there are a number of theories that propose that specific brain changes caused by repeated drug use can explain addiction, but this does not necessarily make it a disease. Prolonged weight training causes changes in the structure and function of your muscles, but that does not mean that Olympic weight lifters are sick. We really need to know more about what these changes in structure and function are.

A similar explanation of addiction will be discussed in the next section on physical dependence as an explanation of addiction. It states that prolonged exposure to a drug will create a state of dependence that motivates more intensive drug use or addiction. Using the reasoning of Leshner, we can see that physical dependence may be thought of as a disease as well, but most people do not normally think of it that way, so it will be discussed in a separate section later in this chapter

Is Addiction a Disease? When the disease idea was first proposed by the social reformers in the mid-nineteenth century, the suggestion was not based on any scientific or medical evidence. In fact their motivations were political. They wanted to remove the stigma of sinner and criminal from inebriates so that they could be treated rather than punished. Over the years this idea has been widely adopted, and it is now quite clear that addictive behavior can be understood in terms of anatomy, physiology, biochemistry, genetics, and behavioral science (diseased or otherwise) rather than morality. It is now widely accepted that addicts need help and treatment rather than punishment and rejection. It may have taken over a century, but the political and social goals of these Victorian reformers have been realized. But does this mean they were right? Is addiction a "disease"? Well, for the purpose of understanding addiction, it does not really matter anymore whether it is a disease or not. However, for some like Leshner, it may still be important for political reasons to remind people that addiction is a process that can be understood in terms of physiology. Leshner, after all, at the time he declared addiction to be a brain disease, was head of the NIDA, an agency of the U.S. government that funds and oversees a vast amount of addiction research and requires the continuing support of politicians and the public.

There has been a great deal of ink spilled in the debate over whether addiction is a disease, but what all these arguments boil down to is how the term *disease* is defined. Addiction may or may not be a disease. We shall spend the rest of this chapter exploring why people use and abuse drugs. Whether you think addiction is a disease will depend on your definition of disease, not on the mechanisms that cause addiction. In general, you will find that there is little to be gained from claiming addiction to be a disease.

DEFINING ADDICTION

We have been talking a lot about addiction, so perhaps it is about time we attempted to define the term, but, as with many concepts in this book, this is difficult. Like the *DSM-IV* and the *ICD-10* descriptions of *dependence* or *abuse*, most modern definitions of addiction have two elements in common: (a) The addicted individual has impaired control over the use of the drug, and (b) the drug use has harmful consequences (West, 2001). Such definitions, however, present a real conceptual problem for scientific investigations of addiction. The problem with the first element (a) is that there is no way to tell the difference between behavior that is controlled and behavior that is not controlled by the individual. If you watch a person in a bar drinking beer, is there any way of detecting whether that person is controlling the beer drinking or whether something else is controlling the drinking? Could that person stop if he or she wanted to? In fact, simply by studying the person's behavior, there is no way of telling the difference. Of course, you could ask the individual, but then you have to depend on self-report, which is often self-serving, inaccurate, and, in this case, not verifiable. It also presents problems using nonhumans to study addiction since nonhuman animals cannot tell you if they have lost control of their behavior. To get around this problem, addiction definitions often say that the behavior must be harmful to the individual. The reasoning here is that self-injurious behavior must be "out of control" because no persons or animals who had control of their behavior would deliberately injure themselves. This reduces the definition of addiction simply to one of doing harm to oneself, which is clearly not adequate.

Like so many other concepts in this book, it is really not possible to come up with an adequate definition of addiction, but we will not let that stop us from trying to understand it.

ADDICTION AS PHYSICAL DEPENDENCE

Background

Early in the twentieth century, addiction researchers drew attention to the sickness that develops when a user of opium or morphine tries to stop. They proposed a hypothetical substance called an *autotoxin*—a metabolite of opium that stayed in the body after the drug was gone. This autotoxin had effects opposite to opium, and when left in the body, it made the person very sick. Only opium or a related drug could antagonize the extremely unpleasant effects of the autotoxin and relieve the sickness. It was believed that the sickness was so unpleasant that the relief provided by opium was

responsible for the continuous craving for more opium seen in addicts (Tatum & Seevers, 1931).

Later the existence of the autotoxin was disproved. The sickness that remained after the drug was gone became known as *withdrawal* or *abstinence syndrome*, and more accurate explanations were developed to account for it (see Chapter 3). Avoidance of withdrawal, however, was still regarded as the explanation for opium use and the compulsive craving for the drug. The term *physical dependence* or *physiological dependence* was used to describe the state in which the discontinuation or reduction of a drug would cause withdrawal symptoms.

Because alcohol was the other major addicting drug at the time and because alcohol also causes severe withdrawal symptoms, it was logical for scientists to consider avoidance of withdrawal as a general explanation for the excessive use of all drugs. The ability of a drug to cause physical dependence (and, consequently, withdrawal) became accepted as the universal indication of an addicting drug, and the presence of physical dependence became the defining feature of an addict and an addiction.

This assumption became crystallized in the language developed to talk about drug use. The term *dependence* came to describe two separate effects that were synonymous in the minds of scientists at the time. Dependence meant both (a) the state in which a drug produces "physical dependence" (i.e., withdrawal symptoms occur when the drug is stopped) and (b) the compulsive self-administration of a drug. In addition, because the development of *tolerance* seems to be a necessary condition for physical dependence (see Chapter 3), many laboratories studied tolerance and presumed that they were, in fact, studying dependence. *Tolerance* became to some degree a synonym for *dependence*, but the term is seldom used in this way today.

This model of drug abuse, which we shall call the *physical dependence model*, is still widely accepted. If you accept that withdrawal sickness is exceptionally unpleasant, this model explains why addicts work so compulsively to get their drug.

Fear of severe withdrawal can also explain why drug abuse is so self-destructive. Drug-seeking behavior is different from normal behavior because the motivation for drugs is so extreme. According to this view, physically dependent individuals are willing to sacrifice almost anything to avoid having to go through withdrawal (Wikler, 1980). This view of the addict is still commonly presented in movies and on television.

The dependence model, however, had a problem. It could explain only addiction to drugs that cause physical dependence.

Habituation. One way of rationalizing addictions to non–dependence-producing drugs was to suggest that a different mechanism was responsible for the use of such drugs. In 1931, Tatum and Seevers suggested that the term *drug habituation* (meaning "habit forming") should be used for drugs that do not create physical dependence. "Habituation is a condition in which the habitué desires a drug, but suffers no ill effects on its discontinuance" (Tatum & Seevers, 1931, p. 108). *Addiction* referred to behavior that was harmful to the individual, but *habituation* was much less serious and caused little harm (Winger, Hoffmann, & Woods, 1992, p. 17). The term was later used by the World Health Organization into the 1950s, but it is not widely used anymore.

Psychological Dependence. In addition to coining the word *habituation*, Tatum and Seevers (1931) suggested the adoption of "some non-committal term such as psychic addiction" (p. 119). This alternative was later developed into the concept of *psychological dependence*. Following the lead of Tatum and Seevers, the term *psychological dependence* became widely used. It expanded the dependence model by assuming that drugs such as cocaine caused unobservable psychological withdrawal symptoms, that is, psychological, or psychic, dependence. In short, psychological dependence presumed that there was some sort of psychological, as opposed to physical, withdrawal that caused a craving for a drug. This psychological withdrawal was not observable;

it took place in the brain and did not have any outward manifestations apart from the fact that the user became highly motivated to take the drug. It was assumed that the brain could not function normally without the drug and that this inability manifested itself subjectively to the user as a craving. Behaviorally, psychological dependence created an "impaired control of psychoactive substance use" (American Psychiatric Association, 1987, p. 166).

Problems with the Physical and Psychological Dependence Theories. There are several problems with the physical dependence model. To begin with, powerful compulsive drug abuse can develop from intake of substances such as cocaine and marijuana, which cause only mild (if any) withdrawal. In addition, research has shown that even with drugs such as heroin, which can cause physical dependence, many people (and laboratory animals) can become heroin addicts without developing physical dependence. It has also been shown that both humans and laboratory animals will sometimes voluntarily stop taking a drug even though they experience withdrawal symptoms. Furthermore, physical dependence cannot explain relapse where people return to the addictive use of a drug long after the physical dependence to that drug has disappeared. In the light of these findings, even the definition of substance dependence in the *DSM IV* recognizes that it is possible to be "dependent" on a substance without being physically dependent. Even though physical dependence seems to offer a compelling and intuitively obvious explanation of addiction, it cannot survive close scientific scrutiny.

In addition, the concept of psychological dependence presents a serious conceptual problem. It cannot be used by itself as an explanation because it is circular. For example, if we say that we know that John is psychologically dependent because he uses a drug excessively, we cannot say that John uses a drug excessively because he is psychologically dependent. The term may be used to describe a state of affairs, but it cannot be used as an explanation. This problem does not arise with physical dependence because there is independent evidence—withdrawal symptoms—that physical dependence exists.

As they were originally conceived, theories that use relief from psychological withdrawal to explain addictive behavior are now no longer tenable, but more recent research has provided evidence that some of the changes that take place in the brain after repeated exposure to drugs or abuse could explain the compulsion to take more drugs. These findings have broken the circularity in the definition of psychological dependence by identifying brain mechanisms that are affected by withdrawal that can be observed independently of addiction in the same way that we can observe physiological withdrawal. In fact, it may be that changes that take place in the brain during withdrawal can explain the compulsion to use drugs better than the physiological distress of withdrawal sickness. Later in this chapter we will describe newer withdrawal theories in the context of the positive reinforcement explanations discussed later.

MODERN BEHAVIORAL AND NEUROSCIENTIFIC EXPLANATIONS

Background

Until the mid-1950s addictive behavior was considered uniquely human. Attempts to create "addictions" in other species had generally been unsuccessful, largely because nearly all these studies provided drugs via the oral route, which creates several problems. Most drugs have a bitter taste that laboratory animals dislike, and animals have a built-in protective mechanism, called *flavor toxicosis learning*, that causes them to reject any taste that is followed by sickness or an alteration in nervous system functioning. Slow absorption from the digestive system also causes a delay between consumption and the effect of the drug on the brain, which can interfere with the development of addiction. The assumption that only humans could become addicted held back the development of new ideas and properly controlled scientific research.

As early as the 1920s, it was shown that laboratory animals could be made physically dependent if they were forced to consume a drug such as morphine or alcohol, but it could never be shown that they would make themselves physically dependent (then believed to be the defining feature of addiction) if a drug were made freely available to them. Even animals made physically dependent by forced consumption seldom continued to consume a drug when alternatives were made available. In 1937, A. R. Lindesmith, a sociologist, wrote, "Certainly from the point of view of social science it would be ridiculous to include animals and humans together in the concept of addiction" (quoted in Laties, 1986, p. 33).

The reluctance of laboratory animals to show the compulsive and self-destructive drug taking that humans so often exhibit or even to show low levels of drug consumption also led people to believe that addiction must be caused by something that makes humans different from animals. This line of reasoning supported an older, moralistic view that because humans had "free will" and nonhumans did not, humans could "sin" by choosing to take drugs and that this sinning was punished by the misery of addiction.

Another more scientific explanation originated in the physical dependence model: Animals could never become addicted to a drug because they were not capable of learning the association between an injection and relief from withdrawal sickness, which occurred 15 or 20 minutes later (S. R. Goldberg, 1976). Whatever the explanation, it was widely accepted that there was no point in using laboratory animals to study the addictive behavior of humans.

In the absence of laboratory techniques that could test it, the physical dependence model seemed to account nicely for addiction and was virtually unchallenged until a few simple technological breakthroughs were made in the 1950s. At that time, a number of researchers began to show that laboratory animals would learn to perform a behavior that resulted in a drug injection. This line of research expanded quickly when the technology was developed that allowed intravenous drug infusions to be delivered to freely moving animals by means of a permanently implanted catheter (see Figure 5-1). With this one development, our whole view of drug self-administration and addiction changed.

Because of the pervasive influence of the physical dependence model, in these early studies it was assumed that physical dependence was essential for drug self-administration. Thus, rats and monkeys were first made physically dependent on morphine by repeated injections. Then they were placed in an operant chamber and were given the opportunity to press a lever that caused a delivery of morphine through a catheter. The animals quickly learned to respond. It became obvious that the drug infusion was acting like a more traditional positive reinforcer, such as food or water (Thompson & Schuster, 1964).

The role of physical dependence in the positive reinforcing effects of drugs was further explored by Charles Schuster and his colleagues, who showed that animals that were not physically dependent would self-administer doses of morphine so low that no physical dependence ever developed (Schuster, 1970). It was also demonstrated that rats would press a lever to give themselves infusions of cocaine and other stimulants that do not cause marked withdrawal symptoms (Pickens & Thompson, 1968).

These and other studies have clearly demonstrated that many of the assumptions of the physical dependence model are not correct. Physical dependence can be an important factor controlling the intake of some drugs, but it is not necessary for drug self-administration and cannot serve as the sole explanation for either drug use or drug abuse.

The model of drug taking that has developed as a result of these studies we shall call the *positive reinforcement model*. This model assumes that drugs are self-administered because they act as positive reinforcers and that the principles that govern behavior controlled by other positive reinforcers apply to drug self-administration. The remainder of this chapter will be devoted to a discussion of the positive reinforcement model and the insights it has provided into drug self-administration and addiction in both human and

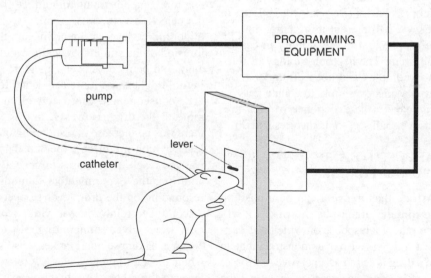

Figure 5-1 A schematic drawing of the drug self-administration preparation for the rat. The rat presses the lever, which causes the activation of the pump by the programming equipment. The pump injects a specific amount of a drug solution through a catheter that has been implanted into the jugular vein near the rat's heart.

nonhuman animals. We will also examine the brain mechanisms involved in positive reinforcement and how they control behavior.

What Is Positive Reinforcement?

Often people use the term *positive reinforcement* interchangeably with pleasure, euphoria, or some sort of positive affect. It is true that stimuli that act as positive reinforcers are often reported to give pleasure, which is then assumed to be a cause of the behavior (e.g., "I do it because it makes me feel good"), but there are plenty of examples of stimuli that can act as positive reinforcers but do not cause pleasure. In fact, there are circumstances in which an electric shock can be a positive reinforcer (Kelleher & Morse, 1964). Traditionally, a positive reinforcer has been defined only in terms of its effect on behavior; that is, *a positive reinforcer is any stimulus that increases the frequency of a behavior it is contingent on* (see Chapter 2). Over the years, there has been much speculation on the nature of positive reinforcement. For example, it has been suggested that it is a result of such things as drive reduction, drive induction, and consummatory behavior (Domjan, 2003). Later in this chapter, we will present information linking positive reinforcement to the activity in certain parts of the brain. The neurophysiology of reinforcement is complex and not well understood; however, it is a mistake simply to equate positive reinforcement with the experience of pleasure, although, as we shall see, some theories still do.

DRUGS AS POSITIVE AND NEGATIVE REINFORCERS

To demonstrate that an event can be a positive reinforcing stimulus, it must be shown that it will increase the rate of a response on which it is contingent. That is, if you wish to demonstrate that an infusion of a drug is acting as a positive reinforcer for lever pressing, it is necessary to show that the frequency of lever pressing will increase if it is reliably followed by an infusion of the drug and will decrease when it is no longer followed by the drug.

To illustrate this point, we will look at a classic experiment performed by Pickens and Thompson and published in 1968. Rats were implanted with catheters so that they could receive infusions of cocaine into the jugular vein. Each rat was then placed in a small chamber that was equipped with two levers and a stimulus light. The rats lived in these chambers permanently and were provided with food and water. From 9:00 A.M. to 11:00 P.M., an infusion of 0.5 mg/kg cocaine was administered to each rat in response to a depression of one of the levers on a continuous reinforcement schedule. Responses on the other lever were recorded but had no effect. Within a few days, each rat was responding at a steady rate of about 8 to 12 infusions per hour on the lever that produced the infusions. There were virtually no responses on the other lever.

Because many people were skeptical about these findings, Thompson and Pickens were careful to design the experiment to show that the drug was acting as a positive reinforcer and that there could be no other explanation. For example, the increases in responding to the drug lever could be due to a general stimulating effect of cocaine on the behavior of the rats. In other words, the rats might hit the lever accidentally, and the resulting infusion of the stimulant cocaine would cause the animal to be more active. This increased activity in turn might cause more accidental lever presses and, consequently, more activation caused by more of the drug. However, in this experiment, there was no increase in responding on the second lever, which might be expected if bar pressing was the result of increases in general activity. In addition, the experimenters demonstrated that responding on the drug lever stopped when they discontinued reinforcing it with cocaine and the rats were given noncontingent infusions of cocaine. Thompson and Pickens also showed that when the contingency was switched from one lever to the other, the rats' choice of levers also switched. This made it clear that behavior was being controlled by the contingency between the lever press and the drug infusion rather than any other property of the drug or the situation.

Thompson and Pickens found that extinction of responding occurred if saline placebo infusions were substituted for the cocaine infusions after each lever press. When the cocaine infusions were stopped, there was a short burst of lever pressing before the rat stopped responding. This pattern is typically observed at the beginning of extinction with other reinforcers. They were also able to show that rats would respond on fixed ratio (FR) schedules for cocaine reinforcement and that the pattern of lever pressing generated by the schedule was similar to the pattern FR schedules generate with other positive reinforcers.

Since these early studies, it has been demonstrated that laboratory animals will self-administer many different drugs. Table 5-1 lists some of these drugs, along with drugs that do not appear to be reinforcers in various nonhuman species.

Self-Administration via Other Routes

Over the years, it has been demonstrated that laboratory animals will administer drugs to themselves through a variety of routes, including *intragastric* (direct injection through a cannula into the stomach), *intracranial* (direct injection of tiny amounts of drug through a cannula into specific parts of the brain), *intraventricular* (injection through a cannula into the ventricles in the brain), and *inhalation*.

Laboratory animals will also consume drugs orally. (Techniques have been developed to overcome the delay in effect and the natural protective mechanisms described earlier.) In addition, the defining characteristics of drug use and abuse are better understood. Much of what we know today about drug use, especially alcohol, has come from experiments with laboratory animals using oral administration (Meisch & Lemaire, 1993).

Drugs as Aversive Stimuli

Before proceeding with a more detailed analysis of drug self-administration, we should note that some drugs do not act as positive reinforcers and that some even have aversive properties; that is, laboratory animals will work to shut off infusions of some drugs or will learn to perform tasks to avoid receiving such infusions. In the avoidance training task described in Chapter 2, laboratory animals are taught to make a response that turns off a stimulus that always precedes an electric shock. To demonstrate that some drugs have aversive properties, a similar procedure is used, except that a drug infusion replaces the shock. Drugs that have been demonstrated to have aversive properties include LSD, antipsychotic drugs such as chlorpromazine, and the antidepressant imipramine.

Problems with the Positive Reinforcement Model

Positive Reinforcement Paradox. The positive reinforcement model seems to account nicely for the "normal" or nonaddictive aspect of drug use, but can we explain addiction using positive reinforcement? The consequences of using some drugs can, indeed, be painful and unhealthy and ought to be punishing enough to make an organism stop using them. For example, when cocaine and amphetamine are made freely available to a monkey for a period of time, very often it will refuse to eat or sleep for extended periods. The drug will cause it to mutilate parts of its body, and ultimately the monkey will die of an overdose or bleed to death from its self-inflicted wounds. This is not unlike the economically and physically destructive behavior motivated by cocaine in some humans. It may seem paradoxical that behavior motivated by positive reinforcement should persist in the face of such punishing consequences. Addicts themselves often acknowledge that continued drug use creates an aversive state they generally would like to avoid or terminate. For this reason, drug users often seek treatment for their addiction. How can an event like the administration of a drug be both positively reinforcing enough to make people continue to use it and at the same time aversive enough to motivate people to stop? As Gene Heyman of Harvard University

TABLE 5-1   Some Drugs Found to Be Self-Administered, Not Self-Administered, and Avoided by Nonhuman Species (Rats, Rhesus Monkeys, Squirrel Monkeys, Dogs, Baboons, Cats, and Pigs)

Drug	Self-Administered	Not Self-Administered	Avoided
Barbiturates:			
amobarbital	X		
pentobarbital		X	
secobarbital	X		
Benzodiazepines:			
chlordiazepoxide	X	X	
diazepam	X	X	
midazolam	X		
triaxolam	X		
Psychomotor stimulants:			
amphetamines	X		
cathinone	X		
cocaine	X		
methylphenidate	X		
phenmetrazine	X		
Opiates:			
codeine	X		
heroin	X		
methadone	X		
morphine	X		
naloxone		X	
Antipsychotics:			
chloropromazine		X	X
haloperidol		X	
Antidepressants:			
atryptyline		X	
imipramine		X	X
Hallucinogens:			
LSD		X	X
PCP	X		
MDA	X		
mescaline		X	
Others:			
aspirin		X	
caffeine	X	X	
ethanol	X		
nicotine	X	X	
procaine	X		
scopolamine	X	X	
THC	X	X	

Sources: Yokel (1987, pp. 4–9); Hoffmeister & Wuttke (1975); Koob (1995, p. 760).

asks, "If addictive drug use is on balance positively reinforcing, then why would a user ever want to stop?" (Heyman, 1996, p. 16).

Such a paradox is not unique to drugs and cannot be used to disqualify drugs as positive reinforcers. More traditional reinforcers such as food can be destructive and cause pain. People often overeat, become obese, and experience physical discomfort, health risks, and social censure and yet continue to overeat. Sexual activity also acts as a reinforcing stimulus. It has positive reinforcing effects, but it also has the potential to cause unpleasant and undesirable consequences, such as sexually transmitted diseases and unwanted pregnancy. In fact, most positive reinforcers, including drugs, can have negative destructive effects that can motivate people to seek treatment to help them quit. The question is, Can this seemingly excessive and self-destructive behavior be explained by what we know about positive reinforcement? In fact, it can.

One of the reasons that positive reinforcing effects continue to control behavior, in spite of punishing effects, is that they are immediately experienced after behavior, whereas the punishing and painful effects are often delayed. One well-understood principle of operant conditioning is that if a consequence is delayed, its ability to control behavior is diminished. Thus, if an intake of alcohol causes pleasure within minutes and a hangover a number of hours later, the pleasure, rather than the hangover, will be more likely to determine whether the person will drink alcohol again. When punishing consequences occur infrequently and after a considerable delay, no matter how severe they might be, they are less likely to exert as much control over behavior as will immediate gratification. This effect is known as the *discounting delay* and will be discussed later in this chapter.

Circularity. Another problem with the positive reinforcement model is that, by itself, it provides a circular explanation of drug use. If we say that a drug is a positive reinforcer because it will increase a behavior on which it is contingent, then we cannot "explain" drug use by saying that a drug is a positive reinforcer (T. E. Robinson & Berridge, 1993). One way out of this dilemma would be to define positive reinforcement in terms of something other than behavior. For example, many have defined it as a stimulus that causes pleasure (or a positive hedonic state, if we want to sound scientific), but this is not a satisfactory solution because, as we have already shown, positive reinforcers need not always be pleasurable. In addition, pleasure is a subjective state, and it is difficult to define the concept

scientifically. Fortunately, there are more acceptable explanations of reinforcement.

We can escape from this dilemma in two ways. First, decades of research have told us a great deal about positive reinforcement. By saying that a drug is a positive reinforcer, we know a lot more than just the fact that it increases behavior. This means that we can use the principles already established for positive reinforcers to understand and predict the way drugs will control behavior. To the extent that drugs conform to these predictions, it is useful to think of them as positive reinforcers. Much of the remainder of this chapter deals with these similarities. It should become apparent that drug use and addiction become more understandable if we think of them in terms of positive reinforcement.

Second, advances in neuroscience have provided considerable insight into the neurological mechanisms of reinforcement. As discussed in Chapter 4 and in the next section of this chapter, there are specific brain systems that are the mechanisms for positive reinforcement and for the motivational effects of stimuli that act as positive reinforcers. Using this neural circuitry, we can now define reinforcement in terms other than the behavior it generates.

SELF-ADMINISTRATION IN HUMANS AND NONHUMANS

Many hundreds of studies have explored the drug-taking behavior of laboratory animals. In fact, we now probably know more about nonhuman drug taking than we do about human drug taking. The success achieved by studying laboratory animals using operant techniques has prompted some scientists to adopt these research strategies to study human behavior (Spiga & Roache, 1997). These techniques were pioneered by Nancy Mello and Jack Mendelson at the McLean Hospital in Belmont, Massachusetts. In this research, paid volunteers live in a hospital ward so that they may be kept under constant medical supervision. Only people who have a history of drug use or previous exposure to a specific drug are generally permitted to participate in these experiments. Their health and their behavior are carefully monitored. They are given the opportunity to perform some operant task, such as pushing a button or riding an exercise bicycle, to earn tokens or points that they are able to exchange for doses of a drug. This arrangement is analogous to the operant task with laboratory animals and can probably tell us a great deal more about drug self-administration than simply observing the behavior of addicts in their natural environment. For example, researchers are able to test and compare the effects of different doses and types of drugs and to contrast drugs with placebos. They can also manipulate other variables, such as availability, route of administration, and work required; check the effects of other drugs administered at the same time; and carefully measure and observe changes in behavior that might be caused by the test drug. The situation is artificial, but it permits researchers to exercise considerable precision and control, which is not possible in any other circumstance (Mello & Mendelson, 1987).

One disadvantage of this method is that it can present an ethical dilemma. It would be unethical to use inexperienced or nonaddicted subjects in research of this type if it involved unrestricted exposure to drugs like heroin, which are known to be habit forming. Such a procedure would introduce subjects to the reinforcing effects of a drug, an experience they might not otherwise have. For this reason this type of research is usually done only on addicted volunteers.

Operant techniques have been further refined to allow some testing of humans outside the laboratory or research ward (Spiga & Roache, 1997). In this research, normal human volunteers report to the laboratory every morning and are asked to swallow a capsule of a particular color. On alternate days, they take a capsule of a different color. Usually, one color is a drug and the other a placebo. When they have been exposed to both, they are asked to choose which one they want to take. If the drug is a reinforcer, it will be chosen

more often than the placebo. This procedure has the advantage of not being carried out in an artificial laboratory environment, but a considerable amount of precision is lost. There are also some ethical restrictions on the types and doses of drugs that can be given.

Similarities and Differences Between Human and Nonhuman Animals

Type of Drug. Comparisons of human and nonhuman behavior in controlled studies like these have made it quite clear that there is not a great deal of difference between species (Griffiths, Bigelow, & Henningfield, 1980). Laboratory animals, including dogs, monkeys, baboons, rats, cats, and mice, will take most of the drugs that humans use, with some interesting exceptions. Nonhumans do not seem to find most of the drugs we classify as hallucinogens, such as LSD, to be reinforcing. Only recently have there been demonstrations that nonhumans do self-administer THC, the active ingredient in cannabis (Tanda, Manzar, & Goldberg, 2000) (see Chapter 15). It has also been shown that both humans and nonhumans will self-administer anabolic steroids (R. I. Wood, 2004).

Patterns of Self-Administration. Not only do nonhumans appear to self-administer similar drugs, but the patterns of self-administration are also similar. Figure 5-2 shows the records of a rhesus monkey self-administering alcohol (ethanol) and a human volunteer in a research ward of a hospital who could earn drinks of alcohol by pressing a button. The records are very similar. Both subjects worked for the alcohol in an erratic pattern, and both subjects voluntarily experienced periods of withdrawal, a pattern quite similar to alcohol consumption patterns of alcoholics in more natural settings. As we proceed through this book and examine the self-administration patterns of humans and nonhumans, many more similarities will become apparent.

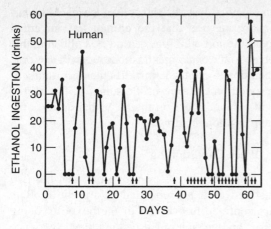

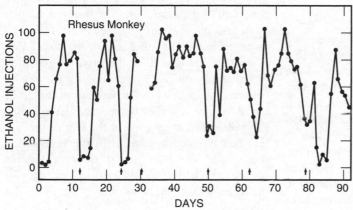

Figure 5-2 The similarity between the patterns of self-administration of ethanol in a human and a rhesus monkey under continuous drug availability. The arrows indicate the occurrence of withdrawal symptoms. *Top:* Data from an experiment in which a volunteer earned tokens by pressing a button. The tokens could be exchanged for drinks. *Bottom:* Intake of ethanol by a rhesus monkey pressing a lever for intravenous infusions. (Adapted from Griffiths et al., 1980, p. 19)

MEASURING THE REINFORCING VALUE OF DRUGS

Like other more conventional reinforcers, the ability of drugs to act as reinforcers is not constant. Food is a conventional reinforcer. Some very palatable foods may be powerful reinforcers, but others that are not so tasty or nourishing may have only limited effectiveness. Similarly, the same food may be an effective reinforcer after an animal has been deprived of food but be ineffective with a food-satiated animal. It is also clear that many other factors can alter the ability of drugs to function as a reinforcer. Similarly, the reinforcing value of drugs may vary, depending on a number

of circumstances. A number of techniques have been developed to assess the reinforcing value of drugs and factors that can influence reinforcing value in both humans and nonhumans.

Rate of Responding

With traditional reinforcers, we know that the greater the reinforcement, the faster an organism will respond. For example, rats will respond faster for three food pellets than they will for one pellet. We might expect that animals will respond faster for drugs that are more reinforcing, but rate of responding has some problems. One is that drugs have different durations of action, and a long-acting drug might well be self-administered at a slower rate than a short-acting drug merely because the effect of each dose lasts longer. In addition, rate of responding depends on the animal's ability to make a response. Many drugs have effects that interfere with self-administration. For example, monkeys will give themselves infusions of anesthetic doses of pentobarbital that immediately cause them to go to sleep. Such a drug may be highly reinforcing, but it could not be self-administered at a high rate. Conversely, many drugs, such as cocaine, could stimulate their own self-administration.

Progressive Ratio

To some extent, these problems can be avoided by using a *progressive ratio schedule*. In this schedule, the subject is required to work for a drug infusion on an FR schedule that consistently gets more demanding. The schedule may start at FR 50. After the first reinforcement is received, it might change to FR 100, then to FR 200 and so on. At some point, known as the *breaking point*, the demand of the schedule will be too high, and the organism will stop responding. Compared to drugs that are not so reinforcing, highly reinforcing drugs will motivate the animal to work harder and will, consequently, have a higher breaking point and greater potential for abuse. Nevertheless, there is evidence that measures of the reinforcing value of drugs, using the progressive ratio schedule, may also be affected by a drug's effect on the ability of an organism to respond (Rowlett, Massey, Kleven, & Woolverton, 1996).

Choice

The choice procedure is fairly simple. With laboratory animals, two levers are presented. In the first session, one lever will cause an infusion of drug A, and the other lever has no consequences. This is followed by a session in which the second lever will cause an infusion of drug B,

and the first lever has no consequences. This procedure ensures that the animal has an equal exposure to both drugs, A and B. Following this phase of the experiment, both levers will dispense their drugs, and the animal has the opportunity to respond on either lever. Presumably, the animal will respond more on the lever that delivers the more reinforcing drug.

Place Conditioning

This technique uses a long box that has two distinctive halves separated by a partition. Rats are confined in one half of the box after being given an injection of a drug, and they experience the effect of the drug there. On an equal number of occasions, they are injected with a placebo and confined in the other half of the box. Later, when they are placed in the box, the partition is removed, and they are allowed to wander between the chambers. The amount of time they spend in each chamber is recorded. Usually, the rats will spend more time in the end of the box that has been associated with the reinforcing drugs, and the strength of their preference for that end of the box is a good indication of the reinforcing value of the drug (Van der Kooy, 1987).

The explanation of this preference is that the location where the drug is given has become a conditioned stimulus that evokes the reinforcing effects of the drug. Therefore, the animal is reinforced for approaching it and spending time there.

FACTORS THAT ALTER THE REINFORCING VALUE OF DRUGS

Reinforcing Value of Different Drugs

Different drugs also are different in their capacity to act as positive reinforcers. This property is sometimes called *abuse potential* or *abuse liability*. It has become important to be able to assess the abuse potential of new drugs as they are developed, and abuse potential is becoming an important consideration in the legal classification of drugs.

These techniques have shown that psychomotor stimulants in general and cocaine in particular are the most robust reinforcers yet encountered. Cocaine is extensively used to train laboratory animals to self-administer drugs, and it has become a standard against which other drugs are often compared (Yanagita, 1975). In the following chapters the reinforcing value of many drugs will be described.

Dose of Drug

These techniques have also demonstrated that larger doses of any drug are generally more reinforcing than smaller doses, although some studies suggest that there may not be much difference between very large doses. In fact, reinforcing ability may decline with some drugs when very large doses are used (Brady et al., 1987; Depoortere, Li, Lane, & Emmett-Oglesby, 1993).

Genetic Differences

Even though the positive reinforcement model of drug self-administration emphasizes that environmental and schedule variables are of primary importance in controlling drug self-administration, the model does not preclude the possibility that biochemical and genetic differences between individuals may be responsible for variations in drug use. In fact, operant drug self-administration techniques can be used to test the reinforcing properties of drugs in different strains of laboratory animals and to test the possibility that certain aspects of an animal's biochemistry could alter drug-taking behavior (F. R. George, Ritz, & Elmer, 1991).

It has been known for some time that different strains of laboratory rats and mice differ in alcohol consumption. In fact, both alcohol-preferring and alcohol-avoiding strains of rats have been selectively bred in the laboratory. In addition, there is now evidence that there is a significant genetic contribution to the risk of becoming alcoholic (Schuckit, 1985, 1992). Men with a family history of alcoholism are at greater risk of becoming alcoholics themselves.

It seems that this genetic predisposition is not unique to alcohol. Frank George at the University of New Mexico and Stephen Goldberg at the National Institute on Drug Abuse in Baltimore have shown that different strains of rats and mice have different preferences for cocaine. Similar genetic differences have been shown in the consumption of opiates (F. R. George, 1997; F. R. George & Goldberg, 1989).

Relief of Unpleasant Symptoms

It would be reasonable to assume that drugs that have therapeutic effects (they relieve unpleasant symptoms) might be self-administered to gain that effect. In fact, it has often been suggested that alcohol is used by some people to relieve the symptoms of stress or depression. Similarly, the motivation for abuse of diazepam (Valium) might be to gain protection against the distress of anxiety. Thus, people experiencing high stress and anxiety might be particularly susceptible to the overuse of alcohol or diazepam.

At the University of Chicago, a research team that includes Harriet de Wit and Chris Johanson has tested some of these assumptions, using a variation on the choice procedure with human subjects. In this procedure, volunteers report to the lab every morning for a number of days. Each day, they are given a capsule to consume at that time. On days 1 and 3 they get a capsule of one color, and on days 2 and 4 they get a capsule of a different color. On the next 5 days, they are given their choice of color. By definition, the more reinforcing pill will be chosen more frequently. Using this technique with normal volunteers as subjects, de Wit and Johanson (1987) found that there is generally no preference for diazepam over a placebo. This result is somewhat surprising because diazepam is an extensively prescribed drug that is suspected of being overused.

The researchers reasoned that diazepam might be preferred and excessively used only by very anxious people, so they screened their subjects by administering a diagnostic test for anxiety. Surprisingly, highly anxious people did not consistently choose diazepam over the placebo, even though the anxious subjects rated the drug more highly than the placebo and reported that the drug reduced their anxiety.

In addition to testing diazepam in various populations, these researchers found that amphetamine, which improves mood and decreases appetite (see Chapter 11), was not preferentially chosen by people who were depressed or overweight (de Wit & Johanson, 1987, p. 568; de Wit, Uhlenhuth, & Johanson, 1987).

In one circumstance, however, anticipated relief of unpleasant symptoms is reinforcing. Opiates will be self-administered to a greater extent by humans if they know that they will experience a painful stimulus (Pirec et al., 1995; Zacny et al., 1996) (see the next section on task demands).

Understanding drug use as a form of self-medication to relieve unpleasant psychological states has considerable intuitive appeal, but as yet there are few studies to support the idea.

Task Demands

It seems clear from human experience that the decision to use or not to use a drug depends on the expected demands of a situation. For example, people may choose not to drink alcohol if they know that they will be driving, or they may take a stimulant if they know that they will be driving long distances at night. Task demand has been systematically examined, by Kenneth Silverman and his colleagues at Johns Hopkins Medical School. They have shown that this variable can affect drug choice in human subjects.

Silverman had volunteers ingest color-coded capsules containing triazolam, a short-acting benzodiazepine tranquilizer (see Chapter 7); d-amphetamine, a stimulant (see Chapter 11); or a placebo. Then they were required to engage in either of two activities: (a) a vigilance task in which they stared at a computer screen for 50 minutes and were required to respond when a star appeared or (b) a relaxation task in which they were required to lie on a bed for 50 minutes without moving. Seven of eight subjects reliably chose the amphetamine capsules when they knew that the vigilance task was to follow, and all eight always chose the triazolam when they knew they would be in the relaxation situation (K. Silverman, Kirby, & Griffiths, 1994).

In a later experiment, K. Silverman, Mumford, and Griffiths (1994) showed that subjects reliably chose a capsule containing 100 mg of caffeine rather than a placebo before the vigilance activity. Subjects will choose an analgesic (nitrous oxide or fentanyl) more often if they are required to undergo the painful experience of immersing their forearms in icy water (Pirec et al., 1995; Zacny et al., 1996). Thus, it appears that task demand can either enhance or diminish the reinforcing value of a particular drug.

Stress

Stress has often been given as an excuse for the use of drugs by humans, but only recently have there been extensive studies of stress and the self-administration of drugs by laboratory animals. From these studies, we know that stress not only enhances the acquisition of the self-administration of a number of drugs, including cocaine, opiates, and alcohol, but also has been shown to increase the reinforcing value of these drugs as determined by rate of responding and progressive ratio (Piazza & Le Moal, 1998). The stressors that produce this effect are of various kinds: tail pinch, social isolation, exposure to aggression by members of the same species, and unpredictable foot shock.

As we shall see later in this chapter, the neurophysiological mechanisms relating stress to the use of drugs shows that the motivation to use drugs is not to gain relief from the stress. It is clear that stress in the present as well as in an individual's past can alter the brain mechanisms that cause all drugs to act as reinforcers.

Other Deprivations and Motivations

Hungry animals will drink more alcohol than satiated animals. It was always assumed that they did so because alcohol has calories that supply the hungry animals with energy. It turns out, however, that hunger also stimulates the self-administration of many other drugs that have no calories, including cocaine and phencyclidine (PCP, a dissociative anesthetic; see Chapter 16), and thirst seems to have the same effect as hunger (Carroll & Meisch, 1984). This may be an expression of the stress effect, discussed in the previous section, because hunger may be thought of as a form of stress. As yet, there have been no studies of deprivation effects on drug self-administration in humans.

Previous Experience with Other Drugs

In general, most research shows that slower-acting drugs in the benzodiazepine family, such as diazepam (Valium), are not self-administered. It turns out that an important determinant of whether diazepam is self-administered is past experience with sedative hypnotic or depressant drugs such as barbiturates. Bergman and Johanson (1985) found that baboons did not self-administer diazepam when they were switched to it from cocaine, but they did self-administer diazepam to some degree when switched to it from pentobarbital.

This difference does not appear to be unique to baboons. Other research using the choice procedure has consistently found no preference for diazepam over a placebo in normal populations of volunteers. In similar experiments conducted with moderate alcohol users, however, people who consumed an average of one drink a day indicated a marked preference for the diazepam. In a different experiment, subjects living on a hospital research ward did work for a benzodiazepine reward

when given the opportunity, but they were all former sedative abusers (de Wit & Johanson, 1987). Similarly, nitrous oxide, a volatile anesthetic sometimes known as laughing gas, is more reinforcing to moderate drinkers than to light drinkers (Cho et al., 1997).

Previous Experience with the Same Drug

In naive laboratory animals, caffeine does not appear to be a robust reinforcer. In one experiment, only two out of six monkeys self-administered caffeine spontaneously. The four monkeys that did not give themselves caffeine were then given automatic infusions of caffeine for a period of time. Caffeine then acted as a reinforcer in three of these four monkeys (Deneau, Yanagita, & Seevers, 1969). In another example, previous exposure to amphetamine will increase the breaking point for self-administered amphetamine on a progressive ratio schedule (Lorrain, Arnold, & Vezina, 2000).

It has been demonstrated repeatedly that a history of either self-administration or passive exposure to a drug can enhance the drug's reinforcing ability (S. R. Goldberg, 1976, pp. 304–305; Samson, 1987). It is likely that the effect of previous exposure to the same or a similar drug is mediated by a general sensitization to the effects of drugs (see Chapter 3 and the section on incentive sensitization later in this chapter).

Physical Dependence

It has been demonstrated that physical dependence is not necessary for drug self-administration, but does it play any role in drug taking? Extensive research has not been attempted, but it appears that withdrawal can influence the strength of the reinforcing effect of many drugs. For example, early research on the self-administration of morphine showed that the rate of self-administration will increase if the animal is denied the opportunity to self-administer for a period of time and is experiencing withdrawal symptoms (Thompson & Schuster, 1964).

In another study, Tomoji Yanagita (1987) compared the breaking points on a progressive ratio for animals that were physically dependent and for animals that were not. Physical dependence was established in some animals by giving them pretreatments with a drug; control animals were pretreated with a placebo. The breaking points on a progressive ratio schedule for the drug were determined for both groups of animals. Yanagita, using this procedure with morphine and codeine, showed that animals that were physically dependent on both drugs had higher breaking points than controls. Physical dependence on ethanol caused only a slight increase in ethanol's breaking point, but the same effect was not seen with diazepam (Valium).

Priming

The priming effect has been studied for many years and appears to occur with many reinforcing stimuli. It has been shown that responding for a reinforcer can be stimulated by a noncontingent presentation of that reinforcer (Reid, 1957). This is also true for drugs (de Wit, 1996).

The priming effect for drugs was demonstrated by J. Stewart and de Wit (1987). They trained monkeys to bar press for an infusion of cocaine or heroin and then extinguished the response by withholding the drug. They then found that a noncontingent infusion of the drug would start the animal bar pressing again. Priming has since been demonstrated with many other drugs.

Priming has been used to explain a phenomenon called "loss of control" in alcoholics. Abstinent alcoholics are warned that if they take just one drink, they will start drinking again and will be unable to control their alcohol consumption (see Chapter 6). It has also been demonstrated that exposure to a formerly abused drug (and even to stimuli associated with the use of the drug) causes both an increased craving and self-administration of the drug, that is, a relapse (see the discussion of incentive sensitization later in this chapter).

In addition to the original training drug, priming can be caused by injections of a different reinforcing drug and by injections of drugs directly into the ventral tegmental area of the mesolimbic system. Priming can also be caused by a stressful stimulus (de Wit, 1996) and stimuli previously associated with drug delivery.

Conditioned Reinforcement

It has long been known that if a neutral stimulus is paired with a reinforcing stimulus, it will acquire reinforcing properties through classical conditioning. In Chapter 3, it was demonstrated that many of the effects of a drug could be conditioned to environmental stimuli. The same is true of the reinforcing effects of drugs. Conditioned reinforcement or conditioned incentive has been demonstrated in a number of different ways, including the conditioned place preference (CPP) described earlier and second-order schedules.

Second-Order Schedules. This is a modification of the standard drug self-administration technique already described. When a drug is administered, it is preceded or accompanied by a distinctive stimulus, such as a light. Eventually, the animal will learn to bar press just to make the light come on; that is, the light acquires reinforcing properties because of its association with the drug. These reinforcing properties can be demonstrated using a *second-order schedule* (Katz & Goldberg, 1987). The light is presented on a schedule of reinforcement such as an FR 10. The FR 10 itself is considered to be a single response in another schedule that is reinforced by a drug infusion—perhaps an FR 20. Thus, the animal gets the light after every 10 responses, and after 20 of these FR 10s are completed, the light and the drug are presented together. Thus, the animal gets the drug after making 200 responses.

Intermittently reinforcing behavior by presenting a stimulus associated with the drug and only occasionally presenting the drug and the stimulus together makes it possible to maintain much more behavior than if the drug were administered alone and no stimulus used (S. R. Goldberg, Spealman, & Goldberg, 1981).

In Chapter 3, it was shown that many of the conditioned effects of a drug are compensatory, or opposite from the unconditioned effect of the drug. If drug-related stimuli cause a compensatory effect, they will reduce the effect of the drug when they are presented along with the drug. This is called *conditioned tolerance*. It does not occur with the conditioned reinforcing effects of drugs. As place preference and second-order schedules show, stimuli paired with a reinforcing drug also acquire reinforcing properties. This means that if the conditioned stimulus and the drug produce the same effect, presenting the drug and the stimulus together will enhance the effect of the drug and cause sensitization (see Chapter 3.)

The role of conditioned reinforcers in maintaining drug self-administration and relapse has long been recognized. Stimuli associated with drug consumption—the sight and smell of cigarettes, the sight of drug injection apparatus, or the environment of the inside of a bar—are all factors that are known to stimulate drug use and precipitate relapse in those who are trying to quit. Some drug therapies deliberately attempt to extinguish the reinforcing effect of these cues by presenting them without the subsequent delivery of a drug (P. B. Silverman & Bonate, 1997).

THE NEUROANATOMY OF MOTIVATION AND REINFORCEMENT

In the 1950s, James Olds and Peter Milner (1954) at McGill University discovered that electrical stimulation of certain areas of the brain would act as reinforcement; that is, rats would learn to perform a task in order to cause the stimulation. In addition, it appeared that these reinforcement centers were associated with the limbic system— the part of the brain that normally controls the expression of "motivational" behavior, such as eating, drinking, and sexual activity. These early experiments led people to believe that there was a single site in the brain that, when activated, would function as reinforcement, a so-called reinforcement center. It has turned out that things are not really that simple. It is now clear that all these circuits are part of a complex brain system that is responsible for learning, motivation, and the control and direction of behavior—that is, a motivation control system. Stimuli that act as reinforcers interact with this motivation control system in complex ways.

This motivation control system handles a number of different functions. It is stimulated when there is an imbalance in the body, such as the need for food (hunger), and it responds by activating behavior and directing that behavior so that the organism approaches objects in the environment and performs acts that have resulted in restoration of that balance in the past. Figure 5-3 summarizes the neurophysiology of such a system and how it is believed to work.

There are two sources of sensory input to the motivation control system. One input monitors the internal state of the organism. When there is an imbalance or deficiency in some system, such as when the organism is hungry, this input stimulates the *ventral tegmental area* (VTA) in the midbrain. Axons from the VTA are connected to the *nucleus accumbens*, and the VTA stimulates the nucleus accumbens by releasing dopamine at its synapses. This connection between the VTA and the nucleus accumbens is known as the *mesolimbic dopamine system*, and it appears to play an important role in reinforcement. Cells in the nucleus accumbens send axons back to the VTA that release a peptide (opiatelike) neurotransmitter there, forming a circuit.

The nucleus accumbens also sends axons to the *basal ganglia*, which, together with parts of the cortex, belong to the *motor loop*. In the absence of any other sensory input, activation of the mesolimbic dopamine system by a homeostatic imbalance such as hunger will stimulate the motor system and cause a general increase in motor activity of the organism. In fact, the output of the nucleus accumbens normally provides continuous inhibition of the motor system. When dopamine is released in the nucleus accumbens, it actually inhibits the inhibitory output to the motor system, and this has the same effect as stimulating the motor system.

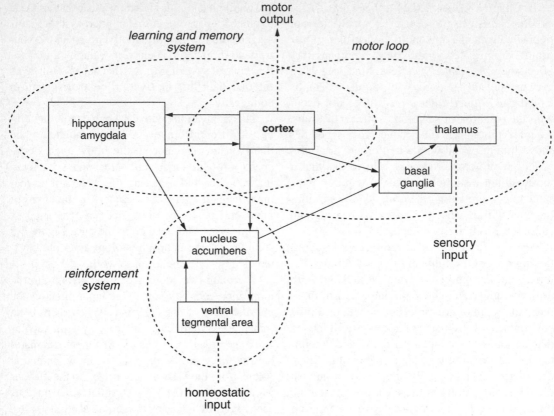

Figure 5-3 The motivation control system of the brain. The reinforcement system stimulates behavior by stimulating the motor loop in response to internal homeostatic input (such as hunger or thirst). Behavior will be directed by sensory input and by memory of the outcome of past behaviors stored in the learning and memory system. Motor behavior can also be stimulated and directed by sensory input to the thalamus, which is compared to past experiences in the learning and memory system. This then activates the reinforcement system. See the text for details.

The motivation control system also receives sensory information about the environment. This information is processed by the *thalamus* and *cortex* and then sent to the *amygdala* and the *hippo-campus*, which are part of a *learning and memory system* that holds the memory of previously experienced stimuli and past actions and their outcomes. With the aid of these memories, it is determined whether these stimuli are biologically significant (e.g., food or a lever that has been followed by food when it has been pressed). Such stimuli are said to

have acquired *incentive salience;* they are easily noticed, and they capture the attention of the organism. If this is the case, the hippocampus and amygdala stimulate the mesolimbic dopamine system via the nucleus accumbens.

The nucleus accumbens then activates the motor loop via the basal ganglia. The motor output that results will be directed toward the significant stimulus (the food or lever), guided by sensory input received via the thalamus. Because behavior is directed toward the significant stimulus, the food will be eaten, or the lever will be pressed and the food that arrives will be eaten. This outcome will then be stored in the learning and memory system and used to modify behavior in the future when the need arises or the appropriate environmental stimuli are present, and the incentive salience of the relevant stimulus will be strengthened.

This motivation control system has evolved so that an organism will be able to show maximum flexibility in a very wide variety of environmental conditions, thus ensuring its survival and increasing the chances that it will pass its genes (including the genes that create this neural circuitry) along to another generation. In general, it works in the following manner.

When a need state occurs (e.g., hunger), it is detected, and the mesolimbic system is activated. This causes an increase in general activity. In the absence of any previous learning or relevant salient stimuli, this activity ensures that the organism will move around its environment and maybe find food accidentally (e.g., find grubs after turning over a rock in a streambed). This outcome is monitored and stored in the cortex and hippocampus. As a consequence, grubs and the streambed acquire incentive salience. In the future, when the organism gets hungry and the nucleus accumbens becomes stimulated, activity will increase, and the stored memories will cause the animal's behavior to be directed toward the rocks in the streambed and the grubs. In addition, the rocks and the streambed, because they have acquired incentive salience, will be readily noticed and attended to (more salient) and will also have the power to activate the nucleus accumbens, so the organism will tend to approach and spend time there even if it is not hungry.

This system of controlling behavior applies to other motivations, including thirst and reproduction, and it provides considerable adaptability in a changing ecology. Suppose there is a drought, the streambed dries up, and no more grubs are to be found there. After turning over a number of rocks and not finding any food, the animal would extinguish the behavior, the streambed would lose its reinforcing and incentive value, and the activation

caused by the hunger would drive the animal to seek food in other places. Such a system clearly contributes to the fitness and survival value of organisms and appears to have done so for a very long time. Even nonmammalian and invertebrate brains have a dopamine system similar to the mesolimbic dopamine system that runs from the midbrain to subcortical structures. In addition, dopamine is known to mediate feeding in a range of organisms, from slugs to humans (Nesse & Berridge, 1997).

"Wanting" Versus "Liking" in Reinforcement

When Olds and Milner first demonstrated the reinforcing properties of stimulation of certain brain centers, people started to call these centers "pleasure centers," partly because when these centers were stimulated in people, they reported experiencing extreme pleasure. They said that they liked it. It was, therefore, reasonable to think that the reinforcing value of this stimulation (and any other reinforcing stimulus) was derived from the pleasure it produced. In fact, many theorists still use the concept of pleasure seeking (*hedonism* means the same thing but sounds more technical) to explain many of these concepts (Koob, Sanna, & Bloom, 1998). They explain reinforcement by saying that food causes a stimulation of the mesolimbic dopamine system, and this means that the organism experiences the sensation of pleasure. The pleasure "reinforces" the behavior of seeking food and is, therefore, repeated.

As discussed earlier, the concept of pleasure seems to make intuitive sense, but it is not necessary for the explanation of reinforcement in behavioral or neurological terms. It may even be misleading because, as we have pointed out, stimuli can act as reinforcers without the sensation of pleasure. In addition, there is evidence that after repeated presentations, activation of the mesolimbic dopamine system occurs more in response to the presentation of stimuli that precede or anticipate a biologically significant stimulus like food rather than to the presentation or consumption of that stimulus itself, which subjectively would seem to be the source of pleasure (Wickelgren, 1997).

Pleasure is a subjective state that often accompanies activation of the mesolimbic dopamine system. However, at the neurological level of analysis, it is unnecessary and inappropriate to use this subjective state as an explanation of its function. It is sufficient to say that the activation of this system alone, not the pleasure, causes behavior to be repeated. In other words, the brain system is there to make you repeat certain actions, not to make you feel good; it is a do-it-again system, not a pleasure system. Any pleasure that is experienced is a subjective by-product of the activation of the mesolimbic dopamine system.

If the nucleus accumbens and the mesolimbic dopamine system do not make up a pleasure or a "liking" system, what are their roles in reinforcement? As we have seen, the mesolimbic dopamine system just described has two roles in motivating behavior. The first role is general activation. This can be thought of as a "pushing" behavior without any general direction. When we do not eat for a while, we get "hungry"—we get up and do something. What we do is controlled by the second function. The second function of the mesolimbic dopamine system is to direct that behavior toward a particular goal. This is done by the process of incentive salience; that is, various stimuli in the environment are given special motivational properties that cause us to notice them, be attracted to them, and do something to them.

There appear to be some stimuli that have natural incentive salience. Such a stimulus might be an attractive member of the opposite sex; our attention is immediately drawn to such a person, we are attracted to him or her, and we enjoy his or her company. Sweet tastes are also naturally attractive and can act as incentives. Neutral stimuli can also acquire incentive salience when they are associated with basic motivations like hunger and sex. The act of pressing the lever in the Skinner box acquires incentive salience when it is repeatedly associated with the delivery of food; rats will approach the lever and begin pressing it when they get the chance. Thus, stimuli and actions associated with these natural incentives acquire incentive value of their own and come to control behavior. This is how reinforcement operates. It is not a matter of the rat remembering that pressing the lever causes food to appear. That may well happen, but the behavior of the rat appears to depend on the attractive motivational properties of the lever and the act of pressing it; that is, the lever becomes "wanted."

The crucial role of the nucleus accumbens in reinforcement is in the formation of incentive salience. It is the nucleus accumbens that is responsible for turning a previously neutral stimulus into a stimulus that we "want," and dopamine appears to be a crucial element in this process. As mentioned previously, natural reinforcers cause the release of dopamine in the nucleus accumbens. Other significant events, even aversive ones, will cause the release of dopamine as well. It has been shown that previously neutral stimuli that regularly precede natural reinforcers also acquire this property and in the process also acquire incentive salience. Thus, the mesolimbic dopamine system and the nucleus accumbens in particular constitute a "wanting" system rather than a pleasure system.

Reinforcing Effects of Drugs. It is now clear that all drugs known to be positive reinforcers are capable of activating the mesolimbic dopamine system either by direct stimulation of the nucleus accumbens or by indirect stimulation of the nucleus accumbens by facilitating excitatory input or blocking inhibitory input to the motivation circuitry (Wise, 1998). It has also been shown that the reinforcing value of drugs of all kinds depends on the integrity of the mesolimbic dopamine system and dopamine receptors located there. Imaging studies and studies of brain chemistry have shown that drugs and natural reinforcers cause an increase in dopamine levels in the nucleus accumbens.

This means that drugs control behavior by using the same brain mechanism as other positive reinforcers (like food). There are, however, some important differences between drug reinforcement and reinforcement by more natural reinforcers. One of the most important differences is that natural reinforcers have a satiation mechanism that terminates their reinforcing effect. Food, for example, is a reinforcer only if we are hungry. After we have eaten a certain amount, food loses its reinforcing value, and we stop eating. The same is true for water, and there are physiological limits on sexual activity as well. Most drugs, on the other hand, do not appear to have any natural limits to their reinforcing ability.

Another difference between drug reinforcement and natural reinforcers is the immediacy and strength of the latter's effect. Drugs are capable of getting to the brain in high concentrations very soon after they are administered. This probably makes drug reinforcement stronger and more immediate than natural reinforcers.

Drugs that reinforce behavior by increasing activity in the mesolimbic dopamine system are not natural reinforcers. Nevertheless, these drugs do control behavior using "natural" mechanisms of positive reinforcement, and this can help us understand and predict their effects and can provide clues to how their ability to control behavior might be diminished.

Stress and Reinforcement. Earlier we saw that stress, both present and in the past, increases the strength of a reinforcing stimulus. This effect of stress is thought to be a result of increased levels of glucocorticoid hormones. These stress hormones cause the release of dopamine in the nucleus accumbens and are known to act as reinforcers. Animals will work for intravenous infusions of them. Because of this connection between stress hormones and dopamine, stress stimulates the mesolimbic dopamine system and intensifies the reinforcing value of drug reinforcers and related stimuli.

Research into sensitization has demonstrated that, like repeated exposure to reinforcing drugs, repeated exposure to stressful stimuli sensitizes the mesolimbic dopamine system. Long-term exposure to stress can increase the incentive value of drugs long after the stressful stimulus has been removed. In fact, it has been shown that there is increased self-administration of amphetamine in rats whose mothers were stressed while they were pregnant (Deminiére et al., 1992; Meaney, 2001)

WHAT HAPPENS DURING ADDICTION?

By considering that drugs act like natural reinforcers, we are able to understand the casual use of drugs that does little harm. But in some individuals this "normal" process seems to escalate into very harmful use where obtaining and using the drug disrupts all other aspects of behavior. We call this state *addiction*. The motivational system in the brain evolved because it increased the survival fitness of organisms in a wide variety of environments, but none of these environments included the availability of refined, high-strength drugs available today or the efficient drug delivery mechanisms we now use. It is not surprising, therefore, that drugs can create special problems that our brains have not evolved to deal with. How drugs alter the functioning of the motivation system and the behavior it controls is not entirely clear, but there are many interesting theories (West, 2001). We will examine several of these theories that make use of the behavioral and neural mechanisms described earlier.

INCENTIVE SENSITIZATION THEORY

The discussion of sensitization in Chapter 3 revealed that when reinforcing drugs are repeatedly administered, there is an increase in behavioral activation. The animal becomes more sensitive to the drug rather than less sensitive. It is now known that the cause of the animal's becoming more active is the increased sensitivity of the mesolimbic dopamine system to the drug.

The *incentive sensitization theory* uses this change in sensitivity to explain addictive behavior.

Incentive Sensitization and Craving

This theory was proposed by Terry Robinson and Kent Berridge (1993, 2003) at the University of Michigan. It was designed to explain the phenomenon of drug craving: "the desire to experience the effect(s) of a previously experienced psycho-active substance" (UNDCP & WHO, 1992). This desire is excessive in people who are considered to be addicted and is often a defining characteristic of addiction. The concept of craving refers to a subjective state, and because researchers have not been able to agree on a definition of craving in behavioral terms (Markou et al., 1993), the concept has been of little use to the scientific investigation of drug abuse. Robinson and Berridge, however, changed that by suggesting that craving could be thought of as the manifestation of incentive salience, which becomes stronger with repeated drug use because of sensitization of the mesolimbic dopamine system to the effects of drugs.

To understand incentive salience, we must return to the general motivating system described earlier in this chapter (refer again to Figure 5-3). Stimuli that activate the mesolimbic dopamine system—either because they are natural reinforcers such as food or because they have been associated with reinforcers in the past—are said to have incentive salience: (a) The stimulus is easily noticed and attended to by the organism, and (b) the stimulus activates behavior that is directed toward the stimulus. When a stimulus with incentive salience such as food is presented to a hungry animal, the food is noticed immediately. The animal becomes more active, and that activity is directed toward the food—the animal approaches the food and eats it. You might say that this activation makes the animal "want" the food. Because drugs activate the mesolimbic system, they are also "wanted," and this makes the drug a positive reinforcer.

With repeated use, a drug will acquire greater incentive value (and be a stronger reinforcer) because of sensitization. Repeated presentation of a reinforcer will also cause the stimuli associated with it to have greater incentive salience as well. Thus, whenever a reinforcing drug—or, more important, stimuli paired with a reinforcing drug—are experienced, the mesolimbic dopamine system in the brain becomes active and creates motivation to approach these stimuli. If the mesolimbic dopamine system has been sensitized, that activation and the attraction of the stimulus are increased. According to incentive sensitization theory, the subjective consequence of activation of this system is "wanting," and the subjective experience of a sensitized system is intense wanting or "craving."

Incentive sensitization theory can explain many aspects of drug use. First, it describes how drug addiction might develop. When a drug is first used or administered casually, it may not be a very strong reinforcer and may not be able to compete with other nondrug reinforcers to control a person's behavior, but with repeated administration, the drug acquires increased reinforcing properties. The more it is used, the more effective a reinforcer it becomes until it has the capacity to control a large amount of behavior.

The theory also explains why stimuli associated with a drug can evoke the craving to use the drug. Because sensitization of the dopamine system is relatively permanent and can become associated with specific stimuli, cravings—or the desire to use a drug—can last a very long time after drug use has stopped. Ex-addicts, even after many years of abstinence, are at a high risk of relapsing, and relapse is often triggered by stimuli associated with the use of the drug. For example, during abstinence, simply visiting the location where they typically administered their choice drug can induce drug craving in addicts and cause relapse into drug taking. Recent brain imaging data suggest that cognitive processing of drug-related cues is biased in addicted and formerly addicted individuals. That is, drug-related stimuli are more attention grabbing and attractive (T. E. Robinson & Berridge, 2000) and receive excessive focus from addicts, as incentive sensitization theory predicts (J. M. G. Williams, Mathews, & MacLeod, 1996).

The technique of using event-related potentials (ERPs) is useful in assessing the direct effect of stimulus presentation on information processing. As we mentioned in Chapter 4, the P300 component of ERP provides an index of the amount of cognitive energy or attention a participant is devoting to perceiving a stimulus. Later components of the ERP (called *slow positive waves*) that appear between 200 and 6,000 ms after stimulus presentation provide an index of sustained attention, or selective cognitive processing, of presented stimuli. Research suggests that these slow waves may be tied to motivational systems in the brain (Cuthbert, Schupp, Bradley, Birbaumer, & Lang, 2000). Using electroencephalography to assess slow positive wave–evoked potentials, researchers presented abstinent heroin addicts and drug-naive participants with neutral-color digital photographs interspersed with images of heroin paraphernalia and people engaged in heroin use. They discovered that abstinent heroin addicts demonstrated increases in slow positive wave amplitude when presented with heroin-associated images, suggesting that these images were selected by the brain for enhanced processing (Franken, Stam, Hendriks, & van den Brink, 2003). Control participants, on the other hand, demonstrated no differences in cognitive processing between neutral and heroin-associated images.

Eliciting drug-related memories in abstinent opiate addicts appears to have a similar effect. Listening to a 2-minute autobiographical script describing a past episode when the participant was experiencing craving for opiates induced current feelings of drug craving in most participants. Positron emission tomography (PET) imaging using [^{15}O]H$_2$O revealed a positive correlation between the intensity of drug craving and the degree of cerebral blood flow in the orbitofrontal cortex (Daglish, Weinstein, et al., 2001). The left anterior cingulate/medial prefrontal region showed increased activation during presentation of the autobiographical script, even in participants who reported no craving. Furthermore, the longer the participant had remained abstinent from opiates, the larger the increase in cerebral blood flow in the left anterior cingulate.

It has also been demonstrated that social users of both alcohol and marijuana are more sensitive to stimuli related to alcohol and marijuana, respectively; they were faster to detect changes that involved drug-related items in a picture of a variety of objects, indicating an information processing bias toward drug-related items (B. C. Jones, Jones, Blundell, & Bruce, 2002; B. T. Jones, Jones, Smith, & Copley, 2003).

This cue-generated craving has recently been linked to brain activity of alcoholics using brain imaging techniques. In long-term alcoholics who remained abstinent for 3 weeks, presentation of alcohol-related pictures induced significant craving for the drug that corresponded with increases in activation of the medial prefrontal cortex and the anterior cingulate cortex measured by functional magnetic resonance imaging (fMRI). Furthermore, PET analysis determined that alcoholics displayed lower levels of D$_2$ receptors in the ventral striatum (including the nucleus accumbens) and that receptor density correlated negatively with the severity of craving and fMRI-measured brain activation. These results are shown in Color Plate A. The authors suggest that the dysfunction of dopamine in the ventral striatum may lead alcoholics to attribute increased amounts of attention to alcohol-related cues and experience greater motivation to consume alcohol (Heinz et al., 2004). Cue-induced activation of the dopamine system also occurs in teenage (14- to 17-year-old) drinkers with only a short (1- to 2-year) history of alcohol abuse. Blood oxygen level–dependent MRI revealed greater activation of the left anterior, limbic, and visual cortices in these teens with the degree of activation positively correlated with the degree of reported craving for alcohol (Tapert et al., 2003). Furthermore, dopaminergic activation in the ventral striatum is increased not only by visual alcohol-related cues but also by olfactory cues, such as the smell of beer and whiskey (Kareken et al., 2004).

Sensitization of incentive salience can also explain the priming effect described earlier wherein a single exposure to a drug can restart more drug use even if it has been extinguished. In priming, a single drug administration stimulates a sensitized reward system that will increase the incentive of the drug and the incentive salience of stimuli associated with it; that is, it causes craving.

Robinson and Berridge are careful to point out that the subjective effect of activation in this brain system is a sensation of "wanting," not of "liking" or pleasure. Pleasure, they say, arises from the drug activating another brain system that shows tolerance rather than sensitization to repeated drug use. This explains why people often crave drugs even as they report that they are miserable and that they get little or no pleasure from the drug.

HEDONIC DYSREGULATION AND ADAPTATION

Another class of theories is based on the physical dependence model described previously. An example of such a theory was proposed by George Koob of the Scripps Research Institute and Mickel Le Moal of l'Universitié de Bordeaux in France (Koob, 2000; Koob & LeMoal, 2001). Their theory is a hedonic, physical/psychological dependence theory; that is, it is based on the presumption that the reinforcement caused by drugs is a result of pleasure created when drugs activate the nucleus accumbens and related structures they call the extended amygdala and the effect of withdrawal on that system. They say that a process similar to that described by Solomon and Corbit (1973) takes place when drugs are repeatedly administered. We discussed Solomon and Corbit in Chapter 3. Solomon and Corbit's theory

is that the activation of euphoria or pleasure is an A process that generates a compensatory B process. The B process is dysphoric and cancels out the A process, and this causes tolerance to the euphoric effect of drugs as described in Figure 3-1 in Chapter 3. As you can see from Figure 3-1, the B process lasts longer than the A process and is the cause of hangover after an acute administration and withdrawal after repeated administration of a drug. Koob and Le Moal also propose that with repeated use of a drug, the level of "happiness" or "pleasure" or "mood" does not return completely to normal, as illustrated in Figure 5-4. This means that repeated use of drugs causes the person to become less and less happy or more and more depressed when they stop using the drug. They describe this as an *allostatic process.*

Allostasis is a fairly new concept in stress physiology and medicine and stands in contrast to *homeostasis,* described in Chapter 3. Homeostasis presumes that physiological processes in the body have a set point, a level that is optimal for the animal, and that through a system of feedback, like a thermostat on a furnace, that level is maintained. Allostasis, on the other hand, refers to situations

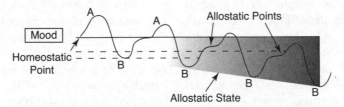

Figure 5-4 This graph is an elaboration of the Solomon and Corbit drawing in Figure 3-1. It shows what happens to the mood (hedonic) set point when a drug such as cocaine is repeatedly administered according to the hedonic dysregulation theory of Koob and Le Moal. When the drug is taken, mood increases above normal (A process), decreases below normal (B process), and then returns to its set point. With repeated administration, the set point gets lower and lower, and the drug used enters an allostatic state. In this state, the new "normal" mood is lower than before the user started to take the drug, and he or she must take more and more of the drug to bring the mood back to the previous normal level. In addition, the ability of all other reinforcers to cause pleasure (act as a reinforcer) is also diminished.

where the set point is not constant but changes in response to changes in the animal's environment (McEwan & Lashley, 2002). As you can see in Figure 5-4, with repeated drug use, new mood set points are established—the user becomes increasingly unhappy and depressed. This new allostatic set point means that a person must take larger and larger doses of the drug to achieve the same degree of euphoria or pleasure as he or she did from the first dose. This sets off a spiral where the user becomes increasingly depressed because the mood set point keeps diminishing. This motivates the user to take larger and larger doses, lowering the set point even further.

Not only does this lowered set point alter the reinforcing effect of the drug, but the reinforcing value of other reinforcers is also diminished. This makes participation in other nondrug activities less and less reinforcing, and eventually their control over behavior diminishes, leaving the field open to the drug, which, because it is more powerful than other reinforcers, becomes the only event capable of acting as a reinforcer. This accelerates the spiral of addiction.

Koob and Le Moal acknowledge that sensitization of the reinforcement system takes place and that this increases the incentive value of drugs in the manner described by Robinson and Berridge, but they suggest that the sensitization contributes to the development of addiction only during the early stages where it stimulates drug intake. Eventually, they say that sensitization is overcome by the processes of *hedonic dysregulation*, the term they use to describe the lowering of the mood set point.

Koob and Le Moal's theory is an example of a modern dependence theory of addiction. It proposes that one of the withdrawal symptoms of all drugs of abuse is *dysphoria* (depression or unhappiness). Because this takes place in the brain and is normally only evident to the drug user, this dysphoria can be thought of as a *psychological withdrawal* syndrome that can be alleviated only by taking more drug in larger quantities. This makes it a mechanism of psychological dependence. Because Koob and Le Moal have identified and measured the changes that take place in the

extended amygdala and in the hormone responses of the brain, they have avoided the circularity of many earlier ideas of psychological dependence described previously.

BEHAVIORAL ECONOMICS: CHOOSING TO USE DRUGS

The theories of both Koob and Le Moal and Robinson and Berridge are based on an understanding of the neurophysiology of the reinforcement system in the brain and what can go wrong, but there are a number of theories that are based on behavioral mechanisms of positive reinforcement alone and do not rely on neurophysiological systems. *Behavioral economic theory* is an example.

In the earlier discussion of factors that alter the reinforcing value of drugs, we looked at choice behavior. In this section, we look at situations in which a choice is made between a drug and a nondrug alternative, and we examine the factors that can influence the choice. It is useful to consider drug use in terms of positive reinforcement, but a single positive reinforcer does not act on behavior in isolation. Nevertheless, the effects of positive reinforcement are often studied in isolation: The organism is in an insulated chamber, only one reinforcing stimulus is available, and only one response, such as pressing a lever, is recorded. This, of course, is a highly contrived and artificial situation. It is useful when we desire to reduce or eliminate the effects of uncontrolled variables on behavior, but it can help us understand only the basic building blocks of behavior. The world we live in and the effects of positive reinforcers are much more complex.

A rat in a Skinner box may press a lever at a high rate, a low rate, or not at all, but when it is not pressing the lever, it does not stop behaving. It may be sniffing, scratching, exploring, sleeping, or engaging in a myriad of other activities, all controlled by reinforcers not immediately apparent to us. Thus, the rate at which a rat presses a lever is influenced not only by the reinforcer we have programmed to follow a lever press but also by all the other reinforcers available to the rat at that instant. In other words, at any given moment, the rat distributes its activity among several possible responses, all controlled by a number of positive or negative reinforcers. How an organism chooses to distribute its behavior among all these alternatives presents a number of interesting and important questions that have been the focus of recent research in behavioral pharmacology laboratories.

The slogan "Just say no to drugs" suggests that doing nothing is the alternative to using a drug. In fact, the choice is not between drug taking and not drug taking but between taking a drug and doing something else. The decision to use a drug may have as much to do with the availability and value of the alternatives as with the availability and incentive value of the drug. To understand drug taking, then, we need to know more than the schedule, availability, and reinforcing value or abuse liability of the drug; we need to know what other activities and reinforcers are available to the organism in its environment. It will also help to understand how people and other animals make choices between alternative reinforcers.

Making Choices

Some time ago, psychologists started studying concurrent schedules of reinforcement. On these schedules, animals are presented with two levers and are free to press either one. Reinforcers are made available on both levers. These levers may vary in the amount of reinforcer delivered and the schedule of reinforcement, and the dependent variable is how the experimental subject distributes its responses between the levers.

For example, a pigeon in a Skinner box may be presented with two response keys. A red key provides a grain reinforcement on a VI 5-minute schedule (a response is reinforced once every 5 minutes on the average). A green key presents the same amount of grain on a VI 10-minute schedule; that is, in the same time period, pecking the red key has the potential to produce twice as many reinforcements as pecking the green key. How does the pigeon handle this situation? It could

peck only the red key and ignore the green key. If it chose this course, however, it would not receive all the reinforcers available to it. On a VI schedule, the longer the pigeon waits after receiving a reinforcement, the more likely it will be reinforced. Thus, the more time it spends pecking the red key, the more likely it will be missing reinforcements from the green key and vice versa. In this situation, the pigeon distributes its responses to each key in proportion to the reinforcements that key produces.

The Matching Law. Richard Herrnstein of Harvard University has proposed that animals distribute their resources (time, money, and effort) to different responses in proportion to the density of reinforcement provided by that response (Domjan, 2003). Thus, a pigeon would respond twice as often on a red key as the green key if the red key were twice as likely to produce a reinforcement as the green key. According to the matching law, the experimenter could easily change the bird's responding on the red key not by altering the reinforcement available on that key but by changing the reinforcement on the green key.

In this key-pecking situation, the matching law makes it easy to predict mathematically how the pigeon will distribute its pecks between two alternatives. Real life is much more complicated. Not only do different stimuli vary in their capacity to function as reinforcers, as we have seen already with drugs, but the reinforcing value of a stimulus can also be modified by numerous factors, including amount, delay, and the current physiological state of the organism. Nevertheless, the same principle applies: An organism will distribute its behavior among different alternatives in proportion to the relative reinforcement each alternative provides.

Thus, in real life, the proportion of a person's behavior that is reinforced by the administration of a drug may have as much to do with the presence and scheduling of other nondrug reinforcers as it does with the reinforcing capacity of a drug. In human terms, this idea suggests that if drugs are available, environmental factors such as boredom, poverty, unemployment, and a lack of economic opportunity or social interaction will contribute to the development of the strength of drug use habits. It is little wonder that drug and alcohol abuse is common in economically depressed inner cities, prisons, and battle zones. An association between economic and social deprivation has been noted many times, and it has usually been attributed to "stress." Rather than stress, however, the crucial variable contributing to drug use in these situations may be the lack of opportunity to obtain reinforcement from any other source.

For example, studies of U.S. service personnel in Vietnam showed that many were using high-grade heroin on a regular basis while assigned there. After their return to the United States, the vast majority stopped using the drug (Robbins, Davis, & Goodwin, 1974), even though many were physically dependent and it was still readily available. It is likely that, apart from drugs, few sources of reinforcement were available in Vietnam, but after the service personnel had returned to the United States, more incompatible activities, such as employment and family activities, were available and competed with drug use. It is easier to say no to drugs if you are busy doing something else. A similar effect has been demonstrated with laboratory animals (Alexander, Beyerstein, Hadaway, & Coambs, 1981).

Looking at drug use in terms of competing activities can also help us understand some of the factors that can lead to the initial use of drugs, how to improve drug therapies, and how to prevent relapse to drug use after therapy (Carroll, 1995). In an environment where the influence of alternative positive reinforcers is minimized because they are difficult to achieve or are unavailable, the impact of introducing a new reinforcer such as a drug might be considerable, and it could easily come to dominate most behavior, especially if it is readily available and not expensive. Once this dominance is established, the effect might be difficult to reverse.

Sudden decreases in the opportunity to obtain competing nondrug reinforcement could also contribute to relapse in former drug users. It has been shown, for example, that former alcoholics are more likely to return to using alcohol at times when there are disruptions in work and family life (Vuchinich & Tucker, 1988, p. 188). Conversely, good therapeutic outcomes are much more likely in individuals with stability in their work situation and their family history (Vaillant, 1992).

Spiral to Addiction. Drug reinforcers have one unique aspect that may contribute to their potential to control large amounts of behavior: They have the capacity to diminish the availability of competing nondrug reinforcers (Heyman, 1996). The use of alcohol, for example, can disrupt relationships with one's spouse or interfere with work and thereby diminish reinforcement normally available from the family or the workplace. The use of many other drugs, especially illegal drugs, often requires a lifestyle that precludes the opportunity to enjoy other reinforcers that may compete with the drug. This diminished availability of competing reinforcement could, in turn, lead to more drinking or increased drug use.

If matching mechanisms control choice to use drugs and if drugs are able to diminish the value and availability of competing activities, drug use can spiral out of control, eventually reaching a state in which the drug controls an addict's life and causes pain, deprivation, and anguish, even though it is a positive reinforcer.

Choice and Time

There are millions of people in North America who smoke tobacco, and it is likely that most of them will admit that they believe that, in the long term, smoking can damage their health, yet they continue to smoke. How can this be? The answer may lie in a phenomenon called *discounting of delay*. This refers to the fact that the perceived value of something decreases the further away it is in time. If you were given the choice of whether you would like to receive $100 or $200 now, the matching law would predict that you would take the $200. If the choice were between $100 now and $200 in 2 years, you would probably take the $100 now. In this way value of future events is discounted by most people.

The nature of the discounting of the value of future events has been extensively studied, and the consequences of the way we discount such events leads to some interesting predictions when it comes to making choices. Figure 5-5 shows what these studies have found. It turns out that the relationship between the length of time in the future a reinforcer will be and how much we discount it in the present is not a straight line. In fact, it is a hyperbolic line; as a distant event approaches, its value increases only slightly, but at a certain point, the value starts to increase rapidly. What this means is that when we have to make choices between two future events, the value of those events can change relative to each other as time passes. At one point, alternative A may be given more value, then, with the passage of time, alternative B may appear to have more value, and our choice will shift as demonstrated in Figure 5-5. This can explain why we change our minds. When two future reinforcers are viewed from a distance in time, we will express a preference for the larger reinforcer, but as the first reinforcer gets closer, we may change our minds and shift our preference to it though it has less value (Bickel & Marsch, 2001).

This sort of delay discounting has been demonstrated in many species and seems to be a fairly universal principle controlling the way most organisms make choices. It can offer some insight into the seeming paradox about why people continue to smoke even when they know it can cause severe health problems in the future. In the case of smoking, a choice has to be made between the immediate value of smoking a cigarette and one's health in the far distant future. Because future health is a distant and elusive concept, its value is discounted so much that it is worth less than a cigarette now. This may explain why most people begin smoking when they are teenagers—future illness seems so far away that it is drastically discounted. As people age, they become more likely to quit smoking. This may well be because their future health is getting closer and closer, and eventually the value of a cigarette drops below the value placed on future health, so they quit. It can also explain the seemingly puzzling behavior of many addicted people in treatment; they claim that they want to give up their drug, but in spite of this, they use the drug as soon as the opportunity arises. For this reason we often say that addicts have lost control, or have no willpower.

There have been a number of studies on the differences between the way addicted and nonaddicted people discount future events. These studies show that addicted people tend to have steeper discount curves than nonaddicted people. For example, it takes 5 years for a nonaddicted person to discount the value of $1,000 by 60 percent, but in an opiate-dependent person, $1,000 is discounted by 60 percent in 1 year. If future events lose their value faster, this means that the behavior of addicted people tends to be controlled more by immediate, small reinforcers than delayed, large reinforcers. This can explain the commonly reported finding that addicts are more impulsive than nonaddicts.

Another interesting difference between addicts and nonaddicts is in the *sign effect*. This refers to

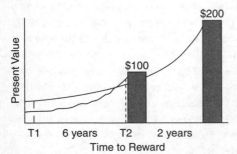

Figure 5-5 This figure shows the relative value of $100 and $200 when both events are in the future. The $100 is 6 years in the future, and the $200 is 8 years away. The lines represent hyperbolic value functions. As you can see at T1, about 6 months from now, the $200 in 8 years has more value than the $100 in 6 years, but as time passes, the relative value of the functions become closer to each other. Eventually, just before T2, the lines cross, and the $100 has more value than $200. This shows that choices between two events will change over time as the events become closer. (Adapted from Bickel & Marsch, 2001)

the finding that normally positive or rewarding events are discounted at a higher rate than losses or negative events of equal value. Thus, the positive value of a $100 payment in a month will be discounted more than the negative value of a $100 fine payable in a month. There is evidence that in addicted people, future negative events or punishers are discounted at the same rate as positive events. This might explain why addicted individuals do not seem to be motivated by factors such as avoiding the distant or potential disruptions in income, health, and occupational and family life caused by using a drug.

BEHAVIORAL ECONOMICS: PRICE AND DEMAND

The study of the factors that contribute to how people distribute their time and money between alternatives has not been solely of interest to psychologists. Economists have investigated similar problems for years. They have especially studied how consumers distribute money among a variety of consumer goods and what happens to the demand for these goods when the price increases and decreases. These lines of inquiry are basically similar, and research in both areas has yielded surprisingly consistent results. The application of economic principles to understanding operant behavior is called *behavioral economics*.

One of the most basic questions in behavioral economics asks how increasing the price of a commodity affects the demand for that commodity. If the price of a commodity—a drug, for example—increases, does the demand for the drug go down, or do consumers of that drug continue to use it to the same extent, in spite of the increased cost?

Economists identify two possibilities here. If consumers continue to spend the same amount (or more) for the drug as before, even though they are not able to purchase as much, demand is said to be *inelastic*. If people start spending less for the drug in response to a price increase, demand is said to be *elastic*. Goods considered necessities—food, water, and shelter—usually show inelastic demand, but

luxury items—entertainment and travel—often show elastic demand. For addicted individuals, the demand for their drug appears to be inelastic; that is, when the price goes up, there is little change in consumption (Bickel & Marsch, 2001).

An experiment conducted by Marilyn E. Carroll (1993) of the University of Minnesota illustrates how this research is done and how the results are often presented. She used rhesus monkeys that were trained to press a lever, on an FR schedule, to receive access to a drinking tube that delivered water containing PCP. She tested the monkeys at a number of different FR values: 4, 8, 16, 32, 64, and 128. The results are shown in Figure 5-6. On each graph, the horizontal axis gives the cost of the drug in terms of the number of responses that must be made to receive each milligram of the drug. The vertical axis on the left panel presents the demand for the drug, that is, the total amount of drug consumed. Both axes are on logarithmic scales (the standard manner of presenting such data). As shown (for now, pay attention just to the open circles), as the cost of each delivery of PCP increases, the demand for PCP drops. The slope of the curve tells whether the demand is elastic or inelastic. If the slope is between 0 and −1.0, the demand does not decline as fast as the price increases (the consumer is spending just as much or more on the commodity); that is, demand is inelastic. Negative slopes with an absolute value greater than −1.0 show that (a) the consumer is spending less and less on the drug as the price goes up and that (b) the decrease is proportionally greater than the price increase; that is, demand is elastic.

The right panel also presents interesting information. The horizontal axis is the unit price in responses per milligram of drug, but the vertical axis is total responses, that is, total expenditure. As cost increased up to 415 responses per milligram of drug, responding also increased. At higher costs, however, responding declined. These results show that at lower costs (up to 415 responses/mg), demand is inelastic (total spending for the drug increased or remained the same), but a point was reached at which demand became elastic (spending

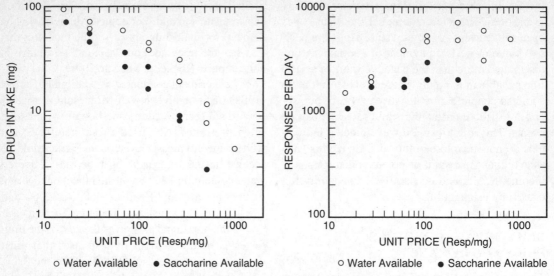

Figure 5-6 Demand curves for monkeys responding on FR schedules of 4, 8, 16, 32, 64, and 128 to receive access to a drinking tube that delivered water containing phencyclidine (PCP). For both graphs, the horizontal axis gives the cost of the drug in terms of the number of responses that must be made to receive each milligram of drug. *Top:* The vertical axis presents the demand for the drug, that is, the total amount of drug consumed per day. *Bottom:* The horizontal axis is also unit price in responses per milligram of drug, but the vertical axis is total responses, that is, total expenditure per day. Both the axes are on logarithmic scales, which have become the standard manner of presenting such data. The open circles indicate responding when water was present, and the closed circles show responding when a sweet-tasting saccharin solution was present (Carroll, 1993). As you can see, the availability of an alternative, nondrug reinforcer, sweet-tasting saccharin, reduced the reinforcing value of the PCP; the demand curve for PCP got steeper (*top*), and the monkey would not work as hard for the drug (*bottom*). This effect was much greater when the cost of the PCP (FR value) was high.

declined). This sort of pattern seems to be typical of many drugs. This situation is analogous to the progressive ratio schedule discussed earlier, in which the schedule requirements for a reinforcer are increased to a point at which the organism stops responding for it. A review by Bickel and his coworkers (Bickel, DeGrandpre, Higgins, & Hughes, 1990) showed a similar function in 10 different experiments using a variety of drugs, including cocaine, barbiturates, d-amphetamine, and ketamine, in rhesus monkeys, squirrel monkeys, and rats.

Research has also found that the slope of the demand curve can be influenced by the availability of other commodities; that is, if an organism has alternatives, it will switch to those alternatives and stop consuming a particular commodity when the price goes up. Thus, the demand curve for beef may well be inelastic if there is no other meat available, but if another meat, such as chicken or pork is available, the demand for beef may drop sharply, showing elasticity.

It appears as though something similar happens with drug and nondrug reinforcers if an alternative activity is made available to a laboratory animal self-administering a drug; making another reinforcer available will decrease the amount of drug the animal takes. In an interesting experiment, rats were allowed to have access to a sweet sugar solution, and their oral consumption of a morphine solution dramatically decreased. When the sweet solution was removed, morphine consumption returned to original levels. Sweet solutions have been shown to reduce amphetamine and ethanol self-administration as well (Carroll, 1993; Kanarek & Marks-Kaufman, 1988), and access to a simple running wheel seems to have the same effect on drug intake as the sweet solution (Kanarek & Marks-Kaufman, 1989).

In the research by Carroll (1993) described previously, when the unit price of PCP was increased, there was a reduction in the use of the drug by rhesus monkeys. The research went on to show that if the monkeys were provided with a nondrug substitute for the PCP—in this case, access to a sweet-tasting saccharin solution—the monkeys did not work as hard for PCP, and the demand for PCP dropped much faster when the saccharin was present. The graphs in Figure 5-6 compare what happened when the substitute was available (solid circles) and when water was available (open circles). When the saccharin was available, the demand for the drug significantly decreased. In the lower panel of Figure 5-6, note that without saccharin, the monkeys increased their responding for PCP up to a cost of 415 responses per milligram (open circles), but when the saccharin was available, responding peaked at 160 responses per milligram (solid circles) and then declined. The fact that saccharin was substituting for PCP was indicated by an increase in saccharin consumption as the PCP consumption declined. This research shows that the effect of a price increase on demand for a commodity depends on the availability of competing commodities that can act as substitutes.

It is worth noting that this effect of the saccharin substitute was much greater when there was a very high work requirement for the PCP. At the lower FR values (FR 4), PCP intake was reduced by only about 21 percent by making the saccharin

available, but the availability of saccharin reduced PCP intake by more than 87 percent at the higher FR values (FR 128).

You will recognize the similarity between this discussion and the discussion of choice. The analysis of behavior in terms of economics—that is, price and demand—essentially boils down to a study of factors that govern how we choose between alternatives. Both lines of research clearly show that an increase or decrease of drug use will depend on the cost (availability) of alternatives (substitutes).

CHAPTER SUMMARY

- Because drug abuse appeared to be particularly compulsive and self-destructive, historically, it was viewed as an abnormal type of behavior that could not be explained by the same rules that govern normal behavior.

- Originally, people who abused drugs were thought to be deficient in willpower or morality, and drug abuse was thought to be a problem for the clergy and the church to handle. Later, the medical profession became involved in attempts to treat people who were abusing opium and morphine because these substances were widely used as medicines. The idea that addiction was a disease was proposed in the mid-1800s but did not become formally recognized as such until the 1950s. Substance dependence is now officially a disorder in the *DSM-IV*.

- Despite explanations involving biochemical deficiency and allergies, the disease of addiction has never been identified. There are two types of disease theories. Predisposition theories say that some people are born with a predisposition to become addicted, and exposure theories that say that excessive exposure to a drug will make you an addict.

- Most definitions of addiction describe drug use that is "out of control"; that is, the addict cannot stop using the drug. The problem with this is that there is no way of defining whether any behavior is controlled.

- The physical dependence model suggests that excessive drug use is motivated by a fear of the withdrawal symptoms that occur when a person stops using a drug. Proponents of the dependence model explain the abuse of drugs that do not cause physical dependence by suggesting that these drugs cause psychological dependence.

- In the 1950s, when it became known that non-humans would give themselves drugs in the same manner as humans, it was easily demonstrated that some assumptions of the disease model and the physical dependence model were not correct.

- Experiments with nonhumans showed that physical dependence was not necessary for self-administration.

- Researchers came to realize that drug administrations could control the behavior of organisms in the same way as more traditional positive reinforcers, such as food and water.

- Some drugs can act as negative reinforcers, and animals will avoid infusions of these drugs.

- A positive reinforcer is any stimulus that will increase the frequency of a response on which it is contingent. It often is accompanied by the experience of pleasure, but this is not necessary.

- The positive reinforcement explanation of drug use and addiction may seem to be circular, but it can be shown that the brain mechanisms of positive reinforcement are similar to those common to all drugs that are used and abused.

- Nearly all the drugs that nonhumans will self-administer are used and abused by humans. The exceptions are most hallucinogens.

- In humans and nonhumans, the pattern of self-administration of particular drugs is similar.

- Rate of responding, progressive ratio schedules, place conditioning, and choice experiments have been used to assess the incentive value or reinforcing properties of drugs. These techniques have shown that the following factors can alter the incentive value of drugs: type of drug, dose, genetics, relief of some unpleasant symptoms, task demands, stress, deprivation, exposure to the same or other drugs, and, to some extent, physical dependence.

- The reinforcing effects of drugs can be conditioned to stimuli paired with drug administration. Two techniques that have demonstrated this are (a) place conditioning and (b) second-order schedules.

- A part of the brain important in motivation is the mesolimbic dopamine system, which is composed of cells in the ventral tegmental area that release dopamine in the nucleus accumbens. This system, in conjunction with the motor loop and the learning and memory system, is responsible for positive reinforcement by giving stimuli incentive salience; that is, these stimuli are easily noticed, and we are attracted to them—we *want* them. This is not a pleasure system.

- All drugs that are self-administered are known to cause a release of dopamine in the mesolimbic dopamine system.

- The incentive sensitization theory proposes that with repeated administration, the reinforcing effects of a drug (incentive value) and related stimuli become sensitized. This means that the drug and related stimuli will have increased incentive salience, which expresses itself as craving for the drug.

- Another neurological theory is the hedonic dysregulation theory, which proposes that with repeated use of a drug, an opponent process or compensatory response increases. This causes tolerance to the pleasurable effect of the drug. In addition, the set point of the pleasure system changes so that the person becomes increasingly insensitive to pleasure. As a result, the person must take increasing amounts of the drug.

- The application of economic principles to understanding operant behavior is called behavioral economics. Drug use can be understood in terms of behavioral economics. It can explain both choice to use drugs and the effect of economic factors, such as price and availability, on the extent of drug use.

- Organisms will distribute their behavior among a number of tasks in accordance with the rate of reinforcement on each task. Known as the matching law, this means that we can alter the reinforcing value of drugs by increasing the other sources of reinforcement available in the environment.

- The value of a reinforcer or a punisher decreases hyperbolically as the event becomes further and further away in time. This can explain why people can make irrational decisions and often change their minds.

- Some drugs can control behavior because the use of those drugs diminishes the availability of other reinforcers that could compete with them, thus starting a spiral of addiction.

- If people spend less on a commodity when the price increases, the demand is said to be elastic. If they do not decrease spending on the drug (or increase spending), the demand is said to be inelastic. For many drugs, demand is inelastic up to a point at which it becomes elastic.

- Providing an alternative reinforcer can greatly diminish the demand for a drug reinforcer. The effect of providing an alternative reinforcer is greatest when the cost of the drug is high.

- Both other drugs and a variety of nondrug reinforcers have been shown to act as alternatives for drug reinforcers.

6

Alcohol

SOURCE OF ALCOHOL

Alcohol is a chemical term that covers a class of substances of which only a few are ever consumed. Some members of this class are *isopropyl alcohol*, used as rubbing alcohol; *methanol* (*methyl alcohol*) or wood alcohol; and *ethanol* (*ethyl alcohol*), the alcohol we drink. The other alcohols can be consumed and have behavioral effects similar to those of ethanol, but they are rather toxic and are normally consumed only by accident. In this book, as in most others, the term *alcohol* will be used to refer to ethanol. Where other alcohols are intended, they will be mentioned by name.

Fermentation

The alcohol we drink is made largely by *fermentation*. When sugar is dissolved in water and left exposed to the air, the mixture is invaded by tiny microorganisms called *yeasts*. Yeasts thrive in this environment; they eat the sugar, and they multiply rapidly. The metabolic processes of the yeasts convert the sugar into ethanol and carbon dioxide (CO_2), which rises to the top in bubbles, and the alcohol remains. More and more yeasts produce more and more alcohol until all the sugar is used up or the yeasts are unable to continue.

The type of beverage you get from fermentation is determined by the source of the sugar. Almost any vegetable material containing sugar may be used, but the most common are grape juice, which is fermented to make wine, and grains, which are fermented to make beer. Modern fermentation is done with special yeasts rather than the wild variety. Yeasts are living organisms; They have been bred and selected over the centuries for particular types of fermentation. Because yeasts can tolerate only low levels of alcohol, fermented beverages do not have alcohol levels much above 10 to 15 percent.

Distillation

There is some debate about the discovery of *distillation*. The Chinese probably were the first to distill alcohol as long ago as 3000 B.C. For a long time the process of distillation, known only to alchemists, was a jealously guarded secret, and little was committed to writing until the Dominican scholar Albertus Magnus described the process in detail in the thirteenth century. The process of distillation is quite simple. It starts with ordinary fermentation of a sugary substance. When fermentation is completed, the mixture is heated. Because alcohol has a lower boiling point than water, the vapor or steam given off will have a higher content of vaporized alcohol than the original product. When this vapor is condensed by cooling, the resulting fluid will also contain a higher percentage of alcohol. There is no reason why the condensed spirits cannot be redistilled again and again until the resulting fluid has the desired level of alcohol. The traditional method among moonshiners for determining whether they have distilled their product sufficiently is to take a teaspoon of the stuff and set it on fire. When the fire has burned off all the alcohol, the spoon is tipped, and if more than a drop of water remains, the liquid is distilled again.

Brandy is the result of distilling wine, and whiskey is distilled from fermented grains. Brandy and whiskey were the first popular spirits. Today, we have rum, distilled from fermented molasses, and schnapps, which traditionally is distilled from fermented potatoes. Gin and vodka are made from a mixture of water, flavoring, and pure alcohol distilled from any source. Distilled spirits, or hard liquor, usually have an alcoholic content of about 40 to 50 percent by volume. In addition to these hard liquors are the liqueurs, which are sweetened and flavored. Some well-known liqueurs are créme de menthe, which is flavored with mint; Cointreau, which has an added flavor of oranges; and the famous Greek drink ouzo, which has an anise flavor.

Midway between the distilled and fermented beverages are the fortified wines, such as sherry, port, madeira, and muscatel, which were developed during the Middle Ages. These are blends of wine with extra alcohol added to boost the alcohol content to about 20 percent. Vermouth is a flavored fortified wine developed in Turin in the eighteenth century.

MEASUREMENT OF ALCOHOL CONTENT

The description of alcohol content has always been confusing. Percentage figures may be given either by volume, as in the United States, or by weight, as in Britain. Alcohol has a specific gravity of about 0.79 (a quantity of alcohol will weigh 79 percent as much as the same volume of water), and, therefore, a ratio based on volumes will have less alcohol than the same ratio based on weight. In other words, a drink that is 50 percent alcohol by volume will be about 40 percent alcohol by weight. In Britain, alcoholic content has customarily been described in terms of *proof*. The term has its origin in the British navy, which traditionally issued all its sailors a ration of rum every day. The navy had to buy vast quantities of rum, and its purchasers developed a rather ingenious way of testing the alcohol content. They would mix the rum with gunpowder and try to light it. If it burned, this was "proof" that it was at least 50 percent alcohol by weight.

In Britain, the Customs and Excise Act of 1952 declared proof spirits (100 proof) to be those in which the weight of the spirits is 12/13 the weight of an equal volume of distilled water at 51 degrees Fahrenheit. Thus, in Britain, 100 proof spirits are 48.24 percent alcohol by weight, or 57.06 percent by volume. Other spirits are designated over or under proof; the percentage of variance is noted.

In the United States, a proof spirit (100 proof) is one containing 50 percent alcohol by volume. Thus, the U.S. proof number is twice the percentage of alcohol by volume.

All this is very confusing. Fortunately, it is becoming more common to have a beverage's percent alcohol content by volume printed clearly on the labels of bottles in unambiguous terms.

ORIGIN AND HISTORY

Alcohol has probably been a part of the human diet and that of our hominin ancestors for millions of years. Many of these ancestors, human and otherwise, were frugivores, eaters of fruit. Fruit contains a high sugar content and would have been an excellent food, but because of the sugar and the presence of yeasts, all fruit, even ripe fruit, contains a small amount of alcohol, and as it matures, the alcohol content increases. The taste and smell of alcohol then would have been associated with food and nourishment throughout a significant proportion of our evolutionary history. As we shall see later, this long-term association has probably had a big influence on physiological and behavioral responses to alcohol (Dudley, 2000, 2002).

While people probably have been brewing alcohol since agriculture began about 10,000 years ago, it was probably small domestic brewing, and there is no record of it. The earliest evidence that humans have been fermenting alcohol are large earthenware jugs found in China that date from 9,000 years ago. There is evidence that they once stored a wine made from rice, honey, and fruit (McGovern, Zhang Tang, et al., 2004).

The earliest written set of laws, the Code of Hammurabi, written in 2225 B.C. in Assyria, sets forth some rules for the keeping of beer and wine shops and taverns. The ancient Egyptians were also known for their drinking. The Egyptian Book of the Dead, from about 3000 B.C., mentions the manufacture of a drink called "hek," a form of beer made from grain (Bickerdyke, 1971). Herodotus, the Greek historian, narrated how, at a rich man's feast in ancient Egypt, it was the custom to have a man carry around the image of a corpse in a coffin and show it to all the guests saying, "Drink and make merry, but look on this for such thou shalt be when thou are dead" (McCarthy, 1959, p. 66). The ancient Egyptians, as well as the Assyrians and the Babylonians, drank beer primarily (their climate was more suitable for the growing of grains than grapes), but they also drank a great deal of wine. The Egyptians probably taught the Israelites to make wine and beer before the Exodus to the Promised Land (Firebaugh, 1972).

There is much evidence that the Greeks, who were supposed to be "temperate in all things," may not always have been so temperate where wine was concerned. Plato had much to say about the effects of alcohol. In *The Law*, Plato said,

When a man drinks wine he begins to be better pleased with himself, and the more he drinks the more he is filled full of brave hopes, and conceit of his powers, and at last the string of his tongue is loosened, and fancying himself wise, he is brimming over with lawlessness and has no more fear or respect and is ready to do or say anything. (Laws I, 649a–b; translation in Jowett, 1931, p. 28)

Although the early Romans had little trouble with wine, there was a great deal of insobriety and debauchery in the declining years of the Roman Empire for which the later Roman emperors, such as Nero, Claudius, and Caligula, became notorious. The fall of the Roman Empire has been blamed on the consumption of wine not so much as a result of the alcohol but because wine at the time was fermented and stored in vessels made of lead, and an additive was put in the wine to enhance the flavor and stop fermentation. This additive had a very high lead content, and it is believed that most of the Roman nobility who drank wine suffered from lead poisoning, of which mental inability is a symptom (Nriagu, 1983).

Before the Romans brought grapes and, subsequently, wine to the British Isles, the main alcoholic beverages were beer made from barley, mead made from fermented wild honey, and cider made from fermented apples. The Romans introduced grapes to Britain, but the vines never thrived in the British climate, and wine, as today, was primarily imported. After the Romans left Britain, so did the grape, but the Saxons carried on the tradition of heavy drinking with mead, ale, and cider. Taverns and alehouses were established in about the eighth century and quickly acquired such a bad reputation that priests were not allowed to enter (French, 1884).

After the Norman Conquest in 1066, drinking became more moderate, and wine was reintroduced, but the English were still heavy drinkers. "You know that the constant habit of drinking has made the English famous among all foreign nations," wrote Peter of Blois (French, 1884, p. 68).

Although distillation had been known for some time, it did not make its presence felt in England until the sixteenth century, when a number of Irish settlers started manufacturing and distributing *usquebaugh*, which became, in English, whiskey. Brandy imported from France was also becoming popular. After the restoration of the monarchy in

1660, distilleries were licensed, and the popularity of gin spread like an epidemic. (Gin is raw alcohol flavored with the juniper berry, which in Dutch is "genever." Through misunderstanding, the drink became known as Geneva dose and later as gin.)

Between 1684 and 1727, the annual consumption of distilled spirits increased from about half a million gallons to over 3.5 million gallons (French, 1884, p. 271). These figures do not include the large quantities of rum and brandy smuggled into the country to avoid paying high duties and tariffs. This epidemic raised such concern that the government passed a desperate series of laws aimed at curtailing the use of liquor, but nothing had much effect. Finally, in 1742, when consumption reached 19 million gallons, Parliament found something that worked: It banned the distillation of grain altogether for a number of years and then closely regulated the manufacture of spirits. By 1782, consumption had dropped to 4 million gallons. But these laws expired, and their enforcement was relaxed over the next 50 years. By the early part of the nineteenth century, things were almost as bad as before.

The English propensity for strong drink was transported across the Atlantic to the colonies. Colonial Americans were hearty drinkers, and alcohol played a large part in their lives.

How highly did the colonies prize booze? Their statutes regulating its sale spoke of it as "one of the good creatures of God, to be received with thanksgiving." Harvard University operated its own brewery, and commencements grew so riotous that rigid rules had to be imposed to reduce "the Excesses, Immoralities and Disorders." Workmen received part of their pay in rum, and employees would set aside certain days of the year for total inebriety (Benjamin Rush, quoted in Kobler, 1973, pp. 25–26).

Before the American Revolution, there had been some success in regulating taverns and drinking, but this control weakened after independence from England was gained.

Americans perceived liberty from the crown as somehow related to the freedom to down a few glasses of rum. Did not both freedoms give a man the right to choose for himself? As a consequence, drinking houses emerged from the war with increased vitality and independence, and the legal regulation of licensed premises waned (Rorabaugh, 1979, p. 35).

Consumption continued to increase to prodigious levels, but a precipitous decline followed between 1830 and 1860. This decline can be attributed to the singular efforts of the temperance movement.

In both England and the United States, there had always been people who openly condemned the use of alcohol, and there were organized movements against drinking and alcohol consumption. In the late 1700s in the United States, the champion of temperance was Dr. Benjamin Rush, a physician who wrote widely about the dangerous physical, social, and moral effects of alcohol. In 1785, Rush published one of the first influential temperance documents, *An Inquiry into the Effects of Ardent Spirits*.

Although Rush's writings were not heeded at the time, they inspired the American temperance movement of the early nineteenth century, which was more successful than any similar movement before or since. The temperance movement was successful because it was philosophically in tune with the moral tenor and ideals of the new republic. Socially, it filled exactly the same function as drinking. "Some men sought camaraderie at the tavern, others in their local temperance organization" (Rorabaugh, 1979, p. 189). In addition, a religious revival was sweeping the United States at the time. Total abstinence provided a symbolic way to express conversion and faith, and booze provided a target for righteous zeal.

The temperance movement was not content to rely on the force of moral persuasion to dry up the country. During this period, the movement attracted enough power to have alcohol prohibition laws enacted in 11 states and two territories. Soon a national Prohibition party was founded, and the temperance reformers set their sights on the federal government. Their vigorous campaign culminated in 1917 with the ratification of the Eighteenth

Amendment to the U.S. Constitution. This was the "noble experiment," Prohibition. It was passed, for the most part, without referendum; most legislatures were paying attention to World War I, and there was little opposition.

Because it did not have widespread public support, the law was virtually unenforceable and provided a vehicle for the rapid development and funding of mobsters and organized crime. Alcohol that was not manufactured in the United States was smuggled in from Canada and elsewhere in vast quantities.

It finally became apparent to both Herbert Hoover and Franklin Roosevelt, the Republican and Democratic candidates, respectively, in the 1932 presidential election, that Prohibition did not have popular support. One month after Roosevelt's victory, a Twenty-First Amendment to the Constitution was drafted that would void the Eighteenth Amendment. Within 2 months, it was passed by both the House and the Senate, and on December 5, 1933, the thirty-sixth state, Utah, ratified it, and it was signed into law. Prohibition had lasted almost 14 years.

After Prohibition ended, alcohol consumption rates increased steadily until they peaked in about 1979. Spurred by movements such as MADD (Mothers Against Drunk Driving), consumption has begun to decline in response to an increasing concern with health and a decreasing public tolerance of drugs in general because of the harm that they do. David Musto, a medical historian at Yale University, is among those who predict that history is likely to repeat itself and that this decline will continue into the early twenty-first century but that it will then be followed by another drinking backlash (Kolata, 1991).

Figure 6-1 shows that American consumption of alcohol appears to go through cycles. Consumption peaks every 60 to 70 years, and these peaks have been followed by declines in use. Historians have pointed out that these periods of decline were accompanied by preoccupation with health and morality and by public concern over the harm that alcohol was doing, but fairly sharp increases in consumption followed. It appears as though the United States has begun a phase of decreasing alcohol use.

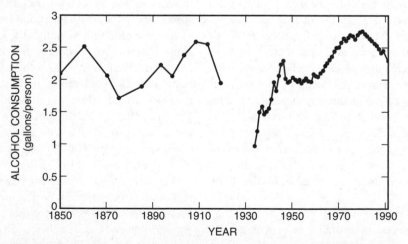

Figure 6-1 Yearly alcohol consumption, in gallons per person, of raw alcohol from 1850 to 1990 in the United States. Note that there are three peaks in consumption about 60 years apart. The gap in the early part of the twentieth century is due to Prohibition. Note the short-lived increase in consumption in the years following World War II. (G. D. Williams, Clem, & Dufour, 1993)

MEASURING ALCOHOL LEVELS IN THE BODY

Alcohol levels are usually measured in terms of the concentration of alcohol in whole blood. This is known as the *blood alcohol level* (BAL), or blood alcohol concentration. The BAL may be measured directly by taking a blood sample, but more often a breath sample is taken and analyzed using a device known as a *Breathalyzer*. It has been well established that alcohol concentration in the breath reliably reflects the concentration in the blood, and so the results of a Breathalyzer are reported as "blood alcohol level" rather than "breath alcohol level."

Metric Measurements and Percentage

The BAL is usually expressed in terms of milligrams (mg) of alcohol per 100 milliliters (ml) of whole blood. (A milligram is 1/1,000 gram; a milliliter is 1/1,000 liter; 100 ml is equal to a deciliter [dl].) The BAL may also be described as a percentage of alcohol in the blood. Conversion between these measures is not difficult; it involves only moving the decimal point three places to the left or right. For example, a BAL of 80 mg per 100 ml (or 80 mg/dl) is the same as 0.08 percent.

SI Units

There has been a recent trend toward reporting drug concentrations in *SI units* (Systéme International d'Unités), and many journals report alcohol concentrations this way. The SI unit for drugs, including alcohol, is millimoles per liter (mmol/l). To convert the metric measures to SI units, one must first convert milligrams of alcohol to millimoles and then convert deciliters of blood to liters. The first step is accomplished by dividing the milligrams by the molecular weight of alcohol, 46.07. Thus, 80 milligrams ÷ 46.07 = 1.74 millimoles. A liter is 10 deciliters; thus, 80 mg/dl is equivalent to 17.4 mmol/l. By combining these steps, milligrams per 100 ml can be converted to mmol/l simply by dividing by 4.607.

ROUTE OF ADMINISTRATION AND PHARMACOKINETICS

Figure 6-2 shows the theoretical time course for the level of alcohol in the blood after taking a single drink. This curve can be considered as being made up of several phases. The part of the curve labeled A is the absorption phase, during which absorption is taking place much more rapidly than excretion. The plateau phase, labeled B and C, is when absorption tapers off and excretion starts to lower alcohol levels. During this phase, blood levels peak. If absorption has been rapid, there may also be a brief period, immediately following the peak, when the decline in blood levels is rapid as a result of the distribution of alcohol out of the blood to other parts of the body. In the excretion phase, D, alcohol is eliminated from the body at a constant rate.

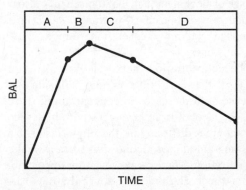

Figure 6-2 Theoretical time course for BAL after taking a single drink. Phase A is the absorption phase, in which absorption is taking place much more rapidly than excretion. Phases B and C form the plateau phase, in which absorption tapers off and excretion starts to lower alcohol levels. During this phase, blood levels peak. If absorption has been rapid, there may also be a brief period, immediately following the peak, when the decline in blood levels is rapid. This rapid decline is caused by the distribution of alcohol out of the blood to other parts of the body. During the excretion phase, D, absorption is complete, and alcohol is eliminated from the body at a constant rate.

ABSORPTION

Alcohol is normally administered orally, and absorption takes place in the digestive tract. Because the molecules of alcohol cannot be ionized, neither the pH of the digestive system nor the pH of the blood has an effect on absorption.

Alcohol readily dissolves in water, and it may pass into the blood from the stomach, intestines, or colon, but it is absorbed most rapidly from the small intestine. In addition, as long as the alcohol stays in the stomach, it is subjected to fairly high levels of alcohol dehydrogenase, the main enzyme that destroys alcohol. In the stomach, alcohol is subjected to considerable *first-pass metabolism* by *alcohol dehydrogenase*. After solid food has been eaten, the digestion process usually keeps the food in the stomach for a period of time before it is released into small quantities. Thus, the longer alcohol stays in the stomach, the more slowly it will be absorbed into the blood, and *first-pass metabolism* will cause less of it to be absorbed. In general, absorption of alcohol is faster on an empty stomach, and more will get into the body. Even though peak blood levels are higher when there is no food in the stomach, the peak will occur at about the same time, and it will take about the same time for blood levels to return to zero (Watkins & Adler, 1993).

Some medicines, such as *cimetidine* (Tagamet) and *ranitidine* (Zantac), which are commonly used to reduce stomach acidity in people who have ulcers, can increase BALs created by a given amount of alcohol. These drugs, known as H_2-receptor antagonists, are widely prescribed. Zantac 75 is ranitidine in nonprescription strength and is available over the counter. These *H_2-receptor antagonists* reduce stomach levels of alcohol dehydrogenase, and this action protects alcohol from first-pass metabolism. One study showed that the amount of alcohol that entered the blood was increased by 17 percent after ranitidine treatment for 1 week. The effect was even greater with cimetidine. The effects of cimetidine and ranitidine are greatest when alcohol is taken on a full stomach. On an empty stomach (or in the case of alcoholics),

there is little first-pass metabolism in the digestive system (DiPadova, Worner, Julkunnen, & Lieber, 1987; DiPadova et al., 1992).

There also appear to be gender differences in first-pass metabolism. Compared to men, women appear to have lower levels of alcohol dehydrogenase in their stomachs; consequently, more of the alcohol a woman drinks gets into the blood, resulting in a higher BAL in a woman than the same amount of alcohol would produce in a man of similar size (Frezza et al., 1990; Whitfield & Martin, 1994). It has been speculated that this difference could be one reason why women are more vulnerable than men to the acute and chronic complications of alcoholism, including alcoholic liver disease.

Interestingly, abstainers reach lower peak BALs than moderate drinkers. The reason for this difference is not clear, but it may have to do with different degrees of first-pass metabolism in people who never drink (Whitfield & Martin, 1994).

The time to reach the maximum blood levels after drinking is highly variable between individuals and situations, but the time to reach the beginning of the plateau (B in Figure 6-2) is usually about an hour, with the peak about 15 minutes later. After a few drinks, however, absorption rates seem to increase, and the peak and plateau will be reached 20 to 25 minutes sooner (Ditmar & Dorian, 1987).

Beer appears to pass out of the stomach more slowly than other alcoholic beverages. For this reason, beer creates lower BALs than the same amount of alcohol consumed in some other beverage. The passage of alcohol through the stomach may also be facilitated by carbonation. Sparkling wines such as champagne and rosé frequently have more "kick" than still wines.

The concentration of the alcohol also contributes to the speed of absorption. Diffusion rates increase with increases in concentration; therefore, the alcohol from beverages with high alcoholic content diffuses into the blood faster than the same amount of alcohol mixed in a weaker concentration. There is, however, an upper limit to this effect. High alcohol concentrations slow down the rate at which the stomach empties its contents into the intestine and, thus, can interfere with absorption. It is probably not a coincidence that the most rapid absorption appears to occur at about 40 percent alcohol, the concentration of most hard liquor.

INHALATION

Normally, alcohol does not evaporate fast enough to be administered by inhalation, but in 2004 a machine called AWOL (Alcohol WithOut Liquid), which vaporizes liquor in oxygen was marketed in the United States and Britain. This mixture is inhaled through a mouthpiece that looks like an asthma inhaler. The vaporized alcohol is absorbed through the lungs and goes directly to the brain, bypassing any first-pass metabolism in the stomach and the liver. These machines are calibrated to administer a shot of alcohol in about 20 minutes, about the same time it might take to drink a shot of liquor. Because of the rapid absorption and the lack of first-pass metabolism, it is likely to cause somewhat higher BALs than drinking the same amount of liquor. It is as yet unknown whether alcohol in those concentrations will cause any damage to lung tissue. This method of alcohol administration is legal in Britain and the United States but has been banned in at least one state (Colorado). Other states are also considering a ban (ABC News Online, 2004; BBC, 2004).

DISTRIBUTION

Because alcohol dissolves much more readily in water than in lipids or fat, alcohol is distributed almost entirely in body water. Therefore, individuals with different proportions of body fat, even though they may weigh exactly the same, may reach different BALs after drinking identical amounts of alcohol. Males, for example, have a lower percentage of body fat than females. Thus, if a man and a woman weigh exactly the same and drink the same amount of alcohol, the woman will have a higher BAL (assuming similar first-pass metabolism). The alcohol she drinks will be more highly concentrated in her body because her body has less water to dilute it.

Age also makes a difference, at least for males. As males age, the percentage of their body fat increases slowly. Even though their total body weight may not change, the same amount of alcohol will result in higher BALs as men get older. Women show a much smaller change in body composition with age.

It is possible to calculate the BAL for an individual after the consumption of a given amount of alcohol. Box 6-1 shows how to make these calculations for any individual.

BOX 6-1   Calculating BALs

Calculating the BAL is relatively simple. You have to know the weight and sex of the individual and the amount of alcohol consumed. To illustrate, let's calculate the BAL of a 175-pound man who has ingested 1 ounce of spirits. Because the BAL is usually given in milligrams per 100 ml of blood, it is easier to do the calculations in metric units rather than in pounds and ounces.

First, we convert the body weight (175 pounds) to kilograms by dividing by 2.2 (1 kg = 2.2 lb). This equals 80 kg. This weight must then be adjusted because not all of the body is capable of absorbing alcohol. The percentage that can absorb alcohol is estimated to be 75 percent in men and 66 percent in women. Therefore, an 80-kg man will have 60 kg to absorb alcohol ($80 \times 0.75 = 60$); 60 kg = 60,000 g or 60,000 ml of fluid because 1 ml of water weighs 1 g.

(Continued)

BOX 6-1

Next, we must convert alcohol to milligrams. One ounce of spirits (100 proof, or 50 percent by volume) will contain 11.2 g of alcohol (0.5 fluid ounce of water weighs 14 g), and alcohol has a specific gravity of 0.8; ($14 \times 0.8 = 11.2$); 11.2 g is 11,200 mg.

Now we can divide the 11,200 mg of alcohol by 60,000 ml of body fluid and multiply by 100. This calculation yields the BAL: 18.6 mg per 100 ml. Our 175-pound man will raise his BAL by 18.6 mg per 100 ml of blood with every ounce of spirits.

Beer is usually about 5 percent alcohol by volume and comes in 12-ounce bottles. One such bottle would contain 13.5 g of alcohol, or 13,500 mg. When this is spread around a 60,000-ml body, it gives a concentration of about 22.5 mg per 100 ml. Our 175-pound man would raise his BAL by 22.5 per 100 ml with each beer. The accompanying table gives the alcohol content of various common drinks so that you can do the appropriate calculations for different sources of alcohol.

To calculate how each of these drinks would affect you, take your weight in pounds and convert it to kilograms by dividing by 2.2. Next calculate the body weight (for your sex) that is capable of absorbing alcohol: male, 75 percent; female, 66 percent. This figure must then be converted to milligrams (and milliliters) by multiplying by 1,000.

Now calculate the amount of alcohol consumed in milligrams, divide it by your weight in milligrams, and multiply by 100. Remember that because the body metabolizes alcohol at a rate of about 15 mg per 100 ml per hour, you can subtract 15 mg per 100 ml for each hour that has passed since your drinking started. Caution: These estimates of your BAL using this technique are just that—estimates. Two factors in this equation are approximations: the percentage of the body that will absorb alcohol and the rate of alcohol metabolism. Both depend on many factors, such as age, health, build, experience with alcohol, and even other drugs in your system. The figures given here are population averages that might not apply to you. In general, however, this technique tends to overestimate BAL, so it should be reasonably safe for most people most of the time. It is not recommended, however, that you bet your life or your driver's license on it.

Alcohol Contents of Some Beverages

Beverage	Alcohol Content Percent (volume)	Alcohol Content (mg)
Spirits (1 fl. oz.*)		
(100 proof)	50	11,200
(89 proof)	43	9,600
(80 proof)	40	8,900
Beer (12 fl. oz.)	5	13,500
Wine (2.5 fl. oz.)	12	8,400

*A shot is 1.25 oz., so that these figures must be increased by 25 percent if "shots" are being used to mix drinks.

Alcohol is distributed rather evenly throughout body water, and it crosses the blood–brain barrier, as well as the placental barrier, without difficulty. Consequently, alcohol levels in most tissues of the body, including the brain and a fetus (if present), accurately reflect the blood alcohol content of the drinker. Alcohol in the blood circulates through the lungs and vaporizes into the air at a known rate, so it is possible to measure the alcohol level in the blood and the rest of the body by measuring the alcohol vapor in exhaled air using a Breathalyzer, as described earlier.

EXCRETION

A small amount of alcohol may be eliminated in breath, sweat, tears, urine, and feces, but over 90 percent of all alcohol consumed is metabolized, mostly in the liver. Because humans have been consuming alcohol throughout a long period of our evolution, we have developed an efficient means of eliminating alcohol and using it as a source of energy. The usual route of metabolism is shown in Figure 1-9. It involves two steps. In the first step, the *rate-limiting step*, alcohol is converted to *acetaldehyde* by the enzyme alcohol dehydrogenase. This is the slowest step in alcohol metabolism. Consequently, the rate at which this conversion takes place limits the speed of the entire process. The conversion rate of alcohol to acetaldehyde is determined by the amount of alcohol dehydrogenase available and is relatively independent of the concentration of alcohol. The metabolism of alcohol, then, usually takes place at a steady rate throughout most BALs. (This rate may vary between individuals and from species to species.)

In the second step, the acetaldehyde is converted into *acetyl-coenzyme A* by several enzymes, the most common of which is *aldehyde dehydrogenase*. Acetyl-coenzyme A is converted mainly into water and carbon dioxide through a series of reactions known as the *citric acid cycle*, during which usable energy is released to the body. Acetyl-coenzyme A is also used in a number of bodily processes, such as the production of fatty acids and steroids. As a result, alcohol consumption and its consequent metabolism can alter a great deal of body chemistry.

Between individuals, there is considerable variability in elimination rates. The range found in one study was from 5.9 to 27.9 mg per 100 ml per hour, with a standard deviation of 4.5 (Dubowski, 1985). For the majority of individuals, the range is usually accepted to be between 10 and 20 mg per 100 ml per hour, with a mean of 15. The rate of metabolism of alcohol also seems to be influenced by drinking

experience. Nondrinkers metabolize alcohol at a slightly slower rate (12–14 mg per 100 ml per hour) than light to moderate drinkers (15–17 mg per 100 ml per hour) (L. Goldberg, 1943; Whitfield & Martin, 1994).

It has also been demonstrated that food can have an effect on the rate of alcohol metabolism as well as its absorption. Ramchandani, Kwo, and Li (2001) have shown that having eaten speeds up the rate of alcohol metabolism from 25 to 45 percent. The increase did not seem to depend on the type of food eaten and is probably a result of increased blood flow to the liver caused by a food in the stomach.

Methanol is also metabolized in the liver by alcohol dehydrogenase, but the metabolic byproducts are *formaldehyde* and *formic acid*, which are very toxic and metabolize very slowly. Methanol alone is not very toxic, but consumption of methanol can result in severe illness, blindness, and death as a result of accumulation of these toxins in the body. Surprisingly, these toxic effects can sometimes be avoided if a great deal of ethanol is consumed at the same time because both alcohols use the same enzyme system. Ethanol competes with methanol for the available enzymes and thereby slows down the formation of formaldehyde, so it may never reach toxic levels.

Although most alcohol is handled by the alcohol dehydrogenase system, another system appears to be in operation as well. This is known as the *microsomal ethanol-oxidizing system* (MEOS). The MEOS normally handles only 5 to 10 percent of the metabolism of alcohol, but its activity increases at higher levels of blood alcohol. The activity of the MEOS may be doubled or even tripled by continuous alcohol consumption. This increase may account for 50 to 65 percent of the increased alcohol metabolism induced by heavy drinking, a change that partly accounts for alcohol tolerance. The MEOS is important for another reason: It is also responsible for the metabolism of a number of other drugs, such as barbiturates. Therefore, if the MEOS is stimulated by continuous alcohol use, the metabolism of these other drugs will also be speeded up and vice versa

(Leiber, 1977; Leiber & De Carli, 1977). Thus, alcoholics usually have a great deal of resistance to the effects of barbiturates and other drugs.

NEUROPHARMACOLOGY

The neuropharmacology of alcohol is complex and involves a number of systems. Even though it has been studied intensively and much is now known, there are still many mysteries. Because there are a number of similarities between the effects of alcohol and the general anesthetics and solvents, it is believed that all have a similar mechanism of action and that what has been learned about anesthetics can tell us much about alcohol (see Chapter 8).

Whatever that mechanism of action might be, it is clear that neither alcohol nor the general anesthetics produce a direct effect on one specific receptor site; they have many different sites of action and mechanisms of action. The molecules of alcohol act directly on the receptor sites of a number of neurotransmitters and the ion channels they control, altering the effect of the transmitter. They may do this by interacting with a "pocket" (an alcohol-sensitive area on the receptor site) or by entering and blocking the ion channel itself (Lovinger, 1997).

One target of the alcohol molecule is glutamate transmission. It has been shown, in several parts of the brain, that acute doses of alcohol at concentrations achieved by normal drinking depress the functioning of the ion channel controlled by glutamate at the NMDA receptor for glutamate. The NMDA receptor site is in the ion channel itself, and alcohol molecules have the effect of blocking the ion channel. As a result of chronic exposure to alcohol, the brain "up-regulates" NMDA receptor-ion channel functioning; that is, the brain becomes more sensitive to glutamate to compensate for prolonged depression by alcohol. It is believed that this increase in sensitivity to the excitatory transmitter glutamate may be responsible for alcohol withdrawal symptoms that occur (Sanna & Harris, 1993) when alcohol is no longer consumed.

Alcohol is also known to stimulate the function of at least one class of serotonin (5-HT) receptor, the 5-HT$_3$ receptor, which opens ion channels and causes rapid-onset depolarization of the membrane. This appears to be an important step in the release of dopamine in the nucleus accumbens and, consequently, in the reinforcing effect of alcohol. It has been shown, for example, that serotonin antagonists will decrease the reinforcing effects and the discriminative stimulus effects of alcohol. Studies using photon emission tomography (PET) show that acute alcohol consumption facilitates serotonin's excitatory effects (Yoshimoto et al., 2000); however, chronic ingestion actually has the opposite effect, reducing serotonin function (Berggren, Eriksson, Fajlke, & Balldin, 2002).

The GABA-receptor-ionophore complex is also involved in the effect of alcohol, particularly ionophores controlled by the GABA$_A$ receptor. These are inhibitory, and alcohol enhances their inhibition (see Chapter 7). PET-detected decreases in brain metabolic activity appear to be related to alcohol-induced stimulation of GABA receptors; interestingly, such stimulation is more pronounced in men than in women (Wang et al., 2003).

Alcohol also has a myriad of other neurophysiological effects. For example, it disrupts second messengers and is known to alter the functioning of monoamine oxidase, the enzyme responsible for the destruction of monoamine neurotransmitters (Tabakoff & Hoffman, 1987). It also has been shown to alter the responsiveness of the endogenous opiate system (Froehlich & Li, 1993).

Alcohol Antagonists

For thousands of years, people have been searching for a substance that would reverse the effects of alcohol. The ancient Greeks believed that the amethyst, a semiprecious stone, had this property, and the term *amethystics* has been used to describe these supposed agents.

In 1985, researchers at Hoffmann–La Roche reported that they had synthesized a substance called *RO 15-4513*, which seemed to be able to antagonize the effects of alcohol. Careful research has shown that the drug antagonizes only some of the effects of alcohol (including self-administration; June et al., 1992), and it does so because it appears to change the effect of GABA in a manner directly opposite to the effect of alcohol. It does not, however, act as a competitive antagonist to alcohol; that is, it does not compete with alcohol for a receptor site. In addition, RO 15-4513 appears to antagonize the effects of barbiturates and benzodiazepines (see Chapter 7) by working directly on the benzodiazepine receptor site (Lister & Nutt, 1987).

There is little likelihood that RO 15-4513 could have any medical use. Although it blocks some of the effects of alcohol, it does not antagonize alcohol's lethal effects, so it cannot be used to treat alcohol overdose. In addition, it seems to possess the ability to cause convulsions, and this would make it unsuitable for treating alcoholism.

As we saw earlier, serotonin blockers are capable of partly blocking the reinforcing and the stimulus properties of alcohol. Opiate antagonists can also block some of alcohol's physiological effects and might be useful in reducing alcohol consumption and preventing relapse in alcoholics after they have received treatment (Froehlich & Li, 1993).

It has generally been widely believed that coffee will sober someone up, especially if it is black coffee. Systematic studies have done little to confirm this belief. Early studies suggested that caffeine might reverse some impairing effects of low levels of alcohol on driving (less than 100 mg alcohol/100 ml blood) but not at higher blood alcohol levels (Muskowitz & Burns, 1981). A more recent study examining the effect of 200 to 400 mg caffeine on impairment produced by alcohol at about 80 mg/100 ml blood found that caffeine was not able to alter a number of effects of alcohol, including the subjective effects. These caffeine doses were able to cause a partial reversal of a slowing of braking speed caused by alcohol but did not return braking speed to normal levels (Liguori & Robinson, 2001).

Because alcohol has so many effects on so many different sites within the body, it is unlikely that a single substance could antagonize all the effects of alcohol.

EFFECTS OF ALCOHOL

Effects on the Body

Alcohol in low and moderate doses causes a dilation of blood vessels in the skin. This is why white persons who are drinkers sometimes have a flushed face (and heavy drinkers, like W. C. Fields, have a red nose). In addition, drinking alcohol makes the skin feel warm. One of the traditional medical uses of alcohol, therefore, was as a remedy for people who had been exposed to cold. Alcoholic beverages, especially brandy, were supposed to warm the body.

By inhibiting the secretion of antidiuretic hormone, alcohol causes a loss of body water through increased urination. This occurs only while the BAL is steady or falling.

Effects on Sleep

Alcohol, like most depressant drugs, acts as a sedative and induces sleep. Studies of acute effects on normal volunteers have shown that alcohol decreases the time it takes to go to sleep, but it does not have an effect on total sleeping time.

Even at very low BALs, alcohol depresses REM sleep. At low levels, this effect is apparent during the first half of a night following drinking. In the second half, there is an increase in REM, so the total REM time during the night might be unaffected. With larger doses of alcohol, REM is depressed throughout the entire night, but after three nights of alcohol consumption, REM depression shows complete tolerance, and REM returns to normal. When alcohol is discontinued after five nights, there is a REM rebound on the sixth night. A REM rebound is a period in which the percentage of REM sleep increases above normal levels, and this causes poor sleep and unpleasant dreams.

When alcoholics stop drinking, they usually have very high percentages of REM sleep (as much as 90 percent) and other disturbances in sleep patterns that may last as long as 200 weeks (W. B. Mendelson, 1979).

EFFECTS ON HUMAN BEHAVIOR AND PERFORMANCE

Perhaps an indication of the importance of inebriation in our culture is the vast number of synonyms for being drunk. In 1737, Benjamin Franklin compiled 228 terms commonly used for being drunk. He might have missed a few, or, more likely, drinkers have continued to actively create more since his time. The *American Thesaurus of Slang*, published in 1952, lists almost 900 such terms. Most of them suggest some sort of violence or damage, such as *crashed, clobbered, bombed, swacked, plastered, tanked, ossified, looped, paralyzed*, and *wiped out*, to cite just a few. Some terms are very old. *Soused*, for example, dates back to sixteenth-century England, and *cut* was used as long ago as 1770 (Levine, 1981).

What does it mean to be ossified or swacked? The body of literature on this subject, dating back to the time of Aristotle, is so vast that it is almost impossible to characterize it in this short space. Systematic observation of drinkers has shown that at BALs between 50 and 100 mg per 100 ml, people are more talkative, use a higher pitch of voice, and show mild excitement. At about 100 to 150 mg per 100 ml, subjects appear talkative, cheerful, and often loud and boisterous; later, they become sleepy. At BALs above 150 mg per 100 ml, subjects frequently feel nauseous and may vomit. This phase is followed by lethargy and, in some cases, stupor. At doses as high as 290 mg per 100 ml, subjects are variously sleepy, noisy, and inattentive.

The problem with dose-related descriptions such as these is that there is such variability in the responses of individuals, depending on drinking history, environment, tolerance, and motivation, that they very seldom describe the behavior of any one individual on any single drinking occasion.

Subjective Effects

Many researchers, using tests such as the POMS and the ARCI, report that alcohol has a biphasic effect with regard to time and dose. At low doses and while the alcohol blood level is rising, alcohol has a stimulant effect, and people describe elation and euphoria; but at high doses and when the blood levels are falling, subjects report primarily feelings of sedation, anger, and depression (Babor, Berglas, Mendelson, Ellingboe, & Miller, 1983). Recent research has indicated that not everyone experiences the stimulation effect; some subjects experience only the sedating effects. Interestingly, those who described stimulant-like effects also reported a greater "drug liking" for alcohol and had more impairment on the digit symbol substitution test. It has been speculated that such individuals may be at greater risk for alcohol abuse (Holdstock & de Wit, 1998).

Perception

Alcohol has a detrimental effect on vision. It increases both the absolute and the difference thresholds but usually only at high doses. A decrease in visual acuity, indicated by a lowering in the critical flicker fusion threshold, is caused by a BAL of about 70 mg per 100 ml. Decreases in peripheral vision have also been reported. Decreases in sensitivity to taste and smell occur at low doses, and a decrease in pain sensitivity is common at BALs of 80 to 100 mg per 100 ml.

Performance

Alcohol slows reaction time by about 10 percent at BALs of 80 to 100 mg per 100 ml, and large consistent deficits are evident with larger doses. Complex reaction-time tasks that require the subject to scan and integrate stimuli from several sources before responding show that at lower doses, both the speed and the accuracy of performance decrease. Deficits are also seen in hand–eye coordination tasks, for example, in which the subject is required to maintain a marker over a moving target. PET analyses show that alcohol consumption decreases blood flow to the cerebellum, a region that controls voluntary movement and coordination, which may explain impairments on tasks requiring hand–eye coordination (Volkow et al., 1988). In general, the more complex the task, the greater the impairment seen at lower doses. Small deficits occur at doses as low as 10 to 20 mg per 100 ml. Alcohol also impairs performance on the digit symbol substitution test.

Drowsiness caused by alcohol also shows up on vigilance tasks, and impairments are noted at doses as low as 60 mg per 100 ml.

One of the most sensitive tests is the *Romberg sway test*. The subject is asked to stand with eyes closed and feet together. BALs as low as 60 mg per 100 ml can cause a 40 percent decrease in steadiness as measured by the amount of swaying. This lack of steadiness makes it difficult for a person to stand on one foot with eyes closed. Before the Breathalyzer, the police used this test to detect impairment. At higher BALs, the lack of steadiness degenerates into staggering and reeling. The increase in sway appears to be a result of the effect of alcohol on the sensitive organs of balance in the inner ear and is also responsible for the sensation that the room is spinning around, which people experience when they lie down after drinking too much. Lack of steadiness can also bring on nausea and vomiting (Money & Miles, 1974).

Many people have demonstrated the impairing effects of alcohol on many tasks, but these effects are sometimes elusive. In many cases, they depend on the expectancy and motivation of the individual. Vogel-Sprott (1992) has shown that, at low doses at least (less than 100 mg/100 ml blood), many response deficits will disappear if subjects are paid or provided with an incentive to overcome the effects of the drug. In addition, subjects who expect that the drug will have an effect are often more impaired than those who do not (Fillmore & Vogel-Sprott, 1998).

Memory and Blackouts. Alcohol is also known to have a detrimental effect on memory. Low and moderate levels of alcohol have been shown to affect both the storage and the retrieval of information, but the storage function seems to be more strongly affected (Birnbaum & Parker, 1977). Impairments in memory encoding and attention are demonstrated in the odd-ball paradigm (described in Chapter 4) using auditory evoked potentials. Ethanol administration reduced P300 amplitude and increased delay both when participants were paying complete attention to the auditory task and when attention was divided by performing the task while listening to a story (Lukas, Mendelson, Kouri, Bolduc, & Amass, 1990). In long-term alcohol abusers, PET analyses using 2-deoxy-2[^{18}F]fluoro-d-glucose show that deficits in verbal and visual memory, as well as attention, correspond with decreased metabolism in the dorsolateral prefrontal cortex and the anterior cingulate cortex (R. Z. Goldstein et al., 2004).

Heavier drinking may also cause periods of amnesia or *blackouts* where people may be unable to remember events that occurred while they were intoxicated. There are two different varieties of blackout. The first type is called a *grayout* or a *fragmentary blackout* and is the most common form of alcohol amnesia. When a grayout occurs, the drinker is able to remember only bits and pieces of events that occurred while drinking. The missing memories usually return, especially if the drinker is reminded of these events or if he or she returns to the place where they occurred. This shows that the problem is primarily one of retrieval—the memories were formed and stored in the brain, but the person has trouble accessing them later when the alcohol is gone. Grayouts are likely to result from dissociation (Overton, 1972; see also Chapter 3).

En bloc blackouts are more serious but less frequent. When this occurs, the drinker is usually able to remember events of a drinking episode up to a particular time and then remembers nothing until another well-defined point in time, usually when he or she wakes up the next morning. All events that occurred during that block of time are not remembered. In fact, there is no evidence that these memories were ever put into long-term storage because they never return, even when the person is reminded. Interestingly, during the period when a blackout is happening, the drinker may appear to behave perfectly normal. He or she can carry on a conversation and carry out many normal behaviors, such as driving a car. They can recall what happened in the past, before they began drinking, but cannot remember what happened 20 minutes ago (Ryback, 1970). They are able to hold things in short-term storage or working memory, but they are unable to form long-term memories. There is good evidence that this is because of the effect of alcohol on the hippocampus, the part of the brain that is needed to form long-term memories (White, 2003).

Effects on Driving

Studies of the effects of alcohol on driving, in simulators and in real cars on closed tracks, have generally confirmed that alcohol begins to affect performance at about 50 to 80 mg per 100 ml (Mitchell, 1985; Starmer, 1990). At 80 mg alcohol per 100 ml blood, participants in a simulated driving study drove at higher speeds and showed a trend toward increased collisions with other cars. These performance deficits corresponded with decreases in activation of the orbitofrontal cortex and motor regions of the brain measured by functional magnetic resonance imaging (fMRI) (Calhoun, Pekar, & Pearlson, 2004).

This finding is reflected in real-life driving accident statistics. Figure 6-3 shows the relative probability of being responsible for a fatal crash at various BALs. The curve starts to rise between 50 and 100 mg per 100 ml. At 100 mg per 100 ml, the probability of being responsible for a fatal crash is seven times greater than if the BAL had been 0. After this point, the curve rises sharply. At a BAL of 200 mg per 100 ml, a driver is 100 times more likely to cause a fatal crash (Organization for Economic Cooperation and Development, 1978).

Statistics such as these establish the rationale for setting legal limits on BAL for driving. In most jurisdictions, the limit is between 80 and 100 mg per 100 ml of blood, the point at which the curve starts to rise sharply. It is important to remember, however, that these curves underestimate the risk for young, inexperienced drivers; older drivers; and people not used to drinking. Their risk of being involved in an accident is considerably elevated even at BALs below the legal limit. Figure 6-4 shows similar curves for people of different ages (Organization for Economic Cooperation and Development, 1978).

It is also interesting to note that the impairment caused by alcohol seems to last beyond the time when alcohol is gone from the body (Starmer, 1990).

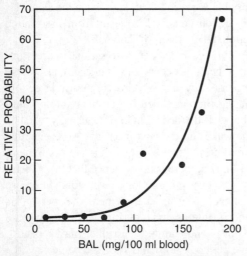

Figure 6-3 The relationship between BAL and the relative risk of being involved in a traffic accident. The risk with a BAL less than 1.0 mg per 100 ml blood is 1.0. (Organization for Economic Cooperation and Development, 1978)

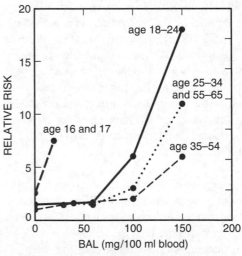

Figure 6-4 The relationship between BAL and the relative risk of being involved in a traffic accident for people of different age-groups. The risk with a BAL of 1.0 mg per 100 ml blood is 1.0. (Organization for Economic Cooperation and Development, 1978)

Disinhibition and Behavior Control

One of the frequently reported effects of alcohol is *disinhibition*, a term that is generally used to mean that under the influence of alcohol, people do things they normally would not do for fear of adverse consequences. This is most evident in conflict situations in which a certain activity has both positive and negative consequences. Alcohol reduces the influence of the negative consequences and appears to release the behavior from inhibition. This was demonstrated in an experiment by Muriel Vogel-Sprott of the University of Waterloo. Subjects made a sequence of responses for which they were given both painful electric shocks and money. The shocks severely depressed the responding of subjects who had been given a placebo but failed to suppress the responding of subjects after they had been given alcohol (BALs of 50 to 80 mg/100 ml; Vogel-Sprott, 1967).

More recent research on the effect of alcohol on behavioral control is often done using a "go stop" task. In this task, a subject is required to make a response when a particular signal, the "go" signal, is presented but must withhold that response if the "go" signal is followed by a "stop" signal. Studies have shown that alcohol at moderate doses does not interfere with responding to the "go" signal, but it selectively interferes with the ability of the "stop" signal to inhibit behavior. Furthermore, fMRI studies of brain activity during these tasks show that alcohol weakens the connections between the frontal areas of the cortex and the striatum, the motor area of the brain (Vogel-Sprott, Easdon, Fillmore, Finn, & Justus, 2001).

It is interesting that this disinhibition effect may actually improve performance on tasks in which anxiety or conflict is interfering with behavior. A practical example might be someone who is afraid to ask the boss for a raise. Conflict exists because the person wants the raise but is afraid of being fired or making the boss angry. After a few drinks, fear of the boss loses its control of the behavior, and the task can be performed.

In summary, perhaps the best way to characterize the effects of alcohol is to retell the old fable about Saint Martin, the monk who was reputed to have brought grapes to France. At first, the vine was hidden in the bone of a bird; then, after outgrowing the bird, it was hidden in the bone of a lion; finally, it was hidden in the bone of a donkey. Later, after the vine had grown and wine was made, the monks who drank it showed the characteristics of the animals used in its transportation. After the first bottle, they sang like birds; after the second, they had the courage of lions; but after the third, they behaved like asses.

EFFECTS ON THE BEHAVIOR OF NONHUMANS

Conditioned Behavior

For various reasons, few studies have been done on the effects of alcohol on positively reinforced behavior, but those that have been done show that the effects are dose dependent; on both fixed interval (FI) and fixed ratio (FR) schedules, alcohol increases the rate of responding at low doses and decreases the rate at higher doses.

Alcohol is similar to tranquilizers and antipsychotic drugs because it depresses shock avoidance at doses that do not interfere with escape (Heise & Boff, 1962).

The effect of alcohol on punished responding is also similar to that of the barbiturates and benzodiazepines but not quite as striking. In an early experiment, Conger (1951) trained rats to run down a runway for food and then gave their paws a shock when they began to eat. He adjusted food deprivation and shock levels carefully until the rats were willing to run partway down the runway but would not touch the food. He found that alcohol would cause the rats to approach and eat the food immediately, but rats given a placebo required many trials. Since then, several researchers have found that ethanol will increase response rates that are suppressed by contingent shock in an operant task. This result is similar to the finding in humans that alcohol tends to reduce the control of aversive consequences on behavior, as demonstrated by Vogel-Sprott's experiment, described earlier.

DISCRIMINATIVE STIMULUS PROPERTIES

Animals can be trained very easily to discriminate alcohol from saline. In a discrimination task, Overton showed that at a dose of 3,000 mg/kg, rats will reach criterion discrimination performance in just three trials. Of the drugs tested, the only drugs that were discriminated faster were phenobarbital and pentobarbital (Overton, 1982; Overton & Batta, 1977).

Using the electrified T-maze, Overton found that rats trained to discriminate alcohol from saline generalized the alcohol response when given a barbiturate and vice versa, indicating that the two drugs produce a similar subjective state. However, in a later series of experiments, Overton (1977) was able to train rats to discriminate between alcohol and barbiturates, showing that although the effects of barbiturates and alcohol are similar, they can be discriminated by rats. It has also been shown that the alcohol response is not generalized to meprobamate (Barry, McGuire, & Krimmer, 1982), chlorpromazine, amphetamine, or atropine (Barry & Kubina, 1972). The alcohol response, however, will generalize to several anesthetics and to the solvents toluene and 1,1,1-trichloroethane (Bowen & Balster, 1997) and to isopropanol (Porcu & Grant, 2004).

The stimulus properties of alcohol can be blocked by 5-HT$_3$ receptor blockers but not by haloperidol, a dopamine D$_2$ blocker—an indication that serotonin rather than dopamine may mediate the subjective effects of alcohol (Grant & Barrett, 1991).

More recent research has shown that the alcohol stimulus is complex and made up of several elements shared with other drugs. Porcu and Grant (2004) used a three-choice discriminative task to separate these elements. They trained rats to discriminate between water ethanol and the benzodiazepine midazolam (a positive GABA$_A$

modulator). Because ethanol is also a positive GABA$_A$ modulator, this forced the rats to discriminate ethanol on the basis of some other property. In this situation, the alcohol cue generalized to dizocilpine, an NMDA receptor blocker, showing that both the effects of ethanol on GABA and the NMDA glutamate receptor have separate stimulus effects that can be separated (Porcu & Grant, 2004).

TOLERANCE

Acute Tolerance

Several studies have shown that many of the effects of alcohol are more pronounced while the BAL is rising than later when the BAL is falling. In the first study of this type, done many years ago, it was shown that while the BAL was rising, subjects first appeared intoxicated at 150 mg per 100 ml, but while the BAL was falling, they appeared sober at 200 mg per 100 ml (Mirsky, Piker, Rosebaum, & Lederer, 1945). Many other effects of alcohol also show acute tolerance (Vogel-Sprott, 1992).

Chronic Tolerance

Chronic tolerance to alcohol appears to develop rapidly in both animals and humans. The extent and speed of tolerance depend on the species studied and the alcohol effect measured. The maximal tolerance develops in a few weeks in humans and reaches a point at which doses have to be increased from 30 to 50 percent to overcome it. Tolerance disappears in rats after 2 or 3 weeks of abstinence but develops again more quickly with repeated exposure (H. Kalant, LeBlanc, & Gibbins, 1971).

Metabolic Tolerance

One effect of heavy drinking is the stimulation of both alcohol dehydrogenase, the major enzyme responsible for the destruction of alcohol, and the MEOS. As described in the section on absorption, light to moderate drinkers are able to metabolize alcohol somewhat faster than abstainers (L. Goldberg, 1943; Whitfield & Martin, 1994). Although such changes certainly decrease the effects of alcohol, they cannot account for the extent of tolerance to alcohol described in the literature.

Behavioral Tolerance

Practice seems to be important in the development of tolerance to some of the effects of alcohol. In one experiment, a group of rats was given alcohol and placed on a treadmill. The rats quickly developed tolerance to the disruptive effects of the drug, but those that were given the same number of alcohol injections after the treadmill sessions did not show any tolerance when tested on the treadmill later under the influence of alcohol (Wenger, Tiffany, Bombardier, Nicoins, & Woods, 1981).

It has also been demonstrated that rats' tolerance to the hypothermic effect of alcohol (decrease in body temperature) is the result of a conditioned hyperthermic effect (increase in body temperature) associated with the specific environment in which the alcohol has been administered (Le, Poulos, & Cappell, 1979). Rats were given alcohol in one environment and saline in another environment. As expected, tolerance developed to the hypothermic effects of the alcohol, but when rats were given the alcohol in the environment where they had previously received only saline, the tolerance was diminished. In addition, rats that were given saline in the alcohol-related environment showed an increase in body temperature. This increase was a conditioned compensatory response to the alcohol effect (see Chapter 3).

WITHDRAWAL

As with most of the depressant drugs, chronic consumption of alcohol can cause withdrawal symptoms. Although the distinction may not always be appropriate, it is customary to think of two separate stages of withdrawal: (a) the early minor syndrome and (b) the late major syndrome, also known as *delirium tremens* or the *DTs*. The early minor symptoms usually appear about 8 to 12 hours after the end of a drinking bout, although many aspects of withdrawal may be seen during the latter part of long drinking sessions even while the drinking is still going on. Withdrawal starts in the form of agitation and tremors; other symptoms, such as muscle cramps, vomiting, nausea, sweating, vivid dreaming, and irregular heartbeats, may also be seen. This stage is usually over within 48 hours.

Fewer than 5 percent of patients hospitalized for alcohol withdrawal go on to show the late major withdrawal symptoms. After 2 days of the minor symptoms, patients show increasing agitation, disorientation, confusion, and hallucinations. Seizures may also occur (Wolfe & Victor, 1972). These major symptoms may last as long as 7 to 10 days. Alcohol withdrawal hallucinations are not usually of the proverbial pink elephant. They frequently involve smaller animals, such as rats, bats, or insects, and can be quite terrifying.

Late major withdrawal can cause death in a substantial number of cases if the symptoms are not treated. A report written at the beginning of the twentieth century, before treatment techniques had been developed, showed a 37 percent (52/140) mortality from alcohol withdrawal (Boston, 1908). Modern estimates are about 2 percent (Naranjo & Sellers, 1986).

In general, the most effective treatment of alcohol withdrawal is a combination of supportive care and the administration of another depressant drug such as diazepam, which suppresses the withdrawal symptoms and has a long duration of action. Other specific symptoms may also be treated with other drugs; for example, hallucinations can be controlled with haloperidol, an antipsychotic. Effective supportive care consists of measures such as reducing sensory stimulation by placing the patient in a dimly lit, quiet room; providing adequate food and water to prevent dehydration; keeping the patient warm and comfortable; and providing reassurance (Naranjo & Sellers, 1986).

SELF-ADMINISTRATION IN NONHUMANS

Oral Self-Administration

When alcohol is freely available to rats and monkeys in conditions in which food and water are also freely available, they will drink the alcohol but not in quantities sufficient to cause obvious intoxication or physical dependence. This type of drinking resembles typical human drinking patterns, but the thrust of this research has been to provide a model of human alcoholism, so there has been considerable research over the years to attempt to find what factors can cause this consumption to increase. Research using oral administration has been hampered because alcohol has a disagreeable taste that most nonhuman species prefer to avoid, and the effects on the central nervous system (CNS) are somewhat delayed because of slow absorption from the digestive system (Meisch, 1977).

One way to increase these low levels of intake is to subject the animal to a period of forced consumption when its only source of food or water is laced with alcohol. After a rat has been forced to consume the alcohol, its voluntary intake may increase. Depriving the animal of food or water will also induce it to consume higher levels of alcohol. Intake will sometimes remain high even after the food or water is returned (see Chapter 5). The animal will learn to press a lever on a reinforcement schedule for access to alcohol. Although some reports claim that food deprivation and other induction procedures are not necessary, they are often used.

It has been noted in these studies that physical dependence is not necessary for alcohol consumption, and when physical dependence exists, it does not increase alcohol intake. Animals that have been made physically dependent will sometimes fail to drink alcohol even while experiencing withdrawal symptoms (Hunter, Walker, & Riley, 1974).

Intravenous Self-Administration

Induction procedures are generally not necessary when alcohol is administered through a cannula implanted in the bloodstream. Giving the alcohol this way avoids the problem of bad taste and slow effect on the CNS, and most animals rapidly learn to self-administer alcohol. When alcohol infusions are freely available, the pattern of self-administration is somewhat erratic. Periods of high-level intake are followed by self-imposed abstinence lasting 2 to 4 days, when withdrawal symptoms may occur. These periods do not seem to follow any regular pattern. (Compare this with the stimulants such as cocaine; see Figure 11-2.) Figure 5-2 shows the intake of a rhesus monkey pressing a lever for intravenous alcohol over a period of 90 days in the laboratory of Jim Woods and his colleagues. The similarity of this pattern to human alcohol intake has already been noted.

SELF-ADMINISTRATION IN HUMANS

Laboratory Studies

In the laboratory, the pattern of alcohol self-administration when freely available is fairly consistent. Alcohol is consumed at high levels for several days. Then follows a self-imposed period of low consumption lasting 2 or 3 days. During this time, withdrawal symptoms may appear. Figure 5-2 shows the drinking pattern of alcoholic volunteers who worked on an operant schedule of button pushing to earn drinks. This pattern is very similar to that of a rhesus monkey under similar conditions and to the typical pattern of many chronic alcoholics under natural conditions (Griffiths, Bigelow, & Henningfield, 1980).

Factors That Affect Consumption

As we have seen in the section on the history of alcohol, its use is almost universal, but some factors are known to modify its use.

Culture. Cross-cultural studies in numerous societies in which alcohol is consumed have revealed some interesting patterns that appear to be consistent across cultures, even in our own. Alcohol consumption is generally a male activity that is practiced socially outside the home among peer groups and not in the company of family members or people of higher status. Drinking is generally more acceptable among warriors and people who must grapple with the environment than among the members of a society who are charged with preserving tradition, such as priests, mothers, and judges (D. Robinson, 1977, p. 63).

Among individuals and cultures, many drinking patterns have been identified. The spree drinker, common in Finland, binges occasionally but stays relatively sober otherwise. A drinker common in France consumes a large fixed amount of alcohol every day steadily over the course of the day and exhibits few symptoms of intoxication. Such differences in national drinking patterns do not seem to influence certain consequences of consumption, such as rate of alcoholism or alcohol-related diseases. However, the difference may be significant when acute intoxication is important; for example, one beer a day may not ever cause a traffic accident, but the same quantity of beer, if consumed on one occasion every 2 weeks, could easily be responsible for traffic accidents.

Gender. Although heavy drinkers are more likely to be male, this fact does not mean that women drink less than men. Studies have shown that women do consume less alcohol than men, but when adjustments are made for differences in body size and ability to absorb alcohol, it turns out that women social drinkers achieve the same BALs as men (W. A. McKim & Quinlan, 1991; Vogel-Sprott, 1984).

Age. People tend to drink less when they get older. A number of studies have shown that although people drink just as frequently as they age, they tend to drink less on each occasion (Vogel-Sprott, 1984), so their total consumption declines. Unlike the difference in consumption between genders, this age-related decline in consumption per occasion cannot be explained by changes in body composition with age (W. A. McKim & Quinlan, 1991).

Behavioral Economics of Alcohol Consumption

Laboratory Studies. Numerous experiments in laboratory settings with both alcoholics and casual drinkers have shown that increases in the cost of alcohol or increases in the work required to get a drink will decrease the amount of alcohol consumed (Mello & Mendelson, 1972). For example, in an experiment by Bigelow and Liebson (1972), two skid-row alcoholics were given the opportunity to earn drinks by pulling a lever. At the lowest cost requirement, one consumed the maximum of 24 drinks a day, and the other consumed 17. At the highest work requirement, both consumed fewer than four drinks per day.

Demand Characteristics of Alcohol. It has been clearly demonstrated that consumption of alcohol is related to price (Seeley, 1960), but what is the exact relationship between price and consumption? Does the demand for alcohol show elasticity when the price changes?

There have been numerous studies of the elasticity of alcoholic beverages in populations when the price of alcohol has changed. Using many different techniques and statistics from a variety of sources, these studies show that the demand characteristics are different for different beverages in different populations. Beer, for example, has an elasticity coefficient of about −0.30 (inelasticity). This means that if the price of beer were to double, consumption would go down by only 20 percent.

Demand for spirits, on the other hand, has much higher coefficients (ranging from −0.57 to −1.95), indicating elasticity. Elasticity of wine varies, depending on the country. In France, where wine is consumed with meals and considered a necessity, it is inelastic (−0.06), but in the United States and Britain, demand appears to be elastic (−1.65 and −1.23, respectively).

Studies on Laboratory Animals. Most studies with laboratory animals have shown that the demand for alcohol is elastic. In an experiment by Carroll, Rodefer, and Rawleigh (1995), rhesus monkeys responding for oral ethanol on FRs ranging from 4 to 128 showed a coefficient of -2.3, indicating elasticity. Heyman (1996), however, in a study with rats with a long history of alcohol consumption, found a coefficient of 0.09, indicating inelasticity. His rats responded on a variable ratio (VR) schedule that ranged from VR 4 to VR 20, and he found inelasticity even though a sucrose substitute was available. His findings suggest that elasticity may vary, depending on the extent of experience with alcohol.

Availability. Changes in price can alter the consumption of alcohol, and it appears that changes in availability can as well. Governments have considerable means of control over the availability of alcoholic beverages: enforcing a legal drinking age, licensing drinking establishments and liquor stores, and regulating the days and/or hours permitted for operation and sale. Considerable research has shown that alcohol consumption increases as alcohol becomes easier to obtain, and it decreases when it is more difficult to get (Single, 1988); that is, it behaves like any other commodity in the marketplace (Babor, 1985; Österberg, 1992; Popham, Schmidt, & de Lint, 1976).

Here are some examples:

- In 1989, when Iceland ended a 75-year prohibition on beer, the consumption of wine and liquor declined by 25 and 18 percent, respectively, but total alcohol consumption from all sources increased by 23 percent (Österberg, 1992).
- Studies of the effects of permitting wine to be sold in grocery stores in four states—Idaho, Maine, Virginia, and Washington—showed that in three of the four states, the change in law resulted in an overall increase in total alcohol consumption (Macdonald, 1986).
- For 8 months, 10 of Finland's liquor monopoly stores were closed on Saturdays on a trial basis. This experiment resulted in a total decrease in alcohol consumption of 3.2 percent and, also decreased public drunkenness and alcohol-related violence (Säilä, as cited in Österberg, 1992).

ALCOHOLISM

When the social reform movement of the nineteenth century was campaigning for better treatment of people who drank too much, they adopted the position that excessive drinking was a disease. Previously drunkenness was known by such terms as *inebriety* or *intemperance*, but more medical-sounding terms were developed, including *alcoholism*, *dipsomania*, and *narcomania*. *Alcoholism* survived and is now the commonly accepted term (Barrows & Room, 1991).

Like the term *dependence*, *alcoholism* may be used in two different ways: (a) as an explanation or (b) as a description of behavior. Many definitions are purely descriptive; they describe a pattern of behavior and then label it alcoholism. What is confusing is that many descriptions are used as though they were explanations. For example, the fourth edition of the *Diagnostic and Statistical Manual of Mental Disorders* (*DSM-IV*) defines substance dependence (see Box 5-1). (The *DSM* defines substance dependence and abuse; this is generally taken to mean alcoholism if the substance is alcohol.) The *DSM-IV* definition is a description of a state of affairs; it is not an explanation. Unfortunately, many writers use such descriptions as though they were explanations. For example, it could be said that an individual is an alcoholic because he or she fits the *DSM-IV* description. This statement is fair enough, but it cannot be said that this individual drinks excessively because he or she is an alcoholic. (This would be a circular argument; we know that person X is an alcoholic because he or she drinks too much, and we know that person X drinks too much because he or she is an alcoholic.) The only way around this circularity is to define the condition of alcoholism in terms other than the behavior of drinking; then the term can legitimately be used as an explanation of the behavior.

Explaining something is considerably more complicated than describing it. Explanations take the form of theories, and good theories must withstand the test of scientific investigation. Over the years, a great number of theories have been proposed to explain alcoholism. In Chapter 4, there was a discussion of several theories of addiction that could be applied to alcoholism, but alcoholism had its own disease theory that has been widely accepted for many years since Jellinek proposed it in 1960. It is a disease theory, and it suffers from the general problems that all disease theories have, but it is so widely accepted that it is worth discussing.

The Disease Explanation

In the 1950s, E. M. Jellinek first clearly proposed that alcoholism was a disease. His arguments were published in his book *The Disease Concept of Alcoholism* (Jellinek, 1960). Jellinek was associated with the *Alcoholics Anonymous* movement, and the increasing prominence of this movement and Jellinek's arguments were effective in convincing both the American Medical Association and the World Health Organization to declare alcoholism a disease. In spite of this, its status as a disease is still the subject of considerable heated debate.

One of the more important assumptions of this disease theory is that alcoholism is not caused by alcohol. Alcoholism is a genetic disease, and people are alcoholics from the time they are born. Everyone, both alcoholic and nonalcoholic, starts drinking in the same way, in a moderate, social manner, but there are some who progress to drink more and more heavily, and eventually they enter the *prodromal phase* of alcoholism, which is characterized by frequent blackouts. Many such people are not "alcoholics." They are "problem drinkers" who either stay that way or eventually stop drinking. Some individuals progress to become *gamma alcoholics* (Jellinek's term). The change from being a problem drinker to a gamma alcoholic is marked by two symptoms: (a) a loss of control over drinking, and (b) physical dependence indicated by high levels of tolerance and withdrawal symptoms such as seizures, hallucinations, and the delirium tremens. It is worth noting that the distinction between problem drinkers and alcoholics is the presence or absence of physical dependence and loss of control, not the amount consumed. Problem drinkers may actually consume more than

alcoholics, but they are not considered alcoholics, and they do not have the disease. Any research on the disease of alcoholism, therefore, must be done on alcoholics, not on problem drinkers. This distinction is responsible for many arguments over data between supporters and opponents of the disease model.

We have already considered the role of physical dependence in alcoholism, so we will now look at some of its other assumptions.

Genetics of Alcoholism. Evidence is clear that the risk of becoming an alcoholic is increased as much as fourfold if a close relative (mother, father, or sibling) is an alcoholic. Families, however, share both genetics and environment, and the challenge to researchers has been to separate these factors.

It is known, for example, that the amount of drinking of identical twins (who have exactly the same genes) is more similar than the drinking behavior of fraternal twins (who have the same genetic similarity as normal siblings). Thus, the closer the genetic makeup, the more similar the drinking pattern. It has also been shown that an adopted person with a biological parent who is an alcoholic has an increased risk of alcoholism, but having an adoptive parent who is alcoholic does not increase the risk of becoming alcoholic (Schuckit, 1992). Unfortunately, twin studies cannot completely disentangle genetics from environment, and adoption studies have serious conceptual and methodological flaws that make it difficult to draw firm conclusions (Searles, 1988). Nevertheless, there is an overwhelming volume of data supporting the heritability of alcoholism. It seems, though, that heritability varies considerably, depending on factors such as gender, the measure of drinking behavior, the definition of alcoholism, and the population studied (Goldman, 1993).

There is no single alcoholism gene, and the influence of genetics is modified by environment. A person with an identical twin who is alcoholic has only a 60 percent chance of being alcoholic, so something more than genetics must be involved. Genetics probably controls some aspects of body chemistry, personality, or brain function that increase the probability that a person will drink in an alcoholic manner in a particular environment. A variety of genetic susceptibilities to alcohol may cause problems only in particular environments. The right combination of environment and genetics may be necessary to make a person drink in an alcoholic manner.

FHP Versus FHN. One method that could be useful in understanding the nature of the disease of alcoholism might be to compare alcoholics with nonalcoholics on a number of measures; any consistent difference in the physiology, biochemistry, personality, or response to alcohol could give a clue as to the nature of alcoholism. A problem with this approach is that it is quite likely that any differences found might be caused by the alcohol consumed, not the alcoholism.

One way to avoid this difficulty is to compare people who are likely to become alcoholics before they start drinking with those who are less likely and to note the differences (remember that according to this theory, an alcoholic is an alcoholic before he or she starts drinking). We know that people who come from families in which there is a history of alcohol problems (*family history positive* [FHP]) are at a greater risk of becoming alcoholic than those who have a family history without alcohol problems (*family history negative* [FHN]). One interesting line of research has attempted to compare high-risk (FHP) and low-risk (FHN) individuals to see whether it is possible to detect markers might be able to identify potential alcoholics or some light on the disease of alcoholism.

Although early studies were encouraging, there not appear to be any consistent differences between FHP and FHN individuals in terms of pharmacokinetics and metabolism of alcohol, and clear-cut differences have been established in cognitive and neuropsychological measures of personality (Searles, 1988) or in alcohol preference, alcohol-liking scores, BALs, or alcohol-induced impairment (de Wit & McCracken, 1990).

Some studies, however, have detected differences between FHN and FHP subjects in electroencephalographic responses, and in some experiments,

FHP subjects may show a greater sensitivity to the subjective and motor-impairing effects of alcohol than FHN subjects (Porjesz & Begleiter, 1987; Schuckit, 1987, p. 1531; Schuckit, 1992).

If alcoholics are really different from nonalcoholics, these differences are rather difficult to establish. They appear to be limited to subtle changes (in the electroencephalogram, hormone levels, and subjective sensitivity) that require large-scale, carefully controlled experiments to detect. It is still not clear how any of these differences contribute to the development of alcoholic drinking, if they do at all.

Loss of Control

According to the disease model, one of the defining characteristics of alcoholism is *loss of control*. It is assumed that exposure to even one or two drinks of alcohol will cause, in the alcoholic, an uncontrollable craving to drink more and more. In other words, the alcoholic will lose control of alcohol consumption; one drink develops into one drunk.

Since the time it was proposed, the loss-of-control theory has never received significant experimental support. In fact, most research has disconfirmed the basic notion (Finagrette, 1988). A number of studies in England (D. L. Davis, 1962) and the United States (Armor, Polach, & Stambul, 1978) have found many cases of alcoholics who have reverted from excess drinking to moderate social drinking and have maintained that level for years. These studies caused a storm of controversy, and many alcoholism experts denounced them as dangerous and unscientific and attacked them on various grounds (Pendrey, Maltzman, & West, 1982).

Some have argued that most of these studies were done with problem drinkers, not with populations of gamma alcoholics, as defined by other characteristics such as physical dependence. In addition, it has been argued that most studies purporting to show that alcoholics can return to controlled drinking do not allow a sufficiently long time frame to detect whether controlled drinking is possible (Maltzman, 1994).

In addition to the research with alcoholics in treatment, laboratory studies have repeatedly shown that alcoholics are perfectly capable of moderating their alcohol intake in response to such manipulations as increased cost, and they virtually never lose control (Mello & Mendelson, 1972). Such laboratory studies are also challenged on the grounds that the laboratory is too artificial to be relevant to alcohol use in a natural setting (Maltzman, 1994).

Perhaps related to the concept of loss of control is the phenomenon of priming (see Chapter 5). It was shown some time ago that noncontingent infusion of the drug would reinstate drug self-administration in laboratory animals that had stopped pressing a lever. De Wit and Chutuape (1993) have shown that social drinkers are much more likely to choose an alcoholic drink and report an increased craving for alcohol after they have been given a priming dose of alcohol. This study was later replicated (Chutuape, Mitchell, & de Wit, 1994), but a more recent study was able to show only an increased desire for alcohol, not an increased choice of alcohol among primed social drinkers (Kirk & de Wit, 2000). Priming has also been demonstrated in laboratory animals. While priming looks like loss of control, it is not clear whether it is analogous to loss of control. Priming is a fairly universal phenomenon that can be seen in many species with many different reinforcers, while loss of control as described by Jellinek is seen only for alcohol and only in alcoholics.

HARMFUL EFFECTS OF AN ACUTE ADMINISTRATION

Alcohol Poisoning

A single dose of alcohol, if large enough, can be lethal. A blood alcohol level of about 300 to 400 mg per 100 ml of blood will usually cause loss of consciousness. In a study of alcohol poisonings, Kaye and Haag (1957) reported that without therapy, people whose BALs reached 500 mg per 100 ml of blood died within an hour or two. The world record for high BAL is probably 1,500 mg per 100 ml, reported in a 30-year-old man whose life was saved by vigorous medical intervention. Later he reported that he had drunk 4.23 liters of beer and an undetermined number of bottles of liquor in the space of 3 hours (O'Neil, Tipton, Prichard, & Quinlan, 1984).

As with most depressant drugs, death by alcohol usually results from respiratory failure. Alcohol is a rather toxic substance, and the lethal dose is uncomfortably close to the usual social dose. A 150-pound male would have to drink 7.5 ounces of liquor to have a BAL of 150 mg per 100 ml of blood. These numbers are at the upper levels of an acceptable social high. Around 25 ounces of liquor would produce a BAL of 500 mg per 100 ml of blood, probably a lethal dose for most people. Thus, the therapeutic index for alcohol is about 3.5 (25/7.5).

Fortunately, alcohol has a built-in safety feature: People vomit or pass out before they can kill themselves. People who die from alcohol poisoning usually drink a large amount quickly and in high concentrations. They are able to get a lethal dose into their bodies before they lose consciousness.

Hangover

The problem of how to avoid a hangover from alcohol has occupied some of history's best minds, as this passage from Plato's *The Dialogues* illustrates:

They were about to commence drinking, when Pausanias said, "And now, my friends, how can we drink with the least injury to ourselves?" I can assure you that I feel severely the effect of yesterday's potations, and must have time to recover; and I suspect that most of you are in the same predicament, for you were of the party yesterday. Consider then: "How can the drinking be made easiest?" (Symposium 176a–b, translation in Jowett, 1931)

Like the ancient Greeks, most drinkers have, at some time, suffered the next day for having had too much the night before. Apart from the puritanical notion that we are getting just what we deserve, there are several explanations for a hangover. These explanations suggest that hangover results from alcohol-produced effects, such as low blood sugar levels, dehydration, and irritation of the lining of the digestive system. There is no doubt that most effects of alcohol contribute to discomfort the next day, but it is probably best to think of a hangover as a miniwithdrawal from alcohol, a rebound excitation of an alcohol-depressed nervous system, that is, a miniwithdrawal symptom. This rebound makes the brain more sensitive to seizures.

For most drinkers, hangovers are not physiologically serious, but for persons with epilepsy, heart disease, or diabetes, hangovers could have serious medical consequences (Gauvin, Cheng, & Holloway, 1993).

The Greeks never did answer Pausanias's question "How can the drinking be made easiest?" apart from concluding that "drinking deep is a bad practice," but over the centuries, a number of cures have been suggested, including eating a spoonful of sugar or drinking lots of water. To the extent that a hangover can be thought of as a withdrawal from alcohol, one cure is to take a "hair of the dog that bit you." Consuming more alcohol relieves the hangover by depressing this rebound excitability in the same way that other depressant drugs are used to treat withdrawal. If the alcohol is taken in small quantities, it might work, but if too much is consumed, it will only postpone withdrawal.

Alcohol-Induced Behavior

Apart from the self-inflicted physical harm that can be done by an acute administration of alcohol, the drug can be responsible for changes in behavior that cause untold social, psychological, financial, and physical harm to the drinker and others. It is not possible to catalog all the manifestations of harm, but most people have been made aware of them in some form. They include accidents caused while drunk or hung over not only while driving but also in industry and at home (Gutjahr, Gmel, & Rehm, 2001), crimes committed under the influence of alcohol, and damage done to families and social relationships. All these effects are difficult to quantify, and some may not be a direct result of alcohol.

They are nonetheless real and must be included in any assessment of the harmful effects of alcohol.

Reproduction

A well-known quote from Shakespeare's *Macbeth* states that drink "provokes the desire, but takes away the performance" in matters sexual. The bard's analysis is essentially correct. Acute alcohol consumption may increase interest by diminishing inhibitions, but, at least in higher doses, it reduces sexual arousal in both males and females. In males, alcohol at lower doses (BAL less than 100 mg/100 ml) may increase the duration of erections and, thus, provide increased opportunities for fulfillment of the partner. This fact may explain why alcohol is often perceived as enhancing sexual performance (Mello, 1978; Rubin & Henson, 1976).

A study with rats showed that increasing doses of alcohol caused increasing disruptions of copulation of male rats with receptive females. In addition, low doses of alcohol that disrupted copulation with receptive females caused male rats to attempt to copulate with unreceptive females, something they would normally not attempt. These findings support the speculation that low doses of alcohol adversely affect uninhibited sexual performance but can stimulate sexual behavior that is normally inhibited (Pfaus & Pinel, 1988).

HARMFUL EFFECTS OF CHRONIC CONSUMPTION

The Liver

Prolonged drinking of alcohol damages the liver. The damage usually starts with a buildup of fat in the liver. Alcoholics also frequently contract alcoholic hepatitis, which usually develops into *cirrhosis*, which means "scarring." The liver becomes filled with scar tissue and is no longer able to function, and the condition is frequently fatal, especially if alcohol consumption is not stopped.

Cirrhosis is present in 8 percent of chronic alcoholics; among nonalcoholics, the condition affects only 1 percent. Alcohol consumption accounts for 40 to 90 percent of liver cirrhosis deaths in the United States. Generally, alcohol consumption of over five drinks a day for at least 5 years is necessary for the development of cirrhosis

The Nervous System

Some alcoholics and heavy drinkers may show a cluster of symptoms that includes a loss of memory for past events, an inability to remember new material, and disorientation and confusion. These symptoms are collectively known as *Korsakoff's psychosis*. They are a result of damage in certain parts of the brain first noted by Wernicke and called *Wernicke's disease*. The condition seems to result from deficiency of thiamin (vitamin B1), which is common among many alcoholics (Victor, Adams, & Collins, 1971). Many of the conditions suffered by alcoholics can be traced to vitamin deficiencies, chiefly because people who drink large quantities of alcohol do not normally have a balanced diet. In addition, alcohol can damage the digestive system and interfere with the normal absorption of some nutrients.

The Wernicke–Korsakoff syndrome is not the only neurological damage associated with heavy drinking. A number of other disorders of both the central and the peripheral nervous system, such as epilepsy, cerebellar syndrome, and alcoholic dementia, are attributable either directly or indirectly to excessive alcohol use (Marsden, 1977, p. 189). Individuals with a chronic history of alcohol consumption exhibit global demyelination of neurons, glial cell loss, loss of neuronal dendrites, neuronal death, and neuronal shrinkage in many different brain regions (Mann et al., 2001). Consistent with this, MRI analysis of chronic alcohol users shows widespread brain tissue loss (Gazdzinski, Durazzo, & Meyerhoff, 2005) and decreases in cerebral blood flow (Demir, Ulug, Lay Ergun, & Erbas, 2002). These effects are partially reversed with prolonged abstinence from alcohol, with the greatest increases in brain volume noted within the first month of withdrawal (Gazdzinski et al., 2005).

Cancer

The use of alcohol is directly related to cancers of the mouth, throat, and liver—the parts of the body that are directly exposed to high alcohol concentrations and susceptible to alcohol damage. This may be a result of the first metabolite of alcohol, acetaldehyde, which is a known *carcinogen*. Acetaldehyde is created in the upper digestive tract by alcohol dehydrogenase, which is present there and is responsible for first-pass metabolism of alcohol.

There is conflicting evidence relating alcohol consumption with breast cancer. In general, there appears to be a weak association in the general population, but alcohol does increase breast cancer in populations that are otherwise at risk, that is, those who have a family history of breast cancer or those postmenopausal women taking estrogen replacement therapy (Gunzerath, Faden, Zakhari, & Warren, 2004)

Reproduction

In males, chronic alcohol consumption is known to cause impotence, shrinking of the testicles, and a loss of sexual interest. Although there have been few studies of the effects of chronic alcohol consumption in females, there is evidence that it can cause menstrual dysfunctions, such as amenorrhea, dysmenorrhea, and premenstrual discomfort (Mello, 1987, p. 1517).

There are ancient beliefs that alcohol might be teratogenic (responsible for birth defects). In ancient Carthage, drinking on wedding days was forbidden; it was believed that it might cause an abnormal child to be born (K. L. Jones & Smith, 1975). Aristotle warned against drinking during pregnancy, and later, at the time of the gin epidemic in England, it was noted that there was an increase in infant deaths. Similar effects associated with alcohol consumption have been reported in the medical literature, and the extent of the problem is now fully appreciated. It is now recognized that the use of alcohol during pregnancy can harm the developing fetus and may result in a number of behavioral, anatomical, and physiological irregularities, which are known as *fetal alcohol syndrome* (FAS) in their more severe form or *fetal alcohol effects* (FAE) or *alcohol-related birth defects* or *alcohol-related neuro-behavioral disorder* if only a few behavioral or neurological symptoms are present.

The manifestations of FAS are mental retardation, poor coordination, loss of muscle tone, low birth weight, slow growth, malformation of organ systems, and peculiar facial characteristics, such as small eyes, drooping eyelids, and a misshapen mouth that looks like the mouth of a fish. These symptoms do not always appear together, but the chances for development of any or all of these effects increase according to the amount of alcohol drunk during pregnancy.

The mechanism by which alcohol affects the developing fetus is not known. Many normal, healthy children are born to women who have drunk heavily during pregnancy, so alcohol alone cannot be entirely responsible. As Abel and Sokol (1989) suggest, alcohol is a necessary but not a sufficient condition for FAS or FAE. Other factors that may be involved include (a) having previous children, (b) being black, (c) having a high score on an alcohol screening test, and (d) having a high percentage of drinking days. It also seems clear that occasional high levels of consumption do more damage than the same amount of alcohol consumed at chronic low levels (Abel & Sokol, 1989; Maier & West, 2001). It has also been suggested that high levels of acetaldehyde may be a factor (Hard, Einarson, & Koren, 2001).

Functional disruption neural of organization may occur in the formation of the cortex. It appears that alcohol is responsible for a disruption of cell migration in the cortex; only four layers, rather than the normal six layers, are formed. In addition, these cells may end up migrating to the wrong layer (Abel, 1989).

Apart from FAS, maternal alcohol consumption can affect growth. At ages 10 and 14, children of women who drank an average of one drink a day during the first 3 months of pregnancy were 4 pounds lighter than children born to nondrinking mothers. (Day et al., 2002).

There does not appear to be any time during pregnancy when it is safe to drink, but it seems clear from both human and nonhuman studies that drinking during early stages of pregnancy is most likely to be harmful. In fact, considerable harm can be done to the fetus before a woman even recognizes that she could be pregnant (Maier & West, 2001).

The only way to be certain of avoiding all these effects is to avoid alcohol completely during pregnancy (and during times when becoming pregnant is possible). If there is any drinking at all, high BALs should be avoided.

Heart Disease

Degeneration of the heart muscle, known as *alcoholic cardiomyopathy*, results directly from the chronic consumption of alcohol. This condition most likely arises from the effect alcohol has on the metabolism of the membrane of the cells of the heart muscle. The result is very similar to cirrhosis of the liver and was once described as "cirrhosis of the heart" (Myerson, 1971, p. 183).

Other Effects

Chronic use of alcohol may also be responsible for a number of other pathologies. These include diseases of the digestive system such as ulcers and cancer, inflammation and other disorders of the pancreas, pneumonia and other diseases of the lungs and respiratory system, abnormalities of the blood, and malnutrition.

It has been observed for some time that alcoholics are more susceptible to many infectious diseases and less responsive to treatment. The reasons for this susceptibility include differences in lifestyle, nutrition, and liver functioning, but it has become clear recently that alcohol has an adverse effect on all aspects of the functioning of the immune system, thus impairing the body's ability to resist and fight infections (Baker & Jerrells, 1993).

BENEFITS OF ALCOHOL CONSUMPTION

It is not unusual for substances that are physiologically stressful and toxic at high doses to be beneficial at low doses. This effect is called *hormesis* (Dudley, 2002). It may reflect an evolutionary adaptation to substances that an organism is naturally exposed to at low doses. The sort of exposure to alcohol experienced by our frugivore ancestors may have favored the evolution of metabolic adaptations to alcohol that maximize its benefits and minimize its harm.

Historically, alcohol has been used as a medicine. Avicenna, the tenth-century Persian physician, recommended wine for his older patients, although he cautioned his younger patients to drink it in moderation. Arnaud de Villeneuve, who reputedly invented brandy in the thirteenth century, hailed it as the water of immortality and called it *aqua vitae*, "water of life." He was convinced that it would increase longevity and maintain youth (W. A. McKim & Mishara, 1987).

There has been a great number of epidemiological studies that have plotted daily dose of alcohol against the relative risk of some or another health problem. Relative risk is calculated by dividing the incidence of a disease in people who use a given amount of alcohol by the incidence of that disease in people who do not consume any alcohol at all. Thus, if 5 percent of alcohol abstainers get cancer and 10 percent of heavy drinkers get cancer, then the relative risk of heavy drinkers is 2.0; that is, they are twice as likely to get cancer than abstainers. The relative risk of abstainers is always 1.0, and numbers less than 1 indicate a reduced risk of the disease. Figure 6-3 shows a plot of the relative risk of having an automobile accident against BALs.

When alcohol consumption is plotted against relative risk of coronary heart disease, the result is in the form of a "J" curve or a "U" curve, depending on the range of doses reported; that is, relative risk drops to numbers less than 1 for moderate consumption (usually defined as one or two drinks a day) but increases to higher numbers as daily consumption increases (Gunzerath et al., 2004). The relative risk of myocardial infarction (heart attack) is reduced by 25 percent in men who consume up to two drinks a day. In fact, it has been suggested that if all drinking of alcohol ceased, there would be about 80,000 more deaths from coronary heart disease each year in the United States (Pearson & Terry, 1994). This protective effect of alcohol is likely a result of the ability of alcohol to lower levels of low-density cholesterol and increase high-density cholesterol.

Another J-shaped risk curve with alcohol consumption has been reported for diabetes; moderate drinking reduces the incidence of type 2 diabetes. One study showed a 60 percent reduction associated with two drinks a day, but at three drinks a day this protective effect disappeared. And the incidence of diabetes increased as alcohol consumption increased above that level (Gunzerath et al., 2004).

Finally, because alcohol reduces blood clotting and reduces levels of low-density cholesterol that can clog arteries, it might be expected that alcohol would be able to increase blood flow to the brain and reduce the risk of ischemic strokes (caused by clots blocking arteries in the brain). In fact, there appears to be some beneficial effect of alcohol on dementia caused by diminished blood flow to the brain in older people but not on dementia caused by Alzheimer's disease. A J curve also has been shown for risk of ischemic strokes in the elderly, with two drinks a day giving the best protection but seven drinks a day increasing relative risk to 3.0 (Gunzerath et al., 2004).

In general, it appears that there are some beneficial effects to low and moderate alcohol consumption, but it seems that most of the conditions where alcohol is beneficial are those associated with aging. Young people are at relatively low risk of coronary heart disease, ischemic stroke, and diabetes. Therefore, they are not likely to benefit from any of the beneficial effects of alcohol but are exposed to all the risks of alcohol consumption, whereas older people are more likely to get some benefit. Research has shown that for those under 60, increased alcohol consumption is related to increased risk of dying from any cause (no J curve), but for those over 60, the relative risk of dying was less for light and moderate drinkers than for heavy drinkers and abstainers. This relationship was the same for both sexes (Rehm & Sempos, 1995). It is possible that all this was foreseen a thousand years ago by Avicenna when he recommended wine for his older patients.

If alcohol has so many health benefits, should it be "prescribed" to abstainers? One article summed up the dilemma this way: "Nowhere in medicine is the double edged sword so sharp on both sides" (Sandridge, Zylstra, & Adams, 2004, p. 670). These authors believe that the beneficial effects could be offset by the risks of addiction, especially in people with a family history of alcoholism. They believe that patients should be informed of all the pros and cons and then be allowed to make a truly informed decision.

It must also be remembered that all this research is correlational, not experimental. It is possible that there is some third factor, such as general health, that correlates with alcohol consumption; for example, people who are generally healthy are less likely to get sick and are also more likely to be moderate alcohol consumers. Timothy Naimi and his colleagues at the Centers for Disease Control and Prevention in Atlanta, Georgia, analyzed the findings of a large-scale population health study and found many factors that correlated with both moderate alcohol consumption and reduced risk of cardiovascular disease. They point out that many of these factors are not measured in those studies that show that moderate alcohol consumption is associated with a lowered risk of cardiovascular disease, so there is no way of assessing their involvement in the relationship (Naimi et al., 2005).

TREATMENTS

Because there has been little agreement over the years about what alcoholism really is and why people drink, many types of treatments have been developed to help those who want to reduce their alcohol intake. It is usually agreed that the first step must be to eliminate physical dependence if it is present. This is usually done in a hospital or a detoxification center where the alcoholic goes through withdrawal under medical supervision until all withdrawal symptoms are over. Following detoxification, an active treatment phase may or may not be followed by a long-term program to prevent the recurrence of drinking (a *relapse*, in the language of physicians).

The nature of the therapy and its outcome goal are determined by how the therapist defines alcoholism. If alcoholism is considered a disease, theoretically it should be possible to cure the underlying disorder. The excessive drinking, which is a symptom, will then disappear. As mentioned earlier, there is little agreement on the nature of the underlying disorder, so this method of cure is not currently possible.

The reinforcement approach described earlier presumes that excessive drinking is a result of normal behavioral processes interacting in a maladaptive way with the environment. Treatments then aim to reestablish acceptable behavior patterns by using the behavioral principles of conditioning and instrumental learning that have been developed to change other abnormal or undesirable behavior patterns.

In practical terms, there is little difference between the disease model approach and the reinforcement approach. Both are aimed at changing the behavior of alcoholics. The disease approach differs from the reinforcement approach in one basic way: The disease approach insists that because the disease cannot be cured, the aim of all therapy must be total abstinence from alcohol.

Alcoholics Anonymous

Alcoholics Anonymous (AA) was founded in 1935. It grew out of the Oxford Movement, a popular Protestant religious movement in which small groups met weekly for prayer, worship, and discussion, with the aim of self-improvement. One Oxford group meeting in Akron, Ohio, was attended by an alcoholic stockbroker and an alcoholic physician, both of whom were seriously but unsuccessfully trying to stop drinking. They found that their fellowship and that of the group helped them to stop drinking. They brought other alcoholics into the group, and many had similar success. In fact, helping other alcoholics to stay sober seemed to be making an important contribution to the maintenance of their own sobriety. As the meetings got bigger, new groups were formed, and eventually they broke away from the Oxford Movement and became AA (Alcoholics Anonymous, 1980).

The organization has grown rapidly and spread around the world. In 1982 there were 20,000 groups in 100 countries, and the estimated world membership was well over 1 million (Maxwell, 1984, p. 2). As of January 1, 2005, AA estimates that there are almost 105,000 groups and a membership of 2 million (Alcoholics Anonymous, 2005).

Although AA broke away from the Oxford Movement, it has retained many of the elements that seemed to be responsible for its effectiveness, including religion, although this aspect can be moderated to suit each individual.

At every meeting of AA, someone reads the 12 steps and the 12 traditions that explain the basic principles and processes the organization has found to be effective over the years (Alcoholics Anonymous, 1998). The AA approach, also known as the 12 steps approach, has been adapted to many other support groups for people who have problems controlling gambling, overeating, and the use of other drugs.

AA is not a temperance organization. The temperance movement is religion based and made up largely of individuals who are not alcoholics and have never had a drinking problem but wish to impose their views about alcohol on others. AA is made up of alcoholics. AA members are not antiliquor and do not seek to impose their views on anyone else. The organization exists only to help alcoholics who want to achieve sobriety.

The AA approach to alcoholism coincides with the disease model discussed earlier. Most AA members believe that to control drinking, the individual must first admit to being "powerless over alcohol" and unable to control drinking without help. AA members believe that drinking can be controlled only by relying on a greater power, often identified as "God," or "God as we have come to understand Him" (or Her) for people who are uncomfortable with the concept. They feel that there is no cure; there are only alcoholics who drink and alcoholics who do not drink. For this reason, members are expected to attend regular meetings for extended periods of time. It is not unusual for new members to attend more than six meetings a week. (In fact, there is a tradition of new members doing "90 meetings in 90 days.") In addition to attending meetings, members often see each other socially outside of meetings and frequently talk on the phone, especially if stress or desire for alcohol is threatening a member's resolve (Maxwell, 1984). For many people, AA is not a treatment at all; it is a long-term commitment and a way of life. It has been estimated that AA is currently helping as many alcoholics in the United States as all medical facilities combined. It has been estimated that about 5 percent of all alcoholics are affiliated with AA (Finagrette, 1988, p. 89).

There can be no doubt that AA is very effective for many drinkers. In fact, it has been claimed that participation in AA is the most effective treatment, but this is a difficult claim to test, largely because AA does not permit itself to be subjected to the same close scientific evaluation that other treatment techniques must undergo. In addition, the persons who try and stick with AA are most likely to have a high socioeconomic status and a stable social situation, are highly motivated to quit, are between ages 40 and 45, and have spouses who help with the treatment (Baekeland, 1977). These are the best candidates for help, no matter what the treatment (Ogbourne & Glaser, 1981).

Vaillant has suggested that one reason why AA works is that it provides alternative sources of reinforcement and keeps the alcoholic busily engaged in activities that are incompatible with drinking alcohol. AA provides a busy schedule of social and service activities with supportive former drinkers, especially at times of high risk (e.g., holidays). AA requires members to "work the program" and encourages returning again and again to group meetings and to sponsors who provide an external conscience (Vaillant, 1992, p. 52).

Treatment with Other Drugs

Antabuse. Antabuse (disulfiram) blocks the action acetaldehyde dehydrogenase. Drinking alcohol with this enzyme out of commission will cause a buildup of acetaldehyde in the body, which makes a person feel very sick. If alcohol is not consumed, the drug has little effect. Therefore, a person taking the enzyme blocker cannot drink without getting sick. It is frequently prescribed for alcoholics as an adjunct to other therapies, but it can work only if the alcoholic takes it regularly. Some studies with disulfiram show fairly high alcohol abstinence rates among those who take the drug regularly, but properly controlled clinical trials with random assignment to groups have failed to show that disulfiram is superior to a placebo (Gorelick, 1993). Antabuse offers some protection from unplanned or spontaneous drinking, but a patient who wants to drink can simply stop taking the drug. Antabuse, however, has proven effective when used in conjunction with treatment programs such as the Community Reinforcement Approach (discussed later in this chapter).

There have been encouraging results from using drugs that specifically operate on the serotonin system. The most studied drugs in this regard are selective serotonin reuptake inhibitors (SSRIs; see Chapter 14), which increase levels of serotonin in the synapse. A series of studies at the Addiction Research Foundation in Toronto found that fluoxetine and sertraline, drugs normally used as antidepressants, reduced alcohol intake by 9 to 14 percent and increased the number of abstinent days in volunteer subjects who were described as heavy social drinkers or early problem drinkers. The result has been replicated with alcoholics (Gorelick, 1993).

A number of other drugs have also been shown to reduce alcohol consumption in both humans and laboratory animals, including drugs that stimulate 5-HT_{1A} receptors (buspirone) and drugs that block either 5-HT_2 (ritanserin) or 5-H_3 receptors (ondansetron). It seems that the SSRIs reduce all consummatory behavior, but the effect of these drugs seems to be more specific in reducing alcohol consumption (Litten & Allen, 1993).

Why do both agonists and antagonists of serotonin receptors show this effect? Many of these drugs are also used clinically as antidepressants, and alcohol abusers are frequently found to be clinically depressed. Interestingly, the alcohol-suppressing effect is evident as soon as the drug is taken, but the antidepressant effects usually do not show up for several weeks (see Chapter 14). Serotonin is involved in a complex way with the neurophysiology of alcohol consumption. In particular, serotonin is involved in the release of dopamine in the mesolimbic dopamine system.

Other Drugs. There is also evidence that the dopamine D_2 receptor agonist (bromocriptine) and the opiate receptor blocker (naltrexone) are effective in reducing alcohol consumption in laboratory animals and in human alcoholics (Litten & Allen, 1993).

Behavior Therapy

Behavior therapists treat alcohol drinking like any other positively reinforced response and try to stop drinking by reinforcing behaviors that are not compatible with drinking (Caddy & Block, 1983).

Community Reinforcement Approach. If competing sources of reinforcement can reduce the use of alcohol, as discussed in Chapter 5, might it be possible to teach people to take advantage of other sources of reinforcement and reduce their dependence on alcohol? Training in social skills (such as how to get and hold a job) or more effective ways of relating to people, teaching and encouraging recreational activities, and improving family relations are often incorporated into treatment programs. Because interpersonal relationships and social support are also seen as important, it is becoming more common to incorporate the entire family of the alcoholic into the therapeutic process (Higgins, 1997).

Relapse Prevention. It is also known that relapse to drinking is more likely to occur in circumstances in which a person (a) feels angry or frustrated with a personal or social situation or (b) is under social pressure to drink. One approach, developed by G. A. Marlatt and his associates (W. H. George & Marlatt, 1983), stresses identification of situations that cause a high risk of relapse to excessive drinking and training of coping responses to each situation so that the individual will feel in control and will not need to resort to alcohol.

CHAPTER SUMMARY

- Ethyl alcohol is created during the fermentation of the sugar contained in fruits and grains. Fermented beverages, such as wine and beer, have a low alcohol content (10 to 15 percent). The concentration of alcohol can be increased by distillation. The result is hard liquor, which usually has an alcohol content of 40 to 50 percent.

- Alcohol content can be given as a percent by weight or volume. Because the specific gravity of alcohol is .79, there is more alcohol in a percent by weight than the same percent by volume.

- Alcohol has been consumed in fermented fruit by our fruit-eating ancestors for millions of years but has been deliberately made for only about the past 10,000 years.

- Alcohol consumption in the United States has cycled through highs and lows. Currently, its use is declining.

- Alcohol levels in the blood can be measured with a Breathalyzer and are usually reported in terms of percentage, or milligrams of alcohol in 100 milliliters of blood, or in SI units.

- Alcohol is consumed orally. It is absorbed quickly and distributed evenly in body water. It easily crosses the blood–brain barrier and the placental barrier.

- Most of the alcohol consumed is metabolized by the enzyme alcohol dehydrogenase at a constant rate, which averages about 15 mg per 100 ml of blood per hour.

- Alcohol does not have a specific receptor site but is known to alter the functioning of neurotransmitters, including glutamate, by blocking the NMDA receptor. GABA and serotonin are also altered by alcohol.

- Even at low levels, alcohol disrupts performance and can interfere with complex activities. It generally causes feelings of happiness and reduces the ability of aversive events to control behavior. Higher doses cause loud, vigorous behavior, and even higher doses cause loss of consciousness and, finally, death.

- Alcohol can cause memory disruption in the form of either a grayout (fragmentary memory loss due to dissociation) or an en bloc blackout (complete loss of the ability to form new memories while intoxicated).

- Increasing BAL is associated with an increased risk of being involved in an automobile accident, and the risk is much higher in young and inexperienced drivers.

- The discriminative stimulus effects are similar to the barbiturates and can be blocked by a serotonin receptor blocker.

- Tolerance develops to the effects of alcohol through many different processes. Alcohol causes physical dependence, and the withdrawal symptoms of the late major type (delirium tremens) can be quite severe and may even cause death if not treated.

- Both humans and nonhumans self-administer alcohol in a similar pattern involving binges and erratic periods of abstinence. Consumption is influenced by culture, gender, age, and availability.

- There are many explanations of excessive drinking or alcoholism. The disease model claims that alcoholism is a disease and that alcoholics are different from nonalcoholics even before they start drinking. In addition, because of "loss of control," alcoholics can never drink in moderation and are unable to control their drinking.

- There is little evidence to support alcohol loss of control in alcoholics, and only small differences have been found between those with a positive family history of alcoholism and those with a negative family history.

- Alcohol can cause physical dependence. It also causes a hangover.

- Alcohol has many harmful effects, including death by respiratory suppression in high doses. Acute effects can cause both industrial and automobile accidents, and continuous use can cause cirrhosis of the liver, Wernicke–Korsakoff syndrome, and various types of cancer and heart disease. In addition, if taken during pregnancy, alcohol can cause various malformations of the fetus known as fetal alcohol syndrome (FAS) or alcohol-related neuro-behavioral disorder (ARND).

- Low to moderate levels of alcohol consumption can have health benefits, including reduction in the risk of cardiac disease and stroke.

- Excessive alcohol use, or alcoholism, can be treated, but success rates are low.

- There are numerous treatments for alcoholism, including Alcoholics Anonymous, treatment with other drugs including disulfiram and SSRIs, community reinforcement, and relapse prevention training.

7

Tranquilizers and Sedative-Hypnotics

INTRODUCTION

The term *tranquilizer* or *anxiolytic* is applied to drugs that are used therapeutically to treat agitation and anxiety. The term *sedative-hypnotic* refers to drugs that are used to sedate and aid sleep (i.e., sleeping pills). There are several categories of drugs that have these effects. The most common in use today is the *benzodiazepines*. Before that, the *barbiturates* were widely used. A number of other substances that are neither barbiturates or benzodiazepines have also been used as sedative-hypnotics or tranquilizers. They include older drugs like *meprobamate* (Miltown) and *methaqualone* (Quaalude), which were widely used in the 1960s but are no longer used today, and newer drugs like *abecarnil* and *alpidem* and a class of drugs sometimes called the *Z drugs*, which include *zolpidem*, *zopiclone*, and *zaleplon*, which were introduced in the late 1990s. The hypnotic, sedating, and tranquilizing properties of all these drugs arise from the same neural mechanism. For the most part the medical use of the drug (i.e., whether it is prescribed as a tranquilizer or as a sedative-hypnotic) is determined by other factors, such as the speed of action and the duration of effect. Fast-acting drugs with short duration of action are useful as sedative-hypnotics, and longer-acting drugs are used as tranquilizers. The newer drugs and the Z drugs, however, are now able to target specific symptoms.

Tranquilizers and sedative-hypnotics share some properties with alcohol (Chapter 6), with inhaled solvents, and with other substances generally called depressants or general anesthetics (see Chapter 8) Although they have other effects on neuronal function, all these drugs facilitate the functioning of the inhibitory transmitter *gamma-aminobutyric acid* (GABA).

GHB (gamma-hydroxybutyrate) is a peculiar substance that occurs naturally in the body and shares many properties and could well have been included with the sedative-hypnotics but also has many unique properties that have caused some to suggest that it is a unique pharmacological entity. For this reason it will be discussed in Chapter 16.

HISTORY

Before the development of the barbiturates, physicians of the nineteenth century had only a few substances that they could use to calm people down or aid sleep. These were alcohol (usually in the form of brandy), bromides, chloral hydrate (otherwise known as chloral), and opium. For the most part, these were marginally effective and had unwanted side effects. Barbiturates were first synthesized in 1864, and for over 100 years they were one of the most useful drugs in the physician's black bag for the treatment of anxiety and insomnia, replacing brandy, bromides, and opium as tranquilizers.

Over the years, thousands of different barbiturates were synthesized, and about 50 have been marketed. Compounds containing barbiturates have been recommended in the treatment of no less than 77 different disorders ranging from arthritis to bed-wetting (Reinisch & Sanders, 1982). By the 1990s, however, benzodiazepines had replaced barbiturates in almost all their medical uses, with only a few exceptions. Phenobarbital is still prescribed to prevent seizures. Butalbital is also used in combination with drugs such as aspirin, caffeine, acetaminophen, and codeine in analgesic preparations such as Fioronal and Fioricet for headaches, and some very short-acting barbiturates are used as anesthetics. The use of barbiturates as sedative-hypnotics has not entirely disappeared. In 1995, phenobarbital appeared in 8.2 percent of sedative-hypnotics sold worldwide (J. Woods & Winger, 1997).

In the 1960s, barbiturates were sold illicitly on the streets as downers. Almost all illicit barbiturates were diverted from medical use, and as the medical use of barbiturates has declined, so has their availability and, consequently, their illicit use.

The first synthesis of the benzodiazepines was a combination of good science and good luck. In the 1930s, Leo Sternback synthesized several substances known as *heptoxdiazines* while working on the chemistry of dyes in Krakow, Poland. But not until the 1950s, when he was working at the Hoffman–La Roche laboratories in the United States, did Sternback and his colleagues do further work with these compounds. Their research was stimulated by an attempt to find a new, safe drug that could be used as a tranquilizer. Their approach was simple; they would pick a class of biologically

active chemicals that was simple to make and easy to change and that no one else had studied. They would then make and test as many derivatives as they could, hoping to discover a useful drug by chance. The heptoxdiazines fitted this description perfectly, so the researchers started to synthesize all sorts of new variations and had them tested for their biological properties.

None of the derivatives they tested had any biological effect. However, one of these derivatives, identified as Ro 5-0690, was not tested at that time; it was assumed to be inactive and was set aside. Not until 1957, after it had been taking up needed space on the worktable for two years, was it finally sent for testing. In fact, one story has it that the reason it was sent for testing rather than being thrown out was that it had "such pretty crystals." To everyone's surprise, the pretty crystals were found to have sedative properties (Sternback, 1973). The researchers finally decided to call Ro 5-0690 *chlordiazepoxide*. After further testing, it was marketed as Librium (Greenblatt & Shader, 1974).

In the years that followed, many more drugs of this type, known as the benzodiazepines, were synthesized and tested, and a number were eventually marketed. One of these was *diazepam* (Valium), which was also developed by Sternback and marketed in 1963. Although all the benzodiazepines have very similar effects in humans, they differ in their relative potency. Some are more potent as sedative-hypnotics, and some are more potent as tranquilizers, and they also differ in their speed of action. Apart from diazepam and chlordiazepoxide, common anxiolytic benzodiazepines are *lorazepam* (Ativan), *chlorazepate* (Trannxene), *alprazolam* (Xanax), and *oxazepam* (Serax). Sedative-hypnotic benzodiazepines are *nitrazepam* (Mogadon), *flurazepam* (Dalmane), *triazolam* (Halcion), and *temazepam* (Restoril). *Clonazepam* (Rivotril) is used as an anticonvulsant.

One benzodiazepine is of particular interest. That is *flunitrazepam* (Rohypnol). Although recreational use of benzodiazepines is not extensive, as was the use of barbiturates, this benzodiazepine is reported to be widely used on the street. The World Health Organization reported in 1995 that illicit use of flunitrazepam was higher than for any other benzodiazepine. As a result, the UN Commission on Narcotic Drugs increased restrictions on flunitrazepam (Mintzer & Griffiths, 1998).

Rohypnol is sold in Europe, Mexico, and South America, but it has never been marketed in the United States. It is smuggled from Mexico to the southern states, and by 1995 it was being used quite extensively by young people, especially in conjunction with alcohol. It is known as *Mexican Valium, roaches*, or *roofies*. Flunitrazepam now has the status of a club drug—a drug used at dance clubs, bars, and all-night dance parties, or *raves*. It also has the reputation of being a *date rape drug* that is slipped into the drinks of young women who are then sexually assaulted.

Drugs that are neither barbiturates or benzodiazepines have been developed. Methaqualone and meprobamate were marketed in the 1960s, but they were widely abused and are no longer used. Several newer ones have also been developed. These are the so-called Z drugs: *zopiclone* (Systemic or Imovane), *zolpidem* (Ambiem), *zaleplon* (Sonata), and *abecarnil* (J. Woods, Katz, & Winger, 1995).

Recent trends in prescribing show an overall decrease in prescriptions for benzodiazepines since a peak in the mid-1970s (Griffiths & Sannerud, 1987, p. 1536). There has been an increase in the use of short-acting benzodiazepines that do not have active metabolites and a decrease in the use of long-acting benzodiazepines such as diazepam that have active metabolites (Busto, Isaac, & Adrian, 1986). Although the use of benzodiazepines as tranquilizers is declining, until recently their use as sedative-hypnotics has remained stable (J. Woods et al., 1995). Since their introduction in their late 1990s, the Z drugs have been slowly replacing the benzodiazepines in the treatment of insomnia, especially in North America.

ROUTE OF ADMINISTRATION AND ABSORPTION

Both barbiturates and benzodiazepines are weak acids. Benzodiazepines have a pKa of about 3.5 to 5.0, and they are readily absorbed from digestive

and parenteral administration. The choice of route depends on the purpose for which the drug is given. If a rapid effect is needed, an intravenous injection would be indicated, but if a long-term effect is wanted, as when diazepam is used to treat anxiety, the oral route is appropriate. Absorption from the digestive system is more rapid than absorption from an intramuscular site, probably because the drugs tend to bind to protein and do so more readily at an injection site than in the digestive system. There are reports that flunitrazepam can cause very rapid effects when the tablets are ground into a powder and administered intranasally (J. Woods & Winger, 1997, p. 3S).

There is a range of lipid solubility in the benzodiazepines and a resulting difference in the speed of absorption of different benzodiazepines. Diazepam, one of the fastest-acting benzodiazepines, reaches a peak in about 30 to 60 minutes. Other fast-acting benzodiazepines are midazolam, temazepam, flunitrazepam, and triazepam. Oxazepam is slower acting and may take several hours to peak (Busto, Bendayan, & Sellers, 1989). Among individuals, there is a great deal of variability in the rate of absorption and the peak blood levels obtained after a given dose of a benzodiazepine. A dose of diazepam given to one person may cause a blood level 20 times higher than the same dose in another person (Garattini, Mussini, Marcucci, & Guaitani, 1973).

Absorption from the digestive system may be greatly increased by the drinking of alcohol. After small amounts of alcohol are ingested, the blood levels of diazepam can be nearly doubled (Laisi, Linnoila, Seppala, & Mattila, 1979).

The Z drugs are readily absorbed from the digestive system and reach a peak in about an hour. There is considerable first-pass metabolism of zaleplon.

DISTRIBUTION AND EXCRETION

Once a barbiturate or benzodiazepine is in the blood, distribution and, consequently, duration of action are determined by the lipid solubility of the particular drug. The highly lipid-soluble drugs pass through the blood–brain barrier quickly, and their effects on the brain are seen quickly. However, the effects can disappear rapidly because their levels in the brain soon fall. This decrease occurs because highly lipid-soluble drugs become redistributed to areas of the body that contain fat. From these fat deposits, the drug is released slowly into the blood and metabolized by the liver. Thus, fast-acting drugs also tend to have a short duration of action, even though they may still circulate at low levels in the blood for a period of time (Busto et al., 1989; Mark, 1971). The redistribution of the benzodiazepines in body fat creates a two-phase excretion curve. During the first phase, there is a rather rapid drop in blood level as the drug is redistributed. This phase has a half-life of 2 to 10 hours. In the second phase, the blood level drops more slowly because the drug remaining in the blood is being metabolized, and as it is metabolized, it is being replaced by the drug, which is slowly being released from body fat. The half-life during this phase varies from 27 to 48 hours, although the half-life of some benzodiazepines, such as oxazepam and triazolam, is much faster, about 1 to 5 hours (Wilder & Bruni, 1981, p. 109). There is considerable variability in the half-lives of benzodiazepines from individual to individual.

The duration of the effect of the benzodiazepines, however, is not always determined by their half-lives because the metabolites of some of the older benzodiazepines (e.g., diazepam, chlordiazepoxide, and flurazepam) are also active. These metabolites have even longer half-lives and may have somewhat different effects. In the development of newer benzodiazepines, consideration has been given to the elimination of these active metabolites. The newer benzodiazepines—oxazepam, triazolam, alprazolam, clonazepam, and lorazepam—do not have any active metabolites (American Society of Hospital Pharmacists, 1987, p. 1141; Rickels, 1983).

The benzodiazepines and barbiturates also cross the placental barrier easily, and they appear in the milk of nursing mothers.

The metabolism of benzodiazepines can be slowed by the consumption of alcohol. It has been shown that the half-life of chlordiazepoxide is increased by 60 percent after a small drink of alcohol (Desmond, Patwardham, Schenker, & Hoyumpa, 1980).

Zaleplon has an extremely short half-life of about 1 hour (Julien, 2001).

NEUROPHYSIOLOGY

The neurophysiology of the barbiturates and benzodiazepines is fairly well understood. Their effects are mediated primarily by their ability to modify the effects of the inhibitory transmitter GABA (see Chapter 4). GABA has two types of receptor sites: $GABA_A$ and $GABA_B$ receptors.

The $GABA_A$ receptor site is directly linked to a gated chloride ion channel in a large protein molecule known as the *GABA receptor–chloride ionophore complex*. (An *ionophore* is another name for an ion channel.) When GABA is released at a synapse, its interaction with the $GABA_A$ receptor directly opens the chloride channel (Haefely, 1983; Paul, 2000). The open channel permits negatively charged chloride ions to flow in and out of the cell in response to changes in the membrane potential caused by excitatory neurotransmitters, and this tends to stabilize the membrane, making the neuron more difficult to fire. In this way, GABA acts as an inhibitory transmitter (see Figure 7-1). GABA receptors are found all over the central nervous system (CNS), both at synapses and elsewhere, and seem to maintain a general level of activity that creates an *inhibitory tone* in the brain, believed to be responsible for preventing too much excitation to develop that could result in seizures.

The barbiturates and benzodiazepines do not modify the effects of GABA by altering the levels of GABA or by interacting directly with its receptor site. Instead, the barbiturates and the benzodiazepines each have their own receptor sites on the GABA receptor–chloride ionophore complex. When barbiturates and benzodiazepines activate their receptors, there is an increase in the ability of GABA occupying the $GABA_A$ receptor to open the chloride ionophore. Drugs that do this are described as *positive GABA$_A$ modulators*. Some drugs like abecarnil and alpidem have a low affinity for the benzodiazepine receptor and have a weak effect. Others, like diazepam, flunitrazepam, midazolam, and triazolam, have a high affinity and a correspondingly greater effect.

The benzodiazepines have the ability only to make GABA more effective; they do not alter the operation of the ionophore directly. At low doses, the barbiturates have the same effect, but at higher doses, the barbiturates seem able to open the ionophore by themselves. Therefore, there is an upper limit on the inhibitory effect of the benzodiazepines on the brain but no upper limit on the inhibitory effect of the barbiturates. High doses of benzodiazepines can cause extreme sedation and grogginess but are not life threatening. High doses of barbiturates produce unconsciousness and anesthesia (Richards, 1980), and they depress breathing by inhibiting the autonomic centers on the brain stem. The respiratory depression caused by barbiturates is similar to the depression caused by alcohol. Barbiturates cause slow, shallow breathing and, at high doses, may prevent breathing altogether. This depression of breathing and a similar depression of the cardiovascular system are the main cause of death in cases of barbiturate overdose. The difference in the potential to cause lethal overdose is the major difference between the barbiturates and the benzodiazepines and is the reason why the benzodiazepines have replaced the barbiturates as tranquilizers and sedative-hypnotics.

As you can see from Figure 7-1, the GABA$_A$ receptor–ionophore is a large complex molecule. It is made up of five subunits that are proteins, or chains of amino acids folded into a complex unit. Each of these subunits is created by a different gene, and there is considerable variability in the composition of each subunit. There are three main subunits designated alpha (α), beta (β), and gamma (γ). There are six varieties of alpha (α_{1-6}), and three each of beta and gamma. These are put together in a variety of combinations, making

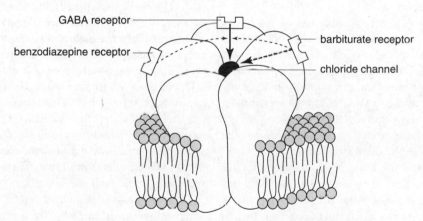

Figure 7-1 A schematic drawing of the GABA receptor–chloride ionophore complex. Three receptor sites are shown: a GABA receptor, a barbiturate receptor, and a benzodiazepine receptor. The solid arrow indicates that the GABA receptor can open the ionophore when it is occupied. The dark, dashed arrow indicates that the barbiturate receptor can also open the ionophore but only at high doses. The light, dashed arrows indicate that both the benzodiazepine and the barbiturate receptors can enhance the ability of GABA to open the ionophore. When the ionophore is open, it permits chloride ions (Cl$^-$) to pass in and out of the cell and makes it more difficult for excitatory neurotransmitters to depolarize the membrane.

many different types of $GABA_A$ receptors possible. What is important is that different configurations of the receptor are associated with different parts of the brain and mediate different functions. For example, the α_1 subtype exists in systems that seem to be responsible for sedation, and the α_2 subunit exists in systems that are responsible for the anxiolytic effects (Möhler, Fritschy, Crestani, Hensch, & Rudolph, 2004).

For the most part, different benzodiazepines affect these receptor subtypes the same way, but the newer Z-type drugs act differently at each subtype. Both zolpidem and zaleplon appear to be effective at the receptors with an α_1 subunit but have a lower affinity for receptors with the α_2 subunit. Therefore, they can act as sedatives without involving the antianxiety mechanisms. Conversely, new drugs are being developed that reduce anxiety without making a person sleepy or interfering with driving by acting at different receptor subtypes (Möhler, Fritschy, & Rudolph, 2002; Rush, 1998). As a result of this line of research many new drugs with selective actions and few side effects are being developed

The $GABA_B$ receptor also has an inhibitory effect but uses a completely different mechanism. It releases a second messenger that opens a potassium channel. The $GABA_A$ receptors are in operation all the time and maintain an inhibitory tone in the brain, whereas the $GABA_B$ receptors appear to be in operation only some of the time. They are not affected by barbiturates and benzodiazepines but may be affected by GHB (see Chapter 16).

Why would the brain have receptor sites for benzodiazepines? It is likely that the body has endogenous substances that use these receptors. A search is under way to find an endogenous benzodiazepine. It is thought that such a substance might be responsible for modulating anxiety. In fact, it has been demonstrated that there is an enhancement in the receptivity of benzodiazepine receptors immediately following periods of stress in laboratory animals. Such an increase would make an endogenous benzodiazepine more effective and increase inhibitory tone, making the organism less sensitive to the physiological and possibly cognitive effects of stress and distress (Hommer, Skolnick, & Paul, 1987, p. 982; Martin & Acre, 1996).

An endogenous benzodiazepine, however, might have exactly the opposite effect. We know that there are some benzodiazepines that work as *inverse agonists* or *negative GABA_A modulators*. They have the opposite of the usual benzodiazepine effect; they decrease GABA's ability to open the ionophore, and they increase feelings of tension, anxiety, and panic (Carvalho, de Greckshk, Chapouthier, & Rossier, 1983; Squires & Braestrup, 1977; Stephenson, 1987). Likewise, there are barbiturate inverse agonists that have this effect and induce seizures (Ticku & Olsen, 1978).

Even though many of the effects of the benzodiazepines and barbiturates can be understood in terms of their modulation of the effects of GABA, their neurophysiology is complex, and other transmitters and neuromodulators may be involved. For example, the benzodiazepines also enhance the effects of adenosine, another inhibitory transmitter, by blocking its reuptake and permitting its accumulation (Phillis & O'Regan, 1988), an effect directly opposite to that of caffeine (see Chapter 10).

Interestingly, the barbiturates and the benzodiazepines are reported to decrease dopamine activity in the nucleus accumbens, exactly the opposite effect of most reinforcing drugs. If this is so, how can they be reinforcing? The effect of dopamine on the neurons of the nucleus accumbens is known to be inhibitory; when dopamine is released, the cells in the nucleus accumbens are inhibited, and so is their output. There are GABA receptors in the nucleus accumbens, and GABA is also inhibitory, so it is likely that GABA has the same effect on these cells that dopamine does, that is, it causes reinforcement (Wise, 1998).

EFFECTS ON THE BODY

Apart from a depression in respiration and a slight drop in blood pressure, barbiturates have few physiological effects at low doses. Unlike the barbiturates, the benzodiazepines do not produce significant depression of respiration in healthy individuals, even at high doses. They also have little effect on heart rate or blood pressure. The benzodiazepines are also reported to increase appetite, and weight gain is sometimes a consequence of continuous use (Greenblatt & Shader, 1974, p. 5; Haney, Comer, Fischman, & Foltin, 1997).

Outside the CNS, the benzodiazepines have very few effects. They have muscle-relaxant properties that are clinically useful and appear to result from the effect of the drug on the brain rather than on the muscles themselves. These properties have made benzodiazepines useful in treating increased muscle tone caused by multiple sclerosis, Parkinson's disease, and brain injury. The benzodiazepines are also reported to be useful in the treatment of backache and muscle strain.

The benzodiazepines are anticonvulsants, and they are useful in treating petit mal seizures and infantile spasms; however, for long-term control of epilepsy, the benzodiazepines are not likely to replace the barbiturate and barbiturate-like drugs now commonly in use.

Effects on Sleep

The benzodiazepines are effective in treating insomnia; flurazepam is widely used in the United States, and nitrazepam is used in Europe for this purpose. Zolpidem is also one of the most widely used hypnotics. These drugs decrease latency to fall asleep, decrease wakefulness during the night, and increase total sleeping time. Unfortunately, benzodiazepines, like the barbiturates, decrease the percentage of time spent in REM as well as in stage 3 and stage 4 sleep. This effect diminishes with continued use, and when the drug is discontinued, after as little as 2 weeks, there is a withdrawal rebound (Griffiths & Sannerud, 1987, p. 1539). With nitrazepam, this rebound reaches a peak about 10 days after the drug is stopped and may last for several weeks. With the increase in REM comes an increase in rebound insomnia, that is, bizarre dreaming, restlessness, and wakefulness during the night (Oswald, Lewis, Tangey, Firth, & Haider, 1973).

The desire to resume taking the drug to get a good night's sleep increases accordingly.

This rebound appears to be a withdrawal symptom that can be eliminated simply by returning to the use of the sleeping pill. As a result, once people have started to use sedative-hypnotics for sleep, they find it difficult to stop. After periods as short as a week, they find that they cannot get a good night's sleep without their pill, and every time they try to stop, the same thing happens. They do not realize that they must go through a period, sometimes as long as a month, of poor sleep before they can sleep well without their pill.

Zopiclone is reported to have little if any rebound effect after short-term use (Hajak, 1999), and no withdrawal or rebound effects were found with zaleplon after 2 to 4 weeks of use (Elie et al., 1999). A number of studies have failed to demonstrate any rebound insomnia after flunitrazepam (J. Woods & Winger, 1997). Zaleplon, because it is relatively fast acting, reduces the time to go to sleep but does not increase total sleeping time (Elie et al., 1999).

EFFECTS ON BEHAVIOR AND PERFORMANCE OF HUMANS

Subjective Effects

Many (although not all) studies of the subjective effect of the benzodiazepines have shown that subjects report euphoria and liking along with sedation and fatigue (de Wit & Griffiths, 1991; Evans, Griffiths, & de Wit, 1996). In one experiment, diazepam and a placebo were given to volunteers who were asked to fill out a Profile of Mood States form at that time and at 1, 3, and 6 hours later. Compared with a placebo, doses of 5 and 10 mg of diazepam caused a decrease in feelings of arousal and vigor and an increase in fatigue and confusion. These effects were seen only at 1 hour with the low dose but were generally seen for up to 3 hours with the high dose. These feelings were considered unpleasant by the subjects, few of whom voluntarily took the drug again when they were given the chance (Johanson & Uhlenhuth,

1980). Positive effects and increased liking scores for benzodiazepines are more likely to be seen in people with a history of sedative or alcohol abuse, moderate alcohol use, or opiate use, including those on methadone maintenance. (Evans et al., 1996). Flunitrazepam seems more likely than other benzodiazepines to increase "liking" and "take again" scores in normal healthy volunteers and in people on methadone maintenance (Garek et al., 2001; Mintzer & Griffiths, 1998).

Benzodiazepines are effective anxiolytics or tranquilizers (i.e., they reduce anxiety in anxious individuals). This is one of their major clinical uses, but they are effective in only 60 to 70 percent of cases. There appear to be a number of factors that can modify their clinical effectiveness. These include current and past exposure to various forms of stress (Haller, 2001).

EFFECTS ON PERFORMANCE

The benzodiazepines and barbiturates increase the critical frequency of fusion threshold, indicating a deficit in visual functioning. Some studies have also reported that the auditory flicker fusion threshold is diminished by the benzodiazepines (J. R. Vogel, 1979).

The benzodiazepines can have severe effects on memory; they cause anterograde amnesia, a loss of memory for events that occurred while under the influence of the drug. These problems occur at low doses that do not cause sedation or impair alertness or motor functioning. Memory problems are sometimes observed in patient populations taking benzodiazepines for anxiety or insomnia. Memory effects do not seem to show tolerance and may persist for months after the drug is discontinued. One reason why flunitrazepam is reputedly used as a date rape drug is because the victim often has trouble remembering incidents surrounding the assault.

Psychologists who study memory sometimes use benzodiazepines as a tool to explore memory processes (Pompéia, Gorenstein, & Curran, 1996). It is often observed that even at low doses, benzodiazepines cause deficits in *explicit memory* but not in *implicit memory*. That is, if people are asked to *use* information they acquired after taking a benzodiazepine (implicit memory), they can do that. But if they are explicitly asked to *recall* that information (explicit memory), they have trouble. There is some evidence that this is a result of the fact that there are usually no retrieval cues in explicit memory tasks, but there are such cues in implicit memory tasks. In any case, it has been shown that benzodiazepine-caused memory problems can often be overcome by providing recall cues and reminders of what happened (Pompéia et al., 1966) in a manner similar to alcohol grayout (see Chapter 6).

Even though the benzodiazepines have a clear effect on the ability to acquire new information, they do not appear to alter the ability to recall information acquired prior to their administration (Taylor & Tinklenberg, 1987).

At higher blood levels, sedation occurs that can be detected by tests such as the digit symbol substitution test (which shows a decrease in working or short-term memory), by tests of attention, and by psychomotor performance tests such as reaction time. These effects can be reversed by administration of the benzodiazepine receptor blocker flumazinil (Bareggi, Ferini-Strambi, Pirola, & Smirne, 1998).

Attention and psychomotor effects may start as soon as 1 hour after oral administration for diazepam or 3 hours for lorazepam. The duration of the impairment will vary, depending on the dose, but can last 24 hours. The time course of the impairment does not reflect the concentration in the blood, and shorter-acting benzodiazepines may actually cause a longer-lasting effect than long-acting benzodiazepines. The degree of impairment is not always evident to the individual, who will frequently report that he or she feels fine (Roache & Griffiths, 1987; Taylor & Tinklenberg, 1987).

It should also be remembered that the benzodiazepines can actually improve performance in some people. Improvements were usually seen in individuals who were highly anxious or were in difficult and stressful situations where anxiety might be expected to interfere with performance (Janke & DeBus, 1968).

Residual Effects

Benzodiazepines are widely used at bedtime to induce sleep. Many have such a long half-life that they are still in the body for some time the next day. Because sleeping pill users may drive to work, operate equipment, and engage in other activities that might be impaired by the drug, it is important to determine whether these residual levels of the drug can affect performance the next day. Many but not all studies show next-day residual effects of benzodiazepines. Not surprisingly, higher doses are more likely to have residual effects than lower doses (J. Woods & Winger, 1997). In an attempt to reduce these residual effects, the benzodiazepines with short-elimination half-lives are now being more widely used as hypnotics.

The residual effects of benzodiazepines also greatly enhance the effect of a single drink of alcohol (Saario & Linnoila, 1976).

Among the newer sedative-hypnotics, no residual effects on reaction time, driving, and memory were seen with zopiclone even when it was administered 4 to 6 hours before in the middle of the night (Verster et al., 2002).

Effects on Driving

Extensive research by a group at the University of Helsinki in Finland has also shown that a 10-mg dose of diazepam will increase collisions in a simulated driving task. This impairment is also greatly increased by alcohol (Linnoila & Hakkinen, 1974). In general, evidence shows that there is a considerable risk of an automobile accident in first-time users of benzodiazepines. The risk is probably amplified by the fact that the individual is often not able to detect the impairment (Taylor & Tinklenberg, 1987). Although some tolerance may develop to this effect, driving impairments and next-day sleepiness have been seen with lorazepam after 7 days of use (van Laar, Volkerts, & Verbaten, 2001). Driving impairments in patients receiving diazepam for anxiety are still apparent 3 weeks into treatment (van Laar, Volkerts, & Willigenberg, 1992).

Many studies show that the benzodiazepines may have residual effects on driving the next morning. One study showed that flunitrazepam and to a lesser extent zopiclone had effects of driving at 9:00 A.M. the day after being used, but zolpidem did not. By 11:00 A.M., flunitrazepam still has effects, but neither zolpidem nor zopiclone did (Bocca et al., 1999). Similar residual effects have been reported with flurazepam but not lormetrazepam, which does not have any active metabolites (Brookhuis, Volkerts, & O'Hanlon, 1990).

In spite of the foregoing evidence, the presence of benzodiazepines in the blood was not found to be a contributing factor in a large sample of road accidents after the effects of alcohol had been accounted for (Benzodiazepine/Driving Collaborative Group, 1993).

EFFECTS ON THE BEHAVIOR OF NONHUMANS

Unconditioned Behavior

One of the first effects noticed in the early screening tests of the benzodiazepines was a "taming" effect. The research animals became more placid, and fighting behavior induced by electric shocks was reduced. It has since been demonstrated that chlordiazepoxide and diazepam are effective in reducing only defensive aggression, that is, aggression that is induced by an attack or provoked by a painful stimulus like a shock. Unprovoked aggression or attack behavior does not seem to be altered at lower-than-toxic doses (DiMascio, 1973). It has been suggested that this change in provoked aggression is a result of the ability of the benzodiazepines to diminish anxiety. Defensive aggression is presumably a result of anxiety or fear caused by being attacked. Attack itself is not motivated by anxiety (Hoffmeister & Wuttke, 1969).

Conditioned Behavior

Benzodiazepines show the classical profile of drugs that are therapeutically useful in the treatment of anxiety. Heise and Boff (1962) showed that doses of benzodiazepine that decrease avoidance responses are one-fourth to one-sixth the size of doses that have any effect on escape responding.

The benzodiazepines also have a spectacular effect on behavior suppressed by punishment: They cause an increase in punished behavior at doses that decrease or have little effect on positively motivated behavior (Hanson, Witloslawski, & Campbell, 1967; Kleven & Koek, 1999). Animals injected with barbiturates continue to make responses that are punished by electric shock at normal, unpunished rates. The reason for their unchanged behavior does not appear to be that they no longer feel the shock; they jump and flinch when it happens, but they nevertheless continue to make the punished response.

DISCRIMINATIVE STIMULUS PROPERTIES

Laboratory animals can be readily trained to discriminate all benzodiazepines from saline. Flunitrazepam and tiazolam appear to be more potent than other benzodiazepines (J. Woods & Winger, 1997).

Animals trained to discriminate a benzodiazepine will generalize the response to other benzodiazepines and barbiturates but not to the antipsychotics or ketamine. The discriminative stimulus effects of benzodiazepines cannot be blocked by stimulant drugs such as amphetamine, caffeine, cocaine, and the hallucinogen mescaline, but they can be blocked by drugs that block the benzodiazepine receptor (Colpaert, 1977; Lelas, Gerak, & France, 1999).

Although the benzodiazepine cue will generalize to the barbiturates, it has been shown that rats can be trained to discriminate chlordiazepoxide from barbiturates and alcohol but not from diazepam. This finding indicates qualitative differences between the subjective effects of all these drugs, even though they are similar enough to generalize to each other (Barry, McGuire, & Krimmer, 1982). It has been shown, however, that alcohol will potentiate the discriminative effects of flunitrazepam (Schechter, 1998). There is some evidence from rats that zolpidem may have slightly different discriminative effects from the benzodiazepines since there is only partial generalization

to many benzodiazepines, and no generalization in rats trained to discriminate alcohol occurs (Rush, 1998).

TOLERANCE

Acute Tolerance

Tolerance to the effects of benzodiazepines can develop during a single administration. Such tolerance seems to be limited in humans to the effect of benzodiazepines on behavior such as digit symbol substitution and tracking and may not be seen in physiological effects. It has also been shown that the acute tolerance can develop to the motor-impairing effects of midazolam (Coldwell et al., 1998). Similarly, studies have shown that phenobarbital has a more powerful effect at a given concentration as the blood level is rising than when the blood level is descending (Ellenwood et al., 1981).

Chronic Tolerance

With repeated administration, benzodiazepines become less and less effective in their ability to modulate the effects of GABA. There is some disagreement, however, whether this is a result of a reduction in the capacity of the benzodiazepines to alter the effect of GABA or whether the sensitivity of the GABA receptor to GABA is reduced. In any case, many behavioral effects of the benzodiazepines show tolerance (A. Hutchison, Smith, & Darlington, 1996).

In laboratory animals, tolerance develops to many of the behavioral effects of the benzodiazepines, including their locomotor, ataxic, muscle relaxant, and anticonvulsant effects. Tolerance to the disruptive effects of chlordiazepoxide on avoidance develops in rats when the drug is administered every day for 6 weeks (Masuki & Iwamoto, 1966). Tolerance to the anxiety-reducing effects in humans is variable and appears to be related to the dosing regime and the specific benzodiazepine used (A. Hutchison et al., 1996).

Tolerance also develops slowly to the anticonvulsant effects of the benzodiazepines as well as to the drowsiness that is seen sometimes at therapeutic doses. Although there are some data to suggest that tolerance does not develop to the hypnotic effects of benzodiazepines and to zolpidem in particular, recent work has shown that tolerance to the sleep-producing effects of these drugs develops after about 4 weeks (Rush, 1998). As mentioned earlier, there has been a tendency to prescribe short-acting benzodiazepines as sleeping pills to avoid next-day residual effects, but it seems that these benzodiazepines have a tendency to develop tolerance faster than the longer-acting benzodiazepines. In addition, they also seem to cause more frequent and more intense rebound insomnia. Among the short-acting hypnotics, however, there are differences. Triazolam appears to cause more rebound insomnia than either midazolam or zolpidem (Soldatos, Dikeos, & Whitehead, 1999).

Cross-Tolerance

There is cross-tolerance between the benzodiazepines and other depressant drugs. The drowsiness sometimes produced by higher therapeutic doses of the benzodiazepines is less often seen in people who have a recent history of barbiturate and alcohol abuse (Greenblatt & Shader, 1974, p. 232).

One study has shown that tolerance develops after only one exposure to the motor-impairing effect of alcohol, barbiturates, and benzodiazepines in mice. Animals that are tolerant to the barbiturates are cross-tolerant to alcohol and the benzodiazepines, and benzodiazepine-tolerant animals are tolerant to the effects of alcohol but show only weak or partial tolerance to the barbiturates. This suggests that the tolerance to barbiturates and benzodiazepines may arise from mechanisms that are similar but not identical (Khanna, Kalant, Chau, & Shah, 1998).

WITHDRAWAL

In laboratory animals, it has been shown that many benzodiazepines will cause physical dependence similar to barbiturates, and there is a cross-dependence between phenobarbital and many benzodiazepines; that is, withdrawal from phenobarbital

can be blocked by benzodiazepines (Gerak et al., 2001).

In humans, barbiturate withdrawal was first described in the medical literature in 1905, 2 years after the introduction of the first barbiturate into medical practice. In spite of this early report, the medical literature on barbiturate withdrawal was contradictory until the 1930s, when the weight of evidence could no longer be denied.

The benzodiazepines have been used widely in medical practice since the early 1960s, but, as with the barbiturates, years passed before their ability to cause physical dependence at therapeutic doses become widely acknowledged. It has been known for some time that withdrawal from relatively high doses of benzodiazepines taken for a long time will cause symptoms similar to those of withdrawal from barbiturates and alcohol: agitation, depression, abdominal pain, delirium tremens, insomnia, and seizures (Greenblatt & Shader, 1974; L. B. Hollister, Motzenbecker, & Degan, 1961) (see Chapter 6). Such dependence was believed to be rare, and most physicians were confident that there was no chance of physical dependence in their patients who received low therapeutic doses. An early study estimated that physical dependence occurred in only 1 percent of patients receiving diazepam for various emotional disorders (Bows, 1965). In fact, physical dependence was considered so unlikely that one group of researchers concluded, "It is time to dispel the myth that the unsuspecting housewife must be protected from the careless prescribing of dangerous drugs likely to produce lifelong addiction" (Rickels, Downing, & Winokur, 1978, p. 403). It soon became apparent, however, that therapeutic doses of benzodiazepines could cause rather unpleasant withdrawal symptoms and could lead to excessive use by some individuals.

In a study by Cosmo Hallstrom and Malcolm Lader (1981), four patients were gradually weaned from a high daily dose (average of 135 mg) of diazepam, and six patients were weaned from a low daily dose (average of 20 mg/day). After the drug was withdrawn, patients in both groups showed symptoms that included anxiety, sleep disturbances, intolerance to bright lights and loud noises, weight loss, unsteady gait, and numbness or tingling feelings. There were also changes in EEG activity and duplication of the increase in the electrical activity of the cortex that follows a loud noise (auditory evoked potential). These changes were similar in both the high- and the low-benzodiazepine subjects. Most of the symptoms peaked in intensity after 5 days and were gone within 2 weeks. Other researchers found similar withdrawal effects with therapeutic doses (Crawford, 1981; Petursson & Lader, 1981). Therapeutic doses were clearly causing problems.

David E. Smith of the Haight-Ashbury Free Medical Clinic and Donald R. Wesson (1983) suggested, on the basis of extensive clinical experience, that there are actually two types of withdrawal from benzodiazepines: *sedative-hypnotic withdrawal* and *low-dose withdrawal*. Each has a different set of symptoms (Griffiths & Sannerud, 1987). Each type has a different time course, and the occurrence of both types of withdrawal may overlap.

Sedative-Hypnotic Type

The sedative-hypnotic type of withdrawal involves tremors, delirium, cramps, and, possibly, convulsions. These are similar to the symptoms of barbiturate and alcohol withdrawal (described in Chapter 6), and they are the symptoms described in studies of the effects of high doses of benzodiazepines. Sedative-hypnotic withdrawal can be expected in people who have taken the drug in higher-than-recommended therapeutic doses for at least a month. Generally, the withdrawal symptoms start within a few days of abstinence and are gone within about 10 days. These withdrawal symptoms are more likely to be seen with benzodiazepines that have short half-lives because blood levels of these drugs fall more rapidly than blood levels of the longer-acting drugs.

Low-Dose Withdrawal

Low-dose benzodiazepine withdrawal symptoms are seen in some individuals after low therapeutic doses have been taken for longer than 6 months. They emerge more slowly and include anxiety, panic, irregular heartbeat, increased blood pressure, impairment of memory and concentration, feelings of unreality, muscle spasm, and a sensitivity to lights and sounds. Patients consistently report feeling as though they are walking on cotton wool, in a mist, or while wearing a veil over their eyes. There are frequent reports of perceptual difficulties, such as sloping walls or floors, and distortion of reality and self-perception: "Everything feels unreal or distant"; "I feel I'm not really me"; "My head feels like a huge balloon" (Ashton, 1984, p. 1138).

Very often these feelings come in cycles or waves; their frequency may vary with each symptom (Ashton, 1984). D. E. Smith and Wesson (1983) suggest that many symptoms cycle every 10 days. There are no consistent data on the duration of withdrawal. It has been reported to last as briefly as 2 weeks (Owen & Tyrer, 1983) and as long as a year (Ashton, 1984; D. E. Smith & Wesson, 1983). It is also not clear how many users of benzodiazepines at therapeutic doses have withdrawal symptoms; estimates range from 15 to 44 percent (Higgitt, Lader, & Fonagy, 1985). Certain people may be more susceptible than others.

As with most withdrawal symptoms, both the sedative-hypnotic type and the low-dose type of symptoms disappear quickly when the withdrawn drug is resumed. The low-dose withdrawal symptoms are especially sensitive to resumption of treatment and can be controlled with only a few milligrams of benzodiazepine.

The benzodiazepine receptor antagonist flumazenil can precipitate these low-dose symptoms in long-term users of benzodiazepines at therapeutic doses (the equivalent of 11.2 mg diazepam/day). The precipitated symptoms are similar to nonprecipitated symptoms except that they are more likely to include panic attacks. The magnitude of the withdrawal symptoms was correlated with the daily dose of benzodiazepine but was not related to the duration of use (Mintzer, Stoller, & Griffiths, 1999).

Individuals who have taken high doses of benzodiazepines for longer than 6 months may well

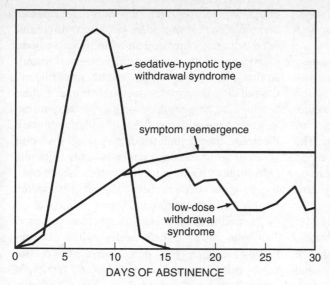

DAYS OF ABSTINENCE

Figure 7-2 Two types of withdrawal symptoms that may be seen after use of the benzodiazepines. The sedative-hypnotic type of withdrawal has severe symptoms but lasts only a few days. The low-dose benzodiazepine withdrawal symptoms are less intense but last much longer and seem to come and go in cycles. Also shown is the reemergence of symptoms that were there before the benzodiazepine was started and may reappear, causing more distress. (Adapted from D. E. Smith & Wesson, 1983, p. 89)

experience both types of withdrawal (see Figure 7-2). Note that other changes may occur when the benzodiazepines are stopped. These changes are due to symptom reemergence—the expression of symptoms that were present before the drug was started and were suppressed while the drug was being used. Reemerging symptoms are not really withdrawal symptoms, but their presence contributes to and complicates benzodiazepine withdrawal.

SELF-ADMINISTRATION IN HUMANS

Laboratory Studies

Choice Experiments. In a study that used normal human subjects and has been replicated several times, Johanson and Uhlenhuth (1980) gave people a choice between capsules of different colors. In an earlier part of the experiment, subjects had been given each of the capsules twice, so they knew what effect each colored capsule would have, even though they did not know what each capsule contained. In this experiment, the subjects chose capsules containing amphetamine much more often than a placebo, but they did not choose diazepam more often than a placebo (Griffiths, Bigelow, &

Henningfield, 1980). In a similar procedure, lorazepam was not chosen more often than a placebo; in fact, at higher doses, subjects chose a placebo more frequently than lorazepam or diazepam (de Wit, Johanson, & Uhlenhuth, 1984; Johanson & Uhlenhuth, 1980).

In a similar study, subjects were selected for high anxiety levels and given the choice between diazepam and a placebo. The highly anxious subjects reported that the capsules containing the diazepam reduced their anxiety, but they did not choose the diazepam capsule more frequently than a placebo. This finding suggests that relief from anxiety is not a motivation for benzodiazepine self-administration and that highly anxious people are not particularly at risk for benzodiazepine abuse (de Wit & Johanson, 1987), although other experiments have not found this latter effect (McCracken, de Wit, Uhlenhuth, & Johanson, 1990).

It has been demonstrated that moderate alcohol users and people with a history of sedative-hypnotic and alcohol abuse would choose benzodiazepines more frequently than a placebo (de Wit & Griffiths, 1991; Evans et al., 1996). In another study, people chose benzodiazepines when the choice was reliably followed by a task that required relaxation and earned them some money (K. Silverman, Mumford, & Griffiths, 1994).

Self-Administration Experiments. In a study conducted by Roland Griffiths and his colleagues (Griffiths, Bigelow, & Lieberson, 1979) at the Johns Hopkins University School of Medicine, pentobarbital was made available to male volunteers in an experimental hospital ward setting. The subjects, all of whom had a history of sedative drug abuse, could earn an administration of a drug by riding an exercise bicycle for 15 minutes. Five of the seven subjects continued to self-administer doses of 90 mg (a high level) of pentobarbital over the 10 days of the experiment, indicating that the drug acted as a positive reinforcer in humans. The same experiment also showed that subjects would not self-administer a placebo. Diazepam was self-administered by some subjects but not as frequently or as reliably as the barbiturate.

Outside the Laboratory

Outside the laboratory, humans show two patterns of benzodiazepine self-administration apart from use for legitimate medical conditions. In the legal or *iatrogenic* (physician-caused) pattern, the drug is prescribed for its effects as an aid to sleep or anxiety problems and is then continued unnecessarily, or the dose is escalated. In the street-use pattern, the drugs are obtained illegally and are taken at high doses. Of these two patterns, the first is more common.

Iatrogenic Use. Benzodiazepines are widely prescribed for a variety of symptoms. In many cases, the prescription and use are entirely consistent with appropriate treatment of medical conditions; however, the use of these drugs often changes in nature and may cause problems for the patient in a couple of different ways. As we have seen, if they are prescribed at too high a dose or for too long, they can cause physical dependence and require special treatment to avoid withdrawal when the drug is discontinued. In addition, a patient may become motivated by the reinforcing effects of the drug and may start exhibiting an inappropriate amount of behavior toward obtaining the drug in increasing amounts. Such a patient may learn exactly how to tailor a medical history so that a physician will predictably prescribe the desired drug or may go "doctor shopping" to find a compliant physician. Some patients may refuse to stop taking a drug and not consider alternative therapies, even though the drug is causing adverse side effects or the doctor recommends stopping. Other signs include a tendency to escalate doses, requests for early refills of the prescription because the prescription was "lost," and so on.

According to the popular stereotype, the typical Valium user is a well-educated, middle-class, suburban housewife who is denied personal or professional fulfillment by her husband and family. In fact, this does not appear to be the case. The Balter survey found that typical long-term users of anxiolytic benzodiazepines tended to be over 50, female, and suffering from substantial anxiety and some significant chronic health problem, such as heart disease or arthritis. This survey showed that, in general, most of the people who are receiving long-term benzodiazepines are receiving them for legitimate medical reasons—usually anxiety. Mellinger, Balter, and Uhlenhuth (1984) showed that at least half of long-term users suffered from high levels of psychic distress (anxiety).

Survey results indicate that large numbers of people who report severe symptoms of anxiety do not report the use of benzodiazepines. Given this information, some observers have concluded that benzodiazepines are underused rather than overused because there appear to be many people who could benefit from benzodiazepine use but are not receiving benzodiazepine treatment (Uhlenhuth, de Wit, Balter, Johanson, & Mellinger, 1988).

The extent of abuse or misuse of the benzodiazepines is not well understood. In one study, 176 people were referred to an outpatient clinic for assessment of benzodiazepine abuse. Fifty-six percent used benzodiazepines in clinically appropriate doses but did so longer than recommended by their physician. Others who took doses larger than prescribed did so in combination with other substances, such as alcohol, opiates, and cannabis (Juergens, 1993). In another study of 136 clinic clients who were found to be benzodiazepine abusers, less than 0.5 percent abused benzodiazepines alone. Most were well-educated Caucasian females more than 30 years old, and they received their benzodiazepines legally from a physician. Diazepam was the preferred benzodiazepine, particularly by primary cocaine and opiate users (Malcolm, Brady, Johnston, & Cunningham, 1993). The use of alprazolam and diazepam is a particular problem for many people on methadone maintenance (Sellers et al., 1993), although some research shows that heroin addicts and those on methadone maintenance have a distinct preference for flunitrazepam (J. Woods & Winger, 1997).

Because flunitrazepam appears to be different from other benzodiazepines in terms of its potential for recreational use, a number of researchers have attempted to discover if there is anything different about it that causes this effect. So far, no special property of flunitrazepam has become apparent (Mintzer & Griffiths, 1998; J. Woods & Winger, 1997).

Street Use. When used for recreational purposes, the benzodiazepines are most often taken in conjunction with some other drug. Often that drug is alcohol, but, surprisingly, it has been reported that 60 to 70 percent of patients on methadone maintenance use benzodiazepines (often to boost the effects of the methadone) (see Chapter 12). Laboratory data also support the claim that diazepam will enhance the subjective and physiological effects of opiates (Griffiths & Sannerud, 1987, p. 1537), although one study showed that diazepam did not alter the blood levels of methadone and vice versa (Preston, Griffiths, Clone, Darwin, & Gorodetzky, 1986).

National surveys in the United States indicated that the illicit use of sedatives and tranquilizers steadily declined from 1975 to 1992, but between 1992 and 2004, the number of students in grade 12 reporting the use of sedatives and tranquilizers within the past 30 days more than doubled, exceeding the levels of the early 1980s. In 2004,

3.1 percent of grade 12 students reported using a tranquilizer within the past 30 days (Johnston, O'Malley, Bachman, & Schulenberg, 2005).

SELF-ADMINISTRATION IN NONHUMANS

Like humans, rats and monkeys will readily work to give themselves infusions of all types of barbiturates, although it appears that the short-acting barbiturates may maintain higher rates of responding than the longer-acting barbiturates (Winger, Stitzer, & Woods, 1975). Response patterns maintained by barbiturates on fixed interval (FI) and fixed response (FR) schedules are similar to typical response patterns maintained by other reinforcers and takes place at doses that do not appear to cause physical dependence (Kelleher, 1976).

Early self-administration research with benzodiazepines had difficulty demonstrating that benzodiazepines were reinforcing, but later research has shown that laboratory animals will self-administer this class of drugs both intravenously and orally (B. S. Stewart, Lamaire, Roche, & Meisch, 1994). The problem may have been that early research used benzodiazepines with rather slow onset and long duration of action. (In general, drugs with these properties are difficult to establish as reinforcers.) Currently, there are many demonstrations of self-administration of both short- and long-acting benzodiazepines (Griffiths, Lamb, Sannerud, Ator, & Brady, 1991; Gerak et al., 2001), although short-acting benzodiazepines like triazolam maintain higher rates of responding than long-acting benzodiazepines (Griffiths, Lucas, Bradford, Brady, & Snell, 1981). Where comparisons have been made, the positive reinforcing effects of benzodiazepines are not as robust as those of barbiturates (Griffiths et al., 1991).

The reinforcing effects of the benzodiazepines, even long-acting ones, can be enhanced by a period of exposure to the drug or to other barbiturates or benzodiazepines. In one study, R. T. Harris, Glaghorn, and Schoolar (1968) gave rats a choice between drinking a solution of chlordiazepoxide and drinking pure water. The rats always chose water. Then, for 25 days, the rats had to drink the chlordiazepoxide in order to obtain food. After this period of forced consumption, the rats showed a preference for the chlordiazepoxide, even when the alternate choice was water. Other research has shown that the effect of prior exposure does not depend on the development of physical dependence (Ator & Griffiths, 1992).

Taken together with the human choice and self-administration laboratory studies that show reinforcing effects in people with a history of sedative-hypnotic abuse, it appears that, at least for the longer-acting benzodiazepines administered orally, a period of forced consumption greatly enhances the reinforcing effect of the drug. In this respect, benzodiazepines are very different from the barbiturates, which are very powerful reinforcers right from the start in humans and nonhumans.

Subjective reports and epidemiological studies suggest that flunitrazepam may have a higher potential for use than any other benzodiazepine because it is preferred by many users, but self-administration and drug discrimination studies with laboratory animals have been unable to find any difference between the effects of flunitrazepam and other short-acting benzodiazepines like midazolam and triazolam (Gerak et al., 2001).

HARMFUL EFFECTS

Reproduction

Initially, it was thought that the benzodiazepines interfered with the menstrual cycle and fertility in women, but such concerns have not been substantiated. In males, chlordiazepoxide has been reported to cause a failure to ejaculate, but this does not appear to be a common problem (Greenblatt & Shader, 1974, p. 231). In fact, there have been reports that the benzodiazepines improve reproductive success in previously infertile couples.

Early epidemiological studies suggested that the benzodiazepines might cause birth defects in humans. These have not been confirmed (Eros et al., 2002), but there is evidence that they may have behavioral teratogenic effects in rats. In one

study with rats, it was shown that pups born to mothers injected with diazepam during the third week of gestation showed an absence of locomotion responses and of the acoustic startle responses seen in normal rats (Kellogg, Tervo, Ison, Paisi, & Miller, 1980). In fact, it appears that exposure to benzodiazepines in the uterus affects the reaction of animals to various stressors, and these effects may be different at different developmental stages throughout the life span and may even extend into old age (Kellogg, 1988).

Withdrawal symptoms have been reported in infants when the mothers used normal therapeutic doses of diazepam during pregnancy. The withdrawal symptoms—tremors, irritability, and hyperactivity—are similar to withdrawal from opiates. They start 2 1/2 to 6 hours after delivery and can be treated with barbiturates (Rementiria & Bhatt, 1977). Even benzodiazepines given during labor have been reported to affect the newborn infant by depressing respiration, creating a reluctance to feed and decreasing the ability to maintain normal body temperature (floppy baby syndrome). Apgar scorers (ratings of cardiac and respiratory functioning at birth) are also depressed. The drug has been detected in the blood of a baby up to 8 days after delivery (Cree, Meyer, & Hailey, 1973).

As with most drugs, it is probably unwise to take benzodiazepines at any time during pregnancy or even if pregnancy is possible. This could be a serious problem because benzodiazepines are prescribed much more frequently for women than for men.

Overdose

The main reason why benzodiazepines have replaced the barbiturates is that they are much safer. The major danger from barbiturate use is overdose, either accidental or deliberate. At one time, more than 15,000 deaths per year in the United States resulted from barbiturate overdose; without doubt, the majority of these were suicides.

Benzodiazepine overdoses are not as dangerous as barbiturate overdoses. About 12 percent of drug overdose emergencies in the United States involve the benzodiazepines, but because benzodiazepines do not cause significant respiratory depression, the outcomes of benzodiazepine overdoses are seldom fatal, and there seem to be no lasting effects. Doses as high as 2,250 mg of chlordiazepoxide have been tolerated with symptoms of sleep and drowsiness. There is no deep coma or severe respiratory depression, and the victims can usually be awakened (Greenblatt & Shader, 1974, p. 251). Most symptoms disappear within 48 hours. Deaths due solely to benzodiazepine overdose are more likely to result from the shorter-acting drugs like nitrazepam, temazepam, and flunitrazepam (Drummer & Ransom, 1996). Hospital emergency rooms will often use flumazenil, the benzodiazepine receptor antagonist, to treat benzodiazepine overdoses.

Although the benzodiazepines are relatively safe by themselves, they intensify the effect of other depressants, such as alcohol and the barbiturates. The benzodiazepines can be and frequently are fatal when combined with high doses of alcohol (Torry, 1976).

TREATMENT

Anyone wishing to discontinue using the benzodiazepines after a long period of use should not attempt it alone because the withdrawal can be severe and may involve convulsions, which require medical treatment. Withdrawal should be done under medical supervision with the aid of a physician who appreciates the problem. Although withdrawal can usually be accomplished on an outpatient basis, hospitalization may be necessary, especially for patients with a history of seizures, psychotic episodes, or high doses of the drug (Higgitt et al., 1985).

The approach to detoxification from a benzodiazepine is similar to detoxification from other sedative drugs and alcohol. If only the low-dose benzodiazepine withdrawal symptoms are anticipated, the best way to proceed is gradually to reduce the daily dose of the benzodiazepine. This

is most successfully done in conjunction with counseling and careful monitoring of the patient's withdrawal symptoms. It is important that the patient be told exactly what symptoms to expect and how long they will last. It is sometimes helpful to seek social support from self-help groups and members of the family. The patient should also be taught various strategies for coping, not only with the withdrawal but also with the reemergence of the symptoms for which the benzodiazepine was prescribed in the first place (Colvin, 1983). The most intense withdrawal and the greatest anxiety and panic are experienced while the last few milligrams of the drug are being withdrawn (D. E. Smith & Wesson, 1983). Treatment of iatrogenic physical dependence is usually successful: 88 to 100 percent of patients stop their benzodiazepine intake (Higgitt et al., 1985).

When withdrawal has been managed, various therapies may be attempted, but it is important to match the patient with an appropriate therapeutic strategy. Options include group therapies with people who have similar problems, education, family involvement, a 12-step program similar to Alcoholics Anonymous in which participants are encouraged to "work" a program of recovery, and the support of peer groups and a physician who understand the process.

An illegal user seldom abuses benzodiazepines except as an adjunct to some other addiction, such as alcohol, heroin, or amphetamine, and treatments usually focus on the primary addiction.

CHAPTER SUMMARY

- Tranquilizers are used to treat agitation and anxiety, and sedative-hypnotics are used to sedate people and help them sleep (i.e., they are sleeping pills).

- The benzodiazepines are a class of drugs that was developed in the 1950s and became popular during the 1960s and 1970s for the control of anxiety and insomnia. Benzodiazepines replaced the barbiturates because they are much safer. There are newer drugs introduced in the late 1990s called Z drugs that appear to be replacing the benzodiazepines.

- These drugs are absorbed readily after oral administration. They may also be injected, depending on the medical reason the drug is being used. Their speed of absorption depends on their lipid solubility. Highly lipid-soluble drugs are redistributed into body fat.

- Benzodiazepines and barbiturates enhance the action of GABA, an inhibitory transmitter found widely throughout the brain. They act as their own receptors, which are located on the $GABA_A$ receptor–chloride ionophore complex. This action potentiates the ability of GABA to stabilize the cell membrane. As a result, they are called positive $GABA_A$ modulators. At higher doses, barbiturates but not benzodiazepines are able to open the ion channel directly.

- The benzodiazepines and barbiturates essentially have similar effects and the speed of action determined their use; fast-acting drugs were used as sedative-hypnotics, while longer-acting drugs were used as anxiolytics.

- The GABA receptor–ionophore complex is made of five different subunits, and there are many different varieties of subunits. Different subunits are located in receptors in different sites that control different systems. The Z drugs appear to selectively affect different subunits, so different drugs can specifically target different symptoms.

- The effects of the benzodiazepines on human performance are similar to those of alcohol. Some of these effects are still evident on the day following the use of barbiturates and benzodiazepines as sleeping pills, although the individual may not be aware of the effects. Some of the newer sedative-hypnotics like zopiclone do not appear to have this residual effect. High doses of barbiturates but not benzodiazepines cause death from respiratory depression, which results from a depression of the respiratory centers in the medulla.

- In low doses, the benzodiazepines cause decreases in arousal and vigor and increases in fatigue and confusion. They also decrease feelings of anxiety—their chief medical use. They interfere with memory and slow reaction time, and the drug impairs other skills, including driving. This effect is potentiated by alcohol.

- The benzodiazepines can cause amnesia for events that occur while they are in effect and have an effect on explicit memories.

- There have been ample demonstrations that the benzodiazepines increase behaviors suppressed by punishment. This effect in nonhumans predicts the antianxiety effect of these drugs in humans.

- Tolerance develops to many of the effects of these drugs, including their therapeutic effects.

- There are two separate patterns of withdrawal from the benzodiazepines: (a) the sedative-hypnotic type, similar to withdrawal from alcohol and the barbiturates, and (b) low-dose benzodiazepine withdrawal, which emerges slowly after therapeutic doses have been stopped. The symptoms of anxiety, panic, irregular heartbeat, and memory impairment come and go in cycles of about 10 days and may last for 6 months to a year.

- Benzodiazepines have reinforcing properties in both humans and nonhumans and are readily self-administered. In humans, there are two patterns of use: (a) iatrogenic or physician-caused use and (b) illegal street use. The illegal pattern is characterized by episodic binges. Benzodiazepines are frequently used in conjunction with other drugs such as heroin, cocaine, or alcohol. Flunitrazepam (Rohypnol) appears to be the most highly preferred benzodiazepine for street use, but researchers have not been able to find anything distinctive about it that can explain this preference.

- Because of their lethal effects, the barbiturates have caused many accidental poisonings. Benzodiazepines are much safer but can be fatal when combined with high doses of alcohol.

8

Solvents, Anesthetics, and Inhaled Substances

INTRODUCTION

The substances discussed in this chapter are normally administered by inhalation. Some of them are gases at normal temperatures and pressures but become liquids when pressurized in containers. Merely releasing them from the container turns them to vapor. More commonly, these substances exist in liquid form at normal temperatures and pressures when kept in a closed container, but they are *volatile*. That is, when exposed to the air, they evaporate rapidly, and the fumes can be inhaled. Some substances, however, may be heated to speed vaporization and increase concentrations in the air. Sometimes they are consumed orally in their liquid form, but this only rarely happens.

A great many substances can be included in this category. They include substances that are called *solvents* because they are used to dissolve greases and oils for cleaning or as a medium for adhesives or paints; *fuels*, such as propane and gasoline; *propellants* used in aerosol spray cans; *anesthetics*, such as ether and chloroform, that are sometimes used as solvents but are rarely available for that purpose;

other anesthetics, such as nitrous oxide, ("laughing gas"), that are normally gases and are never used as solvents but may be used as a propellant in aerosol cans; and other chemicals, such as the *nitrites*, that cannot be included in any of these categories.

This is a diverse group of chemicals that have only two things in common: They are almost always inhaled, and they are self-administered. Apart from this, it is not known how much these substances have in common because knowledge of the similarities and differences in their properties is far from complete (Balster, 1998). It is possible, however, to characterize effects that many inhaled substances have in common and note substances that appear to have distinctly different effects.

SOURCES OF INHALED SUBSTANCES

There is a wide variety of self-administered inhaled substances, and they are available from many different sources. Many of these substances and their sources are listed in Table 8-1.

TABLE 8-1   Inhaled Substances Categorized by Source Product

Adhesives

airplane glue	toluene (methyl benzene), ethyl acetate
other glues	n-hexane, toluene, methyl chloride, acetone, methyl ethyl ketone (MEK), methyl butyl ketone (MBK)
special cements	trichloroethylene (TCE), tetrachloroethylene

Aerosols

spray paint	butane, propane, fluorocarbons, toluene
hair spray	butane, propane
deodorant air freshener	butane, propane
analgesic spray	CFCs (chloroflurocarbons, freon)
asthma spray	CFCc
fabric spray	butane, trichloroethane
computer cleaner	dimethyl ether, hydrofluorocarbons
fire extinguisher propellant	bromochlorodifluoromethane (halon)

Anesthetics

gaseous	nitrous oxide
volatile	ether, chloroform, sevoflurane, isoflurane

Cleaning agents

dry cleaning	tetrachloroethylene (perc), 1,1,1-trichloroethane
spot remover	xylene, petroleum distillates, hydrocarbons
degreaser	tetrachloroethylene, 1,1,1-trichloroethane, TCE, ether, chloroform

Solvents

nail polish remover	acetone, ethyl acetate
paint remover	toluene, methylene chloride (dichloromethane), methanol (methyl hydrate), acetone, ethyl acetate
paint thinner	petroleum distillates esters, acetone
correction fluid and thinner	TCE, 1,1,1-trichloroethane

Fuels

fuel gas	butane, isopropane, gasoline
lighter fuel	butane, isopropane

Food products

whipped cream	nitrous oxide
whippets	nitrous oxide

Room odorizers

Locker Room, Rush, etc.	isoamyl nitrite, isobutyl nitrite, isopropyl nitrite, butyl nitrite, cyclohexyl nitrite

Source: Adapted from Sharp (1992, pp. 3–4); Kurtzman, Otsuka, & Wahl (2001, p. 174).

Solvents

Substances in this category include often called *volatile solvents*. These are commonly available in glues, spray paints, cleaning fluid, correction fluid, hair spray, nail polish, and a variety of other commercially available products. Many of these substances are used as solvents in glues and paints because they evaporate quickly (i.e., they are volatile). Often a single product will contain a mixture of several different solvents. Unfortunately, the labels on a commercial product are not likely to identify anything but the major chemicals used in that product and are not likely to mention the minor but important elements.

Solvents have a bewildering array of names, and it is very easy to get confused when reading about them if you do not have a background in chemistry. What makes things difficult is that many names sound the same. In addition, many substances may have several names, and different sources call the same substance by different names. For example, one of the most common solvents is *toluene*, but it may also be referred to as *toluol, methyl benzene, phenylmethane*, or *methacide*. Toluene is the main solvent in many glues, such as airplane glue. It can be found in paint, paint thinners, varnishes, and cleaning products and is a common solvent in nail polishes.

Another widely used solvent is *tetrachloroethylene*. It is used largely for textile processing and cleaning, for degreasing and drying metal, and for manufacturing other solvents and is a common ingredient in water repellants, such as suede protectors. It is what you smell in a dry-cleaning store. Tetrachloroethylene is also known as *TCEE, tetrachloroethene, perchloroethylene, 1,1,2,2-tetrachloroethylene, ethylene tetrachloride, perchlor, perc, PCE, tetra,* and *perclene*.

Trichloroethylene is used as a degreaser, paint remover and stripper, spot remover, cleaning fluid, and typewriter correction fluid. It is also used as an anesthetic, an analgesic, a disinfectant, and a pet food additive and was used to remove the caffeine in decaffeinated coffee until 1977, when such uses were banned in the United States. It is also called *TCE, TRI, acetylene trichloride*, and *ethylene trichloride*.

Another solvent easily confused with trichloroethylene is *1,1,1-trichloroethane*, also referred to as *TCA*. TCA is also known as *TCEA, TRI, chloroethene, methyltrichloromethane, trichloromethylmethane, alphatrichloroethane*, and *alpha-T*. It is found in building materials, glues, water repellants, spray paints, paint thinners and removers, and video head cleaners.

Other solvents include *methanol (methyl hydrate), xylene, ethyl acetate, n-hexane, methyl chloride, acetone, methyl ethyl ketone* (MEK), *methyl butyl ketone, diethyl ether*, and *chloroform*.

Not all solvents are self-administered. A common paint thinner often known as *mineral spirits, petroleum distillate*, or *Stoddard solvent* is not sufficiently volatile to produce vapors in high enough concentrations to be effective.

Fuels

Fuels include *butane*, which is used in lighters. It is a component of *liquified petroleum gas* (LPG), which also contains propane and isopropane. These are sold under pressure in containers as camp stove fuel.

Gasoline is a mixture of more than 250 different hydrocarbons and additives. Its composition may change according to the type of fuel it is sold as, the time of year, and the country it is sold in. It contains from 1 to 5 percent benzene, 5 to 7 percent toluene, and about 2 to 3 percent n-hexane. The different constituents of gasoline evaporate at different rates, so the vapor given off by gasoline actually contains lower concentrations of benzene and n-hexane than in the liquid fuel. A common additive to gasoline is lead, but this has now been phased out in North America. It has been replaced by ethanol, methanol, or other additives.

Some petroleum distillates, such as kerosene, are used as fuels, but they are not often deliberately inhaled because they are not sufficiently volatile.

Propellants

Chlorofluorocarbons, also known as *freons* or *CFCs*, were very commonly used as propellants in pressurized aerosol cans. Propane has now replaced CFCs as a propellant because CFCs have been shown to damage the ozone layer of the upper atmosphere, and their use is being restricted. CFCs are still being used in refrigerators and air conditioners, although this use is being phased out as well. *Halon* is also a CFC. It is also known as *bromochlorodifluoromethane* and was used in fire extinguishers designed to put out electrical fires. It was phased out for environmental reasons by 2000.

Nitrous oxide is used as a propellant in aerosol cans of whipped cream.

Nitrites

Amyl, butyl, and *isopropyl nitrite (alkyl nitrites)* and, more recently, *cyclohexyl nitrite* are often inhaled deliberately. They are clear or yellow liquids with a distinctive smell that resembles dirty sweat socks and is usually considered unpleasant. These are not normally available in other products and are usually purchased specifically for inhalation, although for legal reasons they are sold as odorants. Nitrites originally came in small glass ampules called "poppers" or "snappers" because they are popped or cracked open, and the contents are then inhaled. They also are available in small sealed bottles and are sold in sex shops, record shops, clubs, and bars under names like Aroma of Men, Rush, Stud, Hardware, Locker Room, Liquid Gold, Thrust, and Climax (Balster, 1998).

Anesthetics

A number of substances have been used at some time or another as anesthetics and are sometimes encountered in industrial and commercial products. These include *gaseous anesthetics* (normally a gas) like nitrous oxide and *volatile anesthetics* (a liquid that evaporates quickly) like ether and chloroform. Some of the substances discussed previously as solvents or propellants have been used at times as anesthetics as well.

The term *ether* (or *aether*) refers to a variety of chemicals, but the one discussed here is ethyl or d thyl ether. Ether was originally made by dis t g ethyl alcohol and sulfuric acid together, a overy said to date back to the thirteenth ury. It was referred to as "sulfuric ether."

Ether and chloroform may be encountered in i istrial settings where they are used as solvents, l nitrous oxide is available as a propellant in c is of whipped cream and can be bought in ca ridges for making whipped cream or blowing up alloons. These cartridges can be bought in stores that sell drug paraphernalia or party supplies. Nitrous oxide is sometimes mixed with automotive fuel in automobile racing, and pressurized canisters of nitrous oxide are sold in some specialty automotive supply stores.

HISTORY

Solvents and Fuels

Before 1959, there are very few reports of anyone deliberately inhaling the vapors of glues, solvents, and fuels, but by the end of the 1960s, the practice of solvent sniffing had become widespread among young people and stimulated widespread public concern, including laws against it. What could have caused this sudden increase in sniffing within the space of a few years? Ironically, the answer seems to have been publicity and widespread public health warnings as described by *The Consumers Union Report on Licit and Illicit Drugs* published in 1972 (Brecher & the Editors of *Consumer Reports*, 1972).

The first known mention of glue sniffing in print was in August 1959, when two reporters for the *Denver Post* reported on their investigations into arrests by police of several children in Tucson, Arizona, and Pueblo, Colorado, for sniffing glue. Their article reported on the arrests and included detailed instructions on how the glue was being inhaled and the fact that it caused "dizziness followed by drowsiness. There is a feeling of suspension of reality. Later there is a lack of coordination of muscle and mind."

Prior to this account, Denver police knew of no cases of deliberate glue sniffing, but by June 1960, they had investigated some 50 cases of glue sniffing. This increase was met with many dire warnings in the media that the practice could cause brain damage and death. These warnings were based entirely on what was known about industrial exposure to or the accidental inhalation over many years, not short-term acute use by inhalation.

This publicity seems to have had an effect opposite to the one intended. In October 1961, the chief probation officer of the Denver juvenile court reported seeing "30 boys a month on this glue sniffing problem," and the Denver police reported 278 arrests in 1961. Since glue sniffing was not illegal, the young people were arrested under juvenile procedures, and the arrests were classed as "drunkenness arrests." It was, however, soon to change in many places.

This story repeated itself in New York, Salt Lake City, and many other American cities. Soon it was covered by national publications such as *Newsweek*, and glue sniffing became a "national drug menace." In 1962, the Hobby Industry Association of America announced it was spending $250,000 a year to combat glue sniffing and produced a 15-minute color film on its dangers. Incidentally, this film also mentioned that cleaning fluid and nail polish also contained solvents that could cause intoxication.

By 1968, public concern was so high that anti–glue-sniffing legislation had been passed by 13 states and 29 counties and municipalities, but this had little effect. Before the 1960s, glue sniffing may have been practiced sporadically by a few individuals who discovered its effect by accident, but by the end of the 1960s, it was estimated (Brecher & the Editors of *Consumer Reports*, 1972) that at least 5 percent of all young Americans graduating from high school had sniffed glue at least once.

In the 1970s, a similar campaign was launched against aerosol sniffing. It started with reports in the media, descriptions of the products that were being used (hair spray, deodorant, household cleaners, and so on), accounts of how they were being administered (sprayed into a paper bag and then inhaled), and what effects they had (a strange, floating kind of high). There were dire warnings of the dangers of the practice by experts and national campaigns by the aerosol industry, including a film distributed to schools. As with glue sniffing, all this publicity seems to have had an effect opposite to what was intended.

In the 1990s, gasoline sniffing seemed to have become the inhalant of choice, although use of solvents and aerosols still continues.

Nitrites

Up until 1968, ampules of amyl nitrite were available over the counter in the United States. They were sold for the treatment of angina, but in the 1960s, it became clear that they were being used for nonmedical purposes. Since that time,

organic nitrites such as nitroglycerine have largely replaced amyl nitrite for treating angina, but amyl nitrite is still available by prescription for treatment of angina and is used in hospitals to treat cyanide poisoning.

After medicinal amyl nitrite was no longer easily available in the United States, an underground market for it and other nitrites developed. Butyl nitrite was manufactured and sold legally in sex shops as an incense or aromatic agent. When the use of all alkyl nitrites was banned, cyclohexyl nitrate was developed. It could be sold legally because it is technically not an alkyl nitrite. Nitrites are not illegal in Great Britain.

As described later, its use has been associated with the spread of HIV/AIDS among gay men, and its popularity has declined in recent years.

Anesthetics

Inhalation anesthesia has been regarded as the most important contribution to medicine made by the United States. Interestingly, inhalation anesthesia would not likely have been discovered if these gases had not first been widely used to produce drunkenness. As noted by David Nagle (1968), who wrote a history of the subject, "Drunkenness was the foundation stone in the development of anesthesia" (p. 36).

Nitrous Oxide. Nitrous oxide (N_2O) was discovered by Sir Joseph Priestly in 1776, and Sir Humphry Davey first synthesized it that same year. Davey found that when he inhaled the gas, it produced a state of excitement and made him laugh loudly. From that time, nitrous oxide became known as "laughing gas." Davey proceeded to hold nitrous oxide parties, which were attended by well-known people, such as the poets Robert Southey, Samuel Taylor Coleridge, and Josiah Wedgwood, the founder of Wedgwood pottery. Davey even considered marketing the gas in competition with alcohol. In 1795, Davey had noticed that the gas had anesthetic properties when he used it to relieve the pain of a toothache but never investigated further.

In the early 1800s, nitrous oxide was used at parties both in Europe and in North America. In 1844, a medical student in Boston, Gardner Quincey Coulton, marketed nitrous oxide for this purpose. He held a public exhibition in Hartford, Connecticut, where volunteers inhaled the gas. A dentist, Horace Wells, while attending Coulton's demonstration, noticed that one of the volunteers gashed his leg and yet seemed to feel no pain. Wells tried out the drug on his patients and found that he was able to make extractions completely painlessly. In 1845, with the assistance of his friend and apprentice, William T. G. Morton, he demonstrated the gas at Massachusetts General Hospital. Unfortunately, the demonstration was not a success because the patient came out of the anesthetic too soon after the extraction and complained loudly of pain. Even though Wells was laughed out of the hospital, he and others continued to use nitrous oxide. It is still used in dental surgery today.

Recreational use of nitrous oxide also continues among those in the medical profession and others who have access to it.

Ether. Ether has been known about for a very long time, and its origins are obscure. It is a liquid but evaporates very quickly when exposed to air and may be either drunk or the fumes inhaled. It derives its name from the Greek word *ether* (or *aether*), meaning "sky" or "air."

Fredrich Hoffman, a German physician who lived from 1660 to 1742, introduced ether to medical practice. He made a mixture of ether and alcohol that he called Anodyne or, generically, ether drops. It was consumed orally and recommended for pain due to kidney stones, gallstones, intestinal cramps, earache, toothache, and painful menstruation. Its use became quite popular and was described in medical texts of the eighteenth century. It is also fairly clear, however, that ether, often in a medical pretext, was being used as an alcohol substitute. "Genteel ladies who would never think of touching sinful whiskey have been known to treat their ills with the drops" (Nagle, 1968, p. 26).

In one famous case, an entire town in Northern Ireland, Draperstown, switched from alcohol to ether. In 1840, a temperance crusade convinced the residents to take the pledge against alcohol. The local doctor also swore to abandon alcohol but realized that the ether he was prescribing seemed to have similar effects. He started consuming ether and spread the information—and ether—to his patients and friends. Shortly thereafter, the British government placed a high tax on alcohol, so even after the zeal of the temperance crusade had died down, the people of Draperstown were still motivated to use ether, which was now considerably cheaper than alcohol. An additional advantage was that intoxication could be achieved several times a day, reputedly without a hangover, and if arrested for drunkenness, the person would be sober by the time he or she reached the police station. The practice of ether drinking is reported to have persisted in Draperstown until the 1920s, when liquor became cheaper and more readily available.

In the early nineteenth century, ether parties known as "ether frolics" became popular in the United States. In this case, ether was inhaled rather than swallowed. It became popular among medical students and professors. Oliver Wendell Holmes Sr., a professor at Harvard Medical School and well-known writer, used ether. It was Holmes who coined the word *anesthesia*, meaning "insensitivity to pleasure and pain," to describe the effects of this class of drugs.

When Crawford Williamson Long was a medical student at the University of Pennsylvania in 1838 and 1839, he witnessed laughing gas demonstrations and participated in a few ether frolics. Like Wells, he noticed that injuries received under the influence of these drugs were seldom noticed by the participants. Later, while practicing in Georgia, he had to perform surgery on a Mr. Venable, who was afraid of the knife but was also a regular ether sniffer. Long invited Venable to sniff ether before and during the surgery for the removal of two cysts from his neck. When the surgery was over, Venable could not believe that the surgery had taken place. He was charged a $2.00 fee for the surgery and the anesthesia.

Ether was also used as an anesthetic by William T. G. Morton, a dentist at Harvard Medical School. He was the friend of Horace Wells, the dentist mentioned earlier who pioneered the use of nitrous oxide in dental practice. Morton used ether for dental surgery at Massachusetts General Hospital in 1846 and encouraged its use in general surgery. An account of Morton's dental extractions and several other surgeries was described in an article in *The Boston Medical and Surgical Journal* in 1846. This account has been cited as the birth of modern inhalation anesthesia (Nagle, 1968), although it was preceded by the demonstrations of both Wells and Long.

Chloroform. Chloroform was discovered by Samuel Guthrie, of Sackets Harbor, New York, in 1831. From the start, chloroform was used both medicinally and as an intoxicant. It had the advantages that it was faster acting than ether, it smelled better, and it was not flammable. Chloroform was recommended for convulsions, tetanus, asthma, and angina, and it was also recommended for the suppression of pain—in particular, the pain of childbirth. As an intoxicant, Guthrie himself preferred it to whiskey and found it to be faster acting than ether and left no hangover like alcohol. It also appeared to be more lethal than ether, and the early literature reported a number of accidental overdose deaths.

Horace Wells, who first successfully used nitrous oxide in dental anesthesia, later experimented with chloroform as an anesthetic. At that time, his friend Morton was being given credit for inventing inhalation anesthesia after his successful demonstrations with ether in 1846. Wells felt betrayed. He began experimenting with chloroform as an anesthetic. Unfortunately, it seems that he also used it extensively as an intoxicant. In 1848, after inhaling chloroform, he was arrested for throwing acid on two prostitutes in the street. He was disgraced, and soon after he committed suicide. Ironically, he did so by holding a chloroform-soaked towel to his face, opening a vein in his leg with a pocket razor, and bleeding to death.

In 1847, chloroform was introduced to Britain by the Scottish obstetrician James Simpson, who used it widely to eliminate pain during childbirth. This sparked considerable controversy because of the admonition in the Bible that women should bring forth children in pain. Simpson replied to the criticism by pointing out that God put Adam to sleep before removing the rib from which he created Eve. Queen Victoria settled the matter when she used chloroform to assist in the delivery of her eighth child.

Chloroform and ether are now seldom used as anesthetics. They have unwanted side effects, and ether is highly explosive. They are rarely used recreationally because they are not readily available in consumer products.

ROUTE OF ADMINISTRATION

The drugs in this class are almost universally inhaled, although some, like ether, that have a liquid form are sometimes swallowed before they vaporize. The usual method of administration is to fill a bag or soak a cloth with the substance and hold the bag or the cloth over the face. The practice of inhaling through the nose is called *sniffing*, but if the fumes are inhaled through the mouth or mouth and nose, it is called *huffing*.

The sort of bag used depends on the substance. Glue and most adhesives are put in a paper bag, but gasoline and other liquids are often put in a plastic bag. Gases under pressure such as nitrous oxide are often put in balloons.

Breathing through a soaked cloth ensures that the user will also get a supply of fresh air mixed with the vapor with each breath. Using a bag has the effect of concentrating the solvent, but it means that the user will usually rebreathe his or her own exhaled air, which is low in oxygen and high in carbon dioxide.

Aerosols and propellants may be sprayed into a bag or are sprayed directly into the mouth and nose.

ABSORPTION DISTRIBUTION AND EXCRETION

All these substances are absorbed quickly and completely from the lungs and are delivered to the brain quickly. The rate of absorption is determined by diffusion so that the substance moves into the blood along the concentration gradient. This means that the concentration in the blood becomes equivalent to the concentration in the breathed air. The solvents tend to be highly lipid soluble. They are delivered to body tissue in relation to the amount of blood flow so that fatty tissue with high blood flow, particularly the brain and liver, receives the highest concentrations. The muscles receive less, and absorption into the body fat is the slowest because not much blood goes to body fat (Kennedy & Longnecker, 1996; Rosenberg & Sharp, 1992).

Substances that are normally gases also pass from the blood to the air in the lungs along their concentration gradient when the person stops breathing the fumes. Thus, the concentration in the blood can drop quickly once sniffing stops. With volatile substances, the rate that they can leave the blood in the lungs is determined both by the concentration gradient and by how fast they can evaporate. Because there is less blood flowing to the muscles and fat, the drug is removed from these places more slowly (see Figure 8-1).

Not every inhaled substance is eliminated this way. As it circulates through the body, much of it passes through the liver, where some metabolism takes place. For gases and highly volatile substances, metabolism accounts for only a negligible amount of elimination, but for others, like toluene, that evaporate more slowly, only 20 percent is exhaled, and the rest is metabolized in the liver. In some cases, the liver creates metabolites that may be active or toxic.

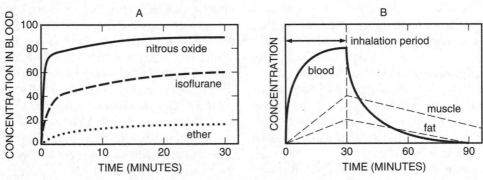

Figure 8-1 Absorption and excretion of inhaled substances. Panel A shows the absorption of ether, isoflurane (a volatile anesthetic), and nitrous oxide (a gaseous anesthetic). The vertical axis shows the concentration in the blood as a percentage of the concentration in the air being breathed. The horizontal axis shows the duration of inhalation. Gases are absorbed more quickly than volatile substances, and there is variability in the rate of absorption of volatile substances. Panel B shows the concentration of an inhaled substance in the blood, muscle, and body fat. During an inhalation period of 30 minutes, the substance reaches high concentrations in the blood and is absorbed more slowly by the muscle and fat. After inhalation ceases, concentrations drop rapidly in the blood as the substance diffuses from the lungs back into exhaled air. It takes much longer for it to be removed from muscle and fat tissue. (Adapted from Kennedy & Longnecker, 1996, p. 299)

NEUROPHYSIOLOGY

Solvents and Anesthetics

The solvents and volatile anesthetics are a diverse group of chemicals, but it seems that they have many similar properties. They are both highly lipid soluble; in fact, ether and chloroform are used as solvents. In addition, toluene and TCE can act as anesthetics in laboratory animals. It is likely, therefore, that solvents share neuropharmacological properties with some volatile anesthetics. Since anesthetics have effects on the central nervous system (CNS) similar to alcohol (Chapter 6) and the barbiturates and benzodiazepines (Chapter 7), it is also likely that all these substances—alcohol, anesthetics, and sedative-hypnotics—have overlapping behavioral effects (Balster, 1998).

Three of the physiological effects of anesthetics seem to be able to account for their behavioral properties: (a) enhancement of the inhibitory transmitter gamma-aminobutyric acid (GABA), (b) enhancement of the effects of glycine, another inhibitory transmitter; and (c) to a lesser extent, the attenuation of the NMDA receptor for the excitatory neurotransmitter glutamate (Balster, 1998; Kennedy & Longnecker, 1996). The enhancement of the effectiveness of the inhibitory neurotransmitter GABA is due to an increase in the affinity of the $GABA_A$ receptor for GABA molecule, and a similar mechanism is probably responsible for the enhancement of glycene functioning. The exact mechanism by which anesthetics do this is not clear, but it probably does not involve a receptor site in the manner of the barbiturates and benzodiazepines (see Chapter 7). More likely, they act like ethyl alcohol and have diverse effects on the configuration of the proteins that make up receptor sites and ion channels, thereby altering their function (Beckstead et al., 2000; Kennedy & Longnecker, 1996).

The ability to block the NMDA glutamate receptor is another function solvents and anesthetics share with alcohol. This effect has been demonstrated for toluene and TCE, but, like the effect on GABA, there does not appear to be a receptor site involved (Balster, 1998). The mechanism of reinforcement is somewhat more obscure, but, like alcohol and the barbiturates, the reinforcing effects of many solvents and anesthetics are probably an indirect result of the enhancement of GABA. Studies of the effect of toluene on the firing rate of dopaminergic neurons in the ventral tegmental area (VTA) of rats have reported both increases and decreases (Balster, 1998, p. 211; Riegel & French, 1999). Toluene inhalation produces rapid increases in dopamine in the frontal cortex (Gerasimov et al., 2002), an area rich in dopaminergic projections from the VTA. Imaging with photon emission tomography (PET) using [11C]toluene injected intravenously into baboons shows rapid uptake of the radiotracer in dopamine-rich brain regions, including the striatum and frontal cortex, as well as other regions, including the cerebellum and thalamus (Gerasimov et al., 2002). Dopamine has also been shown to be involved in the reinforcing effects of ether (Pogorelov & Kovalev, 1999).

Nitrites. Nitrites work outside the CNS to relax smooth muscles, and they also act as a vasodilator. The vasodilation causes a sudden lowering of blood pressure, flushing, and pooling of blood in the lower extremities. This is accompanied by feelings of warmth and a throbbing sensation and lightheadedness. These feelings enhance the beat of the music and light shows at dance clubs where nitrites are sometimes used. They are also commonly used to enhance sexual activity, particularly male homosexual activity, because they enhance penile engorgement and cause smooth muscle relaxation, which facilitates anal intercourse (Goode & Troiden, 1979).

There is no evidence that nitrites have any effect on the CNS, although the possibility has not been extensively investigated.

EFFECTS ON THE BEHAVIOR OF NONHUMANS

Unconditioned Behavior

Acute exposure to different solvents causes somewhat different effects. Most solvents such as toluene and TCE act like classical "depressants," such as barbiturates and alcohol. At low doses they cause an increase in spontaneous motor activity, and at higher doses there is an initial increase followed by a decrease in activity (Bowen & Balster, 1998; Warren, Bowen, Jennings, Dallas, & Balster, 2000). Other behavioral effects include ataxia, falling, head jerking, hind limb paralysis, aimless scratching, and prostration. The paralysis and head jerking are seen only with dichloromethane, and the scratching is seen only with toluene. Isoamyl nitrite does not increase or decrease spontaneous activity over a wide range of doses (Bowen & Balster, 1998).

Some solvents such as n-hexane and n-heptane seem to have the opposite effects on arousal; they produce convulsions at high doses. When toluene is mixed with n-hexane, the convulsions are suppressed. Although the nitrites do not increase spontaneous activity, amyl, ethyl, and butyl acetate seem to cause central nervous system excitation resulting in hyperreactivity to stimuli and convulsions (Bowen & Balster, 1997). These different effects can interact to potentiate or antagonize each other when solvents are taken in conjunction, as they often are.

Thus, whereas many solvents such as toluene and TCE appear to cause effects on behavior similar to the classical CNS "depressants" like alcohol and the sedative-hypnotic/tranquilizers and anesthetics, there are some that do not. Some, like n-hexane, appear to have convulsant properties.

The analgesic effects of nitrous oxide have also been demonstrated in the rat and the squirrel monkey. Wood, Warren, and Weiss (1980) have shown that these animals will tolerate higher shock levels after being exposed to nitrous oxide.

At higher doses, many solvents cause unconsciousness and death.

Conditioned Behavior

A number of early reports found evidence that many solvents like toluene, TCE, and methoxyflurane decrease high rates of responding engendered by a fixed ratio (FR) schedule and have a biphasic effect (increase followed by a decrease) on schedules like fixed interval and differential reinforcement of low rates (DRL) that engender lower rates of responding (Glowa, 1985). These rate-increasing effects, however, are small and not always observed (Bowen & Balster, 1998).

In one study, the effect of long-term exposure was investigated. Rats were exposed to toluene at various concentrations for 1 hour a day for 154 days and then tested for a number of days for residual effects of this exposure. No changes were found in activity and FR performance, but exposed rats took longer to acquire a DRL schedule than control rats (Ikeda, Maehara, Harabuchi, Kishi, & Yokota, 1983).

It has been shown that toluene will reinstate punishment-suppressed behavior in rats in the same manner as the benzodiazepine diazepam. In fact, the two drugs seemed to potentiate each other because the effect of administering them together was greater than the sum total of the effects of each by itself, suggesting that they use similar neural mechanisms (Geller, Hartman, Mendez, & Gauss, 1983). A similar effect has been reported in squirrel monkeys with toluene and m-xylene (Wood, Coleman, Schuler, & Cox, 1984).

EFFECTS ON THE BEHAVIOR OF HUMANS

Subjective Effects

Often the state produced by inhalation of solvents is described as being similar to that produced by alcohol. Users often report exhilaration and euphoria, but unlike alcohol, many young users often describe vivid hallucinations that are primarily visual and frequently involve bright colors, although sometimes there are auditory hallucinations as well. The nature of the hallucination may be either pleasant or unpleasant, and they are rarely sexual in nature. The hallucination often is under the control of the observer who may also be able to participate in the hallucination. Hallucinations are sometimes shared by several people sniffing together.

This is an account published in a 1967 paper. These reports are from interviews with young people ages 8 to 15 years from slum neighborhoods in New York. Some had been admitted to a psychiatric hospital:

My boy (friend) Indio said, "Lucky, come over here and I will show you a trick I invented with glue." Then we started sniffing glue in the hall and he said, "Open the window. Open the window," and the window started opening. I saw it open, I said, "What— This is true, this is true. If you sniff glue and tell the window to open, it opens." I kept sniffing and sniffing and the window opened and I said, "Oh man, this is magic or something— I could rob me a lot of things like this. I could go to a fire escape and open a window like that and go in and rob the apartment." (Preble & Laury, 1967, p. 276)

I dream. It's like television. I see nice things, nice colors—orange, yellow, black. Orange are the clowns. I don't know what they say. When we sniff we don't talk at all about what we see. Only later, or some other day do we talk about it. My friends see animals; it's a real show. At times I see nice girls and toys and big cars, but I don't always see the same. It changes. If I take glue now, I would see different things than last time. (Preble & Laury, 1967, p. 278)

For ethical reasons, laboratory studies with solvents have not been attempted with humans, but some research has been done with gaseous anesthetics like nitrous oxide and with volatile anesthetics like sevoflurane, which are likely more similar to solvents. Nitrous oxide and sevoflurane at subanesthetic doses cause increased feelings of being "high," "drunk," "elated," "light-headed," "sedated," and "stimulated." Subjects generally show a greater degree of drowsiness with the volatile anesthetic than with nitrous oxide (Zacny, Janiszewski, Sadeghi, & Black, 1999). Nitrous oxide is an analgesic at subanesthetic doses, but sevoflurane is not (Janiszewski et al., 1999). Hallucinations have not been reported.

Effects on the Body and Behavior

Acute Effects. Laboratory studies on the acute effects of solvents have not been done for ethical reasons, but clinical observations have identified several stages of intoxication with solvents. The onset of acute effects occurs very quickly and usually disappears rapidly when administration ceases. Intoxication can be maintained for several hours by continuous exposure and administration. Initially, solvent users show an exhilaration and excitation similar to that caused by alcohol. They may also show coughing and wheezing and other signs of the irritating effect of the solvent on the eyes and throat. If sniffing continues, the user will begin to show slurred speech, disorientation, delusions and hallucinations, tremor, weakness, and headache. In later stages, the user will show severe movement difficulties with depressed reflexes and, finally, stupor, coma, seizures, and possibly death (Kurtzman, Otsuka, & Wahl, 2001).

Systematic laboratory studies have been attempted on the behavioral effects of anesthetics. Both the volatile anesthetic sevoflurane and the gaseous anesthetic nitrous oxide impair performance on the digit symbol substitution test, which requires subjects to write symbols in spaces according to code as fast as they can. It is a test of short-term memory and dexterity. Considerably more impairment is caused by sevoflurane (thought to be similar to solvents) than nitrous oxide. For both drugs, this effect disappears within 5 minutes after inhalation ceases (Zacny et al., 1999).

No laboratory studies have been attempted on the effects of solvents on driving. In Norway, a number of drivers arrested on suspicion of driving while intoxicated were tested for drugs in their blood. Twenty-nine cases were found where toluene was the only drug that was detected. For 18 of those cases, it was determined that toluene had impaired their driving (Gjerde, Smith-Kelland, Normann, & Morland, 1990).

Chronic Effects. Chronic effects of solvents include nosebleed, ulcers of the nose, and mouth irritation of the nose and eyes that are a direct result of the irritating effect of the chemical on these organs. Other effects common in heavy long-term users of solvents that persist after the acute effects have gone are short-term memory loss, emotional instability, cognitive impairment, slurred speech, staggering and wide-based gait, tremor, loss of hearing and smell, weight loss, depression, and lethargy, as described in the following section on harmful effects on the nervous system (Pryor, 1992, p. 245). Long-term exposure to solvents is also correlated with abnormal $[^{15}O]H_2O$ PET imaging of frontal lobe activation during a verbal working memory task (Haut et al., 2000) as well as increased P300 latencies (Morrow, Steinhauser, & Hodgson, 1992) and decreased P300 amplitudes in an oddball paradigm (Lindgren, Osterberg, Orbaek, & Rosen, 1997). For the most part, these effects disappear within weeks or months, but there is increasing evidence that, for some, the effects on the nervous system and other organs may not be reversible.

Many of these effects of solvents and gasoline are believed to be a result of toluene, which is the most common ingredient in abused substances, but it is difficult to be sure because commercially available products like glues and cleaners are a mixture of many substances. It is only by systematic investigation in the laboratory using laboratory animals that it will be possible to isolate the offending solvents.

DISCRIMINATIVE STIMULUS PROPERTIES

In drug state discrimination studies, mice trained to discriminate injected toluene from saline generalized the response to inhaled toluene, inhaled ether, and injected phenobarbital but not to morphine (Rees, Kinsey, & Balster, 1987). In a similar experiment, rats were trained to discriminate intraperitoneal injections of toluene. These rats generalized the response to the barbiturate methohexital and to the benzodiazepine oxazepam but not to the antipsychotic chlorpromazine (Kinsey, Rees, & Balster, 1990). Mice trained to discriminate alcohol (ethanol) from saline generalize to the volatile anesthetics halothane and isoflurane, to the solvents toluene, 1,1,1-trichloroethane, and to oxazepam but not to isoamyl nitrite or a convulsant, flurothyl (a drug that induces seizures) (Bowen & Balster, 1997; Rees, Kinsey, Breen, & Balster, 1987). Similarly, phenobarbital-trained rats will generalize to the anesthetic halothane,

1,1,1-trichloroethane, and oxazepam but not to amyl nitrite or fluorothyl (Rees, Kinsey, Balster, Jordan, & Breen, 1987). Toluene will also partially substitute for phencyclidine (PCP) (Bowen, Wiley, Jones, & Balster, 1999).

In summary, all the inhaled solvents tested have a discriminable subjective effect in rats and mice. The stimulus properties of toluene and several other solvents are similar to alcohol and drugs we class as tranquilizers, sedative-hypnotics, and anesthetics but not to opiates, antipsychotics, or convulsants. Some inhaled drugs like isoamyl nitrite do not appear to be part of this group and have different subjective properties.

Alcohol, anesthetics, and the sedative-hypnotics are drugs known to produce some of their effects by enhancing GABA. Many inhaled solvents such as toluene share discriminative stimulus properties with these drugs, suggesting that it is due to similar effect on GABA. In addition, PCP is known to be an antagonist of the NMDA glutamate receptor. The fact that toluene will partially generalize to PCP supports the belief that NMDA antagonism may be another mechanism of action of toluene as discussed.

TOLERANCE AND WITHDRAWAL

It is not clear whether tolerance develops to the effects of solvents in humans because of ethical problems doing such research, but anecdotal reports from areas where ether has been used as an alcohol substitute suggest that a tolerance does indeed develop. It is likely that the development of tolerance depends on the particular substance, on its duration of action, and on the extent of its use. Withdrawal symptoms are most likely to be seen with substances that have long-lasting effects and are used frequently. In practice, withdrawal symptoms to solvents are seldom seen (Howard, Cotter, Compton, & Ben-Abdullah, 2001).

One experiment has demonstrated acute tolerance development to the analgesic effects and drug-liking effects of nitrous oxide but not to other effects on mood or to its psychomotor-impairing effects (Zacny et al., 1996).

Although there have been no systematic investigations, anecdotal reports suggest that inhalants do not cause a hangover in doses usually consumed. It is usual, however, for patients to feel very sick after surgical anesthesia. Thus, hangover, if it occurs, may be related to the specific inhaled substance and the dose.

HARMFUL EFFECTS

Effects on the Nervous System

Solvents. Chronic users who have sniffed solvents for longer than a year sometimes show signs of psychotic behavior, such as delusions of persecution and hallucinations, that may last for several months after they stop sniffing. They also show some negative symptoms of schizophrenia (see Chapter 13), such as loss of initiative and apathy, a state sometimes compared to the "amotivational syndrome" first described in heavy users of marijuana (see Chapter 15). In Japan, where solvent use is widespread, long-term users are often diagnosed with a "solvent psychosis," although this diagnosis is seldom used in North America. It is still not clear whether solvent use actually causes a psychosis or whether solvent use precipitates such symptoms in those with a genetic predisposition to become schizophrenic (Yamanouchi, Okada, Kodama, & Sato, 1998).

Also reported in long-term solvent users are various movement disorders that involve tremors of various sorts, decreases in visual acuity associated with damage to the retina and optic nerve, and cognitive dysfunction.

Chronic exposure to solvents has been shown to cause damage to the cortex and cerebellum. Myelin, the white matter that surrounds axons, seems to be particularly susceptible to damage by solvents such as toluene. In fact, it has been noted that many of the symptoms of the damage done by solvents resemble the effects of multiple sclerosis, a disease of the myelin sheath. There is also evidence of a restriction of blood flow in various parts of the brains of long-term solvent users. Long-term workplace exposure to organic solvents reduces cerebral blood flow to the frontal cortex (measured by SPECT following inhalation of ^{133}Xe) both during resting and during a learning task of associated word pairs (Maximilian, Risberg, Prohovnik, Rehnstrom, & Haeger-Aronsen, 1982).

The neurological damage caused by toluene is primarily to the CNS, which causes mild to severe cognitive impairment or even dementia, tremor, deafness, and ataxia (movement difficulty) associated with damage to the cerebellum and spinal tracts. This nerve damage is correlated with level of impairment and with length of toluene exposure. SPECT, using [^{99}mTc]-ethyl cysteinate dimer, a perfusion tracer, showed decreased blood flow in the cerebral cortex, basal ganglia, and thalamic regions following 8 months of toluene abuse (Ryu et al., 1998). These effects may not be permanent, however, and many heavy chronic users of toluene have no persistent cognitive impairment (Rosenberg & Sharp, 1992), although these symptoms may take many months to dissipate (Yamanouchi et al., 1998). In addition to this CNS damage, toluene can also damage the cranial nerves, which can result in loss of vision, ringing in the ears, and hearing loss.

Rats exposed to toluene, xylene, and styrene in a dose and pattern similar to human abuse develop an irreversible hearing loss that results from damage to the hair cells in the cochlea of the inner ear. The hearing loss is greater at higher auditory frequencies and is related to the extent of exposure (Pryor, 1992).

Metabolites of some glue and paint solvents (methyl butyl ketone and n-hexane) have effects primarily in the peripheral nervous system. A metabolite of these substances, 2-5-hexanedione (2,5-HD), is a neurotoxin that causes axon degeneration of nerves in the peripheral nervous system with a loss of sensation in the hands and feet (Kurtzman et al., 2001). In severely affected individuals, this effect is not reversible (Rosenberg & Sharp, 1992).

Gasoline is a mixture of various organic solvents, some of which like toluene, benzene, and n-hexane have known neurotoxic effects. In addition, much of the toxicity of gasoline appears to be due to the presence of tetraethyllead or its metabolite. High lead levels can cause hallucinations, disorientation, convulsions, ataxia, tremors, and sometimes limb paralysis. Currently in North America, lead is not added to commercially available gasoline.

Nitrites. Nitrites are vasodilators and relax smooth muscles. For this reason, they are often used by gay men to assist in anal intercourse. Nitrites have been implicated in the spread of HIV/AIDS in several ways. Nitrite use by gay men is associated with persistent high-risk sexual behavior (Goode & Troiden, 1979). In addition, nitrites in some studies with laboratory animals have been found to suppress the immune system (although this is not consistently found in human users). Finally, among those who have HIV/AIDS, gay men who use nitrites are likely to develop the cancer Kaposi's sarcoma. Others who have contracted HIV/AIDS by other means, such as needle sharing, are unlikely to develop Kaposi's sarcoma, suggesting that nitrites may be a promoter or cofactor for Kaposi's sarcoma (Haverkos, Kopstein, Wilson, & Drotman, 1994).

Nervous system damage has also been reported in users of nitrous oxide. Chronic nitrous oxide use results in peripheral nerve damage, causing numbness and weakness in the limbs, loss of dexterity, and loss of balance. These are a result of a degeneration in some parts of the spinal cord thought to be caused by the fact that nitrous oxide inactivates vitamin B_{12} which is necessary for normal cell metabolism and growth (Rosenberg & Sharp, 1992).

Effects on Other Organs

Kidney damage, both to the tubules and to the glomerulus of the nephron, can be caused by a variety of solvents, including toluene. Metals such as cadmium and lead in paint sprays and lead in gasoline are also known to damage the kidney. Liver damage has also been reported to arise from the use of methylene chloride combined with other solvents and with trichloroethane. Most liver damage is reversible within a few weeks of abstinence.

Dichloromethane (paint stripper) is metabolized to carbon monoxide that occupies the hemoglobin, making it unable to carry oxygen. This decreased oxygen-carrying capacity of the blood causes stress on the cardiovascular system.

Reproduction

There is some evidence from studies of people (e.g., painters, printers, and dry cleaners) whose work exposes them to various solvents that for men there is a decrease in fertility. There are no data on such effects on recreational users.

Although some have speculated that there may be a "fetal solvent syndrome" similar to fetal alcohol syndrome (FAS) (see Chapter 6), epidemiological studies of solvent-using mothers have not been able to separate the effects of the solvents from risk factors such as poor maternal health, poor prenatal care, and other aspects of the inhalant abuse lifestyle (Jones & Balster, 1998). It is possible, however, that solvents can combine with or potentiate the teratogenic effects of alcohol and cause FAS at lower doses of alcohol.

Studies with laboratory animals, however, are able to show consistent teratogenic effects. Intermittent maternal exposure to trichloroethylene in rats caused reduced brain weight, reduced locomotor activity, and deficits on a number of behavioral tests of strength and coordination in rat pups (Coleman, Mason, Hooker, & Robinson, 1999). In another study, pregnant rats were exposed to toluene. The exposed newborn pups showed a reduced brain size, reduced brain cell size, and reduced mylenation of neurons in several parts of their brains. All these effects reversed themselves during the first 3 weeks after birth except for a reduction in mylenation of cells in the forebrain that appeared to be irreversible (Gospe & Zhou, 1998). Other studies have shown that prenatal exposure to toluene causes abnormal neuron migration and proliferation during development (Gospe & Zhou, 2000).

Lethal Effects

A number of studies have examined deaths due to inhalant use in the United States and other countries. One study examined 39 documented fatalities in Virginia from 1987 to 1996 that were a result of inhalant use (Bowen, Daniel, & Balster, 1999). This study found that victims were most likely to be young (average age 19) Caucasian males. Eighteen of the deaths were associated with the fuels butane and propane, 10 with the CFC freon, and the rest with toluene, gasoline, trichloroethylene, and nitrous oxide. The lethal mechanism was not discussed in this study, but it is clear that in some cases in which the victims were found with a plastic bag over their heads, suffocation was the likely cause.

Inhaled substance deaths may be caused by direct toxic effects of the substance or may arise from the means of administration. Most inhaled substances act as cardiac and respiratory depressants that suppress the breathing reflex. Sniffers use paper and plastic bags and other means to increase the concentration of the substance they are breathing. In doing so, they reduce the amount of fresh oxygenated air they breathe and increase carbon dioxide levels in the blood. This leaves them vulnerable to suffocation, especially if they lose consciousness in the process and their normal breathing reflexes are depressed (Dinwiddie, 1998). Suffocation is also known to occur among nitrous oxide users. Nitrous oxide is sometimes breathed at 100 percent concentration to achieve the maximum effect. Unfortunately, when this is done, the individual may lose consciousness, and, because there is no oxygen in 100 percent nitrous oxide, the person may suffocate. One should never breathe pure nitrous oxide.

There are also reports that some inhaled substance users have been killed by inhaling their own vomit. This type of death has also been reported with excessive use of alcohol and probably results from the suppression of normal swallowing and vomiting reflexes arising from the depression of the autonomic control centers in the brain stem.

Another possible cause of death is cardiac arrhythmia, which is caused by a sensitization of the heart muscle to catecholamines. Such deaths have been reported after using butane, CFCs, trichloroethylene, 1,1,1-trichloroethane, and toluene (Garrott, 1992).

Butane as a fuel and as a propellant is under pressure in canisters. As it is released, it evaporates and cools surrounding materials, including skin. This can cause cold burns and if released into the throat can chill the vagus nerve, causing slowing of the heart and cardiac arrest.

SELF-ADMINISTRATION IN NONHUMANS

Some inhaled substances have been shown to act as positive reinforcers in several nonhuman species. Yanagita, Takahashi, Ishida, and Funamoto (1970) reported that monkeys would self-administer chloroform, toluene, and ether through an intranasal cannula. Later, in a series of studies, Wood (1979) showed that monkeys would inhale toluene and nitrous oxide. In addition, Yavich, Patkina, and Zvartau (1994) have shown conditioned place preference generated by exposure to a mixture of commercial solvents, and Pogorelov and Kovalov (1999) have demonstrated that rats will self-administer ether vapor.

SELF-ADMINISTRATION IN HUMANS

Laboratory Studies

Because of the ethical problems of giving potentially harmful substances to volunteers, there have been no laboratory studies of solvent self-administration in humans, but a number of studies have been done with nitrous oxide and with volatile anesthetics. These studies have generally shown that nitrous oxide will function as a reinforcer in choice studies where it is preferred over a placebo. Preferences, however, are not strong and, like the preference for benzodiazepines, appear to depend on past experience. Zacny and his colleagues have shown that nitrous oxide will function as a reinforcer in people who have a history of moderate drinking (average seven drinks a week) but not in people who are light drinkers (one drink a week) (Zacny, Janiszewski et al., 1997). There is also evidence that nitrous oxide is more likely to function as a reinforcer in people who are informed that they would be receiving nitrous oxide and told about the sort of effects to expect (Zacny, Cho et al., 1997). The volatile anesthetic sevoflurane, however, was not preferred by healthy moderate drinkers (Zacny et al.,1999).

Epidemiology

The use of inhaled substances in the United States is highly age related with the highest use reported by eighth graders with 4.5 percent reporting use in the past 30 days in 2004. Among tenth graders, this drops to 2.4 percent and to 1.5 percent among twelfth graders (see Table 8-2). Several surveys indicate that inhaled substance use among school-age children peaked in 1995 and has been slowly declining since that time (Kurtzman et al., 2001). Table 8-2 suggests that this trend may have bottomed out in 2004. Male use is only slightly higher than female use. In fact, females seem to start sniffing sooner than males but are much less likely to continue using into adulthood.

Solvent sniffers in the United States are often described as belonging to one of three classes (May & Del Vecchio, 1997). The largest class is the experimental youthful use. This involves children in their preteen and early teen years who try solvents because of peer group influence, curiosity about intoxication, attention or thrill seeking, or easy availability. Because this is likely to be their first exposure to an intoxicant, long-term commitment to solvent use is not normally seen. This pattern of use is more prevalent in rural areas than urban areas, and "hot spots" may develop. These are locations where very high levels of sniffing are reported, 60 to 80 percent in some cases. These hot spots may develop in particular communities, neighborhoods, ethnic groups, or schools and are related to physical and social isolation, economic status, family stability, and the availability of solvents and other drugs (Beauvis & Oetting, 1988; Oetting & Web, 1992).

A second category involves older youth, ages 15 to 20, who are multiple substance users and who include inhalants along with many other substances. These youth may start off as experimental users but then gravitate to peer clusters that emphasize recreational drug use including marijuana and alcohol. Unlike the experimental users, users in this group are more likely to have family, school, or psychological problems and go on to more serious drug-related problems.

The rarest type of user is the adult chronic user. The people in this category are in their late teens or older. Solvent use in the other two categories is generally equally distributed between the sexes, but the chronic user is virtually always male. Chronic users inhale solvents daily and attempt to remain intoxicated. Their lives are

TABLE 8-2   Reported Use of Inhalants by High School Students in the United States by Grade and by Year

	Eighth Graders				Tenth Graders				Twelfth Graders			
	1998	2000	2002	2004	1998	2000	2002	2004	1998	2000	2002	2004
Lifetime	20.5	17.9	15.2	17.3	18.3	16.6	13.5	12.4	15.2	14.2	11.7	10.9
Annual	11.7	9.4	7.7	9.6	8.0	7.3	5.8	5.9	6.2	5.9	4.5	4.2
30-day	4.8	4.5	3.4	4.5	2.9	2.6	2.4	2.4	2.3	2.2	1.5	1.5

Source: These data were obtained from Monitoring the Future Survey conducted by the University of Michigan's Institute for Social Research funded by the National Institute on Drug Abuse, National Institutes of Health of the United States. (http://www.nida.nih.gov/Infofax/HSYouthtrends.html)

"Lifetime" refers to use at least once during a respondent's lifetime. "Annual" refers to an individual's drug use at least once during the year preceding his or her response to the survey. "30-day" refers to an individual's drug use at least once during the month preceding his or her response to the survey.

centered on obtaining and using solvents. They usually have serious social or psychological problems. They are unemployed and are not part of a social group. They are loners and do not use the drug socially. By the time the chronic users reach their thirties, they often die or become severely disabled as a result of solvent use and end up in hospital emergency rooms, chronic care wards, or psychiatric hospitals.

One large-scale survey of high school students in Illinois found that sniffers were not typical of adolescents who use other drugs. It was found that inhaled substance use in the upper grade levels is associated with a greater frequency of criminal behavior and that users are more likely to get into trouble for drinking and drug use. The authors suggest that inhaled substance use is more closely related to general delinquency than it is to general drug use (Mackesy-Amiti & Fendrich, 1999), although it is not clear whether the delinquent behavior caused the solvent use or the other way around (Wu, Pilowsky, & Schlenger, 2004).

PREVENTION AND TREATMENT

Prevention

Various methods have been tried to prevent the use of solvents by young people, but none have met with any success. Many jurisdictions have made it illegal to provide inhalants to children, but this seems to have had little effect. For one thing, it is difficult to enforce because potentially abused substances are so widely available in so many forms and have so many legitimate uses in household situations. It is unreasonable to expect retail stores to be able to determine the use their customers make of these products and to be able to restrict sales to adults. In some cities in the United States, bans have been placed on selling toluene-containing glues to adolescents. This had the effect of causing a shift to increased use of lighter fluids and aerosol, considered to be more dangerous than toluene. Attempts have been made to put warning labels on products, but this only seems to have had the effect of identifying sniffable products to potential users. Manufacturers have also tried to add foul-smelling or irritating substances such as oil of mustard to solvents, but often this merely irritates legitimate users and does not deter habitual sniffers (Kerner, 1988).

Educational campaigns may be an effective prevention tool, but they have not been evaluated and may not always work as expected. As Brecher and the Editors of *Consumer Reports* (1972) have described earlier in this chapter, publicity given to solvent sniffing initially had the effect of only increasing use, even though it included dire and often exaggerated warnings about health problems and dangers of sniffing.

In Australia, British Petroleum (BP) has developed a fuel that might provide a solution for remote communities. They noticed that gas sniffing was not a problem in those communities that used aviation fuel for both planes and other gasoline engines. This was often done in smaller communities because it reduced the need for having two storage tanks. The difference between Australian aviation fuel and standard gasoline is that aviation fuel contains a very low percent of toluene and other ring-shaped hydrocarbons, which are responsible for the behavioral and reinforcing effects of gasoline. BP developed a fuel it calls OPAL, which contains a straight-chain hydrocarbon called alkylate rather than toluene. It is now being evaluated (Nowak, 2005).

Treatment

It may be more difficult to treat users of volatile solvents than users of any other type of drug (Jumper-Thurman & Beauvais, 1992). There are a number of reasons for this, not the least being that solvent users usually have a great many other social, financial, family, and behavioral problems concurrent with and contributing to their solvent use. The complexity of the problem means that it requires much in the way of resources, time, and emotional involvement of the therapist. It has also been found that solvent users generally do not seem to benefit from existing treatment modalities and procedures, and very little is known about how best to go about treating them. For this reason, treatment is not very often successful, and programs set up to treat solvent-using young people rarely survive more than a few months before they run out of money and the therapists run out of patience.

Mostly, solvent users do not appear voluntarily for treatment. They are referred by the justice system or by social service agencies, and their participation is secured by some coercive means. An additional difficulty often encountered is that sniffers, because they often are from dysfunctional families, are frequently socially dependent on peer clusters that are highly deviant. Because there are no positive social influences in their lives such as family, school, church, and so on, relapse during treatment is almost inevitable. For this reason, such treatment is better done on an inpatient basis, or some effort must be made to isolate the person from the social environment controlling the solvent use.

The normal first stage of treating people with a drug problem is detoxification, in which the individual is assessed and any effects of the drug, including withdrawal, are treated and allowed to decline. With inhaled substance users, withdrawal is not normally a problem, but the neurological effects of sniffing, including cognitive impairment, often take weeks or months to disappear. Sniffers often are not capable of benefiting from treatments until they have recovered sufficient emotional and cognitive functioning.

Because many personal, social, and emotional problems must be addressed, a wide array of interventions may be needed. Solvent users are most often in need of a variety of skills required for effective living, so intensive social skills training, including personal hygiene, is needed. It is not known how long treatment needs to continue to be most effective, but it may need to be continued for as long as 2 years (Jumper-Thurman & Beauvais, 1992).

CHAPTER SUMMARY

- Substances administered by inhalation are normally gases or the fumes of volatile liquids that evaporate rapidly. They are often solvents, propellants, fuels, anesthetics, and nitrites and are inhaled by a practice known as sniffing or huffing.

- Solvents include toluene and many other substances that are used in paints, adhesives, and cleaners.

- Some substances used as solvents, such as chloroform and ether, have also been used as anesthetics, and anesthetics such as nitrous oxide were used for recreational purposes. Nitrous oxide is also used as a propellant in cans of whipped cream.

- Propane is used as a propellant and as a fuel, and chlorofluorocarbons are used as propellants and in air conditioners. Both are widely self-administered.

- Nitrites were originally used to treat pain from angina but became popular as recreational drugs, particularly among gay men as an erotic aid. Its use has declined particularly since it has been associated with HIV/AIDS.

- Chloroform, ether, and nitrous oxide were widely used as intoxicants and as alcohol substitutes before their use as anesthetics was developed in the United States in the mid-1800s.

- Most inhaled substances are highly lipid soluble and are rapidly absorbed when inhaled. Gases are exhaled rapidly, but volatile substances are absorbed by body fat and may remain in the body for a longer time and be metabolized by the kidney.

- Anesthetics and most solvents have three main neurophysical effects: (a) They enhance the inhibitory effect of GABA, (b) they enhance the effects of the inhibitory transmitter gycline, and (c) they block the NMDA receptor for the excitatory transmitter glutamate. They also increase dopamine levels in the striatum, where the nucleus accumbens is located. Nitrites do not appear to have any effect on the central nervous system. They are vasodilators and cause light-headedness and other effects by a sudden lowering of blood pressure.

- Solvents and anesthetics at subanesthetic doses have effects similar to alcohol and the depressant drugs, except that many users also report hallucinations.

- In nonhumans, most solvents and anesthetics have effects on behavior similar to the depressants, although some solvents, such as n-hexane and n-heptane, may have excitatory effects and cause convulsions.

- Solvents have stimulus effects similar to alcohol, anesthetics, and the depressant drugs and generalize partially to PCP.

- Tolerance develops to the effects of solvents and anesthetics, but withdrawal is not commonly seen except when substances with a long duration of action are used.

- Chronic solvent use can lead to damage to the brain, particularly the myelin sheath of axons. This causes cognitive, perceptual, and movement disorders, which in many cases may or may not be reversible.

- Deaths have been reported from overdoses of solvents, although many deaths are a result of suffocation by a plastic bag being used for administration.

- Laboratory animals will self-administer solvents. In humans, solvents are consumed primarily by young children with peak use reported in grade 8. Solvent use among school children in the United States peaked in 1995 and has been declining.

- Solvent and gas sniffing is difficult to prevent. Treating solvent abuse is lengthy and difficult because of the cognitive impairment and the fact that many users are socially isolated.

9

Tobacco and Nicotine

Tobacco is the only known natural source of *nicotine,* and it is now clear that nicotine is the active ingredient in tobacco. The tobacco plant belongs to the genus *Nicotiana*, of which there are two subgenera, *rustica* and *tabacum*, used for their nicotine content. Both subgenera contain many species and varieties that differ quite widely in physical characteristics. By far the principal source of tobacco today is *Nicotiana tabacum*, which is cultivated in temperate climates all over the world. Species of *rustica* are not grown widely commercially. While it has a higher nicotine content, it is reputedly harder to cultivate. It is interesting to note that cultivated strains of tobacco have a much higher nicotine content than any wild members of the same genus. These facts suggest that the presence of nicotine in tobacco is much more than mere coincidence. The actual nicotine content of the cured tobacco leaf may reach as much as 6.17 percent.

Although some scholars have claimed that tobacco originated in Africa or Asia, it is now certain that its origins are exclusively American and that the aboriginal peoples of North and South America were the first and only users of the drug at the time of the European discovery of the New World. The earliest known illustration of smoking is reproduced in Figure 9-1. This stone carving from a Mayan temple shows a priest smoking what appears to be a cigar or a reed cigarette.

The plants of *N. tabacum* are usually about 2 meters tall and have long, broad, pointed leaves that are harvested two or three at a time from the bottom of the plant as they mature, although for some types of curing the entire plant is cut at one time. In 1809, a French chemist, Louis Nicolas Vauquelin, claimed to have discovered the active ingredient in tobacco (he called it nicotianine), but his extracts were not pure. It was not until 1828 that pure nicotine was isolated by L. Posselt and F. A. Reimann.

PREPARATIONS

The leaves of the tobacco plant are cured and prepared in different ways, depending on the intended use of the tobacco. Tobacco for burning is made into cigars, cigarettes, or pipe tobacco. Tobacco for chewing is specially processed and flavored. Tobacco snuff is made by drying the

Figure 9-1 A priest smoking a cigar or reed pipe: carving found in a Mayan temple. Native American priests and shamans used tobacco in large quantities. Their rituals centered on foretelling the future and curing illness. (From Dunhill, 1954, p. 4)

leaves, grinding them to a very fine powder, and mixing the powder with various aromatic and flavoring agents. The vast bulk of tobacco is consumed as cigarettes or cigars and in pipes, but there has been a resurgence in oral consumption of tobacco, or what is now commonly called smokeless tobacco. This is either the traditional form of chewing tobacco or a product called *moist snuff*, which is not chewed but tucked between the cheek and the gum. Frequent spitting is not required.

Smokeless tobacco has the advantage that it can be used in places where smoking is banned or when both hands are busy, for example, when playing baseball.

HISTORY

One aspect of the life of the native peoples of North America was commented on by every early European explorer from Columbus on: their use of tobacco. At San Salvador, the site of Columbus's first landfall in 1492, the local inhabitants presented him with some "dry leaves," which Columbus concluded "must be a thing much appreciated among them." Later members of his expedition went ashore in search of the Great Khan. They found no Khan, but they did observe the natives smoking cigars, something that they did not appreciate or understand. They reported that the natives were "perfuming themselves" and that they "drink smoke." One of these men, Rodrego de Jerez, was later to become all too familiar with the significance of the activity; he took up smoking and was imprisoned by the court of the Inquisition for this "devilish habit."

Jean Nicot, the French ambassador to Portugal, became convinced of the medical usefulness of the plant and sent seeds to the royal family in France. Because of his great interest in this plant, Nicot's name was given to the genus *Nicotiana* and subsequently to the alkaloid nicotine.

Tobacco use spread as a wonder cure, but it did not take long to catch on as a recreation, although many users were quick to point out that they were really using it to prevent diseases, such as the plague. When Samuel Pepys, the British diarist, encountered houses where victims of the Great Plague had perished, he felt "an ill conception of myself and my smell, so that I was forced to buy some roll-tobacco to smell and to chew, which took away the apprehension" (Brooks, 1952, p. 40). This association of tobacco with healing lasted into the Victorian era.

The English were among the last Europeans to take up tobacco. In the late sixteenth century, British sailors and sea captains, among them

Hawkins, Drake, and Raleigh, carried the habit home from the West Indies. Raleigh's name has long been associated with tobacco not only because he is credited with the introduction of smoking to the English court but also because he founded the colony at Virginia that was later to owe its survival and prosperity to tobacco cultivation.

Although the British were late to take to the drug, they made up for their tardiness in the popularity tobacco acquired. By the end of the sixteenth century, the demand for the leaf was beginning to cause concern in some quarters. In 1604, King James I published an antitobacco essay titled *A Counterblaste to Tobacco*, in which he refuted all the arguments claiming medical benefits from smoking. As a matter of fact, James I anticipated most of the modern antismoking campaigns, even to claiming that smoking affects "the inward parts of man, soiling and infecting them with a vicious and oily kind of Soote, as hath been found in some great tobacco takers, that hath after their death opened" (Arber, 1895, p. 111).

The tobacco that the English were smoking all this time (and that so angered the king) was imported from Spain at great expense, but the English colony at Virginia was to change all that. The colonists, under John Rolfe, had gotten off to a very bad start. They suffered shipwreck and starvation and were on the point of quitting when Rolfe decided to try growing some Spanish tobacco seeds (*Nicotiana tabacum*) in the soil of Virginia. The experiment was a great success. The plants prospered, and in 1616 a shipload of Virginia tobacco was sent to Britain. At first, the English were skeptical, but the quality of Virginia tobacco was obvious, and within a decade it had replaced the Spanish imports. In spite of the king's taxes and other attempts to discourage the tobacco trade, the colony flourished and secured the English colonial presence in North America.

Smoking has been the primary means of administering tobacco throughout most of its European history, but for a time, it was eclipsed by snuffing. Powdered tobacco was either pinched between the fingers or placed on the back of the hand and then sniffed into the nostrils. The result was usually a vigorous sneeze. The early use of snuff was associated with the clergy (Pope Urban VII was an ardent snuffer), who preferred it to smoking because it was not outlawed in churches and its use could be better concealed from disapproving parishioners.

Tobacco chewing was a North American contribution. It was first observed as a habit of the American Indian, but chewing was never very popular in Europe. In the early part of the nineteenth century, however, there was a strong nationalist sentiment in the new United States and a deliberate rejection of European habits and fashions; snuff was rejected, and chewing tobacco was adopted with patriotic fervor. Chewing was democratic; snuff was aristocratic. Snuff and the pipe had "filtered down from the leaders of fashion to the common folk, while chewing was a practice which . . . seeped from the common man upward into the higher ranks of society" (Robert, 1967, p. 103). The popularity of chewing prompted one Englishman, Charles MacKay, to suggest that the national emblem of the United States should be a spittoon rather than an eagle.

Like tobacco chewing, cigarette smoking had its beginnings in America. Early Spanish explorers reported that Mexican Indians smoked tobacco through "reeds." These were hollow canes filled with tobacco and lighted so that they "burned themselves out without causing a flame." For centuries, cigarette smoking was confined to the Spanish and Portuguese empires, and, even there, it accounted for only a small part of tobacco use. Quite suddenly, in the 1840s, it became very popular in France, especially among French ladies, and it was chiefly the enthusiasm women showed for this means of smoking that stimulated its general acceptance. It was also about this time that flue-cured, or *bright*, tobacco was discovered in North Carolina. This low-nicotine, sweet, mild smoke was perfectly suited to the cigarette. Some people considered cigarettes a novelty—a fad that would soon pass—but they were wrong.

Tobacco smoking persisted unabated until the 1960s, when tobacco was dealt a severe but not fatal blow. The U.S. Surgeon General's Report of 1964, for the first time, definitely linked smoking to cancer and other diseases. This was followed in 1971 by a similar report of the Royal College of Physicians of London. The truth could no longer be hidden or ignored: Tobacco smoking was unhealthy. These statements, combined with the environmentalist and naturalist movements, were actually able to stop the growth of smoking and start a decline.

Globally, about one half of the men in the world (47 percent) are smokers, and 12 percent of the women smoke, consuming 15 billion cigarettes a day (American Lung Association, 2004). Although the use of tobacco in the industrialized nations is declining, tobacco consumption has been rising in the developing countries of the world by about 1.4 percent per year. The increase has been most rapid in the western Pacific region. As a result, global cigarette consumption has remained relatively steady at about 1,650 cigarettes per adult throughout the 1980s and early 1990s (World Health Organization, 1996). It appears that tobacco manufacturers, discouraged by the shrinking of their traditional market, turned their attention to populations not so well educated about the health risks of smoking (Fielding, 1985b; Greenlees, 2005). If current trends continue, by the mid-2020s, about 85 percent of the world's smokers will be in poor and developing countries (American Lung Association, 2006).

Legal Status

Even though tobacco contains an active ingredient (nicotine), for various political and economic reasons, tobacco has never been treated as a drug or medicine, and it is not regulated by governments in Western industrialized countries. Tobacco is not even classed as a "consumer product" for purposes of regulation by the U.S. Consumer Product Safety Commission.

In the United Kingdom, tobacco is not governed by the Medicines Act. Until recently, nicotine tobacco products were not regulated by the U.S. Food and Drug Administration (FDA). The FDA is entitled to regulate drugs in the United States, and a drug is defined as a substance intended by its makers (a) to affect the structure or functions of the body or (b) for use in the diagnosis, cure, mitigation, treatment, or prevention of disease. The tobacco industry had escaped FDA control by claiming that tobacco products were sold for smoking pleasure only and not for the effect of nicotine.

In February 1994, after years of planning, the commissioner of the FDA formally requested that the FDA be given the power to regulate cigarettes as drugs. This request led to a series of hearings before a subcommittee of the U.S. House of Representatives. In the course of the hearings, the commissioner outlined the argument that nicotine was addicting and presented evidence that cigarette manufacturers had knowingly manipulated nicotine delivery of tobacco products (Kozlowski & Henningfield, 1995; Schwartz, 1994) and that, in fact, cigarettes were "nicotine delivery systems." The arguments of the FDA did not convince Congress to give it power to regulate tobacco, but in 1996 the administration of President Clinton gave the FDA authority to reduce access and reduce the appeal of tobacco products to children and adolescents. In 1997, a provision went into effect prohibiting sales of tobacco products to anyone under the age of 18, a measure that was ruled legal by a federal district court decision. However, in 2000, the U.S. Supreme Court ruled in a 5 to 4 decision that the FDA cannot regulate tobacco products until given authority by the Congress. The issue is still unsettled.

ROUTE OF ADMINISTRATION

Unlike cocaine from the coca leaf or morphine from opium, nicotine from tobacco was virtually never self-administered in its pure form. Nicotine is a highly toxic poison, and doses must be controlled precisely; too high a dose will have quite unpleasant effects. Because of its diluted concentration in tobacco, precise control of dosage can more easily be achieved when the nicotine is in its natural form.

When tobacco is chewed, the nicotine is absorbed through the membranes of the mouth. It is only rarely swallowed. Usually, the tobacco juice is spit out, so this process does not represent the usual form of oral administration. Nicotine is a weak base with a pKa of about 8, so it will not have many lipid-soluble molecules when dissolved in solutions with a pH lower than 6. Consequently, nicotine is not quickly absorbed from the acidic digestive system. Oral administration of nicotine has another disadvantage because the blood from the capillaries of the digestive tract must pass through the liver before it achieves general circulation throughout the body. Because the metabolism of nicotine is rather fast in the liver, much of the nicotine taken orally is metabolized during this first pass before it can get to the rest of the body. Although nicotine is not normally self-administered orally, a large number of poisonings occur each year among children who eat tobacco. Fortunately, the nicotine that gets into the blood induces vomiting, and the swallowed tobacco is frequently expelled before the nicotine reaches toxic levels.

Tobacco taken in the form of snuff is sniffed into the nostrils. With this route of administration, most of the nicotine is absorbed through the mucous membranes of the nasal cavity, although some tobacco eventually gets into the stomach and lungs.

When tobacco is burned, nicotine vaporizes and can be found in the smoke and particles of ash that dissolve in the mucous membranes of the inside surface of the lungs. About 90 percent of inhaled nicotine is absorbed into the blood in this way (Pierce, 1941). Studies have shown that the major determinant of nicotine absorption is the volume of smoke inhaled and that increasing the duration of the inhalation does not significantly increase nicotine absorption (Zacny, Stitzer, Brown, Yingling, & Griffiths, 1987).

Nicotine from tobacco smoke may be absorbed through membranes of the mouth in a similar fashion, but this route is more readily influenced by changes in the pH of saliva. In general, cigarettes are made from flue-cured tobacco, which has an acidic smoke, and this lowers the pH of saliva to about 5.3. In acidic saliva, nicotine is ionized and absorption reduced. To be absorbed, the nicotine

from cigarette smoke must, therefore, be inhaled into the lungs, which are so efficient that pH has no effect on absorption. By contrast, pipe and cigar tobacco is usually air-cured, and this process results in a more basic or alkaline smoke. Its pH of about 8.5 is well into the range where ionization of nicotine is less than 50 percent, and absorption is facilitated. Consequently, nicotine in the smoke from cigars and pipes can be absorbed from the mouth, and inhalation is not necessary (Armitage, 1973; R. T. Jones, 1987).

Nicotine absorbed from the lungs is carried directly to the heart; from there, much of the blood containing the nicotine goes straight to the brain. Because of this direct route, the nicotine does not get a chance to dissipate, so the high concentration in the lungs after a puff or rapid inhalation of smoke tends to remain in the blood as a nicotine bolus until it reaches the brain (M. A. H. Russell, 1976). Because nicotine is absorbed much more slowly from the capillaries of the mouth and nose, no such bolus occurs if the smoke is not inhaled. The role of the nicotine bolus in nicotine self-administration and dependence will be discussed later in this chapter.

The average cigarette contains 8 to 9 mg of nicotine, of which a typical smoker absorbs 1 mg in the course of taking 10 puffs per cigarette (R. T. Jones, 1987, p. 1592). The amount of nicotine actually delivered to the smoker is determined to a greater extent by the way the cigarette is smoked than by the actual nicotine content of the cigarette; the delivered amount can vary between 0.3 mg and 3.2 mg per cigarette (Benowitz & Henningfield, 1994).

Newer forms of nicotine administration have been developed for the purpose of nicotine replacement therapy in people who have given up smoking. Nicotine chewing gum was the first of these. The fact that nicotine can be absorbed transdermally (through the skin) allowed for the development of the *patch*. Nicotine-containing patches are placed on the skin, and they release nicotine in various concentrations for a period of time. Most recently, a nicotine nasal spray has been tested. Inhalers and lozenges have also been developed.

The patch causes a slow buildup of nicotine in the blood and maintains it at a constant level for hours. The gum will cause rises and falls in blood nicotine levels in response to its use; as a result, it causes patterns in blood nicotine that more closely resemble those caused by smoking, although peak levels reach only one-third that of smoking (Keenan, Henningfield, & Jarvik, 1995). The nasal spray causes the most cigarette-like changes in blood levels. Within 2.5 minutes of administration, nicotine reaches 85 percent of peak levels in the blood (Sutherland et al., 1992). Figure 9-2 shows the blood level of nicotine for 1 hour after administration by these routes.

In 1996, the U.S. FDA approved the use of a nicotine inhaler. It looks like a cigarette and is held between the fingers. It contains small cartridges of vaporized nicotine that is delivered to the mouth and throat when you draw air through it. Absorption is through the membranes of the mouth rather than the lungs and is therefore slow like nicotine gum. It has the advantage, however, of looking very much like a cigarette and permits the user to manipulate something with the fingers and mouth as they would a real cigarette.

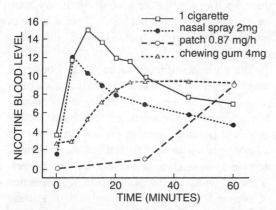

Figure 9-2 Nicotine blood levels for 1 hour after administration of nicotine from various sources. (From de Wit & Zacny, 1995, p. 459)

DISTRIBUTION

The patterns of nicotine distribution in the body depend on the route of administration and the time after administration. When initial high concentrations circulate in the blood, as after inhalation, a high concentration is apparently retained in the brain. After about 30 minutes, the nicotine leaves the brain and is concentrated in the liver, kidneys, salivary glands, and stomach (Schmiterlow & Hanson, 1965).

Nicotine crosses most barriers, including the placenta, and may be found in the sweat, saliva, and milk of nursing women.

EXCRETION

The amount of nicotine excreted by the kidneys depends on the pH of the urine, as described in Chapter 1. Acidic urine (pH less than 7) tends to ionize nicotine and reduce its reabsorption through the nephron wall. Consequently, as much as 30 to 40 percent of administered nicotine may be eliminated in the urine. Reduced ionization at an alkaline pH increases reabsorption into the blood, and the efficiency of the kidneys is reduced, thereby shifting the load of excretion to the enzymes of the liver.

Two pathways in the liver metabolize nicotine to two inactive metabolites, *cotenine* and *nicotine-1'-N-oxide* (Beckett, Gorrod, & Jenner, 1971a). There is evidence that smokers are able to metabolize nicotine faster than nonsmokers and that, among nonsmokers, there may be a difference in nicotine metabolism between males and females (Beckett, Gorrod, & Jenner, 1971b). The half-life of nicotine is variable but is estimated to be about 30 minutes. Nicotine will accumulate in the body of a smoker over the course of a day, but elimination is sufficiently rapid that there will be no day-to-day accumulation (Issac & Rand, 1972).

There appear to be genetic differences in the way people metabolize nicotine. About 16 to 25 percent of the population have a genetic defect in their ability to metabolize nicotine. A given dose of nicotine will reach higher levels and last longer in those people. This appears to offer some protection from becoming a smoker; people with this genetic defect are less likely to become smokers, and if they do smoke, they consume fewer cigarettes (Pianezza, Sellers, & Tyndale, 1998).

NEUROPHYSIOLOGICAL EFFECTS

There are two basic types of cholinergic receptor sites: (a) *muscarinic* and (b) *nicotinic*. Muscarinic receptors are stimulated by muscarine and blocked by anticholinergics such as atropine (see Chapter 4). Nicotinic receptors may be stimulated by nicotine and blocked by curare, a poison used by South American Indian tribes on the tips of their spears and arrows. Another drug that blocks nicotinic receptors but does not appear to be toxic in effective doses is *mecamylamine*. This drug is useful in research with nicotine because if a nicotine effect can be blocked by giving mecamylamine, it is reasonable to conclude that the nicotine effect was a result of its effect on ACh receptors.

Because nicotine occupies and activates nicotinic cholinergic receptor sites, it has traditionally been classified as a nicotinic cholinergic stimulant, but nicotine has a biphasic effect on cholinergic transmission. In low doses, it stimulates these receptors, but it can also block them at higher doses, so it is more accurate to think of nicotine as both a stimulant and a blocker of cholinergic transmission.

What we know about cholinergic receptors is a result of research on the peripheral nervous system. Although muscarinic receptors have been known to exist in the central nervous system for many years, nicotinic receptors were not discovered in the brain until 1980 (Romano & Goldstein, 1980). This research showed that these receptors are part of cholinergic synapses in the brain and are similar to nicotinic cholinergic receptors in the peripheral nervous system. In addition, many nicotinic receptors are found in the synapses and cell bodies of cells in the brain that use DA and NE, and when they are stimulated, they cause a release of DA and NE. Nicotinic receptors of this nature are found in the cortex, the basal ganglia, the ventral tegmental area, and the nucleus accumbens (Balfour, 1991; Levin, 1992).

In addition to its effect on acetylcholine and the catecholamines, nicotine causes the release of serotonin, beta-endorphin, and numerous hormones, such as vasopressin, growth hormone, and prolactin, all known to have effects on behavior (O. F. Pomerleau & Pomerleau, 1984).

EFFECTS OF TOBACCO

Effects on the Body

Peripheral Nervous System. In the peripheral nervous system, nicotinic receptor sites are located primarily in the neuromuscular junctions of striated or voluntary muscles. The poisonous effects of curare result because the drug blocks these junctions, and the muscles become paralyzed; the victim can no longer breathe and dies of suffocation. Nicotine stimulates these receptors, and muscular tremors result. One British surgeon, H. J. Johnson (1965), was motivated to quit smoking when he noticed that an extra cigarette before surgery caused a fine hand tremor. In addition, there may be an inhibition of some reflexes. There is a decrease in the patellar reflex (knee jerk) after a cigarette. This effect, which is due to a lowering in the tone of voluntary muscles, appears to be a direct result of stimulation of inhibitory cells in the motor pools in the spinal cord (Domino, 1973).

The biphasic effect of nicotine on cholinergic transmission is reflected in the ability of nicotine to stimulate and then block transmission in autonomic ganglia. These two effects, however, are modified because nicotine causes the release of other neurotransmitters that affect the peripheral nervous system. One such neurotransmitter is epinephrine, which produces sympathetic stimulation of its own. When this is combined with neuromuscular and parasympathetic stimulation and blocking, the result is a very complicated array of peripheral nervous system changes.

In general, at doses encountered in tobacco smoking, nicotine produces increases in heart rate and blood pressure and causes a constriction of blood vessels in the skin. This constriction causes a drop in skin temperature and is probably responsible for the cold touch that smokers have and the reason that the skin of smokers tends to wrinkle and age faster than that of nonsmokers (Daniell, 1971). The reduced blood flow to the skin also explains why smokers do not blush easily. This lack of skin color prompted one judge in the 1930s to accuse cigarettes of "deadening the sense of shame" and corrupting the morals of young people.

Nicotine also inhibits stomach secretions and stimulates activity of the bowel. For this reason, especially for someone with little tobacco tolerance, a cigarette can act as a laxative.

Central Nervous System. The effects of nicotine in the central nervous system (CNS) are complicated. Apart from its direct effects on synapses, nicotine also stimulates the release of epinephrine from various sites, including the adrenal glands. This causes a CNS arousal resulting in a decrease in the alpha activity shown in the electroencephalogram (EEG). Arousal is also produced by direct stimulation of the reticular activating system. Respiration is increased because of both direct and indirect stimulation of the medullary respiration centers. Respiratory arrest caused by an overdose of nicotine results from a block of these centers as well as of the neuromuscular junctions that control the muscles used in breathing.

Another brain stem center that is stimulated both directly and indirectly by nicotine is the vomiting center. This effect is most noticeable in naive smokers who have no tolerance and do not have the experience to control dosage appropriately. Their initial experience with tobacco makes most young people nauseous and "green about the gills." This effect is subject to tolerance, but even experienced smokers can feel a bit "green" if they consume more than their accustomed amount of tobacco.

Higher in the brain, nicotine causes a general release of NE and DA and activates systems that use these transmitters. Photon emission tomography (PET) imaging using [11C]raclopride, which binds to D_2 receptors, demonstrates a relationship between the pleasurable effects of smoking and binding potential of the radiotracer. Participants who reported increases in euphoria while smoking their usual brand of cigarette during a PET scanning session also demonstrated significant decreases in [11C]raclopride binding potential in the caudate region of the striatum (Barrett, Boileau, Okker, Pihl, & Dagher, 2004). Decreases in radiotracer binding potential demonstrate that receptor sites are occupied by dopamine. Conversely, participants who reported experiencing smoking-induced decreases in euphoria demonstrated increased [11C]raclopride binding in the caudate.

Recent research has shown that the cells in the ventral tegmental area (VTA) that release DA in the nucleus accumbens contain a subtype of nicotinic receptor. Nicotine is not reinforcing in mice that are genetically manipulated, so they do not have these receptors (knockout mice). When the genes that make these receptors are reintroduced into the VTA, nicotine becomes reinforcing (Maskos et al., 2005). This indicates that nicotine increases dopamine activity in the nucleus accumbens by directly stimulating the neurons in the VTA.

Serotonin systems are also altered by nicotine, particularly the system that runs from the Raphé system to the cortex. This system is the primary site of action of the antidepressant drugs (Chapter 14), and nicotine appears to have an effect similar to that of the antidepressants (Balfour, 1991).

It has also become clear that cholinergic systems, both muscarinic and nicotinic, are important in cognitive functioning. In a later section in this chapter, the cognition-enhancing effects of nicotine are discussed.

Effects on Sleep

There is some evidence that intravenous infusions of nicotine may cause REM sleep in cats (Domino & Yamamoto, 1965), but nicotine given intravenously before bedtime did not have any effect on sleep stages in healthy humans (Domino, 1967).

In another study, withdrawal from tobacco did disrupt sleep. Smokers undergoing withdrawal were shown to have a moderate increase in REM sleep time. This increase was accompanied by subjective reports of an increase in dreaming and in the vividness of dreams (Kales, Allen, Preston, & Tan, 1970).

EFFECTS ON THE BEHAVIOR AND PERFORMANCE OF HUMANS

Subjective Effects

Acute Effects. Smoking is a pleasurable experience for many people (de Wit & Zacny, 1995). In one study, nicotine was administered either by tobacco smoke inhalation or by intravenous infusion to volunteers, and their subjective responses were measured using the Addiction Research Center Inventory. Smokers reported increased liking scores and reported subjective effects similar to those caused by morphine and amphetamine. These effects peaked about 1 minute after administration and were gone within a few minutes. Nonsmokers, however, did not enjoy the experience (Henningfield, Miyasato, & Jasinski, 1985; Jasinski, Johnson, & Henningfield, 1984). These subjective effects were blocked by mecamylamine (Henningfield, Miyasato, Johnson, & Jasinski, 1983). In another experiment, smokers were given cigarettes with different levels of nicotine in the morning after being deprived of smoking since the previous evening. They were permitted to smoke the cigarettes themselves and were asked to push a button when they experienced "a rush, a buzz, or a high." Nineteen of 22 subjects experienced at least one such sensation. Frequency and duration of sensations were related to blood nicotine levels. These sensations lasted for about 11 seconds and occurred with a delay of about 30 seconds after a puff (C. S. Pomerleau & Pomerleau, 1992).

Nesbitt's Paradox. In most studies, nicotine appears to cause an arousal in brain wave activity and a release of epinephrine that arouses the sympathetic nervous system, yet most smokers report that they smoke because smoking a cigarette relaxes them. Even people who have given up smoking for a long time report that they feel the need for a smoke during moments of stress. One researcher (Schachter, 1973) has called this unexpected observation Nesbitt's paradox, after a man who first studied it, and it has been the object of considerable research.

There are a number of explanations of Nesbitt's paradox, and all are related to the question of why people smoke. It may be that lighting and holding a cigarette gives people something to do with their hands, and this act calms the nerves, as pressing worry beads does. In fact, one study showed that the act of smoking causes increases in alpha waves, indicating relaxation, but the nicotine causes arousal (Murphree, Pfeiffer, & Price, 1967). It is also possible that the calmness is a result of relief from the nicotine withdrawal symptoms that smokers may experience in a mild form between cigarettes, or stimulation may be caused by low doses and relaxation by high doses, and the smoker can control the desired effect by altering inhalation of the smoke (O. F. Pomerleau & Pomerleau, 1984; Stepney, 1982). One study showed that the effect of smoking on arousal can depend on the stressfulness of the circumstances in which the cigarette is smoked. When subjects were stressed by noise, smoking reduced arousal as measured by the EEG, but under conditions of low arousal, smoking had an activating effect on EEG (Mangan & Golding, 1978). Another study showed that subjective arousal (although not arousal measured by blood pressure and heart rate) was related to baseline arousal levels. Nicotine nasal spray and cigarette smoking increased arousal in people who had low baseline levels but had little effect on those whose arousal levels were already high (Perkins, Grobe, Epstein, Caggiula, & Stiller, 1992).

Chronic Effects. As we shall see later, one theory of why people smoke is that they are using the nicotine in tobacco to control their response to stress and to create a positive mood. There are, in fact, few data to support this. A survey in the United Kingdom has shown that smokers have lower levels of psychological well-being than nonsmokers and ex-smokers (West, 1993). In addition, even though it is typically found that mood worsens when a person stops smoking, it slowly returns to the normal smoking level after 3 or 4 weeks. What's more, it then continues to improve even further during the following 10 weeks, so the person's mood becomes even better than it was while he or she was smoking (Hughes, Higgins, & Hatsukami, 1990).

Effects on Performance. There have been many studies of the effects of nicotine on human performance, and the results have not been entirely consistent. The data are further complicated by the fact that the effects of nicotine appear to be different in smokers and nonsmokers. In general, the major effect of smoking is to improve the performance of regular smokers whose behavior has been degraded by withdrawal from nicotine. In a simulated driving task, for example, it was found that the performance of nonsmokers and of smokers who were allowed to smoke was equal, but an impairment in vigilance and tracking was detected in smokers deprived of nicotine (Heimstra, Bancroft, & De Kock, 1967).

Functional magnetic resonance imaging studies provide an illustration of the cognitive impairments caused in chronic smokers by nicotine abstinence. Using BOLD imaging, researchers presented participants with a visual display of constantly changing letters in which the letter X was the target letter. When the letter X appeared, participants were asked to report which letter had been presented either immediately before, two letters before, or three letters before the letter X. Increasing the number of letters that must be remembered increases cognitive load by taxing working memory. If the participants had smoked nicotine within 1.5 hours prior to testing, activity in the dorsolateral prefrontal cortex was significantly lower when reporting which letter had directly preceded the letter X (1-back) compared to when reporting which letter had occurred two or three

letters before X (2-back and 3-back). However, following 14 hours of nicotine abstinence when participants were experiencing nicotine withdrawal, BOLD imaging showed that participants exhibited high levels of cognitive activity in the dorsolateral prefrontal cortex, regardless of which letter they were asked to report. In other words during nicotine withdrawal, the previously simple 1-back task required as much brain activity as the 2- and 3-back task. They also found that the participants made more errors on all three tasks during nicotine withdrawal (Xu et al., 2005). These effects are shown in Color Plate B.

Other studies, however, have shown that smoking may do more than just eliminate nicotine withdrawal deficits. On tasks that require vigilance and sustained attention, such as driving, it can enhance performance, even beyond the performance of nonsmokers (Tarriere & Hartemann, 1964; Wesnes & Warburton, 1983). In an extensive review of nicotine and human performance, Wesnes and Warburton (1983) concluded that smoking does help sustain performance on monotonous tasks and improves both the speed and the accuracy of information processing.

In addition to speeded information processing, faster motor reaction speeds have also been reported for both cigarette smoking and chewing nicotine gum (Pritchard, Robinson, & Guy, 1992; Sherwood, Kerr, & Hindmarch, 1992).

Smoking can also improve performance on learning tasks. The effects of smoking one cigarette on serial anticipation learning of a list of nonsense syllables was determined in an experiment by Anderson (1975). She showed that the effects of the cigarette were similar to any arousing stimulus: The learning of the list was impaired, but recall of the list 45 minutes later was improved. She suggested that this outcome reflects the fact that arousal at the time of learning causes poor immediate recall because of the interfering effect of an increase in nonspecific activity. The increased arousal, however, aids the process of consolidation and improves recall of the list at a later time. Similar effects on consolidation have also been reported in studies on nonhumans, as we shall see.

Other improvements in memory have been noted, and it has now been demonstrated that some of these effects are not attributable to relief of smoking withdrawal in regular smokers (Warburton, 1992).

Interestingly, nicotine has been shown to improve various aspects of cognitive functioning in patients with Alzheimer's disease and in aging laboratory rats and monkeys (Levin, 1992).

In spite of demonstrations that nicotine can improve performance and learning, there are many more reports that it has no effect or may even interfere with cognitive and performance variables (West, 1993). These divergent findings have led to rather heated debates among researchers. A debate that was reviewed in *Addiction* (1993, Vol. 88, pp. 591–600) is particularly interesting because, as we shall see later, one theory of why people smoke is that they find it improves their performance. This theory is advanced as an alternative to the theory that smoking can be considered similar to addiction to other drugs (J. H. Robinson & Pritchard, 1992).

EFFECTS ON THE BEHAVIOR OF NONHUMANS

Unconditioned Behavior

Spontaneous motor activity (SMA) of rats is initially depressed by 0.8 mg/kg of nicotine, but, after 7 days of testing, this dosage produces an increase in SMA that, during repeated testing, gets greater until the increase is similar to that produced by 0.8 mg/kg of amphetamine. It is believed that the initial depression is a result of the effect of nicotine on ACh transmission in the brain, an effect that disappears with tolerance after a few days. Once the ACh effect decreases, the increase in epinephrine causes an increase in SMA in a manner similar to amphetamine (Morrison & Stephenson, 1972b; Stolerman, Fink, & Jarvik, 1973).

Conditioned Behavior

After an initial suppression of all behavior at higher doses, the effects of nicotine on both positively and aversively motivated behavior are similar to amphetamine: The effect is dependent on control rate; high rates are depressed, and low rates are increased (Morrison, 1967; Pradhan, 1970). Like amphetamine, nicotine does not appear to increase responses that have been suppressed by response-contingent shock (Morrison & Stephenson, 1972a).

It has also been shown that withdrawal from 0.4 mg/kg of nicotine can disrupt the ability of rats to avoid a shock in the same manner that nicotine withdrawal can interfere with the behavior of humans (Morrison, 1974).

This great similarity between the effects of nicotine and amphetamine on operant behavior suggests that many of these effects are likely brought about by a similar mechanism. Because amphetamine increases activity at catecholamine synapses (see Chapter 11) and nicotine causes the general release of epinephrine and stimulates DA and NE synapses, it is possible that many of these behavioral effects of nicotine are a result of the release of catecholamines (Pradhan, 1970). This increase in catecholamine activity, however, depends on the action of nicotine at its receptor sites because most of these behavioral effects can be blocked by pretreating the animal with mecamylamine, a drug that blocks nicotinic receptor sites (Morrison, 1967).

DRUG STATE DISCRIMINATION

Nicotine is an effective cue in a drug state discrimination task in a dosage range similar to one that alters operant behavior. It has been shown that 0.2 mg/kg nicotine can be used as a cue and will not generalize to various doses of epinephrine, pentobarbital, physostigmine, chlordiazepoxide, or caffeine. The stimulus properties of nicotine can be blocked by mecamylamine (Morrison & Stephenson, 1969; Stolerman, Pratt, & Garcha, 1982).

Although it cannot be found consistently, there is some evidence of partial generalization between nicotine and d-amphetamine, and animals trained to discriminate cocaine will sometimes generalize the cocaine response to nicotine (Stolerman,

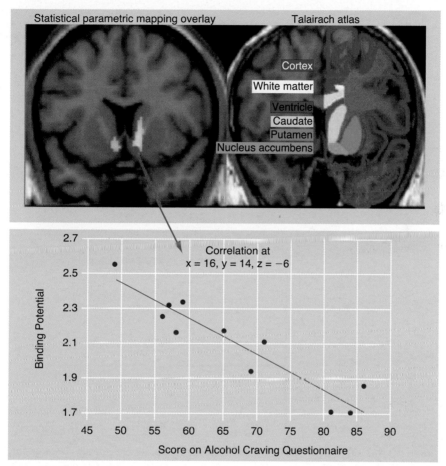

Color Plate A This figure shows the relationship between activity in the ventral striatum (the location of the nucleus accumbens) and craving for alcohol caused by exposure to alcohol-related cues in long-term alcoholics. The yellow brain image at the right shows the area of the brain that was activated when the participants were exposed to the alcohol cues. As you can see, this corresponds to the area of the nucleus accumbens, as shown in the brain image on the left. The lower panel shows the negative correlation between craving and the binding potential for dopamine D_2 receptors in the nucleus accumbens. As you can see, the lower the binding potential at D_2 receptors, the higher the craving induced by the alcohol-related cues. (Heinz et al., 2004; reprinted with permission)

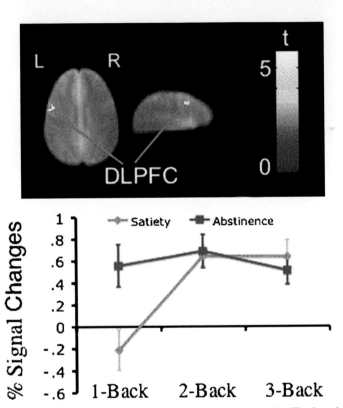

Color Plate B   The top panel of this figure shows the BOLD image of the brain. The location of the dorsal lateral prefrontal cortex (DLPC) is indicated. The color bar at the right indicates the level of activity in the DLP during the task. The lower panel shows the amount of activity in the DLPFC during the 1-, 2-, and 3-back tests when subjects had smoked within the previous 1.5 hours (Satiety) and when they were deprived of nicotine for 14 hours (Abstinence). (Adapted from Xu et al., 2005, fig. 3, p. 147; reprinted with permission)

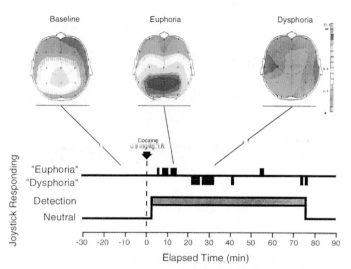

Color Plate C   Behavioral and EEG changes in a participant after receiving a 90 mg/kg cocaine injection. The color bar at the right indicates amount of alpha activity. Euphoria is correlated with increased alpha activity in the occipital and parietal cortex. Below-normal levels of alpha activity occurred when participants reported dysphoria. (Lukas, 1991, chap. 1, fig. 7, p. 14; reprinted with permission)

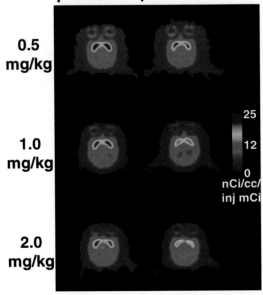

Color Plate D   This figure shows the effect of giving various doses of methamphetamine to baboons four times at 2-hour intervals. These PET images were taken 2 to 3 weeks after the drug treatment. The color bar in the left panel shows the color associated with the amount of binding to the dopamine transporter (DAT), with red showing many transporter molecules and blue showing fewer. The images show the pre- and postmethamphetamine activity in the brain. The yellow and red areas are in the caudate nucleus. You can see a dose-related decrease in DAT binding, indicating that there has been death of some dopamine cells in the area. (Adapted from Villemagne et al., 1998, fig. 1, p. 421; reprinted with permission)

1987). This finding corresponds to the observation made earlier: Humans sometimes describe the effect of intravenous nicotine as being similar to that of cocaine.

It has been shown that humans can discriminate between identical cigarettes that are different only in nicotine content (Kallman, Kallman, Harry, Woodson, & Rosecrans, 1982), although it is not known whether this is done by taste or through a central mechanism.

WITHDRAWAL SYMPTOMS

When most tobacco users attempt to give up their habit, they experience withdrawal symptoms in varying degrees of intensity. If you have ever attempted to quit smoking or have suffered along with someone going through tobacco withdrawal, you are familiar with the symptoms. Withdrawal from nicotine is not as severe physically as withdrawal from heroin, but it is just as stressful psychologically. Indeed, many ex-heroin addicts who have also quit smoking report that they found it harder to give up tobacco than heroin.

Systematic studies of nicotine withdrawal in regular smokers reliably showed the following symptoms: decreased heart rate; increased eating, which caused weight gain; an inability to concentrate; increased awakenings during sleep; craving for cigarettes; and anxiety, anger, aggression, and depression (Hughes, Gust, Skoog, Keenan, & Fenwick, 1991; Hughes, Higgins, & Bickel, 1994). Other symptoms that have been reported are nervousness, drowsiness, light-headedness, headaches, dizziness, tremor, and nausea (Jarvik, 1979, p. 27). EEG recordings of nicotine-dependent individuals who abstain from tobacco for 10 to 24 hours show a slowing in the frequency of alpha waves and an increase in theta wave amplitude and frequency, normally seen during drowsiness or light sleep (Herning, Jones, & Bachman, 1983). These effects are immediately reversed on administration of tobacco, suggesting physical dependence on nicotine. Other researchers have also shown that the application of a transdermal nicotine patch during acute nicotine withdrawal increases EEG brain wave as well as P300 amplitudes (Knott, Bosman, Mahoney, Ilivitsky, & Quirt, 1999).

Most of these symptoms, except for weight gain and craving, are over within a month. For about 25 percent of people, these symptoms may persist as long as 6 months, although there are reports that craving may continue as long as 9 years (Fletcher & Doll, 1969).

Withdrawal symptoms can be relieved by the administration of nicotine from other sources such as gum and transdermal patches. However, unlike withdrawal from many other drugs, the administration of the receptor blocker for nicotine, mecamylamine, does not induce withdrawal in nicotine-dependent smokers (Hughes et al., 1994). Symptoms of nicotine withdrawal can also be reduced, at least temporarily, by the taste and smell of tobacco or the act of smoking itself. One study showed that tobacco withdrawal symptoms were relieved if smokers were allowed to smoke a denicotinized cigarette that delivered no nicotine at all to the smoker (Butschky, Bailey, Henningfield, & Pickworth, 1994).

For a time, nicotine withdrawal can interfere with performance on various cognitive and motor tasks. As we have already seen, nicotine withdrawal interferes with rats' shock avoidance (Morrison, 1974).

Unlike most other drugs that cause physical dependence, withdrawal severity does not seem to be related to dose; heavy and light smokers report equally severe withdrawal. Nor is withdrawal severity related to length of time smoking, previous attempts at quitting, sex, age, education, or alcohol and caffeine use (Hughes et al., 1991).

SELF-ADMINISTRATION IN NONHUMANS

Because self-administration of nicotine in humans is so persistent and widespread, it is surprising that accounts of animal self-administration are rare. There are some anecdotal accounts of tame monkeys smoking. Indeed, Charles Darwin, in *The Descent of Man* (1882), claimed to have seen monkeys "smoke tobacco with pleasure" (p. 7).

Darwin used these observations to support his contention that the sense of taste and the nervous systems of humans and monkeys are similar. Surprisingly, however, systematic research from laboratories has found monkeys to be reluctant smokers (Jarvik, 1973, p. 296). Monkeys have been taught to inhale cigarette smoke, but the procedure involved a period of forced consumption in which the monkeys were reinforced with drinking water for sucking on a tube through which they received tobacco smoke. After this training, some animals seemed to prefer sucking on a tube that delivered tobacco smoke over one that delivered only air. It is doubtful whether this procedure represents a situation similar to human tobacco use. Animals do not normally initiate smoking on their own (Jarvik, 1973).

There are few accounts of animals' working for intravenous infusions of nicotine. Most studies show that if nicotine is self-administered, responding is not robust and is rather slow (Stolerman, 1987). In one study (Deneau & Inoki, 1967), monkeys were given the opportunity to self-administer nicotine through an intravenous cannula. After being given hourly infusions of nicotine for 2 to 5 days, some animals reliably responded for nicotine, but response rates were low, and the pattern was not consistent from day to day. In a later study, S. R. Goldberg, Spealman, and Goldberg (1981) were able to demonstrate reliable intravenous self-administration in monkeys. Using a second-order schedule, they found that if the nicotine infusion was preceded by a colored light, monkeys would respond at a high rate for the light alone, even if it was paired with the nicotine infusion only occasionally. It appears that the stimuli associated with the delivery of nicotine make a very important contribution to the effectiveness of nicotine as a reinforcer. Goldberg and his associates also demonstrated that injections of the nicotine antagonist mecamylamine reduced responding to saline control levels.

In another study, Risner and Goldberg (1983) demonstrated that dogs would self-administer nicotine on a fixed ratio (FR) 10 schedule when a 4-minute time-out was imposed after each infusion. Progressive ratio schedules showed that some nicotine doses would support ratios as high as 510 responses per infusion, much higher than saline but considerably lower than cocaine.

It appears, then, that nicotine infusions do have reinforcing properties in laboratory animals under a restricted range of conditions. Conditions that support nicotine infusion are a period of forced consumption, stimuli paired with the infusion, and a fixed interval or second-order schedule that imposes an abstinence period between opportunities to self-administer.

Intravenous nicotine can also serve as a punisher. In one study, food-reinforced behavior of monkeys was suppressed if it was followed by an infusion of nicotine (S. R. Goldberg & Spealman, 1983). This suppression occurred at the same dose that served as a positive reinforcer for monkeys in other experiments conducted in the same laboratory. It is not clear what might make nicotine a reinforcer under some circumstances and a punisher in others.

SELF-ADMINISTRATION IN HUMANS

There is little doubt that nicotine is a reinforcer in human smokers. In one study, human smokers were attached to an intravenous catheter and could self-administer infusions of nicotine by pressing a lever on an FR 10 schedule. Responding increased on this lever when the nicotine was available and was extinguished when saline infusions were substituted. It was also shown that when larger doses were used, subjects administered fewer infusions, and they increased infusions when the dose was decreased (Henningfield et al., 1987, pp. 582–585; Henningfield, Lucas, & Bigelow, 1986).

Delivery of nicotine is clearly a reinforcer in humans, and humans are capable of adjusting nicotine doses, but the nature of the change in blood nicotine levels that is responsible is not clear. One possibility is that smokers are trying to maintain a constant level of nicotine in the blood, another is that they are trying to achieve sudden high doses delivered to the brain, and a third is that smokers manipulate dose depending on situational factors and the effects that they expect the drug to have on their mood and behavior.

Constant Blood Level Theory

There is evidence that the smoker is trying to maintain a constant level of nicotine in the blood, that is, a dose high enough to avoid withdrawal symptoms but below a level that has toxic or aversive effects.

For some time, it had not been clearly established that nicotine is the ingredient in tobacco that is responsible for tobacco consumption. To show that it is, researchers used the strategy of changing the nicotine content of cigarettes and noting whether the amount of smoking changed as a consequence. Would smokers titrate their dose to achieve a constant level?

Early studies had trouble demonstrating dose compensation when they measured dose by simply counting the number of high-and low-nicotine cigarettes a person smoked. They soon learned that people control nicotine intake not by changing the number of cigarettes they smoke but by changing their smoking behavior; that is, they compensate for low-nicotine cigarettes by taking deeper and more frequent puffs on the cigarette. These variables can be measured precisely by having subjects smoke through a special cigarette holder connected to a computer that monitors total smoke inhalation. Using these techniques, it has been demonstrated that smokers will compensate for increased or reduced doses by increasing and decreasing their puffing behavior, but the compensation is not as complete as when intravenous infusions are used.

One of the predictions of this theory is that the first few puffs on a cigarette will be rapid and deep as the smoker tries to raise blood nicotine levels that have fallen since the previous cigarette was smoked. As the nicotine level increases, the puff rate will decrease, and few puffs will be taken near the end of the cigarette. This change in puff rate has been recorded by several researchers (Chait & Griffiths, 1982). In addition, the theory predicts that people will be highly motivated to smoke when their blood levels are low and that the lowest levels occur after a night of sleeping. A British study showed that 14 percent of smokers light up within 5 minutes of waking in the morning, and 50 percent do so within 30 minutes.

In an elaboration of this theory, Stanley Schachter, at Columbia University, has suggested why smoking increases in times of stress. During stress, the urine becomes acidic. Because nicotine is a weak base, it becomes highly ionized in the acidic urine and, consequently, cannot be reabsorbed into the blood. As a result, the kidneys are very efficient in excreting nicotine, and the blood levels drop rapidly. Schachter (1978) suggested that this rapid drop in blood nicotine is the signal that another cigarette is necessary. In other words, "the smoker's mind is in the bladder." Consequently, smoking increases in times of stress.

Human smokers attempt to prevent their nicotine blood level from falling to the point where withdrawal symptoms occur. Smokers also can make adjustments for the amount of nicotine delivered by their cigarette, but they are unable to compensate completely. Their blood levels then become higher than normal when nicotine content is increased and lower than normal when it is decreased. In addition, increasing blood nicotine levels with nicotine chewing gum will decrease smoking but does not eliminate it. Factors other than constant blood level are controlling nicotine intake as well.

Nicotine Bolus Theory

The *nicotine bolus theory* has been proposed by M. A. H. Russell of the Maudsley Hospital in London to explain some aspects of smoking behavior. Careful observation of a cigarette smoker will show that when smoke is inhaled into the lungs, it is frequently done with one rapid inhalation rather than gradually, as with a normal breath. This sudden filling of the lungs with smoke tends to saturate the blood in the capillaries of the lungs with nicotine at the moment of inhalation. This concentration of nicotine in the blood, known as the *nicotine bolus,* stays together as the blood returns to the heart and is pumped to the brain. This theory suggests that the sudden high level of nicotine in the brain acts as a positive reinforcer and keeps the smoker smoking. It has been established that nicotine stimulates the mesolimbic dopamine system like most other reinforcing drugs, and this is likely responsible for the reports of positive mood and euphoria after its administration. Because the bolus is so pleasurable, it is responsible for the intense craving for tobacco (M. A. H. Russell, 1976). A similar theory has been proposed to explain the addictive nature of intravenous injections of heroin (Dole, 1980) and is consistent with the general finding that the reinforcing properties of drugs can be greatly enhanced by delivering them to the brain rapidly in high concentrations.

Because a nicotine bolus can be achieved only by smoking, this theory explains why the craving for the drug is worse in smokers than in those who take tobacco by other means, but it cannot account for the great popularity of tobacco in its other forms throughout history.

Psychological Tool Theory

Another explanation of smoking is related to Nesbitt's paradox described earlier. It suggests that a smoker uses nicotine as a tool to help cope with daily tasks by manipulating levels of arousal and other psychological functions. As we have seen, nicotine can subjectively both increase and decrease levels of arousal, depending on dose and circumstances. The *psychological tool theory* suggests that the smoker uses smoking as a tool to decrease arousal in times of stress and to increase arousal during fatigue and boredom and, thus, is able to maintain an optimal level of arousal. Changing arousal levels allows performance on tasks to be enhanced as well. Together, these factors increase the psychological comfort of the smoker and provide the motivation for smoking (Balfour, 1982; Hutchison &

Emley, 1973; J. H. Robinson & Pritchard, 1992; Stepney, 1982, pp. 193–196).

This idea has considerable intuitive appeal, and there is some evidence to support it, but most of this evidence is indirect. It has been shown that nicotine can enhance performance on some tasks and can reduce the effects of stress, but these effects are disputed and not easily replicated. In addition, it is difficult to show that beneficial effects of nicotine, even if they do occur, are responsible for nicotine self-administration. Recent studies with amphetamines and sedatives have shown that people will sometimes choose to use a drug that either stimulates them or sedates them, depending on the demands of a task they will be performing (K. Silverman, Mumford, & Griffiths, 1994), but this has not been shown for nicotine. Moreover, many other studies (described in Chapter 5) indicate that, in general, drugs are seldom self-administered for their therapeutic effects. We know that smoking increases in times of stress, but this observation can be explained more simply by other mechanisms, as Schachter has done. In addition, stress-reducing agents such as the benzodiazepines (Librium and Valium) do not appear to be effective in helping people to stop smoking (Jaffe, 1987).

Comparing Theories

These three explanations—the constant blood level theory, the nicotine bolus theory, and the psychological tool theory—are not mutually exclusive. They may all be correct to some extent. Nicotine can act as a positive reinforcer. Constant blood levels that avoid withdrawal may well be reinforcing, and so may the nicotine bolus and the ability to alter arousal and performance. Smokers may be trying to achieve any one or all three at the same time. A combination of all ideas can explain more of the data than a single theory alone. It is also possible that one theory may not be appropriate for all smokers. Different people may smoke for different reasons. Tobacco smoking is a complicated activity.

The debate on the nature of smoking has taken on a political significance since the 1988 U.S. Surgeon General's Report and the 1994 U.S. House of Representatives hearings on whether the tobacco industry in the United States should be regulated by the FDA. The FDA and the surgeon general argue that smoking is addicting in the same sense that cocaine and heroin are; that is, it stimulates reward centers in the brain and is a positive reinforcer. Defenders of the tobacco industry claim that this is not the case. Smoking, they say, is motivated by a desire to control mood and performance; that is, it is a behavior enhancer (J. H. Robinson & Pritchard, 1992). The debate has not been settled on either the scientific or the political front, but the behavior enhancer argument seems to be losing ground on both fronts (Kozlowski & Henningfield, 1995).

Smoking Behavior of Humans

North American native peoples, who were the first to use tobacco, tended to use it as a hallucinogen, and they consumed it irregularly in fairly high doses. It was associated with ceremonies and was often used by shamans. Modern use is quite different. Most cigarette smokers space cigarettes out fairly evenly throughout their waking hours, but a careful analysis shows that there is a regular daily pattern. Smoking is usually greatest in the early afternoon, right after lunch, and after supper (between 7:00 and 10:00 P.M.). Throughout the course of a week, Wednesday and Sunday are the lightest smoking days, and Saturday is the heaviest (Meade & Wald, 1977).

Although the pattern of cigarette smoking is fairly regular over the course of a day or a week for any individual, cigarette intake may increase in particular circumstances. One factor is the presence of cigarettes or of other smokers. Experiments have shown that if smokers are asked to wait in a room, they will light up a cigarette much sooner if other people in the room are smoking (Glad & Adesso, 1976). People are also more likely to smoke if a pack of cigarettes is left in a conspicuous place in the room (Herman, 1974).

Tobacco Chippers. As with other drugs, the amount of nicotine consumed varies considerably among individuals. The average regular smoker consumes about 25 cigarettes a day and shows signs of physical dependence on nicotine, but about 10 percent of regular smokers consume fewer than five cigarettes a day and are clearly not physically dependent. These smokers have been called *tobacco chippers* because their pattern of occasional use without physical dependence resembles a pattern of heroin use called "chipping" (Shiffman, 1989; see also Chapter 12).

Who Smokes?

Tobacco is not used by everyone. Studies of smokers and nonsmokers have revealed some interesting differences. Like drinking, smoking appears to have a genetic component. Studies of twins have shown that identical twins are more likely to have similar smoking habits than fraternal twins. Even when they are not reared together, the smoking behavior of identical twins is highly correlated (Eysenck & Eaves, 1980; Hughes, 1986).

Smokers are more likely than nonsmokers to use other drugs such as caffeine and, especially, alcohol. In addition, smokers are more likely to change their jobs, get married and divorced, have more traffic accidents, be more rebellious, achieve less academically, and be more sexually active than nonsmokers (Ashton & Stepney, 1982, p. 121; Jarvis, 1994).

Before smoking peaked at nearly 80 percent in the middle of the twentieth century, there was no relation between social class, education, and smoking, but now that smoking rates have fallen, distinct effects of social class and economics have become apparent. People who are unemployed, work in unskilled and manual labor jobs, or have less than a high school education are much more likely to smoke than people who work at professional jobs and have a college degree.

Typically, people start to smoke when they are teenagers. At this stage, social class does not seem to have an effect; however, having parents who smoke, a significant other who is a smoker, or poor academic achievement will predict, albeit weakly, who will start smoking. Few people become smokers after the age of 20.

Behavioral Economics

Numerous attempts have been made to determine the price elasticity of cigarettes. Estimates range from −0.4 to −1.3, but the figure is generally accepted to be about −0.7. This indicates a relatively inelastic demand. Further analyses, however, have shown that this inelasticity is not the same for different segments of the population or for different measures of demand. Teenage smokers are more susceptible to price increases than older smokers in terms of both the number of cigarettes smoked and the number of smokers. The slope of the demand curve of participation (number of smokers) was shown to be −1.20 for smokers 12 to 17 years old in the United States, and the quantity (cigarettes smoked per smoker) was −0.25, with a combined demand of −1.40. In this study, the slope of the demand curve for smokers over 20 was −0.42. These figures indicate that demand in young smokers is elastic—that is, increasing the price of cigarettes will have a considerable impact on the initiation rate of young smokers, but it may not have a large effect on the smoking behavior of older, established smokers. Because most people become s okers before the age of 20, price increases will ! a considerable effect. They will decrease ciga- : consumption not only at the time they are put effect but also far into the future (Lewitt, 1989).

Another study of demand elasticity for ciga- r es has shown that elasticities are greater if l g-term effects are measured. A study of ciga- r te prices in the United States from 1955 to 1985 fou nd that a permanent increase of 10 percent in pric e had an immediate effect of reducing consumption by 4 percent. In the long term, however, there was a decrease in consumption of 7.5 percent. In addition, elasticities were much smaller if the price increase was temporary rather than permanent (Becker, Grossman, & Murphy, 1988).

HARMFUL EFFECTS

Heart Disease

Heart disease caused by tobacco smoke appears to be due largely to the combined action of nicotine and carbon monoxide. Nicotine increases the workload of the heart, and carbon monoxide reduces the oxygen-carrying capacity of the blood and, consequently, the oxygen supply to the heart itself. These effects are further complicated by the fact that other constituents in the smoke reduce the lungs' ability to absorb oxygen, so the heart must work even harder to pump more blood through the lungs and satisfy the oxygen needs of the body. In addition, there is a relationship between atherosclerosis and the number of cigarettes smoked per day. Atherosclerosis is a disease wherein plaques, or deposits, build up in blood vessels and eventually stop the circulation of blood. When the blood flow to the heart itself is stopped in this manner, the heart muscle dies, and a heart attack occurs. Atherosclerosis is caused in part by high cholesterol levels in the blood, but smoking doubles the risk of heart attack both in people who have normal cholesterol levels and blood pressure and in those who have raised cholesterol and high blood pressure. Figure 9-3 summarizes how smoking cigarettes contributes to heart disease.

Lung Disease

When tobacco smoke is inhaled, the ash and tars are deposited on the moist membranes on the inside surface of the lung, through which oxygen and carbon dioxide must pass to and from the blood. Normally, particles are cleared from the lungs by small hairs called *cilia*, which agitate and work the pollutants upward until they are ejected by coughing. Another line of defense against inhaled particles is the action of *phagocytes*. The phagocytes attack, surround, and destroy foreign matter in the lungs. Smoking reduces the actions of both the cilia and the phagocytes, leaving the lungs more vulnerable to the toxic effects of inhaled pollutants and infections by bacteria and viruses. As a result, smokers are more susceptible to chronic bronchitis and emphysema.

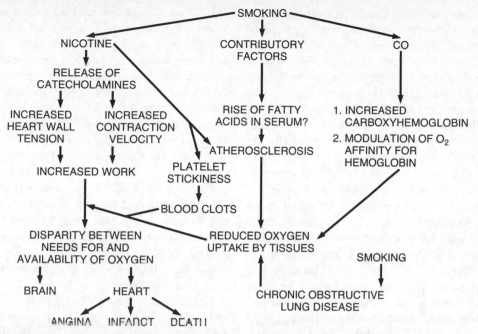

Figure 9-3 The mechanisms by which smoking contributes to heart disease. Smoking increases the demand on the heart by increasing its workload while at the same time decreasing the oxygen the heart muscle receives by increasing carboxyhemoglobin and causing atherosclerosis and lung diseases. (From Van Lancker, 1977, p. 252)

Cancer

The causal link between smoking and cancer is less well established. It is known that smoking greatly increases the risk of cancer of the mouth, lungs, and bladder, but the mechanism by which tobacco smoke actually causes cancer is not entirely understood. A number of substances in tobacco smoke could produce cancerous cells by altering the DNA in normal body cells, but whether this process is what actually takes place in humans has not been conclusively demonstrated. What is known is that smoking greatly increases the risk of cancers produced by other known carcinogens, such as pollutants, asbestos, and alcohol. For example, the risk of smokers getting cancer of the mouth and pharynx is two to six times greater in heavy drinkers than in nondrinkers (Rothman & Keller, 1972).

The risk of lung cancer can be greatly decreased by quitting smoking, and the risk lessens considerably over time after a person stops (Halpern, Gillespie, & Warner, 1993).

Reproduction

There is some debate whether women who smoke are more likely to be infertile than nonsmokers, but the bulk of evidence to date suggests that they are and that the effect is dose related. Women who smoke more than 20 cigarettes per day are 1.7 to 3.2 times more likely to be infertile than nonsmokers. It also appears that the effect is reversible: Fertility returns to normal after cessation of smoking (Baird, 1992).

There is now some evidence that smoking during pregnancy may cause birth defects. Such defects are associated with smoking of both the mother and the father (U.S. Department of Health and Human Services [DHHS], 1990b). In addition, many years of research have clearly established that babies born to women who smoke during pregnancy are likely to be anywhere from 150 to 200 grams lighter at birth than babies born to nonsmoking mothers. This effect is dose dependent and is estimated to be a loss of birth weight of 11 grams per cigarette smoked per day by the mother. The weight loss may occur because smokers do not put on as much weight during pregnancy as nonsmokers do; therefore, their babies are lighter. Another possibility might be that the developing fetus receives less oxygen from the body of a smoking mother because of the reduced oxygen-carrying capacity of her blood (C. S. Russell, Taylor, & Law, 1968). In any case, women who smoke during pregnancy are more likely to spontaneously abort and have babies prematurely, and their children are also more likely to be ill and die (M. S. Kramer, 1987; U.S. DHHS, 1989, 1990a).

Further research has shown that the effects of maternal smoking can last for some time. At 7 years of age, the children of mothers who smoked during pregnancy have lower spelling and reading scores, have shorter attention spans, and are more often hyperactive than children of mothers who did not smoke during pregnancy (Naeye & Peters, 1984). It is not clear, however, whether these effects are due entirely to smoking or to some other factor that correlates with smoking.

It has been estimated that if maternal smoking could be eliminated altogether, the overall infant death rate could be reduced by 10 percent (Haglund & Cnattingius, 1990).

Environmental Tobacco Smoke

Smoking is unhealthy not only for smokers but also for those who work and live with them. In 1992, the U.S. Environmental Protection Agency (U.S. EPA) released a document reviewing what was known at that time about the dangers of being exposed to environmental tobacco smoke (ETS).

ETS comes from two sources: (a) *mainstream smoke* (MS), which the smoker inhales and then breathes back out into the atmosphere, and (b) *sidestream smoke* (SS), which issues from a burning cigarette between puffs. MS is created when the smoker draws air through the cigarette. The flame that creates MS is 200 to 300 degrees hotter than the flame that creates SS. Both types of smoke contain the same carcinogens and toxic substances, but the combustion differences mean that the concentration of these substances is much higher in SS than in MS. For example, the concentration of one carcinogen, 4-ABP, is 30 times greater in SS than in MS. Levels of 4-ABP in the blood of nonsmokers have been measured at 10 to 20 percent that of smokers, even though the smoke they inhale is much less concentrated (U.S. EPA, 1992).

The EPA report concluded that in the United States, carcinogens in ETS are responsible for 3,000 lung cancer deaths per year among nonsmokers. Even though the health dangers of ETS are present for all age-groups, children are particularly vulnerable. The report also concludes that ETS is responsible for between 150,000 and 300,000 cases of bronchitis and pneumonia in infants up to 18 months of age and that ETS exposure worsens the severity of asthma symptoms in 200,000 to 1 million children per year (Spitzer et al., 1990; U.S. EPA, 1992). The report also finds a strong link between ETS and sudden infant death syndrome (SIDS; infants die suddenly and unexpectedly between the ages of 1 month and 1 year). The risk of dying of SIDS is between 1.6 and 7.7 times greater for babies of smoking mothers than for babies of nonsmokers. The risk is also dose dependently higher for babies in homes where the mother smokes more than 20 cigarettes per day (Nicholl & O'Cathain, 1992; U.S. EPA, 1992). It has been estimated that there would be a 27 percent decrease in SIDS if maternal smoking were eliminated (Haglund & Cnattingius, 1990).

The low birth weights created by smoking while pregnant can also occur in nonsmoking women if they are exposed to several hours of ETS daily (U.S. EPA, 1992).

TREATMENTS

Compulsion to Smoke

Perhaps one of the most tragic examples of the strength of the tobacco habit was the founder of psychoanalysis, Sigmund Freud. Freud smoked cigars most of his life in spite of the fact that he suffered from heart pains and cancer of the mouth as a direct result. Toward the end of his life, he was in constant pain after undergoing 33 operations for his cancer yet was still unable to quit. One report concludes,

Freud died of cancer in 1939, at the age of eighty-three. His efforts over a forty-five-year period to stop smoking, his repeated inability to stop, his suffering when he tried to stop, and the persistence of his craving and suffering even after fourteen continuous months of abstinence—a "torture . . . beyond human power to bear" make him the tragic prototype of [the tobacco addict]. (Brecher & Editors of *Consumer Reports*, 1972, p. 215)

Freud, of course, is not alone. In his Statement on Nicotine-Containing Cigarettes in 1994 before the House Subcommittee on Health and the Environment, David Kessler, the commissioner of the FDA, made the following points: (a) Two-thirds of adults who smoke say that they wish they could quit, and (b) 17 million try to quit each year, but fewer than 1 out of 10 succeed. Three out of four adult smokers say they are addicted. By some estimates, as many as 74 to 90 percent are. Eight out of 10 smokers say they wish they had never started.

Tobacco smoking can be a difficult habit to break. Nevertheless, up to 90 percent of former tobacco smokers have quit without the benefit of any treatment. For those who need help, a great variety of therapies is available. One of the most common and most effective is nicotine replacement therapy.

Nicotine Replacement Therapy

This treatment is based on the same strategy as methadone maintenance with heroin addicts (see Chapter 12). It substitutes a relatively safe source of the drug, such as a nicotine patch, gum, or nasal spray, for the more harmful source, tobacco.

When this treatment was originally developed, it was assumed that the primary motivation for smoking was avoidance of the symptoms of nicotine withdrawal. Delivery systems—the nicotine patch and chewing gum—were designed to maintain a constant nicotine blood level. These systems are quite effective, as can be seen in Figure 9-1.

Reports on the use of nicotine gum show that it is significantly more effective than a placebo in reducing cigarette consumption over a period of 2 to 3 weeks. Other reports show that the gum is effective in reducing smoking for a much longer period of time, provided that the smoker continues to use the gum. In addition, it appears that the gum may be more effective for heavy smokers than for light smokers (Stepney, 1982, p. 201).

Gum, however, has the disadvantage that it is difficult to maintain an adequate dose. It is necessary to chew 20 to 30 pieces of gum a day to achieve one half of the nicotine dose of cigarette smoking (Keenan et al., 1995). The transdermal patch does not have this problem and is also effective. A combination of the patch and the gum is better than either alone (Fagerström, Schneider, & Lunell, 1993).

The nicotine bolus theory has suggested that smokers may not be smoking only to avoid withdrawal; they may be obtaining positive reinforcement by delivering high levels of nicotine in the brain. It follows, then, that a nicotine delivery system that mimics this natural pattern of smoking is a more effective substitute. Consequently, a nicotine nasal spray has been developed (Sutherland et al., 1992) and is currently being considered for approval by the FDA (de Wit & Zacny, 1995).

Nicotine replacement may not always lead to smoking cessation, but even if it succeeds only in reducing the number of cigarettes smoked, as it often does, it will have achieved partial success (Keenan et al., 1995). Nicotine replacement therapy should continue for several months with a gradual weaning of dose, although many people continue to use it for a much longer period of time. Those who stop may find it necessary to revert to use of the gum or a patch in circumstances where relapse is likely.

TABLE 9-1 Preference for Different Methods of Smoking Cessation and Success Rates

Method	Preference (%)	Success Rate (%)
Cold turkey/self-help	90.4	<10
Counseling/behavioral	1.3	15
Nicotine patch	4.2	17.7
Nicotine gum	1.6	23.7
Nicotine inhaler	<1	22.8
Nasal spray	0	30.5
Buproprion (Zyban)	1.2	30.5
Other	3.1	Not available

Source: American Lung Association (2006).

Bupropion is another pharmacological treatment but is not a nicotine replacement therapy. Bupropion is an antidepressant drug sold as Zyban (see Chapter 14). It is not clear why it helps people stop smoking, but it appears to be effective. Table 9-1 shows the relative success rates and popularity of different methods of smoking cessation (American Lung Association, 2006).

Immunization

Two pharmaceutical companies, one in England and the other in the United States, have developed and have started clinical trials of a tobacco vaccine. The vaccine, known as TA-NIC or NicVAX, stimulates the body's immune system to create antibodies for molecules of nicotine. The antibodies then block the ability of nicotine to cross the blood–brain barrier. This should greatly diminish the ability of nicotine to act as a reinforcer and should cause smoking behavior to extinguish. The vaccine would need to be given in four or five doses and require a booster shot every few months.

A clinical trial has shown that the vaccine is effective in helping people quit smoking in those where the vaccine was able to create high levels of nicotine antibodies, but this was only one-third of those tested. Before more trials can be conducted, it will be necessary to find a way to increase the ability of the drug to create nicotine antibodies in more people (Maugh, 2005).

CHAPTER SUMMARY

- Nicotine is a drug found exclusively in the tobacco plant, which is consumed either by smoking or chewing or as snuff. It may also be administered in the form of a transdermal patch, nicotine chewing gum, or nasal spray.

- Nicotine is absorbed best from the lungs and is distributed rapidly throughout the body. It is excreted unchanged by the kidneys and metabolized by the liver. It has a half-life of about 30 minutes.

- Nicotine stimulates and then blocks nicotinic cholinergic receptors as dose increases. It has effects on both the central and the peripheral nervous system. It causes elevated levels of catecholamines, and it stimulates dopamine in the mesolimbic dopamine reinforcement system.

- Brain imaging studies show that pleasure reported by people who are smoking is correlated with increased dopamine receptor activation in the striatum, where the nucleus accumbens is located.

- Intravenous nicotine causes euphoric feelings in smokers but may cause unpleasant symptoms in nonsmokers. Even though nicotine increases the arousal level in the brain, smokers report that nicotine causes a feeling of relaxation.

- Some studies have shown that nicotine has little effect on performance, but others have concluded that nicotine at certain levels can enhance performance on some tasks.

- Nicotine's unpleasant withdrawal symptoms include irritability, weight gain, and sleep disturbances. Withdrawal can interfere with performance and has been shown to increase brain activity normally associated with drowsiness.

- Although nicotine is not self-administered by nonhumans as readily as many other drugs, tobacco is a powerful reinforcer for humans. One possible source of the reinforcing effect of nicotine is the sudden high concentration of nicotine that the brain receives after a puff on a cigarette; this is the nicotine bolus theory. Another theory, the psychological tool theory, claims that smokers use nicotine to increase and decrease level of arousal so as to enhance performance. Another theory suggests that smokers try to maintain a constant blood level in order to avoid nicotine withdrawal.

- Population studies show that the demand for cigarettes is inelastic in established smokers. In young smokers, price increases are effective in decreasing the number of smokers and the number of cigarettes they smoke.

- Smoking is not healthy. Tobacco smoking has been linked to heart disease, lung diseases such as emphysema and lung cancer, and cancer of the mouth and bladder. Smoking during pregnancy causes increases in the rate of stillbirths and illness in the newborn. Environmental tobacco smoke—both mainstream smoke (smoke inhaled and expelled by smokers) and sidestream smoke (uninhaled smoke from a burning cigarette)—have been shown to present health hazards to nonsmokers.

- As an aid to quitting, nicotine replacement therapy has been developed. The transdermal patch, nicotine gum, and nicotine nasal sprays are used to replace nicotine normally delivered by smoking. Nicotine replacement therapy appears to improve the success rate of people who quit smoking. Other drugs such as bupropion are also effective.

10

Caffeine and the Methylxanthines

Coffee is useless since it serveth neither Nourishment nor Debauchery.

> —*Anonymous, 1650 (Austin, 1985, p. 236)*

Caffeine is the best-known member of a family of drugs known as the *xanthine stimulants* or the *methylxanthines*. Although there are many methylxanthines besides caffeine, only two others occur naturally and are widely self-administered. These are *theophylline* and *theobromine*. The three have similar molecular structures and similar behavioral and physiological effects. The methylxanthines occur naturally in a number of species of plants belonging to 28 genera and over 17 families, but their most common sources are coffee, tea, and chocolate. Caffeine is also typically added to cola beverages and is an ingredient in many over-the-counter painkillers, cold remedies, and stimulants.

Caffeine was first isolated from coffee in 1820 by Ferdinand Runge, a German chemist, who called it Kaffeebase. It has been suggested that Runge's interest in coffee was stimulated by Wolfgang von Goethe, the author of *Faust*, who was a close friend of Runge's and a great coffee lover. No one is sure where the name *caffeine* came from, but a medical dictionary first used the term in 1823. Theobromine was isolated in 1842 and theophylline in 1888. Most of the basic chemistry of the methylxanthines was worked out and published in 1907 in a book by Emil Fischer, a Nobel prize–winning organic chemist.

SOURCES OF METHYLXANTHINES

Caffeine is available from a wide variety of sources. Table 10-1 gives a summary of some of these sources and an estimate of the amount of caffeine and other methylxanthines they contain.

Coffee

Coffee is made from the fruit of a bush or small tree of the genus *Coffea*. The two most common species are the *arabica* and the *canephora* (also called *robusta*), which together account for 99 percent of the world's coffee. They are native to Ethiopia but are now widely cultivated in Africa and South America and in

TABLE 10-1   Sources of Methylxanthines

Source	Caffeine (mg) Mean	Caffeine (mg) Range	Other Methylxanthines
Coffee (5-oz. cup)			
Instant	60	140	108
Percolated	85	164	124
Drip	112	156	176
Decaffeinated	5	2–5	
Tea (5-oz. cup)			
Bag	40	28–48	Theophylline
Instant	30	24–31	Theophylline
Cola beverages (12 oz.)			
Coca-Cola	45		
Pepsi-Cola	30		
Chocolate (1 oz.)			
Milk	6	11–15	
Sweet	20	15–35	
Baking (bittersweet)	35	18–118	150–300* mg
Chocolate milk (8 oz.)	5	2–7	75–100* mg
Chocolate bar (40–50 g)		40–50	86–240* mg
Over-the-counter analgesics (one tablet)			
Anacin	32		
Dristan	16		
Excedrin	65		
Pre-Mens	66		
Vanquish	32		
Over-the-counter stimulants (one tablet)			
Wake Ups	100		
No-Doz	100		
Ban Drowz	100		
Vivarin	200		

Sources: Barone and Roberts (1984); Gilbert (1976); Mumford et al. (1994); Syed (1976).

* Theobromine.

tropical climates all over the world. The coffee bean is a seed kernel of the coffee berry (or cherry), which grows in clumps along the branches. Each berry contains two seeds within its pulp. Usually, the berry is picked and dried briefly in the sun before the seeds are removed from inside the pulp.

In preparation for making coffee, the beans are roasted. Roasting serves no function other than to enhance the flavor. The roasted beans are then crushed or ground and mixed with boiling water. The caffeine content of a cup of coffee may vary considerably because of a number of factors: the caffeine concentration in the coffee beans (*robusta* has about twice the caffeine content of *arabica*), method of brewing (most brewing methods extract nearly all the available caffeine), and the size of the cup. Actual surveys have shown that the caffeine content of a cup of coffee may range between 40 and 176 mg, but the mean is closer to 85 mg (Barone & Roberts, 1984). However, this estimate is based on a cup size of 5 ounces (150 ml) of coffee. This size may be generally found in restaurants and hospitals, but actual measurements of typical cups used in the home and at work are closer to 7.5 ounces (225 ml). Table 10-1 shows typical sources of caffeine; the 5-ounce cup size is assumed. These figures can be increased by 50 percent. For the sake of convenience, it is usually presumed that a regular cup of coffee contains 100 mg of caffeine.

Tea

Tea is made from the leaves of *Camellia sinensis*, which in its natural form is a large tree but in its commercial cultivated form is more like a bush. For the best-quality teas, only the bud and the first two leaves of each twig are plucked. Inferior-quality teas are made from the third and fourth leaves. Caffeine content, as well as quality, decreases the farther the leaf is from the bud.

A drink may be made from the raw green leaves, but such concoctions are rather bitter. Most of the tea consumed outside of Asia is *black* or *fermented tea* (the process is not really fermentation but *oxidation*). The green leaves are dried slightly and then crushed and left to oxidize. The crushing or rolling breaks the membrane and releases enzymes that cause the oxidation. This turns the leaf black and gives it a particular taste. In *semifermented* or *oolong tea*, the oxidation process is stopped by roasting before it is completed. In *green Chinese tea* or *unfermented tea*, the leaves are steamed soon after picking and before drying to prevent oxidation. Consequently, green tea has quite a different taste from black tea. In the Orient, teas are frequently scented with flower petals. *Jasmine tea* is an example.

The amount of caffeine in a cup of tea is variable, but it is probably less than in a cup of coffee. One study showed a median of 27 mg per 5-ounce cup with a range of 8 to 91 mg. In addition to caffeine, tea contains *theophylline* and *theobromine* (Gilbert, 1976; Graham, 1984).

Cocoa

Cocoa is made from seeds found in the seedpods of the *cacao tree*, *Theobroma cacao*, which is native to the dense, tropical Amazon rain forest. It is cultivated now mainly in Central and South America, the West Indies, and West Africa. The mature tree grows seedpods from the trunk and main branches. These pods, about 6 to 10 inches long and 3 to 4 inches in diameter, contain 20 to 40 seeds surrounded by pulp. The seeds are removed and put in boxes or piles for fermentation. During this process, which lasts 5 to 6 days, the pulp ferments, becomes very watery, and separates from the seed; fermentation heats the beans, causing them to germinate, and then kills them. The beans are then dried in the sun or in commercial driers. All these things are done on the plantation.

At this stage, the dried beans are shipped to manufacturing plants for further processing. The beans are roasted for enhanced flavor and then crushed, and the husks of the shells are removed. The result is sold as unsweetened chocolate, a product that has a high fat content and is not very appealing. In 1828, in the Netherlands, a Dutchman, C. J. Van Houten, invented a press that could remove most of the fat, or cocoa butter. This turned out to be a major breakthrough in the processing of cocoa. In addition to inventing the press, the Dutch also learned to *alkalize* cocoa, which gives it a stronger flavor and a darker color and makes the powder disperse better in water. (The name *cacao* refers to the tree and its seeds; the term *cocoa* is used to refer to the processed products of the bean. Care should be taken not to confuse either of these terms with *coca*, the bush that is the source of cocaine; see Chapter 11.)

In the production of cocoa powder, the unsweetened chocolate is pressed into cakes. This process removes a large part of the cocoa butter. The cakes are then ground to produce the dry cocoa powder. Chocolate is made by mixing the roasted, alkalized, and refined beans with sugar and cocoa butter and, in the case of milk chocolate, with milk or milk solids. The details of the mixing process are complicated and vary according to the type and proposed use of the chocolate being produced (Minifie, 1970).

Chocolate contains both caffeine and theobromine in varying concentrations. It has been estimated that an ounce of sweet chocolate may contain between 75 and 150 mg of combined methylxanthines, and a cup of hot chocolate or chocolate milk may contain 150 to 300 mg.

Other Natural Sources of Methylxanthines

Other natural sources of caffeine are the *ilex plant* of the Amazon region of South America and the *cassina* of North America. The ilex plant, *Ilex paraguayensis*, is a holly (related to the Christmas holly) that contains between 1 and 2 percent caffeine. A tea-like drink called *maté* is made from the leaves and is popular in South America. Each morning, men of the Peruvian Achuar Jivaro tribe are reported to drink a strong herbal tea made from the ilex that contains the caffeine equivalent of five cups of coffee, after which they vomit in order to avoid overdose symptoms. It is considered to be part of a macho ritual passed down through the ages (*Science News*, 1992).

Cassina is another type of holly, *Ilex vomitoria*, from which a beverage known as *youpon*, *cassina tea*, or *black drink* is made. Youpon is not used today, but at one time it was widely consumed by native peoples of the southeastern United States. It was considered a noble beverage, and its use was restricted to great men and chiefs. Cassina tea enjoyed a revival during the American Civil War and World War I, when coffee and tea were either not available or very expensive.

Guarana is a paste made from the seeds of *Paullaina cupana*, which, at 2 to 6 percent caffeine, is the most potent of the natural sources of caffeine. The plant grows in the regions of the Amazon, Orinoco, and Negro rivers in South America. The paste is molded into sticks or bars or even sculptures and dried in the sun. For use, it is powdered and mixed with water. Because it has an acrid taste, like chocolate, it is usually sweetened with sugar.

There are a number of species of the genus *Cola*, a small evergreen tree native to southern Nigeria. Its nuts are edible and contain caffeine and theobromine. Kola trees are now cultivated all over western Africa, and chewing the nut is a widespread habit. The nut is sold commercially to the United States, where it is used to flavor cola beverages such as Coca-Cola and Pepsi-Cola. Most of the caffeine in these beverages, however, does not come from the kola nut but is added later.

Medicines and Food Additives

In addition to being added to cola beverages, caffeine is also added in small quantities for flavor to pudding mixes, baked goods, dairy desserts, and candy (Barone & Roberts, 1984).

Caffeine can be found in hundreds of prescription and over-the-counter medicines. Table 10-1 shows a few of these. They include common analgesics such as Anacin, weight control aids, allergy relief compounds, and stimulants.

Both theophylline and caffeine are used as a respiratory stimulant for newborn babies and people suffering from asthma.

HISTORY OF METHYLXANTHINE USE

Coffee

The coffee bush is native to Ethiopia. Its properties were discovered sometime between the twelfth and fifteenth centuries. From Ethiopia, its use spread across Arabia, Egypt, and North Africa, around the Mediterranean into Turkey, and then to Europe.

William Harvey, the first person to describe the circulation of the blood, was one of the first coffee drinkers in England, and he promoted the beverage for its therapeutic benefits. Two of his students believed that it was a cure for drunkenness (Austin, 1985). The first English coffeehouse opened in Oxford in 1650, and the concept soon spread throughout England. The coffeehouses were referred to as "schools of the cultured," and coffee was "the milk of chess players and thinkers." Along with coffee, this intellectual tradition associated with coffeehouses soon spread throughout Europe.

At one time, coffee drinking gained such popularity in England that the consumption of alcoholic beverages, particularly cheap gin, started to decline. Coffee has remained popular throughout Europe, but in Great Britain it was eventually replaced by tea.

Although tea was the preferred drink in colonial America, coffeehouses were as common as in England and filled the same social function: a meeting place for intellectual and political discussion. Boston coffeehouses such as the Brown, the North End Coffee-House, and the Exchange served as headquarters for Whigs and Tories and were the scenes of much plotting and fighting. One famous coffeehouse, the Green Dragon, is still marked by a plaque at the site where "such adventurous and ardent patriots as Otis, Joseph Warren, John Adams, Samuel Adams, Cushing, Pitts, Molyneux, and Paul Revere met nightly to discuss public affairs" (Cheney, 1925, p. 233).

Tea

There are many legends about the origins of tea. One tale credits the discovery of the beverage to the Chinese emperor Chen Nung. It is known that tea was cultivated and sold commercially in China by 780 A.D., when the book *Ch'a Ching*, or *Tea Classic*, was written. The book was sponsored by a group of merchants, and its purpose was to promote tea drinking (D. Forrest, 1973, p. 16).

Tea was first mentioned in print in Europe in 1559, but it was not until 1606 that the Dutch actually shipped some to Europe. In the 1630s, the Dutch started shipping tea on a regular basis to satisfy a growing demand in their country as well as in Germany and France. Tea was also becoming popular in Portugal, which had an extensive Oriental trade of its own. In the 1640s and 1650s, tea enjoyed a brief phase of popularity in France, but the French turned to coffee in the 1660s.

All this time, tea was not extensively used in England. It did not become fashionable until Charles II married the Infanta Catherine, who brought tea drinking with her from Portugal in 1662. Tea also became popular in the 13 British colonies of North America. In fact, by 1760, tea was the third-largest export from England to the colonies, and this figure represented only a quarter of the total tea imported; the rest was smuggled. The reason for smuggling was the tea tax the English Parliament at Westminster imposed on all tea imported into Britain. When this tea was later shipped to America, the price included this import tax. In 1767, this indirect tax was removed, and a direct tax was imposed. These taxes angered the colonists, and when the British East India Company tried to export a tea surplus to the colonies in 1773, the angry colonists dumped it into Boston Harbor. This "tea party" was the first of many, and it set the stage for the American Revolution.

Cocoa

The Mayas of the Yucatán Peninsula, the Aztecs of Mexico, and the Incas of Peru cultivated the cacao tree long before the European discovery of North America. They believed it to be a gift of the gods. This belief is the origin of the genus name of the cacao bush, *Theobroma*, which is Greek for "food of the gods." Among the Central American Indian tribes, chocolate was a food generally reserved for the wealthy and powerful. It was believed to be an aphrodisiac and was used at wedding feasts and by wealthy noblemen who could afford to support and had to satisfy many wives. It has been reported that Montezuma, emperor of the Aztecs at the time of Cortés, consumed 50 golden goblets of the drink each day. He called it *chocolatl*, but what he downed must have been quite different from modern chocolate. The Aztecs' concoction included maize and spices, such as peppers, but no sugar or milk.

Cortés introduced the drink to the Spanish court in 1520 with the addition of vanilla and sugar, and this sweetened form eventually gained popularity all over Europe. The Spanish managed to keep the source of chocolate secret for 100 years, but eventually the Dutch introduced the plant into the Philippines and Ceylon (now Sri Lanka).

Chocolate was introduced into Europe before coffee and tea and enjoyed a brief popularity, but because it was expensive, its use was restricted to the wealthy and the nobility. In every case, it was displaced by coffee, which remains the most popular xanthine-containing beverage today. (The exception is in England, where coffee was replaced by tea.) In time, chocolate did become cheaper and more readily available. The first chocolate factory in England was founded by S. J. Fry in 1728, when chocolate had become more plentiful, but by that time, tea was the indisputable beverage of the people.

Even though chocolate did not make it as a popular drink, the development of better processing techniques made it successful as a confection.

Today the bulk of the world's supply of cocoa comes from West Africa rather than South America. It is also grown commercially in Indonesia and Sri Lanka. It is perhaps ironic that cocoa, which is native to South America, is now a more profitable crop in Africa. The South Americans, however, have had their revenge many times over. Coffee, a native African plant, is now grown primarily in South America.

ROUTE OF ADMINISTRATION

When consumed in natural products, the methylxanthines are normally taken orally without difficulty, but when given for medical reasons, the purified drugs sometimes cause nausea and gastric irritation, especially in children. In such cases, the drugs may be given in the form of a rectal suppository or by intramuscular or intravenous routes.

ABSORPTION

Although the methylxanthines are absorbed from the stomach, they are absorbed much more rapidly through the walls of the intestine. Factors that decrease stomach-emptying time, such as the presence of food, will slow methylxanthine absorption. The methylxanthines are bases; consequently, when they are dissolved in the acidic environment of the digestive system, they might be expected to be highly ionized and not lipid soluble. However, these drugs have a very low pKa—about 0.5. Consequently, at the pH of the digestive system and any other pH encountered in

the body, the methylxanthines will not be ionized at all and will be free to dissolve in any tissue in accordance with their lipid solubility. The methylxanthines are quite lipid soluble and dissolve poorly in water.

The caffeine in coffee, tea, and chocolate exists and is consumed in its alkaloid form, but for medicinal purposes, the methylxanthines are usually given as salts, which can be absorbed much more readily. Aminophylline is the most widely used methylxanthine preparation. It is a mixture of theophylline and *methylenediamine*. The latter substance is considered therapeutically inert, but it increases the amount of dissolved theophylline 20 times and thereby speeds absorption. *Oxtriphylline* (Choledyl or choline theophylline) is also widely used.

After drinking coffee or tea, a person completely absorbs caffeine from the digestive system, and peak blood levels of caffeine are reached between 30 and 60 minutes later (Arnaud, 1993; Axelrod & Reisenthal, 1953; Marks & Kelly, 1973), although peak absorption may vary between 15 to 120 minutes, depending on the amount of caffeine swallowed and the ingestion of other foods. There is also considerable individual variability in peak blood levels. The same dose may produce a sixfold variation in peak blood levels in different individuals (Dews, 1984). There is no significant first-pass metabolism.

It was once thought that caffeine in cola beverages is absorbed more slowly than caffeine from coffee, but this has been shown not to be the case. Four hundred milligrams of caffeine ingested in either coffee or a cola beverage caused a similar peak caffeine level in saliva at the same time after ingestion. Caffeine absorption from capsules, however, was delayed. There was also no difference in the time course of subjective effects (Liguori, Hughes, & Grass, 1997).

DISTRIBUTION

Caffeine crosses the blood–brain and placental barriers without difficulty and reaches all body organs, although the rates of entering and leaving the organs may vary. About 10 to 30 percent of caffeine in the blood becomes bound to protein and trapped in the circulatory system (Arnaud, 1993; Axelrod & Reisenthal, 1953). Caffeine is present in all body fluids, including breast milk.

EXCRETION

In humans, less than 2 percent of caffeine is excreted unchanged in the urine (Arnaud, 1993). The remainder is converted to various metabolites (Bonati & Garattini, 1984; Burg, 1975). For a given individual, the half-life of caffeine is fairly constant, but this may vary from 2½ to more than 4½ hours in different individuals, with a mean of 3½ hours. There is evidence that the half-life may be dose dependent; that is, the larger the dose, the longer the half-life (Kaplan et al., 1997). In spite of this long half-life, it has been shown that caffeine does not appear to accumulate in the bodies of normal individuals over days if caffeine is not consumed after 6:00 P.M. (Axelrod & Reisenthal, 1953). In nonhumans, the half-life varies considerably, from 11 to 12 hours in the pig and squirrel monkey to 2 hours in the rat (Kihlman, 1977, pp. 20–21).

Caffeine metabolism is slowed by alcohol and speeded by broccoli, and smokers eliminate caffeine twice as fast as nonsmokers (J. J. James, 1991; Parsons & Neims, 1978). In women, metabolism of caffeine is closely related to hormone levels. The caffeine half-life in women is longer during the luteal phase (after ovulation) than during the follicular phase (before ovulation) of the menstrual cycle (Arnaud, 1993). The half-life in women taking oral contraceptive steroids is twice that of women ovulating regularly (Callahan, Robertson, Branfman, McCormish, & Yesair, 1983). Caffeine elimination is also slowed during pregnancy (Neims, Bailey, & Aldrich, 1979). These changes appear to be due to alterations in enzyme levels.

It has also been shown that newborns cannot metabolize caffeine well. They excrete about 85 percent of it unchanged in the urine, with the result that the half-life is about 4 days. The adult pattern of caffeine metabolism is not developed until 7 to 9 months of age (A. Aldrich, Aranda, & Neims, 1979).

Caffeine is metabolized into numerous metabolites, but no other species metabolizes caffeine the way that humans do. For this reason, one must always approach nonhuman studies of the methylxanthines with caution. Some metabolites created in other species may be more active or toxic than those created in humans (Stavric & Gilbert, 1990), and even in humans, there are differences in metabolic pathways between infants and adults. Not only do newborn babies metabolize methylxanthines more slowly, but they also create different metabolites (A. Aldrich et al., 1979).

NEUROPHYSIOLOGY

The effects of methylxanthines on neural functioning are now fairly well understood (Fredholm, 1995). Most of the effects of the methylxanthines appear to arise from the fact that methylxanthines are *adenosine receptor blockers*. There are four types of adenosine receptors—A_1, A_{2a}, A_{2b}, and A_3—and the methylxanthines appear to be effective blockers of the A_1 and A_{2a} types.

Adenosine functions as a neuromodulator and works presynaptically by inhibiting the release of many neurotransmitters. It also reduces the rate of spontaneous firing of neurons. Its general effect is to inhibit the firing of many neurons in the brain. Methylxanthines prevent adenosine's inhibitory action and cause stimulation (Fredholm, 1995; Nehlig, Daval, & Debry, 1992; Snyder, 1981, 1984).

Adenosine receptors are also known to be involved in the postsynaptic effects of dopamine. They increase the activity of the dopamine D_2 receptor (Garrett & Griffiths, 1997), which is known to play a role in the activity of transcription factors and gene expression in some neurons (Fredholm, 1995).

In addition to their effect on adenosine, caffeine and the methylxanthines are known to block benzodiazepine receptors, but this effect seems to require higher doses of caffeine than those that normally cause behavioral effects. At the dose equivalent of 10 cups of coffee, as many as 20 percent of benzodiazepine receptors are blocked (Paul, Marangos, Goodwin, & Slotnick, 1980). Among the different methylxanthines, however, there does not seem to be a correlation between the ability to block benzodiazepine receptors and the drug's effects (Snyder, 1984). It is possible that some of the effects of caffeine, particularly the increases in anxiety seen at high doses, are mediated by the ability of the drug to block benzodiazepine receptors.

Caffeine also appears to cause the release of epinephrine and other catecholamines from brain tissues and from the adrenal gland at usual doses. These indirect effects may contribute to the stimulating effects of the drug. It is also known that large doses (in the range of 500 mg), if taken all at once, cause a response similar to the body's reaction to acute stress: The levels of some hormones drop, and corticosteroid and internal opiate (beta endorphin) levels increase (Spindel & Wurtman, 1984). It is not known whether this effect is mediated by adenosine or benzodiazepine receptors.

Not long ago it was shown that three substances that occur naturally in chocolate resemble anandamide, the endogenous substance that works at cannabinoid receptors (see Chapter 15). In addition, other compounds have been found in chocolate that block the metabolism of anandamide (di Tomaso, Beltramo, & Piomelli, 1996). Although this is not sufficient to cause an obvious high, the presence of these substances could be one reason for the popularity of chocolate beyond the effects predicted by the presence of caffeine.

EFFECTS OF CAFFEINE AND THE METHYLXANTHINES

Effects on the Body

Because the methylxanthines cause the release of epinephrine from the adrenal gland, there is a resultant stimulation of the sympathetic nervous system. However, much of caffeine's effect outside the central nervous system is due to its direct effect on the muscles; smooth muscles tend to relax, and striated muscles are strengthened.

The smooth muscle relaxation results in a dilation of the bronchi of the lungs that decreases airway resistance. Theophylline is the most potent methylxanthine in producing this effect; as a result, it is used clinically in the treatment of asthma. Methylxanthines also reduce the susceptibility of striated (voluntary) muscles to fatigue. The mechanism of this change is probably related to caffeine-caused increases in fatty acids that the muscles can use as fuel (Nehlig & Debry, 1994).

Caffeine has different effects on blood flow in different parts of the body. It causes a constriction of blood vessels in the brain but dilation in the rest of the body. By constricting the blood flow to the brain, caffeine is able to reduce headaches caused by high blood pressure. For this reason, caffeine is found in many over-the-counter headache remedies.

High levels of caffeine stimulate the spinal cord. This is first manifested as an increase in excitability of spinal reflexes. Higher doses lead to convulsions, which are sometimes a cause of death. The regulatory centers of the medulla are also stimulated at high doses, producing an increase in the rate and depth of breathing. This ability of methylxanthines to stimulate respiration makes them useful in the treatment of babies born with breathing difficulties.

Many books suggest that the primary effect of caffeine on the brain is a stimulation of the cortex, but there is little evidence of this effect. Most of the evidence is indirect and based on behavioral studies (Gilbert, 1976).

Effects on Human Performance and Behavior

Textbooks usually give a standard account of the effects of caffeine at low doses (100 to 200 mg). Typically, the following effects are listed: "greater sustained intellectual effort and a more perfect association of ideas" or "a keener appreciation of sensory stimuli" (Ritchie, 1975, p. 367). In reality, there is very little hard evidence that changes of this nature take place. No doubt such accounts are based on subjective experience and the intellectual tradition associated with coffee.

Subjective accounts can be useful in understanding drugs, but they must be interpreted with great caution (see Chapter 2). In an early experiment by A. Goldstein, Kaizer, and Warren (1965), subjects were asked to rate the effects of caffeine on their alertness, physical activity, and wakefulness. Then they were given caffeine and tested on their ability to detect a number in an array of numbers flashed on a screen for 1/32 second. They were also tested on coordination in a line-drawing task. The subjects' assessment of their alertness and physical activeness did not correlate with their real abilities as measured by these various tasks; though all subjects thought they were doing better, caffeine produced no improvement.

There are reports that moderate doses of caffeine can significantly increase visual sensitivity to light, increase the speed of auditory reaction time (Dews, 1984), improve some aspects of driving involving reaction time, and improve performance in a flight simulator (Nehlig et al., 1992). Unfortunately, not all laboratories can replicate these effects, and some find decrements. It seems that the effects of caffeine depend on many factors, including individual susceptibility, dose, time of consumption, and the nature of the task (J. J. James, 1991).

In an extensive review by Weiss and Laties (1962) and another review by Dews (1984), the effects of caffeine on human performance were evaluated. Both reviews concluded that performance on a wide range of activities, with the exception of intellectual tasks, could be enhanced by caffeine. These included athletic activities (see the next section) and perceptual tasks such as monitoring a visual array. It appears, however, that most reports of improved performance occurred only if performance had been degraded by fatigue. The main effect of caffeine was to reduce the effect of drowsiness and boredom. Weiss and Laties also noticed that caffeine caused an improvement in the mood of subjects and in their attitude toward their task, but they were not able to determine whether this improvement in performance caused the mood change. In any case, it appears that coffee breaks may be beneficial, especially for people doing repetitive jobs.

One difficulty with these experiments is that they are usually done on subjects who are regular caffeine consumers and who have been deprived of caffeine for some period of time before the experiment. Under these circumstances, it is difficult to determine whether improvements in performance are a result of relief of withdrawal deficits in performance or net improvements in performance. One recent paper suggests that most reports of improvements can be attributed to relief of caffeine withdrawal (Rogers & Dernoncourt, 1998; Rogers et al., 2005).

Effects on Athletic Performance

Caffeine, in doses of about 6.5 mg/kg (450 mg in a 155-pound person), has been shown to improve some types of athletic performance. It does not seem to improve performance in events that require muscle strength, such as weight lifting, nor does it improve performance that requires intense output over a short duration, such as sprinting and throwing. It does, however, improve performance in tasks that require submaximal output for an extended period of time, such as cross-country skiing, running, or cycling (Nehlig et al., 1992; Ryu et al., 2001). However, even in these events, results are far from consistent, and the effect is moderated by other factors such as body composition. The most likely reason for improved performance on these tasks is that caffeine increases blood levels of fatty acids that can be used as fuel by the muscles. As a result, the muscles use less glycogen, their normal fuel; it is kept in reserve, so the muscles are not fatigued as quickly in endurance events (Tarnopolsky, 1994). These effects are subject to tolerance, and there is a delay between maximal blood levels of fatty acids and caffeine blood levels. For this reason, athletes wanting to take advantage of this effect need to abstain from taking caffeine for 4 days before the event and consume caffeine 3 to 4 hours before the event (Nehlig & Debry, 1994).

Because of the possibility that caffeine is an athletic performance enhancer, for many years caffeine was banned by the International Olympic

Committee (Lombardo, 1986) in urine in concentrations higher than 12 mg per liter (Tarnopolsky, 1994). Only one athlete has ever been disqualified from Olympic competition for exceeding the caffeine limit—a member of the Australian pentathlon team in the 1988 Summer Olympics at Seoul (J. J. James, 1991). The World Anti-Doping Agency lifted this restriction in January 2004, and there are now no legal restrictions on caffeine.

Effects on Sleep

There is little doubt that the methylxanthines can produce insomnia (A. Goldstein, 1964). Their effect seems to be in increasing the "stability of wakefulness" by increasing the length of time it takes to fall asleep and reducing total sleeping time. In one study, 300 mg of caffeine caused an increase in the latency of sleep onset, normally 18 minutes to 66 minutes, and reduced total sleeping time from 475 minutes to 350 minutes compared to control subjects (Brenesova, Oswald, & Loudon, 1975). As can be seen in Table 10-1, caffeine is the major ingredient in many over-the-counter stimulant pills. Most such tablets contain 100 mg of caffeine.

In general, people who take caffeine before going to bed report sleeping less soundly and feeling less rested. Caffeine also lowers the acoustic arousal threshold while sleeping; people wake up more easily in response to a sound in the night. This effect is variable among individuals; habitual coffee drinkers are less affected than coffee abstainers. Recently, it was shown that this difference is probably due to tolerance rather than a preexisting difference between coffee drinkers and coffee abstainers. After 7 days of exposure to a 400-mg dose, measures such as total sleep time and awakenings had returned to baseline levels (Bonnet & Arand, 1992).

It has also been demonstrated that caffeine can counteract the sleep-inducing effects of pentobarbital. A usual sleep-inducing dose of pentobarbital, 100 mg, when given in combination with 250 mg of caffeine, produces the same effect on sleep as a placebo (W. H. Forrest, Bellville, & Brown, 1972).

Effects on Behavior of Nonhumans

Unconditioned Behavior. Caffeine will increase spontaneous motor activity of mice in an open field. Maximum increases are 20 to 40 mg/kg. A dose of 80 mg/kg will greatly decrease spontaneous motor activity. Increases in activity are also produced by theophylline at similar doses, but there is some evidence that theophylline may be slightly more potent than caffeine (C. C. Scott & Chen, 1944). Interestingly, chronic, long-term treatment with caffeine results in a depression of spontaneous activity (Fredholm, 1995).

The LD_{50} of caffeine for both rats and mice is in the neighborhood of 250 mg/kg by intraperitoneal administration (Barnes & Elthrington, 1973). Death may be due to convulsions. Convulsive effects are another example of how chronic treatment has effects opposite to acute treatment. After chronic treatment, there is a decrease in seizure sensitivity (Fredholm, 1995).

Some animals die at lower doses from bleeding as a result of attacking themselves. Automutilation has been observed in rats when caffeine was given at a dose of 185 mg/kg for 14 days. The rats bit their tails and paws, even though they seemed to retain their normal sense of pain. When a ball of wire was placed in their cage, they temporarily attacked it but soon returned to biting themselves. When picked up, they did not bite the hand of the experimenter, but they did attack other rats placed with them in a cage (Peters, 1967).

Operant and Respondent Conditioned Behavior. The first person to experiment with the effects of caffeine on conditioned behavior was Pavlov (1927). He showed that the drug could disrupt conditioned discriminations by increasing responses to the negative stimulus. After ingesting caffeine, the animals responded to stimuli that did not signal food in the same way that they had responded to stimuli that did signal food. He concluded that the drug produced "an increase in excitability of the Central Nervous System."

The profile of effects of caffeine on operant behavior is very similar to but not exactly the same as the profile caused by the psychomotor stimulants (W. A. McKim, 1980). This similarity is probably a result of the increased catecholamine release and dopamine activity caused by caffeine (Garrett & Griffiths, 1997).

There is some evidence that caffeine at 30 mg/kg in a rat will increase food-reinforced responding that has been suppressed by punishment with an electric shock (Morrison, 1969). If this observation is true, it makes this effect of caffeine more similar to the barbiturates than to amphetamine. In general, caffeine appears to increase avoidance responding. Increases were seen on nondiscriminated avoidance responding of squirrel monkeys at a dosage of 1 to 30 mg/kg of caffeine; these increases were almost as great as those seen with amphetamine (T. R. A. Davis, Kensler, & Dews, 1973).

Although the effects of caffeine and the other methylxanthines on conditioned animal behavior have not been extensively investigated, it appears that they are very different from the effects of amphetamine on some types of behavior and very similar to amphetamine on others. These data clearly show that caffeine cannot be thought of as a mild amphetamine; its behavioral properties are quite distinctive and difficult to classify with any other category of drug.

DISCRIMINATIVE STIMULUS PROPERTIES

At a dose of 32 mg/kg, rats can be trained to discriminate between caffeine and saline in a two-lever Skinner box. Rats generalize the state produced by caffeine to lower doses of caffeine and higher doses of theophylline, but there is no generalization to nicotine (Modrow, Holloway, & Carney, 1981).

As with human subjective effects, caffeine appears to share some of the subjective effects of cocaine and amphetamine, at least at low doses. There is partial generalization to cocaine and amphetamine in rats trained to discriminate low but not high doses of caffeine and vice versa. Caffeine will increase the discriminative effects of low doses of cocaine. Dopamine receptor blockers will block the discriminative effects of low but not high doses of caffeine (Garrett & Griffiths, 1997, p. 536).

For some time, there has been a concern over what are known as *look-alike* or *turkey drugs*. These preparations look, in all regards, like controlled psychoactive drugs, such as amphetamine, but instead contain a drug or a combination of drugs that are not prescribed or controlled substances. Turkey drugs designed to mimic amphetamine or cocaine often contain caffeine in combination with other substances such as *ephedrine* and *phenylpropanolamine*. One study has shown that, in rats at least, this combination of drugs can mimic the discriminative stimulus effects of 10 mg/kg of cocaine (Gauvin, Harland, Michaelis, & Holloway, 1989).

Although there is considerable individual variability, humans can discriminate the presence of caffeine in capsules in very low doses. In one experiment, a dose of 1.8 mg of caffeine was detected by one subject, although two others detected a dose of 10 mg, and one subject needed 178 mg. In the same experiment, the same subject who was able to detect 1.8 mg of caffeine detected a dose of 100 mg of theobromine, but two subjects out of seven were unable to discriminate 1,000 mg of theobromine (Mumford et al., 1994).

Subjective Effects

Early studies on the subjective effects of caffeine were confusing. In some studies, subjects reported increased anxiety, jitteriness, and nervousness, but other studies reported no subjective effects at all. Recent studies have found increasingly that subjects experience an array of positive effects, such as increases in feelings of well-being, alertness, energy, motivation for work, and self-confidence. Griffiths and Mumford (1995; Rush, Sullivan, & Griffiths, 1995) report that positive effects are more reliably detected under a restricted set of conditions. First, they are seen when caffeine is administered to people who are not caffeine users or to caffeine users who have been deprived at least overnight. The fact that positive effects are seen in coffee abstainers indicates that these effects are not simply a matter of alleviating caffeine withdrawal (N. J. Richardson, Rogers, Ellman, & O'Dell, 1995). Second, positive effects are more likely to be seen at low doses (from 20 to 200 mg). The higher the dose, the more likely that unpleasant effects will be reported. Finally, positive effects are most likely to be reported by individuals for whom caffeine acts as a positive reinforcer (see the next section).

In a study by Mumford and associates (1994), subjects were given 178 mg of caffeine, and responses to a mood scale were determined at various times afterward. The drug caused increases in well-being, magnitude of drug effect, energy, affection for loved ones, motivation to work, self-confidence, social disposition, alertness, and concentration and decreases in "sleepy" and "muzzy" feelings. These changes were evident within 30 minutes and remained higher than placebo levels for at least 8 hours.

The same study also examined the subjective effects of theobromine. A dose of 100 mg produced positive changes in energy, motivation to work, and alertness but to a much smaller extent than caffeine. The time course for these changes was similar to caffeine, but 5 to 10 hours after ingestion, subjects reported unpleasant effects such as headache and lethargy.

In another experiment, subjects with experience with street drug use, including cocaine, were given intravenous doses of caffeine, and the subjective effects were measured. There was a dose-related increase in ratings of "liking," "drug effect," "high," and "good effects." These occurred 2 minutes after injection and decreased over the following 60 minutes. At high doses, caffeine was identified as "a stimulant (like cocaine or amphetamine)." Most subjects were reasonably certain that they had been given cocaine (Rush et al., 1995).

Tolerance

Studies of adenosine receptors have shown that chronic administration of caffeine causes an increase in the number of adenosine receptors, presumably an attempt to restore the influence of adenosine prior to caffeine (Hirsh, 1984).

Tolerance to the behavioral effects of caffeine has been shown to develop in rats. One study (Wayner, Jolicoeur, Rondeau, & Baron, 1976) showed that bar pressing on an FI schedule could be depressed to about 40 percent saline control rates by a 100-mg/kg injection of caffeine. After eight injections of caffeine, this dose could only depress responding to 75 percent of baseline. It has also been demonstrated, in a study of operant responding in rats, that chronic treatment with caffeine shifted the caffeine dose–response curve to the right by a factor of 6. This means that after exposure to caffeine, a sixfold increase in dose was required to produce the same effect as before the exposure (Carney, 1982).

A number of studies using human subjects have shown that caffeine has less effect on heavy drinkers of coffee than on nondrinkers of coffee. In one experiment (Goldstein et al., 1969), 150 to 300 mg of caffeine produced complaints of jitteriness, nervousness, and upset stomach in nonusers, but users reported increased alertness, decreased irritability, and a feeling of contentedness. It should be pointed out that studies like these, while probably demonstrating tolerance, may simply be showing that individuals who are resistant to the effects of caffeine are the ones who become heavy coffee drinkers.

To demonstrate tolerance to a drug effect, an experimenter must give the drug to one group of subjects and a placebo to a second group for a period of time. The effect must diminish in the drug-exposed group. Furthermore, the placebo group must show the effect when switched to the drug. Tolerance to several effects of caffeine has been demonstrated using this design. Different effects of caffeine at normal doses show tolerance at different rates; for example, cardiovascular effects fade within 2 to 5 days, but caffeine-induced increases in urination may take considerably longer or never show complete tolerance. Similarly, tolerance to various physiological effects has been demonstrated (Griffiths & Mumford, 1995). We have seen that the sleep-disrupting effects of

400 mg of caffeine show tolerance within 7 days. The subjective effects of 300 mg are tolerated within 4 days (Evans & Griffiths, 1992). In general, many effects of caffeine seem to disappear within a week at usual levels of consumption. As was pointed out earlier, some acute effects of caffeine—the effect on spontaneous motor activity and susceptibility to convulsions—actually reverse with chronic treatment.

WITHDRAWAL

Laboratory animals appear to suffer from caffeine withdrawal, although the main symptom is a decrease in locomotor activity and a disruption of ongoing operant responding. In humans, there have been a number of documented cases of caffeine withdrawal dating back to 1833. The most common symptom is a headache. In addition, people report drowsiness, decreased energy, and fatigue that can be described as weakness, letdown, or lethargy. People also report decreased motivation for work and impaired concentration, decreased feelings of well-being and self-confidence, increased irritability, and flu-like feelings such as aches and muscle stiffness, hot and cold spells, heavy feelings in the limbs, and nausea (Griffiths & Mumford, 1995). The severity of symptoms is directly related to dose. In one study, deprivation of normal caffeine consumption in the morning (12 to 28 hours of deprivation) produced withdrawal symptoms at lunchtime testing (e.g., decreased feelings of vigor and well-being and increased feelings of fatigue and light-headedness). No changes in psychomotor performance or reaction time were detected, however (J. D. Lane, 1997; Phillips-Bute & Lane, 1998).

Doses as high as 600 mg per day can cause physical dependence after only 6 to 14 days of exposure. Withdrawal symptoms can also be seen at daily exposures of as little as 100 mg per day over a longer period of time (Griffiths & Mumford, 1995).

Withdrawal symptoms usually start within 12 to 28 hours of the last coffee intake, peak at 20 to 51 hours, and last 2 to 9 days (Griffiths & Mumford, 1995; Griffiths & Woodson, 1988; Juliano &

Griffiths, 2004). Figure 10-1 shows the time-course incidence of headache and scores on an "energy/active" scale of subjects maintained on 100 mg of caffeine and switched to a placebo. As you can see, it took nearly 2 weeks for these scores to return to normal (Griffiths & Mumford, 1995).

Studies have shown that among coffee consumers in the United States who have gone without coffee for 24 hours, 27 to 52 percent report experiencing headaches. Estimates of the number of people who are exposed to caffeine withdrawal (i.e., the number who consume more than 100 mg a day) is enormous. Caffeine withdrawal is often overlooked as a possible diagnosis when people report headache, fatigue, and mood disturbances in circumstances where normal diet, including caffeine, is disrupted. Such circumstances might include fasting before various laboratory tests, operations, or procedures such as endoscopies.

On a more mundane level, caffeine withdrawal may well be responsible for the behavior of people who are grouchy and impossible to get along with until they have had their first cup of coffee in the morning. It is probably also responsible for illnesses and headaches that occur during holidays or weekends or when people interrupt normal routines that include coffee drinking.

In the *DSM-IV-TR*, a revision of the *DSM-IV* put out in 2000 (American Psychiatric Association, 2000), caffeine withdrawal was included on an experimental basis to encourage research into its clinical significance. It has also been included as an official diagnosis in the *ICD-10* (World Health Organization, 1993). However, in 2002, it was suggested that withdrawal symptoms from caffeine could be explained by nonpharmacological factors such as expectations or placebo effects, as described in Chapter 2 (Dews, O'Brien, & Bergman, 2002). This possibility was investigated in 2004 by Juliano and Griffiths (2004), who reviewed the current literature to that date. They pointed out that most of the studies that have found clinically significant withdrawal from caffeine were double-blind studies where the participants did not know that they were experiencing caffeine withdrawal; expectancy and

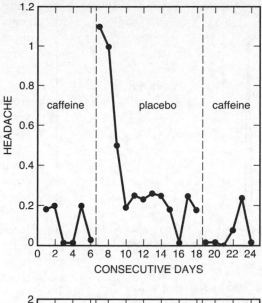

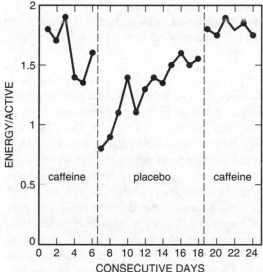

Figure 10-1 Changes in frequency of reported headaches and scores on an "energy/active" scale of subjects for 24 days while they consumed 100-mg caffeine capsules, then a placebo, and then switched back to caffeine. Caffeine withdrawal caused increases in reported headaches and a decrease in energy and activity that lasted as long as a week. (From Griffiths et al., 1990)

placebo effects were not likely to have caused the withdrawal symptoms. In fact, in some studies,

participants did not know that the experiment involved caffeine at all.

SELF-ADMINISTRATION IN NONHUMANS

In laboratory animals, caffeine is not a robust reinforcer. It can serve as a reinforcer but only in a limited number of circumstances, and it does not seem to be able to support a lot of behavior. In one study where bar pressing delivered an intravenous caffeine infusion, only two out of six monkeys self-administered the caffeine spontaneously. The four monkeys that did not give themselves caffeine were then given automatic infusions of caffeine for a period of time. This procedure succeeded in establishing caffeine as a reinforcer in three of the four remaining monkeys (Deneau, Yanagita, & Seevers, 1969). The pattern of self-administration was irregular; there were periods of voluntary abstinence. There was no tendency to increase the dose over time. Other researchers have also demonstrated modest reinforcing effects with caffeine, but they were limited to specific doses and particular animals (Griffiths, Bigelow, & Lieberson, 1979). Other studies have not been able to demonstrate reinforcing effects of caffeine at all, although these studies used only one dose of caffeine or tested for only a short time (Hoffmeister & Wuttke, 1973).

Figure 10-2 shows the pattern of caffeine self-administration in a baboon (Griffiths & Mumford, 1995). This animal is typical of most. Caffeine is administered erratically, and irregular periods of abstinence occur. The reinforcing nature of caffeine is demonstrated, however, because rates of responding decline to near zero when a placebo is substituted.

Similar results have been found when rats have been given the opportunity to consume caffeine orally. Few spontaneously consume caffeine orally, and some period of forced consumption is usually required before caffeine is self-administered (M. V. Vitiello & Woods, 1975).

Even though it may not be a robust reinforcer on its own, caffeine has been shown to potentiate

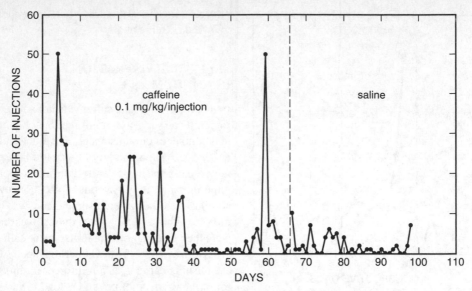

Figure 10-2 Intravenous self-injection rates of caffeine for a baboon with a history of self-administering numerous sedative and stimulant drugs. Caffeine was available on an FR 2 schedule, and a maximum of 50 administrations were available each session. The dotted line indicates that a saline placebo injection was substituted for the caffeine. (From Griffiths & Mumford, 1995)

the reinforcing effects of cocaine (Horger, Wellman, Morien, Davis, & Schenk, 1994), and it will act as a primer for cocaine; that is, an injection of caffeine will reinstate previously extinguished cocaine self-administration in rats (Worley, Valdez, & Schenk, 1994), an effect that can be blocked by the administration of dopamine receptor blockers.

SELF-ADMINISTRATION IN HUMANS

A number of human self-administration preference studies have shown that both caffeinated coffee and capsules containing caffeine will serve as reinforcers in humans. People who have been permitted to consume caffeine freely for 1 week before the test reliably preferred caffeinated coffee, but people who were not permitted to have any caffeine for 1 week and were presumably not physically dependent on caffeine showed considerable individual variation in caffeine preference

(Griffiths & Woodson, 1988). In later research, subjects were given a choice between capsules containing caffeine and a placebo. Of 12 subjects, four showed a clear-cut preference for caffeine. Coffee consumption prior to the experiment did not seem to be related to caffeine preference (Griffiths & Woodson, 1988). Another study, conducted with moderate coffee drinkers, showed that they had a distinct preference for caffeinated coffee over decaffeinated coffee. This preference could be detected in some people at doses as low as 25 mg per cup and was greatest when the subjects reported caffeine withdrawal (Hughes, Higgins, Bickel, & Hunt, 1989; Hughes, Higgins, Gulliver, & Mireault, 1987).

These and other studies (Schuh & Griffiths, 1997) show that the preference for caffeine may be determined by the state of physical dependence on caffeine. In one study (Garrett & Griffiths, 1998), subjects were maintained for 9 to 12 days on a daily dose of caffeine (300 mg/70 kg/day; caffeine dependent) or a placebo (caffeine nondependent).

When dependent on caffeine, subjects showed typical withdrawal symptoms (fatigue and so on) when given a placebo. They were also willing to forfeit money to avoid placebo administration and to pay more money for caffeine than when they were nondependent. When dependent, they were twice as likely to take a dose of caffeine versus a placebo as when they were nondependent. This study shows clearly that people were actively avoiding the caffeine withdrawal as well as seeking the effects of caffeine.

In both humans and nonhumans, the reinforcing properties of caffeine seem to vary considerably from individual to individual, and several factors have been identified as contributing to choosing caffeine. Being physically dependent is one. Another is that the people who usually report positive subjective effects from caffeine also show a caffeine preference, and people who report adverse effects usually avoid it (Griffiths & Woodson, 1988). But these characteristics are not essential. In one experiment, a person who was otherwise a coffee abstainer showed a definite preference for caffeine over a placebo (Griffiths & Mumford, 1995).

Higher doses are not as reinforcing as lower doses. Increasing doses beyond 100 mg usually decreases the rate of self-administration, and doses in the 400- to 600-mg range are usually avoided.

Studies have also shown that caffeine preference may be related to task requirements after ingestion. All subjects, in an experiment in which they were required to participate in a computer vigilance task after taking a capsule, showed a preference for caffeine-containing capsules, but only two of seven subjects had a preference for caffeine when the capsule was followed by a relaxation activity (K. Silverman, Mumford, et al., 1994).

Caffeine Dependence Syndrome?

In Chapter 5, the *DSM-IV* criteria for "substance dependence" were discussed. These criteria are used to make a clinical diagnosis of dependence on a variety of drugs, such as cocaine and heroin. Is it possible to be clinically diagnosed as "dependent" on caffeine? Evidence from case histories suggests that it is. One study, published in the *Journal of the American Medical Association* in 1995, reported on clinical interviews with a number of people recruited through newspaper notices who thought that they were dependent on caffeine. These people were interviewed using a structured clinical interview by a psychiatrist, and 16 were identified as meeting the *DSM-IV* criteria of caffeine "dependence." Of these 16, 94 percent reported withdrawal, 94 percent reported use continuing despite knowledge of persistent or recurrent physical or psychological problems likely to have been caused or exacerbated by caffeine use, 81 percent reported persistent desire or unsuccessful attempts to cut down or control use, and 75 percent reported tolerance. These people reported daily doses of caffeine that ranged between 129 and 2,548 mg per day, and three people diagnosed as dependent had daily doses less than the average daily consumption in the United States. Seven of the 16 primarily consumed soft drinks, one drank tea, and the remainder drank coffee (Strain, Mumford, Silverman, & Griffiths, 1995).

In a laboratory study, coffee and cigarettes were made available to subjects on a fixed ratio (FR) schedule of 100, and then the FR requirement was increased to 1,000 and 2,500 independently for each reinforcer. Coffee demand was relatively inelastic (elasticity index −0.26 and −0.51), meaning that coffee consumption did not decrease in proportion to the price increases. As the price of cigarettes increased, the consumption of both coffee and cigarettes decreased, but as the price of coffee increased and coffee consumption fell, the consumption of cigarettes did not change. This finding suggests that changes in smoking behavior can influence coffee consumption, but people will smoke whether they are drinking coffee or not (Bickel, Hughes, DeGrandpre, Higgins, & Rozzuto, 1992).

Population Studies

It is surprising that nonhumans are reluctant caffeine consumers and that humans do not show a more avid and compelling preference in the laboratory. Caffeine and the other methylxanthines are probably the most widely self-administered drugs in the world. After oil, coffee is the world's most valuable traded commodity.

The Scandinavian countries have the world's greatest partakers of coffee. Their per-capita consumption is about twice that in the United States. Canada ranks quite a bit below the United States, and countries such as Iraq, Sudan, and Japan are at the bottom of the list of coffee consumers. Where tea is concerned, Ireland and Great Britain outconsume Canada by about 4 to 1 and the United States by about 12 to 1. European countries, including the Scandinavian countries, are at the bottom of the tea list.

The average caffeine consumption of the world's population is about 70 mg per person per day, 90 percent of which is consumed in the form of coffee and tea. North American consumption is probably over 200 mg per person per day (Barone & Roberts, 1984). About 60 percent of caffeine consumption is in the form of coffee, 16 percent as tea, 16 percent as soft drinks, and less than 2 percent as chocolate (Gilbert, 1984). Elsewhere, it is estimated that the total consumption of methylxanthines in the United States is more than 230 mg per day. Caffeine accounts for 84 percent, theobromine 17 percent, and theophylline less than 1 percent (Hirsh, 1984).

HARMFUL EFFECTS

Reproduction

At high enough levels, caffeine will damage chromosomes, but it appears that such effects do not occur at the concentrations normally found in the human body, and caffeine is generally considered safe in this regard, although there is some speculation that it might enhance the chromosome-damaging activity of other agents, such as X-rays (Kihlman, 1977, pp. 414–415). Even though it does not damage chromosomes, caffeine can affect the fetus via other mechanisms. For example, caffeine raises the levels of circulating catecholamines, which could affect the unborn child by reducing blood flow to the fetus. Studies in animals

have shown that low levels of caffeine retard both embryonic and neonatal growth in animals (Dunlop & Court, 1981). One study has shown that daily consumption of three cups of coffee moderately increases the risk of miscarriage. It is not clear, however, that this was a result of caffeine because it was not the case for women consuming an equivalent amount of caffeine in the form of caffeinated soft drinks (Dlugosz et al., 1996).

There is now some evidence that caffeine consumption retards fetal growth and lowers birth weight in humans, especially if caffeine consumption exceeds 300 mg per day (Santos, Victoria, Hutty, & Morris, 1998). In addition, it has been shown that caffeine will potentiate the effect that smoking has on reducing birth weight (see Chapter 9; for a review, see E. M. McKim, 1991). In addition, heavy caffeine use during pregnancy (more than four cups of coffee per day) increases the risk of SIDS (sudden infant death syndrome) in infants (Ford et al., 1998). Remember that the rate of caffeine metabolism is considerably delayed during pregnancy, and women who maintain usual consumption will experience higher and higher blood levels of caffeine as their pregnancy progresses, and so will their unborn child.

Methylxanthines are also found in considerable concentrations in breast milk. Considering that the rate of methylxanthine metabolism in newborns is extremely slow, even small amounts acquired in breast milk could accumulate, possibly to toxic levels.

Some claim that there is no reason why pregnant women should be concerned about caffeine consumption during pregnancy, but the majority of expert opinion suggests that until a safe level of consumption can be established, it is probably wiser for pregnant women (and nursing mothers) to abstain from caffeine-containing beverages and medicines (J. J. James, 1991).

Cardiac Disease

Some studies show that caffeine increases blood pressure (e.g., Kaminsky, Martin, & Whaley, 1998), and others do not (e.g., Hofer & Battig, 1994). Even studies that show blood pressure increases report considerable variation among individuals.

The epidemiological evidence linking caffeine consumption to heart disease is still equivocal. In the early 1970s, the Boston Collaborative Drug Surveillance Program published two studies that showed that drinking more than six cups of coffee a day doubled the risk of heart attack. Since that time, numerous studies have failed to replicate the finding. Contradictory results abound. For example, one study of more than 85,000 women in the United States concluded that coffee was not an important cause of heart attacks (Willett et al., 1996); another study of more than 800 women in Boston found that heavy coffee consumption (more than five cups per day) did increase the risk of heart attack (Palmer, Rosenberg, Rao, & Shapiro, 1995).

Factors that may contribute to these divergent findings might be that exposure to caffeine is usually not measured accurately, and, as a result, risk is consistently underestimated (J. J. James, 1991). Another reason might be related to the manner in which coffee is prepared. One study has shown that boiled coffee contains a substance that raises cholesterol levels, but filtered coffee does not contain this factor (Pirich, O'Grady, & Sinzinger, 1993). Even though many have assumed that coffee consumption is not a risk factor in heart disease (Robertson & Curatolo, 1984), the issue is far from settled.

Cancer

Studies with caffeine in laboratory animals have failed to show clearly that caffeine causes cancer. Some studies have found that caffeine may enhance the effect of other cancer-causing agents by inhibiting the ability of the cell to repair damaged DNA. Other studies have actually found that caffeine may inhibit some cancers (J. J. James, 1991).

Epidemiological studies have suffered from the same problems as described for cardiac disease; that is, the ability to measure exposure to caffeine is imprecise. Many studies find increased cancer risk for coffee users as opposed to nonusers but no difference in risk between those who use different amounts of caffeine. Some have suggested that this failure to find a dose effect means that the link between coffee and cancers is circumstantial rather than causal. Nevertheless, it has been pointed out that studies may be examining the wrong measure of coffee exposure. In one study, it was found that the risk of ovarian cancer was 3.4 times greater in women who had drunk coffee for more than 40 years than in women who had never drunk coffee. Among those who did drink coffee, the risk of cancer remained the same no matter how much was consumed. Possibly, the crucial variable is duration of use rather than amount of use—a measure seldom taken in epidemiological studies.

A study in the early 1980s claimed to have found an association between caffeine and pancreatic cancer. This caused considerable concern, but there were methodological flaws in the study, and the effect cannot be consistently replicated. Nevertheless, recent work seems to indicate that caffeine may interact with smoking in causing pancreatic cancer; that is, the risk of cancer for smokers is increased by the consumption of coffee, but coffee has no effect in nonsmokers. Interestingly, the cancer risk for smokers was increased by both regular coffee and decaffeinated coffee. This finding may mean that the important agent was not caffeine, or it may indicate that current drinkers of decaffeinated coffee may have been regular coffee users in the past (J. J. James, 1991).

Inconsistent associations have also been reported between caffeine use and kidney cancer, bladder cancer, testicular cancer, fibrocystic breast disease, and breast cancer (J. J. James, 1991).

Bone Density

Of increasing concern is the effect of caffeine on the rate of bone density in postmenopausal women. One study showed that a daily consumption of two to three cups of coffee accelerated bone loss in the spine and body of postmenopausal women who consumed less than the recommended daily dietary source of calcium (S. Harris & Dawson, 1994).

Abnormal Behavior

At doses of 5 to 10 cups per day, caffeine can cause sensory disturbances, such as ringing in the ears and flashes of light, as well as mild delirium and excitement. These are symptoms of a disorder called *caffeinism*, which is very similar to anxiety neurosis and is frequently diagnosed as such. Caffeinism is usually seen at doses above 1,000 mg per day. Patients report a low-grade fever of about 100 degrees Fahrenheit, which is a result of the drug's action on the body's heat-regulating mechanism in the hypothalamus. Other symptoms include flushing, chilliness, insomnia, irritability, irregular heartbeat, and loss of appetite. Unlike anxiety neurosis, these symptoms do not respond to treatment with tranquilizers. The only cure is to eliminate caffeine from the diet (Greden, 1974).

It has also been shown that caffeine will cause panic attacks and increase anxiety in people with panic and anxiety disorders, but it does not generate them in normal individuals unless used excessively (Carroll, 1998, p. 102).

The psychological basis for these effects appears to lie in the fact that, at high doses, caffeine blocks benzodiazepine receptors. The benzodiazepines are the family of tranquilizers to which chlordiazepoxide (Librium) and diazepam (Valium) belong (see Chapter 7). The benzodiazepines act at a particular type of receptor in the brain that appears to be the site of action of an endogenous form of benzodiazepine that has similar antianxiety properties. The reason caffeine produces anxiety-like symptoms at higher doses is that it blocks these benzodiazepine receptors, and the body's natural benzodiazepine cannot function. When these receptors are blocked, the therapeutic effectiveness of an administered benzodiazepine is also diminished.

There is also evidence that caffeine reduces the effectiveness of the major family of antipsychotic drugs, the phenothiazines, including chlorpromazine (Kulhanek, Linde, & Meisenberg, 1979).

Not only does caffeine interfere with the effectiveness of many psychotherapeutic drugs, but it may also make the symptoms of both neurotic and psychotic patients worse (Greden, Foutaine, Lubetsky, & Chamberlin, 1978). In one experiment (De Freitas & Schwartz, 1979), patients in a psychiatric hospital who were switched to decaffeinated coffee for 3 weeks without their knowledge showed a decrease in anxiety, hostility, irritability, tension, and psychotic symptoms. During a 3-week period after caffeine was restored, all the improvements were reversed. This study, however, has not been replicated (Mayo, Falkowski, & Jones, 1993).

Lethal Effects

Six deaths due to caffeine overdose have been reported (Syed, 1976). The lethal dose in humans has been estimated at between 3 and 8 g (30 to 80 cups of coffee or stay-awake pills) taken orally. Death results from convulsions and respiratory collapse.

EPILOGUE

What Do We Really Know About Caffeine?

Caffeine is big business—even bigger than the tobacco business. You can be sure that any threat to the profits of the coffee industry would be met with resources similar to those that the tobacco industry has put forward in defending itself against the increasing public awareness of the dangers of smoking. Perhaps that threat already has been met.

In an editorial in the British journal *Addiction*, one of the world's foremost caffeine researchers, Jack James of La Trobe University in Bundoora, Australia, warned that the coffee industry has been subtly directing caffeine research away from areas of health problems and manipulating the dissemination of health information about caffeine for many years (J. J. James, 1994). The coffee industry established something called the International Life Sciences Institute (ILSI). This sounds as though it should be a scholarly organization with lofty aims, but in reality it was established to make sure that caffeine retained its status as "generally recognized as safe" by the U.S. Food and Drug Administration. In this regard, it has been successful. Despite increasing numbers of studies that have provided reason to doubt it, caffeine is still considered a "safe" food additive.

How does the ILSI work? Its influence may be seen in the pages of this book. According to James, the ILSI sponsors international conferences attended by prominent scholars by invitation only and then publishes the results. According to James, however, in the publications that deal with the health hazards of caffeine, "evidence is consistently interpreted in a way that is favourable to the interests of the book's sponsors." This approach is given credibility because other publications that do not deal with health issues are balanced, erudite, and scholarly.

In addition, the caffeine industry sponsors research but is careful to sponsor research in "safe" areas, such as the study of compounds in coffee other than caffeine. As James says, "Under the guise of public interest, the industry actively supports continuing research on noncaffeine constituents of coffee, knowing fully that nothing untoward (and nothing of particular interest to the public) is likely to be revealed" (J. J. James, 1994, p. 1579).

CHAPTER SUMMARY

- The three commonly used methylxanthine drugs are caffeine, found mainly in coffee; theophylline, found in tea; and theobromine, found in chocolate. Caffeine is also added to some cola beverages, headache medications, and over-the-counter stimulants.

- Beverages that contain methylxanthines have been used in Europe and North America since the 1600s, and their popularity has made them important commodities. Their trading and taxation have played an important role in commerce and history.

- The methylxanthines are readily absorbed orally and distributed throughout the body. After its oral administration, caffeine reaches peak blood levels in 30 to 60 minutes. It is metabolized in the liver and eliminated slowly, with a half-life of about 3½ hours.

- The main neurophysiological effect of the methylxanthines is that they block receptors of the inhibitory neuromodulator adenosine. They also cause the release of epinephrine and catecholamines.

- Caffeine improves performance on boring and tiring tasks. There are some circumstances in which caffeine can improve athletic performance in endurance events.

- Caffeine can delay sleep. Sleep after caffeine is lighter, and people are more easily awakened.

- In nonhumans, caffeine stimulates spontaneous activity and can cause automutilation at larger doses. Operant analysis of the effects of caffeine has shown that its effects are similar to those of amphetamine, with some important differences.

- Caffeine can act as a discriminative stimulus and will generalize partially to cocaine. Humans can also detect the presence of caffeine in low concentrations.

- Doses of 100 to 200 mg of caffeine administered to people who are not tolerant to caffeine are experienced as pleasant, and when it is given intravenously, people report a "high" similar to cocaine. Higher doses are often reported to be unpleasant.

- Tolerance develops to many of the effects of caffeine in both humans and nonhumans. Withdrawal symptoms, consisting of headaches and restlessness, have been reported at doses as low as 100 mg a day. Withdrawal peaks between 20 and 48 hours and may last as long as a week.

- Although humans consume vast quantities of caffeine, it is not a robust reinforcer in laboratory animals. It usually requires a period of forced administration before it will serve as a reinforcer. Humans will choose beverages and capsules containing caffeine if they report pleasant subjective effects and are physically dependent on caffeine.

- It is possible to meet the *DSM-IV* criteria for "substance abuse" with caffeine.

- The average caffeine consumption in North America is over 200 mg per person per day. Most caffeine is consumed in the form of coffee.

- There is evidence of a detrimental effect of caffeine on reproduction and a possible association with heart disease and cancer. It has not yet been clearly established that there is a link because of difficulties with measuring caffeine consumption and separating its effects from the use of other drugs, such as tobacco.

- At higher doses (10 to 15 cups a day), the drug can cause caffeinism, with symptoms indistinguishable from anxiety neurosis. Even at low doses, caffeine may worsen the symptoms of neurosis and psychosis and diminish the effectiveness of some psychotherapeutic drugs.

11

Psychomotor Stimulants

The drugs known as psychomotor stimulants have one effect in common: They stimulate transmission at synapses that use epinephrine (E), norepinephrine (NE), dopamine (DA), or serotonin (5-HT) as a transmitter. These transmitters are called *monoamines* (MAs) or *biogenic amines*. The first three—E, NE, and DA—are very similar. In fact, the body manufactures E from NE in one chemical step, and NE is made by changing the structure of DA slightly. Together, these three are called *catecholamines* (CAs). The odd monoamine is 5-HT. It is an *indoleamine*, which is chemically different from the CAs but is influenced by many of the same drugs and destroyed by many of the same enzymes (see Chapter 4).

The term *sympathomimetic* is sometimes used to refer to this class of drugs. This term is used because epinephrine is the primary transmitter in the sympathetic nervous system, and these drugs stimulate sympathetic synapses to some extent and mimic sympathetic arousal.

SOURCES

Some psychomotor stimulants occur naturally and have been used for centuries, and some are very new synthetic drugs. The *amphetamines* are synthetic and do not occur naturally; *d-amphetamine* (dextro-amphetamine, or dex-amphetamine) and *l-amphetamine* (levo-amphetamine) have exactly the same chemical structure, but the molecules are mirror images of each other (technically, they are called *optical isomers*). In the amphetamines, the d- isomer is more potent than the l- isomer for most central effects. When the term *dl-amphetamine* or just *amphetamine* is used, it refers to a mixture of the two isomers. The most common trade name of dl-amphetamine was Benzedrine, but neither Benzedrine nor dl-amphetamine is currently in use in the United States or Canada. Dexedrine is a common trade name of d-amphetamine. Another similar drug is *methamphetamine,* which differs slightly in structure and effect from the other two. It was sold under the trade names Methedrine or Desoxyn. Methamphetamine can be synthesized from material legally available, which includes cold medication that contains ephedrine or pseudoephedrine, iodine, hydrochloric acid, ether, and ammonia. It is currently manufactured in large quantities in illegal laboratories and sold in a waxy form known as base or paste or in a tablet or powder. When the powder is recrystalized, it is sold as "crystal," "ice," or "crystal meth." Only slightly different chemically from the amphetamines are two synthetic drugs, *methylphenidate* (Ritalin) and *pipradrol*.

Another psychomotor stimulant is a naturally occurring drug, *ephedrine*. Ephedrine comes from the herb *ma huang* (*Ephedra vulgaris*), which has been used as a medicine in China for centuries. There are also North American varieties of *Ephedra*.

Cocaine is extracted from the leaf of a small tree known as the *coca bush* (*Erythroxylum coca*), which is native to South America. It prefers high elevations and thrives on the slopes of the Andes Mountains. It grows in both wild and cultivated forms from northwestern Argentina to Ecuador.

Cathinone is another naturally occurring cocaine-like drug found in the leaves and shoots of *Catha edulis*, a shrub-like plant that grows in the countries of eastern Africa and southern Arabia. It is called *khat* in Yemen (also spelled *quat* or *qat* and pronounced "cat"). It is also known as *tscaht* in Ethiopia and *miraa* in Kenya (Kalix, 1994). Cathinone is not stable; it degrades shortly after the plant is harvested. For this reason, the plant is used primarily in the area where it is grown, and, unlike cocaine, it is not exported for use elsewhere (United Nations, 1980). However, *methcathinone* (the cathinone equivalent of methamphetamine) is an established abused drug in some countries. In Russia, it is known as *ephedrone* or referred to as *jeff, Jee-cocktail,* or *cosmos,* and abuse of it has been a problem since the early 1980s. In the early 1990s, it appeared in the illicit drug market and was found in clandestine labs in the United States as *cat*. In 1992, it was classified as a Schedule-1 substance (the highest restriction a drug can receive) under the Emergency Scheduling Act (Glennon, Young, Martin, & Dal Cason, 1994).

HISTORY

Cocaine

For centuries, coca leaves have been chewed by various Indian tribes in South America. No one knows how long the coca plant has been used, but it is of great antiquity. Legends of some tribes of Colombian Indians tell how their people came from the Milky Way in a canoe drawn by an anaconda. In addition to a man and a woman, the canoe contained several psychoactive plants, including coca (Schultes, 1987, p. 229). Coca leaves have been found in burial middens in Peru that date back to 2500 B.C. Large stone monolithic idols found in Colombia and dating to 500 B.C. have the puffed-out cheeks of the coca chewer. The Incas started to use the plant when they conquered the region in about the tenth century. Under the Incas, coca became sacred. It was used primarily by the priests and nobility for special ceremonies and was not consumed daily by the common folk.

When the Spanish conquered the Incas, at first they banned coca use, considering it to be idolatrous and pagan, but they changed their minds when they found out how useful it could be. The Spanish did not use coca themselves, but they learned that it had great value as payment for labor in the gold and silver mines in the Andes. In addition to finding coca an item of commerce, the Spanish realized that the Indians could work harder and longer and required less food if they were given coca.

As the Spanish grew more interested in the plant, attempts were made to classify it. In 1749, samples were sent to Europe, where Linnaeus gave the plant its own family, Erythroxylaceae. In 1786, Lamarck named the most important species *Erythroxylon coca* (M. R. Aldrich & Baker, 1976).

Europeans remained unaware of either the medicinal or the psychological effects of the plant, probably because samples sent from South America had deteriorated from age. It is also likely that Europeans were averse to chewing the leaves in the manner of the South Americans. Not until the form of the drug was changed did they show any interest in coca. The first change involved identifying the active ingredient. Earlier attempts had been made with partial success, but the credit for isolating and naming cocaine goes to Albert Niemann of the German university town of Göttingen, who published his results in 1860.

For several years, cocaine was a drug without a medical use until Sigmund Freud became interested and proposed many uses of cocaine, including the treatment of addictions and depression, but it was one of his colleagues, Karl Koller, who discovered the only real medical use of cocaine—it was the world's first local anesthetic.

The isolation of cocaine not only stimulated a search for medical uses for the drug but also made it available in a form that the upper middle class could inject along with morphine, which was popular at the time (see Chapter 12). Around the turn of the twentieth century, cocaine gained favor with writers and intellectuals. Robert Louis Stevenson is reported to have written *The Strange Case of Dr. Jekyll and Mr. Hyde* with the aid of cocaine. Sherlock Holmes, the fictional detective created by Sir Arthur Conan Doyle, was a prototype of the intellectual cocaine user of the time. Over the cautions and objections of the good Dr. Watson, he injected the drug to keep his keen mind stimulated.

In 1863, Angelo Mariani, a Corsican chemist, patented a wine containing coca that became exceedingly popular and made Mariani a very wealthy man. It was probably Mariani's success that inspired a Georgia pharmacist, John S. Pemberton, to produce an American version called "French Wine of Cola, Ideal Tonic." Later, in 1886, he removed the alcohol and replaced it with a kola nut extract, added soda water, and called it Coca-Cola. In its early days, Coca-Cola was promoted as a remedy and a health drink, and it is probably for this reason that soda fountains developed in drugstores in the United States. In 1906, the Pure Food and Drug Act outlawed cocaine, and it was removed from the drink. To this day, Coca-Cola is made from coca leaves from which the cocaine has been removed.

The passage of the Pure Food and Drug Act was a manifestation of a growing backlash against cocaine and other drugs in the early part of the twentieth century in the United States. Cocaine was being injected by professionals and intellectuals, but the drug was associated with corruption and crime in the popular mind. It was no surprise

that cocaine was included with morphine and opium in the Harrison Narcotic Act of 1914, which effectively banned its use. As a result of this inclusion of cocaine in the U.S. law and the influence of the United States on the development of international narcotics control, cocaine was also included with morphine in all international treaties aimed at the control of narcotics and in the internal legislation of many other countries.

The Harrison Act drove cocaine underground, where it was used by the "unconventional rich and the unconventional poor": partygoing, decadent, wealthy whites, and gamblers, musicians, and artists of all colors. For decades, cocaine was not a part of the lives of the vast majority of the population of the United States. Then, during World War II, amphetamines were introduced, so the idea of a stimulant or an "upper" was no longer new and foreign. In the 1960s, things started to change. The use of cocaine increased along with a general increase in the use of other drugs, including marijuana and hallucinogens, at the time (Grinspoon & Bakalar, 1976, p. 49).

Amphetamines

Ephedrine, in the herb ma huang, has been used in China for more than 5,000 years. Legend has it that its medicinal properties were first identified by the emperor Chen Nung, who was also credited with the discovery of tea. Ephedrine was isolated from the herb in the 1880s, but not until 1924 were its properties investigated by two Americans, Ko Kuei Chen and C. F. Schmidt. They pointed out that the structure and actions of ephedrine were similar to those of the neurotransmitter epinephrine, which was known to be a stimulant of the sympathetic nervous system. Epinephrine was used at the time to treat asthma because one of its effects was to dilate the airways in the lungs and make breathing easier. Epinephrine, however, was very unstable; it had to be administered by injection, and its effects were very brief. Ephedrine was far superior because it could be taken in pill form, had a longer duration of action, and was less toxic.

The use of ephedrine became so widespread that there were fears that supplies would run out, and a search was begun for a synthetic substitute. As it happened, such a substitute had already been discovered, but no one knew it. Many years earlier, in 1887, L. Edealeno had synthesized what we now know as amphetamine, but he had failed to explore its properties, and it remained untested until 1910, when G. Barger and Sir H. H. Dale (the proposer of Dale's law; see Chapter 4) published a technical paper showing the effects of amphetamine and other sympathomimetic drugs on the body. The significance of Barger and Dale's paper was not grasped until 1927, when Gordon Alles, a young chemist at a research laboratory in Los Angeles, suggested that amphetamine would probably be the best and cheapest substitute for ephedrine.

In 1937, the American Medical Association sanctioned the use of amphetamine for the treatment of the sleep disorder narcolepsy and as a mild "pick-me-up" or stimulant for depression. By 1943, at least half the sales of the drug were prescribed for weight reduction and diet control, antidepressant or stimulant effects, or extended periods of alertness. Amphetamine was also marketed in inhalers for the treatment of asthma and sold over the counter without a prescription. The pharmaceutical company Smith, Kline, and French held the patents of amphetamine and was doing so well that other companies wanted some of the market, too. It was not long before the Ciba company started marketing methylphenidate as a "nonamphetamine" stimulant (Grinspoon & Hedblom, 1975). To control the indiscriminate prescribing of amphetamines by physicians, most countries now limit the medical conditions for which amphetamines may be prescribed. These conditions are narcolepsy and the treatment of hyperactivity in children and do not include obesity or the need to stay awake. The production and marketing of amphetamines are now carefully monitored.

As medicinal sources of amphetamines dried up, more amphetamine and methamphetamine were being made in illicit labs, which are now the primary source. Apart from illegally manufactured methamphetamine, most stimulant abuse in Western countries is confined to cocaine.

Cathinone (Khat)

Khat use has been known since antiquity. Alexander the Great sent khat to General Harrar to cure his melancholia, and it has been mentioned repeatedly by Arab physicians as a remedy for a variety of disorders. Amda Sion, a fourteenth-century ruler of Ethiopia, was the first recorded khat addict. Khat has been known in Europe since the early 1600s but has only recently been used there because of difficulties transporting the leaf.

The first case of khat psychosis in the United States was reported in 1982. Since then, cases have been reported in the United Kingdom (Giannini, Miller, & Turner, 1992), Europe (Kalix, 1994), and Canada (Kalix, 1994). Public awareness of khat has increased as a result of reports emanating from the UN Mission in Somalia. There has been some concern that U.S. soldiers, after being exposed to khat use because of the interdiction of alcohol in Muslim countries, may have brought the habit back to the United States. There are, however, no reports of such cases.

ROUTES OF ADMINISTRATION AND ABSORPTION

The amphetamines are weak bases and have a pKa of between 9 and 10. When taken orally, they tend to be ionized in the digestive system, which slows the rate of absorption. The drug is more potent when administered by injection, inhalation, or snorting. When given for medicinal purposes or to prevent sleep and fatigue, amphetamines are always taken orally, and the decrease in potency can be compensated for by increasing the dose. The oral route has the advantage that blood levels may be kept fairly constant without too much variation over time. When amphetamines are taken for the rush they produce, they are administered by injection, which causes the sudden high blood levels required for this effect.

The same is true for cocaine, which has a pKa of 8.7. Traditionally, the Indians of the Andes rolled coca leaves into a ball, stuck a wad in the cheek, and sucked it. It is also common for those who take coca in this manner to mix the leaves with lime in the form of wood ashes (Schultes, 1987, p. 225) or ground shells; this practice raises the pH of the saliva and the digestive system and, consequently, reduces ionization and increases absorption. It is very unusual for pure cocaine to be taken orally. It is nearly always injected or sniffed to improve absorption, but recently it has become popular to smoke cocaine, both as a hydrochloride salt and as a freebase.

Most of the cocaine sold in the United States is the salt cocaine hydrochloride (cocaine HCl). It may contain various impurities from the refining process and be deliberately diluted or "cut." One method that was used to determine the purity of this drug was to place some of the powder on a sheet of tinfoil and heat it until it vaporized; pure cocaine HCl leaves little residue. It soon became apparent to those who performed this test that inhaled cocaine has an effect similar to injected cocaine. Soon this method of smoking, called *tooting*, became popular, as did other methods, such as mixing cocaine with tobacco or marijuana.

Freebasing is a process that separates the cocaine molecule from the HCl. It is rather risky because it involves heating highly combustible chemicals. The freebase vapor that is produced has a much stronger effect than the cocaine HCl because of the increased lipid solubility of the freebase form of the drug. Freebasing's popularity was greatly facilitated by the advertising and sale of special pipes and chemical kits for converting the cocaine HCl into the freebase (R. K. Siegel, 1982b). The older and more dangerous methods of making cocaine freebase have now been replaced by making crack cocaine.

Crack is cocaine HCl mixed with a solution of baking soda (sodium bicarbonate). The water is evaporated, leaving crystalline chunks or "rocks" that are heated in pipes or other devices, and the vapors are inhaled. This process accomplishes the same effect as freebasing and is considerably cheaper and safer.

After oral administration of amphetamines, the absorption rate is determined by factors such as the presence of food in the stomach and the degree of physical activity. Peak blood levels may be reached in 30 minutes to 4 hours (Brauer, Ambre, & de Wit, 1996; Vree & Henderson, 1980). After intranasal administration (sniffing) of cocaine, peak blood levels are achieved in 10 to 20 minutes (Javid, Musa, Fischman, Schuster, & Davis, 1983). The rate of absorption of vaporized cocaine HCl and cocaine from vaporized freebase or crack has not been studied, but it is likely extremely rapid because both processes release the cocaine molecule in un-ionized form, making it highly lipid soluble. In fact, crack is a variation on the ancient technique used by the Incas, who mixed coca leaves with lime. This made the saliva basic and enhanced the absorption of the cocaine from the coca leaves using the same chemical principle.

Traditionally, cathinone is taken orally by chewing the leaves of the khat plant in much the same manner as the natives of the Andes have used coca. In Russia, methcathinone is usually administered by injection, but in the United States, sniffing of methcathinone powder seems to be preferred (Glennon et al., 1994).

DISTRIBUTION

The amphetamines, cocaine, and other drugs in this class cross the blood–brain barrier and are concentrated in the spleen, kidneys, and brain.

EXCRETION

The excretion of the amphetamines depends to a very great extent on the pH of the urine. Because it is ionized at acid pHs, amphetamine is not reabsorbed from the nephron in acid urine, but as the urine becomes more basic, more of the drug is reabsorbed and more of the burden of excretion is carried by metabolism in the liver. The half-life of amphetamine may be as short as 7 to 14 hours when the urine is acidic. When the urine is basic, excretion is shifted to metabolic processes, and the half-life may be 16 to 34 hours (Creasey, 1979, p. 180). Amphetamine is also excreted in sweat and saliva (Britton, El-Wardney, Brown, & Bianchine, 1978; Vree & Henderson, 1980).

Amphetamines that are not excreted unchanged are metabolized through several routes that use a variety of enzymes. Many of the metabolites are also behaviorally active and have very long half-lives (Brookes, 1985, p. 265).

Cocaine is excreted much faster than the amphetamines. It has a half-life of about 40 minutes (Javid et al., 1983), although this also depends on the pH of the urine. Cathinone has a half-life of about 90 minutes, intermediate between cocaine and amphetamine (Kalix, 1994).

NEUROPHYSIOLOGY

All the drugs in this chapter are grouped together because they have a common effect on synapses that use a monoamine (MA) as a transmitter, but the mechanisms by which they stimulate these synapses differ. (It may be useful at this point to review the discussion of MA synapses in Chapter 4.)

The amphetamines, cathinone, and methcathinone primarily affect synapses that use serotonin and the catecholamines, epinephrine, norepinephrine, and dopamine (DA) as transmitters or modulators. They have a threefold effect on these s)ses: (a) They cause the transmitter to leak   taneously out of the synaptic vesicles into   synaptic cleft, (b) they increase the amount of   mitter released in response to the arrival of   ction potential at the synapse, and (c) they k the reuptake of the transmitter into the   synaptic cells and prolong the duration and i nsity of their effect. All these actions greatly st ulate the synapse (Carlsson, 1969; Glennon et ..., 1994).

Cocaine does not produce the first two of amphetamine's effects, but it is a reuptake blocker and stimulates the synapse this way (Groppetti & Di Giulio, 1976; Wolverton & Johnson, 1992). Cocaine blocks the reuptake of the neurotransmitter

by working at a receptor site on the transporter molecule (Izenwasser, 1998). Photon emission tomographic (PET) studies suggest that between 60 and 77 percent of dopamine transporters are blocked by doses of cocaine commonly abused by humans and that at least 47 percent of transporters must be blocked for users to experience a cocaine-induced high (Volkow et al., 1997).

In the peripheral nervous system, these drugs stimulate synapses that use epinephrine, the transmitter in the sympathetic nervous system, and cause sympathetic arousal (the fight-or-flight response).

In the central nervous system (CNS), all monoamine systems are known to be affected by the psychomotor stimulants, but most of the behavioral effects appear to be a result of their effect on dopamine systems (see Chapter 13). One is the nigrostriatal system between the substantia nigra and the striatum (basal ganglia), which is important in the control of motor activity. Psychomotor stimulants are known to increase the release of dopamine in the nucleus accumbens, part of the mesolimbic dopamine system, which controls reinforcement and motivation (see Chapter 4 and Kalix, 1994). Another DA system exerts some control over the secretions of the pituitary gland. This DA system inhibits the secretion of *prolactin*, a hormone that controls the release of milk during breast feeding, and also suppresses male sexual activity.

In addition to its abilities as an MA stimulant, cocaine has the ability to block sodium ion channels in membranes. This blocks the conduction of action potentials along nerve axons and is the basis of cocaine's ability to act as a local anesthetic. The local anesthetic action, however, has nothing to do with the MA-stimulating effect of the drug and requires much higher concentrations. Cocaine is seldom used for this purpose today. Procaine (novocaine), a synthetic substitute that has the local anesthetic action of cocaine without its stimulant properties, was developed for this purpose. Even though procaine lacks the stimulant properties of cocaine, it nevertheless acts as a positive reinforcer in rats and monkeys (Ford & Balster, 1977; Yokel, 1987).

The influence of cocaine is still felt in the naming of local anesthetic drugs. It is common to use the ending -*caine* in the formulation of generic and trade names to indicate that the drug has local anesthetic action.

EFFECTS OF PSYCHOMOTOR STIMULANTS

Effects on the Body

Because the psychomotor stimulants activate the sympathetic nervous system, they cause an increase in heart rate and blood pressure and *vasodilation* (a dilation of the blood vessels) and *bronchodilation* (dilation of the air passages in the lungs). Bronchodilation is medically useful for people suffering from asthma. This was the primary motivation for the invention and development of the amphetamines in the first place. However, most of the sympathetic effects are not considered pleasant by people who inject amphetamines for psychological effects. They generally prefer methamphetamine, which has stronger CNS effects and fewer peripheral effects than d- or l-amphetamine.

Studies of laboratory animals have shown that some of the effects of amphetamine are greater if animals are tested in groups rather than alone. One study with humans showed that amphetamine has a tendency to cause higher increases in blood pressure and body temperature in humans tested in groups rather than alone (de Wit, Clark, & Brauer, 1997).

Some patients receiving amphetamines for medical reasons report headaches, dry mouth, stomach disturbances, and weight loss due to depression of appetite.

Effects on Sleep

One reason for the widespread use of amphetamines during World War II and in the 1950s was that they prevented sleep. Amphetamines were used by truck drivers on long trips and by students staying awake to cram for exams. Systematic studies have shown that amphetamine use does cause insomnia.

EFFECTS ON THE BEHAVIOR AND PERFORMANCE OF HUMANS

Subjective Effects

When cocaine and amphetamine are given intravenously, their effects are identical (Fischman et al., 1976).

One of the most noticeable effects of the amphetamines is that they make people feel good; they improve the mood. From the earliest occasions when amphetamines were given to humans, positive mood changes were recorded. There were reports that the drug caused "a sense of well-being and exhilaration," feelings of "high spirits," and "bubbling inside." Most subjects felt a decrease in fatigue and an increase in energy; a clear, organized mind; and a desire to get to work and accomplish things (Grinspoon & Hedblom, 1975, p. 62). Later, systematic double-blind studies confirmed these reports. Figure 11-1 shows the results of such a study. Subjects were given a low dose (5 mg) of d-amphetamine or a placebo and were asked to fill out the Profile of Mood States (POMS) questionnaire. They filled in the POMS again 1, 3, and 6 hours after the drug was taken. As can be seen in Figure 11.1, the drug caused an increase in vigor, friendliness, elation, and positive mood (Johanson & Uhlenhuth, 1980). These effects were greatest 3 hours after administration, and some of the mood changes lasted as long as 6 hours. These euphoric feelings were followed several hours later by a feeling of depression (Gunne & Anggard, 1972). PET studies using radioactive glucose have shown that cocaine-induced euphoria is correlated with a 14 percent global reduction in glucose metabolism in all areas of the neocortex as well as in the basal ganglia, thalamus, midbrain, and hippocampus (London et al., 1990) and that glucose metabolism rebounds to above-normal levels during the first week of withdrawal (Volkow et al., 1991).

Some of the subjective effects of amphetamine are greater if the subject is expecting to receive the drug (Mitchell, Laurent, & de Wit, 1996), but the effects appear to be similar in subjects tested alone or in social groups (de Wit et al., 1997).

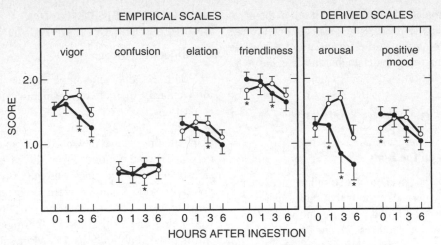

Figure 11-1 Changes in mood after 5 mg of amphetamine. Subjects were given the amphetamine orally and then filled out the POMS after 0, 1, 3, and 6 hours. Statistically significant differences between the drug (open circles) and a placebo (solid circles) are indicated with an asterisk (*). (Adapted from Johanson & Uhlenhuth, 1980, p. 277)

Higher acute doses produce a more intense subjective effect, but acute tolerance to pleasurable effects occurs with one administration or with repeated doses within a single session. Subjective effects tend to be greater when blood levels are rising than when they are falling (Brauer et al., 1996). In one study, humans were permitted to administer cocaine intravenously every 10 minutes for 1 hour. Feelings of positive mood increased after the first infusion but did not increase throughout the session, even though the blood levels of cocaine rose steadily with repeated infusions (Fischman & Schuster, 1982).

In addition to making people feel good, amphetamine at high doses after intravenous or intranasal administration produces intense feelings of euphoria and pleasure, called *rushes.* Rushes are not exclusive to intravenous administration, but this route is extremely efficient at delivering high drug levels to the brain and increasing their intensity. The rush has been described as "being lifted into the air with feelings of extreme happiness." Another account claims, "The heart starts beating at a terrible speed and his respiration is very rapid. Then he feels as if he was ascending into the cosmos, every fiber of his body trembling with happiness." Many people report that the rush has a strong sexual component. "The shot goes straight from the head to the scrotum," as one user put it (Rylander, 1969, p. 254).

The effects of cocaine are similar but shorter acting. Within a couple of minutes after cocaine is snorted, there is a numbing sensation called the *freeze,* which is followed after 5 minutes by a feeling of exhilaration and well-being. As with amphetamine, there is a feeling of energy and a sensation of clear thoughts and perceptions. This lasts for 20 to 30 minutes and is followed by a mild depression called the *comedown* or *letdown.*

When cocaine is injected, there is also a rush that may be felt within seconds and lasts about 45 seconds. This is illustrated in the following experiment. Electroencephalographic (EEG) recordings allow researchers to correlate subjective reports with neurophysiological changes. Since head movements can interfere with EEG recordings, participants were asked to use a microswitch-equipped joystick to report when the effects of cocaine could be detected and when the participant was experiencing cocaine-induced euphoria or dysphoria. Using this technique, researchers discovered that whereas cocaine was "detected" for approximately 75 minutes postinjection, cocaine-induced euphoria occurred only during the first 10 to 15 minutes and correlated with increased alpha activity over the parietal and occipital lobes. During the 20 to 30 minutes postinjection, euphoria was replaced with dysphoria and correlated with a below-baseline level of activity in these brain regions (Lukas, 1991). These findings are shown in Color Plate C.

As with amphetamine, the rush associated with cocaine injection is almost universally described in sexual terms, namely, the orgasm. Unlike snorting, the effects of injected or inhaled are far from subtle and gradual; they take hold of the user immediately. The experience is so intense that it tends to encompass and engross the shooter totally and cuts him or her off from other people who might be nearby (Waldorf, Murphy, Renarman, & Joyce, 1977, p. 35).

With repeated administrations, cocaine-produced rushes show rapid tolerance. When intravenous injections of cocaine were given 70 minutes apart, reports of rushes disappeared over the session, but other measures, such as "feeling good," were unchanged (Kumor, Sherer, Muntander, Jaffee, & Herning, 1988).

It is generally assumed that the feelings of pleasure and euphoria result from the direct effects of these drugs on the mesolimbic dopamine system and that the direct stimulation of this system is also responsible for the powerful reinforcing effects of the psychomotor stimulants (Wolverton & Johanson, 1984). Recent evidence, however, has shown that things may not be quite that simple. For example, drugs that block both D_1 and D_2 receptors do not block amphetamine-induced euphoria, and other drugs known to mimic the effects of cocaine on dopamine synapses do not cause euphoria. Other brain systems are clearly involved in the subjective effects of psychomotor stimulants (Brauer, Goudie, & de Wit, 1997).

Stereotyped Behavior

In 1965, a Swedish psychiatrist, Gosta Rylander, described a peculiar behavior shown by high-dosage users of phenmetrazine, an amphetamine-like drug used for weight reduction. These users ground up phenmetrazine pills and injected them intravenously to experience the rush. The behavior Rylander noticed was what the users called *punding*—the repetitive performance of some (usually useless) act for an extended period. Typical acts were taking apart and putting together a watch or a telephone, sorting and resorting things in a handbag, or cleaning an apartment. When users are punding, they will usually not eat or drink or even go to the bathroom, and they become annoyed if the activity is interrupted (Rylander, 1969). Similar behavior is common among amphetamine users. Punding is considered the human equivalent of stereotyped behavior seen in laboratory animals after high-dose injections of amphetamines. (Stereotyped behavior of nonhumans will be described in detail shortly.)

It is quite likely that both punding and stereotyped behavior are caused by stimulation of the nigrostriatal DA system, which has input into the extrapyramidal motor system (see Chapter 4).

Amphetamine Psychosis

High doses of the amphetamines can cause psychotic behavior in otherwise normal people (Bowers, 1987, p. 820). The psychosis is virtually indistinguishable from true, full-blown paranoid schizophrenia. The symptoms of amphetamine psychosis include auditory and visual hallucinations, delusions of persecution, delusions of grandeur, and, sometimes, hostility and violence triggered by a paranoid belief that danger is imminent.

Amphetamine psychosis can occur in individuals who have no history of psychotic behavior. It usually clears in several days without residual effects (Angrist & Sudilovsky, 1978).

At high doses, cocaine and cathinone are also capable of causing psychotic episodes. Such a cocaine-induced psychosis convinced Sigmund Freud that cocaine was not a wonder drug after all. Freud had been giving cocaine to a friend,

Dr. von Fleischl-Marxow, to treat pain from neural tumors. During the course of treatment, Fleischl found it necessary to increase the dose to high levels, and he started showing the signs that are now known to be typical of a psychosis caused by both cocaine and amphetamines. One of the most distressing symptoms Fleischl experienced was the feeling of creatures—in his case, white snakes—crawling over him. Others have described the feeling as bugs crawling around just under the skin (Brecher & the Editors of *Consumer Reports*, 1972, p. 275). These are known as *cocaine bugs* (crank bugs, if they are caused by amphetamine). This phenomenon is formally called *formication*, from the Latin *formica*, meaning "ant."

Schizophrenia is thought to be, at least in part, a result of excessive DA functioning in the mesolimbic system (see Chapter 13). Drugs such as amphetamine worsen the psychotic symptoms of schizophrenics and create psychotic symptoms in normal persons. We also know that the effectiveness of the antipsychotic drugs (drugs that reduce the symptoms of psychosis) appears to arise from their ability to block DA receptors (Post, Cutler, Jimmerson, & Bunney, 1981) (see Chapter 13). Antipsychotics also diminish psychotic behavior caused by excessive amphetamine.

Violence. Violent behavior has been associated with continued amphetamine use. The violent behavior usually results from changes in the user's personality, which becomes hostile, paranoid, and defensive. Although violent episodes are not especially frequent, they are unpredictable and sudden. Rylander (1969, p. 263) described one such case:

One addict who had just taken a shot stopped his car in a street, not feeling well, leaned backwards and put his feet up on the instrument panel. A bypasser asked if he was sick and offered his help. The addict drew a knife, got out and chased the helpful man. He stumbled and fell just when the addict tried to slash his back.

Sensory Effects

Amphetamines have been reported to raise the critical frequency of fusion threshold, indicating an increase in visual acuity (Simonson & Brozek,

1952). Slight improvements have been reported in auditory flicker fusion as well (Besser, 1967). The passage of time is underestimated; 1 second seems longer than it really is (Goldstone, Boardman, & Lhamon, 1958).

Effects on Performance

The Spanish conquistadores may not have believed the claims of the South American Indians that coca made them stronger, but there seems to be little doubt that amphetamines and cocaine can improve performance on a number of tasks and skills. Most of the early work of this nature was done by the armed forces of several countries during World War II. They found that endurance could be increased and the effects of fatigue could be diminished by amphetamines. In fact, amphetamines are still used in the military for this purpose. They are commonly referred to as *go pills*.

It does not appear that amphetamine will improve reaction time under normal circumstances, but it has been demonstrated many times that the drug will eliminate the effects of fatigue on reaction time, restoring it to normal. This finding also appears to be true for most measures of motor coordination and control. Improvements are more likely to be seen in complex motor tasks than in simple tasks.

Amphetamine has the ability to improve performance in tasks that require vigilance or prolonged attention. One measure of vigilance is the *clock test*. In this test, the subject faces a large dial around which a pointer moves in discrete steps. Every once in a while, the pointer moves two steps rather than one, and the task of the subject is to detect when such events occur. Over a period of 2 hours, the performance of normal subjects deteriorates from 95 to 80 percent accuracy. Subjects given 10 mg of amphetamine prior to this test show no deterioration in accuracy over the 2-hour period (Weiss, 1969). Amphetamine can also overcome deterioration in performance caused by other factors, such as decreased oxygen levels.

Not only does amphetamine return performance to normal levels, but other studies have also shown that in some situations, amphetamine can actually improve performance over normal levels. In a simplified simulated flying task, where subjects are required to move a joystick in order to keep dials from moving off center, it was found that the performance of subjects given a placebo deteriorated over a 4-hour period, but the scores of subjects given 5 mg of amphetamine actually stayed above their normal levels for the test (Weiss, 1969).

Although these drugs can improve performance, this improvement may be limited to overlearned and overpracticed tasks. Some investigators have suggested that stimulants may actually impair performance requiring flexibility and the ability to adopt new strategies (Judd, Squire, Butters, Salmon, & Paller, 1987, p. 1471).

Athletic Performance. In one early study, G. M. Smith and Beecher (1959) gave amphetamine to competitive swimmers who were then timed while performing in the event for which they were training. They found that amphetamine could produce a 1 percent improvement in their best drug-free times. Although 1 percent does not sound like much, in the highly competitive sport of swimming, athletes may train many months to reduce their times by 1 percent. Similar improvements have been seen in such track events as the 600- and 1,000-yard runs and the mile and in such field events as the shot put.

Because the psychomotor stimulants improve athletic performance, their use by athletes is banned by most national sports federations, and urine samples supplied by athletes at sporting events are screened for these drugs. As mentioned earlier, ephedrine is a psychomotor stimulant closely related to amphetamine. Ephedrine and similar drugs act as *bronchodilators* and are found in many cold preparations, cough syrups, and decongestants. Athletes undergoing such testing should be aware of the contents of these medicines before they take them because they could make their urine test positive for a banned substance. Some banned substances found in cold medicines include norpseudoephedrine, methoxphenamine, isoprenaline, isoproterenol, and methylephedrine.

EFFECTS ON THE BEHAVIOR OF NONHUMANS

Unconditioned Behavior

At low and intermediate doses, amphetamines increase spontaneous locomotor and exploratory activity in rats. At higher doses, there is an increase in locomotion at first, but after about an hour, the animals start to show increased sniffing and a variety of stereotyped behavior. The stereotyped behavior is usually some simple, short act with no particular function; it is repeated over and over to the exclusion of other behavior. In rodents, it may take the form of bobbing the head up and down, sniffing in a corner, rearing on the hind legs, or gnawing and biting.

In monkeys, there is a decrease in locomotor activity, and the stereotyped behavior is generally more complex than in rodents. It is also different in different subjects. One monkey may examine its hands; another may move sideways. These behaviors will reappear in the same animals when the drug is given at a later date. In humans, stereotyped behaviors, described earlier as punding, are more complex.

After high doses of amphetamines and cocaine, it is common for both rodents and monkeys to chew and bite at their own bodies. This self-directed biting is called *automutilation*. Animals may sometimes bite off their fingers, toes, or paws. It is likely that automutilation is a form of stereotyped behavior because it appears to be repetitious, but it may also be a result of formication. A sensation of bugs crawling under or on the skin is a symptom of amphetamine or cocaine psychosis in humans. The same sensation, experienced by animals, could cause them to pick at or cut their skin in an attempt to let the bugs out.

Even at low doses, amphetamines and cocaine decrease consumption of both food and water in most species. This is probably a combination of

(a) the effect of the drug on the part of the brain that controls appetite and (b) the fact that the drug increases other behavior sequences and reduces the time available for eating and drinking. We know that appetite suppression is not related to the reinforcing effects of these drugs because fenfluramine, a drug very similar to amphetamine, is very effective in suppressing appetite but does not appear to have any reinforcing effects (Brady et al., 1987).

Conditioned Behavior

In one of the earliest experiments on the effects of amphetamines on operant behavior, Peter Dews (1958) gave methamphetamine to pigeons responding on several schedules of reinforcement for food. Dews found that the drug increased responding on the fixed interval (FI) schedule but decreased fixed ratio (FR) responding at exactly the same dose. In his paper, Dews first demonstrated a relationship between the effect of amphetamine and the rate at which the pigeon was responding. He noticed that methamphetamine increased the rate of responding if it was low, as in the FI, but slowed responding that was normally fast, as in the FR. This effect became known as the *rate dependency effect*. It has since been demonstrated that this rule applies across all amphetamine-type drugs and many others, across many species, and across many types of behavior and schedules of reinforcement (Dews & Wenger, 1977). The significance of this observation cannot be overestimated. It was one of the first demonstrations that a drug interacts dynamically with ongoing behavior. It also showed that it was not appropriate to understand the effect a drug might have by simply classifying it as a "psychomotor stimulant." Whether the drug stimulates or depresses motor activity is a result of the behavior being observed and not entirely determined by the properties of the drug alone.

The rate dependency principle appears not to apply to the effect of amphetamine on behavior suppressed by punishment. Punishment-suppressed behavior usually occurs at a low rate, but most amphetamines and cocaine do not increase the rate.

The effects of cocaine are similar to those of amphetamine, but the rate-increasing effects of cocaine are not as great (C. G. Smith, 1964).

DISSOCIATION AND DRUG STATE DISCRIMINATION

It has been demonstrated that amphetamine causes dissociation; animals trained under the influence of amphetamine cannot completely remember what they learned when the amphetamine has worn off. This may be bad news for people who use amphetamines to help them stay awake and cram for exams (Roffman & Lal, 1972).

Rats can learn to discriminate amphetamine and cocaine from saline with moderate ease, although they are not as easily discriminable as barbiturates or benzodiazepines (Overton, 1982). Animals generalize the amphetamine response to cocaine, methylphenidate, cathinone, and some monoamine oxidase (MAO) inhibitors (see Chapter 14) (Glennon, 1987, p. 1630; Glennon et al., 1994; Huang & Ho, 1974; Porsolt, Pawelec, & Jalfre, 1982; Schechter & Glennon, 1985). In rats, amphetamine responses do not generalize to caffeine, nicotine, the barbiturates, chlorpromazine, atropine, or any of the common hallucinogens (Seiden & Dykstra, 1977, p. 416). Humans can also readily learn to discriminate amphetamine from a placebo (Chait, Uhlenhuth, & Johanson, 1986).

The discriminative effects of amphetamine can be blocked by dopamine D_2 receptors and, in some cases, by D_1 receptors, showing that dopamine systems are involved. It does not appear that norepinephrine or serotonin plays a significant role in amphetamine discrimination (Brauer et al., 1997).

TOLERANCE

Acute Tolerance

As described earlier, with continuous use of cocaine sniffing every 20 or 30 minutes for 10 or 12 hours, cocaine quickly loses its ability to cause rushes and gradually becomes unable to improve mood. This phenomenon, sometimes known as a *coke-out*, is usually why runs come to an end (see the section on self-administration of cocaine later in this chapter). This acute tolerance dissipates rapidly and may be gone within 24 hours (Waldorf et al., 1977). Even though acute tolerance develops to the subjective effects, it does not appear to develop to the effects on blood pressure and heart rate. This suggests that people who increase the frequency of dose of amphetamine or cocaine to maintain a subjective effect may be in danger of reaching levels that could be toxic (Brauer et al., 1996).

Chronic Tolerance and Sensitization

Some effects of cocaine and amphetamines become tolerated with repeated administration. In humans, the appetite-suppressing effect usually disappears in about 2 weeks, and the effects on the heart and blood pressure also diminish. The lethal effects also show tolerance, and chronic amphetamine users are able to increase their dose to extremely high levels. In one such case, a 15,000-mg dose of amphetamine was administered in a 24-hour period; this was 1,000 times the normal therapeutic dose and several times the estimated LD_{50} for nontolerant humans. Some effects, such as the blocking of sleep, show no tolerance.

For some effects, reverse tolerance or sensitization takes place. Stereotyped behavior and psychotic behavior appear more frequently after repeated doses in humans. In rats, chronic administration of cocaine lowers the threshold for convulsions, and some electrical activity within the brain increases with continued use (Stripling & Ellinwood, 1976). With continued administration of cocaine, stereotyped behavior and spontaneous motor activity also increase in frequency and intensity (Post, Weiss, Pert, & Uhde, 1987). As described in Chapter 3, this sensitization is a result of increased sensitivity of the mesolimbic dopamine system (R. C. Pierce & Kalivas, 1997).

WITHDRAWAL

Amphetamine and cocaine are not associated with a severe or medically serious withdrawal when use is discontinued. Depression seems to be the most prominent characteristic of psychomotor stimulant withdrawal.

After a single dose of amphetamine or cocaine, the high is usually followed by a *letdown*—a period of depression and lethargy that can be thought of as a withdrawal symptom. The depression is immediately relieved by another administration of the drug. The letdown occurs within half an hour with cocaine, but its appearance is delayed for a number of hours with amphetamines. The severity of the depression is related to the dose and the duration of the intake period. If the intake period has been long enough to interfere with sleep and eating, there will also be a compensatory increase in sleeping and eating. The nature of the sleep will also change because there will be a rebound of REM sleep that the drug suppressed.

After continuous long-term use of cocaine, a permanent depression in mood may arise from changes in the functioning of the monoamine systems in the brain. These changes appear to be similar to the changes associated with depression and can be treated with antidepressant drugs (Gawin & Kleber, 1987).

When high levels of amphetamine have been continuously used for an extended time, the depression that results may be quite severe and may be accompanied by suicidal thoughts and suicide attempts. Amphetamine withdrawal depression is similar to psychiatric depression except that the latter is characterized by insomnia and decreased appetite, whereas the opposite is true for the amphetamine-induced depression (Angrist & Sudilovsky, 1978).

Withdrawal from psychomotor stimulants can also disrupt performance. In the early stages of abstinence, methamphetamine addicts demonstrate decision-making dysfunctions on tasks that require switching from a losing to a winning strategy in a two-choice procedure. This performance deficit correlates with reduced dorsolateral prefrontal cortex activation and failure to activate the ventromedial cortex, as measured by functional magnetic resonance imaging (fMRI) (Paulus et al., 2002). Following at least 1 year of amphetamine abstinence, PET imaging continued to demonstrate decreased dorsolateral prefrontal cortex activation in association with decision making in risky situations (Ersche et al., 2005).

SELF-ADMINISTRATION IN HUMANS

Cocaine

Cocaine has a long history of self-administration, starting with the native people of South America, who consumed the drug orally, as noted earlier in this chapter. Their pattern of use was very different from the modern North American patterns of self-administration of pure cocaine or amphetamines. With pure cocaine, continuous use is rare. When snorted or injected, cocaine is usually taken in large quantities for brief periods of time that are followed by periods of abstinence. It is usually consumed, with some ceremony and ritual, at parties and in social settings.

Cocaine is often taken in conjunction with other drugs. The most usual mix is the *speed ball*, a combination of cocaine (or amphetamine) and heroin. Users claim that the heroin reduces the jitteriness that cocaine arouses by stimulating the sympathetic nervous system, and the cocaine diminishes the sleepiness or nod caused by heroin. Cocaine is also regularly mixed with depressants such as benzodiazepines or with ketamine or PCP for the same reason.

Amphetamines

Like cocaine, amphetamines are self-administered sporadically rather than continuously, but the pattern may depend on the effect for which the drug is taken. Because it is longer lasting than cocaine, amphetamine allows constant blood levels to be maintained more easily for an extended period of time—for example, when the drug is used by truck drivers or students cramming for finals to enhance behavior or prevent sleep. When the need is over, the drug is usually discontinued, and the person then recovers by making up for the lost sleep.

When amphetamines are used for their euphoric effects, usually much higher doses are taken, and the administration is frequently intravenous. In the 1960s, this type of use was characterized by the *peak user* or *speed freak* who typically injected amphetamine every few hours for days at a time. During such *runs*, users do not sleep, they eat very little, and they may show symptoms of amphetamine psychosis, such as punding and paranoia. Eventually, when they are too exhausted to continue or they run out of the drug, they *crash*—they sleep for an extended period (24 to 48 hours). When they wake up, they are very hungry and will eat ravenously before going out to search for more drugs in order to begin another run. This pattern is now seen with crack addicts.

SELF-ADMINISTRATION IN NONHUMANS

In 1968, Roy Pickens and Travis Thompson, then at the University of Minnesota, published the first detailed account of cocaine self-administration in nonhumans. (The first cocaine self-administration experiments were actually done by G. A. Deneau and his colleagues at the University of Michigan, but these were not published until 1969.) Pickens and Thompson, using two rats implanted with intravenous catheters, showed that the rats would bar press on an FR schedule for cocaine. (This experiment is described in Chapter 5.) For several reasons, this was an important milestone. It was the first demonstration of self-administration of a drug other than morphine, and it established that a drug with no apparent withdrawal symptoms could be a reinforcer, confirming that the reinforcing effect of drugs was not a result of fear of withdrawal. Since the time of this experiment, there have been many demonstrations of cocaine self-administration in many species.

In fact, cocaine may have a more robust reinforcing effect than almost any other drug. Animals learn to self-administer cocaine more easily than any other drug, and they work harder for it. In an experiment reported by Yanagita (1975), the reinforcing potency of cocaine was compared with that of a number of other drugs, using the progressive ratio procedure. In four of six monkeys, cocaine was the most reinforcing drug tested. (One monkey worked the ratio up to 6,400 before stopping.) Cocaine tied for first in a fifth monkey, and the sixth found amphetamine more reinforcing than cocaine.

Figure 11-2 shows data published by Deneau, Yanagita, and Seevers (1969) and demonstrates the erratic pattern of cocaine self-administration in monkeys when the drug is freely available 24 hours a day. A monkey learns quickly to give itself the drug and is soon administering the drug at levels high enough to cause convulsions. The record shows that there is considerable fluctuation from day to day. On some days, no drug is

taken; on others, massive quantities are infused. Often, if monkeys are given unlimited access to the drug, they will administer to the point of killing themselves (Bozarth & Wise, 1984).

Figure 11-2 also shows the typical run–abstinence cycle that is characteristic of human stimulant use. In this case, the monkey actually stopped responding for a 28-hour period on day 17 before resuming injections on day 18.

The pattern of self-administration is quite different when daily access to cocaine is limited. Under these conditions, laboratory animals self-administer cocaine in a steady and regular manner, precisely controlling the amount of drug they receive on any given day (Amed & Koob, 1998). If the work required for each infusion or the dose

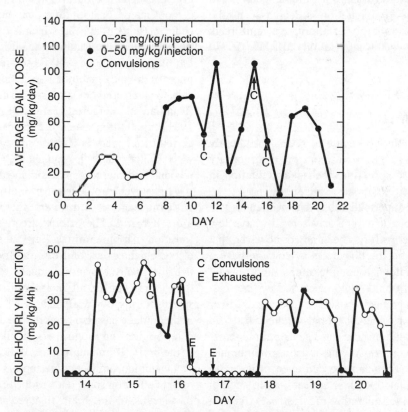

Figure 11-2 The pattern of cocaine self-administration in the monkey. *Top*: Daily intake for 21 days. *Bottom*: Intake in 4-hour periods from day 14 to day 21, illustrating the cycles of intake and abstinence. (Adapted from Deneau, Yanagita, & Seevers, 1969)

per infusion is changed, the behavioral output changes exactly as needed to keep the daily dose constant.

Behavioral economics studies show that the demand for cocaine, like the demand for most drugs, is inelastic when cost is low but becomes elastic when cost is very high (Carroll & Bickel, 1998; Yokel, 1987, p. 15).

Nonhumans readily self-administer all the psychomotor stimulants, using a variety of routes of administration. The patterns and rates are similar to those for cocaine. Cocaine self-administration can be primed by other psychomotor stimulants and by other drugs such as morphine and caffeine. In addition, cocaine self-administration is enhanced by stress, previous experience with cocaine, and the concurrent administration of caffeine, heroin, and alcohol. Self-administration is decreased by the concurrent availability of alternative reinforcers such as sweetened water (Carroll & Bickel, 1998).

HARMFUL EFFECTS

Direct Effects

When methylphenidate is given chronically at low levels in the treatment of hyperactivity in children, it sometimes causes a reduction in growth velocity (Brookes, 1985, p. 267).

There are reports that the Andean Indians who chew the coca leaf regularly seem to have few health problems. It has been noted, however, that these and other regular users of cocaine have a sallow or yellowish complexion, which may be attributable to mild jaundice caused by liver disease. Chronic cocaine use has also caused liver damage in experimental animals (Caldwell, 1976). Chronic cocaine sniffing can also cause inflammation and ulceration of the mucous membranes in the nose. This damage can even progress to the extent that openings appear in the septum (the membrane separating the nostrils). Because cocaine is a local anesthetic, this discomfort in the nose will be relieved by sniffing more cocaine, and in this way it will contribute to the motivation to continue sniffing the drug.

Cocaine sniffing, smoking, or injecting can lead to an intense compulsion to continue until the drug runs out or the user becomes exhausted. During such runs, it is not unusual for vast sums to be spent on the drug (R. K. Siegel, 1982a). People have been known to sell their houses and cars to finance continuous intake. Not only do such binges consume personal finances, but many users report disturbing physiological and psychological symptoms: paranoid feelings, visual hallucinations, cravings, antisocial behavior, attention and concentration problems, blurred vision, and weight loss.

The use of oral amphetamine for short periods (e.g., to stay awake while driving or studying) can have undesirable effects that include restlessness, excessive talking, confusion, and dizziness. If use is continued for too long, paranoid psychotic behavior starts to appear, which is complicated by the lack of sleep. Punding and irrational thinking may also emerge, and these are not likely to improve driving or studying. In susceptible individuals, the increased blood pressure can cause strokes (Rumbaugh, Bergeron, Fang, & McCormack, 1971). In addition, when the drug is stopped, the period of recovery is characterized by depression with suicidal tendencies and lethargy, and the REM rebound will cause sleep disturbances.

High-level chronic use, especially if associated with intravenous administration, is potentially quite harmful. The effects are both direct and indirect. Amphetamines have a strong direct effect on the heart and circulatory system; the irregular heartbeat and increased blood pressure they cause can result in internal bleeding and strokes (Grinspoon & Bakalar, 1979a). Irreversible brain damage has also been reported as a result of deterioration and rupturing of small blood vessels in the brain (Rumbaugh et al., 1971).

In addition, amphetamine appears to have a neurotoxic effect on some parts of the brain, especially those cells in the brain that release dopamine. Nonhuman primate studies demonstrate that damage to brain dopamine neurons can result, not from excessive use but from only four administrations of methamphetamine at doses comparable to those used recreationally by humans. PET imaging with a radiolabeled dopamine transporter ligand revealed that total doses of 2, 4, or 8 mg/kg of methamphetamine injected into baboons over 8 hours on a single day resulted in significant reductions in dopamine transporter density in the caudate and putamen 2 to 3 weeks later. This indicates the death of dopamine cells (Villemagne et al., 1998). The results of this study are shown in Color Plate D.

Indirect Effects

As with so many drugs used excessively, many of the harmful effects of amphetamine are indirect and arise from the user's lifestyle. Because intravenous users rarely use sterile injection apparatus, they frequently contract diseases, particularly hepatitis and AIDS. Their ability to fight diseases is reduced by (a) the poor diet caused by the appetite-suppressing effects of the drug and (b) the fact that they seldom sleep. High-dose amphetamine users are suspicious, antisocial, and prone to violence (Rylander, 1969). The death rate among intravenous amphetamine users is much higher than expected in the general population, but it is about the same as among chronic alcoholics and heroin addicts of the same age group (H. Kalant & Kalant, 1979).

Reproduction

Both amphetamine and cocaine have been used to enhance sexual activity. It has been reported that low doses prolong erections and delay ejaculation in males and enhance desire and enjoyment of orgasms in females. These changes, along with the decrease in sexual inhibitions that is caused by the drug, sometimes lead to changes in sexual orientation and practices while taking these drugs. People who would not normally do such things sometimes engage in marathon sexual acts, group sex, and homosexuality (D. E. Smith, Buxton, & Dammann, 1979). Continuous high doses of cocaine by inhalation of crack or freebase or by injection often lead to a disruption in sexual activity in males and periods of disinterest in sex (R. K. Siegel, 1982a).

Like cocaine, khat initially increases sex drive in males, but continued use can cause decreased sexual interest and impotency (Giannini, Burge, Shaheen, & Price, 1986). It can also inhibit milk production in nursing mothers who continuously abuse the plant.

There have been some studies of the effects of amphetamine-like drugs on fetal abnormalities. Most of these studies were done on women who used these drugs to control their appetite during pregnancy. They provided some evidence linking this chronic, oral, low-dose use with a higher-than-average incidence of birth abnormalities. Evidence from animal studies also indicates that amphetamine used during pregnancy can cause behavioral and physical problems in offspring (Grinspoon & Hedblom, 1975, pp. 146–147).

There is mounting evidence that cocaine use by a pregnant woman is detrimental to the fetus, but the media presentation of *crack babies* was somewhat of an exaggeration. Many studies have found that maternal cocaine use does retard fetal growth; babies are smaller and more likely to be premature (Zuckerman & Frank, 1994). Other studies, however, have found that babies born to mothers who reported using cocaine while pregnant were not more likely to be born prematurely or to have smaller birth weights but were almost 10 times more likely to have *abruptio placentae* (the placenta detaches prematurely; Shiono et al., 1995). Studies of possible long-term developmental and behavioral effects of prenatal exposure to cocaine are plagued with methodological difficulties, not the least of which is accurately measuring cocaine exposure and separating its effect from other concurrent factors such as the use of other drugs and the quality of pre- and postnatal care (Zuckerman & Frank, 1994). It is now becoming clear that such exposure does not necessarily lead to reduced intelligence, as was once thought. Several studies, however, have concluded that children whose mothers used cocaine while pregnant have more behavioral problems, including a decreased ability to pay attention and stay focused, increased aggression, and irritability (G. Vogel, 1997).

Overdose

Cocaine users who take large doses commonly experience muscle weakness and respiratory depression. The user may be unable to stand up or may collapse but not lose consciousness (Crowley, 1987, p. 202).

The lethal dose of cocaine depends to a large extent on the route of administration. Individuals vary greatly, but the LD_{50} in a 150-pound man is about 500 mg. When the drug is taken intranasally, the LD_{50} may be as low as 30 mg. The absolute dose may not be the important variable in determining the lethality; rather, what seems to be important is the sudden increase in drug levels in the brain.

The cocaine-related deaths of several prominent athletes have emphasized that cocaine has intense cardiovascular effects that can be fatal when the drug is injected or inhaled in concentrated form, causing the cocaine sudden-death syndrome. As noted earlier, it is not unusual for laboratory animals to self-administer lethal doses of cocaine. F. R. George and Goldberg (1989) showed that between individual strains of rats and mice, there is considerable variability in sensitivity to various effects of cocaine. One strain of rats, for example, seemed insensitive to the reinforcing effects of usual doses of cocaine but was very sensitive to the lethal effects of cocaine on the heart. If there are similar genetic variations in humans, it is possible that certain individuals might be highly resistant to the euphoric effects of the drug. Such people would be at a considerable risk from cocaine because attempts to reach euphoric doses could easily drive blood levels into the lethal range. Such genetic variations in sensitivity may account for the cocaine sudden-death syndrome (F. R. George & Goldberg, 1989).

The cocaine overdose or *caine reaction* has two phases. An initial excitement is followed by severe headache, nausea, vomiting, and then severe convulsions. This phase is followed by a loss of consciousness, respiratory depression, and cardiac failure causing death. Death may be very rapid, within 2 to 3 minutes, or it may take as long as half an hour. Someone who survives the first 3 hours is likely to recover, but if breathing has been depressed too long, there may be brain damage from loss of oxygen (Gay & Inaba, 1976).

Seizures caused by cocaine overdose can be treated with diazepam, and respiratory depression or arrest can be treated with artificial respiration. Chlorpromazine, an antipsychotic, is also very effective as an antagonist of the toxic effects of cocaine (Crowley, 1987, p. 203).

TREATMENT

The first stage in the treatment of a cocaine abuser involves a period of detoxification during which the direct effects of cocaine are treated. The Haight-Ashbury Free Medical Clinic in San Francisco (Gay & Inaba, 1976) has developed a procedure whereby the acute toxic effects of cocaine are treated directly until the patient is out of danger, and then, for the next 3 to 12 days, depressant drugs are given and are slowly tapered off. For the less seriously afflicted, a period of hospitalization may not be essential.

Following detoxification or for users wishing to stop who are not under the influence of the drug, there are a number of possible long-term treatments. Some of these depend on treatment with other drugs, and some do not.

The initial concern with cocaine abusers seeking treatment is that they will resume using the drug very quickly, before treatment has had a chance to have any effect. Because of drug priming (see Chapter 3), it is particularly important to prevent the patient from using cocaine again, even once. The craving for cocaine increases considerably just 15 minutes after a single cocaine injection (Jaffe, Cascella, Kumor, Sherer, 1989). This fact makes a relapse extremely likely.

A recently developed approach makes use of positive reinforcement in the form of a monetary reward for providing clean urine samples. The reward increases with each succeeding drug-free test. In addition to the money, a relative, spouse, or friend who is involved in the program participates in some previously agreed-on enjoyable activity. These incentives are combined with counseling to help the user avoid situations where there is a risk of relapse, employment counseling, and encouragement to pursue educational or recreational goals. In a test of this strategy, 11 of 13 cocaine users admitted for outpatient treatment remained drug free for a 12-week period of treatment. Only five of 12 patients in a control group that was offered 12-steps counseling remained drug free for the 12 weeks (Higgins et al., 1991). Other cognitive-behavioral techniques are now being developed for methamphetamine users. These techniques combine social support, family education, individual counseling, and urine testing (Rawson et al., 2004).

In addition to these treatments, some drugs, primarily antidepressants, have been found to be helpful. There is some evidence that a period of prolonged cocaine use will cause permanent biochemical changes in the brain that are similar to the biochemical changes associated with depression (see Chapter 14). This depression may be responsible for the craving that ex-users have for cocaine. Relieving the depression with antidepressant drugs could also diminish the craving. In fact, antidepressants have been reported to diminish the craving for cocaine in ex-users with a delay of about 2 weeks after beginning treatment. This is, in fact, the same delay that is often seen with the antidepressants in their therapeutic effect on depression (Gawin & Kleber, 1987).

More recently, a new drug has been tried with some initial success. Topiramate is a drug used to prevent seizures. It works by both stimulating gamma-aminobutyric acid and blocking glutamate. This combination of effects also seems to reduce cocaine craving (Kampman et al., 2004). Drug craving can be experimentally induced and correlated with changes in regional blood flow using PET scanning. Researchers recorded 1-minute audio scripts of cocaine addicts describing detailed personal experiences and subjective effects of cocaine use and replayed the script to the addicts during a PET scanning session. Compared to control conditions in which the scripts described a personal experience in nature, cocaine-related scripts induced sensations of drug craving that correlated with increased cerebral blood flow in the nucleus accumbens, dorsal and ventral regions of the anterior cingulate cortex, and the frontal cortex (Kilts, Gross, Ely, & Drexler, 2004). Topiramate's effects may therefore decrease craving by inhibiting increases in cerebral blood flow in reward-related brain regions.

Another drug that appears to be useful in treating cocaine addicts and preventing early relapse during treatment is modafinil (Dackis et al., 2005). Modafinil is a stimulant drug used to treat narcolepsy. It works by increasing activity of glutamate and dopamine. It has been described as a "mood brightener." The drug may be reversing the dopamine and glutamate depletion caused by excessive cocaine use and thereby blocking the mood depression caused by cocaine withdrawal.

Substitution therapies do not seem to be effective. Attempts to use methylphenidate and phenmetrazine (an appetite suppressant) as maintenance drugs for cocaine abusers, in the same way that methadone is used with heroin users (see Chapter 12), were unsuccessful. A similar technique was tried with amphetamine abusers in the 1960s, but this failed as well (Bergsman & Jarpe, 1969; Gawin & Kleber, 1987, p. 175; Gorelick, 1995). It is possible that modafinil may be able to fulfill this function.

CHAPTER SUMMARY

- All the drugs covered in this chapter—amphetamines (including crystal meth), ephedrine, cocaine, and cathinone—have a similar effect on the nervous system; they all increase activity at synapses that use a monoamine (MA) as a transmitter.

- Cocaine, ephedrine, and cathinone are derived from plant material, but the amphetamines are synthetic.

- Amphetamine and cocaine are weak bases. Although they can be absorbed from the digestive system, they are much more effective when injected, sniffed, or smoked and inhaled. They are easily distributed throughout the body and are extensively metabolized by the liver and excreted in the urine. Cocaine has a much shorter half-life than the amphetamines.

- Crack cocaine is a mixture of cocaine and baking soda. As a consequence, it is not ionized and rapidly absorbed and distributed.

- The amphetamines and cathinone increase activity at MA synapses by stimulating leakage of the transmitter, increasing the amount of transmitter released, and blocking reuptake of the transmitter. Cocaine works by blocking uptake of the transmitter.

- MA systems in the brain are closely related to the mesolimbic dopamine system, which governs reinforcement, and the basal ganglia of the nigrostriatal system, which regulate body movement.

- The psychomotor stimulants improve mood. When amphetamine and cocaine are taken in high doses by inhaling or intravenous injection, they cause intense feelings of pleasure called rushes. After the effects of the psychomotor stimulants have worn off, a period of depression usually ensues.

- When taken continuously at high doses, by humans or nonhumans, the psychomotor stimulants cause stereotyped behavior—the senseless repetition of a meaningless act. In humans, high doses may also cause paranoid behavior and psychosis.

- At low doses, the amphetamines and cocaine can improve performance in certain activities and can eliminate the effect of fatigue on most cognitive and perceptual tasks and on athletic activity.

- The amphetamines can cause dissociation and are readily discriminated from saline. All the psychomotor stimulants and antidepressants will generalize to each other but do not generalize to any other type of drug.

- The discriminative stimulus effects of cocaine and amphetamine appear to be controlled by DA receptors.

- Withdrawal from amphetamines and cocaine is characterized by intense depression, and fMRI and PET studies have detected changes in frontal cortex activity associated with disruption of decision-making capabilities even after a year of abstinence from amphetamine.

- The psychomotor stimulants are readily self-administered by both humans and nonhumans, and the pattern of self-administration is similar in most species. It consists of a run of self-administration lasting for days or hours during which there is very little eating or sleeping, followed by a period of abstinence and recovery. This period is followed by another run. Cocaine and amphetamine are probably more powerful reinforcers than any other drug.

- Excessive cocaine use and the associated lifestyle can be unhealthy. Many who inject cocaine do not use sterile needles, and this contributes to the spread of AIDS. Continuous use of high doses of psychomotor stimulants can make people paranoid and psychotic, retard the development of unborn children, and cause sudden death in susceptible individuals.

- Among the treatments being developed for cocaine and psychomotor stimulant abuse are antidepressant drugs that reduce withdrawal depression. Other drugs that seem to be helpful are modafinil and Topiramate. Alternate therapies offer social and monetary rewards for remaining abstinent.

12

Opiates and Opioids

The patience of a poppy.
He who has smoked will smoke.
Opium knows how to wait.
—*Jean Cocteau (1968, p. 36)*

The drugs in this class are referred to either as *opiates* or *opioids*. These terms refer to any drug, either natural or synthetic in origin, that has properties similar to opium or its main active ingredient, morphine. (Technically, the term *opiate* should be used only to refer to drugs of natural origin, i.e., derived from opium, and *opioid* should be used in reference to all opiate-like drugs, including the opiates and synthetic drugs, but often this distinction is not made.) This text will use the term *opioid* in a generic sense to refer to all drugs in this class.

This family of drugs is also frequently referred to as *narcotic analgesics* or just *narcotics*. Technically, a narcotic is a drug that causes sleep. The narcotic analgesics produce *analgesia* (loss of sensitivity to pain) and make a person sleepy. This name distinguishes these drugs from *nonnarcotic analgesics*, such as aspirin, which do not cause sleep. One difficulty with the word *narcotic* is that over the years, it has acquired a new meaning and is now commonly used to refer to the habit-forming property of a drug. It has also developed a distasteful connotation; calling a drug a *narcotic* immediately conjures up visions of degenerate and depraved addicts who are slaves to the drug and its suppliers. This misuse of the term has been given legal sanction, further increasing the confusion. In the United States, the Harrison Narcotic Act of 1914 defined both marijuana and cocaine as narcotics, along with opiates. In Canada, a so-called Narcotic Control Act regulates the use of many habit-forming drugs, some of which, like marijuana, are not narcotics at all in the sleep-production sense, but in a legal sense they have become "narcotics."

Because it has so many meanings, the term *narcotic* will be avoided here. The term *opioid* will be used instead.

ORIGINS AND SOURCES OF OPIOIDS

Natural and Semisynthetic Opioids

The main natural source of *opium* is a poppy (*Papaver somniferum*). This poppy had its origins in Asia Minor but is now grown in countries with

261

similar climates throughout the world. On only 10 days in its life cycle, the plant manufactures the drug, which must be gathered then. Opium is the sap that exudes out of scratches made in the seedpods of the poppy after the petals have fallen off. The scratches are made one day; the next day, the sap is scraped off and compressed into cakes. This is *opium*.

There are several active ingredients in opium. The two main ones are *morphine*, which accounts for 10 percent of the weight of opium, and *codeine*, which makes up only 0.5 percent. Morphine was first isolated from opium by the German chemist Frederick Serturner. He called it "morphium" after Morpheus, the Greek god of dreams, and published his findings in 1803. The significance of the finding was not immediately recognized, but in 1831, he was awarded a prize by the Institute of France for his discovery. Also in the 1830s, morphine was first manufactured and sold commercially. Codeine was isolated in 1821 by Pierre J. Robiquet while he was experimenting with a new process for isolating morphine.

Heroin is a semisynthetic opiate made by adding two acetyl groups to the morphine molecule (*diacetylmorphine* or *diamorphine*). Heroin is about 10 times more lipid soluble than morphine and, therefore, gets to the brain faster and in higher concentrations.

Morphine is widely used in medicine and is usually sold as a salt under its generic name *morphine sulfate*. In the United States, morphine and codeine are legally available only on prescription. In Canada, the same is true for morphine, but codeine is available in small quantities, without a prescription, in some over-the-counter painkillers and cough medicines. Heroin is illegal and cannot be prescribed or used in the United States. For some restricted purposes, it may be used in Canada on an experimental basis. It may also be prescribed in the United Kingdom under certain conditions.

Synthetic Opioids

A number of drugs bear little chemical resemblance to morphine but appear to have similar pharmacological and behavioral effects and to work at the same receptor, although they are not all as effective at the receptor as morphine, and some are much more effective. The best known of these is *meperidine*, which is sometimes called *pethidine* (Demerol). It is similar to morphine but shorter acting. *Methadone* (Dolophine) and *LAAM* (1-alpha-acetylmethadol) have a much longer duration of action than morphine and are much more effective when given orally. Other synthetics are *fentanyl* (Sublimaze), *levorphanol* (Levo-Dromoran), *pentazocine* (Talwin), *phenazocine* (Narphen), and *propoxyphine* (Darvon). Another opioid that is widely used both as a medicine and on the street is *oxycodone*. It is sold as Percocet (if it is mixed with acetaminophen) or Percodan (if it is mixed with aspirin). A much more notorious formulation of oxycodone is OxyContin, a tablet that contains many times the oxycodone of a regular tablet but in a slow-release form. It is designed to give long-term pain relief to arthritis sufferers, but if the tablet is crushed, dissolved, and injected, it can create severe addiction and has caused many accidental overdoses. All these drugs are available only on prescription in most countries.

Over the years, clandestine laboratories have synthesized many "designer drugs" based on the fentanyl molecule, *China White* being the best known. Another notorious designer drug was created in an attempt to synthesize pethidine. This resulted in the accidental production of MPTP, which was metabolized into a toxin that destroyed the substantia nigra, part of the extrapyramidal motor system that provides dopamine stimulation of the basal ganglia. The result was what has been called the "frozen addict," a person with severe symptoms of Parkinson's disease.

Another opioid of interest is dextromethorphan, a common ingredient in cough-suppressant medicines like Robitussin. Apart from the ability to suppress coughing, dextromethorphan is a unique opioid in that it does not have an effect on opioid receptors. Instead, it appears to have effects similar to PCP (phencyclidine). For this reason it will be discussed separately in Chapter 16.

Opioid Antagonists and Mixed Agonist-Antagonists

Several synthetic drugs act as antagonists to opioids. One, *naloxone*, is a pure antagonist that will block the action of any other opioid. Others, such as *nalorphine* and *cyclazocine*, have some opioid activity of their own but will antagonize other opioids. (We will return to the neurophysiology of opioids and opioid receptors later.)

HISTORY

It is believed that the opium poppy was being cultivated in the western Mediterranean region in the sixth millennium B.C., and opium capsules found in grass bags in Neolithic burial sites in northern Spain dated to about 4200 B.C. (Rudgley, 1995). The earliest written reference to opium is a Sumerian idiogram that is translated as "joy plant." The use of this symbol has been dated to about 4000 B.C. Opium is also mentioned frequently in Assyrian medical tablets dating from the seventh century B.C. These tablets are probably copies of earlier manuscripts. Originally wild, the opium poppy was being cultivated in Assyria and Babylon by the second century B.C. By this time as well, opium use had spread throughout the Middle East and North Africa. It was mentioned in the Ebers Papyri, early Egyptian medical scrolls dating to 1550 B.C. In these early writings, the poppy is mentioned primarily as a medicine, but the nonmedical properties of the plant were certainly appreciated.

The ancient Greeks knew of opium as well. The Greek physician Hippocrates recommended the use of opium for a number of conditions, as did the Roman physicians Pliny and Galen and the Arabian physician Avicenna, who recommended it for diseases of the eye and diarrhea.

The use of opium spread from the Middle East in every direction with the expansion of the Islamic religion. It was carried east to India by Arab traders in the ninth century and then from India to China, where it was used primarily as a medicine and taken orally. Later, when tobacco smoking was banned by a Chinese emperor in 1644, the Chinese filled their pipes with opium and invented the practice of opium smoking, a very efficient drug delivery system that ensured the popularity of the drug in that country.

The Arabs traded opium, along with spices and other goods, with the merchants of Venice. In the early part of the sixteenth century, Europeans became aware of opium primarily through the efforts of traveling physicians. A Swiss doctor known as Paracelsus traveled throughout Europe and carried opium in the pommel of his saddle. He called it "the stone of immortality." Other physicians quickly adopted the drug and prescribed it in various forms to their patients, with great success. John Sydenham, an English physician, wrote in 1680, "Among the remedies it has pleased Almighty God to give to man to relieve his sufferings, none is so universal or so efficacious as opium."

Throughout the seventeenth and eighteenth centuries, the popular use of opiates grew steadily, but in the nineteenth century, there was a drastic increase in the British consumption of opium. In 1825, the opium consumption rate was between 1 and 2 pounds per 1,000 population, but at its peak in 1875 the rate was greater than 10 pounds per 1,000 population. Opium was available in many formulations from food stores, pubs, and even peddlers on the streets. The most popular form in which opium was sold was tincture of opium, or laudanum, which was opium dissolved in alcohol.

About this time, morphine became available. Morphine, however, remained more under the control of the medical profession and, unlike opium, was never widely sold in shops. This restriction did not hinder its popularity; physicians generally prescribed it when requested. Because the lower classes seldom saw a doctor, morphine was more commonly used by the middle and upper classes.

Although many people were openly addicted to the drug, it was not perceived as a medical or social problem at the beginning of the nineteenth century. Not until the 1830s did all this opium use generate any concern, and not until 1868 was any legislative effort made to control it. The regulatory change was brought about by the development of social and political ideas rather than medical research or theory.

The availability of the drug was recognized as the main problem. In 1868, the British Parliament passed the Pharmacy Act, which made pharmacists' shops the only legal source of opiates and was the first of several laws that slowly brought the use of opiates under the control of the medical profession and out of the hands of the people. It also marked the start of the belief—a new idea at the time—that addiction was a medical problem and should be handled by physicians.

The story of opiate use in the United States is somewhat different. Americans were just as fond of opiates as the British. In 1870, when British consumption peaked at over 10 pounds per 1,000 population, American consumption rates were greater than 13 pounds per 1,000. Some of this was consumed orally in the form of patent medicines; the majority was refined into morphine and injected by means of the recently developed hypodermic syringe. This route of administration may have become popular because of the wide use of morphine during the Civil War, when morphine addiction became known as "the army disease." In 1914, Congress passed the Harrison Narcotic Act, which, in effect, made it illegal to be an addict and illegal for physicians to prescribe opiates to addicts.

Heroin

Heroin was invented in 1898 by Heinrich Dreser and marketed by the Bayer company of Germany. Dreser was the inventor of aspirin. He had discovered that if he took salicylic acid, an effective but corrosive painkiller, and added an acetyl group to the basic molecule, he could reduce its corrosive properties. The result was acetylsalicylic acid (ASA, originally trademarked as *Aspirin*). Having made a great deal of money with aspirin, Dreser thought he might try the same trick with the morphine molecule and made *diacetylmorphine* (or diamorphine), which the Bayer company marketed as *Heroin*. The name was derived from the German *heroisch*, meaning "heroic," to imply concentrated power. Early tests showed that heroin was more effective as an analgesic than morphine but did not cause as much nausea and vomiting. It was advertised in newspapers and magazines and sold freely as sort of a superior aspirin. Bayer also claimed that heroin was not addictive, and, surprisingly, this was believed by the medical profession for many years.

It did not take long for the morphine users to discover heroin. They soon found that heroin could be sniffed into the nostrils and did not always require injections. This fact and the relative lack of nausea must have enhanced its appeal to casual users. By the 1920s, the newspapers associated heroin with crime, industrial unrest, and a series of Bolshevik bombings, so in 1924 it was banned totally by Congress. It became illegal for doctors to prescribe it for any reason. This law and the Harrison Act are still in effect today in the United States.

Excellent sources of information on the fascinating history of opiates are J. M. Scott (1969), Latimer and Goldberg (1981), and Berridge and Edwards (1981).

ROUTES OF ADMINISTRATION

Morphine is a base with a pKa of about 8. Consequently, it is not rapidly absorbed from the digestive system because most of its molecules are ionized in acid pHs. Even though opium eating (or drinking) is common and morphine is frequently given in oral medications, opiates given by the oral route are much less effective than the same dose given parenterally. In addition to slow absorption, morphine given orally is subject to significant metabolism on its first pass through the liver, before it can get to the brain (Goth, 1984). Opioids are frequently given as analgesics, and the slowness of the absorption from the digestive system is an advantage because by using this route, it is easier to maintain constant drug levels in the blood (Melzack, 1990).

When the drug is administered for its subjective effects, most users prefer parenteral routes, which cause sudden high levels that appear to be the most reinforcing. Heroin, but not morphine, can be taken intranasally in the form of snuff. Many years ago, the Chinese developed a method of smoking opium in a pipe. More recently, the AIDS epidemic has made many people reluctant to use needles, and a newer form of smoking has been developed, called "chasing the dragon." Oil-rich, relatively pure heroin is heated on metal foil until it vaporizes. The user then inhales it through a tube, chasing the smoke so as not to miss any (Schuckit, 1993). This appears to be an efficient way to get the drug into the body. Anywhere between 17 and 63 percent of heated heroin is vaporized, depending on whether it is a salt or freebase, on the temperature, and on the airflow (Meng, Litchman, Bridgen, & Martin, 1997).

The two most important opioid antagonists, nalorphine and naloxone, are poorly absorbed from the digestive system and are usually administered parenterally. Maximum brain levels are reached in 15 to 60 minutes.

DISTRIBUTION

After absorption into the blood, most opioids are concentrated in the lungs, liver, and spleen, and a large percentage is bound to blood proteins. Opioids readily pass through the placental barrier into the fetus, but most are slow getting through the blood–brain barrier because they have poor lipid solubility.

The heroin molecule is highly lipid soluble and, therefore, gets into the brain quickly and in high concentrations. The heroin molecule is inactive in the brain, but it is rapidly converted into its metabolites, morphine and monoacetylmorphine, in high concentrations. As a result, heroin is about 10 times more potent than morphine (Inturrisi et al., 1983). Codeine also appears to have little direct action on receptors in the brain and has its effect through metabolites, the main one being morphine.

It also appears that the brain is able to eliminate opioids by an active transport mechanism. These two factors combine to keep brain levels of opioid low relative to the levels in other body tissues. Within the brain, opioids are concentrated in the basal ganglia, the amygdala, and the periaqueductal gray, an area closely associated with the sensation of pain. The opioid antagonists enter the brain much more quickly than morphine and reach higher concentrations there.

EXCRETION

About 10 percent of morphine is excreted in the urine unchanged. The remainder is turned into various metabolites that are eliminated in the urine and in the feces through concentration in the bile. The half-life of morphine is about 2 hours; the half-life of codeine is about 3 to 6 hours. Ninety percent of morphine is eliminated within 24 hours of administration (Creasey, 1979).

Meperidine is extensively metabolized in the liver, and the metabolites are eliminated by the kidneys. It has a half-life of 3½ hours. Methadone is not completely metabolized; about 10 percent is eliminated unchanged in the urine. Compared to other opioids, it has an extremely long half-life of 10 to 25 hours because methadone becomes bound extensively to blood proteins and is not available for metabolism. This long duration of action makes methadone ideal for maintenance therapies. At low doses, methadone is excreted primarily in the feces, but at higher doses, more and more methadone is found in the urine. An even longer half-life has been reported for another synthetic opioid, l-alpha-acetylmethadol (LAAM). LAAM itself is not active, but two of its metabolites are.

Naloxone is completely metabolized in the liver and has a half-life of about 1½ hours, although its effects may be shorter than this since the drug is rapidly redistributed to body fat. This may be of concern when naloxone is being used to treat an opioid overdose. Its effects may rapidly disappear, and the opioid overdose effects may unexpectedly return (Clarke, Dargan, & Jones, 2005).

NEUROPHYSIOLOGY

Scientists had been certain for many years that opioids worked at receptor sites because their activity seemed to be related to their molecular configuration, and there was competitive antagonism of their effects. But until the early 1970s, no one had ever found an opioid receptor in the body, nor had any endogenous substance been found in the brain that might work as an opioid receptor. In 1973, however, three laboratories independently identified specific receptors for opioids in the brains of rats. This discovery stimulated considerable research, and there has been a veritable explosion of data on opioid receptors since that time. Opioid receptors have now been found in the brains of most vertebrates, from hagfish to humans.

If the brain is equipped with receptors for opioids, it is likely that the brain has opiate-like substances of its own. A search for such a substance was begun. Within 2 years of the discovery of opioid receptors, six naturally occurring opioids had been isolated from the brains of several different species of animals, including humans. One of the researchers, Eric J. Simon (1981), proposed the name *endorphins* for these substances. He derived this name from the words *endogenous* and *morphine*. The endogenous opioids are derived from a polypeptide: a string of amino acid molecules. Two of these opioid-acting polypeptides are short strings, five amino acids long, called the *enkephalins*. The longer chains are 16 to 30 amino acids long and are more properly referred to as the endorphins. Many more endorphins have now been isolated, and their molecular structure is now understood (Snyder, 1977). All of these strings of amino acids have been identified as segments of a large molecule called *beta-lipotropin*, 91 amino acids long, which is secreted by the pituitary gland.

In general, endorphins are found in the areas of the brain that are rich in opioid receptors and are known to be stored in synaptic vesicles, so it might be reasonable to suppose that endorphins are neurotransmitters, but other roles have been postulated for them as well. It is known that the presence of an endorphin interferes with the release of other neurotransmitters, such as norepinephrine, dopamine, and acetylcholine, and that opioid receptors are located on presynaptic membranes. These discoveries suggest that the endorphins work as neuromodulators by influencing the presynaptic membranes of other synapses. It is also known that endorphins are released into the blood by the pituitary gland for general distribution around the body, like other pituitary hormones. Opioid receptors are known to exist outside the nervous system in areas such as the intestines; these might be the targets for the endorphins acting as hormones.

Opioid Receptors

There appear to be at least three types of opioid receptors in the brain, referred to as mu (m), kappa (k), and delta (δ). These receptors differ in their distributions and in their affinities for endogenous opioids. The mu receptor has a diffuse distribution throughout the limbic system, including the hippocampus and the amygdala, and throughout the thalamus and the locus coeruleus. The delta receptor is also located in the limbic system, including the hippocampus and the amygdala, but in regions that do not overlap with the mu receptor distribution. Delta receptors are also located in the cortex, the hypothalamus, the nucleus accumbens, and some regions of the medulla. The kappa receptor has a third distinct distribution that includes the nucleus accumbens, the ventral tegmental area, the hypothalamus, and specific regions of the thalamus (Mansour et al., 1994).

All of the opioid receptors have their effects either through second messengers or by being taken inside the cell membrane where they activate kinases directly. The mu receptor is responsible for most of the effects of morphine and the drugs described in this chapter. Solomon Snyder and his colleagues have demonstrated that not all opioids bind to mu receptors with the same affinity; some have a strong attraction for the receptor, and some have a much weaker attraction. In general, those with the weakest attraction at the receptor have the greatest effect on the receptor. Morphine, for example, does not have a strong attachment to mu receptors but has a strong effect when it binds with them. In contrast, nalorphine has only a weak effect on the receptor but is bound strongly to it. When these two drugs are mixed together, the nalorphine will be the one to have an effect because it will displace the morphine from the receptor. Because the effect of the nalorphine is only slight, there will be little opioid effect, even though morphine is present. Thus, the nalorphine acts as a competitive antagonist to the morphine, turning off the effect of the morphine and substituting its own mild effect. In this sense, it acts as an antagonist because it blocks the morphine, but it is also an agonist because it stimulates the receptor in a mild, morphinelike way.

An opioid with these properties is known as a *mixed opioid agonist–antagonist*. Nalorphine, pentazocine, and cyclazocine belong to this category. They will terminate the activity of more potent agonist drugs and at the same time have a milder effect of their own (Snyder, 1977).

Naloxone is a pure antagonist. It will displace any other opioid from the mu receptor but has no opioid effect of its own. It is used to treat victims of opioid overdoses because it will immediately terminate the action of all agonists. If naloxone is given to an individual who is physically dependent on opioids, it will immediately cause withdrawal symptoms. Opioid antagonists are used in some forms of treatment of opioid addiction. Naloxone is very important in opioid research because it provides a way of making sure that the effect of a drug is due to its interaction with mu receptors. This can be established simply by giving naloxone and seeing whether the effect is blocked (Garfield, 1983).

Sites of Action in the CNS

The opioids appear to produce their analgesic effects by several mechanisms. They affect areas of the spinal cord that transmit dull, burning pain, and it is believed that they block this incoming sensory information. The periaqueductal or central gray is an area of the brain known to be important in the perception of pain and rich in opioid receptors. When the body undergoes stress and pain, this system is activated, and the pain is reduced. It is believed that opioids cause some of their analgesic effects by stimulating the opioid receptors in this part of the brain.

Pain is a complicated phenomenon. Not only does it have a sensory component, but it has emotional aspects as well. We not only know that a sensation is painful; we also know that we really do not like it.

The sensory component of pain can be broken into several separate sensations. We may experience *thermoceptive pain* (pain caused by extreme heat or cold), *mechanical pain* (pain due to physical damage to the muscles and skin), and *visceral nociception* (pain associated with organ damage). These types of pain can be acute or chronic or may even appear to arise from limbs that have been amputated (*phantom limb pain*). Mu agonists seem to be effective against a broad range of pain, including all the acute types and some chronic types but not phantom pain. Delta agonists are effective against thermal and mechanical pain but are ineffective against visceral pain. Kappa agonists can be used against visceral pain but are effective only against low-intensity thermal and mechanical pain (Millan, 1986, 1990; Schmauss & Yaksh, 1984).

Opioids also reduce the aversive emotional aspect of pain. This effect may be mediated through opioid receptors located in various areas of the limbic system, such as the amygdala. It is believed that in addition to these lower centers, there are opioid systems in the frontal cortex through which opioids relieve pain.

Because of the mu receptors in the ventral tegmental area, opioids also stimulate the mesolimbic dopamine system. Imaging by functional magnetic resonance imaging (fMRI) BOLD in rats has demonstrated heroin-induced increases in signal intensity in the mesolimbic system, amygdala, and hippocampus. These effects are completely prevented by pretreatment with naloxone indicating that they are caused by mu receptors (Xu et al., 2000). This increase in mesolimbic activity is responsible for the reinforcing properties of opioids. Laboratory animals will readily learn to press a lever to deliver minute quantities of morphine directly to the ventral tegmental area.

Opioids depress three important centers in the brain stem. They depress the respiratory center and cause slow, shallow breathing. Death from opioid overdose is usually a result of respiratory depression. The vomiting center is also depressed, and so is the center that causes us to cough. This suppression of the cough center is one reason why opiates have been included in cough medicines for centuries. At one time, most over-the-counter cough medicines contained codeine, but now they contain dextromethorphan, a synthetic opioid without any analgesic effects (Atweh & Kuhar, 1983).

In addition, repeated injection of morphine into the periventricular gray but not the ventral tegmental area will cause the development of physical dependence (Bozarth & Wise, 1984).

EFFECTS OF OPIOIDS

Effects on the Body

When opioids are first administered, two of their most notable effects are nausea and vomiting. These are caused by the stimulation of an area of the brain known as the chemoreceptor trigger zone, which detects impurities in the blood and stimulates a center that causes vomiting. Opioids also depress this vomiting center, and this action blocks vomiting. The result of these two effects is that nausea and vomiting are usually seen only after the first administration of the drug. With continuing doses, these symptoms decrease.

Because opioids constrict the pupils of the eyes, many opioid users have small pupils, and this effect diminishes only slightly with tolerance. Pinpoint pupils are also a symptom of opioid overdose. Opioids have little effect on the functioning of the heart, but there is some lowering of blood pressure due to dilation of the peripheral blood vessels. This dilation causes the face and neck to become flushed and warm and may cause sweating. Profuse sweating is one of the unpleasant side effects of methadone.

One of the first medical uses of opium was in the treatment of diarrhea and dysentery, and it is still used for this purpose. Opioids do not decrease the overall action of the stomach and intestines, but they seem to disrupt the coordination of digestive activity, causing the food to pass very slowly through the system. This effect stops diarrhea but produces constipation instead, and it can be a serious medical complication of opioid addiction. Opioids also interfere with urination by causing contractions of the bladder sphincter, making it difficult to pass urine.

Opioid use is known to decrease the level of sex hormones in both sexes, and this lowered hormone level is thought to be responsible for males' difficulty in maintaining erection and for the reduced sex drive and diminished fertility of both male and female opioid users. Heavy use may even cause atrophy of secondary sex characteristics in males and stop menstruation in women (Cushman, 1981). It has been suggested that opioid addiction is common among prostitutes because they have historically used opioids as a birth control measure.

Effects on Sleep

In spite of the fact that morphine is named after the god of dreams, opioids do not increase sleep. They cause a sleepy sensation and nodding, under normal circumstances, but acute administration of morphine and heroin actually causes insomnia and does not increase sleeping time (Belleville, Forrest, Shroff, & Brown, 1971). The user may doze off but will soon awaken with a start and will not feel rested. When subjects do sleep, they show increased muscular tension, spend more time in the lighter sleep stages, and experience a decrease in slow-wave and REM sleep (Kay, Eisenstein, & Jasinski, 1969). However, opioids are useful in causing sleep in people who are kept awake by pain.

EFFECTS ON HUMAN BEHAVIOR AND PERFORMANCE

Subjective Effects

Many literary figures were known to be users of opium. One of the first people to write about the effects was Thomas De Quincey, the English essayist, critic, and writer, author of the now famous *Confessions of an English Opium-Eater*, published in 1821. De Quincey used opium for much of his life and wrote about its effects on his mind and on his life in *Confessions*. Like most people in the nineteenth century, he first took opium as a medicine but quickly appreciated its euphoric effects. After his first dose, his reaction was as follows:

In an hour, O heavens! What a revulsion! What a resurrection from its lowest depths, of the inner spirit! . . . That my pains had vanished was now a trifle in my eyes; this negative effect was swallowed up in the immensity of those positive effects which had opened before me, in the abyss of divine enjoyment thus suddenly revealed. . . . Here was the secret of happiness, about which philosophers had disputed for so many ages, at once discovered; happiness might now be bought for a penny, and carried in the waistcoat-pocket; portable ecstasies might be had corked up in a pint-bottle and peace of mind might be sent down by the mail. (De Quincey, 1901, pp. 169–170)

De Quincey reported that he had an increased sensitivity in both hearing and vision. The increase was not so much in the loudness of noises and brightness of lights as in the ability of the mind "to construct out of raw organic sound an elaborate intellectual pleasure" (De Quincey, 1901, p. 179).

And finally, the dreams. Opioids at higher doses induce a sleepy, trancelike state called a nod, during which the user sees visions or dreams (hence the expression "pipe dreams"). Unlike the hallucinations from drugs such as LSD, these are more like vivid daydreams:

Whatsoever things capable of being visually represented I did but think of in the darkness . . . which once traced in faint and visionary colour. . . . They were drawn out by the fierce chemistry of my dreams into insufferable splendor that fretted my heart. (De Quincey, 1901, p. 224)

Nor are the dreams always visual. Samuel Taylor Coleridge always claimed that the words to the famous poem Kubla Khan came to him in a trance after he had taken opium. Users of opium are firmly convinced that the creative processes are helped by the drug. As Jean Cocteau, the French poet, playwright, and artist, said,

All children possess the magic power of being able to change themselves into what they wish. Poets, in whom childhood is prolonged, suffer a great deal when they lose this power. This is undoubtedly one of the reasons which drives the poet to use opium. (Cocteau, 1968, p. 71)

De Quincey took opium orally, and though he enjoyed the experience well enough, he missed a subjective effect that is usually experienced only by people who inject morphine or heroin or who smoke opium: the rush. This intense momentary feeling of pleasure is experienced after injecting the drug and is a result of the high concentrations delivered suddenly to the brain. Rushes are usually described as sexual, rather like an orgasm in the stomach or in the entire body. As one 17-year-old addict described it, "It's just the most intense wonderful feeling. . . . I worry that I will always be tempted to feel the heroin rush again, because nothing else I've tried comes close to it" (Weil & Rosen, 1983, p. 87).

Systematic Studies of Mood

Many authors who write about the subjective effects of opioids stress the euphoric effects and the "divine enjoyment" that the drug offers. Such writings and other accounts have frequently led theorists to speculate that the origin of the attraction of opioids is the relief of anxiety and depression, but most of the experiments in which mood and emotional behavior are measured objectively find that positive feelings do not last and are replaced with mood changes and emotions that are mostly negative. In one study conducted at the McLean Hospital in Belmont, Massachusetts, by Roger Meyer, Steven Mirin, and their associates (Meyer & Mirin, 1979), male adult heroin addict volunteers were admitted to the hospital and kept in a ward for 42 days. During that time, for a period of 10 days, they were allowed to earn heroin injections. During their entire stay, the ward staff kept track of their aggressive and social behaviors, and they were administered standardized psychological tests and asked to complete mood scales. This study found that during the first few days of heroin administration, before significant tolerance developed, heroin relieved tensions and produced euphoria. However, as use continued, there was a shift to unpleasant mood states and increased psychiatric symptoms. These unpleasant feelings were relieved for only a brief period of 30 to 60 minutes after each injection. In addition to this deterioration in mood, there was a decrease in physical activity and social interaction and an increase in aggressive behavior and social isolation. These effects diminished when the subjects were maintained on methadone and when the self-administered heroin was blocked by an opioid antagonist.

The effects on mood also differ with whether the drug is given to experienced users or naive subjects. In a classic study, Lasagana and his colleagues at Harvard (Lasagana, Felsinger, & Beecher, 1955) investigated the changes in mood and subjective effects in different populations and found that former addicts were more likely to experience positive feelings after opioids, whereas nonusers reported sedation, mental clouding, and feelings of sickness. In this experiment, 17 out of 30 former users said that they would like to repeat the experience of morphine a second time, whereas only 2 out of 20 nonusers wanted to repeat. Other researchers have not been able to find consistent reports of positive feelings experienced after mu agonists such as heroin (Zacny & Walker, 1998, p. 353).

The subjective effects of morphine are different when given to people experiencing pain. Conley, Toledano, Apfelbaum, and Zacny (1997) gave morphine to subjects who were also experiencing the pain of having their arms immersed in icy water. They found that the pain diminished the feelings of being "spaced out," "high," "sleepy," and "light-headed," which were normally caused by morphine in individuals not experiencing pain.

The mixed opioid agonist–antagonists, like pentazocine, are even more likely to produce unpleasant subjective effects of feeling "confused" and having "difficulty in concentrating" in nondependent opioid users and, to an even greater extent, nonusers. The mixed opioid agonist–antagonists cause withdrawal symptoms in dependent opioid users (Zacny, Hill, Black, & Sadeghi, 1998; Zacny & Walker, 1998).

Some opioids, such as cyclazocine, which have a stronger affinity for kappa receptors, have quite unpleasant subjective effects, including depersonalization, hallucinations, and many symptoms of psychosis in both opioid abusers and nonabusers (Zacny & Walker, 1998).

Performance

In a review of the effects of opioids on human performance (Zacny, 1995), it was concluded that acute administration of opioids to those with little or no experience of the drug can have a moderate effect on performance. In general, performance seems to slow down but does not become more erratic. Partial agonists, or mixed agonist–antagonists such as propoxyphine, cause more impairment than full agonists such as morphine (Zacny et al., 1998). Cognitive performance seems to be less impaired than psychomotor performance.

For most types of tasks, it appears that tolerance develops and that, with moderate dosages of heroin or morphine, addicted individuals can maintain good health and productive work for extended periods. There are numerous cases of individuals who administered opioids in one form or another for years but were still able to pursue successful and even brilliant careers. One such individual was Dr. William Stewart Halstead, one of the founders of Johns Hopkins Medical School and one of the most brilliant surgeons of his day. He pioneered in the development of aseptic surgical techniques and the use of cocaine as a local anesthetic and was known as the "father of modern surgery." Yet during his career, he was addicted to morphine, a fact that he was able to keep secret from all but his closest friends (Brecher & the Editors of *Consumer Reports*, 1972, p. 35).

These observations that tolerance to the detrimental effects of opioids occurs in chronic users have been confirmed. Longtime opioid-dependent users show little, if any, impairment caused by either morphine or the mixed agonist–antagonists. It is still not entirely clear, however, whether this is true for those who use opioids for long-term pain relief, although it has been shown that the detrimental effects of opioids on performance are diminished when given to people experiencing pain (Conley et al., 1997).

Opioid Withdrawal

The only time Dr. Halstead's habit caused him any trouble was when he was attempting to reduce his dosage and started to show withdrawal symptoms. This is similar to the finding by Thompson and Schuster (1964) that food-seeking and shock-avoidance behavior of monkeys was not disrupted while monkeys self-administered morphine but was disrupted when they were not allowed access to morphine and started to experience withdrawal. (This research will be discussed later in this chapter.)

EFFECTS ON THE BEHAVIOR OF NONHUMANS

Unconditioned Behavior

Morphine has a biphasic effect on spontaneous motor activity (SMA). At low doses, there is an increase in movement, but at higher doses, there is a decrease. In mice, this low-dose stimulation causes "running fits," where the mice run blindly and continuously. This effect can be blocked by nalorphine. In rats, low doses cause an increase in SMA. At higher doses, this behavior takes the form of stereotyped responses that differ from the stereotyped behavior caused by amphetamine (see Chapter 11). Morphine-produced stereotyped behavior covers a wide range of behaviors, including social behavior, whereas stereotyped behavior caused by psychomotor stimulants involves only nonsocial behaviors of short duration (Schörring & Hecht, 1979). Still higher doses produce a type of *catalepsy*; the animal's body becomes rigid and can be molded into almost any position, which it will maintain for extended periods. In primates, there does not seem to be an excitatory phase. The main effect is a depression of behavior.

Conditioned Behavior

At low doses, opioids tend to increase response rates of most species of animals responding for positive reinforcers at a low rate, but high doses decrease response rates (Thompson, Trombley, Luke, & Lott, 1970). The rate-decreasing effects of opioid agonists can be blocked by low doses of antagonists, but these antagonists at higher doses have effects very similar to agonists.

As with fixed interval (FI) response rates, there are reports that opioids increased both discrete trials and continuous avoidance of electric shocks at low doses, which is not what might be expected from an analgesic, but at higher doses, opioids slowed avoidance behavior without disrupting escape responding (Heise & Boff, 1962), an effect similar to alcohol and the tranquilizers.

It might be expected that a drug with noted analgesic properties would increase behavior suppressed by punishment, but this is not the case. Opioids usually only decrease response rates already diminished by response-contingent shock (Geller, Bachman, & Seifter, 1963). It would appear that the ability of opioids to diminish pain is not one of the mechanisms by which the drugs change avoidance behavior.

Effects of Self-Administered Opioids

Travis Thompson and Charles Schuster (1964) conducted one of the earliest experiments in which monkeys were maintained on a schedule of self-administered morphine. Monkeys could give themselves intravenous morphine for a brief period every 6 hours. After the self-administration behavior was acquired, Thompson and Schuster placed the monkeys on a fixed ratio (FR) 20 for food and a discrete-trials shock-avoidance schedule between periods of morphine availability. They found that the behavior of the monkeys on these schedules was not impaired by the self-administered drug, even though the doses reached rather high levels. The only time they noticed a deterioration in the avoidance or the FR was when the morphine was no longer available and the monkeys were going through withdrawal. This is similar to the experience of Dr. Halstead, the addicted surgeon described earlier.

DRUG STATE DISCRIMINATION

Opioids are readily discriminated from saline by both rats and monkeys. Morphine is not as discriminable as the barbiturates or marijuana, but it is more easily discriminable than the hallucinogens and the stimulants (Overton, 1973).

Animals trained to discriminate morphine will generalize to all other opioid agonists, such as methadone and codeine, but only partly to mixed opioid agonist–antagonists, such as cyclazocine. In addition, rats can be trained to discriminate between morphine and cyclazocine. Discriminative stimulus control of morphine and cyclazocine can be blocked by opioid antagonists, but cyclazocine requires a dose of antagonist 10 to 30 times higher than morphine. This evidence suggests that these drugs have effects on different populations of opioid receptors (Zacny & Walker, 1998, pp. 349–353). Morphine works at the mu receptor, which can be blocked easily by opioid antagonists, but cyclazocine works at both mu and kappa receptors, so its effects can only be partly blocked by the antagonist.

It has been shown that tolerance to the discriminative effects of morphine in rats can develop in 1 to 3 days and increases with higher doses (Young, Steigerwald, Makhay, & Kapitsopoulos, 1991).

TOLERANCE

As we have seen with many of the behavioral effects of opioids in humans, there is rapid and extensive tolerance to most of their effects. Figure 12-1

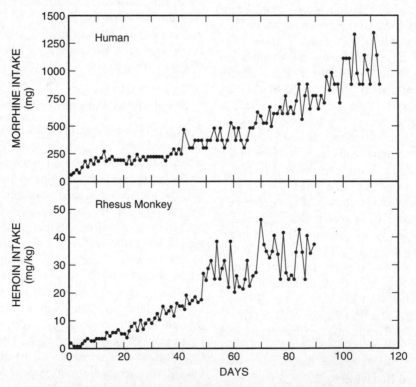

Figure 12-1 Daily intake of morphine and heroin in a human and a rhesus monkey when allowed free access to the drug. In both species, intake slowly increases over time, and there are no periods of abstinence or voluntary withdrawal. (Adapted from Griffiths et al., 1980)

shows the increasing dose self-administered by two species. Within 3 or 4 months of regular use, consumption will increase tenfold or more. In fact, doses taken by a regular user may be sufficiently high to kill a nontolerant individual several times over. Tolerance to different effects develops at different rates and disappears at different rates. For example, complete tolerance to the analgesic and positively reinforcing effects may develop, but the constriction of the pupils only partially disappears with continued opioid use, and the constipating effects never go away.

Some tolerance is due to changes in opioid metabolism, and some is the result of changes in the properties of the opioid receptors. Another likely mechanism of tolerance is learning since tolerance seems, to some extent, to be dependent on the environment in which the drug is given (S. Siegel, 1983). (See the discussion of tolerance in Chapter 3.)

Cross-Tolerance

Generally, when tolerance has developed to any opioid drug, there will be tolerance to all others. This cross-tolerance does not extend to the depressants, stimulants, or hallucinogens, but there is some degree of cross-tolerance between opioids and alcohol.

WITHDRAWAL

Opioid withdrawal is probably one of the most misunderstood aspects of drug use, largely because of the images of withdrawal that have been portrayed in the movies and popular literature for many years. The popular notion of the severity of heroin withdrawal probably came about in the 1920s and 1930s, when heroin addicts had easier access to cheaper sources of the drug and took it in much greater quantities than are common now. Few addicts these days are able to take enough drug to cause the severe withdrawal symptoms that are shown in the movies. Even in its most severe form, however, opioid withdrawal is not as dangerous or

terrifying as withdrawal from barbiturates or alcohol. In fact, withdrawal from alcohol can be fatal, but withdrawal from heroin or any other opioid is never fatal.

Classic heroin withdrawal proceeds in predictable stages. It starts 6 to 12 hours after the last administration of the drug, peaks at 26 to 72 hours, and, for the most part, is over within a week. The first signs are restlessness and agitation. Yawning soon appears and may become quite violent. The person is able to stay still only briefly and paces about with head and shoulders stooped over. The user experiences chills, with an occasional hot flash, and breathes with short, jerky breaths. During this time, goose bumps appear on the skin, which takes on the appearance of the skin of a plucked turkey (this is the origin of the expression "going cold turkey"). At this point, the addict becomes drowsy and will often fall into a deep sleep known as the *yen sleep*, which may last 8 to 12 hours. After awakening, there are cramps in the stomach, back, and legs; vomiting; and diarrhea. There may also be twitching of the extremities, which causes the hands to shake, and a kicking of the legs (this is the origin of the expression "kicking the habit"). There is also profuse sweating; the person's clothes and bed may become saturated with sweat. These symptoms become progressively less severe and soon disappear altogether.

The severity of the withdrawal depends on the daily dose of the addict and is seldom as drastic as this description. For most individuals, withdrawal resembles a bad case of the flu. Even though heroin withdrawal is not life threatening, it is extremely uncomfortable and is not undertaken lightly.

Withdrawal is similar for all opioids, although it is usually less severe with the less potent opioids such as codeine or propoxyphine. The withdrawal symptoms can be stopped almost instantly, at any stage, by the administration of any of the opioid drugs. Opioid withdrawal symptoms can also be reduced by alcohol (Ho & Allen, 1981). Withdrawal in a physically dependent individual can be generated almost instantly by the administration of an opioid antagonist.

SELF-ADMINISTRATION IN HUMANS

We tend to think of all heroin users as addicts, but this assumption is certainly not true. Many people appear to be able to maintain what is called an "ice cream habit" or "*chipping*," in which heroin is taken occasionally when the drug and the opportunities to take it are available. Chipping is a reality, but its extent is unknown because chippers are difficult to detect. They appear to be able to maintain a normal lifestyle and seldom require treatment.

We know a great deal more about the pattern of addicted heroin use, which has been extensively studied. In this pattern, the user is often (though not always) physically dependent and attempts to consume sufficient heroin to experience the rush and to avoid withdrawal—usually at least one injection a day. The addict is preoccupied with "taking care of business" or "scoring"—obtaining and taking the drug. This usually requires most of the addict's attention and money, leaving little time and resources for anything else. A heroin addict typically chooses friends and associates who are also heroin users.

The first exposure to heroin is usually motivated by curiosity and approached with caution. Frequently, the new user is introduced to the drug by someone he or she trusts. Surveys show that the majority of addicts were first given the drug by a friend. Very few were given the drug by a "pusher" or someone unknown to them. It is extremely unlikely that someone could be made into an addict, against his or her will, by an unscrupulous pusher trying to develop new markets.

We have already seen that the initial experience with heroin is considered unpleasant by the majority of first-time users, and it probably requires considerable persistence to acquire a physical dependence. It is not known how many people exposed to opioids do not become addicts and avoid the addicted lifestyle.

At the other end of addiction, there appears to be a *maturing out* of heroin use. Studies have indicated that many addicts spontaneously discontinue use of the drug (Winick, 1962). These addicts usually reach this point in their 30s or 40s after some 5 to 10 years of heroin use. The longer a person has used heroin, the less the chance of maturing out. It is difficult to estimate the number of addicts who eventually mature out; estimates range from more than two-thirds (Winick, 1962) to less than a quarter (Ball & Snarr, 1969). A great many heroin addicts never do manage to leave the habit behind and survive into old age still using heroin. Addiction workers are reporting an increasing number of heroin-addicted seniors (C. Jones, 2005).

Laboratory Studies

Laboratory studies of human opioid self-administration show that opioids act as reinforcers in opioid abusers by a number of different routes of administration. Different drugs have different reinforcing potential. Morphine appears to be more reinforcing than codeine, and both are more reinforcing than propoxyphine. Propoxyphine would be self-administered only in situations where it was available at little or no cost. Not surprisingly, heroin does not function as a reinforcer in opioid abusers when they are pretreated with an opioid antagonist. A study by Lamb et al. (1991) showed that nondependent drug users would self-administer intramuscular morphine at doses so low that the drug had no detectable subjective effect.

There are few studies of self-administration in non–drug-abusing populations. One such study of fentanyl showed that it would not be self-administered unless the subject was experiencing pain from immersing his or her arm in cold water. Thus, it appears that in non–drug users, opioids function as reinforcers only in the presence of pain. This is not surprising given the results of the Lasagana et al. (2005) study mentioned earlier, but more research needs to be done with this population (Zacny & Walker, 1998, pp. 346–349).

Patterns of Use

Studies of nonhumans and humans have shown very similar patterns. In both cases, when the drug is freely available, the amount of self-administered drug is carefully regulated. The daily dose increases gradually and regularly until it reaches a peak and then remains steady. There are no intake–abstinence cycles as with alcohol and stimulants, and withdrawal symptoms are not seen. Figure 12-1 shows data from similar studies. In one study, a human heroin addict self-administered morphine intravenously; in the other, a rhesus monkey gave himself heroin via the same route (Griffiths, Bigelow, & Henningfield, 1980). For the most part, this pattern is similar to that of the opioid addict who attempts to maintain a fairly constant blood level and avoids withdrawal when it is at all possible to do so.

It is tempting to speculate that the gradual increase in dose is a result of tolerance, but this may not be the case. As we have seen in Chapter 3, the reinforcing effects of many drugs, including heroin, become sensitized with repeated rather than diminished administrations. The increase in self-administered drug may be a result of increased reinforcing properties of the drug since it has been shown that up to a point, larger doses are more reinforcing than smaller doses.

SELF-ADMINISTRATION IN NONHUMANS

Morphine was the first drug for which intravenous self-administration was demonstrated in nonhumans. We have already discussed one of the first experiments of this type, conducted by Travis Thompson and Charles Schuster and published in 1964. At the time this research was done, it was assumed that physical dependence was an essential aspect of addiction, so Thompson and Schuster used squirrel monkeys that had been made dependent on morphine by injections four times a day for 30 days. The monkeys were then given the opportunity to bar press for morphine four times a day. The monkeys were placed on an

FI–FR chain schedule; to receive the drug, the monkeys were on an FI 2-minute schedule while a tone was turned on. The first response made after 2 minutes turned off the tone and turned on a white light. While the white light was on, the animals were required to make 25 responses. When this requirement was completed, a red light came on, and an infusion of morphine was given through an intravenous catheter.

The monkeys readily learned this response, and they performed on these schedules in the same manner as they would for any other reinforcer. Thompson & Schuster (1964) also demonstrated that both deprivation from morphine and injections of nalorphine would increase the amount of morphine the monkeys would administer. In later research, they demonstrated that nondependent monkeys would also self-administer morphine (Schuster & Thompson, 1969).

As shown in Figure 12-1, when morphine is freely available, it is self-administered by laboratory animals with great regularity on a daily basis, and the dose slowly increases.

All the mu receptor agonists are self-administered by laboratory animals, although the mixed agonist–antagonists do not seem to be as reinforcing as morphine and heroin. The reinforcing effects of the opioids can be blocked by mu antagonists. The antagonists naloxone and naltrexone are not self-administered. In fact, laboratory animals will learn to respond to avoid administrations of antagonists (Zacny & Walker, 1998, p. 344).

Drugs such as cyclazocine, which stimulate kappa receptors, are not self-administered, and there are reports that laboratory animals will respond to avoid infusions of them. There are also reports that kappa agonists can block the reinforcing effects of both morphine and cocaine, suggesting that the kappa receptor system may interact with the mu system where reinforcement is concerned (Glick, Maisoneuve, Raucci, & Archer, 1995). Delta agonists do not appear to have reinforcing properties.

In humans, heroin is often administered in conjunction with cocaine in what is called a *speedball*. One study with monkeys self-administering vaporized heroin showed that the reinforcing effect of the heroin was enhanced when it was administered in conjunction with vaporized cocaine (Mattox, Thompson, & Carroll, 1997).

HARMFUL EFFECTS

Acute Effects

At very high doses, opioids produce a comatose state with pinpoint pupils and severe depression of breathing, which eventually causes death. Unlike barbiturates, opioids lower the seizure threshold and may also cause convulsions at high doses. Opium has been used historically as a poison, so it is not surprising that people die from time to time from accidental overdoses of opioids. Box 12-1 describes how a derivative of fentanyl was used by the Russian security forces on Chechen rebels who seized a Moscow theater in 2002. The drug killed both the hostage takers and many hostages.

Heroin overdose is the leading cause of death among heroin users. In fact in some communities, it is the leading cause of death in males between the ages of 25 and 54. In Australia, it has been estimated that every year about 2 percent of heroin users die, and the majority of these deaths are due to overdose (Gerostamolous, Staikos, & Drummer, 2001). Most heroin overdose deaths occur in people with 5 to 10 years of experience with using the drug; only about 17 percent are new users. These deaths do not seem to be related to changes in the purity of street heroin (Sporer, 2003).

One mystery related to heroin overdose is that many times, the victim has not used more heroin than usual or more heroin than other people using the drug at the time (Brecher & the Editors of *Consumer Reports*, 1972).

If these deaths were not overdoses, what could be killing so many addicts? There are several explanations. One possibility is quinine, a drug used to cut or dilute the heroin before it is sold on the streets. Quinine can be lethal when given intravenously, and these overdose victims frequently show signs of quinine poisoning, such as froth oozing from the nose and mouth. Another explanation is the mixing of heroin with other drugs. One study showed that 85 percent of those dying from heroin overdose were using another central nervous system depressant, 45 percent were using benzodiazepines, and 36 percent were using alcohol (Gerostamolous et al., 2001). These drugs potentiate the effects of heroin and may make an otherwise normal dose of heroin lethal. Janis Joplin, the rock singer, died of a heroin overdose after some hard drinking with her friends at a nearby bar.

Another possible cause of an unexplained overdose is a loss of tolerance to the drug. Often this loss is due to a period of abstinence. Addicts have seven times the risk of overdose during their first 2 weeks after their release from residential treatment (Sporer, 1999). During treatment, they have lost their tolerance to the lethal effects of the drug, so their usual dose is now fatal.

Another possible reason for the loss of tolerance may be due to conditioned tolerance effects. As described in Box 3-1 in Chapter 3, some tolerance may depend on the specific environment in which the drug is normally given. If the drug is used in a new environment, tolerance is diminished, and what is a normal dose for an addict may suddenly be transformed into a lethal dose.

Chronic Effects

Health. Surprisingly few medical problems arise as a direct result of chronic heroin use. One of these is constipation. Somewhat more serious is a direct link between opioids and cancer. Opioids interfere with the body's ability to repair damaged DNA molecules, and this effect makes them cancer promoters; they enhance the cancer-causing effects of other substances that damage DNA. Like alcohol use, heroin use greatly increases the chance of bladder cancer caused by smoking (Falek, Madden, Shafer, & Donahoe, 1982).

CNS Effects. Opioids do not appear to alter the structural anatomy of the brain. However, SPECT data suggests that chronic heroin use is

BOX 12-1 What Was the Mysterious Gas Used by the Russians to End the Moscow Theater Hostage Taking?

On October 23, 2002, at about 9:00 P.M., 41 Chechen terrorists invaded a popular Moscow theater. They took over 800 people hostage and demanded that the Russians withdraw their troops from Chechnya. The terrorists threatened to start shooting their hostages and blow up the theater with explosives strapped to their bodies. The Russian government refused to negotiate. The standoff lasted 57 hours. Early on the morning of October 27, the Russian Federal Security Service pumped a gas into the theater and then stormed it and took it by force. The gas was effective—it knocked the terrorists out so fast that they were not able to detonate their explosives. Unfortunately, the gas proved lethal to many; 129 of the hostages and all but two of the terrorists were killed by the gas.

At the time, the Russians would not say what gas they had used, but in response to international pressure they announced several days later that the gas had been a fentanyl derivative, but questions still remain. There are several derivatives of fentanyl that could have been used, but the most likely would have been carfentanil, which is more than 30 times more potent than fentanyl and 10,000 times more potent than morphine. Potency would have been an important consideration. Fentanyl and its derivatives like morphine are not normally a gas at room temperature, so the carfentanil must have been nebulized and made into an aerosol, that is, turned into very fine particles and dispersed into the air—a complicated process. The more potent the drug, the less nebulization would have been needed.

But another question remains. Why did so many people die? It turns out that carfentanil and other fentanyl derivatives have a fairly high therapeutic index (TI) compared to morphine. The TI of morphine is about 70, while the TI of carfentanil is 10,600. These numbers suggest that these drugs should have been quite safe. There are two possible answers to this question. The first is that the dose received by each individual would have varied greatly, depending on where each person was. The aerosol was introduced into the theater by the ventilation system, and those close to the air vents would have received a much higher dose. This inability to control the dose is an inherent problem with using gases and aerosols in this manner. But there is another possibility. Another agent may have been mixed with the fentanyl derivative.

One advantage of using an opioid drug is that there is a very effective and fast-acting antidote available, naloxone. After the raid, many victims were treated in nearby hospitals that had been warned to stock up on their supplies of naloxone; unfortunately, the doctors were not told that the gas was an opioid, so many did not use the naloxone. In many cases, however, when it was used, it did not seem to be effective. This has led many to speculate that another agent had been mixed with the fentanyl derivative. Many suspect that it might have been the gaseous anesthetic halothane (see Chapter 8). Many survivors reported a sweet smell as the gas took effect. This is a property of halothane. In addition, a toxicological analysis of a German survivor after returning to Germany showed traces of halothane. If halothane were mixed with the fentanyl derivative, it might explain why there were so many deaths. Halothane has a very low therapeutic index, and, additionally, it does not have any antidote.

In these days of terrorism and hostage taking, there is little doubt that many militaries around the world are developing "calmative" or rapidly acting agents that can incapacitate a person rapidly but not be lethal. Normally such research is never made public, so this incident provides us with a speculative glimpse of where this field may be going (Wax, Becker & Curry, 2003).

associated with widespread reductions in cerebral blood flow to the frontal, parietal, and temporal lobes of patients with the first week of heroin withdrawal. These effects may not be long lasting since perfusion deficits show marked improvement following 3 weeks of heroin abstinence (Rose et al., 1996). Opioid users and former users do show abnormal brain activation patterns during decision making on the *Cambridge risk task*. This task involves choosing among two computer-based decks of cards, one associated with an unlikely high reward and one associated with a likely low reward. As is the case with stimulant addicts, imaging by photon emission tomography (PET) and fMRI completed during the task demonstrates that opioid addicts show reduced activation of the anterior cingulate cortex during errors made on the task (Forman et al., 2004). It is not clear whether this difference was caused by the drug or whether it is a preexisting condition in opioid addicts.

Lifestyle Effects. Although opioids cause some direct health problems, most of the harm done by opioids is indirect and arises from the addicted lifestyles most addicts are forced to adopt. Heroin is expensive, and it may take several hundred dollars a day to support the habit. Because getting the drug takes such priority, housing and nutrition suffer, and so does health. Added to these difficulties is the greatly increased [ex]posure to disease caused by the practice of [sho]oting up" the drug. These injections are sel[dom] done with clean needles and syringes; many [peop]le often use the same equipment, providing [dire]ct access into the body for diseases such as [hep]atitis and HIV/AIDS. Being a heroin addict is [un]healthy.

In a 33-year study of 581 heroin-addicted criminal offenders admitted to the California Civil Addict Program between 1962 and 1964, it was found that by 1997, nearly half the group had died. This represents a death rate 50 to 100 times the death rate among the general population of men the same age. Accidental poisoning and drug overdose were the most common cause of death

(21.6 percent). Nineteen and a half percent were homicide, suicides, and accidents. Liver disease, cancer, and cardiovascular disease accounted for the remaining deaths (Hser, Hoffman, Grella, & Anglin, 2001). Nearly 40 percent of those surviving used heroin within the past year, and nearly 10 percent were in methadone treatment.

Reproduction. In males, chronic opioid use reduces levels of the male sex hormone testosterone. This effect leads to a decrease in sex drive and fertility and may also cause changes in secondary sex characteristics. In women, alteration in hormone levels causes menstrual irregularities, amenorrhea, and a consequent decrease in fertility.

Pregnancies are also complicated by direct and indirect effects of opioids and opioid withdrawal. During pregnancy, the ability of the body to eliminate opioids is increased. The subsequent reduction in circulating levels of opioids leads to increased demand for the drug, and the probability of withdrawal is greater if the drug supply is irregular or uncertain. It is believed that opioid withdrawal during pregnancy can harm the fetus because it causes a decrease in blood oxygen levels. Numerous other medical complications during the pregnancies of addicted women may arise from the problems of the addicts' lifestyle. These complications, which occur in 40 to 50 percent of pregnant addicts, include anemia, cardiac disease, swelling, liver disease, hypertension, pneumonia, tuberculosis, and infections of the urogenital system, such as bladder infections and venereal disease (Kreek, 1982).

Babies born to addicted mothers have low birth weights and are more likely to be premature and to experience illness and complications after birth. In general, these problems are less likely in methadone-maintained mothers than in those using street heroin.

One big problem for babies born to dependent mothers is that right after birth, they have to go through withdrawal because they are no longer exposed to the opioid in the mother's blood. Withdrawal in neonates is similar to adult withdrawal. The symptoms include irritability, respiratory distress, yawning, sneezing, tremors, difficulty in sucking and swallowing, and a peculiar high-pitched cry. Some may even experience seizures. These symptoms start within 72 hours of birth and may last 6 to 8 weeks (Finnegan, 1982).

TREATMENT

Maintenance Therapies

The British System. Maintenance therapies are based on the philosophy that the real harm done by opioids arises from the fact that they are expensive and illegal. It follows that if addicts have a cheap, reliable source of the drug, they will remain healthy, be free to pursue careers and normal lives, and not be forced into a criminal way of life. In England, this approach has been followed for years. An addict can obtain a prescription from a special clinic and have it filled at public expense at any druggist's shop. This approach is known as the *British System*, and it appears to be modestly effective in preventing new cases of heroin addiction, decreasing the death rate in addicts, reducing criminal behavior, and improving the functioning of addicts. It has the added advantage of bringing addicts into regular contact with health professionals and is effective in stopping the spread of AIDS (Bewley, 1974; O'Mara, 1993).

One British writer has suggested that treating addiction as a medical problem in a clinic reduces the glamour of drugs; after all, "Sickness is generally less attractive than sin" (Bewley, 1974, p. 160).

Methadone Maintenance. In the United States, various laws made it impossible for doctors to prescribe heroin to addicts, so methadone has been used to prevent withdrawal (Nyswander, 1967). Methadone has several advantages over heroin as a maintenance drug: (a) It can be taken orally, (b) it prevents withdrawal symptoms for 24 hours, and (c) it acts as an antagonist to heroin. Because it can be taken orally, it is easy to administer and does not have all the associations of shooting up. The fact that it lasts for 24 hours means that it can be administered once a day in a clinic, and the user does not need to take it home. And because it blocks the effects of heroin, addicts on methadone will experience few euphoric effects or rushes if they decide to try heroin. This is probably because methadone occupies mu receptors and blocks mu agonists like heroin. Methadone continues to occupy mu opioid receptors in the thalamus, caudate, anterior cingulate cortex, and middle temporal and frontal cortices at 22 hours postadministration in former heroin users on maintenance therapy. PET imaging with [^{18}F]cylcofoxy, which binds to mu receptors, suggests that receptor availability is reduced by 19 to 32 percent in these regions (Kling et al., 2000). It is also likely that the lack of sensitivity to heroin arises from cross-tolerance between methadone and heroin.

Substitution of methadone for heroin is not considered a therapeutic end in itself. Methadone is always used in conjunction with psychological or social treatments. In fact, the success of methadone treatments depends heavily on the addict's having a good, trusting relationship with a well-trained staff (Weddington, 1995).

In a typical methadone maintenance clinic, patients are screened to ensure that they really are physiologically dependent on heroin. Then, over a period of several weeks, a dosage of methadone is worked out that will maintain the patients free from withdrawal symptoms. Typically, patients must return to the clinic every day for a drink of methadone. In some programs, addicts who demonstrate that they have been free of heroin and other problems are permitted to take the drug home and are required to attend only two or three times a week.

Over the years when methadone has been used as a maintenance drug in the United States, it has been demonstrated that it reduces sickness and death associated with illicit drug use (Sporer, 2003), normalizes disruptions of immune and endocrine functions, reduces the transfer of HIV/AIDS, and reduces criminal activity (Ling, Rawson, & Compton, 1994).

Many addicts choose to stay maintained on methadone indefinitely, but as normal lifestyles develop, there are pressures to detoxify altogether. Methadone patients are discriminated against in insurance, licensing, employment, and housing, and the pressures to attend clinics regularly interfere with travel and vacations. Then, too, methadone has uncomfortable side effects, such as sweating, sexual dysfunction, and constipation. When patients appear ready and motivated to discontinue the drug, doses of methadone are slowly decreased over a period of no less than 6 months, so that withdrawal is minimized. This process is best accomplished at a very gradual rate that is decided on by the user. Even when the methadone reduction is gradual, detoxification becomes difficult when the dosage gets low.

In general, relapse rates in addicts weaned from methadone are similar to those with other methods—80 to 90 percent—but some reports have been quite impressive (Meritz, Kleber, Riordan, & Solbetz, 1978; D. D. Simpson, Joe, & Bracy, 1982; Weddington, 1995). It is estimated that of the 500,000 to 1,000,000 people in the United States who are addicted to heroin, 100,000 receive methadone maintenance therapy in the 750 to 800 clinics across the country (Ling et al., 1994).

LAAM. Like methadone, this new maintenance drug can be taken orally and blocks the effects of heroin, but its effects last longer than methadone (up to 72 hours) and it needs to be taken only three times a week. The addict need not come to the clinic as often, and the clinic need not send any of the drug home with the addict. After many years of extensive testing, LAAM was formally approved in the United States in 1993 as a maintenance drug for heroin addicts.

LAAM appears to work better than methadone for addicts who are unable to get to a clinic on a daily basis because of difficulties with employment, child care, or transportation. Some addicts also have problems stabilizing on a dose of methadone, and some simply refuse to enter methadone treatment. Many of these people report that LAAM "holds" better than methadone (Ling et al., 1994).

Some people believe that LAAM has the capacity to change the face of heroin maintenance

therapy. Methadone may still be used for primary treatment in specialized clinics in inner-city areas, where heroin use flourishes and users require the intensive support of daily clinic visits, but as addicts establish more stable lifestyles, employment, and family lives, it would be more appropriate to switch to LAAM and make it available in a general health care setting (Ling et al., 1994).

Buprenorphine. Buprenorphine has been used as an analgesic and is still used experimentally for heroin dependence. It can be taken orally and has a long half-life, although its effects do not last as long as those of LAAM. Buprenorphine is a mixed agonist–antagonist. Thus, it will block the effects of heroin and causes only mild physical dependence itself. Therefore, it is much easier to stop taking buprenorphine than methadone or LAAM, and it is easier to switch to antagonist therapies without experiencing withdrawal (Ling et al., 1994). In normal circumstances, buprenorphine is given every day, but recently it has been shown that buprenorphine is just as effective when given three times a week (Schottenfield et al., 2000). One problem with buprenorphine pills is that they are sometimes crushed and injected for a more intense effect. To prevent this, naloxone is added to the oral buprenorphine pills, which are administered sublingually (under the tongue). This way, the buprenorphine is absorbed, but the naloxone is not. If crushed and injected, the naloxone blocks the effect of the buprenorphine.

Antagonist Therapies

As mentioned, one of the advantages of methadone over heroin for maintenance is that methadone works as an antagonist to the effects of heroin. In the presence of methadone, the effect of heroin is greatly diminished. This aspect of methadone is considered beneficial, but it is not the main reason why methadone is used. Methadone prevents withdrawal. An implicit assumption of maintenance therapies is that the primary motivation for taking heroin is the fear of withdrawing. Addicts are, therefore, maintained on the drug so that they will not be compelled to use heroin from the streets to prevent withdrawal. As we have seen in Chapter 3, this assumption may not be correct. We know from studies of self-administration with laboratory animals that physical dependence is not necessary to maintain opioid self-administration. Nondependent monkeys will self-administer opioids at a high rate even though they have never experienced withdrawal. This type of research has shown that drug taking is motivated by the positively reinforcing effects of drugs, not the fear of withdrawal. It is little wonder, then, that drug-seeking behavior persists during and after maintenance. It is likely that the heroin-blocking effect of methadone is more important than its ability to avoid withdrawal.

If the reinforcing effect of the heroin is responsible for its use, there is no need to maintain a person in a physiologically dependent state, but it is important to keep the reinforcing effect of heroin blocked. This is where the antagonists can play a role. They are very effective heroin blockers and have only minimal agonist properties.

Patients are first withdrawn from heroin and kept abstinent for 7 to 10 days; otherwise, the antagonist would precipitate withdrawal symptoms. This stage can be difficult, and the dropout rate is very high. As early as possible, addicts are given daily doses of an antagonist—naloxone, naltrexone, or cyclazocine—when they come for therapy, which is usually at an outpatient day program where they also have educational seminars, recreational activities, and group therapy. The best way to get rid of positively reinforced responses is to extinguish them by allowing the responses to occur but removing the reinforcement. The antagonist accomplishes this purpose by blocking the rewarding effects of heroin when it is used so that the heroin is no longer a reinforcer. Because the patients in the antagonist therapy treatment are outpatients who are free to spend their evenings and weekends with their friends, they inevitably attempt to use heroin, but this behavior quickly extinguishes and soon disappears.

Early experimental antagonist programs report success in keeping addicts in treatment. At the end of one year, 70 percent were still in the day program, and fewer than half of these were still taking the antagonist. Urine tests for heroin showed that fewer than 2 percent of the patients used heroin (Kleber, 1974). The results of programs such as these suggest that maintenance on antagonists may be more beneficial than maintenance on agonists.

Even though results have been encouraging (Kleber, 1974), an unexpected difficulty has arisen. When drug users know that they are getting an antagonist, they seldom try to shoot up heroin because they know that it will not have an effect. When they start taking the antagonist, they usually stop using heroin so suddenly that the positive reinforcing effects of the heroin on heroin-seeking behavior never get a chance to extinguish. Consequently, once the antagonist is discontinued, relapse rates will be high (W. R. Martin, Eades, Thompson, Huppler, & Gilbert, 1976). In addition, compliance is also a problem with antagonist therapies—patients often discontinue the antagonist when they want to use heroin. In spite of this problem, research has shown that if a person stays in antagonist therapy for 2 to 3 months or longer, chances of staying heroin free after treatment are considerably increased. Success rates with antagonist therapies are much better with people who are highly motivated to quit, have strong family support, and have legitimate professional careers to pursue or have been ordered by a court to discontinue heroin use (Jaffe, 1987). Antagonist therapy is beneficial, probably because it gives users a chance to decide to remove themselves from the temptation to relapse and permits them to develop other, more socially acceptable sources of reinforcement (Wikler, 1980).

To help overcome the compliance problem, a slow-release implant has been developed that will maintain effective levels of the antagonist on the body for weeks at a time.

CHAPTER SUMMARY

- The opioids are a class of natural and synthetic drugs. Opium, derived from the opium poppy, is the source of morphine and codeine. Heroin is made by slightly altering the morphine molecule to make it more lipid soluble and, consequently, more potent. Synthetic opioids such as pentazocine, methadone, and LAAM have a different chemical structure but have the same site of action and similar physiological effects. These drugs are sometimes referred to as narcotics or narcotic analgesics.

- Opium has been used for centuries in the Middle East. It was spread by Arab traders from there to Africa, China, and Europe, where in the sixteenth and seventeenth centuries it was widely used as a medicine. Its popularity grew until the middle of the 1800s, when legal restrictions were placed on its use in England. In the United States, all opioids were banned by the Harrison Narcotic Act of 1914.

- Most opioids are not well absorbed from the digestive system; they need to be inhaled or injected for full effect. The opioids are metabolized primarily in the liver and have a half-life of 2 to 4 hours, except for some synthetics such as methadone or LAAM, which have much longer half-lives.

- The body uses endogenous opiate-like chemicals called endorphins or enkephalins as both neurotransmitters and neuromodulators. There are several opioid receptors—mu, kappa, and delta. The mu receptor is responsible for reinforcing and many analgesic effects.

- One opioid system involves the spinal cord and a part of the brain known as the periaqueductal or central gray. It is thought that some of the analgesic properties of the opioids are mediated by this mechanism. Opioids also activate the nucleus accumbens and depress the respiratory center.

- Opioids cause a sleepy, dreamy state. When taken intravenously, they cause rushes, or feelings of intense pleasure resembling orgasm.

- Mu agonists cause feelings of pleasure and rushes at high doses in experienced users but often have unpleasant effects on inexperienced subjects.

- Chronic opioid use causes constipation and diminished sex drive and sexual performance, but if doses are not too high, chronic use does not interfere with intellectual or physical abilities.

- The opioids slow the behavior of nonhumans responding on both positively and negatively reinforced schedules. They slow avoidance responding at doses that do not affect escape but do not increase punishment-suppressed behavior.

- Tolerance to the different effects of opioids develops at different rates. Withdrawal symptoms occur after chronic opioid use, and the severity of withdrawal increases with higher chronic doses. These symptoms may last for about 3 days, and although very unpleasant, they are not life threatening.

- Humans and nonhumans will readily self-administer mu agonists whether they are physically dependent or not. The typical pattern is to start at low doses and increase dosage as tolerance develops. Once a stable pattern has been achieved, daily doses seldom change, and there is little variability from day to day. Intake is not cyclic, and voluntary withdrawal symptoms are seldom seen.

- Although chronic opioid use has few serious direct physical effects, the indirect effects of using the drug and the addicted lifestyle can be serious.

- Most attempts to treat chronic heroin use have a very high relapse rate—about 90 percent. The most popular current treatment is maintenance on a long-acting opioid such as methadone or LAAM or buprenorphine.

13

Antipsychotic Drugs

Canst thou not minister to a mind diseased; pluck from the memory a rooted sorrow; raze out the written troubles of the brain; and with some sweet oblivious antidote cleanse the stuff'd bosom of that perilous stuff which weighs upon the heart?

—*Macbeth*

Macbeth asked this question of the doctor treating Lady Macbeth. The doctor's answer was no. Modern physicians are a bit better off when it comes to ministering to a "mind diseased." In fact, modern psychiatry has been revolutionized by many "antidotes" in the form of anxiolytics, antipsychotics, antidepressants, and antimanics. They are not as wonderful as Macbeth envisioned them; they have troublesome side effects, and they do not always work well, but they are probably a good deal better than the treatment that Lady Macbeth was offered.

The drugs that are useful in treating the symptoms of schizophrenic psychoses are called by several names. In North America, they are often referred to as *antipsychotics*; in Europe, the term *neuroleptic* is preferred. They are also referred to as *major tranquilizers*. These three names are derived from three major effects of this class of drugs on behavior.

The drugs are called antipsychotic because their most useful effect is to diminish the symptoms of *psychosis*. There are two basic types of psychosis: (a) *schizophrenia* and (b) *bipolar disorder* (also called manic-depressive psychosis). The drugs referred to as antipsychotic are useful in the treatment of schizophrenic psychosis (described in this chapter) and in the treatment of symptoms of the manic phase of bipolar disorder (described in Chapter 14).

The term *neuroleptic* means "clasping the neuron." It refers to a capacity of these drugs to cause rigidity in the limbs and difficulty of movement similar to that seen in people suffering from Parkinson's disease. As a result, these effects are sometimes called *parkinsonian symptoms*. This property of these drugs is a persistent and bothersome side effect, and it is indeed strange that a family of drugs should be named after a side effect rather than its most useful therapeutic effect. This name may have been chosen because at one time it was believed that both effects were related; that is, people believed that these drugs would not relieve psychosis unless they were causing neuroleptic effects as well. It is now known that the two types of effects are independent (Creese, 1983). In fact, we now have drugs that seem to be effective antipsychotics but have few, if any, neuroleptic (parkinsonian) effects.

The term *neuroleptic* is probably more common than *antipsychotic*, but we will use the latter term here because it seems more appropriate to think of drugs in terms of their useful effects rather than their side effects.

The term *major tranquilizer* is sometimes used to refer to the antipsychotics because they have a sedating effect not only on agitated psychotic patients but also on healthy people. This name is inappropriate because it suggests that these drugs are useful only because they "tranquilize" agitated patients. Even though there is a tranquilizing effect, these drugs seem to produce their antipsychotic effect by directly blocking the symptoms of psychosis. Rather than simply making psychotic people more tranquil or sedated, they cause psychotic people to be less psychotic and, in many cases, less agitated. Another problem is that *major tranquilizer* implies that they are just a stronger version of *minor tranquilizers*, a term sometimes applied to drugs such as the benzodiazepines or barbiturates (see Chapter 7). This terminology is misleading because it implies that both drugs have a similar effect and that one class is more powerful than the other. In fact, there is very little similarity, in chemistry or effect, between the barbiturates and benzodiazepines on the one hand and the antipsychotics on the other.

TYPES OF ANTIPSYCHOTICS

In recent years, a distinction has often been drawn between typical and atypical antipsychotic drugs. The drugs in the older group, the *typical antipsychotics*, were all developed before 1975. They are either *phenothiazines* (e.g., chlorpromazine, fluphenzine) or *phenothiazine-like* (e.g., haloperidol). These drugs tend to cause neuroleptic or parkinsonian symptoms in addition to their

antipsychotic effects, and they seem to be most effective in treating the positive symptoms of psychosis (i.e., the hallucinations and delusional thinking) rather than the negative symptoms, such as flattened affect and alogia. (More on this later.) A number of drugs developed and introduced since 1990 have minimal parkinsonian effects and seem more effective in treating the negative symptoms; these are termed *atypical antipsychotics*. All of the antipsychotics presently under development fit into the atypical class.

TABLE 13-1   Typical and Atypical Antipsychotic Drugs

Generic Name	Trade Name
Typical antipsychotics:	
chlorpromazine	Thorazine, Largactil
promazine	Sparine
triflupromazine	Vesprin
thioridazine	Mellaril
mesoridizine	Serentil
trifluoperazine	Stelazine
fluphenazine	Prolixin
perphenazine	Trilafon
acetophenazine	Tindal
prochlorperazine	Stemetil, Compazine
carphenazine	Proketazine
thiothixene	Navane
chlorprothixene	Taractan, Tarasan
loxapine	Loxitane, Loxapac
haloperidol	Haldol
molindone	Lindone, Moban
Atypical antipsychotics:	
clozapine	Clozaril
respiridone	Resperdal
raclopride*	
remoxipride**	
quetiapine	Seroquel
olanzepine	Zyprexa
pimizide	Orap
sertindole	Serlect
ziprasidone	Zelox
amisulpride	Solian

* Not licensed in the United States or Canada.

** Found to have dangerous side effects and is not used therapeutically but is still used in nonhuman experimentation.

Sources: Churness (1988, pp. 529–530); J. Davis, Janicak, Linder, Maloney, and Avkovic (1983, p. 25); Jarvik (1970, p. 157); Julien (2001).

Typical Antipsychotics

Table 13-1 lists some commonly used antipsychotics alongside some of their more common trade names. Perhaps the best known antipsychotic is *chlorpromazine* (Thorazine or Largactil). Others include *promazine* (Sparine), *trifluoperazine* (Stelazine), *fluphenazine* (Prolixin), and *haloperidol* (Haldol).

Atypical Antipsychotics

Thioridazine (Mellaril) has been used for many years and was recognized as causing few parkinsonian symptoms. It is now often classified as an atypical antipsychotic. The next such drug to be developed was *clozapine* (Clozaril). Since the introduction of this drug, several more have been introduced, and many more are being developed. These include *respiridone* (Risperdal), *sulpride* (Sulmatil and Dolmatil), *amperozide* (Solian), *quetiapine* (Seroquel), and *olanzapine* (Zyprexa). Often these drugs are used in the United Kingdom or other European countries first and are slow to be approved for use in the United States and Canada.

THE NATURE OF PSYCHOSIS AND SCHIZOPHRENIA

At this point, we take a brief look at psychosis, the disorder that these drugs are used to treat. *Psychotic disorders* are characterized by a loss of touch with reality; people with psychosis reach a state where they completely misunderstand and misinterpret the events going on around them, and they respond inappropriately in both an intellectual and an emotional sense. They often experience bizarre hallucinations, and their behavior is guided by delusions, beliefs that have no basis in reality.

Psychoses may be brief and temporary, brought on by drugs or some toxin, and psychotic behavior may arise from diseases such as Alzheimer's, but the major types of psychosis are bipolar disorder (which used to be known as manic-depressive psychosis, discussed in Chapter 14) and schizophrenia.

The term *schizophrenia* itself is often misunderstood. The word is derived from the Greek *schizein*, "to split," and *phren*, "mind." The splitting referred to, however, is not into two different personalities in the same individual. It is a separation between thought and emotion, the different aspects of one personality.

The diagnostic criteria for schizophrenia have been established by the American Psychiatric Association and are published in the *Diagnostic and Statistical Manual of Mental Disorders, Fourth Edition* (1994), which is more commonly referred to as the *DSM-IV*. Box 13-1 presents the characteristic symptoms for schizophrenia as listed in the *DSM-IV*.

The symptoms of schizophrenia are often classified into two types: positive and negative. *Positive symptoms* include hallucinations and delusions or irrational beliefs that can be very complex and highly organized. Feelings of grandeur ("I am being spoken to by God") or paranoia ("The CIA is plotting to kill me because I know too much") are often involved. The disorder in thinking and speech involves a loosening of associations between ideas; thoughts skip from one subject to another, completely unrelated subject, and the speaker is unaware that the topics are unconnected. The speech of such people has been described as "word salad."

Negative symptoms include affective flattening; the person's face is immobile and unresponsive, and he or she shows a diminished range of emotional expressiveness. Another negative symptom is *alogia*, or impoverished speech; replies are brief and uncommunicative and seem to reflect diminished thinking. *Avolition* is an inability to initiate or engage in goal-directed activities. The person sits for long periods of time and shows no interest in participating in work or social activities.

Box 13-2 presents a case study of a patient suffering from catatonic schizophrenia, one form of the disease.

BOX 13-1 *DSM-IV* Diagnostic Criteria for Schizophrenia

A. Characteristic Symptoms: Two (or more) of the following, each present for a significant proportion of time during a 1-month period (or less if successfully treated):

1. delusions
2. hallucinations
3. disorganized speech (e.g., frequent derailment or incoherence)
4. grossly disorganized or catatonic behavior
5. negative symptoms, i.e., affective flattening, alogia (poverty of speech or thought), or avolition (inability to initiate and persist in goal-directed activities)

Note: Only one Criterion A symptom is required if delusions are bizarre or hallucinations consist of a voice keeping up a running commentary on the person's behavior or thoughts, or two or more voices conversing with each other.

Source: Reprinted with permission from American Psychiatric Association. © 1994, DSM-IV Diagnostic Criteria for Schizophrenia.

BOX 13-2 Schizophrenia: A Case Study

This account of a schizophrenic episode was published in the *Journal of Abnormal and Social Psychology* in 1955 ("An Autobiography," 1955). The author is not identified by name, but we are told that she is a college-educated social caseworker and was a 36-year-old mother of three children when she experienced her first schizophrenic episode. Her experience with schizophrenia was at a time before antipsychotic drugs were available, and common treatments were barbiturates (amobarbital) and shock treatment. Compare the symptoms this woman describes with the description of schizophrenia provided in Box 13-1. Do you feel that she fits the criteria for schizophrenia?

Most of what follows is based on an unpublished autobiography written in the spring of 1951 shortly after I returned home from the second of the three episodes of my schizophrenic experiences. . . .

Shortly after I was taken to hospital for the first time in a rigid catatonic condition,* I was plunged into the horror of a world catastrophe. I was being caught up in a cataclysm and totally dislocated. I myself had been responsible for setting the destructive force into motion, although I had acted with no intent to harm, and defended myself with healthy indignation against the accusations of others. If I had done anything wrong, I was suffering the consequences along with everyone else. Part of the time I was exploring a new planet (a marvelous and breathtaking adventure) but it was too lonely. I could persuade no one to settle there and I had to get back to earth somehow. The earth, however, had been devastated by atomic bombs and most of its inhabitants killed. Only a few people—myself and the dimly perceived nursing staff—had escaped. At other times I felt totally alone on the new planet.

After the first few weeks of extreme disorganisation, I began to acquire some relatively stable paranoid delusions. . . .

During the paranoid period I thought I was being persecuted for my beliefs, that my enemies were actively trying to interfere with my activities, were trying to harm me, and at times even trying to kill me. I was primarily a citizen of the larger community. I was trying to persuade people who did not agree with me, but whom I felt could be won over, of the correctness of my belief. . . .

In order to carry through the task which had been imposed upon me, and to defend myself against the terrifying and bewildering dangers of my external situation, I was endowed in my imagination with truly cosmic powers. The sense of power was not always truly defensive but was also connected with a strong sense of valid inspiration. I felt that I had power to determine the weather, which responded to my inner moods, and even to control the movement of the sun in relation to other astronomical bodies. . . . I was also afraid that other people had power to read my mind, and thought I must develop ways of blocking my thoughts from other people. . . .

A mixture of sexual and ethical motivation became apparent during phases when I felt myself to be carrying through a predominantly maternal role and to be symbolically identified with Mary, the Mother of Christ. This identification was poetic; that is, I knew that I was myself and was Mary only in the figurative sense. The "Christ-Child" was apparently the human baby in general, the infant as the symbol of humanity, but I doubt that I would have made this identification if all my children had been girls.

Catatonic schizophrenia is characterized by a state of immobility in which the individual assumes a position without moving for extended periods of time.

HISTORY

Like most of the therapeutically useful drugs described in this book, drugs that treat the symptoms of schizophrenia were discovered by accident. In the 1950s, a French military surgeon, Henri Laborit, was looking for a preoperative medicine that would relieve patients' anxiety and reduce the high death rate that was associated with *surgical shock*, an acute and sometimes fatal state of weakness and reduction in vital functions that occur during surgery. Laborit theorized that shock was caused by excessive release of transmitters such as epinephrine, acetylcholine, and histamine; therefore, he tried out drugs known to block these substances to see if they would reduce the incidence of surgical shock. The drugs he tried included atropine, curare, and antihistamines. The first antihistamine Laborit tested was *promethazine*, which

was supplied by the Rhône-Poulenc company. Like most antihistamines, it has both antihistamine and sedating properties. Laborit was encouraged by the results he got with promethazine. In 1951, Rhône-Poulenc asked Laborit to try another antihistamine that it had synthesized several years earlier but had rejected because its sedating properties had been too strong. This was chlorpromazine.

The results were impressive. Laborit's patients did not lose consciousness but became sleepy and lost interest in everything going on around them (the sedating or tranquilizing effect) and could be anesthetized with a reduced dose of anesthetic. Laborit described the state induced by chlorpromazine as "artificial hibernation." He recognized the significance of this effect and immediately suggested to some psychiatrist friends that the drug might be useful in treating agitated mental patients. Two Parisian psychiatrists named Delay and Deniker learned about these trials and requested samples from Rhône-Poulenc. They administered the drug in higher doses and did not mix it with other drugs as other psychiatrists had been doing. In 1952, they reported some amazing successes; in 1953, the drug was marketed in Europe as Largactil (Sneader, 1985, p. 177; Snyder, 1986, p. 71; Spiegel & Aebi, 1981, p. 33).

Chlorpromazine was marketed in the United States in 1955 as Thorazine and was very successful. At that time, the number of patients in mental hospitals had been climbing steadily, but with the introduction of chlorpromazine, it started to decline dramatically. In the next three decades, the resident population of mental institutions in the United States dropped by 80 percent (Hollister, 1983, p. 3), largely as a result of the use of antipsychotics.

ROUTES OF ADMINISTRATION

The antipsychotics are usually taken orally, but preparations are available to be given in intramuscular or intravenous injections. They are seldom injected when given as antipsychotics, but they are injected when used as a presurgical or preanesthetic medication because the sedating effects appear more quickly when given parenterally. Intravenous injection also avoids any irregularities or delays in effect arising from erratic absorption from the digestive system. It is doubtful, however, that antipsychotic effects can be significantly speeded by giving the drug parenterally; the antipsychotic effects take several days to develop. The antipsychotics may be injected in circumstances where it may be difficult to induce agitated schizophrenic patients to take the drugs orally.

Because antipsychotic drugs are often taken chronically and patients do not always take them reliably, they are sometimes given in the form of a slowly dissolving *depot injection*, as described in Chapter 1. Depot injections release the drug into the system slowly, and a single injection may be effective for as long as 4 weeks (Lemberger, Schildcrout, & Cuff, 1987, p. 1288).

ABSORPTION AND DISTRIBUTION

Most antipsychotics are readily absorbed from the digestive system. Once absorbed, they are distributed throughout the body and easily cross the placental and blood–brain barriers. Blood protein binding is considerable, and the drugs tend to be absorbed into body fat and released very slowly.

EXCRETION

The drugs are destroyed entirely by metabolism, and almost no drug is excreted in the urine. Because of their strong protein binding and their tendency to stay in body fat, antipsychotics have very long half-lives of 11 to 58 hours, and metabolites can be found in the urine months after treatment. There is considerable individual variability in the metabolism of antipsychotics and in the optimal blood concentration. Finding the best dose for any individual is largely a matter of trial and error.

Because of their pharmacokinetics, it is usually appropriate to take them once a day, usually at bedtime, so that their sedating effects will be maximal during sleep.

NEUROPHYSIOLOGY

The *dopamine hypothesis* has been the dominant theory of the neurological basis of schizophrenia since the 1970s. This theory holds that schizophrenia is the result of an excess of dopamine activity in the brain. The theory was developed in response to two major observations: (a) Drugs that increase dopamine function (e.g., cocaine) can cause a state almost indistinguishable from schizophrenia, and (b) the antipsychotics available at the time (the typicals) were all dopamine blockers (more on this later).

As was discussed in Chapter 4, there are two major dopamine systems in the brain: the *mesolimbic system*, which is implicated in motivation and reinforcement, and the *nigrostriatal system* of the basal ganglia, which plays a role in the control of movement. The effect of antipsychotic drugs on the mesolimbic system seems to be responsible for their therapeutic effect, and their effect on the nigrostriatal system seems to be responsible for their main side effect, parkinsonian or neuroleptic effects.

The Mesolimbic Dopamine System

This system has its cell bodies in the ventral tegmental area (VTA) of the lower brain and synapses in the nucleus accumbens in the limbic system (see Figure 13-1). The cell bodies in the VTA also synapse on cells in other parts of the brain, including the frontal cortex and other parts of the limbic system.

The original dopamine hypothesis maintains that psychoses, both schizophrenia and bipolar disorder, are a result of excessive dopamine activity in the mesolimbic dopamine system and that antipsychotic drugs work because they block dopamine receptors in the mesolimbic dopamine system and decrease this excessive activity.

More recently, we have come to understand that the situation is much more complicated. Other neurotransmitters are involved, including serotonin, and other brain systems also play important roles. This is supported by the observation that antipsychotic drugs block dopamine as soon as they are taken, but the therapeutic effect may be delayed for days or weeks. This delay suggests that there is more involved than simply blocking excessive dopamine activity (Carlsson, 1994). The therapeutic effectiveness of antipsychotics may also involve the slow and long-lasting changes in the electrical properties or connectivity of cells, as discussed in Chapter 4.

One clue to the involvement of dopamine in schizophrenia is the observation that psychomotor stimulants like cocaine that increase dopamine levels can cause psychotic symptoms if taken in excess. Other drugs are also known to

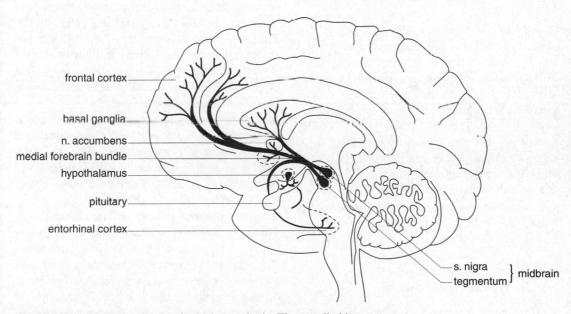

frontal cortex

basal ganglia

n. accumbens
medial forebrain bundle
hypothalamus

pituitary

entorhinal cortex

s. nigra
tegmentum } midbrain

Figure 13-1 Dopamine systems in the human brain. The mesolimbic system originates in the midbrain in the ventral tegmentum and runs to the nucleus accumbens and forward to the forebrain. The nigrostriatal system originates in the midbrain in the substantia nigra and runs forward to the basal ganglia in the striatum.

cause psychotic-like symptoms. These are the hallucinogens, such as LSD, that alter serotonin and PCP, which blocks NMDA receptors for glutamate. So both serotonin and glutamate may have a role to play in psychosis (see Chapter 16). It is also known that there is an interaction between serotonin and glutamate activity. As we shall see, the atypical antipsychotic drugs also alter serotonin functioning. Exactly how dopamine, serotonin, and glutamate interact to cause psychosis is not clear at this time.

The Nigrostriatal System

The integration of smooth movements is thought to be the function of a part of the brain known as the basal ganglia. The basal ganglia consist of the caudate nucleus, the putamen, the globus pallidus, and the substantia nigra. Together, they form part of what is known as the *extrapyramidal motor system* or *motor loop* (see Chapter 4). Cell bodies located in the substantia nigra in the midbrain (close to the VTA) send axons to synapses in the basal ganglia (close to the nucleus accumbens), as shown in Figure 13-1. These synapses use dopamine as the transmitter, and it is known that proper functioning of the extrapyramidal motor system depends on normal levels of dopamine being released at these synapses. When there is a deficiency of dopamine at these synapses, people show symptoms of the movement disorder known as Parkinson's disease. When antipsychotic drugs are given, they block the activity of dopamine in the basal ganglia as well as the mesolimbic dopamine system and can cause parkinsonian movement disorders (sometimes called *extrapyramidal symptoms* or neuroleptic symptoms, as described earlier).

Differences Between Typical and Atypical Antipsychotics

The typical antipsychotics (which were the only antipsychotics available when the dopamine hypothesis was developed) are primarily blockers of D_2 receptors. In fact, if one examines the relationship between the therapeutic dose of a typical antipsychotic and the drug's affinity for the D_2 receptor, there is almost a perfect correlation (Seeman, Lee, Chau-Wing, & Wong, 1976). The weaker the drug's affinity for the D_2 receptor, the larger the dose that is required to have a therapeutic effect. This relationship is powerful evidence that these drugs exert their primary therapeutic effect at the D_2 receptor. But there are other dopamine receptors in the nucleus accumbens.

Atypical antipsychotics avoid the problem of blocking dopamine in the nigrostriatal system because they do not have a high affinity for the D_2 receptor but have high affinities for the D_3 and D_4 subtypes. Neither of these receptor subtypes is found in the basal ganglia in high numbers. The D_3 receptor is localized largely to the nucleus accumbens, the terminal point of the mesolimbic projection with many fewer receptors in the basal ganglia (Landwehrmeyer, Mengod, & Palacios, 1993). The D_4 receptor is localized largely in the cortex, amygdala, and hippocampus—the regions that are important in cognition, emotion, and learning. There are very few, if any, D_4 receptors in human motor systems (Primus et al., 1997). Thus, it is possible for the atypical antipsychotics to depress dopamine activity in the mesolimbic system and treat psychoses without having a great effect on the nigrostriatal system and causing parkinsonian side effects.

Another major difference between the typicals and atypicals is the extent to which they block one of the serotonin receptors, the 5-HT$_{2A}$ receptor. Both classes of antipsychotics have some 5-HT$_{2A}$ blocking activity, but this activity is much higher for the atypicals than for the typicals. Figure 13-2 shows the different profiles of a number of drugs. The typical antipsychotics tend to have greater effects at D_2 receptors than at 5-HT$_{2A}$ receptors (the notable difference is chlorpromazine), and just the opposite is true for atypical antipsychotic drugs. Lieberman et al. (1998) developed a model in which the D_2 blockade leads to parkinsonian symptoms, but an additional blockade of 5-HT$_{2A}$ receptors counteracts the D_2 blockade. Atypical antipsychotics then may avoid parkinsonian side effects three ways: (a) They have a high affinity

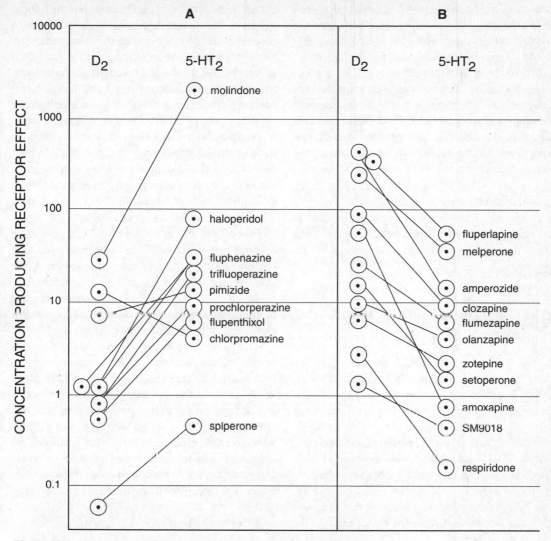

Figure 13-2   Panel A shows the relative effectiveness of various typical antipsychotic drugs on dopamine (D$_2$) and serotonin (5-HT$_2$) receptors (the lower the number, the greater the effect). Most of these drugs, with the exception of chlorpromazine, have a greater effect on dopamine receptors than serotonin receptors. Panel B shows the same analysis for many atypical antipsychotic drugs, which show a greater effect on serotonin than dopamine receptors. (Adapted from Seeman & Van Tol, 1994)

for D$_3$ and D$_4$ receptors; (b) they have a low affinity for D$_2$ receptors; and (c) their 5-HT$_{2A}$ activity cancels out their D$_2$ activity.

There is another reason why the effects of atypical antipsychotic drugs on 5HT$_{2A}$ receptors may be important. Drugs like LSD are agonists at 5HT$_{2A}$ receptors, and this effect causes an increased response of large glutaminergic neurons in the cortex to input. This effect on glutaminergic neurons on the frontal cortex is thought to be important in the hallucinations caused by many LSD-type drugs. By blocking these receptors, the atypical antipsychotic drugs may be reducing psychotic symptoms (see Chapter 16).

All of the antipsychotics have actions at all of these dopamine and serotonin receptors and the receptors of other transmitter systems as well, including acetylcholine and histamine. In addition, they may alter the effects of gamma-aminobutryic acid (GABA) and peptide transmitters, and they block norepinephrine (NE) receptors and increase NE synthesis and release (Roth, 1983, p. 127). In some cases, these effects on other receptor sites appear to be responsible for differences in the effect of various antipsychotic drugs on positive and negative symptoms and in the side effects they cause.

EFFECTS OF ANTIPSYCHOTICS

Effects on the Body

The effects of the different antipsychotics show considerable variation but not as much variability as can be seen among different individuals taking the same drug. Each drug's effectiveness as an antipsychotic and the sort and intensity of side effects will vary considerably from person to person. This is one reason why so many of these drugs are on the market. Psychiatrists may try giving an individual a number of different drugs at different doses until one is found that produces the most favorable therapeutic effect and has the fewest side effects.

As we have already seen, the most pronounced side effect is alterations in movement that resemble the symptoms of Parkinson's disease. This effect is reported in about 40 percent of patients on typical antipsychotics. It includes a dulled expression on the face, rigidity and tremor in the limbs, weakness in the extremities, and very slow movements. In addition, about 20 percent of patients show *akathesia*, a condition characterized by uncontrolled restlessness, constant compulsive movement, and sometimes a protruding tongue and facial grimacing.

After taking the typical antipsychotics for a period of time, about 30 percent of patients show a condition called *tardive dyskinesia*, characterized by involuntary, repetitive movements of the face, such as smacking of the lips and twitching. Unfortunately, for some individuals, the symptoms of tardive dyskinesia are permanent and do not go away even after the drug is stopped (Enna & Coyle, 1983, p. 10).

Antipsychotics also seem to cause the body to have trouble regulating temperature, which becomes easily influenced by changes in the environment. In hot environments, patients are more susceptible to heat stroke; in cold climates, they are more vulnerable to hypothermia.

In certain susceptible individuals, epileptic seizures may increase. Other side effects include reduced food intake, altered pigmentation of the skin, changes in heart rate and blood pressure (due to the effect of these drugs on NE receptors), dry mouth, impaired vision, constipation (due to anticholinergic effects), and jaundice.

The major problem with clozapine is that it is known to cause a disorder called *agranulocytosis*, a potentially fatal suppression of bone marrow activity. It occurs in 1 to 2 percent of all patients receiving clozapine and can happen at any time. For this reason, clozapine is administered only to patients who have not responded to any other antipsychotic drug, and patients on this drug must be carefully and continuously monitored. This serious side effect kept clozapine off the market for many years.

Effects on Sleep

Antipsychotics at therapeutic doses have very little effect on sleep, but some antipsychotics that have sedating effects (e.g., chlorpromazine) will increase sleep time when given at high doses or when first administered. The antipsychotics do not alter sleep cycles or REM sleep (Spiegel & Aebi, 1981, p. 116).

Lethal Effects

The antipsychotics produce many side effects, but these drugs are not lethal. In fact, they are extremely safe and have a high therapeutic index (see Chapter 1), about 100. For some antipsychotics, the therapeutic index is as high as 1,000 (Baldessarini, 1985, pp. 35, 38, 81). It is practically impossible to use antipsychotics to commit suicide.

EFFECTS ON THE BEHAVIOR AND PERFORMANCE OF HUMANS

Subjective Effects

Chlorpromazine, when given to healthy subjects, causes a very pronounced feeling of tiredness. Subjects report slower and confused thinking, difficulty in concentrating, and feelings of clumsiness. They also report a need for sleep, dejection, anxiety, and irritability. Simple tasks such as walking seem to take great effort.

Haloperidol is not as sedating as chlorpromazine, but, along with other atypical antipsychotic drugs, it makes subjects feel internally aroused and externally sedated at the same time; that is, they feel restless and want to do something but also feel restrained and have difficulty moving (Spiegel & Aebi, 1981, p. 62).

The subjective experience of antipsychotics is never described as pleasant. This fact is probably responsible for the poor compliance rates with these drugs; patients often do not take them. This does not appear to be true, however, of many of the atypical antipsychotics, such as clozapine (Meltzer, 1990).

Effects on Performance

Reports on the effects of typical antipsychotics on attention and cognitive performance have been variable. Most studies of the acute effects show impairment probably related to sedative effects. Tolerance to these effects has also been reported to occur within 14 days. Clozapine and remoxipride, both atypical antipsychotics, have been shown to interfere with performance. The findings with sulpride, however, have been mixed (King, 1993).

Surprisingly, few studies of the effects of antipsychotics on cognitive functioning have been conducted. Those that were done have been inconclusive, reporting no effect, deficits, or improvements (Judd, Squire, Butters, Salmon, & Paller, 1987, p. 1469).

EFFECTS ON THE BEHAVIOR OF NONHUMANS

Effects on Unconditioned Behavior

Unlike the antianxiety drugs, such as the benzodiazepines, the most remarkable effect of the antipsychotic drugs is that they suppress spontaneous movement in an open field, and higher doses render most laboratory animals immobile. In fact, these animals take on a sort of *plastic immobility*. Their limbs will remain in any position in which they are placed, as though the animals were made out of modeling clay. This immobility gave rise to the name *neuroleptic*.

At doses that do not seem to have those neuroleptic effects, antipsychotic drugs diminish the frequency and intensity of attack behaviors in most species. This decrease in aggression coincides with an overall decrease in activity, so it is possible that it results from an overall debilitation in motor abilities (Miczek & Barry, 1976).

Effects on Conditioned Behavior

In general, the antipsychotic drugs cause a decrease in responding on schedules maintained by positive reinforcement, although at lower doses there are reports that low response rates may be increased. This rate-dependent effect is similar to the effect seen with many other drugs, including amphetamine.

As far back as 1953, when chlorpromazine was first being tested on humans by Laborit, Simone Courvousier and her associates at the Rhöne-Poulenc company (Courvousier, Fournel, Ducrot, Kolsky, & Koetschet, 1953) discovered that the drug would decrease avoidance at doses that would have no effect on escape from a shock, an effect now known to be shared by antianxiety drugs such as barbiturates and benzodiazepines. In fact, this was the first time that this technique had been adopted for use in testing drugs, and it has since become one of the most widely used screening devices for new psychotherapeutics (Laties, 1986, p. 27).

DRUG STATE DISCRIMINATION AND DISSOCIATION

It has been demonstrated that chlorpromazine will cause dissociation. In one study, rats trained on an avoidance task under the influence of chlorpromazine were unable to remember what they had learned when tested under saline but could recall the task when returned to the drug state again (Otis, 1964). This finding has caused some concern among psychotherapists because psychotherapy involves learning, and patients often receive psychotherapy while they are being treated with these drugs. Consequently, when they are taken off the drugs, they may not recall what they learned in psychotherapy.

In drug state discrimination studies, the antipsychotics are not well discriminated. For an antipsychotic to act as a discriminative stimulus, large doses are required, and many more training trials are needed, compared with most other behaviorally active drugs (Overton, 1987; Overton & Batta, 1977).

Once an animal has been trained to discriminate an antipsychotic, the response will generalize to most other antipsychotics at sufficiently high doses. There are some exceptions. For example, a rat trained to discriminate clozapine will not generalize to haloperidol or chlorpromazine (Goas & Boston, 1978). There is no generalization between the antipsychotics and the antidepressants or any other class of drugs (J. Stewart, 1962).

TOLERANCE

There is no evidence that tolerance develops to the antipsychotic effects of these drugs. Once a patient has been established on a therapeutically effective dose, it is often maintained for years without any decrease in effectiveness. Tolerance seems to develop to the sedating effects of the drugs seen when it is first given, and tolerance also seems to develop to the parkinsonian effects.

WITHDRAWAL

Physical dependence, if it occurs at all, is rare. There are reports of muscular discomfort, exaggeration of psychotic symptoms and movement disorders, and difficulty in sleeping when some antipsychotics are suddenly withdrawn, but such effects are not normally seen even after years of use at normal doses. It is possible that the failure to notice withdrawal symptoms is due to the extremely slow excretion of the drug from the body (Baldessarini, 1985, p. 38).

SELF-ADMINISTRATION IN HUMANS AND NONHUMANS

As we have seen in Chapter 5 (see Table 5-1), chlorpromazine is not self-administered by laboratory animals. In fact, these drugs appear to be aversive. In one experiment, monkeys learned to bar press to avoid infusions. At first, the monkeys did not respond to avoid chlorpromazine; after a week, they were successfully avoiding 90 percent of the programmed infusions. It appears that the aversive properties of chlorpromazine develop slowly, with repeated doses (Hoffmeister & Wuttke, 1975, p. 424).

Experience with humans is similar. The antipsychotics are never abused; in fact, they are a class of drugs that have considerable compliance problems. *Compliance* refers to the extent to which a patient adheres to a regimen of medical treatment. In the case of typical antipsychotics, most schizophrenic patients show poor compliance: They often stop taking their medication, with the usual result that their symptoms reappear. For this reason, various administration techniques have been developed that do not depend on the patient's compliance. Among them is administration of depot injections, which slowly release the drug and maintain the appropriate blood levels. Noncompliance is less of a problem with the atypical antipsychotics.

HARMFUL EFFECTS

Reproduction

Apart from the movement disorders already described, the antipsychotic drugs can have serious effects on reproductive functions.

In males, the antipsychotics reduce sexual interest, an effect that may arise from their sedative properties. Sexual performance may also be impaired. The primary difficulty is a failure to ejaculate; erection and orgasm are unaffected. These problems arise from both anticholinergic properties of the antipsychotics and their effect on hormone levels (N. F. Woods, 1984, p. 440). Figure 13-1 shows that there is a short dopamine pathway running from the hypothalamus to the pituitary. When this system is activated, it suppresses the release of *prolactin*, a hormone that suppresses male sexual activity. Drugs like cocaine, which activate this system, can stimulate male sexual performance by suppressing prolactin release, but drugs like antipsychotics, which block dopamine, have the opposite effect. Atypical antipsychotics do not seem to alter prolactin release.

In females, there may be abnormal menstrual cycles and infertility. In both males and females, there is sometimes an enlargement of the breasts, and fluid will sometimes ooze from the nipples (N. F. Woods, 1984, p. 441).

OTHER THERAPEUTIC EFFECTS OF ANTIPSYCHOTIC DRUGS

Antipsychotic drugs are useful in the treatment of other medical problems. They are effective *antiemetics*; that is, they prevent nausea and vomiting and are useful in the treatment of motion sickness. In addition, they were originally developed by Laborit as presurgical and preanesthetic medications and are still used for that purpose.

A number of movement disorders thought to result from excessive dopamine activity in the brain can, not surprisingly, be treated effectively with antipsychotics. These disorders include *Huntington's chorea*, an inherited degenerative disease. Huntington's is fatal, but antipsychotics

help control some of the symptoms. Antipsychotics are also useful in treating *Tourette's syndrome*; Tourette patients show involuntary muscle tics, twitches, and vocalizations (often swearing). Surprisingly, antipsychotics are also used to treat tardive dyskinesia.

Antipsychotics have also been used to treat hiccups, stuttering, and delirium tremens caused by alcohol withdrawal (Van Woert, 1983) and psychotic behaviors induced by psychomotor stimulants, LSD, and other hallucinogens.

CHAPTER SUMMARY

- Antipsychotic drugs are also referred to as neuroleptic drugs or major tranquilizers. They are used in the treatment of schizophrenia and bipolar disorder.

- Extrapyramidal motor effects (also known as parkinsonian effects or neuroleptic effects) are common side effects of antipsychotic drugs. These effects constitute a movement disorder similar to Parkinson's disease.

- People suffering from schizophrenia lose touch with reality. They misunderstand events going on around them and make inappropriate intellectual and emotional responses to those events. Positive symptoms include hallucinations and delusions. Negative symptoms include a loss of initiative, flattening of affect, and alogia (impoverished speech and thought).

- Typical antipsychotic drugs are effective only against positive symptoms, but the newer, atypical antipsychotic drugs are effective on both positive and negative symptoms and have fewer side effects on movement.

- Chlorpromazine was marketed in 1955. Along with other similar antipsychotics, it dramatically reduced the number of patients in mental hospitals throughout the world.

- Antipsychotics are administered orally and are distributed throughout the body. They easily cross the placental and blood–brain barriers. Because they are highly lipid soluble, they have very long half-lives.

- Antipsychotics work by blocking the dopamine D_2 receptors in the mesolimbic system. They cause parkinsonian movement disorders and tardive dyskinesia by blocking D_2 receptors in the nigrostriatal system.

- Newer, atypical antipsychotic drugs have a low affinity for D_2 receptors but a high affinity for D_3 and D_4 receptors that are not located in the nigrostriatal system. They also block a serotonin receptor that has the effect of diminishing the activity of glutaminergic activity in the cortex. These differences may explain why the atypical drugs do not have serious extrapyramidal side effects and are effective in treating negative symptoms.

- When given to normal people, antipsychotics cause a feeling of tiredness, and the effects are never described as pleasant.

- Antipsychotics decrease general activity levels of nonhumans and have a rate-dependent effect on operant behavior. They decrease avoidance behavior in doses that have no effect on escape behavior.

- Tolerance to the antipsychotic effect of these drugs does not appear to develop, and withdrawal symptoms are rare. They are never self-administered by nonhumans and are not abused by humans.

- Antipsychotics can depress sexual interest and performance in males and interfere with menstruation in females.

14

Antidepressants and Mood Stabilizers

There are several types of antidepressants. The first drugs that were successfully used to treat depression were the *monoamine oxidase inhibitors* (MAOIs) and the *tricyclic antidepressants* (TCAs). Consequently, they are sometimes referred to as *first-generation antidepressants*. Newer drugs have been developed that do not belong to either of these categories, and they are often called *second-generation antidepressants*. This diverse group of chemicals includes the *selective serotonin reuptake inhibitors* (SSRIs), inhibitors of norepinephrine reuptake (NARIs or sometimes SNRIs) and dopamine reuptake, and drugs that selectively block or stimulate specific serotonin and norepinephrine receptors.

The first MAOI to be used was *iproniazid*, but it is no longer in use. Others include *phenelzine* (Nardil), *tranylcypromine* (Parnate), and *moclobemide* (Ludiomil, available in the United Kingdom and Canada but not in the United States).

The tricyclic antidepressants are so called because their molecular structure contains three rings. Common TCAs are *imipramine* (Tofranil), *amitriptyline* (Elavil), *desipramine* (Norpramin),

nortriptyline (Aventyl), *doxepin* (Adapin), and *mirtazapine* (Remeron).

Some second-generation antidepressants are *maprotiline* (Manerex), *amoxapine* (Asendin), *trazodone* (Desyrel), *mianserin* (Tolvon, not used in the United States), *nomifensine* (Merital, now withdrawn), *buproprion* (Wellbutrin or Zyban, a DA reuptake inhibitor), and *reboxetine* (Edronax or Vestra, a NARI not available in the United States). Although many second-generation antidepressants have been used in Europe, strict drug development laws have delayed or prevented their use in the United States.

The SSRIs include *fluoxetine* (Prozac), *fluvoxamine* (Luvox), *sertraline* (Zoloft), *paroxetine* (Paxil), and *citalopram* (Celexa).

The element *lithium* is used to treat and prevent the bipolar disorder. It is usually sold as the salt *lithium carbonate* under many different trade names, including Carbolith, Eskalith, Lithonate, and Lithotabs. Lithium has many troublesome side effects and poor compliance, so when it was found that drugs originally developed as anticonvulsants to treat epilepsy and seizure disorders were effective in treating bipolar disorder, its use declined substantially. These drugs include *carbamazepine* (Tegretol), *valproic acid* (Depakine), and *lamotrigine* (Lamictal). Anticonvulsant drugs are now more widely used to treat bipolar disorder than lithium.

THE NATURE OF DEPRESSION AND MANIA

From time to time, we all feel sad or "depressed" as a result of things that happen to us or to those we love, but this condition is not usually accompanied by physical symptoms, and it does not last. For some people, depression is much more serious; there may be no cause in their environment, but their depression is deep, and either it does not go away or it keeps returning for no apparent reason. These people also show a loss of appetite, loss of interest in normally pleasurable activities, loss of energy, problems sleeping, exaggerated feelings of worthlessness and guilt, and haunting thoughts of death and suicide. Box 14-1 presents a summary of the *DSM-IV* criteria for a major depressive episode.

An interesting characteristic of depression is that it can occur in persons who do not actually feel depressed. Often older people show many of the physical symptoms of depression—insomnia,

BOX 14-1 *DSM-IV* Criteria for a Major Depressive Episode

A. Five (or more) of the following symptoms have been present during the same two-week period and represent a change from previous functioning; at least one of the symptoms is either (1) depressed mood or (2) loss of interest in pleasure.

  (1) depressed mood most of the day, nearly every day, as indicated by either subjective report (e.g., feels sad or empty) or observation made by others (e.g., appears tearful)

  (2) markedly diminished interest in pleasure in all, or almost all, activities most of the day, nearly every day

  (3) significant weight loss when not dieting or weight gain (e.g., a change of more than 5% body weight in a month) or decrease or increase in appetite nearly every day

  (4) insomnia or hypersomnia nearly every day

  (5) psychomotor agitation or retardation nearly every day

  (6) fatigue or loss of energy nearly every day

  (7) feelings of worthlessness or excessive or inappropriate guilt nearly every day

  (8) diminished ability to think or concentrate, or indecisiveness, nearly every day

  (9) recurrent thoughts of death (not just fear of dying), recurrent suicidal ideation without a specific plan, or a suicide attempt or a specific plan for committing suicide

B. The symptoms do not meet the criteria for a Mixed Episode.*

C. Symptoms cause clinically significant distress or impairment in social, occupational, or other important areas of functioning.

D. Symptoms are not due to direct physiological effects of a substance (e.g., a drug of abuse or medication) or a general medical condition.

E. Symptoms are not better accounted for by bereavement, i.e., after the loss of a loved one, the symptoms persist for longer than 2 months or are characterized by marked functional impairment, morbid preoccupation with worthlessness, suicidal ideation, psychotic symptoms, or psychomotor retardation.

*A mixed episode is where both manic and depressive symptoms occur at the same time.

Source: Reprinted with permission from American Psychiatric Association. © 1994, DSM-IV Criteria for a Major Depressive Episode.

weight loss, and so on—but do not seem to feel sad. They may, however, show *anhedonia*, a loss of interest in activities that are normally pleasurable. This "clinical depression" or "depressive illness" can be treated with antidepressants.

Depression is classified as an *affective disorder* or *mood disorder*. Traditionally, mild depression was labeled "neurotic depression," but serious depression accompanied by physical symptoms was considered a psychosis. *DSM-IV* no longer makes this distinction or considers depression as psychotic, but it does recognize that depression (see Chapter 13) may be associated with schizophrenia. In such cases, the depressed person will also exhibit hallucinations, delusions, or other symptoms of psychosis.

Depression has been called the common cold of mental illness because large segments of the population experience it at some time in their lives. Modest estimates suggest that within any 6-month period, 3 percent of the population of the United States is experiencing a mood disorder, and about 6 percent have one at some point during their lives. (Some estimates range as high as 26 percent.) In Western cultures depression is more frequent in every generation since World War II.

Compared to men, women are twice as likely to suffer from depression, but there are no gender differences in bipolar disorder. Only about 20 percent of those with depressive illness receive help from a mental health professional (Lickey & Gordon, 1991, p. 149). The resulting disability in the form of health care utilization, absenteeism (172 million working days annually), injuries at work, and the like costs an estimated $26 billion annually in the United States (Janicak, Davis, Preskorn, & Ayd, 1993, p. 207). There are other costs, too. The overall mortality rate for depressed people is higher than for normal people, and the probability of suicide is 20 times greater in depressed people.

Accounts of depressive illness were recorded by the ancient Greeks, and depression is common in contemporary cultures and societies. Similar symptoms are reported except that in non-Western societies, depressed people are more likely to report physical symptoms and less likely to express feelings of guilt and self-reproach (Lickey & Gordon, 1991, p. 175).

Depression is a chronic illness. Eighty-eight percent of those who suffer from depression and receive drug therapy improve within 6 months, but less than one-third of these remain well.

For most individuals, depression comes in cycles that may alternate with normal periods, but it may also alternate with *mania*. Mania is the exact opposite of depression. The person becomes excessively elated and hyperactive and takes on many ambitious and grandiose projects. The need for sleep is decreased, the sense of self-esteem is inflated, and behavior is often reckless. Manic individuals become very talkative, and ideas race through their heads. They are easily distracted, and conversation will switch from topic to topic. Manic people often become reckless and foolhardy, engaging in foolish investments or sexual indiscretions. Box 14-2 gives the *DSM-IV* criteria for a manic episode. The condition in which depression alternates with mania was called *manic-depressive psychosis*, but the *DSM-IV* now prefers the term *bipolar disorder*.

It has been known for some time that mood is related to the functioning of the monoamines (MAs), in particular, serotonin (5-HT) and norepinephrine (NE), although dopamine (DA) may also play a role. Drugs like cocaine and amphetamine make people feel good because they enhance transmission at these synapses, and drugs like reserpine, which depletes the brain of MAs, often cause severe depression. The *monoamine theory* of depression in its original form suggested that depression was a result of reduced levels of activity in these monoamine systems. As we shall see, this theory is no longer tenable in its simple form (Jimerson, 1987; Ordway, Klimek, & Mann, 2002; van Praag, de Kloet, & van Os, 2004, pp. 91–143). All of the three MAs are probably involved in some aspect of mood, and they interact with each other in complex ways, but it is now fairly clear that decreased activity in the serotonin system, although it may not be the direct cause of

BOX 14-2   *DSM-IV* Criteria for a Manic Episode

A. A distinct period of abnormally and persistently elevated, expansive, or irritable mood, lasting at least one week (or any duration if hospitalization is necessary).

B. During the period of mood disturbance, three of the following symptoms have persisted (four if the mood is only irritable) and have been present to a significant degree:

(1) inflated self-esteem or grandiosity

(2) decreased need for sleep

(3) more talkative than usual or pressure to keep talking

(4) flight of ideas or subjective experience that thoughts are racing

(5) distractibility (attention easily drawn to unimportant or irrelevant external stimuli)

(6) increase in goal-directed activity or psychomotor agitation

(7) excessive involvement in pleasurable activities that have a high potential for painful consequences (e.g., engaging in unrestrained buying sprees, sexual indiscretions, or foolish business investments)

C. The symptoms do not meet the criteria for Mixed Episode.

D. The mood disturbance is sufficiently severe to cause a marked impairment in occupational functioning or in usual social activities or relationships with others, or to necessitate hospitalization to prevent harm to self or others, or there are psychotic features.

E. The symptoms are not due to the direct physiological effects of a substance (e.g., a drug of abuse or medication, or other treatment) or a general medical condition.

Source: Reprinted with permission from American Psychiatric Association. © 1994, DSM-IV Criteria for a Manic Episode.

---

depression, certainly renders an individual vulnerable to depression. All treatments that have been shown to be effective in relieving depression have one thing in common: They ultimately change (almost always increase) transmission at serotonin synapses (Blier & de Montigny, 1994). It is clear, however, that these increases in serotonin transmission may be caused by, and may in turn cause changes in, activity of other transmitter systems—even some that do not use MAs (Charney, Southwick, Delgado, & Krystal, 1990; Janicak et al., 1993). An increase in serotonin transmission appears to be a necessary but not sufficient condition for effectiveness against depression (Leonard, 1993). Activity at specific serotonin synapses may in fact be only one link in a long and complex chain of neurological deficiencies that cause depression and mania.

Three brain systems that use MA transmitters have been implicated in some aspect of mood. All have centers in the midbrain or upper brain stem and send projections forward to the various parts of the limbic system and the forebrain through the *medial forebrain bundle*: (a) NE fibers that arise in the *locus coeruleus* in the midbrain, (b) serotonergic fibers that originate in areas of the *Raphé system*, and (c) dopaminergic fibers of the mesolimbic system that originate in the *ventral tegmental area.*

HISTORY

The antidepressant properties of the MAOI iproniazid were discovered accidentally. The drug was developed as a treatment for tuberculosis, but its significant effect on the mood of patients was soon discovered; it relieved depression and made patients feel better. Later research determined that this effect was separate from relief of the symptoms of tuberculosis. When MAOIs were first introduced in the 1950s, they became widely used, but in a few years, the initial enthusiasm waned because of several factors. To begin with, iproniazid was taken off the market soon after it was released because of reports that it caused liver damage. It turned out that the liver damage occurred only because the doses used were too high. In addition, some clinical studies concluded that MAOIs were ineffective. Once again, these reports were unfounded. The studies used inadequate research design, and we now know that the doses used were too low. MAOIs were also known to interact with many other drugs and some foods. It is now known that MAOIs are just as effective as any other treatment for depression (more effective in some types of patients) and that they do not cause liver damage at therapeutic doses. New MAOIs have also been developed. They are more specific in their actions, reversible, and much less likely to interact with diet. This class of drugs is regaining a role as an effective and relatively safe treatment for depression (Kurtz, 1990).

The tricyclic antidepressants were also discovered by accident, during research on antipsychotic drugs (see Chapter 13). In the hope of finding better antipsychotics, many new drugs based on the antipsychotic drug molecule were synthesized; one of these was imipramine. In the late 1950s, imipramine was tested on psychiatric patients, and although it did not improve schizophrenic patients, it did elevate the mood of depressed patients. Because the tricyclics are safer than the early MAOIs, many more have been developed, and their use has become common in the treatment of depression.

The popularity of the tricyclics has been overshadowed by the second-generation antidepressants, which are safer and have fewer of the bothersome side effects of the tricyclic and MAOI drugs (Enna & Eilson, 1987; Feighner & Boyer, 1991; Leonard, 1993; Shopsin, Cassano, & Conti, 1981), although second-generation antidepressants do not seem to be more effective or to work faster in the treatment of depression. Like the TCAs and MAOIs, many second-generation antidepressants were developed for other purposes, and their antidepressant properties were discovered later.

The first SSRI, fluoxetine (more widely known by its trade name Prozac), was introduced in the United States in 1987 and soon received considerable attention in the popular media because it was being used not to treat depression but as a means of altering personality (more on this later). The media also carried reports that the drug could precipitate violent aggressive acts and suicide. If such adverse effects occur, however, they are extremely rare. The use of fluoxetine and other SSRIs continues to increase both in the treatment of depression and as a personality "cosmetic."

Lithium, when given in the form of one of its salts, also works well in preventing both the mania and the depression that come in cycles in bipolar disorder. This effect was also discovered accidentally. In the 1940s, John Cade, an Australian psychiatrist, was testing a theory he had—that is, a toxin in the blood of manic patients caused their disease. He proposed that uric acid might protect experimental rats from the effects of this toxin, so he tried to inject rats with uric acid to see if it protected them from the lethal effects of being injected with the urine from manic patients. Unfortunately (or fortunately), he found that the uric acid did not readily dissolve, so he mixed it with lithium to make a soluble salt. He noticed that this mixture calmed the rats and did seem to offer them some protection. Later, he found that any salt of lithium would do the same thing, and he concluded that it was the lithium, not the uric acid, that was effective (Sneader, 1985, p. 185; Snyder, 1986). When he tested the lithium with his manic patients, he achieved amazing success. The lithium not only decreased symptoms but also prevented the recurrence of both mania and depression if taken regularly.

In spite of clear demonstrations of its effectiveness, lithium was slow to be used and was not available commercially in the United States until 1970.

Lithium is particularly effective in the treatment of bipolar disorder because it relieves mania and blocks the recurrence of depression. It is, however, not effective in treating depression once it occurs. For this reason, lithium is not classed as an antidepressant. It may be referred to as an *antimanic* drug or a *mood stabilizer*. Antidepressants alone are not often used to treat bipolar disorder. They may relieve depression, but they sometimes can induce a manic episode. Lithium is often used in conjunction with an antidepressant in patients with bipolar disorder and may also be used with an antidepressant when the antidepressants are not effective by themselves.

ABSORPTION

The MAOIs, the tricyclic antidepressants, and many second-generation antidepressants have similar absorption pharmacokinetics. The TCAs reach maximal blood concentrations in 1 to 3 hours (although some TCAs may take as long as 8 hours). The absorption of SSRIs is slower; 4 to 8 hours are needed to reach maximum concentrations. Antidepressants generally have high levels of protein binding (over 95 percent for fluoxetine; DeVane, 1998).

A significant proportion of a dose of most antidepressants is destroyed by the digestive system and liver before it reaches the bloodstream. This first-pass metabolism is inhibited by alcohol; as a result, alcohol will greatly increase the amount of drug absorbed from a specific dose. Overdoses of TCAs are much more serious when taken in conjunction with alcohol. SSRIs are an exception; they appear to have little interaction with alcohol. In fact, SSRIs have been suggested as a treatment for alcoholism (Lejoyeux, 1996).

Orally administered lithium is rapidly absorbed. Peak levels in the blood occur between a half hour and 2 hours after consumption. However, lithium is much slower in getting inside cells, and this fact probably accounts for the drug's delayed therapeutic effect (Hollister, 1983, p. 181).

Lithium has a low therapeutic index of about 3 (Baldessarini, 1985, p. 35), so it is important to keep blood levels from becoming too high at any one time. Because lithium is absorbed rapidly, it peaks in the blood at high levels, and these

peaks often exceed the therapeutic window (see Chapter 1). It is also excreted rapidly; several daily doses are needed to maintain the therapeutic level. This problem is often handled by using slow-release capsules in which the lithium is embedded in a material that dissolves slowly. This alternative prevents rapid-rise and high-peak blood levels and allows dosage to be cut back to two administrations per day (Cooper, 1987, p. 1366).

DISTRIBUTION

Antidepressants readily cross the blood–brain and placental barriers. They tend to be concentrated in the lungs, kidneys, liver, and brain. Some antidepressants can be found in significant quantities in breast milk.

Lithium enters and leaves the brain relatively slowly, reaching a peak after more than 24 hours. It seems to be concentrated in some parts of the brain. There is no protein binding. Lithium readily crosses the placental barrier, and because it easily finds its way into breast milk, it should not be used by breast-feeding mothers.

EXCRETION

The MAOIs have a short half-life of 2 to 4 hours (Preskorn, 1993). Some MAOIs may be taken once a day because they have an irreversible effect on MAO, and their effects persist long after they are eliminated from the body. Newer MAOIs like moclobemide have a reversible effect, and two or three daily doses are required. The TCAs have a half-life of about 24 hours and, in most people, reach a steady-state level after about 5 days. Usually, only a single daily dose is needed.

Most second-generation antidepressants have shorter half-lives than the tricyclics and often require more frequent dosing (Rudorfer & Potter, 1987). Newer SSRIs generally have a short to medium half-life (15 to 20 hours) and do not have active metabolites. With these drugs, a steady-state blood level can be achieved in a few days with single daily dosing. One major exception, fluoxetine, has an extremely long half-life and an active metabolite that blocks the enzyme responsible for its destruction. Fluoxetine has a half-life of 6 days, and its active metabolite, norfluoxetine, has a half-life of 16 days. It may take as long as 75 days for the drug and its metabolite to reach a steady-state level in the body. It can also take this long for the drug and its metabolite to be completely eliminated from the body after the drug is discontinued (R. Lane & Baldwin, 1997).

There is considerable variability between individuals in the pharmacokinetics of the antidepressants. After a fixed daily dose of a tricyclic, individual steady-state blood levels may be as much as 36 times higher in some individuals than in others because some people have a genetic deficiency in one of the enzymes the body uses to destroy these drugs. In these people, antidepressants can have extremely long half-lives (Preskorn, 1993, Rudorfer & Potter, 1987). Thus, doses vary for individuals, and in many cases, blood levels must be monitored (G. M. Simpson & Singh, 1990). Swanson, Jones, Krasselt, Denmark, and Ratti (1997) have reported two deaths caused by tricyclics taken at normal clinical doses. The individuals seem not to have cleared the metabolites as rapidly as most people, and the metabolites built up to a toxic level. Like many other genetic factors, the distribution of the enzyme can be associated with ethnicity (Sramek & Pi, 1996).

Lithium is excreted unchanged in the urine and has a half-life of between 12 and 21 hours (Hollister, 1983, p. 181). The excretion rate varies considerably among individuals and increases with age to as long as 36 hours (Baldessarini, 1985, p. 96). For this reason, the blood levels must be carefully monitored when a patient is started on lithium therapy.

NEUROPHYSIOLOGY

Antidepressants

Antidepressants generally work by increasing the activity of one or more of the MA systems of the brain. There are several ways that they can do this, and antidepressants are usually classified by the way in which they work.

The MAOIs do exactly what their name implies—they block the activity of monoamine oxidase, the enzyme that destroys the MAs: dopamine DA, NE, and 5-HT. With this enzyme blocked, MA transmitters released into the synaptic cleft will not be metabolized, and the level of transmitter can rise as the transmitter accumulates. Activity at the synapse will increase unless the synapse has some other means of adjusting its activity. The effect of the older MAOIs is not selective, and the level of all MAs is affected. Some newer MAOIs, however, selectively affect NE and 5-HT and have little effect on DA.

As their name suggests, the selective 5-HT reuptake inhibitors (SSRIs) block the ability of presynaptic cells to reabsorb and recycle 5-HT and have the effect of causing a buildup of 5-HT at synapses. This action is specific to 5-HT; the SSRIs have minimal effect on other MAs.

At one point it was believed that all the tricyclics worked in the same way; that is, that they prevented the reabsorption or uptake of monoamines after they were released into the cleft, but there are now many drugs that have the three-ring structure of the tricyclics but have various effects on functioning of other MAs (Ordway et al., 2002). For this reason we can talk about some tricyclics along with newer or second-generation antidepressants.

Nortriptyline, amoxapine, and venlafaxine are MA reuptake blockers with varying degrees of selectivity for the different MAs. Reboxetine and malprotiline are selective blockers of NE reuptake (NARIs). Amitriptyline is an antagonist at $5-HT_2$ and NE $alpha_2$ receptors. Bupropion is known to block some MA reuptake, particularly DA, but it is not known whether this is responsible for its antidepressant properties. Bupropion is also widely sold as Zyban, an aid to smoking cessation. Nefazodone and terazodone are potent antagonists of the $5-HT_{2a}$ receptor but also have MA reuptake blocking action.

A side effect of the tricyclics is that they act as anticholinergics, blocking transmission at cholinergic synapses. The effect on 5-HT and

NE is believed to be responsible for their therapeutic action, and the anticholinergic effect is responsible for many of the side effects, such as dry mouth and blurry vision, of some antidepressants.

A few second-generation antidepressants, such as amisulpride and sulpride, appear to exert their primary effects not at serotonergic synapses but at dopaminergic synapses in the mesolimbic system through blockade of D_2, D_3, and D_4 receptors. These drugs are sometimes also used as antipsychotic drugs. Finally, a new type of antidepressants are direct agonists at $5-HT_1$ receptors. This final class includes buspirone, ipsapirone, and gepirone (Bonhomme & Esposito, 1998). These drugs may also be used as anxiolytics.

We know that antidepressants have an immediate effect; they increase transmitter levels in MA synapses. In the context of the monoamine theory, which states that depression is a result of diminished MA activity, this makes sense. But, as with antipsychotic medications, there is a substantial problem. The effect on reuptake is immediate—it takes place as soon as the drug gets to the synapse—but the antidepressants need to be taken continuously for 2 to 3 weeks before there is any relief from depression.

This delay must mean one of two things: (a) increased activity at MA synapses does not relieve depression and the MA theory of depression is wrong, or (b) antidepressants do not immediately increase activity at the MA synapses because something delays the effect for about 2 weeks.

When a synapse is overstimulated for a period of time, the postsynaptic cell may reduce the number or the sensitivity of receptor sites. This change, called *down-regulation* of receptors, depends on long-term changes in protein synthesis, as described in Chapter 4. It has been pointed out that down-regulation of some receptors has a time lag of about 2 weeks—the same delay as the therapeutic effect of antidepressants. This similarity has led to speculation that depression might be caused by supersensitivity of MA systems rather than low levels of transmitter and that

the antidepressants work by reducing this supersensitivity, that is, by causing the receptors to down-regulate (Lickey & Gordon, 1991, p. 226; Mobley & Sulser, 1981; Sulser, Vetulani, & Mobley, 1978).

Another possibility—and one that is now widely accepted—is that in serotoninergic synapses at least, increased levels of transmitter do not result in an immediate increase in firing. The presynaptic cell is equipped with an autoreceptor, a receptor that detects excessive amounts of transmitter in the cleft. When the autoreceptor detects excessive transmitter caused by the drug, it inhibits the release of more 5-HT (typically by reducing the influx of calcium at the terminal). Thus, reuptake inhibitors like the SSRIs do not cause an immediate increase in conduction at 5-HT synapses. It takes about 2 weeks for the autoreceptors to habituate to the presence of excess 5-HT, and only then does serotoninergic conduction at the synapse actually increase (Blier & de Montigny, 1994). Studies of the electrical activity at serotoninergic synapses have shown that acute administration of SSRIs does not increase activity; only after 2 weeks of chronic treatment will the electrical activity increase greatly. The delay experienced with other types of antidepressants may be a result of similar adjustment mechanisms.

The bulk of evidence supports the theory that (a) depression is a result of diminished activity in the 5-HT system in the brain, which runs from the Raphé nuclei through the medial forebrain bundle to the forebrain, and (b) mania is a result of excessive activity in this system. The situation is very complicated, however, and many other explanations of depression and mania exist. Alternate theories involve different neurotransmitters, such as GABA, ACh, and DA, and the balance achieved among levels of these neurotransmitters. Other theories suggest the involvement of second messengers, biological rhythms, hormone levels, stress, and the immune system (Janicak et al., 1993, pp. 211–219; Leonard, 1993; Maes & Meltzer, 2000; Ordway et al., 2002).

Mood Stabilizers and Antimanics

No one knows how lithium works, but it appears to stabilize the neurochemical mechanisms that control mood and to keep them from swinging radically between extremes. Lithium is known to do several things in the brain, including (a) altering the balance of ions such as Cl^- and K^+, which are important in the formation of resting and action potentials and post synaptic potentials, (b) altering the functioning of many transmitters, such as 5-HT, NE, DA, ACh, and GABA, and (c) inhibiting the second-messenger cyclic AMP. Lithium also has been shown to cause a down-regulation of some NE receptors (Bunney & Garland-Bunney, 1987). It is still not known which of these effects, if any, is responsible for the therapeutic effect of lithium, but the augmentation of serotonin and its effect on second-messenger activity are the promising candidates. Lithium is also known to stabilize membranes; that is, it makes membranes less excitable. This is a property it shares with the anticonvulsant drugs, and likely arises from (a) listed previously.

The anticonvulsant mood stabilizers valproic acid and carbamazepine and lamotrigine have different neurological effects. Valproic acid increases GABA levels in the brain by blocking *GABA-transaminase*, the enzyme that destroys GABA, but carbamazepine and lamotrigine prevent seizures by blocking sodium channels and inhibiting the release of glutamate and aspartate. Clearly membrane stabilization or inhibition is important in the effectiveness of drugs in treating bipolar disorder, but it is still not clear why.

EFFECTS OF ANTIDEPRESSANTS AND MOOD STABILIZERS

Effects on the Body

Unlike the psychomotor stimulants, the tricyclics do not stimulate the sympathetic nervous system. Instead, their anticholinergic effects block the parasympathetic nervous system, which uses ACh as a transmitter. These effects are characterized by symptoms such as dry mouth, constipation, dizziness, irregular heartbeat, blurred vision, ringing in the ears, and retention of urine. Excessive sweating is also common. Tremors are seen in about 10 percent of patients receiving the tricyclics. Side effects are usually worse during the first 2 weeks of treatment or when the dose is increased suddenly. Older patients are also more likely to show confusion and delirium; incidence can be as high as 50 percent in patients over 70 (Baldessarini, 1985, p. 191). Extrapyramidal symptoms or parkinsonian symptoms, similar to the side effects of antipsychotics (see Chapter 13), are unusual with tricyclics but have been reported (Gill, DeVane, & Risch, 1997).

The SSRIs may cause nausea, headache, nervousness, and insomnia, all of which, apart from the insomnia, tend to disappear with time. More serious is the danger of *serotonin syndrome*, which is caused by an acute increase in serotonergic transmission. Serotonin syndrome is characterized by such cognitive symptoms as disorientation, agitation, and confusion, in addition to autonomic symptoms such as fever, shivering, or diarrhea. Extrapyramidal symptoms (see Chapter 13) may also be part of the symptomology. Serotonin syndrome can be caused by SSRIs alone, but it is most often seen when antidepressants are coprescribed with other medications that alter serotonergic activity or when patients taking antidepressants combine them with psychostimulants such as amphetamine or cocaine. In some cases, an insufficient *washout time* (the time allowed for a drug to be eliminated from the body) when medications are changed can cause serotonin syndrome (R. Lane & Baldwin, 1997). This may happen when patients are changed to another antidepressant from fluoxetine, which has a particularly long half-life.

Patients taking the tricyclics often report an increase in appetite and an increased preference for sweets, accompanied by an increase in body weight. One study reported an increase of 1.3 to 2.9 pounds per month. In fact, excessive weight gain has been reported to be the major reason why patients stop taking these drugs. The MAOIs and lithium also cause weight gain, but the opposite effect has been reported with the SSRIs, which are sometimes used to treat obesity and help with weight loss (Boyer & Feighner, 1991, p. 142).

MAOIs alone do not have very marked effects apart from a lowering of blood pressure and *postural hypotension* (fainting or dizziness when moving to a standing position after being seated or lying down). Unfortunately, MAOIs interact with many other drugs. Drugs like amphetamines, decongestants, and nose drops that cause the release of NE (see Chapter 11) are potentiated by MAOIs because they block the metabolism of NE, which then accumulates. In some cases, they block the metabolism of the other drugs or may interact with them in unexplained ways. Drugs potentiated by MAOIs include alcohol and some opiates.

Another problem with MAOIs is that MAO not only destroys the MAs but also is responsible for the digestion of some substances in food. One of these substances is *tyramine*, which is found in aged cheese, pickled herring, beer, wine, and chocolate. After eating such foods when MAO is inhibited, tyramine accumulates in the body and causes high blood pressure, which in turn can cause headaches, internal bleeding, and even stroke or death. As a consequence, people on MAOIs have always had to watch their diet closely and were at some risk.

There are actually two types of MAO: *MAO-A* is responsible primarily for the breakdown of the 5-HT and NE, and *MAO-B* is most active in metabolizing DA. MAO-A is located in the intestine and normally metabolizes the tyramine just after it is consumed. Any tyramine missed by the intestinal MAO-A is destroyed by MAO-B in the liver and the lungs before it gets into general circulation throughout the body. Normally, less than 1 percent of tyramine gets past this MAO and into the system (Fitton, Faulds, & Goa, 1992). The older MAOIs blocked both forms of MAO, but new MAOIs like moclobemide selectively block MAO-A and have a minimal effect on MAO-B. As a result, tyramine that gets past the inhibited MAO-A in the intestine can still be metabolized by the MAO-B in the liver and lungs. Selective MAO-A inhibitors are, therefore, much safer, and patients do not have to be as careful with their diet (Fitton et al., 1992). It also helps if the pill is taken after eating, allowing any dietary tyramine to be metabolized before the MAOI has its maximum effect.

As many as 90 percent of patients on lithium have complaints about unwanted physical effects. The most common are hand tremors, increased thirst, nausea and vomiting, diarrhea, swelling, and weight gain. After extended treatment, patients may experience fatigue and muscle weakness. Another problem associated with long-term use is kidney damage.

The anticonvulsant drugs used as mood stabilizers—carbamazepine and valproic acid and lamotrigine—can cause frequent urination, nausea, and vomiting and in higher doses can cause tremors (Calabrese & Bowen, 2000). Other side effects include weight gain, hair loss, and dizziness, and lamotrigine causes a rash in about 10 percent of patients (Julien, 2001).

Effects on Sleep

Strangely, the tricyclics cause sleepiness, although this may have more to do with their anticholinergic properties than their MA-stimulating effects. Unlike the antidepressant effect, which takes days to develop, a single dose of a tricyclic can cause drowsiness and is sometimes prescribed to treat insomnia. The drug does not, however, increase total sleeping time. High doses of tricyclics at bedtime can cause nightmares.

Many antidepressants, like fluoxetine and venlaxafine, reduce REM time significantly, although some do not seem to have any effect on REM (Spiegel & Aebi, 1981, p. 116). Bupropion actually increases REM sleep (DeVane, 1998). Reduction in REM sleep may be associated with a drug's antidepressant effects because it has been shown that sleep deprivation, particularly REM deprivation, can actually decrease symptoms of depression temporarily, and sleep can make depression worse (Janicak et al., 1993, p. 322).

Fluoxetine is reported by some patients to increase the vividness of their dreams. While some enjoy this side effect, others find it disturbing.

EFFECTS ON THE BEHAVIOR AND PERFORMANCE OF HUMANS

Subjective Effects

The antidepressants do not produce euphoric or even pleasant effects. At low doses, imipramine's effects are similar to those of the antipsychotics. It causes feelings of tiredness, apathy, and weakness. Higher doses produce impaired comprehension and a confusion that is described as unpleasant. Amitriptyline causes feelings of calmness and relaxation (Spiegel & Aebi, 1981, p. 64).

Lithium has few, if any, subjective effects apart from those associated with side effects such as nausea. Subjects sometimes report a feeling of mental slowing and difficulty in concentration (Judd, Squire, Butters, Salmon, & Paller, 1987, p. 1467).

Effects on Performance

Acute doses of the tricyclic antidepressants imipramine and amitriptyline can have detrimental effects on vigilance tasks and can cause cognitive, memory, and psychomotor impairment that seems to be related to sedation. These drugs should not be used by people who must drive, use heavy equipment, or do intellectual work. Some studies have shown improvement in cognitive functioning after chronic drug treatment, suggesting that these impairments show tolerance. Other studies, however, have not (Lickey & Gordon, 1991, p. 230).

There is evidence that moclobemide impairs psychomotor performance, but there is no evidence of any impairment by the SSRIs (Mattila, Mattila, & Nuotto, 1993, p. 181).

Extensive systematic studies of mental abilities after acute and chronic lithium administration indicate a small but significant slowing of mental processes. There appear to be few effects on performance of tasks and reaction time. The difficulty appears to be in a slowing of information processing and memory (Judd et al., 1987, p. 1468; Kocsis et al., 1993). The anticonvulsant drugs also cause a slowing of cognitive function and learning and can be sedating.

Effects on Personality

In 1990, fluoxetine (Prozac) attracted national attention by appearing on the cover of *Newsweek*. Quoted in that issue was a psychiatrist, Peter Kramer, who had written about giving fluoxetine to people not to treat depression but to modify their personalities. Prozac "seemed to give social confidence to the habitually timid, to make the sensitive brash, and to lend the introvert the social skills of a salesman" (P. D. Kramer, 1993, p. xv). Kramer quoted one of his patients as saying that the drug had made him feel "better than well." He also coined the term *cosmetic psychopharmacology*, suggesting that people could take drugs such as fluoxetine to cover, by neurochemical means, some aspect of their personality that they were not satisfied with in the same way that facial blemishes could be hidden by makeup or the shape of a nose could be made more attractive by cosmetic surgery.

It has been established that fluoxetine and other SSRIs are useful in treating people with diagnosed personality disorders, such as obsessive-compulsive personality, and with compulsive behaviors (Gitlin, 1993). However, the use of fluoxetine and SSRIs as a personality cosmetic for people who do not have a diagnosed disorder but are not happy with their personality is a matter of some debate. It raises a number of interesting issues, not the least of which concerns the origins of personality. If a drug can cause such immediate and profound changes in personality, this effect has far-reaching implications for the way we view personality. Is our personality determined by our past, our childhood experiences, and the like, as many theorists have believed for years, or is it determined by 5-HT levels in the Raphé nuclei (P. D. Kramer, 1993)?

Some patients who have used fluoxetine as a personality cosmetic have become disenchanted with the changes in themselves over a period of time and have discontinued the drug because they felt that it had taken some of the edge or tension out of their lives and made them too bland.

Effectiveness in Treating Depression

There is little doubt that antidepressants are effective in treating depression. Numerous clinical trials have shown that many of these drugs are more effective than a placebo, although there is often a strong placebo effect seen in these studies. A recent meta-analysis of clinical trials with antidepressants has shown that the percentage of patients with major depressive disorder that responded to antidepressant treatment was 50.1 percent, while the percentage in the placebo control group was 29.7 percent. Interestingly, this study found that the percentage of responders in the placebo group has been increasing over the past 20 years (Walsh, Seidman, Sysko, & Gould, 2002).

There are considerable individual differences in the effectiveness of different drugs as well as differences in the way that different types of depression respond to different antidepressants. There are also considerable differences in the severity of different side effects in different individuals. This is one reason why there are so many different antidepressant drugs. It is often necessary to change a drug treatment several times to find a drug and a dose that works for a specific person (Rush & Ryan, 2002).

Advances in antidepressant drugs have usually involved the development of drugs which have fewer side effects rather than drugs with new or novel mechanisms of action, greater therapeutic effectiveness, or faster onset (Ordway et al., 2002).

There has been a considerable interest lately in the use of antidepressants in treating depression in children and adolescents. A number of studies have shown that the TCAs are generally not effective in this population, but the SSRIs do work with children. As with adults, children show a very high rate of placebo effect (between one-third and one-half of the patients in the placebo group improve). Fluoxetine is the only SSRI that

has been shown to be effective at a higher rate than placebos, but there are problems. It is been observed in these studies that there is a higher rate of adverse symptoms in the SSRI group than in the placebo group (1 to 6 percent vs. 0 to 4 percent). These include agitation, hyperactivity, and symptoms of mania.

EFFECTS ON THE BEHAVIOR OF NONHUMANS

Conditioned Behavior

Tricyclic antidepressants are more effective than methamphetamine in increasing operant response rates. They even appear to increase high rates where amphetamine tends to decrease them (Dews, 1962).

The tricyclic antidepressants tend to decrease avoidance behavior at doses that have no effect on escape behavior (McMillan & Leander, 1976), thus making them similar to the antianxiety drugs and the antipsychotics. The tricyclics also do not increase punishment-suppressed behavior. If anything, they tend to decrease it. The tricyclics are similar to amphetamine and the psychomotor stimulants in this regard.

DISCRIMINATIVE STIMULUS PROPERTIES

Neither the MAOIs nor the tricyclics are discriminable at doses that produce most of their behavioral effects. However, at very high but sublethal doses, they can be discriminated. Lithium does not appear to have any discriminative stimulus properties (Overton, 1982, 1987). There does not appear to be any generalization between the antidepressants and the antipsychotics or any other drug class (J. Stewart, 1962).

The SSRIs and the NARIs, however, do have discriminate stimulus properties at therapeutic doses. Dekeyne and Millan (2003) trained rats to discriminate citalopram (an SSRI), bupropion (a dopamine reuptake inhibitor), and reboxetine (an NARI). They also found that antidepressants that blocked both serotonin and norepinephrine would substitute for either citalopram or reboxetine, but SSRIs generalize only to citalopram. Bupropion, the DA uptake inhibitor, did not substitute for either citalopram or reboxetine. Taken together with the observation that the MAOIs and the tricyclics do not appear to have any discriminable properties, this suggests that the stimulus properties of antidepressant drugs do not arise from their antidepressant properties.

The stimulus properties of citalopram were blocked by drugs that block 5-HT_{2C} receptors, and the reboxetine cue was blocked by NE alpha$_1$ antagonists, showing that the stimulus properties of these drugs arise from interactions with very specific receptors (Dekeyne & Millan 2003).

TOLERANCE

There are reports that the therapeutic effectiveness of some drugs may show tolerance in some individuals after a few months of use, but the extent to which this happens and its clinical significance is not clear (Baldessarini, 1985, p. 143).

Tolerance to the many of the side effects of the antidepressants usually occurs within several weeks, although tolerance may not develop to the tiredness reported to the SSRIs.

WITHDRAWAL

Sudden discontinuation of high doses of the tricyclics can cause withdrawal symptoms, which include restlessness, anxiety, chills, muscle aches, and akathesia, a feeling of a compulsion to move (Baldessarini, 1985, pp. 143, 192). For this reason, these drugs should not be discontinued abruptly.

Withdrawal from SSRIs has been reported. The symptoms include dizziness, light-headedness, insomnia, fatigue, anxiety, nausea, headache, and sensory disturbances. These symptoms may last for 3 weeks and can be relieved by resuming

antidepressant medication (Zajecka, Tracy, & Mitchell, 1997).

SELF-ADMINISTRATION IN HUMANS AND NONHUMANS

Neither the tricyclic antidepressants nor the MAOIs are self-administered unless prescribed by a physician for the treatment of depression. They are seldom sold illicitly on the street and do not appear to be used nonmedically. Apart from their medical application, neither the tricyclic antidepressants nor the MAOIs appear to be reinforcing to either humans or nonhumans (Griffiths, Bigelow, & Henningfield, 1980).

To determine whether imipramine has aversive effects, an experiment was conducted in which monkeys were able to avoid infusions of various doses of imipramine by pressing a lever. Imipramine was avoided only at very high doses. It appears to be one of the few drugs tested that has neither positive nor negative reinforcing properties (Hoffmeister & Wuttke, 1975, p. 425).

Interestingly, some of the second-generation antidepressants, particularly the SSRIs, have been successfully used to treat addiction to other drugs, including alcohol. Buproprion is marketed as Wellbutrin as an antidepressant but also as Zyban, a drug to aid people who want to quit smoking.

Compliance

Because depression is a chronic disorder, it is important to find effective ways of preventing relapses. If taken chronically, lithium is effective in preventing relapse. Chronic administration of therapeutic doses of most antidepressants has been shown to be an effective way of preventing relapse. Patients, however, must be willing to tolerate the side effects of the drug over an extended period of time. Comparative trials have shown that the SSRIs are far superior to any other antidepressants in terms of patients' remaining compliant to chronic drug regimens. This success was due to the comparatively low rate of unwanted side effects of the SSRIs (Tollefson, 1993).

HARMFUL EFFECTS

Reproduction

Early studies indicated that the tricyclic antidepressants can interfere with male sexual functioning, but they suggested that the problems are not extensive (Harrison et al., 1986). A later study, however, found evidence that the problem may be more serious than first thought. Monteiro, Noshirvani, Marks, and Elliott (1987) compared a group of patients of both sexes who were receiving the tricyclic clomiprimine for obsessive-compulsive disorder with a placebo control group. In response to general questions about sexual functioning, there did not appear to be any difference between the drug group and the controls, but when questioned more closely in a structured interview about changes in sexuality, nearly all (96 percent) of the drug group reported severe difficulties in achieving orgasm. No difficulties were reported in the control group. This effect did not seem to be a result of sedation or fatigue and did not show any tolerance. Delayed or impaired ejaculation has also been reported with the MAOIs (N. F. Woods, 1984, p. 439). Also, patients on SSRIs frequently report delayed ejaculation and loss of interest in sex.

ere is little evidence that the antidepressants any adverse effects to the fetus during preg- y in humans, but a teratogenic effect has noted in laboratory animals. As a general , antidepressants should be discontinued during pregnancy. In one study, pregnancy outcomes vomen on fluoxetine and tricyclic antidepres- ts were compared with a matched control g p. There were no differences in fetal malformations between the groups, but the women in the fluoxetine and tricyclic antidepressant groups were nearly twice as likely as controls to miscarry (Pastuszak et al., 1993).

Some antidepressants have been detected in breast milk of nursing mothers, but usually there is no evidence of the drug in the blood of the baby. It appears that the first-pass metabolism of the baby is able to get rid of the drug before it gets into its system.

Lithium is known to cause cardiac malformations in the developing fetus if taken early in pregnancy (Hollister, 1983, p. 195), so its use should be avoided if pregnancy is possible. Since it readily passes into breast milk, it should not be taken by nursing mothers. The anticonvulsants are also known to have teratogenic properties.

Violence and Suicide

Soon after fluoxetine was introduced to the U.S. market, there were reports that it induced intense, violent, suicidal preoccupations in some patients (Teicher, Glod, & Cole, 1990). In fact, Prozac-induced violence became a defense in some courtrooms and was the subject of extensive coverage by television talk shows. There have since been many high-profile court cases where fluoxetine in particular has been blamed by the defense for causing many terrible crimes.

The scientific evidence suggesting a link between fluoxetine and violence and suicide has largely been in the form of case studies. On the other hand, large-scale drug trials have actually shown that fluoxetine reduces the incidence of suicide and violence. The issue has not been clearly settled because it is difficult to research. Such drugs are often prescribed for people who are very agitated, depressed, and suicidal anyway. Suicide and violence after taking an antidepressant drug may represent only a lack of effect—an inability to prevent a suicide, not a drug-induced effect (Walsh & Dinan, 2001). In addition, if this drug causes suicide and violence in only a small number of people but reduces these acts in most others, large-scale studies that average across everyone would not detect it.

After being taken for 3 to 4 weeks, fluoxetine may induce an activating effect with racing thoughts, nervousness, and tremor (Boyer & Feighner, 1991). Sometimes this develops to the point where it is called *akathesia*, a movement disorder characterized by restlessness, agitation, an inability to sit still, and a compulsion to be continuously active. Akathesia is also one of the movement disorders seen after the administration of antipsychotics (see Chapter 13). Reports of violence and suicide seem to be associated with akathesia in certain individuals (Rothschild & Locke, 1991). Even though many large-scale studies have not shown increased akathesia caused by fluoxetine in the general population, studies with fluoxetine and teenagers and children have shown that it does occur more often after fluoxetine than a placebo (Vitiello & Swedo, 2005); consequently, the U.S. Food and Drug Administration and drug regulatory agencies in other countries have insisted that a warning be placed on SSRIs and other antidepressants that they could cause increased suicidal thoughts in children.

For most people, fluoxetine is relatively safe and effective, but, like any drug, it has the capacity to cause serious problems for some patients, and its use and dosage should be monitored closely, especially for the first few weeks.

Overdose

As described earlier, SSRIs in combination with other antidepressants or psychomotor stimulants can cause serotonin syndrome. If this syndrome is unrecognized and untreated, it can ultimately cause respiratory, circulatory, and kidney failure.

The tricyclics are the third most common cause of drug-related deaths, exceeded only by alcohol drug combinations and heroin. The toxicity of the tricyclics is due primarily to their effect on the contractility of the heart muscle. They have a therapeutic index of around 10 to 15. This is a serious concern, especially when these drugs are prescribed for people who are seriously depressed and contemplating suicide. There is considerable variability in the death rates attributed to drugs within the same class. Among the tricyclics, clomiprimine is relatively safe, but many deaths have been attributed to amitriptyline. Tranylcypromine, an MAOI,

is responsible for a high rate of deaths, but the rate of isocarboxazide fatalities is low (Leonard, 1993).

The SSRIs are considerably safer. No overdose deaths have been attributed to fluoxetine (Boyer & Feighner, 1991; Leonard, 1993).

CHAPTER SUMMARY

- There are two types of first-generation antidepressants: (a) monoamineoxidase inhibitors (MAOIs) and (b) tricyclic antidepressants. Second-generation antidepressants make up a diverse group that includes the selective serotonin reuptake inhibitors (SSRIs), norepinephrine reuptake inhibitors, dopamine reuptake inhibitors, and a variety of others. In addition, the element lithium is used in the treatment of bipolar disorder (formerly called manic-depressive psychosis) as well as drugs that were originally developed as anticonvulsants.

- Depression has symptoms such as loss of appetite, loss of energy, sleeping problems, intense feelings of guilt or worthlessness, and thoughts of suicide. For some, depression comes in cycles and alternates with mania, a state of elated hyperactivity. This condition is called bipolar disorder.

- The antidepressants are absorbed orally and reach peak blood levels in about 4 hours.

- Most tricyclics have very long half-lives; the half-lives of the second-generation antidepressants are usually shorter.

- All agents that act as antidepressants have the effect of increasing transmission at serotonergic synapses. There is a delay of about 2 weeks in the start of the therapeutic effect of the antidepressants. This could be due to serotonin receptor down-regulation or habituation of a serotonin autoreceptor.

- The MAOIs also block the destruction of toxic substances found in some foods. People taking MAOIs should not eat foods like pickled herring and some types of cheese; they can cause a buildup of tyramine. This is less of a problem with newer, reversible MAO-A inhibitors. Lithium also causes unwanted side effects such as thirst, tremor, and nausea.

- Clinical trials show that there is a high rate of placebo effect for antidepressants, but antidepressants are more effective than a placebo. SSRIs are the only antidepressants that have been shown to be effective in children, although there is a high rate of side effects.

- Increases in violence and suicide have been reported with SSRIs after they have been taken for several weeks. This is sometimes associated with restlessness and akathesia, especially in children and young people.

- Tolerance develops to many of the effects of antidepressants. Withdrawal symptoms are sometimes seen when the drug is discontinued abruptly.

- Antidepressants do not appear to be reinforcing in nonhumans and are never abused or taken for recreational purposes.

- The tricyclics and SSRIs have been shown to cause problems in sexual functioning; both sexes report difficulty in achieving orgasm. Lithium has been shown to cause cardiac malformations in the fetus when taken by the mother early in pregnancy.

15

Cannabis

At first, a certain absurd, irresistible hilarity overcomes you. The most ordinary words, the simplest ideas assume a new and bizzare aspect. This mirth is intolerable to you; but it is useless to resist. The demon has invaded you . . .

—*Charles Baudelaire*

The hemp plant, or *Cannabis sativa*, was given its name and classification by Linnaeus in 1753. It is not known where the plant originated, but it was probably somewhere in central Asia. There are a great many varieties of cannabis, from small shrubs to bushy 20-foot-high plants. Commonly, the plants can be identified by their distinctive leaves, which are frequently long and slender and have serrated edges. There are male and female plants. The female plants are bushy and may grow quite tall. The male plants are smaller and not as bushy or vigorous. The female plant must be fertilized by pollen from the male flower to produce seeds. To help collect the wind-borne pollen, the female exudes a sticky resin from its flowering top. The resin also protects the seeds from heat and insects.

Since Linnaeus first classified *C. sativa*, there has been speculation about whether there was more than one species. Based on differences in form and potency, some botanists have identified three species: *C. sativa*, *C. indica*, and *C. ruderalis* (Grinspoon & Bakalar, 1993). Otherwise, it is speculated that there is only one species, *C. sativa*, of which there are two phenotypes (subspecies or varieties). One is traditionally cultivated in northerly areas for its fiber. It matures rapidly, has a low content of active ingredients, and is often called *hemp*. The other type is slow maturing, is traditionally cultivated in more southerly and tropical regions for its intoxicating properties, and has a relatively high content of psychoactive ingredients (Small, 1979).

THE CANNABINOIDS

The active ingredient in cannabis is usually reported as *delta-9-tetrahydrocannabinol* (delta-9-THC or $\triangle^9$-THC), but the chemistry of cannabis is much more complex. An entire family of drugs, called the *cannabinoids*, is found exclusively in cannabis, and each may contribute, directly or indirectly, to the behavioral effects of the cannabis plant. Over 60 cannabinoids have been identified (Grinspoon & Bakalar, 1997). The most common is delta-9-THC. Another cannabinoid is *delta-8-THC*, but there is relatively little delta-8-THC in cannabis compared to the delta-9-THC content. (The numbers in these names refer to the places where different parts of the molecule are attached. Because there are two different conventions for numbering the parts of the molecules, the same chemical can have two names. For this reason, you will sometimes see the active ingredients in cannabis called *delta-1-THC* and *delta-6-THC*. These are exactly the same as delta-9 and delta-8, respectively.) Other cannabinoids are drugs such as *cannabinol* (CBN) and *cannabidiol* (CBD), but by themselves these are not believed to have any important behavioral effects. The story, however, is not quite this simple because the amount of active ingredients appears to depend on preparation and route of administration, and these inactive ingredients may alter the potency or metabolism of more active ingredients.

Cannabis is sometimes taken orally, but usually it is burned and the smoke inhaled. It has been shown that burning changes many of the cannabinoids and appears to create new ones with increased potencies and effects. It is known, for example, that people can get high from smoking marijuana that contains virtually no delta-9-THC but is rich in CBD. Studies have shown that the inactive CBD is converted into delta-9-THC when the plant is burned, and new cannabinoids of unknown potency are also created (Kephalis, Burns, Michael, Miras, & Papidakis, 1976; Salimenk, 1976).

Not only are new cannabinoids created during burning, but more are created during digestion when the drug is taken orally and still more during metabolism. It is still not clear what effects each of these drugs has, how much each contributes to the effect that cannabis has on behavior, or how each of the cannabinoids interacts with the effects of other cannabinoids. Consequently, the effect of a particular cannabis plant cannot be predicted simply on the basis of the results of an analysis of its ingredients. As if things were not complicated enough, the content of marijuana changes over time, especially if exposed to light and air. With time, THC is apparently converted into CBN (Mechoulam et al., 1976). Recent research has shown that the major effects of marijuana smoke on mice—analgesia, hypothermia, and catalepsy—can be explained entirely by the presence of delta-9-THC and that these effects and blood levels of THC are not modified in any way by any of the other ingredients of marijuana smoke (Vavel, et al., 2005).

Cannabis Preparations

All parts of the cannabis plant contain THC, and the plant is prepared for consumption in various ways. The most familiar to North Americans is *marijuana*. The term *marijuana* is a Mexican–Spanish word that originally referred to a cheap tobacco but later came to refer to the dried leaves and flowers of the cannabis plant. Marijuana is usually smoked in a cigarette, cigar, or pipe but is sometimes baked into cookies or brownies.

In India, a distinction is made between *bhang* and *ganja*. Bhang is similar to marijuana. It is the dried leaves of uncultivated cannabis plants or female plants from which the resin has been removed. Generally, bhang is not very potent. Ganja, made from the tops of female plants from which the resin has not been removed, is three to four times more potent than bhang. In the West Indies, cannabis was imported directly from India, and the Indian term *ganja* rather than the North American *marijuana* is used. In Jamaica, *ganja* refers to the entire cannabis plant, and no distinction is made between ganja and bhang.

Hashish, also known as *charas* in India, refers to the dried resin from the top of the female plant. It is a pale yellow sap when harvested but turns almost black when dried. It may be consumed in a number of ways. Frequently, it is smoked, either alone or in a mixture with tobacco, or it may be baked in candies or cookies.

A purified variation of hashish is *hash oil* or *red oil*, which is prepared by boiling the hashish in alcohol (or some other solvent), filtering out the residue, and then permitting the alcohol to evaporate. The cannabinoids are highly soluble in alcohol, which extracts them from the hashish and concentrates them. Depending on the degree of purity, hash oil may range from black or red to light amber. Hash oil is much more concentrated than hashish. It may contain up to 60 percent cannabinoids, and because it is easier to smuggle, it is becoming more popular. Hash oil may be consumed in several ways. It is common to place a drop on the paper of a regular tobacco cigarette, which may then be smoked inconspicuously. Other ways involve placing a drop on hot tinfoil and inhaling the smoke.

Marijuana samples seized in the 1960s contained, on average, 1.5 percent THC, but the average THC content increased throughout the 1980s to 3.0 to 3.5 percent (U.S. Department of Health and Human Services, 1995). In 1994, it was 3.5 percent THC. Since that time, there appears to have been about a 50 percent average increase in potency. Data from the Potency Monitoring Project indicate that the average THC content of commercial-grade marijuana was 5.03 percent in 2001 and 5.14 percent in 2002. The THC content in crossbred and hydroponically grown marijuana such as *sinsemilla* can be as high as 11.4 percent (National Drug Intelligence Center, 2005a). The increase in average potency is a result of the increased frequency of sinsemilla and high-potency marijuana found in police seizures. Between 1994 and 2002, samples of marijuana testing at higher than 9 percent THC increased more than 600 percent according to data from the Potency Monitoring Project (National Drug Intelligence Center, 2005a).

Extracted and Synthetic Cannabinoids

Pharmaceutical companies have developed cannabinoids for use as medicines. Some of these contain natural cannabinoids extracted and purified from the cannabis plant. One of these is *Sativex*, developed by a British company and granted a license for use in Canada in 2005 for treatment of neuropathic pain associated with multiple sclerosis. It contains THC, which the company calls *tetranabinex*, and cannabidiol, which they call *nabidiolex*. Sativex is administered in the form of a spray squirted under the tongue.

Several synthetic drugs similar to the cannabinoids have been developed, and some are licensed for commercial use. The first was *synhexyl* (called *parahexyl* in Great Britain). *Nabilone* is now used clinically to alleviate nausea and distress in patients receiving chemotherapy for cancer, and a synthetic THC, *dronabinol* (Marinol), is used for the same purpose. Other substances such as *levonantradol* have been developed but not marketed (Consroe & Sandyk, 1992). Another synthetic cannabinoid, *WIN 55212-2*, is now widely used in research. *SR-141716A*, more recently called *rimonabant*, is a synthetic that blocks the main cannabinoid receptor in the central nervous system (CNS) and is an antagonist to cannabinoids (D. Smith, 1998).

HISTORY

It is believed that cannabis originated in central Asia, but its early history is difficult to trace because it was cultivated and widely dispersed long before recorded history. The spread of cannabis appears to have occurred in the middle of the second century B.C. The people responsible were the Scythians, a warlike and mobile Middle Eastern tribe related to the Semites. The word *cannabis* is a Scythian word, and the Greek historian Herodotus described the Scythians as having used cannabis. He explained how the Scythians would enter their tents, throw hemp seeds on heated stones, inhale the vapors, and "howl with joy." This procedure was used as a cleansing ceremony after funerals (Benet, 1975).

The Scythians spread cannabis into Egypt by way of Palestine and northward into Russia and Europe, where the Scythian custom of burning cannabis seeds after funerals still remains (Benet, 1975).

In China, cannabis has been known since Neolithic times, about 6,000 years ago. The Chinese word for hemp, *ma*, has been in use for at least 3,000 years. The plant was cultivated for its fiber; for its seed, which was a staple grain; for its intoxicating effects; and for its medicinal effects (Li, 1975, p. 56).

Cannabis has been used for centuries in India. Its use spread there directly from China rather than from the Middle East. From India, the drug was introduced to Africa by Arab traders who sailed along the east coast of Africa in the twelfth century. It spread across Africa along with the cultural influence of Islam. In Africa, it is known as *bangi* or *dagga* (Toit, 1975). Hemp was introduced into Russia and Eastern Europe by the Scythians. From there, it spread into Western Europe, where it was grown for centuries without its intoxicating properties being widely recognized. It was grown chiefly for its fiber, from which rope was made. It was also commonly used as a medicine.

Despite the fact that cannabis has been used as a folk remedy wherever it has been grown, scientific medical attention was not directed toward the drug until 1839 when W. B. O'Shaughnessy, a young chemistry professor at the University of Calcutta, tried it out on various ailments. He reported that hemp was an effective anticonvulsant and an appetite stimulant. There followed a series of papers that expounded the usefulness of hemp in the treatment of a number of disorders, including tetanus, neuralgia, dysmenorrhea, asthma, gonorrhea, and migraine. It was also reported to be useful in treating addiction to alcohol, opium, and chloral hydrate, and there were claims that hemp might be useful in the treatment of mental illness. One of the earliest of these claims was made in 1845 by the French physician J. J. Moreau de Tours, who used it to treat melancholia, hypomania, and other forms of mental illness (Moreau, 1973). In England, Sir John Russell Reynolds, president of the Royal College of Physicians and physician to Queen Victoria, used marijuana extensively in the treatment of neurological disorders (Consroe & Sandyk, 1992).

In general, the intoxicating effects of the drug remained unnoticed by Europeans until the publication of *Le Club des Hachichins* by the French writer Théophile Gautier in 1846. Gautier was a romantic and flamboyant writer who once offered a reward to anyone who could invent a new pleasure. The reward was earned (but we do not know whether he ever collected) by J. J. Moreau de Tours, the physician just mentioned. Dr. Moreau introduced Gautier to Le Club des Hachichins and gave him his first hashish with the words, "This will be subtracted from your share in Paradise." Gautier's account of the effects is now a classic description of the drug experience.

The drug that Gautier used was imported from the Middle East and North Africa. No one made the association between hashish and the quantities of hemp that were being grown at that time all over Europe to make rope. Even though he recognized that the two plants were related, Moreau believed that hemp and hashish were different. (What the members of the club received was not cannabis resin or what we now call hashish. Moreau used the term *hashish* to refer to a product made by boiling the plant in butter.)

In the era of European imperialism, rope was a very important item. Empires were built on naval strength, and ships could not sail without rope. Hemp did not grow well in England, so its production was encouraged in the American colonies. Sir Walter Raleigh was ordered to grow hemp in his Virginia colony, and consequently a crop was planted alongside tobacco in 1611, the colony's first season. American hemp proved to be of good quality, and hemp became a staple crop of the American colonies for more than 200 years. One of the better-known hemp growers was George Washington.

It is believed that the use of the cannabis plant for smoking and the word *marijuana* were introduced into the United States by Mexican laborers in the early twentieth century. Marijuana smoking spread slowly through the United States, but only among racial minorities and jazz musicians. This association did much to shape the perceptions of white legislators and to motivate opponents. In the 1920s, marijuana started to attract the attention of the authorities and the public, which almost universally condemned it. Alarmist stories appeared in newspapers attributing criminal activity to the drug, especially crimes of violence.

Because there was a shortage of reliable scientific data to the contrary, these accusations went unchallenged. By 1937, most states had laws against marijuana, and the U.S. government had passed the Marijuana Tax Act, which imposed prohibitive taxes on possession and use, effectively eliminating the legitimate medical use of marijuana, and driving recreational users underground. Soon, most other Western countries had antimarijuana laws. In Canada, marijuana is classed as a "narcotic" and included in the Narcotic Control Act with the opiate drugs (and cocaine).

The medical profession, represented by the American Medical Association, has always supported the position of the U.S. government. In 1970, one result was the Controlled Substances Act, which ignored the previous century of accumulating medical evidence and declared that marijuana had no potential medical use but had a high potential for abuse.

In spite of these laws (or perhaps because of them), the popularity of marijuana continued to grow until it reached its peak in the 1970s and started to level off. Throughout the 1980s and early 1990s, use in the United States declined considerably, but that decline may be coming to an end (see the discussion later in this chapter).

ABSORPTION

Oral Administration

THC is a weak acid with a pKa of 10.6; consequently, it is not ionized at body pHs. The cannabinoids are extremely lipid soluble—in fact, they will hardly dissolve in water. When marijuana is taken orally, the cannabinoids are absorbed from the digestive system rather slowly. Oral absorption may be aided by adding oil to the plant material before consumption. This is often done by baking it in a food, such as cookies or brownies. When THC is taken orally in the form of a pill (Marinol is a synthetic THC dissolved in sesame oil), absorption is also incomplete and erratic, and there is considerable first-pass metabolism (D. Smith, 1998, p. 128). For this reason, the dose must be doubled or tripled to have the same effect as when inhaled (Institute of Medicine, 1982, p. 21).

The peak effects after oral administration usually occur 1 to 3 hours after ingestion and may last 5 hours or longer (Agurell, Lindgren, Ohlsson, Gillispie, & Hollister, 1984; Paton & Pertwee, 1973). Oral administration is also more likely to cause nausea or vomiting (Grinspoon, 1969).

With an interest in the use of cannabinoids for medicinal purposes, pharmaceutical companies are developing ways of delivering cannabis preparations that have more rapid absorption. Sativex, for example, is delivered as a spray under the tongue, but absorption is still not as fast as with inhalation. Cannabis inhalers are being developed, but none are commercially available.

Inhalation

Smoking cannabis plant material is an efficient route of administration. Usually the material is hand-rolled in a paper and the *joint* consumed in the manner of a tobacco cigarette. Hashish is often mixed with tobacco and smoked as a joint, but more often it is smoked in a pipe. A water pipe known as a *bong* is often used. It cools the smoke and prevents the loss of the drug through sidestream smoke. Hash oil is placed on joints or tobacco cigarettes or heated on tinfoil, and the fumes are inhaled.

Normal smoking causes about 10 to 25 percent of the cannabinoids in a marijuana cigarette to enter the lungs, and virtually all of that enters the body (Agurell et al., 1986). Blood levels of THC peak within 15 minutes. Effects may begin to be felt within a few minutes and reach a peak after 30 to 60 minutes.

Because of a widespread belief that absorption increases with the duration of each puff, experienced marijuana smokers will take a deep draw on the marijuana cigarette and then hold the smoke in the lungs for 10 to 20 seconds. Actually, holding the smoke in the lungs may not contribute much to absorption of THC. It appears that the depth of an inhalation is much more important than duration in determining THC absorption (Azorlosa, Greenwald, & Stitzer, 1995).

DISTRIBUTION

Because of their high lipid solubility, the cannabinoids are distributed to all areas of the body according to blood flow but tend to become concentrated in the lungs, the kidneys, and the bile of the liver. Only about 1 percent of the administered dose at peak blood concentrations actually enters the brain. This amounts to 2 to 44 micrograms (Adams & Martin, 1996).

Figure 15-1 shows the rated "high" produced by different doses of THC administered by different routes. This peak high lags behind the peak blood levels of THC (Adams & Martin, 1996). The effect may be delayed because THC levels in the brain continue to increase for several hours after the drug has been consumed.

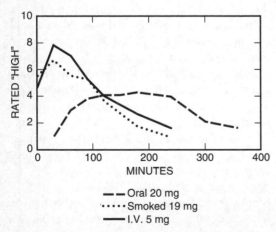

Figure 15-1 The time course for intensity of a subjective "high" after consuming various doses of THC via different routes of administration. (Adapted from Agurell et al., 1986)

EXCRETION

Metabolism starts as soon as the cannabinoids enter the body. There is some metabolism in the lungs if the drug is inhaled and some in the intestines if the drug is taken orally, but most of the metabolism takes place in the liver. Delta-9-THC is converted primarily into *11-hydroxy-delta-9-THC*, a substance that is believed to be more active than delta-9 and that penetrates the blood–brain barrier more easily (Adams & Martin, 1996). These substances are then rapidly converted into numerous other metabolites, some of which may have effects of their own. Some of these effects may be similar to those of THC, but others may be different. Most of these metabolites are less lipid soluble and are more easily excreted (Mechoulam et al., 1976).

CBD is thought to have only a slight effect of its own, but it appears to have a direct effect on the metabolism of THC. It blocks the enzyme that metabolizes delta-9-THC, slows its metabolism, and prolongs its duration of action. By contrast, CBN may speed the metabolism of THC (Mechoulam et al., 1976). It is also possible that CBD and CBN interact with THC in other ways. For example, these substances may alter the distribution of THC by displacing it from binding sites in the blood and increasing the amount of THC available for distribution to the brain (Siemens, Kalant, & Nie, 1976).

Blood levels of delta-9-THC and its main metabolites fall rather rapidly at first. This initial decline, due to redistribution, has a half-life of about 30 minutes in humans, but this is followed by a phase with a much slower rate of decline and a half-life of 20 to 30 hours (Agurell et al., 1986). During this phase, the rate of metabolism is limited by the rate at which the THC is released from body fat into the blood, which is quite slow. Traces may be detected in the body as long as 30 days later (Institute of Medicine, 1982, p. 20; Smith-Kielland, Skuterud, & Mørland, 1999).

It is still not clear whether regular cannabis users metabolize and excrete the cannabinoids faster than nonusers (Adams & Martin, 1996; Agurell et al., 1986). Research with laboratory animals has not shown that the development of tolerance is related to any change in cannabinoid absorption, distribution, or metabolism (Agurell et al., 1986; Dewey, Martin, & Harris, 1976).

NEUROPHARMACOLOGY

Until the late 1980s, the mechanism by which cannabinoids alter neural functioning was a mystery. There was plenty of evidence that they work at a receptor site, but receptor sites for cannabinoids had never been identified. In 1990, an announcement was made that a receptor for cannabinoids had been identified by two scientists at the National Institute of Mental Health in Bethesda, Maryland. The scientists had been working on different problems independently in adjacent labs in the same building.

Researchers in the laboratory of Miles Herkinham had been working with the synthetic cannabinoid levonantradol, which had been made radioactive so that its location could be mapped in the brain of rats. Using this technique, the scientists in Herkinham's lab were creating a map of where levonantradol ended up in the brain and presumed that it was binding to a cannabinoid receptor at these sites.

In the neighboring laboratory of Tom I. Bonner, Linda Matsuda had discovered a gene that would make a receptor. The goal was to find a receptor for substances that modulate pain, but their receptor did not bind any known pain neurotransmitter; in fact, it did not seem to bind any known neurotransmitter. Matsuda knew, however, exactly where in the brain these receptors were found. She had made a map. When Matsuda heard of Herkinham's map, she went down the hall, and they compared maps. It was apparent in an instant that the two maps were similar; the mystery receptors were in exactly the same place in the brain where the radiolabeled levonantradol ended up. It did not take long for the two researchers to confirm that Matsuda's receptor was in fact a cannabinoid receptor (Restak, 1993).

Subsequent work has isolated at least two types of receptors, both of which are coupled to second-messenger systems that use cyclic AMP as the second messenger. The CB_1 receptor, the one identified by Herkinham and Matsuda, is found primarily in the CNS; the CB_2 receptor is located mainly outside the nervous system altogether (B. Martin, 2000; Munro, Thomas, & Abushaar, 1993).

The maps of Herkinham and Matsuda showed that CB_1 cannabinoid receptors are concentrated primarily in the cortex, hippocampus, cerebellum, and basal ganglia but occur also in the hypothalamus, brain stem, and spinal cord (Howlett, Evans, & Houston, 1992). CB_2 receptors are found in the spleen and the immune system (Mechoulam, Hanus, & Martin, 1994). These receptors are structurally different from those found in the brain, and they seem to be associated with the effects of cannabinoids on immune functions. This peripheral cannabinoid receptor also appears to be affected by CBN. These discoveries raise the possibility that there may be many other types of cannabinoid receptors, as there are with the receptors for other neurotransmitters and neuromodulators. Different types of cannabinoid receptors could mediate different cannabinoid effects and make it possible to develop medicines that selectively produce medically useful cannabinoid effects with a minimum of side effects.

Like the discovery of the opioid receptor, the discovery of the cannabinoid receptor has stimulated research into the nature of the endogenous ligand, the substance (or substances) that occurs naturally in the body and acts as the receptor. Such endogenous substances have been referred to as *endocannabinoids* (Di Marzo, Melck, Bisogono, & Di Petrocellis, 1998). The first endocannabinoid was identified by William Devane and Raphael Mechoulam at the Hebrew University of Jerusalem. They called it *anandamide* after the Sanskrit word *ananda*, meaning "internal bliss" (Mechoulam et al., 1994; Restak, 1993). These researchers have also found two more. One of these is *2-arachidonylglycerol*, more conveniently referred to as *2-AG*. THC is longer lasting and had a much greater effect on the cannabinoid receptors than the endocannabinoids.

These discoveries stimulated an explosion of research. Its full impact has yet to be felt, but it will likely lead to new drugs and medicines as well as a better understanding of where and how THC and the cannabinoids alter the functioning of the brain and change behavior.

Cannabinoid receptors and their endogenous ligand appear to function more as neuromodulators of many different neurotransmitters than as neurotransmitters themselves. CB_1 receptors are located mostly in neurons on the terminal boutons. That is, they are presynaptic, and the enzyme that destroys the endocannabinoids is located in the cell body and dendrites of the postsynaptic cell. This indicates that the endocannabinoids are a signaling mechanism between the postsynaptic cell and the presynaptic cell. What seems to be happening is that when the membrane of the postsynaptic cell is depolarized, this triggers the release of an endocannabinoid that acts at the CB_1 receptors on the presynaptic membrane, causing ion channels to open and consequently blocking the action potentials as they arrive. The result is that the presynaptic neuron is disabled. Thus, the postsynaptic neuron is able to shut down the presynaptic neuron. If the neurotransmitter released by the presynaptic neuron is inhibitory, this effect is called *depolarization-induced suppression of inhibition* or (DSI). If the transmitter is excitatory, it is called *depolarization-induced suppression of excitation* (DSE). This effect lasts for tens of seconds and affect other synapses in the area.

When THC is administered, it would have the same effect of shutting down both excitatory and inhibitory transmission in neurons that have these CB_1 receptors in the entire brain for a much longer period of time.

DSI and DSE operate on neurons that use many different neurotransmitters, including norepinephrine (NE), dopamine (DA), serotonin (5-HT), acetylcholine (ACh), histamine, opioid peptides, gamma-aminobutyric acid (GABA), and prostaglandins. In addition, cannabinoids are known to increase synthesis of NE, DA, 5-HT, and GABA. They can potentiate the actions of NE, ACh, GABA, and opiate peptides, and they can alter the functioning of receptors for NE, DA, and ACh. Not all of these effects, however, are likely to be mediated via the cannabinoid receptor; some may be achieved directly by other means (Pertwee, 1992).

Cannabinoid receptors are found in the nucleus accumbens, and it is clear that the THC increases DA levels and activity in the mesolimbic DA reward system. They perform this function by potentiating the effects of endogenous opioid peptides, which in turn function as neuromodulators of DA transmission. This effect appears to be responsible for the reinforcing effects of cannabinoids (Gardner, 1992; Tanda, Pontieri, & Chiara, 1997).

Cannabinoid receptors are also found in the cerebellum and basal ganglia, other parts of the extrapyramidal motor system, and the hippocampus. These anatomical findings correspond to what we know about the effects of cannabinoids on movement and memory.

The endocannabinoid system within the nervous system appears to contribute to many functions, particularly those involved in stress recovery. One review article concluded, "Thus, 'relax, eat, sleep, forget and protect' might be some of the messages that are produced by the actions of endocannabinoids, alone or in combination with other mediators" (Di Marzo et al., 1998, p. 528). There is also evidence that CB_1 receptors are important to the reinforcing effects and the development of physical dependence on opiate drugs such as morphine and heroin (Ledent et al., 1999).

Few cannabinoid receptors are found in the medulla in the brain stem. This is not surprising since we know that they have little effect on the breathing reflex (B. Martin, 2000).

EFFECTS OF CANNABIS

Effects on the Body

Low and moderate doses of marijuana have predictable physiological effects on most people. The most common effect is bloodshot eyes, caused by dilation of the small blood vessels in the whites of the eyes. This effect, which reaches a peak about an hour after smoking, causes no discomfort to the user. Heavy marijuana use can sometimes be detected because the user looks stoned—an appearance marked by a slight droop in the eyelids (Domino, Rennick, & Pearl, 1974).

Another effect is the sensation of having a dry mouth and a compulsion to drink, which frequently induces some users to drink alcoholic beverages while smoking marijuana. An intense feeling of hunger, known as the *munchies*, is strongest about 3 hours after smoking, when other effects have declined. This increase in appetite eventually appears to show tolerance; after a few weeks of continuous marijuana use, appetite is actually depressed.

Smoking marijuana also causes a reliable increase in heart rate, which can go as high as 160 beats per minute in some individuals. There are also unpredictable fluctuations in blood pressure and body temperature. Nausea and vomiting sometimes result, especially after the user has been moving around. At higher doses, headaches are sometimes reported (Paton & Pertwee, 1973).

Effects on Sleep

Marijuana causes drowsiness and increases sleeping time in humans, but higher doses interfere with sleep, causing restlessness and insomnia (Tart & Crawford, 1970). Habitual users may have difficulty getting to sleep (Paton & Pertwee, 1973). Low doses of marijuana cause slight changes in sleep-stage patterns, and many studies have found no effect on sleep. At higher doses, marijuana disrupts normal sleep stages, but when marijuana is discontinued, this does not cause the poor quality of sleep, frequent wakening, or nightmares often seen with barbiturate withdrawal (Feinberg, Jones, Walker, Cavness, & Floyd, 1975).

Medically Useful Effects

Some effects on the body that are not normally noticed have some medical usefulness. For example, THC reduces the pressure of the fluid in the eyeball. *Glaucoma*, a condition in which pressure in the eyes is too high, has been successfully treated with marijuana. In a rather famous case in the United States, a young man with glaucoma was prosecuted for growing marijuana but won his case by arguing that it was necessary to break the law in order to treat his glaucoma (Grinspoon, 1971, p. 397; Grinspoon & Bakalar, 1993, 1997, pp. 48–58).

THC can act as an *antiemetic* (a drug that stops nausea and vomiting). Nabilone and Marinol are now frequently used to treat the nausea and sickness of people receiving chemotherapy for cancer.

THC has been shown to be effective in treating movement disorders and *spasticity* (Braude & Szara, 1976, vol. 2; S. Cohen & Stillman, 1976; Institute of Medicine, 1982). People with damaged spinal cords and people suffering from diseases like multiple sclerosis often experience uncontrollable muscle spasms, loss of motor control, and pain. Clinical studies clearly show that cannabinoids are an effective treatment for this spasticity (Earleywine, 2000).

The cannabinoid system has recently been implicated in the modulation of pain responses. Synthetic cannabinoids can decrease the amount of glutamate released by neurons in culture (Shen, Piser, Seybold, & Thayer, 1996). CNS neurons in pain centers become less responsive to pain-inducing stimuli after administration of synthetic cannabinoids (W. R. Martin, Eades, Thompson, Huppler, & Gilbert, 1976). Finally, blockade of CB_1 receptors in the spinal cord increases sensitivity to pain as measured by the hot plate test (J. D. Richardson, Aanonsen, & Hargreaves, 1998). Together, these results suggest that endocannabinoids play a role as a natural analgesic by shutting off pain signals. Natural or synthetic cannabinoids may mimic this effect.

In a review of the literature on medical marijuana, Earleywine (2002) concluded that cannnabinoid drugs have been proven effective for the following conditions: glaucoma (although alternative treatments work better), nausea (although alternative methods work better but cost more), pain, spasticity, and diminished appetite and weight loss experienced by people with cancer and AIDS. Cannabinoids have a potential for use as a treatment for anxiety, arthritis, dystonia, insomnia, microbial infections, seizures, Tourette's syndrome, and tumors.

Many people who use cannabis for medicinal purposes inhale cannabis smoke. The rapid absorption of the cannabinoids allows them to get rapid effects and to titrate the dose they receive so that they can get maximum medicinal effect without side effects (for medicinal purposes, getting high is usually considered an undesirable side effect). Commercially manufactured cannabinoids such as Nabilone and Marinol are taken as pills and absorbed slowly, and have a delayed effect, making titration difficult. This is one reason why many users of medicinal cannabis prefer smoking marijuana to taking pills. In an effort to overcome this problem, newer medicinal cannabinoid preparations like Sativex are administered as a spray under the tongue and are absorbed much faster, making titration easier. Cannabinoid inhalers that would have much faster effects are also being developed.

Now that cannabinoid receptors have been identified, an increased understanding of how the cannabinoids produce their various effects may soon make it possible to isolate specific medically useful effects and design cannabinoids that will produce them without side effects (Consroe & Sandyk, 1992).

EFFECTS ON BEHAVIOR AND PERFORMANCE OF HUMANS

Subjective Effects

The first European writer to describe the effects of cannabis was Théophile Gautier, who was a member of Le Club des Hachichins of Paris in the middle of the nineteenth century (Gautier, 1966). Gautier's accounts must be considered with some skepticism because they were written primarily to entertain rather than inform. Gautier was an artist, not a scientist, and a rather creative and romantic artist at that. And again, the drug that Gautier and the other club members took was not what we know as hashish but the very potent *dawamesc*, made by boiling the cannabis plant in oil or butter. In addition, dawamesc contains *cantharis* (a supposed aphrodisiac also known as *Spanish fly*), which has unpredictable toxic effects (Grinspoon, 1971, p. 58). Gautier's experiences are, therefore, not typical of contemporary North American use, but much of what he reports is characteristic of the hallucinogenic effects of cannabis intoxication at high doses. Gautier's account is a classic, and in spite of its embellishments and inaccuracies, it has shaped the expectancies and prejudices of users and opponents through the years.

Later, Charles Baudelaire, another member of the club, published his accounts of the hashish experience. Other classical descriptions were written by Fitzhugh Ludlow, the American son of an abolitionist minister and friend of Mark Twain, and the American traveler and diplomat Baynard Taylor (Ebin, 1961; Solomon, 1966).

Mood Changes and Getting High

A more typical experience with marijuana is characterized by swings of mood from euphoric gaiety with hilarious laughter to placid dreaminess. The experience is nearly always pleasant—a feeling of well-being and joyfulness is usually referred to as being high—but occasionally there are feelings of anxiety and foreboding, even at low doses in hospitable surroundings.

When cannabis is consumed socially, as it often is, there is frequent laughing and good humor. Almost anything seems funny, and the most innocent event or statement may ignite gales of contagious laughter. If the drug is taken alone or in a quiet setting, the user may spend time predominantly in a dreamy state getting off, or concentrating on, the subjective experience. It is frequently felt that perceptions are keener and that sensory effects are more intense and are enjoyed more. Just as slightly funny things seem hilarious, mundane thoughts and insights may take on great significance and importance. Artists and musicians frequently feel that their creativity is enhanced.

Although physical activity sometimes increases and users feel that their actions are effortless, they generally avoid tasks requiring effort and prefer instead to remain passive.

In spite of consistent reports from users that marijuana elevates mood, when subjective changes in feelings are measured systematically by a test like the POMS, findings are not at all clear-cut. Both positive and negative changes in mood have been reported (de Wit, Kirk, & Justice, 1998; R. T. Jones & Benowitz, 1976; Rossi, Babor, Meyer, & Mendelson, 1974), and the pattern of responding to mood scales appears to be unique. For example, in one study, smoking marijuana caused an increase in scales indicating stimulation and at the same time increased scores on scales associated with sedation. There were no changes in scales indicating euphoria or positive mood states (Chait et al., 1988). The subjective effects of smoked marijuana and oral THC are similar, except for their time course (Chait & Zacny, 1992) (see Figure 15-1).

Many researchers believe that the reason for variability in subjective ratings between studies is that environment can have a considerable influence on how the drug changes mood. The effects of surroundings on mood have been investigated, but differences such as smoking in a neutral as opposed to a psychedelic environment or while watching television, listening to rock music, or carrying on a conversation had no effect on subjective self-ratings. One factor that does seem to be important, however, is the mood of others. In an experiment in 1978, mood self-ratings were not correlated with ratings of intoxication, but after subjects took marijuana, mood ratings were highly correlated with the mood of the other subjects in the experiment, whether they were high or not. Thus, it would seem that after smoking marijuana, a person becomes more susceptible to being influenced by the mood of others (Rossi, Kuehnle, & Mendelson, 1978).

Mood changes have been studied extensively in experienced users, but almost no attempts have been made to study the subjective effects of marijuana in naive subjects, even though one's first experience with the drug seems to be an important determinant of later use. One study of college students showed that those who reported positive effects at first experience were more likely to use the drug sooner the second time and use it regularly later (Davidson & Schenk, 1994).

Perception

One of the subjective effects of the cannabinoids is an increased sensory sensitivity, but subjective testing of sensory thresholds has found only decreases in sensitivity or no change in auditory, visual, and tactile thresholds (R. T. Jones, 1978). The cannabinoids also cause a loss of sensitivity to pain, which indicates that the drug has analgesic properties.

The time-distorting effect of cannabis has been demonstrated experimentally (Domino, Rennick, & Pearl, 1976). Weil, Zinberg, and Nelson (1968) found that three subjects out of nine judged a 5-minute speech to be 10 minutes long. Increases in subjective time rate (people experience time passing more quickly) is one of the most reliable behavioral effects of cannabis (Chait & Pierri, 1992).

Memory

Marijuana appears to have no effect on the ability to recall material already well learned or on recognition memory (the ability to recognize words or figures), but it does disrupt the ability to recall words or narrative material (Chait & Pierri, 1992). The problems occur primarily in short-term memory, in which information is held actively in the brain for short periods. While intoxicated with cannabis, people frequently show what has been called *temporal disintegration*— they lose the ability to retain and coordinate information for a purpose. If they are required to hold information in the brain for any length of time, it frequently gets lost before it can be used. It is not unusual, for example, for people under the influence of cannabis to start a sentence and then stop halfway through because they forgot what they started to say. When such things happen, others who have been using the drug are not likely to remember the initial idea either, and some very disjointed conversations result (Weil & Zinberg, 1969). Some users have described this inability to hold things in short-term storage by saying that thoughts come so quickly that it is difficult to keep from being distracted by them. It is quite likely that the deficits in short-term memory and the distorted time sense are related since memory helps with judging the passage of time.

It has been pointed out that the effects of cannabis on memory are similar to the symptoms of Korsakoff's psychosis, a neurological disorder seen in long-term alcoholics (see Chapter 6). Among the symptoms of Korsakoff's psychosis are a memory disorder and a disorientation in time that is caused by damage to the limbic system and hippocampus. This similarity has led to speculation that cannabis affects memory by blocking the functions of the hippocampus (L. L. Miller & Drew, 1974). This is a likely hypothesis in light of the fact that cannabinoid receptors are found in high concentrations in the hippocampus.

Attention

There also appears to be a deficit on tasks requiring vigilance or sustained attention, particularly if the task takes more than 50 minutes (Chait & Pierri, 1992). Just as cannabis creates an inability to retain thoughts, it also appears to make attention more distractible. Many researchers report that subjects are not able to concentrate on the tasks they are doing after being given marijuana. They are easily distracted, usually by events in their own minds. Being easily distracted can interfere with many different types of tasks (De Long & Levy, 1974).

Creativity

One of the subjective effects of cannabis is that it helps to improve appreciation of art, even art produced by the user. The widespread belief that the drug increases the creativity of artists may have arisen largely because the drug was widely used by musicians and artists. Nevertheless, there is no consistent evidence from objective research that creativity is enhanced (Chait & Perri, 1992) or that artists who use marijuana are more successful than artists who are not users (Grinspoon, 1971, p. 157).

Performance

Any attempt to summarize the effects of cannabis on the various measures of performance is nearly impossible. There is no doubt that certain tasks are impaired by high doses of the drug, but results are so variable that it is difficult to be specific. As we have seen, variability among experimental findings can arise from differences such as experience of subjects, instructions, motivation, setting, and dosage. These are only a few of the factors that can contribute to the confusion—and no doubt have done so (Chait & Pierri, 1992).

An example of this confusion can be found in experiments on hand–eye coordination, using a pursuit rotor wherein subjects are required to track a moving target manually. One experiment found that marijuana impaired this ability in novice subjects, but the performance of experienced subjects actually improved with marijuana (Weil et al., 1968). Findings like these are not unusual.

Another factor complicates the findings in performance tasks: Deficits in performance may not indicate a loss of the specific ability being measured. Many (but not all) experiments show an increase in mean reaction time. A careful analysis of the data, however, shows that the slowing is a result of a few rather long reaction times in an otherwise normal performance. These occasional long latencies appear to be due to lapses in attention and an inability to concentrate on the task rather than an inability to move the hand. In another experiment, subjects were required to pursue a moving dot on an oscilloscope screen with another dot that they could control by hand. Marijuana interfered with performance, but the interfering factor was a lack of motivation and interest in the task, not a lack of coordination.

One subject stopped following the moving dot and drew patterns on the screen with the dot that he controlled (Manno, Manno, Kiplings, & Forney, 1974).

Simple reaction time appears to be unaffected by marijuana. In complex and choice-reaction-time tests, accuracy but not speed is likely to be affected. Marijuana is often reported to impair hand–eye coordination tasks such as the pursuit rotor and tasks that measure both psychomotor and memory tests (e.g., the digit symbol substitution test) (de Wit et al., 1998).

Driving

Numerous studies have been conducted on the effects of marijuana on driving and flying, and most have reported impaired performance, although such effects are not reported for all individuals (Chait & Pierri, 1992; Klonoff, 1974).

Studies in a driving simulator have shown that marijuana has little effect on the ability to control a car, but it impairs the driver's ability to attend to peripheral stimuli. Thus, marijuana-intoxicated drivers might be able to stop a car as fast as they normally could, but they may not be as quick to notice things that they should stop for, probably because they are attending to internal events rather than to what is happening on the road (Moskowitz, Hulbert, & McGlothlin, 1976). One recent study of the effects of THC on driving in real traffic showed significant impairment caused by low doses of THC (100 and 200 micrograms/kg body weight). These effects were greatly amplified when small doses of alcohol were consumed as well (Ramaekers, Robbe, & O'Hanlon, 2000).

Performance Screening Tests

One concern raised about marijuana and driving is that it is not possible to do a roadside screening test for THC in the same manner as a breathalyzer test for alcohol. The State Police of Victoria in Australia have been developing a performance screening test for marijuana intoxication based on the test developed for alcohol in the 1970s called the *Standardized Field Sobriety Test*.

It consists of tests of *gaze nystagmus* (eye movements as someone follows a moving object with their eyes), the *walk and turn test* (where the subject walks heel to toe up and down a line), and a one-leg stand (where the subject stands on one leg and counts out loud). Performance on all these tasks is scored using objective criteria. This test was administered to three groups. One had been given a placebo, and the other two had smoked marijuana with low and high THC content. The test identified 2.5 percent of the placebo group as being intoxicated and 38.5 percent of the low-THC group and 56.4 percent of the high-THC group as being intoxicated. These results suggest that it should be possible to develop a reliable screening test for THC intoxication (Papafotiou, Carter, & Strough, 2005).

EFFECTS ON THE BEHAVIOR OF NONHUMANS

Unconditioned Behavior

THC has a biphasic effect on spontaneous motor activity (SMA); in many species, there is an increase in activity followed by a depression in behavior. The depressant effect is more powerful, appears in more species, lasts longer, and is more resistant to tolerance. Interestingly, the stimulatory effects appear to be an exaggerated response to environmental stimuli rather than a general increase in activity (de Wit et al., 1998). At high doses, the decrease in motion is called *ataxia* and is accompanied by a loss of motor control and by fine tremors. Laboratory animals assume one posture without moving for long periods. Monkeys stare into space or look at their hands and occasionally appear as though they are hallucinating (Paton & Pertwee, 1973).

One effect was noticed early in animal experimentation: a taming effect, or a reduction in aggression. Animals that were normally aggressive and hard to handle became tame and placid after receiving THC. THC will reduce the attack behavior of the dominant member of a pair of rats and will also diminish the ability of a submissive rat to defend itself in a fight. Predatory attack behavior of several species is also reduced.

In rats, THC causes a decrease in food intake and a subsequent weight loss. THC is about half as potent as amphetamine in suppressing food intake, but unlike amphetamine, THC causes an increased preference for sweet sugar solutions. This may be related to the munchies effect in humans (Sofia, 1978).

THC is as potent as morphine in reducing the response of laboratory rats to painful stimuli, as measured by a number of tests. CBN also has analgesic effects but is only as potent as aspirin. No analgesic effects were found for CBD (Sofia, 1978). The metabolites of THC are probably more potent than the parent compound. At one time, it was believed that these effects were dependent on interactions with the opiate system, but now it has been shown that the analgesic effects are mediated through systems in the brain and spinal cord and are independent of opiate pain control (de Wit et al., 1998).

Conditioned Behavior

As with humans, THC appears to interfere with tasks that require short-term memory, such as the radial maze and the *matching-to-sample test*, in which the animal is required to remember a stimulus for a brief period of time. These deficits in memory are correlated with suppression of firing of cells in the rat's hippocampus and can be caused by direct injection of THC into the hippocampus (Heyser, Hampson, & Deadwyler, 1993). THC has also been reported to interfere with schedules and tasks that require timing. Performance on other tasks appears normal until higher doses, which suppress all behavior, are reached.

Like the barbiturates and the benzodiazepines, THC decreases avoidance responding at doses that do not alter escape responding in a discriminated avoidance task, an effect it shares with the tranquilizers, anesthetics, and alcohol. One might expect that a drug that has both antianxiety and analgesic effects would increase punished behavior, but neither delta-9-THC nor delta-8-THC appears to increase behavior suppressed by punishment with electric shock (McMillan & Leander, 1976). In this regard, THC is very unlike the tranquilizers, anesthetics, and alcohol.

DISSOCIATION

Both delta-9-THC and delta-8-THC cause dissociation of an avoidance task in rats. Rats were unable to transfer to a nondrug state what they had learned in a drug state, and there was a symmetrical inability to transfer to the drug state what they had learned in the nondrug state (Henricksson & Järbe, 1971). Dissociation has also been demonstrated in humans using marijuana. In one study, subjects were asked to learn a list of words after taking a placebo and then to recall the list after smoking marijuana and vice versa. When the subjects acquired information in one state, they had difficulty transferring it to the other state. This effect was not very powerful because the loss of recall could be overcome by prompting and cuing the subjects by reminding them of word categories (Stillman, Eich, Weingartner, & Wyatt, 1976). In another study, only *asymmetrical dissociation* was found. Information acquired while the subjects were not intoxicated was remembered after smoking marijuana, but information acquired during marijuana intoxication was not remembered when sober (Darley & Tinklenberg, 1974).

Dissociation has not been demonstrated for motor skill and perceptual tasks such as card sorting, or on the pursuit rotor task or signaled avoidance, even though marijuana impaired performance on those tasks (Järbe & Mathis, 1992).

DRUG STATE DISCRIMINATION

Rats are easily able to discriminate THC from placebo when it is administered intravenously, intraperitoneally, or orally. The stimulus properties are evident as early as 7½ minutes after injection and peak at 30 minutes but are still reliable at 60 minutes. A training dose of delta-9-THC would generalize to delta-8-THC and the 11-hydroxy metabolite but would not generalize to CBD

(Balster & Ford, 1978), although some generalization occurs to CBN (Järbe & Mathis, 1992). Interesting interactions have been noted with these other naturally occurring cannabinoids; in some experiments, CBD has been shown to enhance and prolong the stimulus effects of THC (Järbe & Mathis, 1992).

Many other drugs have been tested to learn whether the THC response generalizes to them. There appears to be partial generalization to sedative drugs and no generalization to drugs of any other class, including stimulants, hallucinogens, and opiates. Cannabinoid discriminations can be blocked by the cannabinoid receptor antagonist SR-414716A. Interestingly, animals trained to discriminate THC generalized poorly to anandamide and then only when anandamide was given in high doses (de Wit et al., 1998).

Experienced marijuana smokers can easily learn to distinguish marijuana cigarettes containing 0 percent THC from marijuana cigarettes containing 2.7 percent THC. In one study, they were able to make the discrimination within 90 seconds of taking the first puff. They were successful in identifying marijuana containing 1.7 percent THC, but they identified a sample with 0.09 percent THC as a placebo (Chait et al., 1988).

TOLERANCE

In laboratory animals, tolerance to the effects of THC on operant behavior develops rapidly. Depending on the dose and the route of administration, complete tolerance may develop after 5 or 6 days of repeated injections of THC (Abel, McMillan, & Harris, 1974). This tolerance lasts for more than a month, and there is cross-tolerance between delta-9-THC and its 11-hydroxy metabolite (Kosersky, McMillan, & Harris, 1974). Tolerance also develops within a few days to increases in motor activity, but the progress is much slower for the depression in activity. There is no tolerance at all to the anorexia effects or the discriminative stimulus effects. There is also tolerance to the lethal effects in pigeons; a dose of 180 mg/kg had no effect on tolerant animals but was lethal in

naive pigeons (B. Martin, 2000). Tolerance does not appear to be due to alterations in absorption, metabolism, or distribution of the drug (Dewey et al., 1976). Instead, it is known that tolerance is associated with a decrease in the number of cannabinoid receptors in selected brain areas (B. Martin, 2000).

There is some disagreement about the development of tolerance in humans. Many marijuana users have reported a sensitization or *reverse tolerance* to the drug—they become more sensitive to the effects, rather than less sensitive, with repeated use. Reverse tolerance has never been shown in laboratory studies with nonhumans or humans. For several reasons, reverse tolerance is observed only outside the laboratory. One likely reason is a matter of dosage. In laboratory studies, dosage is carefully measured. Outside the laboratory, users calculate their consumption in terms of the number of joints they smoke. With experience, users learn to inhale more efficiently so that they are able to get more drug into their bodies from a given amount of marijuana. Therefore, they will require fewer joints to get high. In addition, experience may be required to learn not only how to get high but also the activities, situations, and company that contribute to the high. All these factors could contribute to the observation that over time, fewer joints are needed to get high.

Early experiments showed that tolerance to the subjective effects of THC and marijuana would develop only if the drug was given in high doses for an extended period of time (Frank, Lessin, Tyrrell, Hahn, & Szara, 1976; R. T. Jones & Benowitz, 1976), but more recent studies have shown that the subjective effects of both high and low doses of orally administered THC and high-potency smoked marijuana administered four times a day showed a considerable drop over 4 consecutive days (Haney, Ward, Comer, Foltin, & Fischman, 1999a, 1999b). In the same experiment, no tolerance to increased food consumption was seen.

WITHDRAWAL

Withdrawal symptoms have been seen after prolonged administration of high doses in nonhumans. These symptoms are not severe and frequently appear as an increase in motor behavior. Recently, it has been reported that cessation of chronic cannabinoid injection causes a marked withdrawal in rodents, but this withdrawal is usually masked by the long half-life of THC and its metabolites. If animals receive high doses of a synthetic cannabinoid for 2 weeks, no withdrawal is seen after administration stops. If the animals receive an injection that blocks cannabinoid receptors, however, withdrawal does occur as measured by release of stress hormones (de Fonseca, Carrera, Navarro, Koob, & Weiss, 1997).

Withdrawal symptoms, without the use of cannabinoid blockers, have been reported with humans. In an early study, human volunteers took high doses of oral THC every 4 hours for 12 days. When the drug was stopped, the subjects reported a sense of "inner unrest" after 6 hours. By 12 hours after the last dose of THC, subjects reported a variety of symptoms, including hot flashes, sweating, runny nose, loose stools, hiccups, and loss of appetite. Other symptoms that were noticed by the experimenters were irritability, restlessness, and insomnia (R. T. Jones & Benowitz, 1976).

More recent research, however, has shown withdrawal symptoms to smoked marijuana and oral THC after four doses per day for only 4 days. During the withdrawal period, subjects reported increased anxiety and irritability and decreased food intake and quality and quantity of sleep (Haney et al., 1999a, 1999b).

SELF-ADMINISTRATION
IN HUMANS AND NONHUMANS

THC is self-administered by humans, but until recently there have been no demonstrations of nonhuman self-administration (Griffiths, Bigelow, & Henningfield, 1980). Tanda, Manzar, & Goldberg (2000) trained squirrel monkeys to give themselves low does of THC, but it was necessary to train them to self-administer cocaine first. The problem seems to be that THC is not readily soluble in water, and this makes it difficult to administer just the right dose intravenously. After all, humans never inject THC. More success has been achieved with water-soluble synthetic cannabinoids like WIN55212-2, which is self-administered by mice (Lident et al., 1999). THC has also been shown to create a conditioned place preference in rats (Lepore, Vorel, Lowinson, & Gardner, 1995).

It is seldom difficult to get humans to take cannabis. In a hospital ward setting, Mendelson and his associates (H. H. Mendelson, Kuehnle, Greenberg, & Mello, 1976) conducted an experiment in which subjects were required to press a button to gain points with which they could buy marijuana cigarettes. A joint could be earned for about 30 minutes of work. Extra points could be saved for money at the end of the experiment. In this experiment were two groups of subjects: casual users and heavy users of marijuana. The number of joints smoked by each group was far less than the number available but showed a slight increase over the 26 days of the experiment. Casual users smoked about two joints per day at the beginning and increased to three by the end of the experiment. Heavy users started at four a day and ended at about seven. Apart from this slight increase, the amount consumed was fairly stable from day to day; no cyclic patterns or periods of abstinence were noted, although there was a big increase on the last day that marijuana was available. No evidence of withdrawal was seen when use was stopped. In this study, there seemed to be a level of high that most users tried to achieve, and they stopped when they achieved it. In other words, they appeared to titrate the dose.

Marijuana self-administration in humans in experimental settings has been demonstrated a number of times since then, but, curiously, it has not yet been shown that THC content is important. In one recent experiment (Kelly, Foltin, Mayr, & Fishman, 1994), marijuana cigarettes with 0 and 2.3 percent THC were smoked with equal frequency, even though self-reports of "high," "potency," and "liking" were higher for the THC-containing marijuana.

Titration

The ability of users to titrate the dose was studied in another experiment. Experienced marijuana users were given joints of different potencies and asked to smoke until they achieved a "nice high." To some extent, these experienced users did smoke fewer high-potency joints than low-potency joints before they stopped, but the compensation was far from perfect. The subjects smoked 60 percent more of the weak marijuana than the strong marijuana, but even after this compensation, they administered a 250 percent higher dose to themselves when the strong joints were available (Cappell & Pliner, 1974). On the basis of this experiment, even experienced users seem unable to adjust their intake accurately in the face of variations in the potency of the marijuana they are smoking. Doubt is also cast on the notion that there is such a thing as a "social high" that can be determined on the basis of an administered dose. Factors other than dosage must control marijuana intake.

Even though people in experiments will smoke an equal number of marijuana cigarettes with 0 percent THC and with 2.4 percent THC (Kelly et al., 1994), choice experiments have shown that the reinforcing effect of marijuana increases with higher THC content. In a preference study, experienced users sampled marijuana of two different potencies (0.63 and 1.95 percent THC). During the choice phase of the experiment, subjects chose the high-potency marijuana much more often than the low-potency marijuana (Chait & Burke, 1994).

EPIDEMIOLOGY

In North America, cannabis is a social drug. In the 1970s, most marijuana was smoked in groups. On some occasions, it may have been consumed in large public gatherings such as rock concerts or large parties, but most of the gatherings were of close friends and acquaintances. The drug was consumed in an almost ritualistic manner. A pipe or joint was passed from one person to another in a circle. Each person took a drag or, if already sufficiently high, passed it along. More recently, solitary use of the drug has become more common, and the ritualism has declined.

The social nature of marijuana may also be responsible for initiation to marijuana use. A very small percentage of users first smoke marijuana alone. There can be no doubt that the strong social reinforcement and the feelings of shared pleasure and intimacy contribute considerably not only to the start of drug use but to its continuation as well.

In some countries where cannabis is a traditional drug with a long history, the pattern and extent of use are quite different than in Europe and North America, where cannabis use is comparatively recent. In countries such as India, Egypt, Greece, Morocco, and Jamaica, the majority of cannabis users take extensive doses every day, and there is little casual use. In the United States, the vast majority of users are casual, and only a small percentage use it daily. Compared with other countries, relatively small amounts are consumed in North America. It has been estimated that a casual cannabis user can get "stoned" on 5 to 6 mg of THC, and the average daily user in the United States consumes about 50 mg of THC per day. The average daily user in Eastern countries consumes 200 mg per day. In addition, marijuana use is not as persistent in the United States as in other countries. Most westerners who start using cannabis eventually decrease their use and stop. In countries where use is more extensive, it may persist for 20 to 40 years.

According to the National Household Survey on Drug Abuse, between 1985 and 1992 the number of marijuana users in the United States declined from 9.3 percent of the population to 4.3 percent, and the number of frequent marijuana users (once a week or more) dropped from 4.6 to 2.4 percent (U.S. Department of Health and Human Services, 1994). This decline bottomed out between 1992 and 1994 (U.S. Department of Health and Human Services, 1995). While marijuana did not substantially increase between 1995 and 2000, marijuana disorders of abuse and dependence as diagnosed by the *DSM-IV* has increased

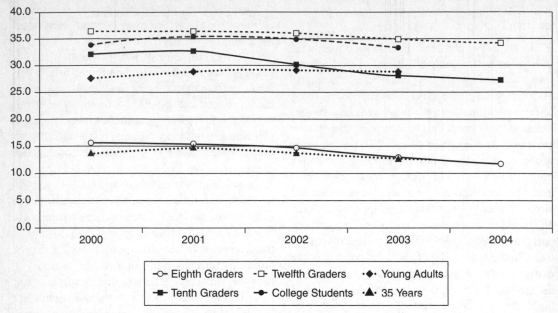

Figure 15-2 Trends in marijuana use in the United States for different age-groups between 2000 and 2004. (Adapted from National Drug Intelligence Center, 2005b)

(Compton et al., 2004). Marijuana was also increasingly involved in hospital emergency room cases during that time. The Drug Abuse Warning Network reported a 126 percent increase in marijuana-related incidents between 1995 and 2000 (NIDA, 2001). The increased potency of marijuana described earlier may have been causing problems for those who continue to use the drug.

Figure 15-2 shows changes in the percent of people in different age-groups in the United States who report using marijuana in the past year from 2000 to 2004. As can be seen, there appears to be a gradual but steady decrease since 2001.

HARMFUL EFFECTS

Cannabis is a drug of great controversy. Probably no other drug in recent times has generated more public concern and debate or stimulated more research into its safety (or lack of it). This body of scientific literature is highly specialized, confusing,

and often contradictory, and it is often misrepresented in the popular media, which have tended to publicize only selected research findings and to ignore others. Nonexperts have had difficulty keeping track of it all. People generally are confused, and those with particular biases have no trouble supporting their position.

The debate on the harmful effects of cannabis products has taken on a new dimension in recent times with the move to use cannabis as a medical treatment for numerous diseases and the tendency to "decriminalize" its use in countries like Holland and Canada.

Marijuana has been accused of having many harmful effects, some of which we shall discuss. It will be obvious to anyone who has read this section that cannabis, like any other drug, has a great number of effects on many systems of the body, some of which have the potential for great harm. It should also be obvious that even though the potential for harm exists, especially at high doses, there are very few hard data to show that the drug really does any harm. The lack of data may mean that there is no harm, but it may also mean that reliable data are difficult to collect.

Violence and Aggression

One of the oldest beliefs about cannabis is that it directly causes violence and aggression and is associated with crime, but there are absolutely no systematic data to support the myth. In long-term studies where marijuana was given to individuals in controlled hospital ward settings, increases in violence were never reported. In addition, mood rating scales generally showed decreases in feelings of hostility and increases in friendliness.

Numerous surveys and field studies, using a variety of techniques, have compared criminal behavior and crimes of violence in groups of marijuana users and nonusers, and in the vast majority of these studies no connection has been found. In fact, if there was a correlation, it was with a decrease in violence. For example, one study showed that among a certain population of young criminal males, marijuana was used specifically to reduce aggression rather than to increase it (Tinklenberg, 1974). Although there may be isolated cases of idiosyncratic or unusually violent reactions among some individuals after taking marijuana, these ordinarily occur in people with a prior psychiatric disturbance or when other drugs are used at the same time.

Mental Disturbance

When the drug is taken in larger doses than usual, the user may be overcome with overwhelming anxiety and paranoid feelings. Such a state often leads to a trip to a hospital emergency department. At higher doses, another reaction to cannabis is an *acute psychotic reaction*, a panic that arises from hallucinations and perceptual distortions. This effect is commonly referred to as a *freak-out*. Users lose touch with reality and feel that they may be going insane, and they panic. Freak-outs usually occur when the drug is taken in unusual and stressful circumstances, if more drug is consumed than the user is accustomed to, or if the cannabis is mixed with other drugs. Freak-outs are much more common with hallucinogens such as LSD than with cannabis. Patients usually can be effectively treated by being quietly "talked down," but in severe cases, a benzodiazepine tranquilizer can be effective (Dinwiddie & Farber, 1995).

What is not so clear is whether cannabis use can cause psychotic or schizophrenia-like illness in later life. A number of studies have shown that heavy cannabis users have an increased risk of suffering from schizophrenia in later life, but later research has suggested that this trend can be explained by the fact that cannabis may precipitate or speed up the emergence of schizophrenic symptoms in people who would have developed the disease in any case (Iverson, 2005). There is little evidence that cannabis use will generate psychoses in users unless they have a predisposing tendency to become schizophrenic. In fact, a study in Australia over a 30-year period has shown that the incidence of schizophrenia did not increase in spite of a drastic increase in cannabis use during that time (Degenhardt, Hall, & Lynskey, 2003).

Permanent Intellectual Impairment and Brain Damage

It is known that long-term heavy use of alcohol results in brain damage and a loss of mental functions; recently, there have been reports that the same outcomes might occur with marijuana. In North Africa and other places where cannabis is used for long periods at high doses, there are reports of *cannabis dementia*. One British study has even reported evidence of a shrinking of the brain, along with the loss of functions seen in alcoholics.

There is conflicting evidence from laboratory studies and experiments with nonhuman animals that exposure to high levels of cannabis might cause damage to nerve cells (Chan, Hinds, Impey, & Storm, 1998; Collins, Pertwee, & Davies, 1994; Silkker, Paule, Ali, Scarlett, & Baily, 1992), but there is no evidence that heavy cannabis use causes any irreversible damage to humans.

In an exhaustive review of the literature, Solowij (1998) concluded that in humans there is little evidence that long-term heavy use produces any severe or grossly debilitating impairment of cognitive functioning. However, the long-term use of cannabis may produce more subtle impairments in the higher cognitive functions of memory, attention, and the organization and integration of complex information. The nature and extent of these problems are related to the duration and extent of use. It is still not known the extent to which these deficits are reversible after abstinence (Solowij, 1998, p. 9).

Most of the research showing that cognitive effects of marijuana are reversible have been conducted in adults, but because so much marijuana is being consumed by teenagers and preteens, there is concern that marijuana use may have irreversible effects on a developing brain. One study suggests that these effects may be reversible. Fried, Watkinson, James, & Gray (2002), compared the IQ of a group of young people when they were 9 years old with their IQ at ages 17 to 19. Those who were using cannabis at the later time showed a decline in IQ, but there was no decline in IQ in people who had been heavy users and had stopped taking the drug. The IQ measure used, however, may not have been able to detect the subtle deficits described by Solowij. This is one area that requires further research.

Amotivational Syndrome

It has sometimes been observed that when a young person starts smoking marijuana, systematic changes occur in that person's lifestyle, ambitions, motivation, and, possibly, personality. These changes have been collectively referred to as the *amotivational syndrome*. Its symptoms are apathy, loss of effectiveness, and a diminished capacity or willingness to carry out complex long-term plans, endure frustration, concentrate for long periods, follow routines, or successfully master new material. Verbal facility is often impaired in both speaking and writing.

Such individuals exhibit greater introversion, become totally involved with the present at the expense of future goals, and demonstrate a strong tendency toward regressive, childlike, magical thinking (McGlothlin & West, 1968, p. 372).

There is no doubt that many young individuals have changed from clean, aggressive, upwardly mobile achievers into the sort of person just described at about the same time as they started smoking marijuana. What is not clear, however, is a causal relationship between the loss of middle-class motivations and cannabis. There is considerable evidence showing that users of cannabis is correlated with reduced educational achievement (Macleod et al., 2003).

Evidence for the existence of an amotivational syndrome has been found in an experiment in which rhesus monkeys were exposed to the smoke from marijuana cigarettes every day for a year (Silkker et al., 1992). These monkeys pressed a lever for banana-flavored food pellets on a progressive ratio schedule. Each time the pellet was received, the ratio requirement increased, and more presses were required (see Chapter 2). Silkker and associates found that during exposure to marijuana smoke, breaking points were considerably lower than they were for controls, and they returned to normal when exposure to the smoke was discontinued. Thus, the monkeys exposed to marijuana smoke were not as willing to work hard for an attractive food as nonexposed monkeys. Because the animals responded normally on other tasks for the same food pellets, the researchers argued that this result was analogous to the amotivational syndrome seen in humans and was not a result of either loss of the ability to respond or loss of appetite.

Laboratory studies with humans have found conflicting effects of cannabis on motivation. In an early experiment by Mendelson, Kuchnle, Greenberg, & Mello (1976), hospitalized volunteers worked on an operant task to earn money and marijuana for 26 days. Smoked marijuana did not influence the amount of work done by either the casual-user group or the heavy-user group; all remained motivated to earn and take home a significant amount of money in addition to the work they did for the marijuana. However, a more recent experiment by Cherek, Lane, & Dougherty (2002) found that cannabis did have a detrimental effect on the motivation of participants to earn money.

The issue is not settled, but even if there is no specific motivational effect, it is clear that cannabis affects attention and memory, and these are intellectual capacities usually considered necessary for success in educational institutions. Achievement motivation must be high indeed in any individual who combines high levels of cannabis use with a successful academic career or job.

Progression to Other Drugs

There are claims that marijuana is a *gateway drug* or a stepping-stone toward the use of more dangerous drugs. In support of this gateway theory are studies that show that virtually all heroin users had used marijuana before they adopted heroin (Golub & Johnson, 1994). In addition, studies have shown that the more a person uses marijuana, the greater is the probability that the person will use other drugs as well (Mullins, Vitola, & Michelson, 1975).

These data suffer from the same difficulty as the research on the amotivational syndrome: No causal relationship can be established. The fact that marijuana is used before heroin does not mean that marijuana use caused heroin use. Most people drink soda pop before they drink alcohol, but this fact does not mean that soda pop causes alcohol drinking.

At the heart of the progression hypothesis is the idea that users develop tolerance to "mild" drugs, become bored with their effects, and escalate to more powerful drugs. If this were true, we might expect that users would abandon marijuana when they progress to other drugs, but this does not appear to be the case. Marijuana is seldom abandoned in favor of other drugs. Instead, the usual pattern is to adopt the use of other drugs along with marijuana.

Even though a causal relationship cannot be proved, we cannot dismiss the correlation between the use of marijuana and other drugs; there must be an explanation, and, like the amotivational

syndrome, it probably has more to do with sociology than with pharmacology. Heavy marijuana use provides the social settings, motivation, and opportunity to use other drugs. In addition, the personality traits of curiosity and risk taking that might motivate a person to use marijuana are also likely to motivate the use of other drugs as well.

As was described in Chapter 5, experience with one drug can sensitize the mesolimbic dopamine system and increase the reinforcing value of another drug. Although specific experiments have not been attempted with THC, we know that THC increases dopamine levels, and it is possible that its use could act to increase use of other drugs.

Reproduction

Although not all researchers have been able to replicate the finding, marijuana seems to lower the levels of the male sex hormone testosterone in both human and nonhuman males. However, it is not yet apparent whether this finding has any biological significance. The levels of testosterone vary greatly from one individual to another and within the same individual throughout the course of a day. We do not know as yet whether a marijuana-induced suppression of testosterone will make any difference in the face of this great natural variability.

There has been some speculation on problems that might be caused by low testosterone levels. These effects include a reduction in fertility (Hembree, Zeidenberg, & Nahas, 1976) and a disruption in the sexual differentiation of males during embryonic development (Kolodny, 1975). In general, little reliable data have been collected to show that these effects occur more frequently among chronic cannabis users.

Studies in mice have shown that anandamide is a chemical messenger between the embryo and the uterus during implantation of the embryo in the uterine wall. It is, in fact, the first communication that occurs between the mother and the child. It is possible that THC might block cannabinoid receptors and interfere with this signal and prevent this process from occurring (Wang, Paria, Dey, & Armant, 1996).

In a large-scale study between 1984 and 1989, more than 7,000 pregnant women in the United States were studied, and their drug use histories were recorded. Eleven percent of these women reported using marijuana during pregnancy. Marijuana use was not associated with low birth weight or prematurity. By comparison, 35 percent of the women smoked tobacco, and this history was associated with low birth weight (Shiono et al., 1995).

Some functional differences, however, have been detected in children exposed prenatally to cannabinoids through maternal marijuana smoking. One study showed abnormal sleep patterns in newborns that persisted at least until the age of 3 years in cannabis-exposed children (Dahl, Scher, Williamson, Robles, & Day, 1995). There is some evidence that prenatal exposure to cannabis may have effects that do not show up for several years. These effects include hyperactivity, impulsiveness, and learning disorders. These effects are small, however, and it is impossible to demonstrate any causal connection to marijuana use (Earleywine 2002, p. 162).

Immunity

It has been clearly established that marijuana reduces activity in the body's immune system, which fights invading microorganisms and disease. This reduction has even caused speculation that THC might be effective in stopping the body's rejection of tissue after transplant operations. Again, the clinical significance of this effect has not been determined. We might suspect that marijuana users would be more susceptible to disease than nonusers, but adequate statistical data on this issue are difficult to obtain and have not been collected (Munson, 1975).

Cancer

Evidence is clear that tobacco smoke is associated with cancer. What about marijuana smoke? Even though marijuana users typically inhale much less smoke than tobacco users, the smoke from marijuana contains 50 to 70 percent more carcinogenic material than tobacco smoke, and marijuana smokers typically inhale more deeply and hold the smoke in the lungs longer than tobacco smokers. Surprisingly, little research has been done in this area, and results are frequently confounded by the fact that most marijuana smokers also smoke tobacco. It seems likely that marijuana accelerates the carcinogenic effects of tobacco smoke. Even though the median age for developing cancer is between 55 and 65, one study of people under age 45 with lung cancer found that almost all smoked both tobacco and marijuana (Sridhar et al., 1994). On the other hand, there are reports that cannabidiol and delta-9-THC are potent antioxidants (Hampson, Grimaldi, Axelrod, & Wink, 1998). Antioxidants are compounds that neutralize free radicals that damage DNA, which, in turn, can lead to cancer. A lot more work needs to be done in this area.

EPILOGUE

Psychopharmacological McCarthyism?

When Lester Grinspoon began studying marijuana in 1967, he claimed that he had no doubt that he would find it was a harmful drug used by more and more foolish people. He took as his job the task of revealing the dangers of marijuana. Instead, after 3 years of study, he concluded that he had been wrong and that his belief that the substance was dangerous was unfounded. In 1971, he wrote a book titled *Marihuance Reconsidered* (Grinspoon, 1971) in which he said so. He naively believed that people would come to understand that marijuana was much less harmful than legal drugs such as alcohol and tobacco and, consequently, that marijuana would be legal within 10 years.

Not only was he wrong, but in another book published in 1993, he comments that there is something special about illicit drugs: "If they don't always make the user behave irrationally, they certainly cause many nonusers to behave that way" (Grinspoon & Bakalar, 1993, p. ix). Grinspoon points out that instead of legalization, the climate has deteriorated so seriously that we are now in a period of what he calls "psychopharmacological McCarthyism"; it is not even acceptable to state in public that a drug like marijuana might have beneficial effects. He points to the widespread public condemnation of published research that found that adolescents who had engaged in some drug experimentation with marijuana were better adjusted than those who had not.

As another example of psychopharmacological McCarthyism, Grinspoon points to mandatory drug testing. In the McCarthy era, people were forced to take loyalty oaths or else risk losing their jobs or reputations. Grinspoon calls drug testing a "chemical loyalty oath." Just as loyalty oaths did little to enhance the national security of the United States, mandatory drug testing is of little use in preventing or treating drug abuse; instead, Grinspoon claims that it is little more than shotgun harassment designed to enhance outward conformity.

CHAPTER SUMMARY

- There may be three species of cannabis plant, although many believe that there is only one species, *Cannabis sativa*, with two distinct phenotypes. One, widely called hemp, has low levels of active ingredient. The other phenotype grows in warmer climates, has a high content of active ingredient, and is used primarily as an intoxicant.

- Although there are a great many cannabinoids, the primary active ingredient in cannabis is delta-9-tetrahydrocannabinol (THC). A number of synthetic cannabinoid-like drugs have also been developed for medical applications.

- Marijuana is made from the dried leaves and flowers of the cannabis plant and is not very potent. Hashish is the resin from the flowering tops of the female plant and is 10 times more potent than marijuana. Hashish can be refined and concentrated into a liquid called hash oil or red oil.

- THC is absorbed very poorly from the digestive system and is usually inhaled in the form of smoke, which is a much more efficient system of administration. After inhalation, effects may begin in 30 to 60 minutes. The effects disappear within an hour or so.

- In the late 1980s, a receptor for THC was isolated and located in many parts of the brain. Later, an endogenous cannabinoid, anandamide, was discovered. Cannabinoid receptors are located on presynaptic neurons and serve to modulate neurotransmitter release in response to endogenous cannabinoids released from the postsynaptic neuron.

- THC has several physiological effects. It causes bloodshot eyes, decreases the pressure in the eyeball, increases appetite and heart rate, and can act as an antiemetic and an anticonvulsant.

- At high doses, cannabis acts like a hallucinogen, but at the low doses common in North American use, the drug is reported to cause a pleasurable high. Cannabis causes temporal disintegration; that is, the user loses the ability to store information in the short term and is easily distracted.

- Cannabis can interfere with driving performance. Roadside screening tests for marijuana intoxication are being developed.

- THC has distinctive stimulus properties and will cause dissociation in both humans and nonhumans. The stimulus properties will generalize to other cannabinoids but not to any other drug.

- Tolerance develops to most of the effects of the cannabinoids.

- Withdrawal symptoms have been reported in humans and nonhumans but are usual only after continuous administration of fairly high doses. Some of the withdrawal symptoms reported are hot flashes, runny nose, loose stools, and sweating.

- Cannabinoids are self-administered by nonhumans. Humans will work to earn marijuana and will titrate dosage, though not very accurately. The use of marijuana in the United States has been steadily decreasing in recent years.

- The belief that cannabis causes violence and aggression has no support in research. It is known to interfere with immune processes and to lower the levels of testosterone in males, but the exact clinical significance of these findings for reproduction and susceptibility to disease in marijuana users is not known.

16

Hallucinogens, Phantasticants, and Club Drugs

The drugs discussed in this chapter do not have a lot in common. At one time in the past, they all might have been referred to as *hallucinogens*. It may be true that many of these drugs can cause hallucinations at high enough doses, but some of these drugs are not often taken in such high doses that hallucinations result—other effects seem to be important to the user.

Many of these drugs have a profound emotional effect. They make the user feel in touch either with others around them or with their inner selves, feel closer to God or the universe, or just feel ecstatic, enhancing the enjoyment of music and dancing and being with other people. For this reason a variety of other names have been suggested that describe some of the other effects. These include *phantasticants, psychedelics* (mind manifesters), *entactogens* (touching within), and *empathogenics* (empathy creators). The latter three were proposed in an attempt to describe an effect of these drugs that causes the user to achieve insights into him- or herself and achieve a closer empathy with others. They have been proposed by those who feel that these drugs are useful tools in psychotherapy (Metzner, 1993). Because the mental state created by some of these drugs is superficially similar to psychosis (and almost identical in others), the name *psychotomimetics* (psychosis mimics) is also sometimes used. More recently, some of these drugs have become associated with the club scene and are used to enhance the pleasure of music, dancing, and being with others. When used this way they are simply referred to as *club drugs*.

Note that cannabis could have been included in this chapter because it has many effects in common with these drugs, but in this book it has been given a chapter of its own. This separate treatment does not reflect any special property of cannabis. Cannabis was given a chapter of its own because of its widespread use and the abundance of information on it.

LSD AND THE MONOAMINE-LIKE DRUGS

The molecular structure of many drugs with hallucinogenic and phantasticant properties bears a resemblance to the monoamine neurotransmitters: serotonin, dopamine, and norepinephrine. *LSD* (lysergic acid diethylamide) and many other drugs are similar to serotonin, which is an indoleamine. Mescaline has a structure similar to the catecholamines dopamine and norepinephrine. Even though they differ somewhat in structure, there is a considerable overlap between the effects of these *indoleamine-like* and *catecholamine-like* drugs, so they can be discussed together. In the next section we will discuss ecstasy, which is a cross between mescaline and amphetamine and has properties of both.

All the indoleamine-like drugs have effects that are similar to LSD and differ from LSD mainly in potency and duration of action. These include *psilocybin*, the ingredient in magic mushrooms; *lysergic acid amide*, found in morning glory seeds; *DMT*, found in the bark of a tree in the jungles of South and Central America; *bufotenine*, found in plants and in the venom on the backs of toads; and *harmine* and *harmaline*, which are found in a tropical vine that grows in South America and is used by the native peoples in the area to make an intoxicating drink (W. McKim, 2003).

Mescaline is a catecholamine-like drug. It, too, has many effects in common with LSD but is about 1/2,000th as potent. It is the active ingredient in a cactus known as the *peyote* (*Lephophora williamsii*), which is native to the deserts of Mexico and the southwestern United States. The peyote is a small, spineless cactus that barely sticks out of the ground and has a thick, tuberous root. It has been used for centuries in Mexico and was a sacred plant of the Aztecs.

Since LSD is the most widely used and studied member of the monoamine-like drugs, it will be discussed in detail as a representative of this class. In fact, it also shares some effects with ecstasy and some other drugs in this chapter.

History of LSD

LSD is a synthetic drug; however, a number of similar chemicals occur naturally in the *ergot fungus* that infects grains, especially rye. During the Middle Ages in Europe, there were outbreaks of what is now called *ergotism*, a reaction caused by eating the fungus-infected grain. There were two kinds of effects caused by different fungi. One kind severely constricted blood flow to the limbs and made them feel excessively warm. Eventually, this condition would lead to gangrene, and the limb would just fall off. In 1039, a religious order was formed in France to treat people afflicted with this kind of ergotism. The patron saint of this order was St. Anthony, and the disease became known as *St. Anthony's fire* because of the sensation of heat. The other type of ergotism was characterized by convulsions, delirium, and hallucinations. That these afflictions were caused by the fungus was not discovered until more than 700 years later, in 1777. In fact, St. Anthony's fire was caused by derivatives of lysergic acid in the ergot fungus.

The story of LSD begins in the twentieth century. One of the effects of the lysergic acid derivatives in ergot was contractions of the uterus, a fact that was known to midwives who used it to aid in childbirth. This prompted Albert Hofmann of the Sandoz Laboratories in Basel, Switzerland, to experiment with the derivatives of lysergic acid in the hope of finding a new medicine. He had no inkling that he was dealing with a hallucinogen. In 1938, he synthesized a series of lysergic acid compounds but found none of them particularly interesting and went on to other things. Five years later, in 1943, Hofmann made a new batch of the twenty-fifth derivative (which he called LSD 25) and tried some new experiments, but he began to feel very peculiar and had to go home. He suspected that the reason for his strange sensations was that he had accidentally taken some of the LSD-25. To test this theory, a few days later he deliberately ingested 0.25 mg (250 micrograms), which he thought was an extremely small dose. His plan was to start with a dose that was so small that it would have no effect and slowly work up, but he did not know the extreme potency of LSD. A quarter of a milligram is a rather large dose, several times what is required to cause a powerful hallucinatory effect. Hofmann experienced the first LSD trip.

Sandoz did not know what to do with LSD, so the drug was distributed for testing to laboratories in Europe and the United States. It was thought that it might be useful in the treatment of mental disorders and alcoholism or at least as a means of studying psychotic behavior. Some researchers, like Humphry Osmond at the University of Saskatchewan, believed that LSD offered the power to provide great personal insights and possessed considerable psychotherapeutic potential. LSD was used in experiments in mental hospitals and laboratories until the mid-1960s, when it broke out of the laboratory and into the street.

Timothy Leary, a research professor in the Department of Social and Human Relations at Harvard University, was always considered by his colleagues to be a bit unconventional and radical in his views. The psychedelic revolution began for Leary in 1960. While he was in Mexico, he ate some mushrooms containing psilocybin, which caused him to have a "full-blown conversion experience." When he returned to Harvard, he and his colleague, Richard Alpert, distributed psilocybin to as many people as they could get to take it. In 1961, they tried LSD, started a new religion, and adopted LSD as a sacrament. In 1963, Leary and Alpert were dismissed from Harvard, a move that generated considerable publicity for them and the drug. They coined the phrase that was to become the philosophy of the hippie movement of the 1960s: "Turn on, tune in, drop out."

LSD had its heyday during the 1960s and early 1970s, the years of the hippie movement, which reached its peak at the Woodstock Music Festival in 1969. LSD has not vanished since then, but the pattern of its use is now somewhat different. In the 1960s, LSD was used as a true psychedelic: High doses were consumed in order to achieve vivid hallucinations and personal or cosmic insights. Using these high doses was not always a pleasurable experience. Gordon Wasson, who explored the religious use of many hallucinogenic plants, was asked once why he did not take hallucinogens all the time. He replied, "Ecstasy is hard work." It has been suggested that drug users in more recent years are not as interested in insight as they are in pleasure (Baumeister & Placidi, 1983).

LSD is now taken in smaller doses. The effect is a euphoric high similar to that of marijuana, and powerful mind-altering states are neither desired nor achieved. LSD is now used more as a phantasticant or entactogen than as a hallucinogen.

Dosage and Sources

LSD is sold on the street as *hits*. In the 1970s, a hit contained about 100 micrograms of LSD with a range of 0 to 300 micrograms (S. H. James & Bhatt, 1972) and does not appear to have changed much over time. There has always been great variation in the dosage available in a hit.

Hits of LSD have traditionally been absorbed in blotting paper, which may be plain or are printed with various cartoons or mosaic patterns. More recent variations include the *gel tab*, LSD in gelatin that is set in molds of various shapes or flat squares called *window panes*. LSD is also now available in candies or tiny pills called *microdots*. There is usually a larger dose of LSD in gelatin than in blotting paper because the gelatin protects the drug from deterioration caused by light and exposure to air.

Pharmacokinetics

LSD is usually taken orally and is effective by this route. Effects usually begin between 30 and 90 minutes after ingestion. Only 1 percent of the drug ever reaches the brain. The half-life of LSD is about 110 minutes in humans. It is extensively metabolized in the liver, and the metabolites are secreted into the digestive system in the bile and excreted in the feces. Mescaline is also readily absorbed from the digestive system and has a similar half-life (Brown, 1972).

Effects on the Body

There are few physical side effects of LSD, the most consistent being a dilation of the pupils. Mescaline often causes a period of nausea during the early stages of its effect.

Neurophysiology

Even though LSD has been around for a long time and has been studied extensively, its effects on the nervous system are still not clear. While it is a serotonin receptor blocker in the peripheral nervous system, in the central nervous system (CNS) it appears to be a selective agonist at some serotonin receptors, particularly the 5-HT_{2A} receptor. This is also true for other indoleamine-like hallucinogens and the catecholamine-like hallucinogens. This effect on 5-HT_{2A} receptors is one of the few effects all these drugs have in common and seems to be responsible for the subjective effects of both classes of drugs (Marek & Aghajanian, 1999).

There are two regions of the brain that appear to be involved: the locus coeruleus (LC) and the cortex. The LC is located in the lower brain and receives input from many sensory sources throughout the body, and it sends axons to almost every area of the brain including the cortex, where it releases NE (see Chapter 4). It is involved in fear and emotional responses and appears to function as a novelty detector. Stimulation of 5-HT_{2A} receptors by both indoleamine- and catecholamine-like hallucinogens has two indirect effects on the LC. First, they suppress output of the LC, although they do so via different mechanisms. In addition— and perhaps more important—they also enhance the response of the LC to novelty. This might explain some of the effects hallucinogenic drugs of this type have on perception. As we see later, after taking mescaline, for example, people often report that it is like seeing things for the first time.

In the cortex, these drugs change the response of large glutaminergic neurons to synaptic input by prolonging excitatory postsynaptic potentials. This effect is mediated through their effect on serotonin synapses. This effect is most prominent in the medial prefrontal cortex, where there is a large concentration of 5-HT_{2A} receptors. This area of the cortex is important in information processing and perception and may be involved in hallucinations.

Subjective Effects

Hallucinogenic Effect. How does a scientist go about studying hallucinations? Hallucinations are, by definition, in the realm of subjective experience, and one of the first principles of scientific inquiry is that all scientific data must be public and observable to anyone. It is, however, possible to study the verbal reports of people who are experiencing or have experienced hallucinations, but then arises the problem of how to organize such a mass of words into something meaningful. Heinrich Kluver (1966), who started his work in the 1920s, combined reports of subjects in his own experiments on mescaline and those of other researchers and noticed that there were consistencies. Mostly, these people described vivid visual images, and the researchers were aware that the images were not real. If they closed their eyes, they would see these images against a black background; if they opened their eyes, the images would be projected on whatever they were looking at. Kluver noticed that the images were frequently geometric patterns, and he identified four types of patterns that resembled (a) a grating or lattice; (b) a cobweb; (c) a tunnel, funnel, or cone; and (d) a spiral. Kluver remarked that images of these types also appear in fever deliriums, insulin hypoglycemia, and states that occur just before drifting off to sleep (*hypnogogic states*). Unfortunately, what Kluver described was only the first of two stages of imagery; the second stage, described by others, is more complex and involves meaningful images of people, animals, and places. Even during this phase, there are some common elements among individuals. For example, 60 to 70 percent of all subjects report seeing small animal or human figures that are friendly and caricature-like, and 72 percent of all subjects report religious imagery.

Despite the great interest surrounding these observations, no comprehensive, systematic, or scientific work on them was attempted until the 1970s. The problem was tackled with surprising ingenuity and success by Ronald K. Siegel (R. K. Siegel & Jarvik, 1975) of the University of California at Los Angeles (UCLA). Siegel adopted a variation of the technique of trained introspection, which had been used by the early German schools of psychology. Siegel trained his observers to use a code to describe their experiences. They were able to code images, colors, and movement by using a series of letters and numbers that they could express as fast as the images appeared. When they demonstrated that they were well trained, Siegel gave them a series of blind tests in which they were given placebos or any of a number of drugs in random order and left in a darkened room to report their experiences. Neither the subjects nor the researchers scoring the imagery codes knew what drug had been given.

Whereas the subjects given placebos saw a predominance of random forms, those getting the hallucinogenic drugs saw far more lattice and tunnel forms, confirming the observations of Kluver. During control sessions, subjects saw primarily black and violet forms, but in hallucinogenic sessions, they saw more colors, ranging into the yellow, orange, and red end of the spectrum. Finally, in all conditions, aimless and pulsating movement was reported, but in hallucinogenic sessions there was an increase in "explosive" movement.

After demonstrating that all of these drugs appeared to create similar types of images, Siegel was also able to show that at higher doses, people sometimes go through a phase where they see themselves being swept up into their own hallucination. This is followed by a stage where the images lose their geometric quality and become meaningful pictures of real objects. These images can change rapidly, as fast as 10 times a second, but the changes are not without a pattern. Each image appears to be related to the one before it. Figure 16-1 illustrates this point. Siegel also noted that the images during this stage were related to the subject's surroundings; for example, sounds such as footsteps induced an image of someone walking. Another interesting finding was that the colors appeared to shift from the blue end of the spectrum to the red end as the effect of the drug increased in intensity.

Because all these drugs have such similar effects, Siegel wondered whether the similarities might be due to cultural factors since all his subjects came from a similar culture (UCLA). To answer this question, he visited a remote tribe of Huichol Indians in the Sierra Madre range of Mexico. These Indians make brightly colored pictures of their peyote visions from colored yarn. Siegel found that the experiences represented by

Figure 16-1 This series of drawings (read from top to bottom, column by column) illustrates the systematic changes in complex meaningful imagery reported after taking mescaline. Note that each scene contains an element of the previous one. Pen and ink drawings by David Sheridan. (From R. K. Siegel & Jarvik, 1975.)

the Huichols in their yarn pictures were identical to those reported by the subjects in his laboratory.

Siegel postulated that the nature and structure of hallucinations must be determined by the nature and structure of the visual system and the brain, not by the drug, because (a) these hallucinatory experiences are similar among vastly different drugs; (b) the experiences resemble the effects produced by other nondrug hallucinations, such as those from fever, hypoglycemia, and migraine headaches; and (c) the experiences are similar between cultures. In other words, the hallucinations are a result of nonspecific interference in brain functioning; the drug intensifies what might be considered normal background noise in the perceptual systems, and this noise is then organized, by the normal processes of perception and cognition, into images and patterns (R. K. Siegel, 1977; R. K. Siegel & Jarvik, 1975).

Siegel's study addressed only the visual property of the hallucinogenic experience, but LSD can cause entactogenic and empathogenic effects as well. These experiences often have a profound effect on emotions, insights, and feelings, which are not as easily studied and can be conveyed only by less scientific modes of expression, as we shall see.

Phantasticant and Perceptual Effects. These drugs can cause users to feel that the experiences they are having are of great emotional significance. Often these experiences can be religious in nature. It is for this reason that drugs like LSD have been widely used in traditional religions. The religious nature of the hallucinogenic experience is described here by R. Gordon Wasson (1972) in this account of his participation in a Mazatec Indian psilocybe mushroom rite:

It permits you to see more clearly than our perishing mortal eyes can see, vistas beyond the horizons of this life, to travel backwards and forwards in time, to enter other planes of existence, even (as the Indians say) to know God. It is hardly surprising that your emotions are profoundly affected and you feel that an indissoluble bond unites you and the others who have shared in this sacred agape. All that you see during this night

has a pristine quality; the landscape, the edifices, the carvings, the animals—they look as though they had come straight from the Maker's workshop. (p. 197)

Another commonly reported experience is the greatly enhanced pleasure derived from viewing art and, especially, listening to music:

Ordinarily I am not particularly susceptible to music. This time, lying on the cot, I became acutely aware of the Montoya record playing. This was more than music: the entire room was saturated with sounds that were also feeling—sweet, delicious, sensual—that seemed to be coming from somewhere deep down inside me. I became mingled with the music, gliding along with the chords. Everything I saw and felt was somehow inextricably interrelated. This was pure synesthesia, and I was part of the synthesis. I suddenly "knew" what it was to be simultaneously a guitar, the sounds, the ear that received them, and the organism that responded, in what was the most profoundly consuming aesthetic experience I have ever had. (J. Richardson in Aaronsen & Osmond, 1970, p. 33)

Club drugs appear to have a similar effect when it comes to the music played at raves and in clubs. It has a loud, strong, repetitive beat and creates the urge to dance, which is enhanced by this effect of drugs like LSD and ecstasy.

Entactogenic and Empathogenic Effects. Another commonly reported effect is that the hallucinogens seem to provide insight into one's past and one's own mind, revealing repressed thoughts and unrecognized feelings. Such insights are similar to those that psychoanalysis attempts to achieve through psychotherapy. It was this effect that inspired Humphry Osmond to suggest that hallucinogens might be useful tools in psychotherapy and prompted the use of the term *entactogenic* (touching within) to describe this effect. Here is a description of the experiences of psychologist Bernard Aaronson, who took LSD as part of an experiment:

We sat on the bench under the trees and talked about the loneliness of being, and talked about how people are forever needing things they expect you to provide. For what seemed a long time, I cried as I have not cried since I was a baby, for all the people in the world who need things and whose needs cannot be met. I cried too for all the people around me that I botched in the giving or to whom I cannot give because I am depleted. . . . I expressed great hostility toward both my parents and with H.'s help analyzed my feelings as they derived from my relationship with each of them. I analyzed my relationship with my next older brother, and examined the meaning in my life of my relationship with that friend whom I love the most. (Aaronson & Osmond, 1970, pp. 47–48)

A more complete account of the subjective experiences of hallucinogens is beyond the scope of this book. A good selection of accounts of drug experiences may be found in Grinspoon and Bakalar (1979b).

Perception

As we have seen, people who use LSD frequently report that their perceptions are much keener and that their sight and hearing have become more acute. There have been a few studies of the effects of LSD on visual sensory thresholds, but their results are not consistent. In general, however, impairments of sensory functions attributable to LSD are reported more often than improvements (Hollister, 1978).

It 's clear that LSD increases the enjoyment of music, but it has not yet been established whether there are any changes in auditory thresholds. The perception of the passage of time is distorted in individuals; however, the direction of distortion is not consistent. In most cases, time is perceived as slowing down (10 seconds seem more 20), but in some experiments the reverse has n reported (Hollister, 1978).

Behavior and Performance

One of the difficulties with measuring human performance under the influence of hallucinogens is maintaining the motivation of the subject to cooperate. Like marijuana, hallucinogens frequently cause subjects to become inattentive to the task and so caught up in internal experiences that they lose their motivation to perform, as well as they are able, tasks that they may feel are irrelevant at the time. It has been suggested that Carlos Castaneda (1973), an anthropology student who wrote extensively about his experiences after taking several different types of hallucinogens, could not have had the experiences he describes because he claims to have been able to continue to take notes while under the influence of the drugs (R. K. Siegel, 1981).

The available data show mostly that LSD impairs reaction time. Oddly enough, performance on a pursuit rotor task may be improved by LSD (Rosenbaum, Cohen, Luby, Gottlieb, & Yellen, 1959).

Functioning on intellectual tasks is also impaired. Like THC, LSD causes a deficit in short-term, or working, memory. Other impairments are seen in problem-solving and cognitive functions such as mental addition and subtraction, color naming, concentration, and recognition (Hollister, 1978, p. 397).

Claims have been made that LSD-like hallucinogens improve creativity, but again, as with THC, these are difficult to substantiate experimentally. There is little doubt that LSD changes the sort of work done by artists, but it is debatable whether these changes are improvements.

Discriminative Stimulus Properties

Nonhumans readily learn to discriminate LSD from saline. The stimulus cue of LSD is not blocked by cholinergic blockers such as atropine, opiate antagonists such as naloxone, or dopamine blockers such as chlorpromazine. Although there is some variability between drugs and laboratories, it appears that the stimulus properties of LSD can be blocked by central-acting serotonin agonists but not by peripheral serotonin agonists; these findings confirm that serotonin receptors in the CNS are involved in the subjective effects of LSD. Serotonin is further implicated in studies in which rats were trained to perform a response when given electrical stimulation of the

Raphé nuclei, a serotonin-containing system implicated in sleep (see Chapter 4). Later this response was performed by rats given LSD, indicating that the Raphé stimulation was regarded as being similar to LSD. In addition, LSD injected directly into the Raphé system produces the same stimulus effects as when given intraperitoneally: All these data support the notion that the subjective effects of LSD depend on serotonin receptors in the Raphé system (Hirschorn, Hayes, & Rosecrans, 1975).

Tolerance

In humans, tolerance to the effects of LSD and psilocybin and related drugs develops rapidly. If LSD is taken repeatedly, its effects disappear within 2 or 3 days; no amount of drug will be effective. This tolerance dissipates quickly, and sensitivity returns within a week. This is one reason why these drugs are seldom taken continually. The ability of LSD to disrupt the operant behavior of nonhumans also shows rapid tolerance. There is cross-tolerance between LSD and psilocybin and mescaline but no cross-tolerance between LSD and d-amphetamine or THC (Brown, 1972, p. 50).

Withdrawal

No withdrawal symptoms to LSD or any similar drugs have been found. This may be because they are seldom taken continuously for any period of time.

Self-Administration

Nonhumans. It is widely accepted that LSD and similar monoamine-like hallucinogens are not self-administered by nonhumans. In fact, they appear to have aversive effects. It has been demonstrated that laboratory animals will work to avoid being given LSD. In one experiment, rhesus monkeys learned to press a lever to turn off a stimulus that normally preceded an infusion of LSD and, thus, prevented the infusion (Hoffmeister & Wuttke, 1975). Nevertheless, a study done in 2004 did show transient self-administration of DMT, mescaline, and psilocybin in some monkeys with a history of self-administering MDMA (discussed later in this chapter; Fantegrossi, Woods, & Winger, 2004). This suggests that the occasional use of these drugs may be reinforcing in some individuals. This may explain why, outside the laboratory, there are reports that nonhumans will, from time to time, consume plants that contain LSD-like drugs. There are also reports that dogs in Hawaii enjoy eating mushrooms that contain psilocybin and that mongooses prefer to eat the species of toad that contains bufotenine (R. K. Siegel & Jarvik, 1975).

Humans. The self-administration of hallucinogens like LSD in human cultures is almost universal and very ancient, but its use is different from the use of most other drugs. First, they are never continuously consumed. They are indulged in sporadically and on special occasions. The use of hallucinogens in most cultures is usually associated with religious ceremonies. Frequently, the drugs are taken only by priests and shamans for the purpose of divination, talking to the dead, or seeking direction from a deity. Even in modern Western culture, hallucinogens are usually taken episodically. At the height of LSD's popularity in the 1960s, some people used it as often as possible and organized their lives around its use, but the rapid development of tolerance prevented a continuous trip. These "acid heads" were likely a phenomenon of the hippie lifestyle. Unlike other heavily used drugs such as alcohol, LSD use, for most people, does not increase over time. Initially, there may be a period during which a user will take the drug more frequently, but after a few years, most hallucinogen users mature out; people seem to get tired of the experience, and hallucinogen use decreases or stops altogether.

LSD use among teenagers in the United States remained fairly high throughout the 1990s but has been steadily declining. In 1996, 8.8 percent of grade 12 students reported using LSD within the past 30 days. In 2004 this number had dropped to 2.2 percent (Johnston, O'Malley, Bachman, & Schulenberg, 2005).

Harmful Effects

The media have given great attention to the behaviors that may be provoked by the acute effects of such drugs. For example, stories appear occasionally about young LSD users who jump out of windows because they believe that they can fly. There are also reports of murders being committed under the influence of the drug. Events such as these undoubtedly occur, but they are extremely rare and probably occur with no greater frequency under the influence of LSD than under the influence of alcohol or any other drug.

Much more common but of less concern is the *acute psychotic reaction* or *freak-out*, which occurs when the user is having a bad trip, an unpleasant experience. Freak-outs happen when the experience is unpleasant and the user forgets that the experience is caused by a drug. The user fears going permanently insane, and the reaction is panic. Panic reactions are not normally seen in experienced users, are frequently a result of an unusually high dose (or a mixture) of drugs, and do not constitute a serious medical emergency. Panicky trippers can usually be talked down: Put in close contact with someone who talks to them constantly, reassuring them that their state is drug induced and will get better. If their attention can be concentrated on this fact, the effects of the drug can be decreased and the panic dispelled. For example, after one young man was talked down from a freak-out, he reported that the drug was causing every object in his entire world to melt and change shape. He concentrated on the person talking to him; that person was the only object that remained constant.

One disturbing effect of many hallucinogens is that some of their effects may be experienced briefly at various times long after the drug has worn off. These episodes are called *flashbacks*. In a similar effect, called *trailing phenomena*, objects seem to move in a jerky, discontinuous fashion as though being illuminated by stroboscopic light. No one understands flashbacks or trailing phenomena. They may occur unpredictably for years after only a single use of LSD. They normally last only a few seconds or minutes and are frequently associated with the use of other drugs such as ecstasy or marijuana or with times of emotional stress. One theory of flashbacks is that they are manifestations of a temporal lobe seizure, but there is little evidence to support this view (Hollister, 1978).

Psilocybin, LSD, and mescaline are not very toxic. There are no recorded cases of anyone dying from an overdose of any of these drugs.

ECSTASY AND SYNTHETIC MESCALINE-LIKE DRUGS

The structure of the mescaline molecule has been altered to form a family of drugs that is a combination of catecholamine-like hallucinogens and amphetamine. These drugs are all synthetic, and many such drugs have been discovered. Much of this research was done in the hope of finding a drug with a medically useful property. So far, the only use for these new substances has been in the drug subculture. Perhaps the best known of these is ecstasy.

The term *ecstasy* usually refers to *MDMA* (3,4-methylenedioxymethamphetamine) but may also refer to a mixture of *MDMA* and *MDEA* (N-ethyl-3,4-methylenedioxyamphetamine) and *MDA* (3,4-methylenedioxyamphetamine), drugs with similar potencies and effects (H. Kalant, 2001). It was originally synthesized by the Merck drug company and was patented in 1914. It was never developed or used for any purpose until the late 1960s, when it first appeared on the drug scene (R. K. Siegel, 1986). It also has been known as *X, Adam, MDM, M&M, e, xtc*, and *beanies*.

During the 1960s, many other synthetics were invented and manufactured in clandestine labs in an attempt to circumvent the law, which identified only specific chemicals as illegal. At that time, slight changes in the molecule could make a drug legal until such time as there was specific legislation against it. Such drugs have become known as *designer drugs*, and they appeared on the street with a bewildering variety of names such as DMA, DOM, DOET, and so on. For the most part, these substances are more potent and considerably more toxic than mescaline, and they cause more unpleasant side effects, such as headaches and nausea. Unlike commercially developed drugs, many designer drugs were not screened for adverse effects, and some had extremely toxic effects and caused a number of deaths. Most of these designer drugs based on mescaline have virtually disappeared, but some, like ecstasy, are still around and are used more widely than ever.

Prior to July 1985, when it was reclassified by the governments of the United States, the United Kingdom, and Canada, some psychiatrists gave MDMA to their patients because it seemed to enhance intimacy and communication between the patient and the therapist (the terms *entactogen* and *empathogen* were invented with ecstasy in mind) (Adler, Abramson, Katz, & Hager, 1985; Verebey, Alrazi, & Jaffe, 1988). When it was reclassified in 1985, its use, even for psychotherapeutic purposes, was banned because it was discovered that the drug had neurotoxic effects; it was shown that a dose of about four times the normal effective dose causes a depletion of serotonin in the brain of rats 1 week after a single administration, a finding now confirmed in humans (Baggott, Jerome, & Stuart, 2001).

Ecstasy is sold in white or colored tablets that may or may not be marked with a symbol. Each pill may contain up to 100 mg or more of MDMA and may also contain varying amounts of MDEA, MDA, PMA (paramethyoxyamphetamine), and MBDB (3,4-methhlenedioxy-phenyl-N-methylbutanamine). A review of the purity of ecstasy tablets showed that in the late 1990s, as many as 20 percent of tablets did not contain MDMA at all; many contained only drugs like caffeine, ephedrine, or ketamine. However, these purity problems have not persisted into the 2000s, and non-MDMA tablets are now infrequent (Parrott, 2004).

Pharmacokinetics

Ecstasy can be taken orally and reaches a peak blood level in about 2 hours. The majority of the drug is either excreted unchanged or metabolized to MDA. It has a half-life of about 8 hours, thus taking about 40 hours for 95 percent of the drug to be eliminated. For this reason, many of its effects persist for several days after use.

Ecstasy is most often used by teens and young adults attending dance clubs and all-night dances or raves, although its use is associated with an increasing number of other activities such as sex. It produces a marked increase in wakefulness, endurance, and energy, and it creates in the user euphoria, an increased sense of well-being, sharpened sensory perception, greater sociability and extroversion, and a heightened sense of closeness to other people. As with LSD, these effects are subject to rapid acute tolerance, which generally means that ecstasy is unlikely to be used continuously. As with LSD, this tolerance dissipates within a few days.

Neurophysiology

Ecstasy and similar synthetics increase transmission at synapses that use serotonin, norepinephrine, and, to a lesser extent, dopamine. It works primarily by causing the release of the neurotransmitter and blocking transmitter reuptake.

Behavior and Performance

A dose of 75 to 100 mg induces a state similar to that caused by marijuana or low doses of phencyclidine (PCP), with no hallucinations, and an enhanced awareness of emotions and sensations—effects similar to the entactogenic effects described earlier in the section on LSD (Lamb & Griffiths, 1987; R. K. Siegel, 1986).

Effects of ecstasy include increased muscular tension, which causes jaw clenching and tooth grinding (*bruxism*) and a restless movement of the legs. Body temperature goes up in a warm environment, and there may be a stiffness in the back and legs for a few days. There often is a loss of appetite, headache, nausea, blurred vision, and insomnia (Kalant, 2001). For a few days after use, people often report a difficulty in concentration, fatigue, and depression similar to the crash or comedown after use of amphetamine and cocaine (see Chapter 11).

Discriminative Stimulus Properties

Although not as much is known about mescaline and the synthetic mescaline-like drugs, it appears that increased serotonin activity is important in their stimulus effects. Rats trained to discriminate saline from MDMA will generalize the response to a serotonin (5-HT$_{1A}$) agonist. It has also been shown that MDMA will enhance the stimulus effects of LSD. This might be the basis of *candy flipping*, the practice of taking ecstasy and LSD together (Glennon & Young, 2000). MDMA stimulus properties do not generalize to cocaine or mescaline.

Tolerance

Similar to LSD, psilocybin, and mescaline, tolerance to the effects of ecstasy develops rapidly in humans.

Self-Administration

Nonhumans. It has been shown that, unlike LSD, MDMA is readily self-administered by primates (Lamb & Griffiths, 1987). Research with rhesus monkeys has shown that the reinforcing effects of MDMA follow an inverted U-shaped function with lower doses and higher doses not being effective reinforcers (Fantegrossi, Ullrich, Rice, Woods, & Winger, 2002). In this experiment, the reinforcing effects could be blocked by a drug that selectively blocked 5-HT$_{2A}$ receptors, but this drug would not block the reinforcing effects of cocaine and methamphetamine, suggesting that the reinforcing effects of MDMA are mediated by a different mechanism from the one used by the psychomotor stimulants. This is odd considering that other drugs that increase serotonin activity at these receptors, such as LSD

and the selective serotonin reuptake inhibitors (SSRI's), are not self-administered.

Human Epidemiology. The use of ecstasy steadily increased among young people in the United States and Europe throughout the 1990s until 2000. In the United States, ecstasy use increased in high school students, and the number of mentions of ecstasy in emergency room admissions about doubled between 1994 and 1999 (NIDA, 2001). A similar trend was seen in the United Kingdom and Canada (Morgan, 2000). But ecstasy use has undergone a drastic decline since peaking in 2000, when 3.6 percent of grade 12 students in the United States reported using the drug in the previous 30 days. In 2004, that figure dropped to 1.2 percent. This decline was accompanied with a general increase in perceived risk of using the drug. (Johnston et al., 2005).

Withdrawal

Ecstasy is known to have hangover effects but, like LSD, is never taken repeatedly, so withdrawal effects are not seen.

Harmful Effects of Ecstasy

Earlier reports of dopamine neurotoxicity have been shown to be in error (see Box 16.1), but there is good evidence that after chronic use, there is depletion in serotonin in the brain that is in proportion to the extent and intensity of use and that appears to be irreversible. There is considerable evidence from studies of chronic users that this depletion in serotonin shows up as problems in many of the areas of behavior known to be associated with serotonin in the brain. Chronic users show sleep disorders, depression, persistent anxiety, impulsiveness and hostility, and selective impairment of memory and attention (Wareing, Fisk, & Murphy, 2000). The cognitive deficits seem to dissipate about 6 months after use is stopped, but the anxiety and hostility may remain for years. It is likely that the recovery is due to an up-regulation of serotonin receptors or some other regulatory adjustment to compensate for the decreased serotonin in the brain (Morgan, 2000).

BOX 16-1   Making Mistakes in Science

In September 2003, a study was published by George Ricuarte and his colleagues at Johns Hopkins Medical School showing that doses of ecstasy in the range of human usage also caused severe dopamine neurotoxicity in two species of nonhuman primates (Ricaurte, Yuan, Hatzidimitriou, Cord, & McCann, 2002). The reason this particular study is remarkable is that it was later retracted by the authors. After publication they were unable to replicate the findings and discovered that there had been a mix-up in the labeling of a bottle; the drug that was used was not ecstasy but methamphetamine (Ricaurte, Yuan, Hatzidimitriou, Cord, & McCann, 2003). This retraction caused quite a stir in many circles since the study had been given wide publicity by antidrug organizations. Many have been left with the impression that all the cautionary studies with ecstasy are not to be trusted and that ecstasy is, in fact, safe to use. On the contrary, this retraction illustrates the way that science works and the importance of replication. We cannot expect every published result to be free from all errors, but the ultimate test is whether a research finding can be reliably reproduced. If it cannot be replicated, this often leads to an investigation that identifies the errors, and, as in the case of this experiment, the results are retracted. More often than not, erroneous findings are eventually ignored if they cannot be replicated. In any case, none of this affects the finding that ecstasy causes serotonin depletion in humans and nonhumans.

One of the more troubling and dangerous effects of ecstasy is the loss of heat regulation in the body, causing an increase in body temperature. This may not be serious in many circumstances, but at a rave where the user is dancing vigorously in a warm environment, it can cause symptoms similar to heatstroke, muscle tissue damage, kidney failure, and liver damage. In addition, if one is dancing vigorously, this also causes profuse sweating, and the body can become dehydrated and lose large amounts of salt. Dancers often attempt to compensate by drinking large amounts of water that, without replacement salt, can dilute the blood and create an electrolyte imbalance. This in turn can cause organs, including the brain, to swell, resulting in epilepsy-like seizures.

Lethal Effects

The therapeutic index of ecstasy is about 15 (Gable, 2004); however, there is a great range of doses that have been known to cause death, some within the range of recreational drug use. Death may result from a number of different mechanisms. In one study of 87 ecstasy-related deaths, eight were related to the heart or circulatory system, four were caused by liver damage, nine were caused by swelling of the brain resulting from blood dilution, 30 were caused by overheating, 14 were caused by suicide or accident, and in 22 cases the cause could not be determined (Kalant, 2001).

A complicating factor is that there is nothing in the way of quality control in the clandestine labs that manufacture ecstasy, and the pills may also contain amphetamine, ephedrine, and other substances like PMA. PMA was developed in a clandestine lab in Canada in the early 1970s and was distributed in the illicit drug market in the United States and Canada. This drug is extremely potent, second only to LSD, but it is also very toxic and has a therapeutic index of 2.5, making it very dangerous to use (Schmidt, 1987). A number of deaths were attributed to PMA before warnings could be spread about it.

In addition, in many ecstasy-related fatalities, other drugs have also been consumed, often alcohol or amphetamine or other club drugs like GHB.

DISSOCIATIVE ANESTHETICS: PHENCYCLIDINE AND KETAMINE

Phencyclidine, also known as PCP, is a synthetic drug that was developed by the Parke-Davis Company as an analgesic and anesthetic in 1963 and marketed as Sernyl. For this purpose, it proved very effective and safe because it did not depress the heart, blood pressure, or respiration. It caused a trance-like state rather than a loss of consciousness. It has been classified as a *dissociative anesthetic* because it seemed to separate people from sensory experience. In 1965, it was withdrawn from the market because patients reported that while they were recovering from the drug, they experienced a delirium, disorientation, and agitation referred to as *emergence delirium*. It was then marketed as Sernylan, and its use was restricted to nonhumans. It started to be sold on the street in 1965 under the names *crystal*, *angel dust*, *hob*, and *horse tanks*, but it did not become popular during the 1960s.

Ketamine was first synthesized in 1962 and marketed as Ketalar in 1969 as a safer replacement for PCP. It is a more potent anesthetic, has a shorter duration of action than PCP, and has milder emergence effects. Ketamine continues to be used as an anesthetic for children and as a veterinary anesthetic under the name Ketaset and Vetalar. It has the street names of *K*, *Special K*, or *kitkat*. It is now widely used as a club drug at dance clubs and all-night dance parties or raves. It also has the reputation of being used as a date rape drug.

Ketamine sold on the street is probably diverted from legitimate veterinary use. It comes in liquid form and is colorless and tasteless. It may be swallowed or injected. Often the liquid is heated and turned to a white powder that is snorted.

Pharmacokinetics and Dose

PCP and ketamine are weak, lipid-soluble bases and are effective orally. They are readily absorbed through most moist tissues and so can be absorbed through the nasal membranes when snorted.

A normal dose of PCP is 5 to 10 mg. The effects of PCP are felt rapidly, within a minute after inhalation and intravenous injection and from 20 to 40 minutes after oral administration. The duration of the peak effect varies from 10 to 90 minutes, and the effects may last from 4 to 8 hours. Drug levels fall rapidly at first as the drug is absorbed into body fat, but then low levels may persist in the body for several weeks as the drug is released from body fat (Gorelick & Balster, 2000).

Ketamine can be snorted, injected, or taken orally. Oral administration is slowly absorbed and subject to first-pass metabolism, so the drug is often administered intranasally. Ketamine is rapidly absorbed, and effects last from 35 to 40 minutes. A normal dose of ketamine is called a *bump* and contains about 75 to 125 mg. A typical oral dose of ketamine is 175 mg, and a typical intranasal dose is 50 mg (Gable, 2004).

Neurophysiology

The dissociative anesthetics alter the functioning of norepinephrine, dopamine, acetylcholine, and serotonin, but it is believed that the principal effect responsible for their reinforcing properties is that they block NMDA receptors for glutamate and aspartate, which are excitatory transmitters in many parts of the brain, including the cortex (K. M. Johnson, 1987). PCP and ketamine have a receptor site located in the ion channel normally activated by an NMDA receptor. When occupied by PCP or ketamine, this receptor blocks the ion channel and makes these transmitters ineffective in the same manner as the alcohol molecule (Dinwiddie & Farber, 1995; Gorelick & Balster, 2000; see also Chapter 6).

These drugs appear to act as reinforcers by directly decreasing the output of the neurons of the nucleus accumbens that are normally inhibited by dopamine (Wise, 1998), although they do so without directly altering dopamine activity (Carlezon & Wise, 1996) in a manner similar to the barbiturates and benzodiazepines (see Chapter 7).

There may be an endogenous substance that acts at the PCP/ketamine receptor, but its existence remains uncertain.

Behavior and Performance

The available data mostly show that PCP impairs reaction time and disrupts performance on a pursuit rotor task (Rosenbaum et al., 1959).

The dissociative anesthetics are known to cause amnesia for events that occur while under the influence of the drug. Although no studies of the effects of PCP on memory in humans have been conducted, PCP does seem to be more disruptive of memory in nonhumans than LSD, THC, opiates, and other psychoactive drugs (Balster, 1987). It is known that integrity of NMDA receptors are vital in the formation of long-term memories, and so it is not surprising that drugs like PCP and ketamine that block NMDA receptors are powerful amnesic drugs. In addition, it has been demonstrated that ketamine induces a type of thought disorder very similar to that seen in schizophrenic patients (Adler et al., 1999).

PCP and ketamine are not hallucinogenic in the sense that LSD is. Taken at usual doses, the dissociative anesthetics cause relaxation, warmth, a tingling feeling, and a sense of numbness. There are euphoric feelings, distortions in body image, and a feeling of floating in space. When these effects wear off, they are sometimes followed by a mild depression that may last from 24 hours to a week. At higher doses, the user may become stuporous or even comatose. Psychotic behavior occurs frequently and may include anything from manic excitation to catatonia, in which the user assumes one position and does not move for a prolonged period of time. There may be sudden mood changes accompanied by laughing and crying; disoriented, confused, and delusional thought; drooling; and repetitive (stereotyped) actions. This psychotic state may slowly disappear as the drug level declines, but sometimes the psychosis requires hospitalization and lasts for weeks.

Stimulus Properties

Dissociative anesthetics appear to have unique stimulus properties. Animals trained to discriminate PCP and ketamine do not generalize this response to any other class of drugs, including stimulants, depressants, and hallucinogens, and no drug has been shown to antagonize their stimulus properties. They generalize only to other drugs known to block NMDA receptors, such as dextromethorphan (see later in this chapter), indicating that this effect is likely the basis for their stimulus properties.

Tolerance

Traditionally, PCP is used sporadically, like LSD, but continuous use became common in the 1970s and 1980s. When the drug is used every day, tolerance develops, and there is some evidence of dependence and withdrawal symptoms (Grinspoon & Bakalar, 1979b). Users frequently need only a few puffs of a PCP-laced cigarette to get high when they first try the drug, but within 2 to 6 weeks, they may be smoking two joints at a time to accomplish the same effect. Tolerance also seems to develop to the analgesic effects in burn patients. Tolerance has also been demonstrated in nonhumans and appears to take place at physiological and behavioral levels rather than in pharmacokinetics (Balster, 1987; Gorelick & Balster, 2000). Rapid tolerance also develops to the reinforcing effects and discriminative stimulus properties of ketamine in rats (Rocha et al., 1996).

Withdrawal

Research with nonhumans has shown that there may be some withdrawal after continual use of PCP. The symptoms include vocalizations, grinding of the teeth, diarrhea, difficulty staying awake, anxiety, confusion, and tremors. No systematic studies of PCP withdrawal in humans have been done (Gorelick & Balster, 2000).

Self-Administration

Nonhumans. PCP is self-administered by monkeys, dogs, baboons, and rats either by intravenous infusion or orally (Balster, 1987; Carroll, 1993; Griffiths, Bigelow, & Henningfield, 1980). PCP injected directly into a part of the nucleus accumbens and the frontal cortex has been shown to be reinforcing, an effect that is not diminished by a dopamine antagonist, showing that this effect is independent of dopamine transmission (Carlzon & Wise, 1996). It has also been demonstrated that ketamine is self-administered intravenously by both rats and monkeys (Moreton, Meisch, Stark, & Thompson, 1977) and that tolerance develops fairly rapidly to ketamine's reinforcing effects in the rat (Rocha et al., 1996).

Human Epidemiology. Patterns of PCP use are similar to LSD. Most use is experimental or occasional, but, unlike LSD, some occasional users become heavy chronic users. Unfortunately, even though tolerance does develop to the reinforcing effects of dissociative anesthetics, the tolerance is not complete enough to discourage continuous use as is the case with LSD (Linder, Lerner, & Burns, 1981).

Not until the decline of LSD in the 1970s did PCP use start to increase. Before PCP became popular in its own right, it was more widely used than most people suspected because it was often mixed with other drugs or sold as something else, like THC, mescaline, or psilocybin. Even today it is sold as "embalming fluid" and sometimes turns up in pills reputed to be ecstasy. While its use has declined, it is still popular in some metropolitan areas and among certain groups who continue to take it by itself or mixed with marijuana or cocaine (Gorelick & Balster, 2000). Since the mid-1990s, even these small numbers have declined. In 2004, less than half of 1 percent of high school students in the United States reported using PCP within the past 30 days (Johnston et al., 2005).

Ketamine was little used until it entered the club scene in the 1980s and its popularity expanded. Its use, however, appears to have leveled off. Ketamine use among high school students in the United States has shown little change since 2000 with about 2 percent of grade 12 students reporting use within the past 12 months (Johnston et al., 2005).

Harmful Effects

PCP and kertamine have the reputation of causing people to be violent and to commit violent, uncontrolled acts toward other people. A recent, careful examination of the literature on the drug has not found any systematic evidence that these drugs specifically cause violent or criminal behavior. It is true that the psychotic state induced by large doses of dissociative anesthetics causes disorientation, agitation, and hyperactivity, and these effects are difficult to manage and have the potential for injury to the individual and others nearby. However, PCP and ketamine do not seem to turn normal, innocent people into dangerous and violent criminals (Brecher, Wang, Wong, & Morgan, 1988; Gorelick & Balster, 2000). Research and experience with laboratory animals even suggest that PCP has a taming effect on normally aggressive animals (Balster, 1987).

Long-lasting psychotic behavior has been reported after PCP use, even in individuals without any psychotic tendencies. This PCP psychosis may last several months in some individuals.

Acute behavioral effects of PCP and ketamine can sometimes be responsible for injury and death. For example, users have drowned in pools or hot tubs while trying to swim to increase a sensation of floating. In addition, because the drugs are anesthetics, rather severe injuries have been tolerated or self-inflicted without pain or any effort at avoidance. Although the exact frequency of this sort of event has not been documented, it is probably more likely to happen with PCP than with LSD and the other serotonin-like and norepinephrine-like hallucinogens.

Genetic Damage and Reproduction. It does not appear that PCP or ketamine are teratogenic, but PCP has been shown to slow the growth of the fetus, precipitate labor, and cause fetal distress. Children born to mothers who use PCP often show muscle stiffness, tremor, irritability, and impaired attention and behavior control that may last for several years, although it is difficult to be sure that these effects are due specifically to PCP because of other maternal drug use (Gorelick & Balster, 2000).

Lethal Effects

A lethal dose of the ketamine is 25 times the effective dose for intranasal administration (Gable, 2004). Although toxic effects may vary, high doses cause coma, convulsions, and respiratory arrest. Brain hemorrhage and kidney failure have also been reported. The lethal effects of PCP and ketamine are potentiated by the presence of depressant drugs such as alcohol or barbiturates in the body.

DEXTROMETHORPHAN

Dextromethorphan is a synthetic, opiate-like drug that appears to have no effect on any opiate receptor. Many years ago it was tested for abuse potential by comparing it with opiates and was found to be very dissimilar to the opiates and, therefore, considered safe. Recently, however, there have been numerous reports of people consuming large quantities of Robitussin (in Canada, cough medicines that contain dextromethorphan often end with a "-DM") and other over-the-counter cough medicines for their psychological effects, a practice sometimes called *roboing* (Darboe, Keenan, & Richards, 1996). This has led to a more careful reexamination of dextromethorphan's behavioral pharmacology (Nicholson, Hayes, & Balster, 1999). Also of interest is *dextrophan*, a metabolite of dextromethorphan.

Neurophysiology

Although it has no effect on opiate receptors, dextromethorphan and dextrophan have been shown to bind with low affinity to the PCP receptor of the NMDA receptor complex, where they also act as channel blockers in a manner similar to alcohol and the dissociative anesthetics (see Chapter 4). This means that they have pharmacological properties similar to the dissociative anesthetics, PCP, and ketamine. Dextrophan has a 5-fold to 10-fold greater affinity for the receptor than dextromethorphan and, consequently, has a much greater PCP-like effect.

Pharmacokinetics

In most cases, dextromethorphan is converted rapidly to dextrophan during first pass through the liver. Because the effects of dextrophan are greater than dextromethorphan, the most intense effects of consuming dextromethorphan may be delayed until this transformation occurs. Since first-pass metabolism is greatest after oral administration, oral consumption may be the most effective route of administration.

Population studies have shown that there is considerable individual variation in the ability to metabolize dextromethorphan to dextrophan. Some are rapid metabolizers and should be able to experience the effects of dextrophan rapidly, but others are slow metabolizers, so the metabolite will not reach high levels, and the effects will be diminished. About 5 to 10 percent of Caucasians and around 4 percent of African Americans are poor metabolizers (He, Daniel, Hajiloo, & Shockley, 1999). Such differences in metabolism can cause considerable individual variation in the effects of taking dextromethorphan.

Discriminative Stimulus Properties

Rats and, to some extent, rhesus monkeys trained to discriminate PCP will generalize fully to dextrophan and partially to dextromethorphan. Generalization is dose and training specific, and this has led researchers to believe that dextromethorphan and dextrophan are not identical to PCP and other full NMDA receptor blockers. They may have their effect on a different subset of NMDA receptors.

Self-Administration

It appears that rats and monkeys will readily self-administer both dextromethorphan and dextrophan.

Behavioral Effects

Nonhumans. The effects of dextromethorphan and dextrophan have been investigated in rats. Dextromethorphan caused a decrease in locomotor activity, whereas dextrophan caused an increase along with stereotyped behavior at higher doses. Some memory impairment was seen with dextromethorphan but not with dextrophan. The two drugs appeared to have different effects, with dextromethorphan's effect resembling that of sedatives and dextrophan resembling PCP (Dematteis, Lallement, & Mallaert, 1998).

Humans. Dextromethorphan has been used as a cough suppressant for over 30 years. At normal therapeutic doses, it has few side effects and no PCP-like effects, but at higher doses, its effects are similar to PCP and ketamine and include ataxia, dizziness, euphoria, and tactile and visual hallucinations.

GHB

GHB (gamma-hydroxybutyrate) occurs naturally in the body as a metabolite of gamma-aminobutyric acid (GABA) and appears to be a neurotransmitter or neuromodulator. It has its own receptor site. GHB is now being developed to be sold under the trade name Xyrem as a treatment for narcolepsy (Nicholson & Balster, 2001).

GHB was initially isolated and investigated in 1960 by Henri Laborit (the researcher credited with the discovery of the antipsychotic drugs; see Chapter 13). It has been widely used in Europe as a medicine and in the United States as a dietary supplement. It received little attention from public health officials until the early 1990s, when its use became more widespread as a growth promoter among bodybuilders, as a sedative, and as a recreational drug used along with ecstasy and ketamine (see Chapter 16) as a club drug at raves and dance parties. It also gained a reputation as a date rape drug. In 1993, the actor River Phoenix collapsed and died outside the Viper Room in Los Angeles. Although it was never confirmed, the rumor that GHB was responsible created a lot of interest in the drug (O'Connell, Kay, & Plosay, 2000).

In 1990, the U.S. Food and Drug Administration declared GHB unsafe and banned it from public sale. This effort was not entirely effective because GHB continued to be sold on the Internet and in some stores. To get around the legislation, kits were sold that contained GBL, a metabolic precursor of GHB, along with instructions on how to convert it into GHB. GHB has many street names, including *liquid X, GBH* (grievous bodily harm), *scoop, cherry meth, blue nitro, easy lay*, and more than 30 others (O'Connell, et al., 2000).

The legal status of GHB remains unclear. In February 2000, the U.S. attorney general was voted authority by the U.S. Congress to make GHB a Schedule I drug; that is, it has abuse potential but no medical use. GHB products now being tested for medical purposes were to be classed as Schedule III drugs. This is similar to the classification of Marinol, a preparation containing THC (the active ingredient in marijuana) that has medical use (see Chapter 15). This ambiguity has not yet been resolved. GHL and kits for making GHB, however, are now illegal in the United States.

Pharmacokinetics and Dose

GHB and GBL, its precursor, are considered to be pharmacologically equivalent except that GBL is more readily absorbed. GHB is rapidly absorbed orally and its effects begin in 15 to 30 minutes and peak between 25 and 45 minutes. It has a half-life of 30 to 50 minutes. Endogenous GHB is taken into cells via an active reuptake mechanism from the synaptic cleft, where it is rapidly metabolized.

A minimum dose is about 10 mg/kg body weight and will produce muscle relaxation. A therapeutic dose for sleep is in the range of 15 to 30 mg/kg, and a high dose of 60 mg/kg will cause unarousable sleep or coma lasting for 1 to 5 hours. A lethal dose may be anywhere between 300 and 900 mg/kg. This gives it a therapeutic index of between 20 and 60.

GHB-associated deaths have been reported, but most have involved the coadministration of another drug, such as heroin or ecstasy

Neuropharmacology

GHB binds to its own receptors, which are located in the CNS. Even though there are high levels of endogenous GHB outside the CNS, all GHB receptors appear to be inside the CNS. The GHB receptor is part of a complex that has its effect by releasing a second messenger inside the membrane.

GHB acts both presynaptically and postsynaptically to modulate activity of other neurotransmitters. Its main effect seems to be on dopamine synapses, where it inhibits dopamine release and causes the accumulation of excess dopamine in the presynaptic neuron. It has also been reported that after a period of inhibition or at higher doses, there is a surge in dopamine activity.

GABA does not bind to the GHB receptor, but GHB does bind to the $GABA_B$ receptor. This appears to happen only at GHB concentrations higher than those that occur naturally in the body. GHB also appears to have a modulatory effect on GABA levels, in some cases decreasing GABA, and, because it is also a GABA precursor, it can also increase GABA levels.

Effects on Behavior

Nonhumans. GHB has sedative properties and at high doses acts as an anesthetic, but there are significant differences between GHB and the other drugs discussed in this chapter. The anesthetic state it induces appears to be more similar to a cataleptic state than anesthesia; the EEG shows seizure-like activity that can be blocked with anticonvulsant drugs like valproic acid. The nonresponsive state achieved at high levels of GHB is more similar to a petit mal seizure than anesthesia. At higher doses, jerks and seizure-like activity can be seen.

Humans. Users report that GHB causes alcohol-like intoxication without a hangover. They report increased feelings of relaxation and euphoria. GHB is sometimes used in conjunction with alcohol and various club drugs like ketamine and ecstasy to enhance their effects. It is also reputed to be an aphrodisiac, increasing libido and increasing and enhancing sexual pleasure.

Amnesia for events both during and after drug use have also been reported (Miotto et al., 2001). At higher doses, before passing out, people show many of the signs of alcohol intoxication, they appear confused, speech is incoherent, and they have poor balance and coordination. Driving ability is clearly impaired (Couper & Logan, 2001).

Effects on Sleep. Unlike the barbiturates and benzodiazepines (or almost any other drug for that matter), GHB normalizes sleep patterns and increases stage 3 and 4 and REM sleep. This effect is the basis for its development as a treatment for *narcolepsy*. In narcolepsy, normal sleep does not occur at night, so the narcoleptic falls into uncontrollable sleep during the day. The benzodiazepine and barbiturate hypnotics alter normal nighttime sleep patterns and are consequently not useful, but GHB appears to be an effective treatment.

Anxiolytic Properties. There is conflicting evidence that GHB has anxiolytic effects. Some studies report that it increases punished responding, but others do not. It is clear, however, that GHB is not as effective an anxiolytic as the barbiturates or benzodiazepines.

Drug State Discrimination

Animals trained to discriminate GHB from saline only partially generalize to morphine, LSD, and chlordiazepoxide and generalize even less to amphetamine and ethanol and do not generalize at all to barbital and PCP-like compounds, indicating a unique subjective effect.

Any generalization to other drugs seems to be highly dose specific. At high training doses of GHB, animals will generalize to drugs that are $GABA_B$ agonists, suggesting that this effect is probably responsible for its subjective effect, but at low doses, the subjective effect appears to be mediated by its activity at its own receptor. Similarly, alcohol-trained rats only generalize to GHB at a very narrow range of intermediate doses.

Self-Administration

Nonhumans. GHB will create a place preference in rats, but it requires more trials than with cocaine. There are no convincing studies that show rats or monkeys will reliably self-administer GHB. On the other hand, there is evidence that GHB will reduce the self-administration of alcohol in both rats and humans, with humans reporting a reduction in craving for alcohol. This may be a result of the dopamine-blocking effect of GHB, but this effect needs further study.

Human Epidemiology. Clearly GHB is used by humans, but little data are available on the extent of its use. The Drug Abuse Warning Network is a system that tracks drug use by frequency of the number of times it is mentioned in cases seen in hospital emergency rooms in the United States and Canada. In 1992 there were 20 mentions of GHB, but in 1998 it was mentioned on nearly 1,300 occasions. This cannot be taken as an indication of how often the drug is used, but it does suggest a drastic increase in use. It remains to be seen whether the newly introduced legislation will be able to reduce its availability and the extent of its use (Nicholson & Balster, 2001).

Prevalence of GHB use among high school students in the United States does not appear to have changed much since 2000. In 2004, 2 percent of grade 12 students reported using GHB (Johnston et al., 2005).

Tolerance and Withdrawal

Tolerance develops to the motor-impairing effects of GHB in rats following high doses for 9 days. These rats were cross-tolerant with alcohol on the same effect. Tolerance has also been demonstrated to the sedating and anesthetic effects of GHB.

Case reports suggest that many chronic users report insomnia that lasts for no more than 3 days after discontinuing using GHB. Anxiety has also been reported. One study, however, has reported more severe cases of withdrawal after continuous consumption every 3 to 4 hours. Initially, patients reported anxiety and tremor. This developed into severe delirium with auditory and visual hallucinations that took 5 to 15 days to resolve (Dyer, Roth, & Hyma, 2001).

GHB will alleviate withdrawal symptoms of alcohol in humans and nonhumans, and it has been used in treating alcoholics who report reduced use of alcohol and reduced craving. GHB is also effective in reducing withdrawal effects from opiates.

CHAPTER SUMMARY

- Hallucinogens are a class of drugs that cause hallucinations. Other drugs discussed in this chapter may be called many names depending on why they are taken. These include phantasticants, psychedelics (mind manifesters), entactogens (touching within), and empathogens (empathy creators). Many are used as club drugs.

- The indoleamine-like drugs include LSD, psilocybin, and DMT, and the catecholamine-like drugs include mescaline and ecstasy.

- LSD is an extremely potent hallucinogen that resembles serotonin. It was synthesized in 1943 but did not become popular until the 1960s, when it was extensively used.

- LSD is sold on the street as hits in blotters, gelatin, and sugar cubes. It is effective orally.

- The indoleamine-like and catecholamine-like drugs all are agonists at a specific serotonin receptor, and this increases the responses of glutaminergic neurons in the cortex.

- In general, the hallucinatory experience starts out with colored visions of tunnel, spiral, and lattice shapes that move. Meaningful images start to become incorporated into these images, and finally there is a rapid succession of meaningful scenes.

- LSD also has empathogenic effects, and people often experience profound feelings of a mystical or religious nature.

- Tolerance develops and dissipates rapidly to the effects of LSD and psilocybin.

- Indeolamine-like hallucinogens are only rarely self-administered by nonhumans, but human use is widespread among many cultures. In the United States, its use has been dropping since 1996.

- There are a large number of synthetic drugs that combine the properties of catecholamine-like drugs and amphetamine. The best known is ecstasy, also known as MDMA.

- Ecstasy enhances social intimacy and is considered an empathogen and entactogen and is widely used as a club drug.

- Ecstasy is taken orally, is absorbed in 2 hours, and has a half-life of about 8 hours. It enhances the release and blocks the reuptake of catecholamines, primarily serotonin.

- Ecstasy is self-administered by nonhumans. Its use among young people in the United States is declining.

- Heavy use of ecstasy causes a depletion of serotonin in the brain and the effects of this last for months and cause sleep disorders, depression, and anxiety. Acute doses at raves cause a loss of heat regulation accompanied by dehydration and heat-stroke symptoms.

- Phencyclidine (PCP) and ketamine are dissociative anesthetics. They can be snorted, injected, or taken orally. Their effects are felt within minutes.

- The dissociative anesthetics block NMDA receptors for glutamate in the cortex. They can block memories for events during their effect and can induce thought disorders. They induce numbness, relaxation, and analgesia. With continuous use, tolerance develops, and there are withdrawal symptoms.

- Nonhumans self-administer dissociative anesthetics. The use of PCP by young people in the United States has declined, but ketamine use is staying steady at a low level.

- Psychosis caused by the dissociative anesthetics can sometimes last long after the drug has been used, and there have been a number of accidental deaths reported.

- Dextromethorphan is widely used in over-the-counter cough suppressants. Both it and its metabolite dextrophan block the NMDA receptor for glutamate and have effects similar to the dissociative anesthetics.

- Dextrophan is more potent than dextromethorphan, so speeded metabolism enhances its effect.

- Nonhumans readily self-administer dextromethorphan.

- GHB is a metabolite of GABA. It was used as a medicine in Europe and became available in health food stores as a dietary supplement. It was made illegal in the United States in 1990, but it also has a legitimate medical use. Its legal status has not been resolved.

- GHB is taken orally. Its effects begin in 15 to 30 minutes and peak between 25 and 45 minutes. It has a half-life of 30 to 50 minutes. Low doses cause relaxation and sleep. High doses cause unarousable sleep or coma.

- GHB has its own receptor in the CNS and modifies the activity of many other neurotransmitters.

- GHB acts like an anesthetic, but it seems to be causing a cataleptic state. It causes an alcohol-like intoxication with amnesia. At therapeutic doses it causes normal sleep with normal EEG patterns and can be used to treat narcolepsy.

- GHB is not self-administered by nonhumans. In the United States, its use increased in the 1990s but appears to have leveled off. Tolerance and withdrawal effects have been reported.

References

ABC News Online. (2004). http://www.abc.net.au/news/newsitems/200408/s1182205.htm, July 29, 2005.

Abel, E. L., McMillan, D. E., & Harris, L. S. (1974). Delta-9-tetrahydrocannabinol: Effects of route of administration on onset and duration of activity and tolerance development. *Psychopharmacologia, 35,* 29–38.

Abel, E. L., & Sokol, R. J. (1989). Alcohol consumption during pregnancy: The dangers of moderate drinking. In H. W. Goode & D. P. Agarwal (Eds.), *Alcoholism: Biomedical and genetic aspects* (pp. 216–227). New York: Pergamon Press.

Adams, I. B., & Martin, B. R. (1996). Cannabis: Pharmacology and toxicology in animals and humans. *Addiction, 91,* 1585–1614.

Adler, C. M. (1999). Comparison of ketamine-induced thought disorder in healthy volunteers and thought disorder in schizophrenia. *American Journal of Psychiatry, 156,* 1643–1649.

Adler, C. M., Malhotra, A. K., Elma, I., Goldberg, T., Egan, M., Pickar, D., & Breier, A. (1999). Comparison of ketamine-induced thought disorder in healthy volunteers and thought disorder in schizophrenia. *American Journal of Psychiatry, 156,* 1646–1649.

Adler, J., Abramson, P., Katz, S., & Hager, M. (1985, April 15). Getting high on "Ecstasy." *Newsweek,* p. 96.

Agurell, S., Halldin, M., Lindgren, J., Ohlsson, A., Widman, M., Gillespie, H., et al. (1986). Pharmacokinetics and metabolites of D1-tetrahydrocannabinol and other cannabinoids with emphasis on man. *Pharmacological Reviews, 38,* 21–43.

Agurell, S., Lindgren, J., Ohlsson, A., Gillispie, H. K., & Hollister, L. (1984). Recent studies in the pharmacokinetics of delta-1-tetrahydrocannabinol in man. In S. Agurell, W. L. Dewey, & R. E. Willett (Eds.), *The cannabinoids: Chemical, pharmacological, and therapeutic aspects* (pp. 165–184). Orlando: Academic Press.

Alcoholics Anonymous. (1980). *Dr. Bob and the good oldtimers.* New York: Author.

Alcoholics Anonymous. (2005). *AA Fact File.* Available at http://www.aa.org/en_pdfs/m-24_aafactfile.pdf

Aldrich, A., Aranda, J. V., & Neims, A. H. (1979). Caffeine metabolism in the newborn. *Clinical Pharmacology and Therapeutics, 25,* 447–453.

Aldrich, M. R., & Baker, R. W. (1976). Historical aspects of cocaine use and abuse. In S. J. Mule (Ed.), *Cocaine: Chemical, biological, clinical, social and treatment aspects* (pp. 1–12). Boca Raton, FL: CRC Press.

Alexander, B. K., Beyerstein, B. I., Hadaway, P. F., & Coambs, R. B. (1981). Effects of early and later colony housing on oral ingestion of morphine in rats. *Pharmacology, Biochemistry and Behavior, 15,* 571–576.

Alexander, B. K., & Schweighofer, A. R. F. (1988). Defining "addiction." *Canadian Psychology, 29,* 151–162.

Amed, S., & Koob, G. (1998). Transition from moderate to excessive drug intake: Change in hedonic set point. *Science, 282,* 298–300.

American Lung Association. (2004). *Trends in tobacco use.* Available at http://www.lungusa.org/site/pp.asp?c=dvLUK9OOE&b=33347

American Lung Association. (2006). Trends in tobacco use 2006. Available at http://www.lungusa.org/site/pp.asp?c=dvLUK9OOE&b=33309#latest

American Psychiatric Association. (1987). *Diagnostic and statistical manual of mental disorders* (3rd ed., Rev.). Washington, DC: Author.

American Psychiatric Association. (1994). *Diagnostic and statistical manual of mental disorders* (4th ed.). Washington, DC: Author.

American Psychiatric Association. (2000). *Diagnostic and statistical manual of mental disorders* (4th ed., Text Revision). Washington, DC: Author.

American Society of Hospital Pharmacists. (1987). *Drug information '87*. Bethesda, MD: Author.

Anderson, K. (1975). Effects of cigarette smoking on learning and retention. *Psychopharmacologia, 41*, 1–5.

Angrist, B., & Sudilovsky, A. (1978). Central nervous system stimulants. In L. L. Iverson, S. D. Iverson, & S. H. Snyder (Eds.), *Handbook of psychopharmacology* (Vol. 11, pp. 95–165). New York: Plenum Press.

Anonymous. (1955). An autobiography of a schizophrenic experience. *Journal of Abnormal and Social Psychology, 512*, 677–689.

Arber, E. (1895). *English reprints: A counterblaste to tobacco (by James I of England)*. Westminster: A. Constable.

Armitage, A. K. (1973). Some recent observations relating to the absorption of nicotine from tobacco smoke. In W. L. Dunn (Ed.), *Smoking behavior: Motives and incentives* (pp. 83–91). Washington, DC: Winston.

Armor, D. J., Polach, J. M., & Stambul, H. B. (1978). *Alcoholism and treatment*. New York: Wiley.

Arnaud, M. J. (1993). Metabolism of caffeine and other components of coffee. In S. Garattini (Ed.), *Caffeine, coffee and health* (pp. 43–95). New York: Raven Press.

Ashton, C. H. (1984). Benzodiazepine withdrawal: An unfinished story. *British Medical Journal, 288*, 1135–1140. Also available at http://www.benzo.org.uk/ashunfi.htm

Ashton, H., & Stepney, R. (1982). *Smoking: Psychology and pharmacology*. London: Travistock.

Ator, N., & Griffiths, R. R. (1992). Oral self-administration of triazolam, diazepam and ethanol in the baboon: Drug reinforcement and benzodiazepine physical dependence. *Psychopharmacology, 108*(3), 301–312.

Atweh, S. F., & Kuhar, M. J. (1983). Distribution and physiological significance of opioid receptors in the brain. *British Medical Bulletin, 39*, 47–52.

Austin, G. A. (1985). *Alcohol in Western society from antiquity to 1800*. Santa Barbara, CA: ABC-Clio Information Services.

Axelrod, J., & Reisenthal, J. (1953). The fate of caffeine in man and a method for its estimation in biological materials. *Journal of Pharmacology and Experimental Therapeutics, 107*, 519–523.

Azorlosa, J. L., Greenwald, M. K., & Stitzer, M. L. (1995). Marijuana smoking, effects of varying puff volume and breathhold duration. *Journal of Pharmacology and Experimental Therapeutics, 272*(2), 560–569.

Babor, T. F. (1985). Alcohol, economics and the ecological fallacy: Toward an integration of experimental and quasi-experimental research. In E. Single & T. Storm (Eds.), *Public drinking and public policy* (pp. 161–190). Toronto: Addiction Research Foundation.

Babor, T. F., Berglas, S., Mendelson, J. H., Ellingboe, J., & Miller, K. (1983). Alcohol: Effect on the disinhibition of behavior. *Psychopharmacology, 80*, 53–60.

Badaiani, A., & Robinson, T. E. (2004). Drug-induced neurobehavioral plasticity: The role of environmental context. *Behavioral Pharmacology, 15*, 327–339.

Baekeland, F. (1977). Evaluation of treatment methods in chronic alcoholism. In B. Kissen & H. Begleiter (Eds.), *The biology of alcoholism* (Vol. 5, pp. 385–440). New York: Plenum Press.

Baggott, M., Jerome, L., & Stuart, R. (2001). 3,4-methylenedioxymethamphetamine (MDMA): A review of the English-language scientific and medical literature. Available at http://www.maps.org/research/mdma/protocol/litreview.html

Baird, D. D. (1992). Evidence for reduced fecundity in female smokers. In D. Poswillio & E. Alberman (Eds.), *Effects of smoking on the fetus, neonate and child* (pp. 5–22). Oxford, England: Oxford University Press.

Baker, R. C., & Jerrells, T. R. (1993). Immunological aspects. In M. Galanter (Ed.), *Recent developments in alcoholism* (Vol. 11, pp. 249–271). New York: Plenum Press.

Baldessarini, R. J. (1985). *Chemotherapy in psychiatry: Principles and practice*. Cambridge, MA: Harvard University Press.

Baldessarini, R. J., Ghaemi, S. N., & Viguera, A. C. (2002). Tolerance in antidepressant treatment. *Psychotherapy and Psychosomatics, 71*, 177–179.

Balfour, D. J. K. (1982). The pharmacology of nicotine dependence: A working hypothesis. *Pharmacology and Therapeutics, 15*, 239–250.

Balfour, D. J. K. (1991). The influence of stress on psychopharmacological responses to nicotine. *British Journal of Addiction, 86*, 489–493.

Ball, J. C., & Snarr, R. W. (1969). A test of the maturation hypothesis with respect to opiate addiction. *United Nations Bulletin on Narcotics, 21*, 9–13.

Balster, R. L. (1987). The behavioral pharmacology of phencyclidine. In H. Y. Meltzer (Ed.), *Psychopharmacology: The third generation of progress* (pp. 1573–1579). New York: Raven Press.

Balster, R. L. (1998). The neural basis of inhalant abuse. *Drug and Alcohol Dependence, 51*, 207–214.

Balster, R. L., & Ford, R. D. (1978). The discriminative stimulus properties of cannabinoids: A review. In B. T. Ho, D. W. Richards, & D. L. Chute (Eds.), *Drug discrimination and state dependent learning* (pp. 131–147). Orlando: Academic Press.

Bareggi, S., Ferini-Strambi, L., Pirola, R., & Smirne, S. (1998). Impairment of memory and flunitrazepam levels. *Psychopharmacology, 140*, 157–163.

Barnes, G., & Elthrington, L. G. (1973). *Drug dosage in laboratory animals: A handbook.* Berkeley: University of California Press.

Barone, J. J., & Roberts, H. (1984). Human consumption of caffeine. In P. B. Dews (Ed.), *Caffeine: Perspectives from recent research* (pp. 59–73). Berlin: Springer-Verlag.

Barrett, R. J., & Smith, R. L. (2005). Evidence for PTZ-like cues as a function of time following treatment with chlordiazepoxide: Implications for understanding tolerance and withdrawal. *Behavioural Pharmacology, 16*, 147–153.

Barrett, S. P., Boileau, I., Okker, J., Pihl, R. O., & Dagher, A. (2004). The hedonic response to cigarette smoking is proportional to dopamine release in the human striatum as measured by positron emission tomography and [^{11}C]raclopride. *Synapse, 54*, 65–71.

Barrows, S., & Room, R. (1991). Social history and alcohol studies. In S. Barrows & R. Room (Eds.), *Drinking: Behavior and belief in modern history* (pp. 1–25). Berkeley: University of California Press.

Barry, H., III, & Kubina, R. K. (1972). Discriminative stimulus characteristics of alcohol, marijuana and atropine. In J. M. Singh, L. Miller, & H. Lal (Eds.), *Drug addiction: Experimental pharmacology* (Vol. 1, pp. 3–16). Mt. Kisco, NY: Futura.

Barry, H., III, McGuire, M. S., & Krimmer, E. C. (1982). Alcohol and meprobamate resemble phenobarbital rather than chlordiazepoxide. In F. C. Colpaert & J. F. Slangen (Eds.), *Drug discrimination: Applications in CNS pharmacology* (pp. 219–233). Amsterdam: Elsevier Biomedical.

Baumeister, R. F., & Placidi, K. S. (1983). A social-history and analysis of the LSD controversy. *Journal of Humanistic Psychology, 23*, 25–60.

BBC. (2004). http://news.bbc.co.uk/1/hi/england/bristol/3497307.stm

Beauvais, F., & Oetting, E. (1988). Inhalant abuse by young children. In R. A. Crider & B. A. Rouse (Eds.), *Epidemiology of inhalant abuse: An update* (pp. 30–48). (NIDA Research Monograph 85). Rockville, MD: U.S. Department of Health and Human Services.

Becker, G. S., Grossman, M., & Murphy, K. M. (1988). An empirical analysis of cigarette addiction. *American Economic Review, 84*, 396–418.

Beckett, A. H., Gorrod, J. W., & Jenner, P. (1971a). Analysis of nicotine-1′-N-oxide in urine in the presence of nicotine and cotenine, and its application to the study of in vivo nicotine metabolism in man. *Journal of Pharmacy and Pharmacology, 23*, 55S–61S.

Beckett, A. H., Gorrod, J. W., & Jenner, P. (1971b). The effects of smoking on nicotine metabolism in vivo in man. *Journal of Pharmacy and Pharmacology, 23*, 62S–67S.

Beckstead, M. J., Weiner, J. L., Eger, E. I., Gong, D. H., & Mihic, S. (2000). Glycine and gamma-aminobutyric acid(A) receptor function is enhanced by inhaled drugs of abuse. *Molecular Pharmacology, 57*, 1199–1205.

Belleville, J. W., Forrest, W. H., Shroff, P., & Brown, B. W. (1971). The hypnotic effects of codeine and secobarbital and their interactions in man. *Clinical Pharmacology and Therapeutics, 2*, 607–612.

Benet, S. (1975). Early diffusion and folk use of hemp. In V. Rubin (Ed.), *Cannabis and culture* (pp. 31–50). The Hague: Mouton.

Benowitz, N. L., & Henningfield, J. E. (1994). Establishing a nicotine threshold for addiction. *New England Journal of Medicine, 331*, 123–125.

Benzodiazepine/Driving Collaborative Group. (1993). Are benzodiazepines a risk for road accidents? *Drug and Alcohol Dependence, 33*, 19–22.

Berggren, U., Eriksson, M., Fajlke, C., & Balldin, J. (2002). Is long-term heavy alcohol consumption toxic for brain serotonergic neurons? Relationship between years of excessive alcohol consumption and serotonergic neurotransmission. *Drug and Alcohol Dependence, 65*, 159–165.

Bergman, J., & Johanson, C. E. (1985). The reinforcing properties of diazepam under several conditions in rhesus monkeys. *Psychopharmacology, 86*, 108–113.

Bergsman, A., & Jarpe, G. (1969). Comments on free prescription of central stimulants and narcotic drugs. In F. Sjoquist & M. Tottie (Eds.), *Abuse of central stimulants* (pp. 275–279). Stockholm: Almqvist & Wiksell.

Berridge, V., & Edwards, G. (1981). *Opium and the people*. London: St. Martin's Press.

Besser, G. (1967). Some physical characteristics of auditory flicker fusion in man. *Nature, 214*, 17–19.

Bewley, T. H. (1974). Treatment of opiate addiction in Great Britain. In S. Fisher & A. M. Freeman (Eds.), *Opiate addiction: Origins and treatment* (pp. 141–161). New York: Wiley.

Bickel, W. K., DeGrandpre, R. J., Higgins, S. T., & Hughes, J. R. (1990). Behavioral economics of drug administration: 1. Functional equivalence of response requirement and drug dose. *Life Sciences, 47*, 1501–1510.

Bickel, W. K., Hughes, J. R., DeGrandpre, R. J., Higgins, S. T., & Rozzuto, P. (1992). Behavioral economics of drug self-administration: 4. The effects of response requirement on the consumption of and interaction between concurrently available coffee and cigarette. *Psychopharmacology, 107*, 211–216.

Bickel, W. K., & Marsch, L. A. (2001). Toward a behavioral economic understanding of drug dependence: Delay discounting process. *Addiction, 96*, 73–86.

Bickerdyke, J. (1971). *The curiosities of ale and beer*. New York: Blom.

Bigelow, G., & Liebson, I. (1972). Cost factors controlling alcoholic drinking. *Psychological Record, 22*, 305–314.

Birnbaum, I., & Parker, E. (1977). Acute effects of alcohol on storage and retrieval. In I. M. Birnbaum & E. S. Parker (Eds.), *Alcohol and human memory* (pp. 99–107). Hillsdale, NJ: Erlbaum.

Blier, P., & de Montigny, C. (1994). Current advances and trends in the treatment of depression. *Trends in Pharmacological Science, 15*, 220–226.

Bocca, M., Le-Doz, F., Ftard, O., Pottier, M., L'Hoste, J., & Denise, P. (1999). Residual effects of zolpidem, 10 mg and zopiclone, 7.5 mg versus flunitrazepam, 1 mg and placebo on driving performance and ocular saccades. *Psychopharmacology, 143*, 373–379.

Boer, G. J., Feenstra, M. G. P., Mirmiran, M., Swaab, D. F., & Van Haaren, F. (1988). *The biochemical basis of functional teratology: Progress in brain research* (Vol. 73). Amsterdam: Elsevier.

Bonati, M., & Garattini, S. (1984). Interspecies comparison of caffeine disposition. In P. B. Dews (Ed.), *Caffeine: Perspectives from recent research* (pp. 48–56). Berlin: Springer-Verlag.

Bonhomme, N., & Esposito, E. (1998). Involvement of serotonin and dopamine in the mechanism of action of novel antidepressant drugs: A review. *Journal of Clinical Psychopharmacology, 18*, 447–454.

Bonnet, M. H., & Arand, D. L. (1992). Caffeine use as a model of acute and chronic insomnia. *Sleep, 15*, 526–536.

Boston, L. N. (1908). Delirium tremens (mania e potu). *Lancet, 1*, 18.

Bowen, S., & Balster, R. (1997). Desflurane, enflurane, isoflurane and ether produce ethanol-like discriminative effects in mice. *Pharmacology, Biochemistry and Behavior, 57*, 191–198.

Bowen, S., & Balster, R. (1998). A direct comparison of inhalant effects on locomotor activity and schedule controlled behavior in mice. *Experimental and Clinical Psychopharmacology, 6*, 235–247.

Bowen, S., Daniel, J., & Balster, R. (1999). Deaths associated with inhalant use in Virginia from 1987 to 1996. *Drug and Alcohol Dependence, 53*, 239–245.

Bowen, S., Wiley, J., Jones, H., & Balster, R. (1999). Phencyclidine- and diazepam-like discriminative stimulus effects of inhalants in mice. *Experimental and Clinical Psychopharmacology, 7*, 28–37.

Bowers, M. B., Jr. (1987). The role of drugs in the production of schizophreniform psychosis and related disorders. In H. Y. Meltzer (Ed.), *Psychopharmacology: A third generation of progress* (pp. 819–823). New York: Raven Press.

Bows, H. A. (1965). The role of diazepam (Valium) in emotional illness. *Psychosomatics, 6*, 336–340.

Boyer, W. F., & Feighner, J. P. (1991). Side effects of the selective serotonin re-uptake inhibitors. In J. P. Feighner & W. F. Boyer (Eds.), *Selective serotonin re-uptake inhibitors* (pp. 133–152). Chichester, England: Wiley.

Bozarth, M. A., & Wise, R. A. (1984). Anatomically distinct opiate receptor fields mediate rewards and physical dependence. *Science, 244*, 516–517.

Brady, J. V., Griffiths, R. R., Heinz, R. D., Ator, N. A., Lucas, S. E., & Lamb, R. J. (1987). Assessing drugs for abuse liability and dependence potential in laboratory primates. In M. A. Bozarth (Ed.), *Methods of assessing the reinforcing properties of abused drugs* (pp. 45–86). New York: Springer-Verlag.

Braude, M. C., & Szara, S. (1976). *Pharmacology of marijuana* (2 vols.). Orlando: Academic Press.

Brauer, L., Ambre, J., & de Wit, H. (1996). Acute tolerance to the subjective but not cardiovascular effects of d-amphetamine in normal, healthy men. *Journal of Clinical Psychopharmacology, 16*, 72–76.

Brauer, L., Goudie, A., & de Wit, H. (1997). Dopamine ligands and the stimulus effects of amphetamine: Animal models versus human laboratory data. *Psychopharmacology, 130*, 2–13.

Brecher, E. M., & the Editors of *Consumer Reports*. (1972). *Licit and illicit drugs*. Mt. Vernon, NY: Consumers Union.

Brecher, E. M., Wang, B. W., Wong, H., & Morgan, J. P. (1988). Phencyclidine and violence: Clinical and legal issues. *Journal of Clinical Psychopharmacology, 8*, 397–401.

Brenesova, V., Oswald, I., & Loudon, J. (1975). Two types of insomnia: Too much waking or not enough sleep. *British Journal of Psychiatry, 126*, 439–445.

Britton, D. R., El-Wardnay, Z. S., Brown, C. P., & Bianchine, J. R. (1978). Clinical pharmacokinetics of selected psychotropic drugs. In L. L. Iverson, S. D. Iverson, & S. H. Snyder (Eds.), *Handbook of psychopharmacology* (Vol. 13, pp. 299–344). New York: Plenum Press.

Brookes, L. G. (1985). Central nervous system stimulants. In S. D. Iverson (Ed.), *Psychopharmacology: Recent advances and future prospects* (pp. 264–277). Oxford, England: Oxford University Press.

Brookhuis, K., Volkerts, E., & O'Hanlon, J. (1990). Repeated dose effects of lormetrazepam and flurazepam upon driving performance. *European Journal of Clinical Pharmacology, 39*, 83–87.

Brooks, J. E. (1952). *The mighty leaf: Tobacco through the centuries*. Boston: Little, Brown.

Brown, F. C. (1972). *Hallucinogenic drugs*. Springfield, IL: Thomas.

Bunney, W. E., & Garland-Bunney, B. L. (1987). Mechanism of actions of lithium in affective illness: Basic and clinical implications. In H. Y. Meltzer (Ed.), *Psychopharmacology: A third generation of progress* (pp. 553–565). New York: Raven Press.

Burg, A. W. (1975). Physiological disposition of caffeine. *Drug Metabolism Reviews, 4*, 199–228.

Busto, U., Bendayan, R., & Sellers, E. (1989). Clinical pharmacokinetics of non-opiate abused drugs. *Clinical Pharmacokinetics, 16*, 1–26.

Busto, U., Isaac, P. D., & Adrian, M. (1986). Changing patterns of benzodiazepine use in Canada [Abstract]. *Clinical Pharmacology and Therapeutics, 23*, 184.

Butschky, M. F., Bailey, D., Henningfield, J. E., & Pickworth, W. B. (1994). Smoking without nicotine delivery decreases withdrawal in 12-hour abstinent smokers. *Pharmacology, Biochemistry and Behavior, 50*, 91–96.

Caddy, G. R., & Block, T. (1983). Behavioral treatment methods for alcoholism. In M. Galanter (Ed.), *Recent developments in alcoholism* (pp. 139–165). New York: Plenum Press.

Calabrese, J., & Bowen, C. (2000). Lithium and the anticonvulsants in bipolar disorder. In *Psychopharmacology: The fourth generation of progress*. Available at http://www.acnp.org/g4/GN401000106/Default.htm

Caldwell, J. (1976). Physiological aspects of cocaine usage. In S. J. Mule (Ed.), *Cocaine: Chemical, biological, clinical, social and treatment aspects* (pp. 187–200). Boca Raton, FL: CRC Press

Calhoun, V. D., Pekar, J. J., & Pearlson, G. D. (2004). Alcohol intoxication effects on simulated driving: Exploring alcohol-dose effects on brain activation using functional MRI. *Neuropsyhopharmacology, 29*, 2097–2107.

Callahan, M. M., Robertson, R. S., Branfman, A. R., McCormish, M. F., & Yesair, D. W. (1983). Comparison of caffeine metabolism in three non-smoking populations after oral administration of radio-labelled caffeine. *Drug Metabolism and Disposition, 11*, 211–217.

Campbell, J. C., & Seiden, L. S. (1973). Performance influence on the development of tolerance to amphetamine. *Pharmacology, Biochemistry and Behavior, 1*, 703–708.

Cappell, H., & Pliner, P. (1974). Cannabis intoxication: The role of pharmacological and psychological variables. In L. L. Miller (Ed.), *Marijuana: Effects on human behaviour* (pp. 233–264). Orlando: Academic Press.

Carlezon, W. A., & Wise, R. A. (1996). Rewarding actions of phencyclidine and related drugs in nucleus accumbens shell and frontal cortex. *Journal of Neuroscience, 16*(9), 3112–3122.

Carlsson, A. (1969). Biochemical pharmacology of amphetamines. In F. Sjoquist & M. Tottie (Eds.), *Abuse of central stimulants* (pp. 305–310). Stockholm: Almqvist & Wiksell.

Carlsson, A. (1994). The search for the ideal medications: Developing a rational neuropharmacology. In N. C. Andreasen (Ed.), *Schizophrenia: From mind to molecule* (pp. 161–172). Washington, DC: American Psychiatric Press.

Carney, J. M. (1982). Effects of caffeine, theophylline and theobromine on schedule controlled responding in rats. *British Journal of Pharmacology, 75,* 451–454.

Carroll, M. E. (1993). The economic context of drug and nondrug reinforcers affects acquisition and maintenance of drug reinforced behavior and withdrawal effects. *Alcohol and Drug Dependence, 33,* 201–210.

Carroll, M. E. (1995). Reducing drug abuse by enriching the environment with alternative drug reinforcement. In L. Green & J. H. Kagel (Eds.), *Advances in behavioral economics* (Vol. 3, pp. 37–68). Norwood, NJ: Ablex.

Carroll, M. E. (1998). Psychological and psychiatric consequences of caffeine. In R. E. Tarter, R. T. Ammerman, & P. J. Ott (Eds.), *Handbook of substance abuse: Neurobehavioral pharmacology* (pp. 97–110). New York: Plenum Press.

Carroll, M. E., & Bickel, W. (1998). Behavioral-environmental determinants of the reinforcing effect of cocaine. In S. T. Higgins & J. L. Katz (Eds.), *Cocaine abuse: Behavior, pharmacology and clinical applications* (pp. 81–106). San Diego: Academic Press.

Carroll, M. E., & Meisch, R. A. (1984). Increases in food reinforced behavior due to food deprivation. In T. Thompson, P. B. Dews, & J. E. Barrett (Eds.), *Advances in behavioral pharmacology* (Vol. 4, pp. 47–88). Orlando: Academic Press.

Carroll, M. E., Rodefer, J. S., & Rawleigh, J. M. (1995). Concurrent self-administration of ethanol and an alternative nondrug reinforcer in monkeys: Effects of income (session length) on demand for drug. *Psychopharmacology, 120,* 1–9.

Carvalho, L. P., de Greckshk, G., Chapouthier, G., & Rossier, J. (1983). Anxiogenic and non-anxiogenic benzodiazepine antagonists. *Nature, 301,* 64–66.

Castaneda, C. (1973). *The teachings of Don Juan.* Los Angeles: Simon & Schuster/University of California Press.

Chait, L. D., & Burke, K. A. (1994). Preference for high- versus low-potency marijuana. *Pharmacology, Biochemistry and Behavior, 49,* 643–647.

Chait, L. D., Evans, S. M., Grant, K. A., Kamien, J. B., Johanson, C. E., & Schuster, C. R. (1988). Discriminative stimuli and subjective effects of smoked marijuana in humans. *Psychopharmacology, 94,* 206–212.

Chait, L. D., & Griffiths, R. R. (1982). Differential control of puff duration and interpuff interval in cigarette smokers. *Pharmacology, Biochemistry and Behavior, 17,* 155–158.

Chait, L. D., & Pierri, J. (1992). Effects of smoked marijuana on human performance: A critical review. In L. Murphy & A. Bartke (Eds.), *Marijuana/cannabinoids: Neurobiology and neurophysiology* (pp. 387–424). Boca Raton, FL: CRC Press.

Chait, L. D., Uhlenhuth, E. H., & Johanson, C. E. (1986). The discriminative stimulus and subjective effects of d-amphetamine, phenmetrazine and fenfluramine in humans. *Psychopharmacology, 89,* 301–306.

Chait, L. D., & Zacny, J. P. (1992). Reinforcing and subjective effects of oral Δ9-THC and smoked marijuana in humans. *Psychopharmacology, 107,* 255–262.

Chan, G. C.-K., Hinds, T. R., Impey, S., & Storm, D. R. (1998). Hippocampal neurotoxicity of Δ9-tetrahydrocannabinol. *Journal of Neuroscience, 18,* 5322–5332.

Charney, D. S., Southwick, S. M., Delgado, P. L., & Krystal, J. H. (1990). Current status of the receptor sensitivity hypothesis of antidepressant action. In J. D. Amsterdam (Ed.), *Psychopharmacology of depression* (pp. 13–34). New York: Marcel Dekker.

Cheney, R. H. (1925). *Coffee.* New York: New York University Press.

Cherek, D. R., Lane, S. D., & Dougherty, D. M. (2002). Possible amotivational effects following marijuana smoking under laboratory conditions. *Experimental Clinical Psychopharmacology, 10,* 26–38.

Cho, A., Coalson, D., Klock, P., Klafta, J., Marks, S., Toledano, A., et al. (1997). The effects of alcohol history on the reinforcing, subjective and psychomotor effects of nitrous oxide in healthy volunteers. *Drug and Alcohol Dependence, 46,* 63–70.

Choudhuri, S., & Valerio, L. G. (2005). Usefulness of studies on the molecular mechanism of action of herbals/botanicals: The case of St. John's wort. *Journal of Biochemical and Molecular Toxicology, 19,* 1–11.

Churness, V. H. (1988). Antipsychotic agents. In C. L. Bare & B. R. Williams (Eds.), *Clinical pharmacology and nursing* (pp. 522–533). Springhouse, PA: Springhouse.

Chutuape, M. A., Mitchell, S., & de Wit, H. (1994). Ethanol preloads increase ethanol preference under concurrent random ratio schedules in social drinkers. *Experimental and Clinical Psychopharmacology, 2,* 310–318.

Clarke, S., Dargan, P., & Jones, A. (2005). Naloxone in opioid poisoning: Walking the tightrope, *Emergency Medicine Journal, 22,* 612–616.

Cocteau, J. (1968). *Opium: The diary of a cure* (M. Crossland & S. Road, Trans.). London: Peter Owen.

Cohen, S., & Stillman, R. C. (1976). *The therapeutic potential of marijuana.* New York: Plenum Press.

Coldwell, S., Kaufman, E., Milgrom, P., Kharasch, E., Chen, P., Mautz, D., & Ramsay, D. (1998). Acute tolerance and reversal of the motor control effects of midazolam. *Pharmacology, Biochemistry and Behavior, 52,* 537–545.

Coleman, C., Mason, T., Hooker, E., & Robinson, S. (1999). Developmental effects of intermittent prenatal exposure to 1,1,1-trichloroethane in the rat. *Neurotoxicology and Teratology, 21,* 699–708.

Collins, D. R., Pertwee, R. G., & Davies, S. N. (1994). The action of synthetic cannabinoids on the induction of long-term potentiation in the rat hippocampal slice. *European Journal of Pharmacology, 259,* R7–R8.

Colloca, L., & Benedetti, F. (2005). Placebos and painkillers: Is mind as real as matter? *Nature Reviews/ Neuroscience, 6,* 545–552.

Colpaert, F. C. (1977). Discriminative stimulus properties of benzodiazepines and barbiturates. In H. Lal (Ed.), *Discriminative stimulus properties of drugs* (pp. 93–106). New York: Plenum Press.

Colvin, M. (1983). A counselling approach to outpatient benzodiazepine detoxification. *Journal of Psychoactive Drugs, 15,* 105–108.

Compton, W. M., Grant, B. F., Colliver, J. D., Glantz, M., & Stinson, F. S. (2004). Prevalence of marijuana use disorders in the United States: 1991–1992 and 2001–2002. *Journal of the American Medical Association, 291,* 2114–2121.

Conger, J. (1951). The effect of alcohol on conflict behavior in the albino rat. *Quarterly Journal of Studies on Alcohol, 12,* 1–29.

Conley, K. M., Toledano, A. Y., Apfelbaum, J. L., & Zacny, J. P. (1997). Modulating effects of a cold water stimulus on opioid effects in volunteers. *Psychopharmacology, 131,* 313–320.

Consroe, P., & Sandyk, R. (1992). Potential role for cannabinoids for therapy of neurological disorders. In L. Murphy & A. Bartke (Eds.), *Marijuana/ cannabinoids neurology and neurophysiology* (pp. 459–524). Boca Raton, FL: CRC Press.

Cooper, T. B. (1987). Pharmacokinetics of lithium. In H. Y. Meltzer (Ed.), *Psychopharmacology: A third generation of progress* (pp. 1365–1375). New York: Raven Press.

Costa, E. (1985). Preface. In D. Kemali & G. Racagni (Eds.), *Chronic treatments in neuropsychiatry: Advances in biochemical pharmacology* (Vol. 40, pp. 5–6). New York: Raven Press.

Couper, F., & Logan, B. (2001). GHB and driving impairment. *Journal of Forensic Sciences, 26,* 919–923.

Courvousier, S., Fournel, J., Ducrot, R., Kolsky, M., & Koetschet, P. (1953). Propriétés pharmacodynamiques du chlor-hydrate de chloro-3 (diméthylamino-3′ propyl)-10-phenorthiazine (4.560 R. P.). *Archives Internationales de Pharmacodynamie et de Thérapie, 92,* 305–361.

Crawford, R. J. M. (1981). Benzodiazepine dependency and abuse. *New Zealand Medical Journal, 94,* 195.

Creasey, W. A. (1979). *Drug disposition in humans.* New York: Oxford University Press.

Cree, J. E., Meyer, J., & Hailey, D. K. (1973). Diazepam in labor: Its metabolism and effect on clinical condition and thermogenesis of the newborn. *British Medical Journal, 4,* 251–255.

Creese, I. (1983). Receptor interactions of neuroleptics. In J. T. Coyle & S. J. Enna (Eds.), *Neuroleptics: Neurochemical, behavioral, and clinical perspectives* (pp. 183–222). New York: Raven Press.

Crowley, T. J. (1987). Clinical issues in cocaine abuse. In S. Fisher, A. Raskin, & E. H. Uhlenhuth (Eds.), *Cocaine: Clinical and behavioral aspects* (pp. 193–211). New York: Oxford University Press.

Cushman, P. (1981). Neuro-endocrine effects of opioids. *Advances in Alcohol and Substance Abuse, 1*(1), 77–99.

Cuthbert, B. N., Schupp, H. T., Bradley, M. M., Birbaumer, N., & Lang, P. J. (2000). Brain potentials in affective picture processing: Covariation with autonomic arousal and affective report. *Biological Psychology, 52,* 95–111.

Dackis, C., et al. (2005). A double-blind placebo controlled trial of modafinil for cocaine dependence. *Neuropsychopharmacology, 30*(1), 205–211.

Dahl, R. E., Scher, M. S., Williamson, D. E., Robles, N., & Day, N. (1995). A longitudinal study of prenatal marijuana use: Effects on sleep and arousal at age three years. *Archives of Pediatric and Adolescent Medicine, 149*(2), 145–150.

Daniell, H. W. (1971). Smoker's wrinkles: A study in the epidemiology of "crow's feet." *Annals of Internal Medicine, 75,* 873–880.

Darboe, M., Keenan, G., & Richards, T. (1996). The abuse of dextromethorphan-based cough syrup: A pilot study of the community of Waynesboro, Pennsylvania. *Adolescence, 31,* 633–644.

Darley, C. F., & Tinklenberg, J. R. (1974). Marijuana and memory. In L. L. Miller (Ed.), *Marijuana: Effects on human behavior* (pp. 73–102). Orlando: Academic Press.

Darwin, C. (1882). *The descent of man.* New York: Appleton.

Davidson, E. S., & Schenk, S. (1994). Variability in subjective responses to marijuana: Initial experiences of college students. *Addictive Behaviors, 19*(5), 531–538.

Davis, D. L. (1962). Normal drinking in recovered alcohol addicts. *Quarterly Journal of Studies on Alcohol, 23,* 94–104.

Davis, J., Janicak, P., Linder, R., Maloney, J., & Avkovic, I. (1983). In J. T. Coyle & S. J. Enna (Eds.), *Neuroleptics: Neurochemical, behavioral and clinical perspectives* (pp. 15–64). New York: Raven Press.

Davis, T. R. A., Kensler, C. J., & Dews, P. B. (1973). Comparison of behavioral effects of nicotine, d-amphetamine, caffeine and dimethylheptyltetrahydrocannabinol in squirrel monkeys. *Psychopharmacologia, 32,* 51–65.

Day, N. L., Leech, S. L., Richardson, G. A., Cornelius, M., Robles, N., & Larkby, C. (2002). Prenatal alcohol exposure predicts continued deficits in offspring size at 14 years of age. *Alcohol: Clinical and Experimental Research, 26,* 1584–1591.

De Angelis, C., Drazen, J. M., Frizelle, F. A., Huag, C., Hoey, J., & Horton, R. et al. (2004). Clinical trials registration: Statement from the International Committee of Medical Journal Editors. *New England Journal of Medicine, 351*(12), 1250–1251.

de Fonseca, F. R., Carrera, M. R. A., Navarro, M., Koob, G. F., & Weiss, F. (1997). Activation of corticotropin-releasing factor in the limbic system during cannabinoid withdrawal. *Science, 276,* 2050–2054.

De Freitas, B., & Schwartz, G. (1979). Effects of caffeine in chronic psychiatric patients. *American Journal of Psychiatry, 136,* 1337–1338.

Degenhardt, L., Hall, W., & Lynskey, M. (2003). Testing hypotheses about the relationship between cannabis use and psychosis. *Drug and Alcohol Dependence, 71,* 37–48.

Dekeyne, A., & Milne, M. (2003). Discriminative stimulus properties of antidepressant agents: A Review. *Behavioural Pharmacology, 14,* 391–407.

De Long, F., & Levy, B. I. (1974). A model of attention describing the cognitive effects of marijuana. In L. L. Miller (Ed.), *Marijuana, effects on human behavior* (pp. 103–120). Orlando: Academic Press.

Dematteis, M., Lallement, G., & Mallaert, M. (1998). Dextromethorphan and dextrophan in rats: Common antitussives—Different behavioral profiles. *Fundamental and Clinical Pharmacology, 12,* 526–537.

Deminiére, J. M., Piazza, P. V., Guegan, G., Abrous, N., Maccari, S., Le Moal, M., et al. (1992). Increased locomotor response to novelty and propensity to intravenous amphetamine self-administration in adult offspring of stressed mothers. *Brain Research, 586,* 135–139.

Demir, B., Ulug, B., Lay Ergun, E., & Erbas, B. (2002). Regional cerebral blood flow and neuropsychological functioning in early and late onset alcoholism. *Psychiatry Research, 115,* 115–125.

Deneau, G. A., & Inoki, R. (1967). Nicotine self-administration in monkeys. *Annals of the New York Academy of Sciences, 142,* 277–279.

Deneau, G. A., Yanagita, T., & Seevers, M. H. (1969). Self-administration of psychoactive substances by the monkey: A measure of psychological dependence. *Psychopharmacologia, 16,* 30–48.

Depoortere, R. Y., Li, D. H., Lane, M. W., & Emmett-Oglesby, M. W. (1993). Parameters of self-administration of cocaine in rats under a progressive-ratio schedule. *Pharmacology, Biochemistry and Behavior, 45,* 539–548.

De Quincey, T. (1901). *The confessions of an English opium-eater.* London: Macmillan.

Desmond, P. V., Patwardham, R. V., Schenker, S., & Hoyumpa, A. M. (1980). Short-term ethanol administration impairs the elimination of chlordiazepoxide (Librium) in man. *European Journal of Clinical Pharmacology, 18,* 275–278.

DeVane, C. L. (1998). Differential pharmacology of newer antidepressants. *Journal of Clinical Psychiatry, 59* (Suppl. 20), 85–93.

Dewey, W. L., Martin, B. R., & Harris, L. S. (1976). Chronic effects of delta-9-THC in animals: Tolerance and biochemical changes. In M. C. Braude & S. Szara (Eds.), *Pharmacology of marijuana* (Vol. 2, pp. 585–594). Orlando: Academic Press.

de Wit, H. (1996). Priming effects with drugs and other reinforcers. *Experimental and Clinical Psychopharmacology, 4*, 5–10.

de Wit, H., & Chutuape, M. A. (1993). Increased ethanol choice in social drinkers following ethanol preload. *Behavioral Pharmacology, 4*, 29–36.

de Wit, H., Clark, M., & Brauer, L. (1997). Effects of d-amphetamine in grouped versus isolated humans. *Pharmacology, Biochemistry and Behavior, 57*, 333–340.

de Wit, H., & Griffiths, R. R. (1991). Testing the abuse liability of anxiolytic and hypnotic drugs in humans. *Drug and Alcohol Dependence, 28*(1), 83–111.

de Wit, H., & Johanson, C. E. (1987). A drug preference procedure for use with human volunteers. In M. A. Bozarth (Ed.), *Methods of assessing the reinforcing properties of abused drugs* (pp. 559–572). New York: Springer-Verlag.

de Wit, H., Johanson, C. E., & Uhlenhuth, E. H. (1984). Reinforcing properties of lorazepam in normal volunteers. *Drug and Alcohol Dependence, 13*, 31–41

de Wit, H., Kirk, J., & Justice, A. (1998). Behavioral pharmacology of cannabinoids. In R. E. Tarter, R. T. Ammerman, & P. J. Ott (Eds.), *Handbook of substance abuse: Neurobehavioral pharmacology* (pp. 131–146). New York: Plenum Press.

de Wit, H., & McCracken, S. G. (1990) Ethanol self-administration in males with and without an alcoholic first-degree relative. *Alcoholism: Clinical and Experimental Research 14*, 63–70.

de Wit, H., Pierri, J., & Johanson, C. E. (1989). Assessing pentobarbital preference in normal human volunteers using a cumulative dosing procedure. *Psychopharmacology, 99*, 416–421.

de Wit, H., Uhlenhuth, E. H., & Johanson, C. E. (1987). The reinforcing properties of amphetamine in overweight subjects and subjects with depression. *Clinical Pharmacology and Therapeutics, 42*, 127–136.

de Wit, H., & Zacny, J. (1995). Abuse potential of nicotine replacement therapies. *CNS Drugs, 4*, 456–468.

Dews, P. B. (1958). Studies on behavior: 4. Stimulant actions of methamphetamine. *Journal of Pharmacology and Experimental Therapeutics, 122*, 137–147.

Dews, P. B. (1962). A behavioral output enhancing effect of imipramine in pigeons. *International Journal of Neuropharmacology, 1*, 265–272.

Dews, P. B. (1984). Behavioral effects of caffeine. In P. B. Dews (Ed.), *Caffeine: Perspectives from recent research* (pp. 86–103). Berlin: Springer-Verlag.

Dews, P. B., O'Brien, C. P., & Bergman, J. (2002). Caffeine: Behavioral effects of withdrawal and related issues. *Food and Chemical Toxicology, 40*(9), 1257–1261.

Dews, P. B., & Wenger, G. R. (1977). Rate dependency of the behavioral effects of amphetamine. In T. Thompson & P. B. Dews (Eds.), *Advances in behavioral pharmacology* (Vol. 1, pp. 167–227). Orlando: Academic Press.

Di Marzo, V., Melck, D., Bisogono, T., & Di Petrocellis, L. (1998). Endocannabinoids: Endogenous cannabinoid receptor ligands with neuromodulatory action. *Trends in Neuroscience, 21*, 521–528.

DiMascio, A. (1973). The effects of benzodiazepines on aggression: Reduced or increased? In S. Garattini, E. Musi, & L. O. Randall (Eds.), *The benzodiazepines* (pp. 433–440). New York: Raven Press.

Dinwiddie, S. H. (1998). The pharmacology of inhalants. In A. Graham & T. Schultz (Eds.), *Principles of addiction medicine* (pp. 187–193). Chevy Chase, MD: American Society of Addiction Medicine.

Dinwiddie, S. H., & Farber, N. B. (1995). Pharmacological therapies of cannabis, hallucinogens, phencyclidine and volatile solvent addiction. In N. S. Miller & M. S. Gold (Eds.), *Pharmacological therapies for alcohol and drug addiction* (pp. 213–216). New York: Marcel Dekker.

DiPadova, C., Roine, R., Frezza, M., Gentry, R. T., Baraona, E., & Lieber, C. S. (1992). Effects of ranitidine on blood alcohol levels after ethanol ingestion: Comparison with other H2-receptor antagonists. *Journal of the American Medical Association, 267*(1), 83–86.

DiPadova, C., Worner, T. M., Julkunnen, R. J. K., & Lieber, C. S. (1987). Effects of fasting and chronic alcohol consumption on the first-pass metabolism of ethanol. *Gastroenterology, 92*, 1169–1173.

Ditmar, E. A., & Dorian, V. (1987). Ethanol absorption after bolus ingestion of an alcoholic beverage: A medico-legal problem: Part II. *Canadian Society of Forensic Sciences Journal, 20*(2), 61–69.

di Tomaso, E., Beltramo, M., & Piomelli, D. (1996). Brain cannabinoids in chocolate. *Science, 382*(6593), 677–678.

Dlugosz, L., Belanger, K., Hellenbrand, K., Holford, T. R., Leaderer, B., & Bracken, M. B. (1996). Maternal caffeine consumption and spontaneous abortion: A prospective cohort study. *Epidemiology, 7*, 250–255.

Dole, V. P. (1980). Addictive behavior. *Scientific American, 234*(6), 138–154.

Domino, E. F. (1967). Electroencephalographic and behavioral arousal effects of small doses of nicotine: A neuropsychopharmacological study. *Annals of the New York Academy of Sciences, 142*, 216–244.

Domino, E. F. (1973). Neuropsychopharmacology of nicotine and tobacco smoking. In W. L. Dunn (Ed.), *Smoking behavior: Motives and incentives* (pp. 5–32). Washington, DC: Winston.

Domino, E. F., Rennick, P., & Pearl, J. H. (1974). Dose-effect relations of marijuana smoking on various physiological parameters in experienced male users: Observations on limits on self-titration intake. *Clinical Pharmacology and Therapeutics, 15*, 514–520.

Domino, E. F., Rennick, P., & Pearl, J. H. (1976). Short-term neuropsychopharmacological effects of marijuana smoking in experienced male users. In M. C. Braude & S. Szara (Eds.), *Pharmacology of marijuana* (Vol. 1, pp. 585–594). Orlando: Academic Press.

Domino, E. F., & Yamamoto, K. I. (1965). Nicotine: Effect on the sleep cycle of the cat. *Science, 150*, 637–638.

Domjam, M. (2003). *Principles of learning and behavior* (5th edition). Belmont, CA: Thomson/Wadsworth.

Drummer, O., & Ransom, D. (1996). Sudden death and benzodiazepines. *American Journal of Forensic Medicine and Pathology, 17*, 336–342.

Dubowski, K. M. (1985). Absorption, distribution and elimination of alcohol: Highway safety aspects. *Journal of Studies on Alcohol, 10*(Suppl.), 98–108.

Dudley, R. (2000). Evolutionary origins of human alcoholism in primate frugavory. *Quarterly Review of Biology, 75*, 3–15.

Dudley, R. (2002). Fermenting fruit and the historical ecology of ethanol ingestion: Is alcoholism in modern humans an evolutionary hangover? *Addiction, 97*, 381–388.

Dunhill, A. H. (1954). *The gentle art of smoking*. New York: Putnam.

Dunlop, M., & Court, J. M. (1981). Effects of maternal caffeine ingestion on neonatal growth in rats. *Biology of the Neonate, 39*, 178–184.

Dyer, J., Roth, B., & Hyma, B. (2001). Gamma-hydroxybutyrate withdrawal syndrome. *Annals of Emergency Medicine, 27*, 147–153.

Earleywine, M. (2002). *Understanding marijuana*. New York: Oxford University Press.

Ebin, D. (1961). *The drug experience*. New York: Orion Press.

Eikelboom, R., & Stewart, J. (1982). Conditioning of drug-induced physiological responses. *Psychological Reviews, 89*, 529–572.

Elie, R., Ruther, E., Farr, I., Emilien, G., & Salinas, E. (1999). Sleep latency is shortened during 4 weeks of treatment with zaleplon, a novel nonbenzodiazepine hypnotic. *Journal of Clinical Psychiatry, 60*, 536–544.

Ellenwood, E. H., Linnoila, M., Angle, H. V., Moore, J. W., Skinner, J. T., III, Easler, M., et al. (1981). Use of simple tasks to test for impairment of complex skills by a sedative. *Psychopharmacologia, 73*, 350–354.

Enna, S. J., & Coyle, J. T. (1983). Neuroleptics. In J. T. Coyle & S. J. Enna (Eds.), *Neuroleptics: Neurochemical, behavioral, and clinical perspectives* (pp. 1–14). New York: Raven Press.

Enna, S. J., & Eilson, M. S. (1987). Second-generation antidepressants. In L. L. Iverson, S. D. Iverson, & S. H. Snyder (Eds.), *Handbook of pharmacology* (Vol. 19, pp. 609–632). New York: Plenum Press.

Eriksson, P. S., Perfilieva, E., Björk-Eriksson, T., Alborn, A., Nordberg, C., Peterson, D. A., et al. (1998). Neurogenesis in the adult human hippocampus. *Nature Medicine, 4*, 1313–1317.

Eros, E., Czeizel, A., Rockenbauer, M., Sorensen, H., Olsen, J. (2002). A population-based case-control teratogenic study of nitrazolam, medazepam, tofisopam, alprazolam and clonazepam treatment during pregnancy. *European Journal of Obstetrics and Gynecology and Reproductive Biology, 101*(2), 147–154.

Ersche, K. D., Fletcher, P. C., Lewis, S. J. G., Clark, L., Stocks-Gee, G., London, M., et al. (2005). Abnormal frontal activations related to decision-making in current and former amphetamine and opiate dependent individuals. *Psychopharmacology, 180*, 612–623.

Evans, S. M., & Griffiths, R. R. (1992). Caffeine tolerance and choice in humans. *Psychopharmacology, 108*, 51–59.

Evans, S. M., Griffiths, R. R., & de Wit, H. (1996). Preference for diazepam, but not buspirone, in moderate drinkers. *Psychopharmacology, 123*, 145–163.

Eysenck, H. J., & Eaves, L. J. (1980). *The causes and effects of smoking*. London: Maurice Temple Smith.

Fagerström, K. O., Schneider, N. G., & Lunell, E. (1993). Effectiveness of nicotine patch and nicotine gum as individual versus combined treatments for nicotine withdrawal symptoms. *Psychopharmacology, 111*, 271–277.

Falek, A., Madden, J. J., Shafer, D. A., & Donahoe, R. M. (1982). Opiates as modulators of genetic damage and immunocompetence. *Advances in Alcohol and Substance Abuse, 1*(3/4), 5–20.

Fantegrossi, W., Ullrich, T., Rice, K., Woods, J., & Winger, G. (2002). 3,4-methylenedioxymethamphetamine (MDMA, "ecstasy") and its stereoisomers as reinforcers in rhesus monkeys: Serotonergic involvement. *Psychopharmacology, 161*, 356–364.

Fantegrossi, W., Woods, J., & Winger, G. (2004). Transient reinforcing effects of phenylisopropylamine and indolealkylamine hallucinogens in rhesus monkeys. *Behavioural Pharmacology, 15*(2), 149–157.

Fehr, K. A., Kalant, H., LeBlanc, A. E., & Knox, G. C. (1976). Permanent learning impairment after chronic heavy exposure to cannabis or ethanol in the rat. In G. G. Nahas (Ed.), *Marijuana: Chemistry, biochemistry and cellular effects* (pp. 495–506). New York: Springer-Verlag.

Feighner, J. P., & Boyer, W. F. (1991). *Selective serotonin re uptake inhibitors.* Chichester, England: Wiley.

Feinberg, I., Jones, R., Walker, J., Cavness, C., & Floyd, T. (1975). Effects of marijuana extract and tetrahydrocannabinol on electroencephalographic sleep patterns. *Clinical and Pharmacological Therapy, 19*, 782–794.

Ferguson, G. A. (1966). *Statistical analysis in psychology and education.* New York: McGraw-Hill.

Fielding, J. E. (1985). Smoking: Health effects and control (second of two parts). *New England Journal of Medicine, 313*, 555–561.

Fillmore, M., & Vogel-Sprott, M. (1992). Expected effect of caffeine on motor performance predicts the type of response to placebo. *Psychopharmacology, 106*, 209–214.

Fillmore, M., & Vogel-Sprott, M. (1998). Behavioral impairment under alcohol: Cognitive and pharmacokinetic factors. *Alcoholism: Clinical and Experimental Research, 22*, 1476–1482.

Finagrette, H. (1988). *Heavy drinking: The myth of alcoholism as a disease.* Berkeley: University of California Press.

Finnegan, L. P. (1982). Outcome of children born to women dependent on narcotics. *Advances in Alcohol and Substance Abuse, 1*(3/4), 55–101.

Firebaugh, W. C. (1972). *The inns of Greece and Rome.* New York: Blom.

Fischman, M. W., & Schuster, C. R. (1982). Cocaine self-administration in humans. *Federation Proceedings, 41*, 204–209.

Fischman, M. W., Schuster, C. R., Resnekov, L., Shick, J. F. E., Krasnegor, N. A., Fennell, W., et al. (1976). Cardiovascular and subjective effects of intravenous cocaine administration in humans. *Archives of General Psychiatry, 33*, 983–989.

Fitton, A., Faulds, D., & Goa, K. L. (1992). Moclobemide: A review of its pharmacological properties and therapeutic use in depressive illness. *Drugs, 43*(4), 561–596.

Fletcher, C., & Doll, R. (1969). A survey of doctors' attitudes to smoking. *British Journal of Social and Preventive Medicine, 23*(3), 145–153.

Ford, R. D., & Balster, R. L. (1977). Reinforcing properties of intravenous procaine in monkeys. *Pharmacology, Biochemistry and Behavior, 6*, 289–296.

Ford, R., Schulter, P., Mitchell, E., Taylor, B., Scragg, R., & Stewart, A. (1998). Heavy caffeine intake in pregnancy and sudden infant death syndrome: New Zealand cot death study group. *Archives of Disease in Childhood, 78*, 9–13.

Forman, S. D., Dougherty, G. G., Casey, B. J., Siegle, G. J., Braver, T. S., Barch, D. M., et al. (2004). Opiate addicts lack error-dependent activation of rostral anterior cingulate. *Biological Psychiatry, 55*, 531–537.

Forrest, D. (1973). *Tea for the British.* London: Chatto & Windus.

Forrest, W. H., Jr., Bellville, J. W., & Brown, B. W., Jr. (1972). The interaction of caffeine with pentobarbital as a nighttime hypnotic. *Anesthesiology, 36*, 37–41.

Frank, I. M., Lessin, P. J., Tyrrell, E. D., Hahn, P. M., & Szara, S. (1976). Acute and cumulative effects of marijuana smoking on hospitalized subjects: A 36-day study. In M. C. Braude & S. Szara (Eds.), *Pharmacology of marijuana* (Vol. 2, pp. 673–680). Orlando: Academic Press.

Franken, I. H. A., Stam, C. J., Hendriks, V. M., & van den Brink, W. (2003). Neurophysiological evidence for abnormal cognitive processing of drug cues in heroin dependence. *Psychopharmacology, 170*, 205–212.

Fredholm, B. B. (1995). Adenosine, adenosine receptors and the actions of caffeine. *Pharmacology and Toxicology, 76*, 93–101.

French, R. V. (1884). *Nineteen centuries of drink in England.* London: Longman.

Frezza, M., DiPadova, C., Pozzato, G., Terpin, M., Baraona, E., & Leiber, C. S. (1990). High blood alcohol levels in women: The role of decreased gastric alcohol dehydrogenase activity and first-pass metabolism. *New England Journal of Medicine, 322*(2), 95–99.

Fried, P., Watkinson, B., James, D., & Gray, R. (2002). Current and former marijuana use: Preliminary findings of a longitudinal study of effects on IQ in young adults. *Canadian Medical Association Journal, 166*, 887–891.

Froehlich, J. C., & Li, T.-K. (1993). Opioid peptides. In M. Galanter (Ed.), *Recent developments in alcoholism* (Vol. 11, pp. 187–205). New York: Plenum Press.

Gable, R. (2004). Acute toxic effects of club drugs. *Journal of Psychoactive Drugs, 36*(1), 303–313.

Garattini, S., Mussini, E., Marcucci, F., & Guaitani, A. (1973). Metabolic studies on benzodiazepines in various animal species. In S. Garattini, E. Mussini, & L. O. Randall (Eds.), *The benzodiazepines* (pp. 75–97). New York: Raven Press.

Gardner, E. L. (1992). Cannabinoid interactions with brain reward systems: The neurobiological basis of cannabinoid abuse. In L. Murphy & A. Bartke (Eds.), *Marijuana/cannabinoids neurology and neurophysiology* (pp. 275–336). Boca Raton, FL: CRC Press.

Garek, L., Wolverton, W., Nadir, M., Patrick, G., Harris, L., Winger, G., et al. (2001). Behavioral effects of flunitrazepam: Reinforcing and discriminative stimulus effects in rhesus monkeys and prevention and withdrawal signs in pentobarbital treated rats. *Drug and Alcohol Dependence, 63*, 39–49.

Garfield, E. (1983). Current comments. *Current Contents, 18*, 5–14.

Garrett, B. E., & Griffiths, R. R. (1997). The role of dopamine in the behavioral effects of caffeine in animals and man. *Pharmacology Biochemistry and Behavior, 57*, 533–541.

Garrett, B. E., & Griffiths, R. R. (1998). Physical dependence increases the relative reinforcing effects of caffeine versus placebo. *Psychopharmacology, 139*, 195–202.

Garrott, J. (1992). Death among inhalant abusers. In E. R. Ottering & F. Beauvais (Eds.), *Inhalant abuse: A volatile research agenda* (pp. 181–191). (NIDA Monograph No. 129). Rockville, MD: U.S. Public Health Service.

Gautier, T. (1966). The hashish club. In D. Solomon (Ed.), *The marijuana papers* (pp. 163–178). New York: New American Library.

Gauvin, D. V., Cheng, E. Y., & Holloway, F. A. (1993). Behavioral correlates. In M. Galanter (Ed.),

Recent developments in alcoholism (Vol. 11, pp. 281–300). New York: Plenum Press.

Gauvin, D. V., Harland, R. D., Michaelis, R. C., & Holloway, F. A. (1989). Caffeine-phenylethylamine combinations mimic the cocaine discriminative cue. *Life Sciences, 44*, 67–73.

Gawin, F. H., & Kleber, H. (1987). Issues in cocaine abuse treatment research. In S. Fisher, A. Raskin, & E. H. Uhlenhuth (Eds.), *Cocaine: Clinical and behavioral aspects* (pp. 174–192). New York: Oxford University Press.

Gay, G. R., & Inaba, D. S. (1976). Acute and chronic toxicology of cocaine abuse: Current sociology, treatment and rehabilitation. In S. J. Mule (Ed.), *Cocaine: Chemical, biological, clinical, social and treatment aspects* (pp. 245–252). Boca Raton, FL: CRC Press.

Gazdzinski, S., Durazzo, T. C., & Meyerhoff, D. J. (2005). Temporal dynamics and determinants of whole brain tissue volume changes during recovery from alcohol dependence. *Drug and Alcohol Dependence, 78*, 263–273.

Geller, I., Bachman, E., & Seifter, J. (1963). The effects of reserpine and morphine on behavior suppressed by punishment. *Life Sciences, 4*, 226–231.

Geller, I., Hartman, R., Mendez, V., & Gauss, E. (1983). Toluene inhalation and anxiolytic activity: Possible synergism with diazepam. *Pharmacology, Biochemistry and Behavior, 19*, 899–903.

George, F. R. (1997). The behavioral genetics of addiction. In B. A. Johnson & J. D. Roache (Eds.), *Drug addiction and treatment: Nexus of neuroscience and behavior* (pp. 187–204). Philadelphia: Lippincott-Raven Press.

George, F. R., & Goldberg, S. R. (1989). Genetic approaches to the analysis of addiction processes. *Trends in Pharmacological Science, 10*, 78–83.

George, F. R., Ritz, M. C., & Elmer, G. I. (1991). The role of genetics in vulnerability to drug dependence. In J. Pratt (Ed.), *The biological basis of drug tolerance and dependence* (pp. 265–295). London: Academic Press.

George, W. H., & Marlatt, G. A. (1983). Alcoholism: The evolution of a behavioral perspective. In M. Galanter (Ed.), *Recent developments in alcoholism* (Vol. 1, pp. 105–138). New York: Plenum Press.

Gerasimov, M. R., Ferrieri, R. A., Shiffer, W. K., Logan, J., Gatley, S. J., Gifford, A. N., et al. (2002). Study of brain uptake and biodistribution of [^{11}C]toluene in non-human primates and mice. *Life Sciences, 70*, 2811–2828.

368   REFERENCES

Gerasimov, M. R., Schiffer, W. K., Marsteller, D. A., Ferrieri, R. A., Alexoff, D., & Dewey, S. (2002). Toluene inhalation produces regionally specific changes in extracellular dopamine. *Drug and Alcohol Dependence, 65,* 243–251.

Gerostamolous, J., Staikos, V., & Drummer, O. H. (2001). Heroin-related deaths in Victoria: A review of cases for 1997 and 1998. *Drug and Alcohol Dependence, 61*(2), 123–127.

Giannini, A. J., Burge, H., Shaheen, J. M., & Price, W. A. (1986). Khat: Another drug of abuse. *Journal of Psychoactive Drugs, 18,* 155–158.

Giannini, A. J., Miller, N. S., & Turner, C. E. (1992). Treatment of khat addiction. *Journal of Substance Abuse Treatment, 9,* 379–382.

Gilbert, R. M. (1976). Caffeine: A drug of abuse. In R. J. Gibbins, Y. Israel, H. Kalant, R. E. Popham, W. Schmidt, & R. G. Smart (Eds.), *Research advances in alcohol and drug problems* (Vol. 3, pp. 49–176). New York: Wiley/Interscience.

Gilbert, R. M. (1984). Caffeine consumption. In A. Spiller (Ed.), *The methylxanthine beverages and foods: Chemistry, consumption and health effects* (pp. 185–213). New York: Liss.

Gill, H. S., DeVane, C. L., & Risch, S. C. (1997). Extrapyramidal symptoms associated with cyclic antidepressant treatment: A review of the literature and consolidating hypotheses. *Journal of Clinical Psychopharmacology, 17,* 377–389.

Gitlin, M. J. (1993). Pharmacotherapy for personality disorders: Conceptual framework and clinical strategies. *Journal of Clinical Psychopharmacology, 13*(5), 343–353.

Gjerde, H., Smith-Kelland, A., Normann, P., & Morland, J. (1990). Driving under the influence of toluene. *Forensic Science International, 44,* 77–83.

Glad, W., & Adesso, V. J. (1976). The relative importance of socially induced tension and behavioral contagion for smoking behavior. *Journal of Abnormal Psychology, 85,* 119–121.

Glennon, R. A. (1987). Psychoactive phenylisopropylamines. In H. Y. Meltzer (Ed.), *Psychopharmacology: A third generation of progress* (pp. 1627–1634). New York: Raven Press.

Glennon, R., & Young, R. (2000). The MDMA stimulus generalization to the 5-HT(1A) serotonin agonist 8-hydroxy-2-(di-n-propylamino)tetralin. *Pharmacology, Biochemistry and Behavior, 66,* 483–488.

Glennon, R. A., Young, R., Martin, B. R., & Dal Cason, T. A. (1994). Methcathinone ("cat"): An enantiometric potency comparison. *Pharmacology, Biochemistry and Behavior, 50*(4), 601–606.

Glick, S. D., Maisonneuve, I., Raucci, J., & Archer, S. (1995). Kappa opioid inhibition of morphine and cocaine self-administration in rats. *Brain Research, 681,* 147–152.

Glowa, J. (1985). Behavioral effects of volatile organic solvents. In L. S. Seiden & R. L. Balster (Eds.), *Behavioral pharmacology: The current status* (pp. 537–552). New York: Alan R. Liss.

Goas, J. A., & Boston, J. E. (1978). Discriminative stimulus properties of clozapine and chlorpromazine. *Pharmacology, Biochemistry and Behavior, 8,* 235–241.

Goldberg, L. (1943). Quantitative studies on alcohol tolerance in man: The influence of ethyl alcohol on sensory, motor, and psychological functions referred to blood alcohol in normal and habituated individuals. *Acta Physiologica Scandanavica, 16*(Suppl.), 5.

Goldberg, S. R. (1976). The behavioral analysis of drug addiction. In S. D. Glick & J. Goldfarb (Eds.), *Behavioral pharmacology* (pp. 283–316). St. Louis, MO: Mosby.

Goldberg, S. R., & Spealman, R. D. (1983). Suppression of behavior by intravenous injections of nicotine or by electric shocks in the squirrel monkey: Effects of chlordiazepoxide and mecamylamine. *Journal of Pharmacology and Experimental Therapeutics, 244,* 334–340.

Goldberg, S. R., Spealman, R. D., & Goldberg, D. M. (1981). Persistent behavior at high rates maintained by intravenous self-administration of nicotine. *Science, 214,* 573–575.

Goldman, D. (1993). Genetic transmission. In M. Galanter (Ed.), *Recent developments in alcoholism* (Vol. 11, pp. 232–248). New York: Plenum Press.

Goldstein, A. (1964). Wakefulness caused by caffeine. *Naunyn-Schmiedebergs Archiv für Experimentelle Pathologie und Pharmakologie, 284,* 269–278.

Goldstein, A., Kaizer, S., & Warren, R. (1965). Psychotropic effects of caffeine in man: 2. Alertness, psychomotor coordination and mood. *Journal of Pharmacology and Experimental Therapeutics, 150,* 146–151.

Goldstein, A., Kaizer, S., & Whitby, O. (1969). Psychotropic effects of caffeine in man: 4. Quantitative and qualitative differences associated with habituation to coffee. *Clinical Pharmacology and Therapeutics, 10,* 489–497.

Goldstein, R. Z., Leskovjan, A. C., Hoff, A. L., Hitzemann, R., Bashan, F., Khalsa, S. S., et al. (2004). Severity of neuropsychological impairment in cocaine and alcohol addiction: Association with metabolism in the prefrontal cortex. *Neuropsychologia, 42*, 1447–1458.

Goldstone, S., Boardman, W., & Lhamon, W. (1958). The effects of quintal barbitone, dextroamphetamine, and placebo on apparent time. *British Journal of Psychology, 49*, 324–328.

Golub, A., & Johnson, B. D. (1994). The shifting of importance of alcohol and marijuana as gateway substances among serious drug abusers. *Journal of Studies on Alcohol, 55*(5), 507–514.

Goode, E., & Troiden, R. (1979). Amyl nitrite use among homosexual men. *American Journal of Psychiatry, 13*, 1067–1069.

Gorelick, D. A. (1993). Pharmacological treatment. In M. Galanter (Ed.), *Recent developments in alcoholism* (Vol. 1, pp. 413–427). New York: Plenum Press.

Gorelick, D. A. (1995). Pharmacological therapies for cocaine addiction. In N. S. Miller & M. S. Gold (Eds.), *Pharmacological therapies for alcohol and drug addiction* (pp. 143–158). New York: Marcel Dekker.

Gorelick, D. A., & Balster, R. L. (2000). Phencyclidine (PCP). In F. E. Bloom & D. J. Kupfer (Eds.), *Psychopharmacology: The fourth generation of progress*. New York: Raven Press. Available at http://www.acnp.org/g4/GN401000171/Default.htm

Gospe, S., & Zhou, S. (1998). Toluene abuse embryopathy: Longitudinal neurodevelopmental effects of prenatal exposure to toluene in rats. *Reproductive Toxicology, 12*, 119–126.

Gospe, S., & Zhou, S. (2000). Prenatal exposure to toluene results in abnormal neurogenesis and migration in rat somatosensory cortex. *Pediatric Research, 47*, 362–368.

Goth, A. (1984). *Medical pharmacology: Principles and concepts*. St. Louis, MO: Mosby.

Graham, H. N. (1984). Tea: The plant and its manufacture: Chemistry and consumption of the beverage. In G. A. Spiller (Ed.), *The methylxanthine beverages and foods: Chemistry, consumption and health effects* (pp. 29–74). New York: Liss.

Grant, K. A., & Barrett, J. E. (1991). Blockade of the discriminative stimulus effects of ethanol with 5-HT$_3$, receptor antagonists. *Psychopharmacology, 104*, 451–456.

Greden, J. F. (1974). Anxiety of caffeinism: A diagnostic dilemma. *American Journal of Psychiatry, 131*, 1089–1092.

Greden, J. F., Foutaine, P., Lubetsky, M., & Chamberlin, K. (1978). Anxiety and depression associated with caffeinism among psychiatric in-patients. *American Journal of Psychiatry, 135*, 963–966.

Greenblatt, D. J., & Shader, R. I. (1974). *The benzodiazepines in clinical practice*. New York: Raven Press.

Greenlees, D. (2005, March 15). Philip Morris makes $5.2 billion bid in Asia. *International Herald Tribune*. Available at http://www.iht.com/articles/2005/03/14/business/tobacco.html

Griffiths, R. R., Bigelow, G. E., & Henningfield, J. E. (1980). Similarities in animal and human drug taking behavior. In N. K. Mello (Ed.), *Advances in substance abuse* (Vol. 1, pp. 1–90). Greenwich, CT: JAI Press.

Griffiths, R. R., Bigelow, G. E., & Lieberson, I. (1979). Human drug self-administration: Double-blind comparison of pentobarbital, diazepam, chlorpromazine and placebo. *Journal of Pharmacology and Experimental Therapeutics, 210*, 301–310.

Griffiths, R. R., Evans, S. M., Heishman, S. J., Preston, K. L., Sannerud, C. A., Wolf, B., et al. (1990). Low dose caffeine physical dependence in humans. *Journal of Pharmacology and Experimental Therapeutics, 225*, 1123–1132.

Griffiths, R. R., Lamb, R. J., Sannerud, C. A., Ator, N., & Brady, J. V. (1991). Self-injection of barbiturates and benzodiazepines. *Psychopharmacology, 103*(2), 154–161.

Griffiths, R. R., Lucas, S. E., Bradford, L. K., Brady, J. V., & Snell, J. D. (1981). Self-injection of barbiturates and benzodiazepines in baboons. *Psychopharmacology, 75*, 101–109.

Griffiths, R. R., & Mumford, G. K. (1995). Caffeine: A drug of abuse? In F. E. Bloom & D. J. Kupfer (Eds.), *Psychopharmacology: The fourth generation of progress*. New York: Raven Press. Available at www.acnp.org/g4/GN401000/65/Default.htm

Griffiths, R. R., & Sannerud, C. A. (1987). Abuse and dependence on benzodiazepines and other anxiolytic/sedative drugs. In H. Y. Meltzer (Ed.), *Psychopharmacology: The third generation of progress* (pp. 1535–1542). New York: Raven Press.

Griffiths, R. R., & Woodson, P. (1988). Caffeine physical dependence: A review of human and laboratory animal studies. *Psychopharmacology, 94*, 437–451.

Grinspoon, L. (1971). *Marihuana reconsidered.* Cambridge, MA: Harvard University Press.

Grinspoon, L., & Bakalar, J. B. (1976). *Cocaine.* New York: Basic Books.

Grinspoon, L., & Bakalar, J. B. (1979a). The amphetamines: Medical uses and health hazards. In D. R. Smith (Ed.), *Amphetamine use, misuse and abuse* (pp. 260–274). Boca Raton, FL: CRC Press.

Grinspoon, L., & Bakalar, J. B. (1979b). *Psychedelic drugs reconsidered.* New York: Basic Books.

Grinspoon, L., & Bakalar, J. B. (1993). *Marijuana, the forbidden medicine.* New Haven, CT: Yale University Press.

Grinspoon, L., & Bakalar, J. B. (1997). *Marijuana, forbidden medicine* (Rev. and Exp. Ed.). New Haven, CT: Yale University Press.

Grinspoon, L., & Hedblom, P. (1975). *The speed culture.* Cambridge, MA: Harvard University Press.

Groppetti, A., & Di Giulio, A. M. (1976). Cocaine and its effect on biogenic amines. In S. J. Mule (Ed.), *Cocaine: Chemical, biological, clinical, social and treatment aspects* (pp. 93–102). Boca Raton, FL: CRC Press.

Gunne, L. M., & Anggard, E. (1972). *Pharmacokinetic studies with amphetamines: Relationship to neuropsychiatric disorders.* Paper presented at the International Symposium on Pharmacological Kinetics, Washington, DC.

Gunzerath, L., Faden, V., Zakhari, S., & Warren, K. (2004). National Institute on Alcohol Abuse and Alcoholism report on moderate drinking. *Alcoholism: Clinical and Experimental Research, 28*(6), 829–847.

Gutjahr, E., Gmel, G., & Rehm, J. (2001). Relation between average alcohol consumption and disease: An overview. *European Addiction Research, 7*, 117–127.

Haefely, W. (1983). The biological basis of benzodiazepine actions. *Journal of Psychoactive Drugs, 15*, 19–40.

Haertzen, C. A., & Hickey, J. E. (1987). Addiction Research Center Inventory (ARCI): Measurement of euphoria and other effects. In M. A. Bozarth (Ed.), *Methods of assessing the reinforcing properties of abused drugs* (pp. 489–524). New York: Springer-Verlag.

Haglund, B., & Cnattingius, L. (1990). Cigarette smoking as a risk factor for sudden infant death syndrome. *American Journal of Public Health, 80*(1), 29–32.

Hajak, G. (1999). A comparative assessment of the risks and benefits of zopiclone: A review of 15 years' clinical experience. *Drug Safety, 21*, 457–469.

Haller, J. (2001). The link between stress and the efficacy of anxiolytics: A new avenue of research. *Physiology and Behavior, 73*, 337–342.

Hallstrom, C., & Lader, M. H. (1981). Benzodiazepine withdrawal phenomenon. *International Pharmacopsychiatry, 16*, 235–244.

Halpern, M. T., Gillespie B. W., & Warner K. T. (1993). Patterns of absolute risk of lung cancer mortality in former smokers. *Journal of the National Cancer Institute, 17*(85), 457–464.

Hampson, A. J., Grimaldi, M., Axelrod, J., & Wink, D. (1998). Cannabidiol and (-)Δ9-tetrahydrocannabinol are neuroprotective antioxidants. *Proceedings of the National Academy of Sciences USA, 95*, 8268–8273.

Haney, M., Comer, S., Fischman, M., & Foltin, R. (1997). Alprazolam increases food intake in humans. *Psychopharmacology, 123*, 311–314.

Haney, M., Ward, A., Comer, S., Foltin, R., & Fischman, M. (1999a). Abstinence symptoms following oral THC administration to humans. *Psychopharmacology, 141*, 385–394.

Haney, M., Ward, A., Comer, S., Foltin, R., & Fischman, M. (1999b). Abstinence symptoms following smoked marijuana in humans. *Psychopharmacology, 141*, 395–404.

Hanson, H. M., Witloslawski, J. J., & Campbell, E. H. (1967). Drug effects in squirrel monkeys trained on a multiple schedule with a punishment contingency. *Journal of the Experimental Analysis of Behavior, 10*, 565–569.

Hard, L., Einarson, R., & Koren, G. (2001). The role of acetaldehyde in pregnancy outcome after prenatal alcohol exposure. *Therapeutic Drug Monitoring, 23*, 427–435.

Harris, R. T., Glaghorn, J. L., & Schoolar, J. C. (1968). Self-administration of minor tranquilizers as a function of conditioning. *Psychopharmacologia, 13*, 81–88.

Harris, S., & Dawson, H. (1994). Caffeine and bone loss in healthy post menopausal women. *American Journal of Clinical Nutrition, 60*, 573–578.

Harrison, W. M., Rabkin, J. G., Erhardt, A. A., Stewart, J. W., McGrath, T. J., Ross, D., et al. (1986). Effects of antidepressant medication on sexual function: A controlled study. *Journal of Clinical Psychopharmacology, 6*(3), 144–148.

Haut, M.W., Leach, S., Kuwabara, H., Whyte, S., Callahan, T., Ducatman, A., et al. (2000). Verbal working memory and solvent exposure: A positron emission tomography study. *Neuropsychology, 14*, 551–558.

Haverkos, H., Kopstein, A., Wilson, H., & Drotman, P. (1994). Nitrite inhalants: History, epidemiology and possible links to AIDS. *Environmental Health Perspectives, 102*, 858–861.

He, N., Daniel, H., Hajiloo, L., & Shockley, D. (1999). Dextromethorphan O-demethylation polymorphism in an African-American population. *European Journal of Clinical Pharmacology, 55*, 475–479.

Heimstra, N. W., Bancroft, N. R., & De Kock, A. R. (1967). Effects of smoking on sustained performance on a simulated driving task. *Annals of the New York Academy of Sciences, 142*, 295–307.

Heinz, A., Siessmeier, T., Wrase, J., Hermann, D., Klein, S., Grusser-Sinopoli, S. M., et al. (2004). Correlation between dopamine D2 receptors in the ventral striatum and central processing of alcohol cues and craving. *American Journal of Psychiatry, 161*, 1783–1789.

Heise, G. A., & Boff, E. (1962). Continuous avoidance as a baseline for measuring the behavioral effects of drugs. *Psychopharmacology, 3*, 264–282.

Hembree, W. C., III, Zeidenberg, P., & Nahas, G. G. (1976). Marijuana's effect on human gonadal functions. In G. G. Nahas (Ed.), *Marijuana: Chemistry, biochemistry and cellular effects* (pp. 521–532). New York: Springer-Verlag.

Hemby, S., Co, C., Koves, T., Smith, J., & Dworkin, S. (1997). Differences in extracellular dopamine concentrations in the nucleus accumbens during response-dependent and response-independent cocaine administration in the rat. *Psychopharmaco-logy, 133*, -16.

Henningfield, J. E., Johnson, R., & Jasinski, D. (1987). Clinical procedures for the assessment of abuse potential. In M. A. Bozarth (Ed.), *Methods of assessing the reinforcing properties of abused drugs* (pp. 573–590). New York: Springer-Verlag.

Henningfield, J. E., Lucas, S. E., & Bigelow, G. E. (1986). Human studies of drugs as reinforcers. In S. R. Goldberg & I. P. Stollerman (Eds.), *Behavioral analysis of drug dependence* (pp. 69–122). Orlando: Academic Press.

Henningfield, J. E., Miyasato, K., & Jasinski, D. R. (1985). Abuse liability and pharmacodynamic characteristics of intravenous and inhaled nicotine. *Journal*

of Pharmacology and Experimental Therapeutics, 234, 1–12.

Henningfield, J. E., Miyasato, K., Johnson, R. E., & Jasinski, D. R. (1983). Rapid physiological effects of nicotine in humans and selective blockade of effects by mecamylamine. In *Problems of drug dependence* (NIDA Monograph No. 43). Washington, DC: U.S. Government Printing Office.

Henricksson, B. G., & Järbe, T. U. (1971). The effect of two tetrahydrocannabinols (delta-9-THC and delta-8-THC) on conditioned avoidance learning in rats and its transfer to normal state conditions. *Psychopharmacologia, 22*, 23–30.

Herman, C. P. (1974). External and internal cues as determinants of the smoking behavior of light and heavy smokers. *Journal of Personality and Social Psychology, 30*, 664–672.

Herning, R. I., Jones, R. T., & Bachman, J. (1983). EEG changes during tobacco withdrawal. *Psychophysiology, 20*, 507–512.

Heyman, G M. (1996). Resolving the contradictions of addiction. *Behavioral and Brain Sciences, 19*(4), 561–610.

Heyser, C. J., Hampson, R. E., & Deadwyler, S. A. (1993). Effects of delta-1-tetrahydrocannabinol on delayed match to sample performance in rats: Alterations in short-term memory associated with changes in task specific filing of hippocampal cells. *Journal of Pharmacology and Experimental Therapeutics, 264*, 294–307.

Higgins, S. (1997). Applying learning and conditioning theory to the treatment of alcohol and cocaine abuse. In B. A. Johnson & J. D. Roache (Eds.), *Drug addiction and its treatment: The nexus of neuroscience and behavior* (pp. 367–385). Philadelphia: Lippincott-Raven Press.

Higgins, S. T., Delaney, D. D., Budney, A. J., Bickel, W. K., Hughes, J. R., Foerg, F., et al. (1991). A behavioral approach to achieving initial cocaine abstinence. *American Journal of Psychiatry, 148*(9), 1218–1224.

Higgitt, A. C., Lader, M. H., & Fonagy, P. (1985). Clinical management of benzodiazepine dependence. *British Medical Journal, 291*, 688–690.

Hirschorn, I. D., Hayes, R. L., & Rosecrans, J. A. (1975). Discriminative control of behavior by electrical stimulation of the dorsal Raphé-nucleus: Generalization to lysergic acid diethylamide (LSD). *Brain Research, 84*, 134–138.

Hirsh, K. (1984). Central nervous system pharmacology of the dietary methylxanthines. In G. A. Spiller (Ed.), *The methylxanthine beverages and foods: Chemistry, consumption and health effects* (pp. 235–301). New York: Liss.

Ho, A. K. S., & Allen, J. P. (1981). Alcohol and the opiate receptor: Interactions with the endogenous opiates. *Advances in Alcohol and Substance Abuse, 1*(1), 53–75.

Hofer, I., & Battig, K. (1994). Cardiovascular, behavioral, and subjective effects of caffeine under field conditions. *Pharmacology Biochemistry and Behavior, 48*, 899–908.

Hoffmeister, F. H., & Wuttke, W. (1969). On the actions of psychotropic drugs on the attack and aggressive-defensive behavior of mice and cats. In S. Garattini & E. G. Sigg (Eds.), *Aggressive behavior* (pp. 273–280). New York: Wiley/Interscience.

Hoffmeister, F. H., & Wuttke, W. (1973). Self-administration of acetylsalicylic acid and combinations with codeine and caffeine in rhesus monkeys. *Journal of Pharmacology and Experimental Therapeutics, 186*, 266–275.

Hoffmeister, F. H., & Wuttke, W. (1975). Psychotropic drugs as negative reinforcers. *Pharmacological Reviews, 27*, 419–428.

Holdstock, L., & de Wit, H. (1998). Individual differences in the biphasic effect of alcohol. *Alcoholism: Clinical and Experimental Research, 22*, 1903–1911.

Hollister, L. E. (1978). Psychotomimetic drugs in man. In L. L. Iverson, S. D. Iverson, & S. H. Snyder (Eds.), *Handbook of psychopharmacology* (Vol. 11, pp. 389–425). New York: Plenum Press.

Hollister, L. E., Motzenbecker, F. P., & Degan, R. O. (1961). Withdrawal reactions from chlordiazepoxide ("Librium"). *Psychopharmacologia, 2*, 63–68.

Hommer, D. W., Skolnick, P., & Paul, S. M. (1987). The benzodiazepine/GABA receptor complex and anxiety. In H. Y. Meltzer (Ed.), *Psychopharmacology: The third generation of progress* (pp. 977–983). New York: Raven Press.

Horger, B. A., Wellman, P. J., Morien, A., Davis, B. T., & Schenk, S. (1994). Caffeine exposure sensitizes to the reinforcing effects of cocaine. *Motivation, Emotion, Feeding, Drinking, Sexual Behavior, 2*, 53–56.

Howard, M., Cotter, L., Compton, W., & Ben-Abdullah, A. (2001). Diagnostic concordance of DSM-III-R, DSM-IV, and ICD 10 inhalant use disorders. *Alcohol and Drug Dependence, 61*, 223–228.

Howlett, A. C., Evans, D. M., & Houston, D. B. (1992). The cannabinoid receptor. In L. Murphy & A. Bartke (Eds.), *Marijuana/cannabinoids: Neurobiology and neurophysiology* (pp. 35–72). Boca Raton, FL: CRC Press.

Hser, Y., Hoffman, V., Grella, C., & Anglin, M. (2001). A 33-year follow-up of narcotics addicts. *Archives of General Psychiatry, 58*, 503–508.

Huang, J., & Ho, B. T. (1974). Discriminative stimulus properties of d-amphetamine and related compounds in rats. *Pharmacology, Biochemistry and Behavior, 2*, 669–673.

Hughes, J. R. (1986). Genetics of smoking: A review. *Behavior Therapy, 17*, 335–345.

Hughes, J. R., Gust, S. W., Skoog, K., Keenan, R. M., & Fenwick, J. W. (1991). Symptoms of tobacco withdrawal: A replication and extension. *Archives of General Psychiatry, 48*, 52–59.

Hughes, J. R., Higgins, S. T., & Bickel, W. K. (1994). Nicotine withdrawal versus other drug withdrawal syndromes: Similarities and differences. *Addiction, 89*, 1461–1470.

Hughes, J. R., Higgins, S. T., Bickel, W. K., & Hunt, W. K. (1989, May). *Caffeine is a reinforcer in humans.* Paper presented to the Behavioral Pharmacology Society, Annapolis, MD.

Hughes, J. R., Higgins, S. T., Gulliver, S., & Mireault, G. (1987, June 6). *Dependence on caffeine in moderate coffee drinkers.* Paper presented to the International Study Group Investigating Drugs as Reinforcers, Philadelphia.

Hughes, J. R., Higgins, S. T., & Hatsukami, D. (1990). Effects of abstinence from tobacco: A critical review. In L. T. Kozlowski (Ed.), *Advances in alcohol and drug problems* (Vol. 10, pp. 317–398). New York: Plenum Press.

Hunter, B. E., Walker, D. W., & Riley, J. N. (1974). Dissociation between physical dependence in volitional ethanol consumption: The role of multiple withdrawal episodes. *Pharmacology, Biochemistry and Behavior, 2*, 523–529.

Hutchison, A., Smith, P., & Darlington, C. (1996). The behavioral and neuronal effects of the chronic administration of benzodiazepine anxiolytic and hypnotic drugs. *Progress in Neurobiology, 48*, 73–97.

Hutchison, R. R., & Emley, G. S. (1973). Effects of nicotine on avoidance, conditioned suppression and aggression response measures in animals and man.

In W. L. Dunn (Ed.), *Smoking behavior: Motives and incentives* (pp. 171–196). Washington, DC: Winston.

Ikeda, M., Maehara, T., Harabuchi, I., Kishi, R., & Yokota, H. (1983). Slow learning in rats due to long term inhalation of toluene. *Neurobehavioral Toxicology and Teratology, 5,* 541–548.

Institute of Medicine. (1982). *Marijuana and health.* Washington, DC: National Academy Press.

Inturrisi, C. G., Schultz, M., Shin, S., Umas, J. G., Angel, L., & Simon, E. J. (1983). Evidence from opiate binding studies that heroin acts through its metabolites. *Life Sciences, 33*(Suppl. 1), 773–776.

Issac, P. F., & Rand, M. J. (1972). Cigarette smoking and plasma levels of nicotine. *Nature, 236,* 308–310.

Iverson, L. (2005). Long-term effects of exposure to Cannabis. *Current Opinion in Pharmacology, 5,* 96–72.

Izenwasser, S. (1998). Basic pharmacological mechanisms of cocaine. In S. T. Higgins & J. L. Katz (Eds.), *Cocaine abuse: Behavior, pharmacology and clinical applications* (pp. 1–11). New York: Academic Press.

Jaffe, J. H. (1987). Pharmacological agents in the treatment of drug dependence. In H. Y. Meltzer (Ed.), *Psychopharmacology: The third generation of progress* (pp. 1605–1616). New York: Raven Press.

Jaffe, J. H., Cascella, N. G., Kumor, K. M., & Sherer, M. A. (1989). Cocaine-induced cocaine craving. *Psychopharmacology, 97,* 59–64.

James, J. J. (1991). *Caffeine and health.* London: Academic Press.

James, J. J. (1994). *Caffeine, health and commercial interests* [Review]. *Addiction, 89,* 1595–1599.

James, S. H., & Bhatt, S. (1972). Analysis of street drugs. *Journal of Drug Education, 2,* 197–210.

Janicak, P. G., Davis, J. M., Preskorn, S. H., & Ayd, F. J., Jr. (1993). *Principles and practice of pharmacology.* Baltimore: Williams & Wilkins.

Janiszewski, D., Galinkin, J., Klock, P., Coalson, D., Pardo, H., & Zacny, J. (1999). The effects of subanesthetic concentrations of servoflurane and nitrous oxide, alone and in combination, on analgesia, mood and psychomotor performance in healthy volunteers. *Anesthesia and Analgesia, 88,* 1149–1154.

Janke, W., & DeBus, G. (1968). In H. E. Efron (Ed.), *Experimental studies on antianxiety agents with normal subjects: Methodological considerations and a review of the main effects, 1957–1967* (pp. 205–208). Washington, DC: U.S. Government Printing Office.

Järbe, T. U. C., & Mathis, D. A. (1992). Dissociative and discriminative stimulus functions of cannabinoids/cannabinometics. In L. Murphy & A. Bartke (Eds.), *Marijuana/cannabinoids neurology and neurophysiology* (pp. 425–458). Boca Raton, FL: CRC Press.

Jarvik, M. E. (1970). Drugs used in the treatment of psychiatric disorders. In L. S. Goodman & A. Gillman (Eds.), *The pharmacological basis of therapeutics* (pp. 51–203). London: Collier-Macmillan.

Jarvik, M. E. (1973). Further observations on nicotine as the reinforcing agent in smoking. In W. L. Dunn (Ed.), *Smoking behavior: Motives and incentives* (pp. 33–50). Washington, DC: Winston.

Jarvik, M. E. (1979). Biological influences on cigarette smoking. In N. E. Krasnegor (Ed.), *The behavioral aspects of smoking* (pp. 7–45) (NIDA Research Monograph No. 26) Washington, DC: U.S. Government Printing Office.

Jarvis, M. J. (1994). A profile of tobacco smoking. *Addiction, 89,* 1371–1376.

Jasinski, D. R., Johnson, R. E., & Henningfield, J. E. (1984). Abuse liability assessment in human subjects. *Trends in Pharmacological Sciences, 5,* 196–200.

Javid, J. I., Musa, M. N., Fischman, M., Schuster, C. R., & Davis, J. M. (1983). Kinetics of cocaine in humans after intravenous and intranasal administration. *Biopharmaceutics and Drug Disposition, 4,* 9–18.

Jellinek, E. M. (1960). *The disease concept of alcoholism.* New Haven, CT: Hillhouse Press.

Jimerson, D. V. (1987). The role of dopamine mechanism in affective disorders. In H. Y. Meltzer (Ed.), *Psychopharmacology: A third generation of progress* (pp. 505–512). New York: Raven Press.

Johanson, C. E., & Uhlenhuth, E. H. (1980). Drug preference and mood in humans: Diazepam. *Psychopharmacology, 71,* 269–273.

Johnson, H. J. (1965). A case history: A surgeon's cure of tobacco habituation. *Medical Times, 93,* 437.

Johnson, K. M., Jr. (1987). Neurochemistry and neurophysiology of phencyclidine. In H. Y. Meltzer (Ed.), *Psychopharmacology: The third generation of progress* (pp. 1581–1588). New York: Raven Press.

Johnston, L. D., O'Malley, P. M., & Bachman, J. G. (2001). *Monitoring the future national survey results on drug use. 1975–2000: Vol.1. Secondary school students* (NIH Publication No. 01-4924). Bethesda, MD: National Institute on Drug Abuse.

Johnston, L. D., O'Malley, P. M., Bachman, J. G., & Schulenberg, J. E. (2005). *Monitoring the future national results on adolescent drug use: Overview of key findings, 2004* (NIH Publication No. 05-5726). Bethesda, MD: National Institute on Drug Abuse.

Jones, K. L., & Smith, D. W. (1975). The fetal alcohol syndrome. *Teratology, 12*, 1–10.

Jones, C. (2005, December 8). Senior drug addicts increasing. *USA Today*. Available at http://www.usatoday.com/news/health/2005-01-21-senior-addicts_x.htm

Jones, B. C., Jones, B., Blundell, L., & Bruce, G. (2002). Social users of alcohol and cannabis who detect substance-related changes in a change blindness paradigm report higher levels of use than those detecting substance-neutral changes. *Psychopharmacology, 165*, 93–96.

Jones, B. T., Jones, B., Smith, H., & Copley, N. (2003). A flicker paradigm for inducing change blindness reveals alcohol and cannabis information processing bias in social users. *Addiction, 98*, 235–244.

Jones, H., & Balster, R. (1998). Inhalant abuse in pregnancy. *Obstetrics and Gynecology Clinics of North America, 25*, 153–167.

Jones, R. T. (1978). Marijuana: Human effects. In L. L. Iverson, S. D. Iverson, & S. H. Snyder (Eds.), *Handbook of psychopharmacology* (Vol. 12, pp. 373–412). New York: Plenum Press.

Jones, R. T. (1987). Tobacco dependence. In H. Y. Meltzer (Ed.), *Psychopharmacology: The third generation of progress* (pp. 1589–1595). New York: Raven Press.

Jones, R. T., & Benowitz, N. (1976). The 30-day trip: Clinical studies of cannabis tolerance and dependence. In M. C. Braude & S. Szara (Eds.), *Pharmacology of marijuana* (Vol. 2, pp. 627–642). Orlando: Academic Press.

Jowett, B. (1931). *The dialogues of Plato* (Vol. 5, 3rd ed.). London: Oxford University Press.

Judd, L. J., Squire, L. R., Butters, N., Salmon, D. P., & Paller, K. A. (1987). Effects of psychotropic drugs on cognition and memory in normal humans and animals. In H. Y. Meltzer (Ed.), *Psychopharmacology: A third generation of progress* (pp. 1467–1475). New York: Raven Press.

Juergens, S. M. (1993). Benzodiazepines and addiction. *Psychiatric Clinics of North America, 16*(1), 75–86.

Juliano, L. M., & Griffiths, R. R. (2004). A critical review of caffeine withdrawal: Empirical validation if symptoms and signs, incidence, severity, and associated features. *Psychopharmacology, 176*, 1–29.

Julien, R. (2001). *A primer of drug action*, (9th ed.). New York: Worth Publishers.

Jumper-Thurman, P., & Beauvais, F. (1992). Treatment of volatile solvent abusers. In E. R. Ottering &

F. Beauvais (Eds.), *Inhalant abuse: A volatile research agenda* (pp. 203–213) (NIDA Monograph No. 129). Rockville, MD: U.S. Public Health Service.

June, H. L., Colker, R. E., Domanagu, K. R., Perry, L. E., Hicks, L. H., June, P. L., et al. (1992). Ethanol self-administration in deprived rats: Effects of RO-4513 alone and in combination with flumazenil (RO 15 1788). *Alcoholism: Clinical and Experimental Research, 16*, 11–16.

Kalant, H. (2001). The pharmacology and toxicology of "ecstasy" (MDMA) and related drugs. *Canadian Medical Association Journal, 165*, 917–928.

Kalant, H., & Kalant, O. J. (1979). Death in amphetamine users: Causes and rates. In D. R. Smith (Ed.), *Amphetamine use, misuse and abuse* (pp. 169–188). Boca Raton, FL: CRC Press.

Kalant, H., LeBlanc, E., & Gibbins, R. J. (1971). Tolerance to, and dependence on, ethanol. In Y. Israel & J. Mardonez (Eds.), *Biological basis of alcoholism* (pp. 235–269). New York: Wiley/Interscience.

Kales, J. D., Allen, C., Preston, T., & Tan, T. (1970). Changes in REM sleep and dreaming with cigarette smoking and following withdrawal. *Psychopharmacology, 7*, 347, 348.

Kalix, P. (1994). Khat, an amphetamine-like stimulant. *Journal of Psychoactive Drugs, 26*(1), 69–74.

Kallman, W. M., Kallman, M. J., Harry, G. J., Woodson, P. P., & Rosecrans, J. A. (1982). Nicotine as a discriminative stimulus in human subjects. In F. C. Colpaert & J. L. Slangen (Eds.), *Drug discrimination: Applications in CNS pharmacology* (pp. 211–218). Amsterdam: Elsevier Biomedical

Kaminsky, L., Martin, C. A., & Whaley, M. H. (1998). Caffeine consumption habits do not influence the exercise blood pressure response following caffeine ingestion. *Journal of Sports Medicine and Physical Fitness, 38*, 53–58.

Kampman, K., Pettinati, H., Lynck, K., Lynch, K., Dakis, C., Sparkman, T., et al. (2004). A pilot trial of topriamate for the treatment of cocaine dependence. *Drug and Alcohol Dependence, 75*, 233–240.

Kanarek, R. B., & Marks-Kaufman, R. (1988). Dietary modulation of oral amphetamine intake in rats. *Physiology and Behavior, 44*, 501–505.

Kanarek, R. B., & Marks-Kaufman, R. (May 1989). *Environmental modulation of drug self-administration*. Paper presented to the Behavior Pharmacology Society, Annapolis, MD.

Kaplan, G. B., Greenblatt, D. J., Ehrenberg, B. L., Goddard, J. E., Cotreau, M. M., Harmatz, J. S., et al. (1997). Dose-dependent pharmacokinetics and psychomotor effects of caffeine in humans. *Journal of Clinical Pharmacology, 37*, 693–703.

Kareken, D. A., Claus, E. D., Sabri, M., Dzemidzic, M., Kosobud, A. E. K., Radnovich, A. J., et al. (2004). Alcohol-related olfactory cues activate the nucleus accumbens and ventral tegmental area in high-risk drinkers: Preliminary findings. *Alcoholism: Clinical and Experimental Research, 28*, 550–557.

Katz, J., & Goldberg, S. R. (1987). Second order schedules of drug injection. In M. A. Bozarth (Ed.), *Methods of assessing the reinforcing properties of drugs* (pp. 105–115). New York: Springer-Verlag.

Kay, D. C., Eisenstein, R. B., & Jasinski, D. R. (1969). Morphine effects on human REM state, waking state and NREM sleep. *Psychopharmacologia, 14*, 404–416.

Kaye, S., & Haag, H. B. (1957). Terminal blood alcohol concentration in ninety-four fatal cases of acute alcoholism. *Journal of the American Medical Association, 165*, 451–452.

Keenan, R. M., Henningfield, J. E., & Jarvik, M. E. (1995). Pharmacological therapies: Nicotine addiction. In N. S. Miller & M. S. Gold (Eds.), *Pharmacological therapies for alcohol and drug addiction* (pp. 239–264). New York: Marcel Dekker.

Kelleher, R. T. (1976). Characteristics of behavior controlled by scheduled injections of drugs. *Pharmacological Reviews, 27*, 307–323.

Kelleher, R. T., & Morse, W. H. (1964). Escape behavior and punished behavior. *Federation Proceedings, 22*, 808–817.

Kellogg, C. K. (1988). Benzodiazepines: Influence on the developing brain. In G. R. Boer, M. G. P. Feenstra, M. Mirmiran, D. F. Swaab, & F. Van Haaren (Eds.), *Biochemical basis of functioning neuroteratology: Permanent effects of chemicals on the developing brain* (Vol. 73, pp. 207–228). Amsterdam: Elsevier Biomedical.

Kellogg, C. K., Tervo, D., Ison, J., Paisi, T., & Miller, R. K. (1980). Prenatal exposure to diazepam alters behavioral development in rats. *Science, 207*, 205–207.

Kelly, T. H., Foltin, R. W., Mayr, M. T., & Fishman, M. W. (1994). Effects of delta-9-tetrahydrocannabinol and social context on marijuana self-administration by humans. *Pharmacology, Biochemistry and Behavior, 49*(3), 763–768.

Kennedy, S. K., & Longnecker, D. E. (1996). History and principles of anesthesiology. In J. G. Hardman & L. E. Limbird (Eds.), *Goodman and Gillman's pharmacological basis of therapeutics* (pp. 295–306). New York: McGraw-Hill.

Kephalis, T. A., Burns, J., Michael, C. M., Miras, C. J., & Papidakis, D. P. (1976). Some aspects of cannabis smoke chemistry. In G. G. Nahas (Ed.), *Marijuana: Chemistry, biochemistry and cellular effects* (pp. 39–50). New York: Springer-Verlag.

Kerner, K. (1988). Current topics in inhalant abuse. In R. A. Crider & B. A. Rouse (Eds.), *Epidemiology of inhalant abuse: An update* (pp. 8–29). (NIDA Research Monograph No. 85). Rockville, MD: U.S. Department of Health and Human Services.

Khanna, J., Kalant, H., Chau, A., & Shah, G. (1998). Rapid tolerance and cross tolerance to motor impairment effects of benzodiazepines, barbiturates and ethanol. *Pharmacology, Biochemistry and Behavior, 59*, 511–519.

Kihlman, B. A. (1977). *Caffeine and chromosomes*. Amsterdam: Elsevier.

King, D. J. (1993). Measures of the neuroleptic effects on cognition and psychomotor performance in healthy volunteers. In I. Hindmarch & P. D. Stonier (Eds.), *Human psychopharmacology: Measures and methods* (Vol. 4, pp. 195–209). Chichester, England: Wiley.

Kilts, C. D., Gross, R. E., Ely, T. D., & Drexler, K. P. G. (2004). The neural correlates of cue-induced craving in cocaine-dependent women. *American Journal of Psychiatry, 161*, 223–241.

Kinsey, J., Rees, D., & Balster, R. (1990). Discriminative stimulus properties of toluene in the rat. *Neuroscience and Biobehavioral Reviews, 15*, 233–241.

Kirk, J., & de Wit, H. (2000). Individual differences in the priming effect of ethanol in social drinkers. *Journal for Studies on Alcohol, 61*, 64–71.

Kleber, H. D. (1974). Clinical experiences with narcotic antagonists. In S. Fisher & A. M. Freeman (Eds.), *Opiate addiction: Origins and treatment* (pp. 211–220). New York: Wiley.

Kleven, M., & Koek, W. (1999). Effects of benzodiazepine agonists on punished responding in pigeons and their relationship with clinical doses in humans. *Psychopharmacology, 141*, 206–212.

Kling, M. A., Carson, R. E., Borg, L., Zametkin, A., Matochik, J. A., Schluger, J., et al. (2000). Opioid receptor imaging with positron emission tomography and [18F]cyclofloxy in long-term, methadone-treated former heroin addicts. *Journal of Pharmacology and Experimental Therapeutics, 295*, 1070–1076.

Klonoff, H. (1974). Effects of marijuana on driving in a restricted area and on city streets: Driving performance and physiological changes. In L. L. Miller (Ed.), *Marijuana: Effects on human behavior* (pp. 359–397). Orlando: Academic Press.

Kluver, H. (1966). *Mescal and mechanisms of hallucinations*. Chicago: University of Chicago Press.

Knott, V., Bosman, M., Mahoney, C., Ilivitsky, V., & Quirt, K. (1999). Transdermal nicotine: Single dose effects on mood, EEG, performance, and event-related potentials. *Pharmacology Biochemistry and Behavior, 63,* 253–261.

Kobler, J. (1973). *Ardent spirits: The rise and fall of prohibition*. New York: Putnam.

Kocsis, J. H., Shaw, E. D., Stokes, P. E., Wilner, P., Elliot, A. S., Sikes, C., et al. (1993). Neuropsychologic effects of lithium discontinuation. *Journal of Clinical Psychopharmacology, 13,* 268–275.

Kolata, G. (January 1, 1991, 1993). Temperance: An old cycle repeats itself. *New York Times*, pp. 35, 40.

Kolodny, R. C. (1975). Research issues in the study of marijuana and male reproductive physiology in humans. In J. R. Tinklenberg (Ed.), *Marijuana and health hazards* (pp. 71–81). Orlando: Academic Press.

Koob, G. (2000). Drug addiction. *Neurobiology of Disease, 7,* 543–545.

Koob, G., & Le Moal, M. (2001). Drug addiction, dysregulation of reward and allostasis. *Neuropsychopharmacology, 24,* 97–129.

Koob, G. F., Sanna, P. P., & Bloom, F. E. (1998). Neuroscience of addition. *Neuron, 21,* 467–476.

Kosersky, D. S., McMillan, D. E., & Harris, L. S. (1974). Delta-9-tetrahydrocannabinol and 11-hydroxy-delta-9-tetrahydrocannabinol: Behavioral effects and tolerance development. *Journal of Pharmacology and Experimental Therapeutics, 189,* 61–65.

Kozlowski, L. T., & Henningfield, J. E. (1995). Thinking the unthinkable: The prospect of regulation of nicotine in cigarettes by the United States government. *Addiction, 90,* 165–167.

Kramer, M. S. (1987). Determinants of low birth weight: Methodological assessment and meta-analysis. *Bulletin of the World Health Organization, 65,* 663–737.

Kramer, P. D. (1993). *Listening to prozac*. New York: Viking.

Kreek, M. J. (1982). Opioid disposition and effects during chronic exposure in the perinatal period in man. *Advances in Alcohol and Substance Abuse, 1*(3/4), 21–53.

Kulhanek, F., Linde, O. K., & Meisenberg, G. (1979). Precipitation of antipsychotic drugs in interaction with coffee or tea. *Lancet, 2,* 1130.

Kumor, K., Sherer, M., Muntander, C., Jaffee, J. H., & Herning, R. (1988). Pharmacological aspects of cocaine rush. In L. S. Harris (Ed.), *Problems of drug dependence, 1988* (NIDA Research Monograph No. 90). Washington, DC: U.S. Government Printing Office.

Kurtz, N. M. (1990). Monoamine oxidase inhibiting drugs. In J. D. Amsterdam (Ed.), *Pharmacotherapy of depression* (pp. 93–109). New York: Marcel Dekker.

Kurtzman, T., Otsuka, K., & Wahl, R. (2001). Inhalant abuse by adolescents. *Journal of Adolescent Health, 28,* 170–180.

Laisi, U., Linnoila, T., Seppala, J. J., & Mattila, M. J. (1979). Pharmacokinetic and pharmacodynamic interactions of diazepam with different alcoholic beverages. *European Journal of Clinical Pharmacology, 16,* 263–270.

Lamb, R. J., & Griffiths, R. R. (1987). Self-injection of d,1-3,4-methylenedioxy-methamphetamine (MDMA) in the baboon. *Psychopharmacology, 91,* 268–272.

Lamb, R. J., Preston, K., Schindler, C., Meisch, R. A., Davis, F., Katz, J. L., et al. (1991). The reinforcing and subjective effects of morphine in post-addicts: A dose response study. *Journal of Pharmacology and Therapeutics, 259,* 1165–1173.

Landwehrmeyer, B., Mengod, G., & Palacios, J. M. (1993). Dopamine D3 receptor mRNA and binding sites in human brain. *Brain Research: Molecular Brain Research, 18,* 187–192.

Lane, J. D. (1997). Effects of brief caffeinated-beverage deprivation on mood, symptoms, and psychomotor performance. *Pharmacology, Biochemistry and Behavior, 58,* 203–208.

Lane, R., & Baldwin, D. (1997). Selective serotonin reuptake inhibitor-induced serotonin syndrome [Review]. *Journal of Clinical Psychopharmacology, 17,* 208–221.

Lankester, E. R. (1889). Mithradatism. *Nature, 40,* 149.

Lapore, M., Vorel, S. R., Lowinson, J., & Gardner, E. (1995). Conditioned place preference induced by delta 9-tetrahydrocannabinol: Comparison with cocaine, morphine and food rewards. *Life Science, 56,* 2073–2080.

Lasagana, L., Felsinger, J. M., & Beecher, H. K. (1955). Drug-induced mood changes in man. *Journal of the American Medical Association, 157,* 1006–1020.

Laties, V. G. (1986). Lessons from the history of behavioral pharmacology. In N. K. Krasenegor, D. B. Gray, & T. Thompson (Eds.), *Developmental behavioral pharmacology: Advances in behavioral pharmacology* (Vol. 5, pp. 21–42). Hillsdale, NJ: Erlbaum.

Latimer, D., & Goldberg, J. (1981). *Flowers in the blood*. New York: Franklin Watts.

Le, A. D., Poulos, C. X., & Cappell, H. (1979). Conditioned tolerance to the hypothermic effect of ethyl alcohol. *Science, 206,* 1109.

Ledent, C., Valverde, O., Cossu, G., Petitet, F., Aubert, J. F., Beslot, F., et al. (1999). Unresponsiveness to cannabinoids and reduced addictive effects of opiates in CB1 knockout mice. *Science, 283,* 401–404.

Leiber, C. S. (1977). Metabolism of alcohol. In C. S. Leiber (Ed.), *Metabolic aspects of alcoholism* (pp. 1–30). Baltimore: University Park Press.

Leiber, C. S., & De Carli, L. M. (1977). Metabolic effects of alcohol on the liver. In C. S. Leiber (Ed.), *Metabolic aspects of alcoholism* (pp. 31–80). Baltimore: University Park Press.

Lejoyeux, M. (1996). Use of serotonin (5-hydroxytryptamine) reuptake inhibitors in the treatment of alcoholism. *Alcohol, 31*(Suppl. 1), 69–75.

Lelas, S., Gerak, L., & France, C. (1999). Discriminative stimulus effects of triazolam, and midazolam in rhesus monkeys. *Behavioral Pharmacology, 10,* 39–50.

Lemberger, L., Schildcrout, S., & Cuff, G. (1987). Drug delivery systems: Applicability to neuropsychopharmacology. In H. Y. Meltzer (Ed.), *Psychopharmacology: A third generation of progress* (pp. 1285–1295). New York: Raven Press.

Leonard, B. E. (1989). From animals to man: Advantages, problems and pitfalls of animal models in psychopharmacology. In I. Hindmarch & P. D. Stonier (Eds.), *Human psychopharmacology: Measures and methods* (Vol. 2, pp. 23–66). Chichester, England: Wiley.

Leonard, B. E. (1993). The comparative pharmacology of new antidepressants. *Journal of Clinical Pharmacology, 54*(8, Suppl.), 3–15.

Lepore, M., Vorel, S. R., Lowinson, J., & Gardner, E. L. (1995). Conditioned place preference induced by delta 9-tetrahydrocannabinol: Comparison with cocaine, morphine, and food reward. *Life Sciences, 56,* 2073–2080.

Levin, E. D. (1992). Nicotinic systems and cognitive function. *Psychopharmacology, 108,* 417–431.

Levine, H. G. (1981). The vocabulary of drunkenness. *Journal of Studies on Alcohol, 42,* 1038–1051.

Lewitt, E. M. (1989). U.S. tobacco taxes: Behavioral effects and policy implications. *British Journal of Addiction, 84,* 1217–1235.

Li, H. (1975). The origin and use of cannabis in eastern Asia. In V. Rubin (Ed.), *Cannabis and culture* (pp. 51–62). The Hague: Mouton.

Lickey, M. E., & Gordon, B. (1991). *Medicine and mental illness: The use of drugs in psychiatry*. New York: Freeman.

Lieberman, J. A., Mailman, R. B., Duncan, G., Sikich, L., Chakos, M., Nichols, D. E., et al. (1998). Serotonergic basis of antipsychotic drug effects in schizophrenia. *Biological Psychiatry, 44,* 1099–1117.

Liguori, A., Hughes, J. R., & Grass, J. A. (1997). Absorption and the subjective effects of caffeine from coffee, cola and capsules. *Pharmacology, Biochemistry and Behavior, 58,* 721–726.

Liguori, A., & Robinson, J. II. (2001). Caffeine antagonism of alcohol-induced driving impairment. *Drug and Alcohol Dependence, 63,* 123–129.

Linder, R. L., Lerner, S. E., & Burns, R. S. (1981). *PCP: The devil's dust*. Belmont, CA: Wadsworth.

Lindgren, M., Osterberg, K., Orbaek, P., & Rosen, I. (1997). Solvent-induced toxic encephalopathy: Electrophysiological data in relation to neurophysiological findings. *Journal of Clinical and Experimental Neuropsychology,19,* 772–783.

Ling, W., Rawson, R. A., & Compton, M. A. (1994). Substitution pharmacotherapies for opioid addiction: From methadone to LAAM and buprenorphine. *Journal of Psychoactive Drugs, 26*(2), 119–128.

Linnoila, M., & Hakkinen, T. (1974). Effects of diazepam and codeine alone and in combination with alcohol, on simulated driving. *Clinical Pharmacology and Therapeutics, 15,* 368–373.

Lister, R. G., & Nutt, D. J. (1987). Is RO 15-4513 a specific alcohol antagonist? *Trends in Neuroscience, 10,* 223–225.

Litten, R. Z., & Allen, J. P. (1993). Reducing the desire to drink: Pharmacology and neurobiology. In M. Galanter (Ed.), *Recent developments in alcoholism* (Vol. 1, pp. 325–344). New York: Plenum Press.

Lombardo, J. A. (1986). Stimulants and athletic performance (part 1 of 2): Amphetamines and caffeine. *The Physician and Sportsmedicine, 14*(11), 128–140.

London, E. D., Cascella, N. G., Wong, D. F., Phillips, R. L., Dannals, R. F., Links, J. M., et al. (1990). Cocaine induced reduction of glucose utilization in human brain: A study using positron emission tomography and (fluorine 18)-fluorodeoxyglucose. *Archives of General Psychiatry, 47*, 567–574.

Lorrain, D., Arnold, G., & Vezina, P. (2000). Previous exposure to amphetamine increases incentive to obtain the drug: Long-lasting effects revealed by the progressive ratio schedule. *Behavioural and Brain Research, 107*(1–2), 9–21.

Lovinger, D. M. (1997). Alcohols and neurotransmitter gated ion channels: Past, present and future. *Naunyn-Schmiedberg's Archives de Pharmacologie, 356*, 267–282.

Lowe, G. (1988). State dependent retrieval effects with social drugs. *British Journal of Addiction, 83*, 99–103.

Lukas, S. E. (1991). Topographic brain mapping during cocaine-induced intoxification and self-administration. In G. Racagni, N. Brunello, & T. Fukuda (Eds.), *Biological Psychiatry* (Vol. 2, pp. 25–29). New York: Excerpta Medica.

Lukas, S. E., Mendelson, J. H., Kouri, E., Bolduc, M., & Amass, L. (1990). Ethanol-induced alterations in EEG alpha activity and apparent source of the auditory P300 evoked response potential. *Alcohol, 7*, 471–477.

Macdonald, S. (1986). The impact of increased availability of wine in grocery stores on consumption: Four case histories. *British Journal of Addiction, 81*, 381–387.

Mackesy-Amiti, M. E., & Fendrich, M. (1999). Inhalant use and delinquent behavior among adolescents: A comparison of inhalant users and other drug users. *Addictions, 94*, 555–564.

Macleod, J., Oakes, R., Copello, A., Crome, I., Egger, M., Hickman, M., et al. (2004). Psychological and social sequelae of cannabis and other illicit drug use by young people: A systematic review of longitudinal general population studies. *Lancet, 363*, 1579–1588.

Maes, M., & Meltzer, H. (2000). The serotonin hypothesis of major depression. In *Psychopharmacology: Fourth generation of progress.* Published online at http://www.acnp.org/g4/GN401000094

Maier, S. E., & West, J. R. (2001). Drinking patterns and alcohol-related birth defects. *Alcohol Research & Health, 25*, 168–174.

Malcolm, R., Brady, K. T., Johnston, A. L., & Cunningham, M. (1993). Types of benzodiazepines abused by chemically dependent inpatients. *Journal of Psychoactive Drugs, 25*(4), 315–319.

Maltzman, I. (1994). Why alcoholism is a disease. *Journal of Psychoactive Drugs, 26*, 13–31.

Mangan, G. L., & Golding, J. (1978). An "enhancement" model of smoking maintenance? In R. E. Thornton (Ed.), *Smoking behaviour: Physiological and psychological influences* (pp. 87–114). Edinburgh: Churchill Livingstone.

Mann, K., Agartz, I., Harper, C., Shoaf, S., Rawlings, R. R., Momenan, R., et al. (2001). Neuroimaging in alcoholism: Ethanol and brain damage. *Alcoholism, Clinical and Experimental Research, 25*, 104S–109S.

Manno, J. E., Manno, B. R., Kiplings, G. F., & Forney, R. B. (1974). Motor and mental performance with marijuana: Relationship to dose of delta-9-tetrahydrocannabinol and its interaction with alcohol. In L. L. Miller (Ed.), *Marijuana: Effects on human behavior* (pp. 45–72). Orlando: Academic Press.

Mansour, A., Fox, C., Burke, S., Meng, F., Thompson, R. C., Akil, H., et al. (1994). Mu, delta and kappa opioid receptor mRNA expression in rats CNS: An in situ hybridization study. *Journal of Comparative Neurology, 350*, 412–438.

Marek, G. J., & Aghajanian, G. K. (1999). 5-HT2A receptor or alpha 1-adrenoceptor activation induces excitatory postsynaptic currents in layer V pyramidal cells of the medial prefrontal cortex. *European Journal of Pharmacology, 367*, 197–206.

Mark, L. C. (1971). Pharmacokinetics of barbiturates. In H. Matthew (Ed.), *Acute barbiturate poisoning* (pp. 75–84). Amsterdam: Excerpta Medica.

Markou, A., Weiss, F., Gold, L. H., Caine, S. B., Schulteis, G., & Koob, G. (1993). Animal models of drug craving. *Psychopharmacology, 112*, 163–182.

Marks, V., & Kelly, J. F. (1973). Absorption of caffeine from tea, coffee, and Coca-Cola. *Lancet, 1*, 827.

Marlatt, G. A., & Rohsenow, D. J. (1980). Cognitive processes in alcohol use: Expectancy and the balanced placebo design. In N. K. Mello (Ed.), *Advances in substance abuse: Behavioral and biological research* (pp. 159–199). Greenwich, CT: JAI Press.

Marsden, C. D. (1977). Neurological disorders induced by alcohol. In G. Edwards & M. Grant

(Eds.), *Alcoholism: New knowledge and new responses* (pp. 189–198). London: Croom Helm.

Martin, B. (2000). Marijuana. In *Psychopharmacology: The fourth generation of progress*. Published online at http://www.acnp.org/g4/GN401000170

Martin R., & Acre, A. (1996). Benxodiazepine receptors increase induced by stress and maze learning performance in chick forebrain. *Pharmacology, Biochemistry and Behavior, 53*, 581–584.

Martin, W. R., Eades, C. G., Thompson, J. A., Huppler, R. E., & Gilbert, P. E. (1976). The effects of morphine- and nalorphine-like drugs in the non-dependent and morphine-dependent chronic spinal dog. *Journal of Pharmacology and Experimental Therapeutics, 197*, 517–532.

Maskos, U., Molles, B. E., Pons, S., Besson, M., Guiard, B., Guilloux, J.-P., et al. (2005). Nicotine reinforcement and cognition restored by targeted expression of nicotinic receptors. *Nature, 436*(7), 103–107.

Masuki, K., & Iwamoto, T. (1966). Development of tolerance to tranquilizers in the rat. *Japanese Journal of Pharmacology, 16*, 191–197.

Mattila, M. J., Mattila, M. E., & Nuotto, E. (1993). Measuring drug-alcohol and drug-drug interactions of psychotropic on human skilled performance. In I. Hindmarch & P. D. Stonier (Eds.), *Human psychopharmacology: Measures and methods* (Vol. 4, pp. 21–38). Chichester, England: Wiley.

Mattox, A., Thompson, S., & Carroll, M. (1997). Smokes heroin and cocaine base (speedball) combinations in rhesus monkeys. *Experimental and Clinical Psychopharmacology, 5*, 113–118.

Maugh, T. H. (2005, July 13). Nicotine vaccine shows promise. *E Commerce Times*. Available at http://ecommercetimes.com/story/43120.html

Maximilian, V. A., Risberg, J., Prohovnik, I., Rehnstrom, S., & Haeger-Aronsen, B. (1982). Regional cerebral blood flow and verbal memory after chronic exposure to organic solvents. *Brain and Cognition, 1*, 196–205.

Maxwell, M. A. (1984). *The Alcoholics Anonymous experience: A close up view for professionals*. New York: McGraw-Hill.

May, P. A., & Del Vecchio, A. M. (1997). Three common behavioral patterns of inhalant/solvent abuse: Selected findings and research issues. In F. Beauvis & J. Trimble (Eds.), *Sociocultural perspectives on volatile solvent use* (pp. 3–37). New York: Haworth Press.

Mayo, K. M., Falkowski, W., & Jones, C. A. (1993). Caffeine: Use and effects in long-stay psychiatric patients. *British Journal of Psychiatry, 162*, 543–545.

McCarthy, R. G. (1959). *Drinking and intoxication*. New York: Free Press.

McCracken, S., de Wit, H., Uhlenhuth, E. H., & Johanson, E. (1990). Preference for diazepam in anxious adults. *Journal of Clinical Psychopharmacology, 10*, 190–196.

McEwan, B., & Lashley, E. (2002). *The end of stress as we know it*. Washington, DC: Joseph Henry Press.

McGlothlin, W. H., & West, L. J. (1968). The marijuana problem: An overview. *American Journal of Psychiatry, 125*, 370–378.

McGovern, P. E., Zhang, J., Tang, J., Zhang, Z., Hall, G. R., Moreau, R. A., et al. (2004). Fermented beverages of pre- and proto-historic China. *Proceedings of the National Academy of Sciences USA, 101*(51), 17593–17598.

McKim, E. M. (1991). Caffeine and its effects on pregnancy and the neonate. *Journal of Nurse-Midwifery, 36*(4), 226–231.

McKim, W. A. (1980). The effects of caffeine, theophylline and amphetamine on the operant responding of the mouse. *Psychopharmacology, 68*, 135–138.

McKim, W. (2003). *Drugs and behavior*, (5th ed.). Upper Saddle River, NJ: Prentice Hall.

McKim, W. A., & Mishara, B. L. (1987). *Drugs and aging*. Toronto: Butterworths.

McKim, W. A., & Quinlan, L. T. (1991). Changes in alcohol consumption with age. *Canadian Journal of Public Health, 82*, 231–234.

McMillan, D. E., & Leander, J. D. (1976). Effects of drugs on schedule-controlled behavior. In S. D. Glick & J. Goldfarb (Eds.), *Behavioral pharmacology* (pp. 85–139). St. Louis, MO: Mosby.

Meade, T. W., & Wald, N. J. (1977). Cigarette smoking patterns during the working day. *British Journal of Preventive and Social Medicine, 31*(1), 25–29.

Meaney, M. (2001). Maternal care, gene expression, and the transmission of individual differences in stress reactivity across generations. *Annual Review of Neuroscience, 24*, 1161–1192.

Mechoulam, R., Hanus, L., & Martin, B. (1994). The search for endogenous ligands of the cannabinoid receptor. *Biochemical Pharmacology, 48*(8), 1537–1544.

Mechoulam, R., McCallum, N. K., Lander, N., Yagen, B., Ben Zvi, Z., & Levy, S. (1976). Aspects of cannabis chemistry and metabolism. In M. C. Braude & S. Szara (Eds.), *Pharmacology of marijuana* (Vol. 1, pp. 39–46). Orlando: Academic Press.

Meisch, R. A. (1977). Ethanol self-administration in infrahuman species. In T. Thompson & P. B. Dews (Eds.), *Advances in behavioral pharmacology* (Vol. 1, pp. 35–84). Orlando: Academic Press.

Meisch, R. A., & Lemaire, G. A. (1993). Drug self-administration. In F. Van Haaren (Ed.), *Drug self-administration* (pp. 257–300). Amsterdam: Elsevier Science.

Mellinger, G. D., Balter, M. B., & Uhlenhuth, E. H. (1984). Prevalence and correlates of long-term regular use of anxiolytics. *Journal of the American Medical Association, 25,* 375–379.

Mello, N. K. (1978). Alcoholism and the behavioral pharmacology of alcohol, 1967–1977. In M. A. Lipton, A. Di Mascio, & K. F. Killam (Eds.), *Psychopharmacology: A generation of progress* (pp. 1619–1637). New York: Raven Press.

Mello, N. K. (1987). Alcohol abuse and alcoholism. In H. Y. Meltzer (Ed.), *Psychopharmacology: The third generation of progress* (pp. 1515–1520). New York: Raven Press.

Mello, N. K., & Mendelson, J. H. (1972). Drinking patterns during work-contingent and non-contingent alcohol acquisition. *Psychosomatic Medicine, 34,* 139–164.

Mello, N. K., & Mendelson, J. H. (1987). Operant analysis of human drug self-administration: Marijuana, alcohol, heroin, and polydrug use. In M. A. Bozarth (Ed.), *Methods for assessing the reinforcing properties of abused drugs* (pp. 525–558). New York: Springer-Verlag.

Meltzer, H. Y. (1990). Clozapine: Pattern of efficacy in treatment resistant schizophrenia. In H. Y. Meltzer (Ed.), *Novel antipsychotic drugs* (pp. 33–46). New York: Raven Press.

Melzack, R. (1990). The tragedy of needless pain. *Scientific American, 262,* 27–33.

Mendelson, H. H., Kuehnle, J. C., Greenberg, I., & Mello, N. K. (1976). The effects of marijuana use on human operant behavior: Individual data. In M. C. Braude & S. Szara (Eds.), *Pharmacology of marijuana* (Vol. 2, pp. 643–653). Orlando: Academic Press.

Mendelson, W. B. (1979). Pharmacologic and electrophysical effects of ethanol in relation to sleep. In E. Majchrowitz & E. P. Noble (Eds.), *Biochemistry and pharmacology of ethanol* (Vol. 2, pp. 467–484). New York: Plenum Press.

Meritz, M., Kleber, H. D., Riordan, C. E., & Solbetz, F. W. (1978). A follow-up study of patients successfully detoxified from methadone maintenance: Year two. In A. Schecter, H. Alksne, & E. Kaufman (Eds.), *Drug abuse: Modern trends, issues and perspectives* (pp. 308–315). New York: Dekker.

Metzner, R. (1993). Letter to MAPS. *Newsletter of the Multidisciplinary Association for Psychedelic Studies,* 4. Available at http://www.maps.org/news-letters/v04n1/04143met.html

Meyer, R. E., & Mirin, S. M. (1979). *The heroin stimulus.* New York: Plenum Press.

Miczek, K. A., & Barry, H., III. (1976). Pharmacology of sex and aggression. In S. D. Glick & J. Goldfarb (Eds.), *Behavioral pharmacology* (pp. 176–257). St. Louis, MO: Mosby.

Millan, M. J. (1986). Kappa-opioid receptors and analgesia. *Trends in Pharmacological Sciences, 11,* 70–76.

Millan, M. J. (1990). Multiple opioid systems and pain. *Pain, 27,* 303–347.

Miller, L. L., & Drew, W. G. (1974). Cannabis: Neural mechanisms and behavior. In L. L. Miller (Ed.), *Marijuana: Effects on human behavior* (pp. 158–188). Orlando: Academic Press.

Minifie, B. W. (1970). *Chocolate, cocoa and confectionary science and technology.* Westport, CT: Avi.

Mintzer, M., & Griffiths, R. (1998). Flurazepam and triazolam: A comparison of behavioral effects and abuse liability. *Drug and Alcohol Dependence, 53,* 49–66.

Mintzer, M., Stoller, K., & Griffiths, R. (1999). A controlled study of flunazemil-precipitated withdrawal in chronic low-dose benzodiazepine users. *Psychopharmacology, 147,* 200–209.

Miotto, K., Darakjian, J., Basch, J., Murray, J., Zogg, J., & Rawson, R. (2001). Gamma-hydroxybutyric acid: Patterns of use, effects and withdrawal. *American Journal on the Addictions, 10,* 232–241.

Mirsky, I. A., Piker, P., Rosebaum, M., & Lederer, H. (1945). "Adaptation" of the central nervous system to various concentrations of alcohol in the blood. *Quarterly Journal of Studies on Alcohol, 2,* 35.

Mitchell, M. C. (1985). Alcohol-induced impairment of central nervous system function: Behavioral skills involved in driving. *Journal of Studies on Alcohol, 10*(Suppl.), 109–116.

Mitchell, S., Laurent, C., & de Wit, H. (1996). Interaction of expectancy and the pharmacological effects of d-amphetamine: Subjective effects and self-administration. *Psychopharmacology, 125*, 371–378.

Mobley, B. L., & Sulser, F. (1981). Down-regulation of the central noradrenergic receptor system by antidepressant therapies: Biochemical and clinical aspects. In S. J. Enna, J. B. Malick, & E. Richelson (Eds.), *Antidepressants: Neurochemical, behavioral and clinical perspectives* (pp. 31–51). New York: Raven Press.

Modrow, H. E., Holloway, F. A., & Carney, J. M. (1981). Caffeine discrimination in the rat. *Pharmacology, Biochemistry and Behavior, 14*, 683–688.

Möhler, H., Fritschy, J. M., Crestani, F., Hensch, T., Rudolph, U. (2004). Specific GABA(A) circuits in brain development and therapy. *Biochemical Pharmacology, 68*(8), 1685–1690.

Möhler, H., Fritschy, J. M., & Rudolph, U. (2002). A new benzodiazepine pharmacology, *Journal of Pharmacology and Experimental Therapeutics, 300*, 2–8.

Money, K. E., & Miles, W. S. (1974). Heavy water nystagmus and the effects of alcohol. *Nature, 247*, 404–405.

Monteiro, W. O., Noshirvani, I. M., Marks, I. M., & Elliott, P. T. (1987). Anorgasmia from clomipramine in obsessive-compulsive disorder: A controlled trial. *British Journal of Psychiatry, 151*, 107–112.

Moreau, J. J. (1973). Hashish and mental illness (H. Peters & G. G. Nahas, Eds., and G. J. Barnett, Trans.). New York: Raven Press. (Original work published 1845)

Moreton, J. E., Meisch, R. A., Stark, L., & Thompson, T. (1977). Ketamine self-administration in the rhesus monkey. *Journal of Pharmacology and Experimental Therapeutics, 203*, 303–309.

Morgan, J. (2000). Ecstasy (MDMA): A review of its possible persistent psychological effects. *Psychopharmacology, 152*, 230–248.

Morrison, C. F. (1967). The effects of nicotine on operant behavior of rats. *International Journal of Neuropharmacology, 6*, 229–240.

Morrison, C. F. (1969). The effects of nicotine on punished behavior. *Psychopharmacologia, 14*, 221.

Morrison, C. F. (1974). The effects of nicotine and its withdrawal on the performance of rats on signalled and unsignalled avoidance schedules. *Psychopharmacologia, 38*, 25–35.

Morrison, C. F., & Stephenson, J. A. (1969). Nicotine injections as the conditioned stimulus in discrimination learning. *Psychopharmacologia, 15*, 351–360.

Morrison, C. F., & Stephenson, J. A. (1972a). Effects of stimulants on observed behavior of rats on six operant schedules. *Neuropharmacology, 12*, 297–310.

Morrison, C. F., & Stephenson, J. A. (1972b). The occurrence of tolerance to a central depressant effect of nicotine. *British Journal of Pharmacology, 45*, 151–156.

Morrow, L. A., Steinhauer, S. R., & Hodgson, M. J. (1992). Delay in P300 latency in patients with organic solvent exposure. *Archives of Neurology, 49*, 315–320.

Moskowitz, J., Hulbert, S., & McGlothlin, W. H. (1976). Marijuana: Effects on simulated driving performance. *Accident Analysis and Prevention, 8*, 45–50.

Mullins, C. J., Vitola, B. M., & Michelson, A. E. (1975). Variables related to cannabis use. *International Journal of Addictions, 10*, 481–502.

Mumford, G. K., Evans, S. M., Kamiski, B. J., Preston, K. L., Sannerud, C. A., Silverman, K., et al. (1994). Discriminative stimulus and subjective effects of theobromine and caffeine in humans. *Psychopharmacology, 115*, 1–8.

Munro, S., Thomas, K. L., & Abu-Shaar, M. (1993). Molecular characterization of a peripheral receptor for cannabinoids. *Nature, 365*(6441), 61–65.

Munson, S. E. (1975). Marijuana and immunity. In J. R. Tinklenberg (Ed.), *Marijuana and health hazards* (pp. 39–46). Orlando: Academic Press.

Murphree, N. B., Pfeiffer, C. C., & Price, L. (1967). Electroencephalographic changes in man following smoking. *Annals of the New York Academy of Sciences, 142*, 245.

Muskowitz, H., & Burns, M. (1981). The effects of alcohol and caffeine alone and in combination, on skilled performance. In L. Goldberg (Ed.), *Alcohol, drugs and traffic safety* (Vol. 3, pp. 969–983). Stockholm: Almqvist & Wiksell.

Myerson, R. M. (1971). Effects of alcohol on cardiac and muscular function. In Y. Israel & J. Mardones (Eds.), *Biomedical basis of alcoholism* (pp. 183–208). New York: Wiley/Interscience.

Naeye, R. L., & Peters, C. E. (1984). Mental development of children whose mothers smoked during pregnancy. *Obstetrics and Gynecology, 64*, 601–607.

Nagle, D. R. (1968). Anesthetic addiction and drunkenness: A contemporary social history. *International Journal of the Addictions, 3*, 25–39.

Naimi, T. S., Brown, D. W., Brewer, R. D., Giles, W., Mensah, G., Serdula, N. L., et al. (2005). Cardiovascular risk factors and confounders among nondrinking and moderate-drinking U.S. adults. *American Journal of Preventative Medicine, 28*, 369–373.

Naranjo, C. A., & Sellers, E. M. (1986). Clinical assessment and pharmacology of the alcohol withdrawal syndrome. In M. Galanter (Ed.), *Recent developments in alcoholism* (Vol. 4, pp. 265–281). New York: Plenum Press.

National Drug Intelligence Center. (2005a). http://www.usdoj.gov/ndic/pubs8/8731/marijuana.htm#Top

National Drug Intelligence Center. (2005b). http://www.usdoj.gov/ndic/pubs11/12620/marijuana.htm.

Nehlig, A., Daval, J.-L., & Debry, G. (1992). Caffeine and the central nervous system: Mechanisms of action, biochemical, metabolic and psychostimulant effects. *Brain Research Reviews, 17*, 139–170.

Nehlig, A., & Debry, G. (1994). Caffeine and sports activity: A review. *International Journal of Sports Medicine, 15*(5), 215–223.

Neims, A. H., Bailey, J., & Aldrich, A. (1979). Disposition of caffeine during and after pregnancy. *Clinical Research, 20*, 236A.

Nesse, R., & Berridge, K. (1997). Psychoactive drug use in evolutionary perspective. *Science, 278*, 63–66.

Nicholl, J., & O'Cathain, A. (1992). Antenatal smoking, postnatal passive smoking and sudden infant death syndrome. In D. Poswillio & E. Alberman (Eds.), *Effects of smoking on the fetus, neonate and child* (pp. 138–170). Oxford, England: Oxford University Press.

Nicholson, K., & Balster, B. (2001). GHB: A new and novel drug of abuse. *Drug and Alcohol Dependence, 63*, 1–22.

Nicholson, J., Hayes, B., & Balster, R. (1999). Evaluation of the reinforcing properties and phencyclidine-like discriminative stimulus effects of dextromethorphan and dextrophan in rats and rhesus monkeys. *Psychopharmacology, 146*, 49–59.

NIDA. (2001, June). *Epidemiologic trends in drug abuse advance report*. Available at http://www.nida.nih.gov/CEWG/AdvancedRep/601ADV/601adv.html

Nowak, R. (2005, June 11–17). Petrol-lite stops sniffers getting high. *New Scientist*, p. 28.

Nriagu, J. O. (1983). Saturnine gout among the Roman aristocrats. *New England Journal of Medicine, 308*, 660–663.

Nutt, D. J. (1997). Neuropharmacological basis for tolerance and dependence. In B. A. Johnson & J. D. Roache (Eds.), *Drug addiction and its treatment: The nexus of neuroscience and behavior* (pp. 171–186). Philadelphia: Lippincott-Raven Press.

Nyswander, M. (1967). The methadone treatment of heroin addiction. *Hospital Practice, 2*(4), 27–33.

O'Brien, C. P. (1976). Experimental analysis of conditioning factors in human narcotic addiction. *Pharmacological Reviews, 27*, 533–543.

O'Connell, T., Kaye, L., & Plosay, J. (2000). Gamma-hydroxybutyrate (GHB): A newer drug of abuse. *American Family Physician, 62*, 2478–2482.

Oetting, E., & Web, J. (1992). Psychosocial characteristics and their links with inhalants: A research agenda. In E. R. Ottering & F. Beauvais (Eds.), *Inhalant abuse: A volatile research agenda* (pp. 59–96). (NIDA Monograph No. 129). Rockville, MD: U.S. Public Health Service.

Ogbourne, A. C., & Glaser, F. B. (1981). Characteristics of affiliates of Alcoholics Anonymous. *Journal of Studies on Alcohol, 42*, 661–675.

Olds, J., & Milner, P. M. (1954). Positive reinforcement produced by electrical stimulation of the septal area and other regions of the rat brain. *Journal of Comparative and Physiological Psychology, 17*, 419–427.

O'Mara, R. (1993, September 19). Maintenence isn't cure, but it is limiting HIV, crime in Britain's drug picture. *The Sun*, p. 6A.

O'Neil, S., Tipton, K. F., Prichard, J. S., & Quinlan, A. (1984). Survival after high blood alcohol levels: Association with first order elimination kinetics. *Archives of Internal Medicine, 144*, 641–642.

Ordway, G. A., Klimek, V., & Mann, J. J. (2002). Neurocircuitry of mood disorders. In K. L. Davis, D. Cherney, J. T. Coyle, & C. Nemeroff (Eds.), *Psychopharmacology: A fifth generation of progress* (pp. 1052–1065). Nashville, TN: American College of Neuropsychopharmacology.

Organization for Economic Cooperation and Development. (1978, September). *Road research: New research on the role of alcohol and drugs in road accidents*. Paris: Author.

Österberg, E. (1992). Effects of alcohol control measures on alcohol consumption. *International Journal of the Addictions, 27*, 209–225.

Oswald, I., Lewis, S. A., Tangey, J., Firth, H., & Haider, I. (1973). Benzodiazepines and human sleep. In S. Garattini, E. Mussini, & L. O. Randall (Eds.), *The benzodiazepines* (pp. 613–625). New York: Raven Press.

Otis, L. S. (1964). Dissociation and recovery of a response learned under the influence of chlorpromazine or saline. *Science, 143*, 1347–1348.

Overall, J. E. (1987). Introduction: Methodology in psychopharmacology. In H. Y. Meltzer (Ed.), *Psychopharmacology: A third generation of progress* (pp. 995–996). New York: Raven Press.

Overton, D. A. (1972). State-dependent learning produced by alcohol and its relevance to alcoholism. In B. Kissen & H. Begleiter (Eds.), *The biology of alcoholism* (Vol. 2, pp. 193–217). New York: Plenum Press.

Overton, D. A. (1973). State-dependent learning produced by addicting drugs. In S. Fisher & A. M. Freeman (Eds.), *Opiate addiction: Origins and treatment* (pp. 61–67). New York: Wiley.

Overton, D. A. (1977). Comparison of ethanol, pentobarbital and phenobarbital using drug vs. drug discrimination training. *Psychopharmacology, 53*, 195–199.

Overton, D. A. (1982). Comparison of the degree of discriminability of various drugs using the T-maze drug discrimination paradigm. *Psychopharmacology, 76*, 385–395.

Overton, D. A. (1987). Applications and limitations of the drug discrimination method for the study of drug abuse. In M. A. Bozarth (Ed.), *Methods of assessing the reinforcing properties of abused drugs* (pp. 291–340). New York: Springer-Verlag.

Overton, D. A., & Batta, S. K. (1977). Relationship between abuse liability of drugs and their degree of discriminability in the rat. In T. Thompson & K. R. Unna (Eds.), *Predicting dependence liability of stimulant and depressant drugs* (pp. 125–135). Baltimore: University Park Press.

Owen, R. T., & Tyrer, P. (1983). Benzodiazepine dependence: A review of the evidence. *Drugs, 25*, 385–398.

Palmer, J., Rosenberg, L., Rao, R., & Shapiro, S. (1995). Coffee consumpton and myocardial infarction in women. *American Journal of Epidemiology, 141*, 724–731.

Papafotiou, K., Carter, J. D., & Stough, C. (2005). An evaluation of the sensitivity of the Standardized Field Sobriety Tests (SFSTs) to detect impairment due to marijuana intoxication. *Psychopharmacology, 180*, 107–114.

Parrott, A. C. (2004). Is ecstasy MDMA? A review of the proportion of ecstasy tablets containing MSMA, their dosage levels and changing perceptions of purity. *Psychopharmacology, 173*(3), 234–241.

Parsons, W. D., & Neims, A. H. (1978). Effects of smoking on caffeine clearance. *Clinical Pharmacology and Therapy, 24*, 40–45.

Pastuszak, A., Schick-Boschetto, B., Zuber, C., Feldkamp, M., Pinelli, M., Sihn, S., et al. (1993). Pregnancy outcome following first-trimester exposure to fluoxetine (Prozac). *Journal of the American Medical Association, 269*(17), 2246–2248.

Paton, W. D. M., & Pertwee, R. C. (1973). The actions of cannabis in animals. In R. Mechoulam (Ed.), *Marijuana* (pp. 192–287). Orlando: Academic Press.

Paul, S. (2000). GABA and glycine. In *Psychopharmacology: The fourth generation of progress*. Published online at http://www.acnp.org/citations/GN401000008

Paul, S. M., Marangos, P. J., Goodwin, F. K., & Slotnick, P. (1980). Brain-specific benzodiazepine receptors and putative endogenous benzodiazepine-like compounds. *Biological Psychiatry, 15*, 407–428.

Paulus, M. P., Hozack, N. E., Zauscher, B. E., Frank, L., Brown, G. G., Braff, D. L., et al. (2002). Behavioral and functional neuroimaging evidence for prefrontal dysfunction in methamphetamine-dependent subjects. *Neuropsychopharmacology, 26*, 53–63.

Pavlov, I. (1927). *Conditioned reflexes*. New York: Dover.

Pearson, T. A., & Terry, P. (1994). What to advise patients about drinking alcohol. *Journal of the American Medical Association, 272*, 967–968.

Pendrey, M. L., Maltzman, I. M., & West, L. J. (1982). Controlled drinking by alcoholics? New findings and a reevaluation of a major affirmative study. *Science, 217*, 169–175.

Perkins, K. A., Grobe, J. E., Epstein, L. H., Caggiula, A. R., & Stiller, R. L. (1992). Effects of nicotine on subjective arousal may be dependent on baseline subjective state. *Journal of Substance Abuse, 4*(2), 131–141.

Pertwee, R. G. (1992). In vivo interactions between psychotropic cannabinoids and other drugs involving central and peripheral neurochemical mediators. In L. Murphy & A. Bartke (Eds.), *Marijuana/cannabinoids: Neurobiology and neurophysiology* (pp. 165–218). Boca Raton, FL: CRC Press.

Peters, J. M. (1967). Caffeine-induced haemorrhagic automutilation. *Archives Internationales de Pharmacodynamie et de Therapie, 169*, 139–146.

Petursson, H., & Lader, M. H. (1981). Withdrawal from long-term benzodiazepine treatment. *British Medical Journal, 283*, 643–645.

Pfaus, J. G., & Pinel, P. J. (1988). Alcohol inhibits and disinhibits sexual behavior in the male rat. Unpublished manuscript.

Phillips-Bute, B. G., & Lane, J. D. (1998). Caffeine withdrawal symptoms following brief caffeine deprivation. *Physiology and Behavior, 63*, 35–39.

Phillis, J. W., & O'Regan, M. H. (1988). The role of adenosine in the central actions of the benzodiazepines. *Progress in Neuro-Psychopharmacology and Biological Psychiatry, 12*, 384–404.

Pianezza, M., Sellers, E., & Tyndale, R. (1998). Nicotine metabolism defect reduces smoking. *Nature, 393*(6687), 750.

Piazza, P. V., & Le Moal, M. (1998). The role of stress in drug self-administration. *Trends in Pharmacological Science, 19*, 67–74.

Pickens, R., & Thompson, T. (1968). Cocaine-reinforced behavior in rats: Effects of reinforcement magnitude and fixed ratio size. *Journal of Pharmacology and Experimental Therapeutics, 161*, 122–129.

Pierce, I. H. (1941). Absorption of nicotine from cigarette smoke. *Journal of Laboratory and Clinical Medicine, 26*, 1322–1325.

Pierce, R. C., & Kalivas, P. W. (1997). A circuitry model of the expression of behavioral sensitization to amphetamine-like psychostimulants. *Brain Research: Brain Research Reviews, 25*, 192–216.

Pirec, V., Coalson, D. W., Lichtor, J. L., Klafta, J., Young, C., Rupani, G., et al. (1995). Cold water immersion modulates the reinforcing effects of nitrous oxide in healthy volunteers. *Experimental and Clinical Pharmacology, 3*, 148–155.

Pirich, C., O'Grady, J., & Sinzinger, H. (1993). Coffee, lipoproteins and cardiovascular disease. *Weiner Klinische Wochenschrsft, 105*, 306.

Pogorelov, V., & Kovalev, G. (1999). Dopaminergic involvement in the process of reinforcement from diethyl ether vapor in rats. *Progress in Neuro Psychopharmacology and Biological Psychiatry, 23*, 1135–1156.

Pomerleau, C. S., & Pomerleau, O. F. (1992). Euphoriant effects of nicotine in smokers. *Psychopharmacology, 108*, 460–465.

Pomerleau, O. F., & Pomerleau, C. S. (1984). Neuroregulators and the reinforcement of smoking: Toward a biobehavioral explanation. *Neuroscience and Biobehavioral Reviews, 8*, 503–513.

Pompéia, S., Gorenstein, C., & Curran, H. (1996). Benzodiazepine effects on memory tests: Dependence on retrieval cues? *International Clinical Psychopharmacology, 11*, 229–236.

Popham, R. E., Schmidt, W., & de Lint, J. (1976). The effects of legal restraint on drinking. In B. Kissen & H. Begleiter (Eds.), *The biology of alcoholism* (Vol. 4, pp. 579–625). New York: Plenum Press.

Porcu, P., & Grant, K. A. (2004). Discriminative stimulus effects of ethanol in rats using a three-choice ethanol-midazolam water discrimination. *Behavioral Pharmacology, 15*(8), 555–567.

Porjesz, B., & Begleiter, H. (1987). Evoked brain potentials and alcoholism. In O. A. Parsons, N. Butters, & P. E. Nathan (Eds.), *Neuropsychology of alcoholism* (pp. 45–63). New York: Guilford Press.

Porsolt, R. D., Pawelec, C., & Jalfre, M. (1982). Use of a drug discrimination procedure to detect amphetamine-like effects of antidepressants. In F. C. Colpaert & J. L. Slangen (Eds.), *Drug discrimination: Applications in CNS pharmacology* (pp. 193–210). Amsterdam: Elsevier Biomedical.

Post, R. M., Cutler, N. R., Jimmerson, D. C., & Bunney, W. F., Jr. (1981). Dopaminergic mechanisms in affective illness. In B. Angrist, G. D. Burows, M. Lader, O. Lingjaerde, G. Sedvall, & D. Wheatly (Eds.), *Recent advances in neuropsychopharmacology* (pp. 55–62). Oxford, England: Pergamon Press.

Post, R. M., Weiss, S. R. B., Pert, A., & Uhde, T. W. (1987). Chronic cocaine administration: Sensitization and kindling effects. In S. Fisher, A. Raskin, & E. H. Uhlenhuth (Eds.), *Cocaine: Clinical and behavioral aspects* (pp. 109–173). New York: Oxford University Press.

Poulos, C. X., & Cappell, H. (1991). Homeostatic theory of drug tolerance: A general model of physiological adaptation. *Psychological Review, 98*, 390–408.

Pradhan, S. N. (1970). Effects of nicotine on several schedules of behavior in rats. *Archives Internationale de Pharmacodynamie, 183*, 127–138.

Preble, E., & Laury, G. (1967). Plastic cement: The ten cent hallucinogen. *International Journal of the Addictions, 2*, 271–281.

Preskorn, S. H. (1993). Pharmacokinetics of antidepressants: Why and how they are relevant to treatment. *Journal of Clinical Psychiatry, 54*(Suppl. 9), 14–33.

Preston, K. L., Griffiths, R. R., Clone, E. J., Darwin, W. D., & Gorodetzky, C. W. (1986). Diazepam and methadone blood levels following concurrent administration of diazepam and methadone. *Alcohol and Drug Dependence, 18*, 195–202.

Preston, K. L., Walsh, S. L., & Sannerud, C. A. (1997). Measures of interoceptive stimulus effects: Relationship to drug reinforcement. In B. A. Johnson & J. D. Roache (Eds.), *Drug addiction and its treatment: The nexus of neuroscience and behavior* (pp. 91–114). Philadelphia: Lippincott-Raven Press.

Primus, R. J., Thurkauf, A., Xu, J., Yevich, E., McInerney, S., Shaw, K., et al. (1997). II. Localization and characterization of dopamine D4 binding sites in rat and human brain by use of the novel, D4 receptor-selective ligand [3H]NGD 94-1. *Journal of Pharmacology and Experimental Therapy, 282*, 1020–1027.

Pritchard, W. S., Robinson, J. H., & Guy, T. D. (1992). Enhancement of continuous performance task reaction time by smoking in non-deprived smokers. *Psychopharmacology, 108*, 437–442.

Pryor, G. (1992). Animal research on solvent abuse. In E. R. Ottering & F. Beauvais (Eds.), *Inhalant abuse: A volatile research agenda* (pp. 233–258). (NIDA Monograph No. 129). Rockville, MD: U.S. Public Health Service.

Ramaekers, J., Robbe, H., & O'Hanlon, J. (2000). Marijuana, alcohol and actual driving performance. *Human Psychopharmacology (Clinical and Experimental), 15*, 551–558.

Ramchandani, V. A., Kwo, P. Y., & Li, T. (2001). Effect of food and food composition on alcohol elimination in healthy men and women. *Journal of Clinical Pharmacology, 41*, 1345–1350.

Rawson, A., Marinelli-Casey, P., Anglin, M., Dickow, A., Frazier, Y., Gallagher, C., et al. (2004). A muilt-site comparison of psychosocial approaches for the treatment of methamphetamine dependence. *Addiction, 99*, 708–717.

Rees, D., Kinsey, J., & Balster, R. (1987). Discriminative stimulus properties of toluene in the mouse. *Toxicology and Applied Pharmacology, 88*, 97–104.

Rees, D., Kinsey, J., Balster, R., Jordan, S., & Breen, T. J. (1987). Pentobarbital-like discriminative stimulus properties of halothane, 1,1,1-trichloroethane, isoamyl nitrite, fluothyl and oxazepam in mice. *Journal of Pharmacology and Experimental Therapeutics, 241*, 507–515.

Rees, D., Kinsey, J., Breen, T. J., & Balster, R. (1987). Toluene, halothane, 1,1,1-teichloroethane and oxazepam produce ethanol-like discriminative stimulus effects in mice. *Journal of Pharmacology and Experimental Therapeutics, 243*, 931–937.

Rehm, J., & Sempos, C. T. (1995). Alcohol consumption and all-cause mortality. *Addiction, 90*, 471–480.

Reid, R. L. (1957). The role of the reinforcer as a stimulus. *British Journal of Psychology, 49*, 292–299.

Reinisch, J. M., & Sanders, S. A. (1982). Early barbiturate exposure: The brain, sexually dimorphic behavior and learning. *Neuroscience and Biobehavioral Reviews, 6*, 311–319.

Rementiria, J. L., & Bhatt, K. (1977). Withdrawal symptoms in neonates from intrauterine exposure to diazepam. *Journal of Pediatrics, 90*, 123–126.

Rennie, D. (2004). Trial registration: A great idea switches from ignored to irresistible. *Journal of the American Medical Association, 292*, 1359–1362.

Restak, R. (1993, September/October). Brain by design. *The Sciences*, 27–33.

Ricaurte, G. A., Yaun, J., Hatzidimitriou, G., Cord, B. J., & McCann, U. D. (2002). Severe dopaminergic neurotoxicity in primates after a common recreational dose regimen of MDMA ("Ecstasy"). *Science, 297*(5590), 2260–2263.

Ricaurte, G. A., Yaun, J., Hatzidimitriou, G., Cord, B. J., & McCann, U. D. (2003). Retraction. *Science, 301*(5639), 1479.

Richards, C. D. (1980). In search of the mechanisms of anesthesia. *Trends in Neuroscience, 3*, 9–13.

Richardson, J. D., Aanonsen, L., & Hargreaves, K. M. (1998). Hypoactivity of the spinal cannabinoid system results in NMDA-dependent hyperalgesia. *Journal of Neuroscience, 18*, 451–457.

Richardson, N. J., Rogers, P. J., Ellman, N. A., & O'Dell, R. J. (1995). Mood and performance effects of caffeine in relation to acute and chronic caffeine deprivation. *Pharmacology, Biochemistry and Behavior, 52*, 313–320.

Rickels, K. (1983). Benzodiazepines in emotional disorders. *Journal of Psychoactive Drugs, 15*, 49–54.

Rickels, K., Downing, R. W., & Winokur, A. (1978). Antianxiety drugs: Clinical use in psychiatry. In L. L. Iverson, S. D. Iverson, & H. S. Snyder (Eds.), *Handbook of psychopharmacology* (Vol. 13, pp. 395–430). New York: Plenum Press.

Riegel, A., & French, E. (1999). An electrophysiological analysis of rat ventral tegmental dopamine neuronal activity during acute toluene exposure. *Pharmacology and Toxicology, 85*, 37–43.

Risner, M. E., & Goldberg, S. R. (1983). A comparison of nicotine and cocaine self-administration in the dog: Fixed ratio and progressive ratio schedules of intravenous drug infusion. *Journal of Pharmacology and Experimental Therapeutics, 224*, 319–326.

Ritchie, M. J. (1975). The xanthines. In L. S. Goodman & A. Gillman (Eds.), *The pharmacological basis of therapeutics* (pp. 367–378). London: Collier-Macmillan.

Roache, J. D., & Griffiths, R. R. (1987). Lorazepam and meprobamate dose effects in humans: Behavioral effects and abuse liability. *Journal of Pharmacology and Experimental Therapeutics, 243*, 978–988.

Robbins, L. N., Davis, D. H., & Goodwin, D. W. (1974). Drug use by U.S. Army enlisted men in Vietnam: A follow up on their return home. *American Journal of Epidemiology, 99*, 235–249.

Robert, J. C. (1967). *The story of tobacco in America.* Chapel Hill: University of North Carolina Press.

Robertson, D., & Curatolo, P. W. (1984). The cardiovascular effects of caffeine. In P. B. Dews (Ed.), *Caffeine: Perspectives from recent research* (pp. 77–85). Berlin: Springer-Verlag.

Robinson, D. (1977). Factors influencing alcohol consumption. In G. Edwards & M. Grant (Eds.), *Alcoholism: New knowledge and new responses* (pp. 60–77). London: Croom Helm.

Robinson, J. H., & Pritchard, W. S. (1992). The role of nicotine in tobacco use. *Psychopharmacology, 108*, 397–407.

Robinson, T. E., & Berridge, K. C. (1993). The neural basis of drug craving: An incentive-sensitization theory of drug addiction. *Brain Research Reviews, 18*, 274–291.

Robinson, T. E., & Berridge, K. C. (2000). The psychology and neurobiology of addiction: An incentive-sensitization view. *Addiction, 95*, S91–S117.

Robinson, T. E., & Berridge, K. C. (2003). Addiction. *Annual Review of Psychology, 54*, 25–53.

Rocha, B. A., Ward, A. S., Egilmez, Y., Lutle, U., & Emmett-Ogelsby, M. (1996). Tolerance to the discriminative stimulus and reinforcing effects of ketamine. *Behavioural Pharmacology, 7*, 160–168.

Roffman, M., & Lal, H. (1972). Role of brain amines in learning association with "amphetamine state." *Psychopharmacology, 25*, 196–204.

Rogers, P. J., & Dernoncourt, C. (1998). Regular coffee consumption: A balance of adverse effects and beneficial effects for mood and psychomotor performance. *Pharmacology, Biochemistry and Behavior, 59*, 1039–1045.

Rogers, P. J., Heatherley, S. V., Hayward, R. C., Seers, H. E., Hill, J., & Kane, M. (2005). Effects of caffeine and caffeine withdrawal on mood and cognitive performance degraded by sleep restriction. *Psychopharmacology, 179*, 742–751.

Romano, C., & Goldstein, A. (1980). Stereospecific nicotine receptors on rat brain membranes. *Science, 210*, 647–649.

Room, R. (1983). Sociological aspects of the disease concept of alcoholism. In R. C. Smart, F. B. Glassier, Y. Israel, H. Kalant, R. E. Popham, & W. Schmidt (Eds.), *Research advances in alcoholism and drug problems* (Vol. 7, pp. 47–91). New York: Plenum Press.

Rorabaugh, W. J. (1979). *The alcoholic republic.* New York: Oxford University Press.

Rose, J. S., Branchey, M., Buydens-Branchey, L., Stapleton, J. M., Chasen, K., Werrell, A., et al (1996). Cerebral perfusion in early and late opiate withdrawal: A technetium-99m HMPAO SPECT study. *Psychiatry Research: Neuroimaging, 67*, 39–47.

Rosenbaum, G., Cohen, B. D., Luby, D. E., Gottlieb, J. S., & Yellen, D. (1959). Comparison of Sernyl with other drugs: Simulation of schizophrenic performance with Sernyl, LSD-25, and amobarbital (Amytal) sodium: 1. Attention, motor function, and proprioception. *Archives of General Psychiatry, 1*, 651.

Rosenberg, N., & Sharp, C. (1992). Solvent toxicity: A neurological focus. In E. R. Ottering & F. Beauvais (Eds.), *Inhalant abuse: A volatile research agenda* (pp. 117–171). (NIDA Monograph No. 129). Rockville, MD: U.S. Public Health Service.

Rossi, A. M., Babor, T. F., Meyer, R. E., & Mendelson, J. H. (1974). Mood states. In J. H. Mendelson, A. M. Rossi, & R. E. Meyer (Eds.), *The use of marijuana: A psychological and physiological inquiry* (pp. 115–133). New York: Plenum Press.

Rossi, A. M., Kuehnle, J. C., & Mendelson, J. H. (1978). Marijuana and mood in human volunteers. *Pharmacology, Biochemistry and Behavior, 8,* 447–453.

Roth, R. H. (1983). Neuroleptics: Functional neurochemistry. In J. T. Coyle & S. J. Enna (Eds.), *Neuroleptics: Neurochemical, behavioral, and clinical perspectives* (pp. 119–165). New York: Raven Press.

Rothman, K., & Keller, A. (1972). The effects of a joint exposure to alcohol and tobacco on risk of cancer of the mouth and pharynx. *Journal of Chronic Diseases, 25,* 711–716.

Rothschild, A. J., & Locke, C. A. (1991). Reexposure to fluoxetine after serious suicidal attempts by three patients: The role of akathesia. *Journal of Clinical Psychiatry, 52*(12), 491–493.

Rowlett, J. K., Massey, B. W., Kleven, M. S., & Woolverton, W. L. (1996). Parametric analysis of cocaine self-administration under a progressive ratio schedule in rhesus monkeys. *Psychopharmacology, 125,* 361–370.

Rubin, H. B., & Henson, D. B. (1976). Effects of alcohol on male sexual responding. *Psychopharmacologia, 47,* 123–134.

Rudgley, R. (1995). The archaic use of hallucinogens in Europe: An archaeology of altered states. *Addiction, 90,* 63–64.

Rudorfer, M. V., & Potter, W. Z. (1987). Pharmacokinetics of antidepressants. In H. Y. Meltzer (Ed.), *Psychopharmacology: A third generation of progress* (pp. 1353–1363). New York: Raven Press.

Rumbaugh, C. L., Bergeron, C. L., Fang, H. C., & McCormack, R. (1971). Cerebral anginographic changes in the drug abuse patient. *Radiology, 101,* 335–344.

Rush, A. J., & Ryan, N. D. (2002). Current and emerging therapeutics for depression, in 5th gen, pp. 1082–1096.

Rush, C. (1998). Behavioral pharmacology of zolpidem relative to benzodiazepines: A review. *Pharmacology, Biochemistry and Behavior, 61,* 253–269.

Rush, C. R., Sullivan, J. T., & Griffiths, R. R. (1995). Intravenous caffeine in stimulant drug abusers: Subjective reports and physiological effects. *Journal of Pharmacology and Experimental Therapeutics, 273,* 351–358.

Russell, C. S., Taylor, R., & Law, C. E. (1968). Smoking in pregnancy: Maternal blood pressure, pregnancy outcome, baby weight and growth, and other related factors. *British Journal of Preventive Social Medicine, 22,* 119.

Russell, M. A. H. (1976). Tobacco smoking and nicotine dependence. In R. J. Gibbins, Y. Israel, H. Kalant, R. E. Popham, W. Schmidt, & R. G. Smart (Eds.), *Research advances in alcohol and drug problems* (Vol. 1, pp. 1–48). New York: Wiley.

Ryback, R. S. (1970). Alcohol amnesia: Observations in seven drinking inpatient alcoholics. *Quarterly Journal of Studies on Alcohol, 31,* 616–632.

Rylander, G. (1969). Clinical and medico-criminological aspects of addiction to central stimulating drugs. In F. Sjoquist & M. Tottie (Eds.), *Abuse of central stimulants* (pp. 251–274). Stockholm: Almqvist & Wiksell.

Ryu, S., Choi, S. K., Joung, S. S., Stjh, H., Cha, Y. S., Lee, S., et al. (2001). Caffeine as a lipolytic food component increases endurance performance in rats and athletes. *Journal of Nutritional Science and Vitaminology, 47,* 139–147.

Ryu, Y. H., Lee, J. D., Yoon, P. H., Jeon, P., Kim, D. I., & Shin, D. W. (1998). Cerebral perfusion impairment in a patient with toluene abuse. *Journal of Nuclear Medicine, 39,* 632–633.

Saario, I., & Linnoila, M. (1976). Effects of subacute treatment with hypnotics, alone and combination with alcohol, on psychomotor skills related to driving. *Acta Pharmacologica et Toxicologica, 38,* 382–392.

Salimenk, C. A. (1976). Pyrolysis of cannabinoids. In G. G. Nahas (Ed.), *Marijuana: Chemistry, biochemistry and cellular effects* (pp. 31–38). New York: Springer-Verlag.

Samson, H. H. (1987). Initiation of ethanol-maintained behavior: A comparison of animal models and their implication to human drinking. In T. Thompson, P. B. Dews, & J. E. Barrett (Eds.), *Advances in behavioral pharmacology: Vol. 6. Neurobehavioral pharmacology* (pp. 221–248). Hillsdale, NJ: Erlbaum.

Sandridge, J., Zylstra, R., & Adams, S. (2004). Alcohol consumption: An overview of benefits and risks. *Southern Medical Journal, 97,* 664–672.

Sanna, E., & Harris, A. (1993). Neuronal ion channels. In M. Galanter (Ed.), *Recent developments in alcoholism* (Vol. 11, pp. 169–186). New York: Plenum Press.

Santos, I., Victoria, C., Hutty, S., & Morris, S. (1998). Caffeine intake and pregnancy outcomes: A meta-analytic review. *Cadernos de Saude Publica, 14,* 523–530.

Schachter, S. (1973). Nesbitt's paradox. In W. L. Dunn (Ed.), *Smoking behavior: Motives and incentives* (pp. 147–155). Washington, DC: Winston.

Schachter, S. (1978). Pharmacological and psychological determinants of smoking. In R. E. Thornton (Ed.), *Smoking behaviour: Physiological and psychological influences* (pp. 208–228). Edinburgh: Churchill Livingstone.

Schechter, M. (1998). Rohypnol ("roofies") control of drug discrimination: Effect of coadministered ethanol or flumenazil. *Pharmacology, Biochemistry and Behavior, 59,* 19–25.

Schechter, M. D., & Glennon, R. A. (1985). Cathinone, cocaine and methamphetamine: Similarity of behavior effects. *Pharmacology, Biochemistry and Behavior, 22,* 913–916.

Schmauss, C., & Yaksh, T. L. (1984). In vivo studies on spinal opiate receptor systems mediating antinociception· II Pharmacological profiles suggesting a differential association of mu, delta and kappa receptors with visceral chemical and cutaneous thermal stimuli in the rat. *Journal of Pharmacology and Experimental Therapeutics, 228,* 1–12.

Schmidt, C. J. (1987). Psychedelic amphetamine, methylendioxymethamphetamine. *Journal of Pharmacology and Experimental Therapeutics, 240,* 1–7.

Schmiterlow, C., & Hanson, E. (1965). The distribution of C-14 nicotine. In E. S. Von Euler (Ed.), *Tobacco alkaloids and related compounds* (pp. 75–86). New York: Macmillan.

Schörring, E., & Hecht, A. (1979). Behavioral effects of low, acute doses of morphine in nontolerant groups of rats in an open-field test. *Psychopharmacology, 64,* 67–71.

Schottenfield, R., Parkes, J., O'Conner, P., Chewarski, M., Oliveto A., & Kostenet, T. (2000). Thrice weekly versus daily buprenorphine maintenance. *Biological Psychiatry, 47,* 1072–1079.

Schuckit, M. A. (1985). Genetics and the risk of alcoholism. *Journal of the American Medical Association, 254,* 2614–2617.

Schuckit, M. A. (1987). Biology of risk for alcoholism. In H. Y. Meltzer (Ed.), *Psychopharmacology: The third generation of progress* (pp. 1527–1533). New York: Raven Press.

Schuckit, M. A. (1992). Advances in understanding the vulnerability to alcoholism. In C. E. O'Brien &

J. H. Jaffe (Eds.), *Addictive states* (pp. 93–108). New York: Raven Press.

Schuh, K. J., & Griffiths, R. R. (1996). Caffeine reinforcement: Role of withdrawal. In L. S. Harris (Ed.), *Problems of drug dependence* (NIDA Research Monograph No. 162:292). Washington, DC: U.S. Government Printing Office.

Schuh, K. J., & Griffiths, R. R. (1997). Caffeine reinforcement: The role of withdrawal. *Psychopharmacology, 130,* 320–326.

Schultes, R. E. (1987). Coca and other psychoactive plants: Magico-religious roles in primitive societies of the world. In S. Fisher, A. Raskin, & E. H. Uhlenhuth (Eds.), *Cocaine: Clinical and behavioral aspects* (pp. 212–250). New York: Oxford University Press.

Schuster, C. R. (1970). Psychological approaches to opiate dependence and self-administration by laboratory animals. *Federation Proceedings, 29,* 1–5.

Schuster, C. R., Dockens, W. S., & Woods, J. H. (1966). Behavioral variables affecting the development of amphetamine tolerance. *Psychopharmacologia, 9,* 170–182.

Schuster, R. M., & Thompson, T. (1969). Self-administration and behavioral dependence on drugs. *Annual Review of Pharmacology, 9,* 483–502.

Schwartz, J. (1994, June 27–July 3). Smoking under siege. *Washington Post,* National Weekly Edition, pp. 6–9.

Science News. (1992). And you thought you hated mornings. *Science News, 141,* 28.

Scott, C. C., & Chen, K. K. (1944). Comparison of the action of l-thyl theobromine and caffeine in animals and man. *Journal of Pharmacology and Experimental Therapeutics, 82,* 89–97.

Scott, J. M. (1969). *The white poppy.* New York: Funk & Wagnalls.

Searles, J. S. (1988). The role of genetics in the pathogenesis of alcoholism. *Journal of Abnormal Behavior, 97,* 153–167.

Seeley, J. R. (1960). Death by liver cirrhosis and price of beverage alcohol. *Canadian Medical Association Journal, 83,* 1361–1366.

Seeman, P., Lee, T., Chau-Wing, M., & Wong, K. (1976). Antipsychotic drug dose and neuroleptic/dopamine receptors. *Nature, 261,* 717–718.

Seeman, P., & van Tol, H. H. (1994). Dopamine receptor pharmacology. *Trends in Pharmacological Sciences, 15,* 264–270.

Seiden, L. S., & Dykstra, L. A. (1977). *Psychopharmacology: A biochemical and behavioral approach*. New York: Van Nostrand-Reinhold.

Sellers, E. M., Ciraulo, D. A., DuPont, R. L., Griffiths, R. R., Kosten, T. R., Romach, M. K., et al. (1993). Alprazolam and benzodiazepine dependence. *Journal of Clinical Psychiatry, 54*(10, Suppl.), 64–75.

Sharp, C. (1992). Introduction to inhalant abuse. In E. R. Ottering & F. Beauvais (Eds.), *Inhalant abuse: A volatile research agenda* (pp. 1–11). (NIDA Monograph No. 129). Rockville, MD: U.S. Public Health Service.

Shen, M., Piser, T. M., Seybold, V. S., & Thayer, S. A. (1996). Cannabinoid receptor agonists inhibit glutamatergic synaptic transmission in rat hippocampal cultures. *Journal of Neuroscience, 16*, 4322–4334.

Sherwood, N., Kerr, J. S., & Hindmarch, I. (1992). Psychomotor performance in smokers following single and repeated doses of nicotine gum. *Psychopharmacology, 108*, 432–436.

Shiffman, S. M. (1989). Tobacco "chippers": Individual differences in tobacco dependence. *Psychopharmacology, 97*, 539–547.

Shiono, P. H., Klebanoff, M. A., Nugent, R. P., Cotch, M. F., Wilkins, D. E., & Rollins, D. E. (1995). The impact of cocaine and marijuana use and low birthweight and preterm birth: A multicenter study. *American Journal of Obstetrics and Gynecology, 172*, 19–27.

Shopsin, B., Cassano, G. B., & Conti, L. (1981). An overview of new "second generation" antidepressant compounds: Research and treatment implications. In S. J. Enna, J. B. Malick, & E. Richelson (Eds.), *idepressants: Neurochemical, behavioral and nical perspectives* (pp. 219–252). New York: Raven Press.

el, R. K. (1977). Hallucinations. *Scientific nerican, 237*(4), 132–140.

el, R. K. (1981). Inside Castenedas's pharmacy. *urnal of Psychoactive Drugs, 13*, 325–332.

el, R. K. (1982a). Cocaine and sexual dysfunction: The curse of Mama Coca. *Journal of Psychoactive ugs, 14*, 71–74.

Siegel, R. K. (1982b). Cocaine smoking. *Journal of Psychoactive Drugs, 14*, 271–359.

Siegel, R. K. (1986). MDMA: Medical use and intoxication. *Journal of Psychoactive Drugs, 18*, 349–353.

Siegel, R. K., & Jarvik, M. E. (1975). Drug-induced hallucinations in animals and man. In R. K. Siegel &

L. J. West (Eds.), *Hallucinations: Behavior, experience, and theory* (pp. 81–162). New York: Wiley.

Siegel, S. (1975). Evidence from rats that morphine tolerance is a learned response. *Journal of Comparative and Physiological Psychology, 89*, 489–506.

Siegel, S. (1982). Drug dissociation in the nineteenth century. In F. C. Colpaert & J. L. Slangen (Eds.), *Drug discrimination: Applications in CNS pharmacology* (pp. 257–262). Amsterdam: Elsevier Biomedical.

Siegel, S. (1983). Classical conditioning, drug tolerance and drug dependence. In Y. Israel, F. B. Graser, H. Kalant, W. Popham, W. Schmidt, & R. G. Smart (Eds.), *Research advances in alcohol and drug problems* (Vol. 7). New York: Plenum Press.

Siegel, S., Hinson, R. E., Krank, M. D., & McCully, J. (1982). Heroin "overdose" death: Contribution of drug-associated environmental cues. *Science, 216*, 436–437.

Siemens, A. J., Kalant, H., & Nie, J. C. de. (1976). Metabolic interactions between delta-9-tetrahydrocannabinol and other cannabinoids in rats. In M. C. Braude & S. Szara (Eds.), *Pharmacology of marijuana* (Vol. 1, pp. 77–92). Orlando: Academic Press.

Silkker, W., Jr., Paule, M. G., Ali, S. F., Scarlett, A. C., & Baily, J. R. (1992). Behavioral, neurochemical and neurophysiological effects of chronic marijuana smoke on the nonhuman primate. In L. Murphy & A. Bartke (Eds.), *Marijuana/cannabinoids neurology and neurophysiology* (pp. 219–274). Boca Raton, FL: CRC Press.

Silverman, K., Kirby, K. C., & Griffiths, R. R. (1994). Modulation of drug reinforcement by behavioral requirements following drug ingestion. *Psychopharmacology, 114*(2), 243–247.

Silverman, K., Mumford, G. K., & Griffiths, R. R. (1994). Enhancing caffeine reinforcement by behavioral requirements following drug ingestion. *Psychopharmacology, 114*(3), 424–432.

Silverman, P. B., & Bonate, P. L. (1997). Role of conditioned stimuli in addiction. In B. A. Johnson & J. D. Roache (Eds.), *Drug addiction and treatment: Nexus of neuroscience and behavior* (pp. 115–133). Philadelphia: Lippincott-Raven Press.

Simon, E. J. (1981). Opiate receptors and endorphins: Possible relevance to narcotic addiction. *Advances in Alcohol and Substance Abuse, 1*(1), 13–31.

Simonson, E., & Brozek, J. (1952). Flicker fusion frequency. *Physiological Review, 32*, 349–378.

Simpson, D. D., Joe, G. W., & Bracy, S. A. (1982). 6-year follow-up of opioid addicts after admission to treatment. *Archives of General Psychiatry, 39,* 1318–1326.

Simpson, G. M., & Singh, H. (1990). Tricyclic antidepressants. In J. D. Amsterdam (Ed.), *Pharmacotherapy of depression* (pp. 75–91). New York: Marcel Dekker.

Singer, S. J., & Nicholson, G. L. (1972). The fluid mosaic model of the structure of cell membranes. *Science, 175,* 720–731.

Single, E. W. (1988). The availability theory of alcohol-related problems. In C. D. Chaudron & D. A. Wilkinson (Eds.), *Theories on alcoholism* (pp. 325–352). Toronto: Addiction Research Foundation.

Small, E. (1979). *The species problem in Cannabis.* Toronto: Corpus.

Smith, C. G. (1964). Effects of d-amphetamine upon operant behavior of pigeons: Enhancement of reserpine. *Journal of Pharmacology and Experimental Therapeutics, 146,* 167–174.

Smith, D. (1998). Review of the American Medical Association Council on Scientific Affairs report on medical marijuana. *Journal of Psychoactive Drugs, 30,* 127–136.

Smith, D. E., Buxton, M. E., & Dammann, G. (1979). Amphetamine abuse and sexual dysfunction: Clinical and research considerations. In D. R. Smith (Ed.), *Amphetamine use, misuse and abuse* (pp. 228–248). Boca Raton, FL: CRC Press.

Smith, D. E., & Wesson, D. R. (1983). Benzodiazepine dependency syndromes. *Journal of Psychoactive Drugs, 15,* 85–96.

Smith, G. M., & Beecher, H. K. (1959). Amphetamine sulfate and athletic performance. *Journal of the American Medical Association, 170,* 542.

Smith, H. W. (1961). *From fish to philosopher.* Garden City, NY: Doubleday.

Smith-Kielland, A., Skuterud, B., & Mørland, J. (1999). Urinary excretion of 11-nor-9-carboxy-Δ9-tetrahydrocannabinol and cannabinoids in frequent and infrequent users. *Journal of Analytical Toxicology, 23,* 323–332.

Sneader, W. (1985). *Drug discovery: The evolution of modern medicines.* Chichester, England: Wiley.

Snyder, S. H. (1981). Adenosine receptors and the actions of methylxanthines. *Trends in Neuroscience, 4,* 242–244.

Snyder, S. H. (1977). Opiate receptors and internal opiates. *Scientific American, 236,* 44–56.

Snyder, S. H. (1984). Adenosine as a mediator of the behavioral effects of caffeine. In P. B. Dews (Ed.), *Caffeine: Perspectives from recent research* (pp. 129–141). Berlin: Springer-Verlag.

Snyder, S. H. (1986). *Drugs and the brain.* New York: Scientific American Library.

Sofia, R. D. (1978). Cannabis: Structure-activity relationships. In L. L. Iverson, S. D. Iverson, & S. H. Snyder (Eds.), *Handbook of psychopharmacology* (Vol. 12, pp. 319–371). New York: Plenum Press.

Soldatos, C., Dikeos, D., & Whitehead, A. (1999). Tolerance and rebound insomnia with rapidly eliminated hypnotics: A meta-analysis of sleep laboratory studies. *International Clinical Psychopharmacology, 14,* 287–303.

Solomon, D. (1966). *The marijuana papers.* Indianapolis: Bobbs-Merrill.

Solomon, R. L., & Corbit, J. D. (1974). An opponent-process theory of motivation: I. Temporal dynamics of affect. *Psychological Review, 81,* 119–145.

Solowij, N. (1998). *Cannabis and cognitive functioning.* Cambridge, England: Cambridge University Press.

Spear, L. P. (1997). Neurobehavioral abnormalities following exposure to drugs of abuse during development. In B. A. Johnson & J. D. Roache (Eds.), *Drug addiction and its treatment: The nexus of neuroscience and behavior* (pp. 233–255). Philadelphia: Lippincott-Raven Press.

Spiegel, R., & Aebi, H. J. (1981). *Psychopharmacology: An introduction.* Chichester, England: Wiley.

Spiga, R., & Roache, J. D. (1997). Human drug self-administration: A review and methodological critique. In D. A. Johnson & J. D. Roache (Eds.), *Drug addiction and treatment: Nexus of neuroscience and behavior* (pp. 39–71). Philadelphia: Lippincott-Raven Press.

Spindel, E. R., & Wurtman, R. J. (1984). The neuroendocrine effects of caffeine in rat and man. In P. B. Dews (Ed.), *Caffeine: Perspectives from recent research* (pp. 119–128). Berlin: Springer-Verlag.

Spitzer, W. O., Lawrence, V., Dales, R., Gill, G., Archer, M. C., Clarke, P., et al. (1990). Links between passive smoking and disease: A best evidence synthesis. *Clinical and Investigative Medicine, 13,* 17–42.

Sporer, K. (1999). Acute heroin overdose. *Annals of Internal Medicine, 130,* 584–590.

Sporer, K. (2003). Strategies for preventing heroin overdose, *British Medical Journal, 22,* 442–444.

Squires, R. F., & Braestrup, C. (1977). Benzodiazepine receptors in the brain. *Nature, 266,* 732–734.

Sramek, J. J., & Pi, E. H. (1996). Ethnicity and antidepressant response. *Mount Sinai Journal of Medicine, 63*, 320–325.

Sridhar, K. S., Ruab, W. A., Weatherby, N. L., Metsch, L. R., Jurratt, H. L., Inciardi, J. A., et al. (1994). Possible role of marijuana smoking as a carcinogen in development of lung cancer at a young age. *Journal of Psychoactive Drugs, 26*(3), 285–288.

Starmer, G. A. (1990). Alcohol and car driving: Impairment and per se limits for drivers. In I. Hindmarch & P. D. Stonier (Eds.), *Human psychopharmacology: Measures and methods* (Vol. 3, pp. 183–201). Chichester, England: Wiley Ltd.

Stavric, B., & Gilbert, S. G. (1990). Caffeine metabolism: A problem in extrapolating results from animal studies to humans. *Acta Pharmacologica Jugoslavica, 40*, 475–489.

Stephenson, F. A. (1987). Benzodiazepines in the brain. *Trends in Neuroscience, 10*(5), 185–186.

Stepney, R. (1982). Human smoking behavior and the development of dependence on tobacco smoking. *Pharmacology and Therapeutics, 15*, 181–206.

Sternback, L. H. (1973). Chemistry of the 1,4-benzodiazepines and some aspects of the structure-activity relationship. In S. Garattini, E. Mussini, & L. O. Randall (Eds.), *The benzodiazepines* (pp. 1–26). New York: Raven Press.

Stewart, B. S., Lamaire, G. A., Roche, J. D., & Meisch, R. A. (1994). Establishing benzodiazepines as oral reinforcers: Midazolam and diazepam self-administration in rhesus monkeys. *Journal of Pharmacology and Experimental Therapeutics, 271*(1), 200–211.

Stewart, J. (1962). Differential responses based on the physiological consequences of pharmacological agents. *Psychopharmacologia, 3*, 132–138.

Stewart, J., & Badiani, A. (1993). Tolerance and sensitization to the behavioral effects of drugs. *Behavioral Pharmacology, 4*, 289–312.

Stewart, J., & de Wit, H. (1987). Reinstatement of drug-taking behavior as a method of assessing incentive motivational properties of drugs. In M. A. Bozarth (Ed.), *Methods of assessing the reinforcing properties of abused drugs* (pp. 211–227). New York: Springer-Verlag.

Stillman, R., Eich, J. E., Weingartner, H., & Wyatt, R. J. (1976). Marijuana-induced state-dependent amnesia and its reversal by cuing. In M. C. Braude & S. Szara (Eds.), *Pharmacology of marijuana* (Vol. 4, pp. 453–456). Orlando: Academic Press.

Stolerman, I. P. (1987). Psychopharmacology of nicotine: Stimulus effects and receptor mechanisms. In L. L. Iverson, S. D. Iverson, & S. H. Snyder (Eds.), *Handbook of psychopharmacology: New directions in psychopharmacology* (Vol. 19, pp. 241–265). New York: Plenum Press.

Stolerman, I. P., Fink, R., & Jarvik, M. E. (1973). Acute and chronic tolerance to nicotine as measured by activity in rats. *Psychopharmacologia, 30*, 329–342.

Stolerman, I. P., Pratt, J. A., & Garcha, H. S. (1982). Further analysis of the nicotine cue in rats. In F. C. Colpaert & J. L. Slangen (Eds.), *Drug discrimination: Applications in CNS pharmacology* (pp. 203–210). Amsterdam: Elsevier Biomedical.

Strain, E. C., Mumford, G. K., Silverman, K., & Griffiths, R. R. (1995). Caffeine dependence syndrome, evidence from case histories and experimental evaluations. *Journal of the American Medical Association, 272*(13), 1043–1048.

Stripling, J. S., & Ellinwood, E. H., Jr. (1976). Cocaine: Physiological effects of acute and chronic administration. In S. J. Mule (Ed.), *Cocaine: Chemical, biological, clinical, social and treatment aspects* (pp. 165–186). Boca Raton, FL: CRC Press.

Sulser, F., Vetulani, J., & Mobley, P. L. (1978). Mode of action of antidepressant drugs. *Biochemical Pharmacology, 27*, 257–261.

Sutherland, G., Stapleton, J. A., Russell, M. A., Jarvis, M. J., Hajek, P., & Belcher, M. (1992). Randomized control trial of nasal nicotine spray. *Lancet, 340*(8815), 324–329.

Swanson, J. R., Jones, G. R., Krasselt, W., Denmark, L. N., & Ratti, F. (1997). Death of two subjects due to imipramine and desipramine metabolite accumulation during chronic therapy: A review of the literature and possible mechanisms. *Journal of Forensic Science, 42*, 335–339.

Syed, I. B. (1976). The effects of caffeine. *Journal of American Pharmaceutical Association, 10*, 568–572.

Tabakoff, B., & Hoffman, P. L. (1987). Biochemical pharmacology of alcohol. In H. Y. Meltzer (Ed.), *Psychopharmacology: The third generation of progress* (pp. 1521–1526). New York: Raven Press.

Tanda, G., Manzar, P., & Goldberg, S. R. (2000). Self-administration behavior is maintained by the psychoactive ingredient of marijuana in squirrel monkeys. *Nature Neuroscience, 3*, 1073–1074.

Tanda, G., Pontieri, F., & Chiara, G. (1997). Cannabinoid and heroin activation of mesolimboc dopamine transmission by a common 1 opioid receptor mechanism. *Science, 276*, 2048–2050.

Tapert, S. F., Cheung, E. H., Brown, G. G., Frank, L. R., Paulus, M. P., Schweinsburg, A. D., et al. (2003). Neural response to alcohol stimuli in adolescents with alcohol use disorder. *Archives of General Psychiatry, 60*, 727–735.

Tarnopolsky, M. A. (1994). Caffeine and endurance performance. *Sports Medicine, 18*, 109–125.

Tarriere, C., & Hartemann, F. (1964). *Investigation into the effects of tobacco smoke on a visual vigilance task* (pp. 5225–5230). Ergonomics: Proceedings of the Second International Congress on Ergonomics, Dortmund, Germany.

Tart, C. T., & Crawford, H. J. (1970). Marijuana intoxication: Reported effects on sleep. *Psychophysiology, 7*, 348.

Tatum, A. L., & Seevers, M. H. (1931). Theories of drug addiction. *Physiological Review, 11*, 107–120.

Taylor, J. L., & Tinklenberg, J. R. (1987). Cognitive impairment and benzodiazepines. In H. Y. Meltzer (Ed.), *Psychopharmacology. The third generation of progress* (pp. 1449–1454). New York: Raven Press.

Teicher, M. H., Glod, C. C., & Cole, J. O. (1990). Emergence of intense suicidal preoccupation during fluoxetine treatment. *American Journal of Psychiatry, 147*, 207–210.

Thompson, T., & Schuster, C. R. (1964). Morphine self-administration, food reinforced and avoidance behaviour in rhesus monkeys. *Psychopharmacologia, 5*, 87–94.

Thompson, T., Trombley, J., Luke, D., & Lott, D. (1970). Effects of morphine on behavior maintained by four simple food reinforcement schedules. *Psychopharmacologia, 17*, 182–192.

Ticku, M. K., & Olsen, R. W. (1978). Interaction of barbiturates with dihydropicrotoxin binding sites related to the GABA receptor-ionophore system. *Life Sciences, 22*, 1643–1652.

Tinklenberg, J. R. (1974). Marijuana and human aggression. In L. L. Miller (Ed.), *Marijuana: Effects on human behavior* (pp. 339–358). Orlando: Academic Press.

Toit, B. M. du. (1975). Dagga: The history and ethnographic setting of Cannabis sativa in southern Africa. In V. Rubin (Ed.), *Cannabis and culture* (pp. 81–118). The Hague: Mouton.

Tollefson, G. D. (1993). Adverse drug reactions/interactions in maintenance therapy. *Journal of Clinical Psychiatry, 54*(8), 48–58.

Torry, J. M. (1976). A case of suicide with nitrazepam and alcohol. *Practitioner, 217*, 648–649.

UNDCP & WHO. (1992). UNDCP and WHO Informal Expert Committee on the Drug-Craving Mechanism Report of the United Nations International Drug Control Programme and World Health Organization. Technical report series (No. V. 92-54439 T).

Uhlenhuth, E. H., de Wit, H., Balter, M. B., Johanson, C. E., & Mellinger, G. D. (1988). Risks and benefits of long-term benzodiazepine use. *Journal of Clinical Pharmacology, 8*(3), 161–167.

United Nations. (1980). Special issue devoted to Catha edulis (khat). *Bulletin on Narcotics, 32*(3).

U.S. Department of Health and Human Services. (1989). *Reducing the health consequences of smoking: 25 years of progress: A report of the surgeon general.* Rockville, MD: U.S. Department of Health and Human Services, Centers for Disease Control, Center for Chronic Disease Prevention and Promotion.

U.S. Department of Health and Human Services. (1990a). *Alcohol, tobacco, and other drugs may harm the unborn.* Rockville, MD: U.S. Department of Health and Human Services, Public Health Service, Alcohol, Drug Abuse, and Mental Health Administration, Office for Substance Abuse Prevention.

U.S. Department of Health and Human Services. (1990b). *The health benefits of smoking cessation: A report of the surgeon general.* Washington, DC: Author.

U.S. Department of Health and Human Services. (1994). *Preliminary estimates from the 1993 national household survey on drug abuse, advance report number 7.* Washington, DC: U.S. Department of Health and Human Services, Substance Abuse and Mental Health Services Administration.

U.S. Department of Health and Human Services. (1995). *Preliminary estimates from the 1994 national household survey on drug abuse, advance report number 10.* Washington, DC: U.S. Department of Health and Human Services, Substance Abuse and Mental Health Services Administration.

U.S. Environmental Protection Agency. (1992). *Respiratory health effects of passive smoking: Lung cancer and other disorders.* Washington, DC: Office of Research and Development, Office of Health and Environmental Assessment.

Vaillant, G. E. (1992). Is there a natural history of addiction? In C. E. O'Brien & J. H. Jaffe (Eds.), *Addictive states* (pp. 41–56). New York: Raven Press.

Van der Kooy, D. (1987). Place conditioning: A simple and effective method for assessing the motivational properties of drugs. In M. A. Bozarth (Ed.), *Methods of assessing the reinforcing properties of abused drugs* (pp. 229–240). New York: Springer-Verlag.

Van Laar, M., Volkerts, E., & Verbaten, M. (2001). Subchronic effects of the GABA-agonist lorazepam and the 5-HT2A/2C antagonist ritanserin on driving performance, slow wave sleep and daytime sleepiness in healthy volunteers. *Psychopharmacology, 154*, 189–197.

Van Laar, M., Volkerts, E., & Willigenberg, A. (1992). Therapeutic effects on actual driving performance of chronically administered buspirone and diazepam in anxious outpatients. *Journal of Clinical Psychopharmacology, 12*, 86–95.

Van Lancker, J. L. (1977). Smoking and disease. In M. E. Jarvik, J. W. Cullen, E. R. Gritz, T. M. Vogt, & L. J. West (Eds.), *Research on smoking behavior* (pp. 230–280) (NIDA Research Monograph No. 17, DHEW Pub. No. ADM 78 581). Washington, DC: U.S. Government Printing Office.

van Praag, H. M., de Kloet, E. R., & van Os, J. (2004). *Stress, the brain and depression.* Cambridge, England: Cambridge University Press.

Van Woert, M. H. (1983). Neuroleptics in neurological disorders. In J. T. Coyle & S. J. Enna (Eds.), *Neuroleptics: Neurochemical, behavioral, and clinical perspectives* (pp. 65–74). New York: Raven Press.

Varvel, S. A., Bridgen, D. T., Tao, Q., Thomas, B., Martin, B. R., & Lichtman, A. H. (2005). Delta9-tetrahydrocannbinol accounts for the antinociceptive, hypothermic, and cataleptic effects of marijuana in mice. *Journal of Pharmacology and Experimental Therapeutics, 314*, 329–337.

Verebey, K., Alrazi, J., & Jaffe, J. H. (1988). The complications of "ecstasy" (MDMA) [Letter]. *Journal of the American Medical Association, 259*, 1649–1650.

Verster, J., Volkerts, E., Schreuder, A., Eijken, E., van Heuckelum, J., Veldhuijzen, D., et al. (2002). Residual effects of middle-of-the-night administration of zaleplon and zolpidem on driving ability, memory functions, and psychomotor performance. *Journal of Clinical Psychopharmacology, 22*, 576–584.

Victor, M., Adams, R. D., & Collins, G. H. (1971). *The Wernicke-Korsakoff syndrome.* Philadelphia: Davis.

Villemagne, V., Yuan, J., Wong, D. F., Dannals, R. F., Hatzidimitriou, G., Mathews, W. B., et al. (1998). Brain dopamine neurotoxicity in baboons treated with doses of methamphetamine comparable to those recreationally abused by humans: Evidence from [11C]WIN-35,428 positron emission tomography studies and direct *in vitro* determinations. *Journal of Neuroscience, 18*, 419–427.

Vitiello, M. V., & Woods, S. C. (1975). Caffeine: Preferential consumption by rats. *Pharmacology, Biochemistry and Behavior, 3*, 147–149.

Vitiello, B., & Swedo, S. (2005). Antidepressant medication in children. *New England Journal of Medicine, 350*, 1489–1491.

Vogel, G. (1997). Cocaine wreaks subtle damage on developing brains. *Science, 287*, 38–39.

Vogel, J. R. (1979). Objective measurement of human performance changes produced by antianxiety drugs. In S. Fielding & H. Lal (Eds.), *Anxiolytics* (pp. 343–374). Mt. Kisco, NY: Futura.

Vogel-Sprott, M. (1967). Alcohol effects on human behavior under reward and punishment. *Psychopharmacologia, 11*, 337–344.

Vogel-Sprott, M. (1984). Response measures of social drinking: Research implications and application. *Journal of Studies on Alcohol, 44*, 817–836.

Vogel-Sprott, M. (1992). *Alcohol tolerance and social drinking: Learning and the consequences.* New York: Guilford Press.

Vogel-Sprott, M., Easdon, G., Fillmore, M., Finn, P., & Justus, A. (2001). Alcohol and behavioral control: Cognitive and neural mechanisms. *Alcoholism: Clinical and Experimental Research, 25*, 117–121.

Volkow, N. D., Fowler, J. S., Wolf, A. P., Hitzemann, R., Dewey, S., Bendriem, B., et al. (1991). Changes in brain glucose metabolism in cocaine dependence and withdrawal. *American Journal of Psychiatry, 148*, 621–626.

Volkow, N. D., Mullani, N., Gould, L., Adler, S., & Krajeswski, K. (1988). Effects of acute alcohol intoxication on cerebral blood flow measured by PET. *Psychiatry Research, 24*, 201–209.

Volkow, N. D., Wang, G. J., Fischman, M. W., Foltin, R. W., Fowler, J. S., Abumrad, N. N., et al. (1997). Relationship between subjective effects of cocaine and dopamine transporter occupancy. *Nature, 386*, 827–830.

Volkow, N. D., Wang, G-J., Ma, Y., Fowler, J., Zhu, W., Maynard, L., et al. (2003). Expectation enhances the regional brain metabolic and reinforcing effects of stimulants in cocaine abusers. *Journal of Neuroscience, 23*, 11461–11468.

Vree, T. B., & Henderson, P. T. (1980). Pharmacokinetics of amphetamines: In vivo and in vitro studies of factors governing their elimination. In J. Caldwell (Ed.), *Amphetamines and related stimulants: Chemical, biological, clinical and sociological aspects* (pp. 47–68). Boca Raton, FL: CRC Press.

Vuchinich, R. E., & Tucker, J. A. (1988). Contributions from the behavioral theory of choice to an analysis of alcohol abuse. *Journal of Abnormal Psychology, 97*, 181–195.

Waldorf, D., Murphy, S., Renarman, C., & Joyce, B. (1977). *Doing coke: An ethnography of cocaine users and sellers*. Washington, DC: Drug Abuse Council.

Walsh, B., Seidman, S., Sysko, R., & Gould, M. (2002). Placebo response in studies of major depression: Variable, substantial, and growing. *Journal of the American Medical Association, 287*, 1840–1847.

Walsh, M-T., & Dinan, T. (2001). Selective serotonin reuptake inhibitors and violence: A review of available evidence. *Acta Psychiatrica Scandanavica, 104*, 84–91.

Wang, G. J., Volkow, N. D., Fowler, J. S., Franceschi, D., Wong, C., Peppas, N., et al. (2003). Alcohol intoxication induces greater reductions in brain metabolism in male than in female subjects. *Alcoholism: Clinical and Experimental Research, 27*, 909–917.

Wang, J., Paria, B., Dey, S., & Armant, D. (1999). Stage-specific excitation of cannabinoid receptor exhibits differential effects on mouse embryonic development. *Biology of Reproduction, 60*, 839–844.

Warburton, D. M. (1992). Nicotine issues. *Psychopharmacology, 108*, 393–396.

Wareing, M., Fisk, J., & Murphy, P. (2000). Working memory deficits in current and previous users of MDMA ("ecstasy"). *British Journal of Psychology, 91*, 181–188.

Warren, D., Bowen, S., Jennings, W., Dallas, C., & Balster, R. (2000). Biphasic effects of 1,1,1-trichloroethane on the locomotor activity of mice: Relationship to blood and brain solvent concentrations. *Toxicological Sciences, 56*, 365–373.

Wasson, R. G. (1972). The divine mushroom of immortality. In P. T. Furst (Ed.), *Flesh of the gods* (pp. 185–200). New York: Praeger.

Watkins, R. L., & Adler, E. V. (1993). The effect of food on alcohol absorption and elimination patterns. *Journal of Forensic Sciences, 38*(2), 285–291.

Wax, P., Becker, C., & Curry, S. (2003). Unexpected "gas" casualties in Moscow: A medical toxicology perspective. *Annals of Emergency Medicine, 41*, 700–705.

Wayner, M. J., Jolicoeur, F. B., Rondeau, D. B., & Baron, F. C. (1976). Effects of acute and chronic administration of caffeine on schedule dependent and schedule induced behavior. *Pharmacology, Biochemistry and Behavior, 5*, 343–348.

Weddington, W. W. (1995). Methadone maintenance for opioid addiction. In N. S. Miller & M. S. Gold (Eds.), *Pharmacological therapies for alcohol and drug addiction* (pp. 411–418). New York: Marcel Dekker.

Weil, A. T., & Zinberg, N. E. (1969). Acute effects of marijuana on speech. *Nature, 222*, 434–437.

Weil, A. T., & Rosen, W. (1983). *Chocolate to morphine: Understanding mind-acting drugs*. Boston: Houghton Mifflin.

Weil, A. T., Zinberg, N. E., & Nelson, J. M. (1968). Clinical and psychological effects of marijuana in man. *Science, 192*, 1234–1242.

Weiss, B. (1969). Enhancement of performance by amphetamine-like drugs. In F. Sjoquist & M. Tottie (Eds.), *Abuse of central stimulants* (pp. 31–60). Stockholm: Almqvist & Wiksell.

Weiss, B., & Laties, V. G. (1962). Enhancement of human performance by caffeine and the amphetamines. *Pharmacological Review, 14*, 1–36.

Wenger, J. R., Tiffany, T. M., Bombardier, C., Nicoins, K., & Woods, S. C. (1981). Ethanol tolerance in the rat is learned. *Science, 213*, 575–576.

Wesnes, K., & Warburton, D. M. (1983). Smoking, nicotine and human performance. *Pharmacology and Therapeutics, 21*, 198–208.

West, R. (1993). Beneficial effects of nicotine: Fact or fiction. *Addiction, 88*, 589–590.

West, R. (2001). Theories of addiction. *Addiction, 96*, 3–15.

White, A. M. (2003). What happened? Alcohol, memory blackouts, and the brain. *Alcohol Research and Health, 27*(2), 186–196.

White, H. R. (1993). Sociology. In M. Galanter (Ed.), *Recent developments in alcoholism* (Vol. 11, pp. 7–27). New York: Plenum Press.

Whitfield, J. B., & Martin, N. G. (1994). Alcohol consumption and alcohol pharmacokinetics: Interaction within the normal population. *Alcoholism: Clinical and Experimental Research, 18*, 238–243.

Wickelgren, I. (1997). Getting the brain's attention. *Science, 278*, 35–37.

Wickler, A. (1980). *Opioid dependence: Mechanisms and treatment.* New York: Plenum Press.

Wilder, B. J., & Bruni, J. (1981). *Seizure disorders: A pharmacological approach to treatment.* New York: Raven Press.

Willett, W., Stampfer, M., Manson, J., Colditz, G., Rosner, B. A., Speizer, F. E., et al. (1996). Coffee consumption and coronary disease in women. A ten-year follow-up. *Journal of the American Medical Association, 275*, 458–462.

Williams, G. D., Clem, D., & Dufour, M. C. (1993). *Surveillance report #27. Apparent per capita alcohol consumption: National, state, and regional trends, 1977–1991.* Rockville, MD: National Institute on Alcohol Abuse and Alcoholism, Division of Biometry and Epidemiology.

Williams, J. M. G., Mathews, A., & MacLeod, C. (1996). The emotional Stroop task and psychopathology. *Psychological Bulletin, 120*, 3–24.

Winger, G., Hoffmann, F. G., & Woods, J. H. (1992). *A handbook on alcohol and drug abuse* (3rd ed.). New York: Oxford University Press.

Winger, G., Stitzer, M. L., & Woods, J. H. (1975). Barbiturate-reinforced responding in rhesus monkeys: Comparisons of compounds with different durations of actions. *Journal of Pharmacology and Experimental Therapeutics, 195*, 505–514.

Winick, C. (1962). Maturing out of narcotic addiction. *Bulletin on Narcotics, 14*(1), 1–8.

Wise, R. A. (1998). Drug activation of reward pathways. *Drug and Alcohol Dependence, 51*, 13–22.

Wise, R. A. (1998). Drug-activation of brain reward pathways. *Drug and Alcohol Dependence, 51*, 13–22.

Wolfe, S. M., & Victor, M. (1972). The physiological basis of the alcohol withdrawal syndrome. In N. K. Mello & J. H. Mendelson (Eds.), *Recent advances in the study of alcoholism* (pp. 188–199). Washington, DC: U.S. Government Printing Office.

Wolverton, W., & Johanson, C. (1984). Preference in rhesus monkeys given a choice between cocaine and d,1-cathinone. *Journal of the Experimental Analysis of Behavior, 41*, 35–43.

Wolverton, W., & Johnson, K. M. (1992). Neurobiology of cocaine abuse. *Trends in Pharmacological Sciences, 13*, 193–200.

Wood, R. (1979). Reinforcing properties of inhaled substances. *Neurobehavioral Toxicology, 1*(Suppl. 1), 67–72.

Wood, R. I. (2004). Reinforcing aspects of androgens. *Physiology and Behavior, 83*, 279–291.

Wood, R., Coleman, J., Schuler, R., & Cox, C. (1984). Anticonvulsant and antipunishment effects of toluene. *Journal of Pharmacology and Experimental Therapeutics, 230*, 407–412.

Wood, R. W., Warren, P. H., & Weiss, B. (1980). Attenuated aversiveness of electric shock during nitrous oxide exposure. *Journal of Pharmacology and Experimental Therapeutics, 213*, 128–132.

Woods, J., & Winger, G. (1997). Abuse liability of flunitrazepam. *Journal of Clinical Psychopharmacology, 17*(Suppl. 2), 1S–57S.

Woods, J., Katz, J., & Winger, G. (1995). Abuse and therapeutic use of benzodiazepines and benzodiazepine-like drugs. In F. E. Bloom & D. J. Kupfer (Eds.), *Psychopharmacology: The fourth generation of progress* (pp. 1777–1791). New York: Raven Press.

Woods, N. F. (1984). *Human sexuality in health and illness.* St. Louis, MO: Mosby.

World Health Organization. (1996). *The tobacco epidemic: A global public health emergency* (Fact Sheet N118). Geneva: Author.

World Health Organization. (1993). *The international statistical classification of diseases and related health problems (ICD-10).* Geneva: Author

Worley, C. M., Valdez, A., & Schenk, S. (1994). Reinforcement of extinguished cocaine-taking by cocaine and caffeine. *Pharmacology, Biochemistry and Behavior, 48*, 217–221.

Wu, L., Pilowsky, D., & Schlenger, W. (2004). Inhalant abuse and dependence among adolescents in the United States. *Journal of the American Academy of Child and Adolescent Psychiatry, 43*, 1206–1214,

Xu, H., Li, S-J., Bodurka, J., Zhao, X., Xi, Z. X., & Stein, E. A. (2000). Heroin-induced neuronal activation in rat brain assessed by functional MRI. *NeuroReport, 11*, 1085–1092.

Xu, J., Mendrek, A., Cohen, M. S., Monterosso, J., Rodriguez, P., Simon, S. L., et al. (2005). Brain activity in cigarette smokers performing a working memory task: Effects of smoking abstinence. *Biological Psychiatry, 58*, 143–150.

Yamanouchi, N., Okada, S., Kodama, K., & Sato, T. (1998). Central nervous system impairment caused by chronic solvent abuse—A review of Japanese studies on the clinical and neuroimaging aspects. *Addiction Biology, 3*, 15–27.

Yanagita, T. (1975). Some methodological problems in assessing dependence-producing properties of drugs in animals. *Pharmacological Reviews, 27*, 503–510.

Yanagita, T. (1987). Prediction of drug abuse liability from animal studies. In M. A. Bozarth (Ed.), *Methods for assessing the reinforcing properties of abused drugs* (p. 189). New York: Springer-Verlag.

Yanagita, T., Takahashi, S., Ishida, K., & Funamoto, H. (1970). Voluntary inhalation of volatile anesthetics and organic solvents by monkeys. *Japanese Journal of Clinical Pharmacology, 1*, 13–16.

Yavich, L., Patkina, N., & Zvartau, E. (1994). Experimental estimation of addictive potential of a mixture of organic solvents. *European Neuropsychopharmacology, 4*, 111–118.

Yokel, R. A. (1987). Intravenous self-administration: Response rates, the effects of pharmacological challenges, and drug preferences. In M. A. Bozarth (Ed.), *Methods of assessing the reinforcing properties of abused drugs* (pp. 1–34). New York: Springer-Verlag.

Yoshimoto, K., Ueda, S., Kato, B., Takeuchi, Y., Kawai, Y., Moritake, K., et al. (2000). Alcohol enhances characteristic release of dopamine and serotonin in the central nucleus of the amygdala. *Neurochemistry International, 37*, 369–376.

Young, A. M., & Goudie, A. J. (1995). Adaptive processes regulating tolerance to the behavioral effects of drugs. In F. E. Bloom & D. J. Kupfer (Eds.), *Psychopharmacology: The fourth generation of progress* (pp. 733–742). New York: Raven Press.

Young, A. M., Steigerwald, E., Makhay, M., & Kapitsopoulos, G. (1991). Onset of tolerance to discriminative stimulus effects of morphine. *Pharmacology, Biochemistry and Behavior, 39*, 487–493.

Yun Meng, Lichtman, A. H., Bridgen, D. T., & Martin, B. R. (1997). Inhalation studies with drugs of abuse. In *Pharmacokinetics, metabolism, and pharmaceutics of drugs of abuse* (pp. 201–224) (NIDA Research Monograph No. 201). Rockville, MD: U.S. Department of Health and Human Services.

Zack, M., & Vogel-Sprott, M. (1995). Behavioral tolerance and sensitization to alcohol in humans: The contribution of learning. *Experimental and Clinical Psychopharmacology, 3*, 396–401.

Zacny, J. P. (1995). A review of the effects of opioids on psychomotor and cognitive functioning in humans. *Experimental and Clinical Psychopharmacology, 3*, 432–466.

Zacny, J., Cho, A., Coalson, D., Rupani, G. G., Young, C., Klafta, J., et al. (1996). Differential acute tolerance development to the effects of nitrous oxide in humans. *Neuroscience Letters, 209*, 73–76.

Zacny, J., Cho, A., Tolendano, A., Galinkin, J., Coalson, D., Klock, P., et al. (1997). Effects of information on the reinforcing and psychomotor effects on nitrous oxide in health volunteers. *Alcohol and Drug Dependence, 48*, 85–95.

Zacny, J. P., Hill, J., Black, M., & Sadeghi, P. (1998). Comparing the subjective, psychomotor and physiological effects of intravenous pentazocine and morphine in normal volunteers. *Journal of Pharmacology and Experimental Therapeutics, 286*, 1197–1207.

Zacny, J., Janiszewski, D., Sadeghi, P., & Black, M. (1999). Reinforcing, subjective and psychomotor effects of sevoflurane and nitrous oxide in moderate-drinking healthy volunteers. *Addiction, 94*, 1817–1828.

Zacny, J. P., McKay, M., Toledano, A., Marks, S., Young, C. J., & Apfelbaum, J. L. (1996). The effects of cold water immersion stressor on the reinforcing and subjective effects of fentanyl in health volunteers. *Drug and Alcohol Dependence, 42*, 133–142.

Zacny, J. P., Stitzer, M. L., Brown, F. J., Yingling, J. E., & Griffiths, R. R. (1987). Human cigarette smoking: Effects of puff and inhalation parameters on smoke exposure. *Journal of Pharmacology and Experimental Therapeutics, 240*, 554–563.

Zacny, J. P., & Walker, E. A. (1998). Behavioral pharmacology of opiates. In R. E. Tarter, R. T. Ammerman, & P. J. Ott (Eds.), *Handbook of substance abuse* (pp. 343– 362). New York: Plenum Press.

Zajecka, J., Tracy, K. & Mitchell, S. (1997). Discontinuation symptoms after treatment with serotonin reuptake inhibitors: A literature review. *Journal of Clinical Psychiatry, 58*, 291–297.

Zuckerman, B., & Frank, D. A. (1994). Prenatal cocaine exposure: Nine years later. *Journal of Pediatrics, 124*(5, Pt. 1), 731–733.

Index

Pages on which there is a definitive discussion of each concept are indicated in boldface type.

dopamine hypothesis, 288–89
dopamine receptor blockers, 234
dopamine receptors, 291
dopamine transporter, 257
dorsal horn, **74**
dorsolateral prefrontal cortex, **79**, 207, 253–54
dosages, **2**
dose–effect curve, **2**
dose–response curve, **2**
double-blind procedure, **29**
downers, 32, 162
down-regulation, 304
doxepin, 297
DRC, **2**
dreaming, 206, 268
Dristan, 221
driving, 33, 108, 169, 255
DRL, **52**, 188
dronabinol, **315**
drug, **1**, 55
Drug Abuse Warning Network, 330, 354
drug binding, 83
drug self-administration, 98
DSE (*see* depolarization-induced suppression of excitation)
DSI (*see* depolarization-induced suppression of inhibition)
DSM (DSM-IV), **92**–93, 95, 97, 232, 235, 285–86, 299, 300, 329
   substance abuse, **94**
   substance dependence, **94**
DSST (*see* digit symbol substitution test)
dysphoria, 118
dystonia, 322

e, 344
E (*see* epinephrine)
easy lay, 352
ecstasy (*see also* MDMA), **344–48**
   acute tolerance, 345
   alcohol withdrawal, 354
   aphrodisiac, 353
   cognitive deficits, 346
   craving for alcohol, 354
   dehydration, 347
   depletion in serotonin, 345–46
   discriminative stimulus properties, 346
   driving, 353
   electrolyte imbalance, 347
   entactogenic effects, 345
   epidemiology, 346
   half-life, 345
   harmful effects, 346
   heat regulation, 347
   lethal effects, 347
   narcolepsy, 353
   neurophysiology, 345
   opiates withdrawal, 354
   performance, 345
   pharmacokinetics, 345
   place preference, 354
   raves, 345
   REM sleep, 353

   self-administration, 346
   tolerance, 346
   withdrawal, 346
ED$_{50}$, **4, 39**
EEG, 32, **81**, 117, 173, 205, 209, 248
EEG waves, 81
   advantages, 88
   amplitude, **81**
   beta waves, 81
   delta waves, **81**
   disadvantages, 88
   frequency, **81**
effectiveness, **5**
electrostatic charge, **59**
elevated plus maze, **34**
emergence delirium, **348**
empathogen, **336, 345**
empathogenic effects, 341
emphysema, 214
endocannabinoids, **319–20**
endocytosis, **72**
endogenous benzodiazepine, 166
endogenous opiate system, 138
endogenous opioid peptides, 320
endorphins, **69**, 72, **266**
enkephalins, **69**, 72, 77, **266**
entactogen, **336, 345**
entactogenic effects, 341
entorhinal cortex, 289
enzyme, **17**
enzyme induction, **19**
Ephedra vulgaris, **242**
ephedrine, **68**, 204–5, 208, 227, 230, 241–43, 246
epidermis, 14
EPSP (*see* excitatory post synaptic potential)
ergot fungus, 337
ergotism, **337**
ERPs, 116
Erythroxylon coca, **242**
escape, 271, 293
ethanol (*see also* alcohol), 105, 110, 353
ether, 180, 182, 193
   frolics, 182
   history, 184
ethyl acetate, 180, 181
ethylene trichloride, 181
ETS, **215**
euphoria, 205
event related potentials (ERP), **82**, 116
evoked potentials, **82**, 117–18
Excedrin, 221
excipients, **2**
excitation, **64**
excitatory postsynaptic potential, **64**, 339
excretion, **6**,16
expectancy, **54–55**
expectation mechanism, 55
experimental control, **25**
experimenter bias, **29**
explicit memory, **168**
extended amygdala, 118

manic-depressive psychosis, 283, 299
manic episode, 300
MAO, 71
MAO-A, **306**
MAO-B, **306**
MAOIs (*see also* antidepressants), 252, 297, 300–301,
    303–4
    half-life, 302
maprotiline, 297
marijuana, 83, 117, 272, **314–16**, 318, 320
    cigarettes, 327–28
    cognitive functioning, 332
    decriminalization, 330
    IQ, 332
    National Household Survey on Drug Abuse, 329
    schizophrenia, 331
Marinol, **317**, 322
matching law, **120**
maté, 223
maturing out, 274
MBDB, **345**
MBK, 180, 191
MDA, 344
MDEA, 344
MDM, 344
MDMA, 344 (*see also* ecstasy)
mecamylamine, **204**, 206, 208
medial forebrain bundle, **76**, 78, 289, 300, 304
median effective dose, **4**
median lethal dose, **4**
medulla, **75**
MEK, 181
MEOS, 137, 144
meperidine, **262**, 265
meprobamate, 161
mescaline, 170, 337, 339, 343–44, **345**–46
mesolimbic dopamine system, 55, **78**, **111–12**, 113–14, 116,
    118, 267, 288–90
mesoridizine, 284
metabolism, **16**
metabolites, **17**
methacide, 181
methadone, 174, 258, **262**, 272
    half-life, 265
methadone maintenance, 168, 279
methamphetamine, 83, **241**, 244, 308, 347
methanol (methyl hydrate), 181
methaqualone, 161
methcathinone, 242
methoxphenamine, 251
methoxyflurane, 188
methyl benzene, 180–81
methyl butyl ketone, 180–81, 191
methyl chloride, 180–81
methyl ethyl ketone, 181
methylenediamine, **225**
methylephedrine, 244, 251, 258
methylphenidate, **242**
methyltrichloromethane, 181
methylxanthines (*see also* caffeine, theophylline and
    theobromine), **220**

athletic performance, 228–29
conditioned behavior, 229–30
consumption, 235–36
dependence syndrome, 235
discriminative stimulus properties, 230
harmful effects, 236–38
human performance, 227–29
lethal effects, 238
neurophysiology, 226–27
pharmacokinetics, 225–26
pKa, 225
routes of administration, 225
self-administration, 233–35
sleep, 229
sources, 220–23
subjective effects, 230–31
tolerance, 231–32
unconditioned behavior, 229
withdrawal, 232–33
Mexican Valium, 163
mianserin, 297
microdots, **338**
microsomal ethanol-oxidizing system (*see* MEOS)
midazolam, 163, 165, 170–71
migraine, 341
millivolts, **58**
mineral spirits, 181
minor tranquilizers, 284
mirtazapine, 297
mithradatism, **42**
mixed opioid agonist–antagonist, 267, 270
moclobemide, 297, 302, 307
modadifinil, **258**
moist snuff, 199
molindone, 284
monoacetylmorphine, 265
monoamines, **68**, **71**, 241, 246, 253, 299, 303
monoamine-like hallucinogens, **336**
monoamine oxidase (*see* MAO)
monoamine oxidase, 138
monoamine oxidase inhibitors (*see* MAOIs)
monoamine theory, 304
mood brightener, 258
mood disorder, 299
mood stabilizers, **302**
    effects on the body, 306
    neurophysiology, 305
morning glory seeds, **337**
morphine, 72, **77–78**, 83, 125, 190, 206, **262**, 267, 270,
    272, 320, 353
    dreams, 268
    first-pass metabolism, 264
    half-life, 265
    overdose, 50
    pKa, 264
    stereotyped behavior, 271
    tolerance, 49
motoneurons, 74
motor cortex, 76
motor loop, **111**, 290
MPTP, 262

VI (*see* variable interval schedule)
Vietnam, 121
vigilance task, 108
visual cortex, **79**
vitamin B12, 192
Vivarin, 221
volatile solvents, **180**
volatility, **179**
vomiting, 321
vomiting center, **75**, 205
VR (*see* variable ratio schedule)
VTA (*see* Ventral Tegmental Area)

Wake Ups, 221
walk and turn test, **325**
wanting system, 114
washout, 304
white matter, **73**
WIN 55212-2, **315**, 328
window panes, 338
withdrawal, **45**, 96, 98–99, 171, 206

withdrawal rebound, 167
World Health Organization, 93, 162

X, 344
xtc, 344
xylene, 180–81, 191
Xyrem, **352**

yeasts, 128
yen sleep, 273
youpon, 223

zaleplon, 161, 163, 166, 167
z-axis, **85**
Z drugs, **161**, 163, 166
    pharmacokinetics, 163
    neurophysiology, 166
    sleep, 167
    performance, 16
zolpidem, 161, 163, 167, 169, 170–71
zopiclone, 161, 163, 167, 169